Biondo Flavio's
Italia Illustrata

Text, Translation, and Commentary

Biondo Flavio's Italia Illustrata

Text, Translation, and Commentary

Catherine J. Castner

VOLUME II

CENTRAL AND SOUTHERN ITALY

Global Academic Publishing
Binghamton University
Binghamton, New York
2010

A Global Academic Publishing Book

Published by
State University of New York Press, Albany

Library of Congress Cataloging-in-Publication Data

Biondo Flavio, 1392–1463.
[Italia illustrata. English & Latin]
Biondo Flavio's Italia illustrata / text, translation, and commentary
Catherine J. Castner.
p. cm.
English and Latin.
Includes bibliographical references and index.
ISBN: 978-1-58684-278-9 (pbk. : alk. paper)
1. Italy--Description and travel--Early works to 1800. 2. Italy--History--To 1500--Early works to 1800. 3. Humanism--Italy--Early works to 1800. 4. Italy--Biography--Early works to 1800. 5. Italy--Genealogy--Early works to 1800. I. Castner, Catherine J., 1949– II. Title.
DG422.B56 2005b
911'.45--dc22

2005022178

For information, contact State University of New York Press, Albany, NY

www.sunypress.edu

Contents

Acknowledgments vii
Credits for Illustrations ix
Introduction to Volume II xi

Part I, Central Italy

Regio II, Tuscany xvi
Regio III, Lazio 60
Regio IV, Umbria 138
Regio V, March of Ancona 174

Part II, Southern Italy

Regio XII, Abruzzo 206
Regio XIII, Campania 278
Regio XIV, Puglia 346

Commentary 357

Bibliography 443

General Index 449

Index of Places 465

Plates

I. Cenotaph of Bishop Guido Tarlati di Pietramala 371
II. Grotto at Palazzolo 385
III. Licenza in Sabine territory 394
IV. Valley of the Farfa river 395
V. General map of Campania (detail) 417
VI. General map of Campania (detail) 418
VII. Lacus Lucrinus and Portus Iulius 435

Acknowledgments

In addition to the gratitude expressed in the first volume for repeated support from my university at various stages of the research and production of this book, it is a pleasure to thank Dean Mary Anne Fitzpatrick of the College of Arts and Sciences for her generous subvention of the publication and indexing costs of this second volume. In 2001 I received a College of Liberal Arts Scholarship Support grant for travel to Italy to conduct research for this second volume. I am especially grateful to Dean Gordon Baylis for his advocacy in obtaining that indispensable support. This volume entailed work in areas of Italy unfamiliar to me. I am grateful to Francesca Gleason of John Cabot University, Rome, for her assistance in my visit to Lago di Patria; and to Gregorio Palumbo, vulcanologist at the University of Naples, for organizing my visit to the site of the "villa of Scipio," and his valuable comments on the geomorphological changes in the area.

Several colleagues made important contributions in areas beyond my competence, for which I express my heartfelt gratitude. Faust Pauluzzi was instrumental in obtaining permission to publish illustrations from Italian sources. Virginia Brown provided crucial help in obtaining permission to publish the illustration of the grottoes at Palazzolo (Plate II). Vera von Falkenhausen provided expert assistance with place names in Calabria. Charles Mack, who many years ago provided the original impetus to begin my work on Biondo Flavio, read the chapter "Tuscany" and contributed comments and perspective on a region of Italy with which he is deeply familiar. Keith McGraw skillfully improved on my unpromising raw material to create the images in the plates. Kristina Stefanic-Brown prepared the indices for this volume as well as for the first.

I am grateful also to the anonymous reader for the press who pointed out errors and inconsistences in my typescript. To Lori Vandermark-Fuller, editor at Global Academic Publishing, I owe a particular debt of gratitude for her patient, meticulous, and expert work on the production of this and the previous volume. Whatever errors remain are my responsibility alone.

Catherine J. Castner
Columbia, South Carolina, USA
July, 2010

Credits for Illustrations

I am grateful to Dott. Luigi Devoti for permission to publish an illustration from his book, *Splendori dei Castelli Romani: Espressioni artistiche dal secolo XVII al secolo XX* (Rome and Velletri: Edizioni tra 8 e 9, 1992), Plate II. The maps of Sabine territory (Plates III and IV, map No. 144-II-SE) are reproduced here with the permission of the Istituto Geografico Militare, Florence, Italy. I am grateful to Dr. Nicholas Purcell for permission to publish the maps of Campania (Plates V–VII) from *Campania* by Martin W. Frederiksen, edited by Nicholas Purcell (British School at Rome, 1984).

Introduction

The first volume of this work, organized geographically, presented the regions of northern Italy in Biondo Flavio's *Italia illustrata*.[1] The present volume treats Biondo's description of the regions of central and southern Italy: Tuscany (Biondo's second region), Lazio (3), Umbria (4), March of Ancona (5), Abruzzo (12), Campania (13), and Puglia (14).

Like *Italia illustrata* as a whole, the chapters describing central Italy show a disparity in length and importance, reflecting the generally greater significance of "Tuscany" and "Lazio" in terms of ancient history, contemporary culture, and Biondo's own direct observation and familiarity through residence in the regions. However, all four chapters describing central Italy contain evidence of Biondo's antiquarian interests and direct observation in his correlations of ancient toponyms with modern sites, as well as his observation of natural phenomena that excited curiosity and marvel in people of his day (*e.g.*, gorges like the Gola del Furlo and that at Incisa in Val d'Arno).

In 1450, during the composition of "Lazio" and "March of Ancona" and perhaps the other two central regions as well, lacking the support of any powerful patron, Biondo resided at his farm in San Biagio, near Ferrara, and was thus not living in any of these four regions while writing their descriptions. His descriptions of the regions of central Italy are thus not informed by the same immediacy that pervades the sixth region, "Romandiola." Eugenius IV had died in 1447, but Biondo is still cognizant of much gratitude to this pope, and inserts mentions of him frequently when a town or city connected with him presents itself along his written route. At the same time, the bishop of Siena, Aeneas Silvius Piccolomini, who will become Pope Pius II (r. 1458–1464), appears as a promising source of friendship and support, and receives several complimentary mentions in these chapters.

---

[1] Castner, Catherine. *Biondo Flavio's Italia illustrata: Text, Translation, and Commentary. Volume I: Northern Italy*. Binghamton, NY: Global Academic Publishing, 2005. For an extended introduction to this book, including Biondo's biography, see the introduction to Volume I, xiii–xxxv.

Long past by the time of *Italia illustrata*'s composition are Biondo's intoxicating days at Florence in the 1430s. This period of intellectual growth had produced the *De verbis Romanae locutionis* (1435), a dialogue represented as taking place in Eugenius IV's chambers. Florence nonetheless occupies a dominant place in "Tuscany" (as "Tuscany" and "Lazio" do in the description of central Italy), and Biondo provides detailed descriptions of its buildings and famous men which generally conform to traditional assessments of their importance.

Biondo's concern with patronage is especially apparent in "Lazio:" the prosopography of famous men of the region traces the humanist's connections in the Curia, and the chapter abounds in flattering remarks about the Colonna and especially the cardinal Prospero, to whom Biondo may have intended to dedicate this chapter separately and from whom he had requested assistance in the composition of the entire treatise. Not only are even the smallest possessions of the Colonna mentioned specifically, but Biondo evidences direct observation of many small towns and fortified villages, and his antiquarian interests, shared with the cardinal, provide narratives of visits to Anzio and Mt. Soracte, and of the famous attempt to raise one of the Roman ships from Lago di Nemi.

Despite Umbria's important center of Perugia, the evidence of Propertius, the sensational rite of the *barilotto,* the strategic importance of the Marches to the papal state, some spectacular natural phenomena resulting from their rivercourses and mountain formations, and Biondo's detailed elaboration of the location of Horace's villa, the impression made by "Umbria" and "March of Ancona" is muted in comparison with Biondo's vivid personal reminiscences of, and the cultural brilliance associated with, the regions of the second and third chapters.

The southern regions remained unfinished. In addition to very full descriptions of Abruzzo and Campania, and the abbreviated treatment of Puglia, Biondo planned to cover Calabria, Lucania, and Bruttium. According to Biondo, an enemy's plagiarism of the entire work forced him to premature publication of *Italia illustrata* without the remaining southern regions. The three southern regions are disparate in form: only Campania displays a full and typical account of the region. As Clavuot (68) notes, the historical excursus on southern Italy (**[389B–395D]**) which occupies the long initial portion of "Abruzzo" was designed as an introduction and a unifying bracket for the seven southern regions combined in the Regno.

Since my first volume appeared from this press, several important contributions to the study of Biondo Flavio's *Italia illustrata* have appeared. Chief among them is Jeffrey White's *Italy illuminated.*[2] White's first volume covers the regions of Liguria, Tuscany, Lazio, Umbria, Piceno, and Romagna. This groundbreaking contribution provides the first modern critical edition of the Latin text of *Italia illustrata.* Although my Latin text is that of the early printed edition of Froben (Basle 1559) and this work was substantially complete before the appearance of White's first volume, my commentary is indebted to White's *Notes to the Translation* for the regions of Tuscany, Lazio, Umbria, and Piceno; and for a number of toponyms in my English translation in cases where White has identified the modern Italian equivalents of Biondo's Latin place names.

Ottavio Clavuot's 1990 book remains the most important comprehensive analysis of *Italia illustrata* and a pervasive contribution to the second volume of my work. Clavuot's "Verzeichnis" and White's "Notes to the Translation" provide an exhaustive account and identification of Biondo's citations of his sources. Recently Clavuot has expanded his analysis to the prosopographical area in two important articles to which this volume is also indebted.[3] Recent prosopographical attention has also focused on art history. P. Pontari's article on "Gli Artisti" is a substantial contribution in this area.[4]

The reader is referred to the Introduction and Bibliography in Volume I for a full appreciation of *Italia illustrata* in the context of Biondo's life and work; and for citations of works also cited in this volume.

---

[2] *Biondo Flavio, Italy Illuminated,* edited and translated by Jeffrey White. The I Tatti Renaissance Library. Cambridge, MA and London: Harvard University Press, 2005.

[3] Clavuot, Ottavio. *Biondos »Italia illustrata«: Summa oder Neuschöpfung? Über die Arbeitsmethoden eines Humanisten.* Bibliothek des Deutschen historischen Instituts in Rom 69. Tübingen: Max Niemeyer Verlag, 1990; "Verzeichnis" 307–322. *Idem,* "Flavio Biondos *Italia illustrata.* Porträt und historisch-geographische Legitimation der humanistischen Elite Italiens," in *Diffusion des Humanismus: Studien zur nationalen Geschichtsschreibung europäischer Humanisten,* edd. J. Helmrath et al. (Göttingen: Wallstein Verlag, 2002): 55–76; and "Italien entdeckt sich selbst-Über die historischen und antiquarischen Studien des Biondo Flavio (1392–1463)" in *Feconde venner le carte: Studi in Onore di Ottavio Besomi* (Bellinzona: Casagrande, 1997): 145–159.

[4] Pontari, Paolo. "Gli artisti nel *Catalogus Virorum Illustrium* dell' *Italia illustrata* di Biondo Flavio," *Letteratura e Arte* 1 (2003): 80–110.

PART ONE

CENTRAL ITALY

Regio Secunda
Etruria

Etruria ad Macram sequitur, regio Italiae secunda vel inde notissima, quod priscum semper servavit nomen. Eius sunt notissimi etiam nunc fines: Macra et Tiberis amnes centum et septuagintaquattuor milibus inter se distantes; Apenninus mons et inferum mare, eius maris pars, quae a dictorum amnium ostiis longitudine et ad Sardiniam usque **[300E]** latitudine terminata fuit, quandoque Tuscum, quandoque Tyrrhenum pelagus dicta est.

Etenim Tuscorum gens, sicut Iustinus a Trogo tradit, ex Lydia Asia provincia veniens, pulsis Umbris incoluit hanc Italiae partem, quae primo Tyrrhenia ab eorum rege Tyrrheno, mox Etruria a multo ac frequentato deorum per tura cultu est appellata. Leonardus autem Arretinus primo Historiarum dicit Etruscos venisse ex Moeonia, unde Lydi gens maxima navibus in Italiam advecti sunt.

Huius provinciae vetustatem dignitatemque Livius Patavinus libro sexto sic ostendit:

> Tuscorum ante Romanorum imperium late terra marique opes patuere, mari infero superoque quibus Italia modo insulae cingitur quantum potuerint, nomina sunt argumento, quod alterum Tuscum communi vocabulo gentis, alterum Adriaticum mare ab Adria Tuscorum colonia vocare Italicae gentes, Graeci eadem Tyrrhenum atque Adriaticum vocant. Et in utrumque mare vergentes incoluere urbibus duodenis terras, prius cis Apenninum ad inferum mare, postea trans Apenninum, totidem quot capita originis erant missis coloniis, et trans Padum omnia excepto Venetorum angulo quae sinum **[300F]** circumcolunt maris usque ad Alpes tenuere.

Duodecim autem urbes, quibus Etrusci incoluerint Etruriam singulis magistratibus ann[u]is quos vocabant lucumones creatis, qui omnem

Second Region
Tuscany

Tuscany follows at the Magra river, the second region of Italy, and perhaps the most famous, because it has kept its ancient name. Even now its borders are well-known: the one hundred seventy-four miles between the Magra and Tiber rivers; the Apennines, and the Tyrrhenian Sea. Part of that sea has sometimes been called the Tuscan, sometimes the Tyrrhenian Sea; its length extends from the mouths of these rivers and its width extends **[300E]** to Sardinia.

Justin, relying on Trogus, says that the Etruscans came from the province of Lydia, in Asia Minor, drove out the Umbrians, and settled this part of Italy which was first called Tyrrhenia, after its king Tyrrhenus, and a little later Etruria, after their worship, which involved much use of incense. But Leonardo Bruni, in the first book of his *Histories*, says that the Etruscans came from Maeonia, from where the Lydian people came in great numbers by ship to Italy. We know of this province's antiquity and greatness from Livy's sixth book:

> Before the time of the Roman empire, the Etruscan empire extended its power widely on land and on sea. The names of the upper and lower seas, which surround Italy like an island, are a testament to Etruscan power: for the Italian races call one of them "Tuscan," and the other "Adriatic," from Adria, an Etruscan colony; and the Greeks call the same seas "Tyrrhenian" and "Adriatic." In the lands which slope on either side towards each of these seas, they had inhabited twelve cities; first, the twelve on this side of the Apennines, towards the lower sea; to which afterwards they added the same number beyond the Apennines, by establishing as many colonies as there were original cities. Thus they possessed all the Transpadane region (except the corner belonging to the Veneti, who dwell around **[300F]** the gulf) as far as the Alps.

But the twelve Etruscan cities which originally settled Etruria elected annually individual magistrates, called *lucumones*; and through these officials, the Etruscans governed the entire province. The twelve cities were

provinciam gubernabant, has fuisse invenimus: Lunam, Pisas, Populoniam, Volaterram, Agillinam, Faesulas, Russellanam, Arretium, Perusiam, Clusium, Faleriam, et Vulsiniam, quarum quattuor tantummodo integrae exstant. Etruscorum vero dignitatem fuisse maximam hinc constat, quod Livius tradit Romanos ab his accepisse praetextam, trabeas, phaleras, anulos, togas pictas et palmatas, currus triumphales, fasces, lictores, tubas, sellam curulem. Additque Livius Romanos consuevisse pueros mittere ad disciplinam, sicut postea in Graeciam fuerunt missi. Potentiae etiam Etruscorum maximum est argumentum, quod saepius ob Etruscum quam aliud bellum Romae trepidatum est, saepius dictator est dictus.

Subacti vero sunt Romanis Etrusci ad annum urbis conditae septuagesimum et quadringentesimum, cum apud Vadimonis lacum, ingenti proelio superati essent. Bis tamen Romano populo rebellare conati sunt. Primum Hannibalis tempore ducibus Arretinis, de **[300G]** quibus scribit Livius XXVIII: "Cornelius consul in Etruria iudiciis agitavit eos, qui ad Magonem respiciebant, et animos rebelles prae se ferebant." Secunda rebellio intentata fuit bello Marsico sive sociali, quae quidem rebellio Arretinorum, Faesulanorum, et Clusinorum multo sanguine atque urbium Arretii et Clusii vastatione sopita est.

Paruitque postmodum Etruria Romanis quietissime per annos circiter septingentos, usque ad Arcadii et Honorii tempora, quando Romani imperii inclinatio inchoavit. Multas postmodum passa calamitates, quarum minores fuerunt quas Gothi intulerunt, a Longobardis vero crudeliter oppressa fuit, quam sicut libro Historiarum octavo ostendimus, principio adventus in Italiam sui supra ceteros omnes afflixerunt, adeo ut unicus eorum magistratus gastaldio Etruriae appellatus, gubernationi illius satisfacere potuerit. Longobardis vero eiectis cum Caroli Magni et filiorum temporibus Etruria, sicut et aliae Italiae regiones respirare coepisset, eam Lodovicus Caroli filius cum Pascali Romano pontifice partitus est, ut Arretium, Volaterrae, Clusium, Florentia, Pistorium, Luca, Pisae, et Luna imperio, ceterae omnes pontifici **[300H]** Romano parerent.

Luna, Pisa, Populonia, Volaterrae, Agillina, Faesulae, Rusellana, Arretium, Perusia, Clusium, Faleria, and Vulsinia. Only four of them now exist undamaged. That the authority of the Etruscans was very great we know from Livy, who informs us that the Romans took from them the customs of the *toga praetexta*; the robe of state; trappings for horses; the rings; the embroidered toga and toga embroidered with palms; the triumphal chariot; the *fasces* and lictors; the trumpet; and the curule chair. Livy adds that the Romans were accustomed to send their sons to the Etruscans for learning in the same way that in later ages boys were sent to Greece to be educated. The most convincing proof of the great power of the Etruscans is that the Romans were more frightened by the Etruscan wars than by any other, and turned to a dictator more often in these confrontations.

The Etruscans were, however, subdued by the Romans in the 470th year after Rome's foundation, when they were defeated in the great battle of Lake Vadimonis. They nevertheless tried twice to rise up against the Roman people. The first time, under the leadership of Arretium, was when Hannibal was in Italy. Livy gives the account **[300G]** in book 28: "While in Etruria, the consul Cornelius vexed with his judicial investigations the Etruscans who were dependent on Mago and had betrayed rebellious attitudes." The second insurrection was directed against the Romans during the Marsic or Social War by the people of Arretium, Faesulae, and Clusium; it was put down with much bloodshed and the cities of Arretium and Clusium were devastated.

For about 700 years afterwards, Etruria was a peaceful subject of the Romans, until the decline of the Roman empire began, in the time of Arcadius and Honorius. Then Etruria was visited by many disasters. Those inflicted by the Goths were less severe than the region's cruel oppression by the Lombards: as I mentioned in the eighth book of my *Histories*, at the beginning of the Lombards' invasion of Italy they devastated Etruria more than the other regions, with the result that a single one of the Lombards' magistrates, called the gastald of Etruria, sufficed to govern that region. After the Lombards had been expelled, in the time of Charlemagne and his sons, Etruria and the other regions of Italy began to breathe again; but Louis, Charlemagne's son, and Pope Paschal II divided it up in such a way that Arretium, Volaterrae, Clusium, Florence, Pistorium, Luca, Pisa, and Luna were subject to the Empire, while all the rest were **[300H]** subjects of the Pope.

Postquam vero Caroli Magni stirpis reges ab Italia sunt eiecti, Berengariusque Italicensis imperator et Lotharius eius filius rex Italiam administrare coeperunt, maximas Italia atque horrendas incurrit calamitates, in quarum una ad annum salutis quadragesimum supra nongentesimum, Ioanne decimo pontifice Romano Ungari Etruriam omnem spoliarunt. Et mortales, qui caedibus superfuerant, utrumque sexum in Ungariam asportarunt. Aelius Spartianus de eadem Etruria honoratius scribit, qui Hadrianum dicit imperatorem in Etruria praeturam gessisse.

Sed iam ad nostrum revertamur ordinem. Secus Macram amnem vetusta interiit Luna, inter capita Etruriae numerata, quae Eutichianum pontificem Romanum patre maximo genuit, eius vero urbis desolationem, quam nunc habet diutissime antea inchoasse indicat Lucanus in primo, his versibus:

Hoc propter placuit Tuscos de more vetusto
Acciri vates, quorum qui maximus aevo
Arruns incoluit desertae moenia Lunae.

Indicatque Martialis poeta eius urbis regionem caseo abundasse his versibus:

Caseus Etruscae signatus imagine Lunae
Praestabit pueris prandia mille tuis.

Eius tamen urbis retinet denominationem regio Lunensis appellata, Genuensibus maiori ex parte subiecta.

Est ad Macrae dexteram supra Lunam Sarzana, cuius arçem Sarzanellum appellatam Thomas **[301A]** Fregosus Genuensis, vir sicut ostendimus illustris et egregie communivit, et intus lautissime ac splendidissime exaedificavit. Sunt etiam ad eandem dexteram Castrum Novum, Fossa Nova, Ortus Novus, Villa Francha. Torrens Bagnonus cum oppido eius nominis, Filatera, Malgratum. Et in Apennini radicibus, Pontremulum, nobile regionis oppidum. Sunt quoque interius hinc Fivizanum, Verucula, et Gragnola. Inde Montionum, Chararia Massa et aliquot minora castella in montibus, olim Violatum Tiguliorum, et Segaunorum, ac Appuanorum populorum olim Ligustinorum appellatis. Qui montes ab Apennino in litus inferi maris trans-

After Charlemagne's family were thrown out of Italy, Berengar, the emperor, and his son Lothar, the king, began to manage the rule of Italy. Then great disasters afflicted Italy, for example the complete devastation of Etruria by the Hungarians in 940, during the papacy of John X. Those of either sex who survived the slaughter were transported to Hungary. Aelius Spartianus, writing more favorably about Etruria, says that the emperor Hadrian exercised the office of praetor in Etruria.

But let me now return to the order of my work. Ancient Luna has perished, the city beside the Magra river, numbered among the capital cities of Etruria. It was the home of Pope Eutychianus, son of a very great man. This city's desolation is longstanding, as Lucan shows in these verses from his first book:

> For this, soothsayers were summoned by the Etruscans according to their ancient custom; the oldest of them, Arruns, lived within the deserted city of Luna.

And the poet Martial attests in the following verses that the area around this city was an abundant source of cheese:

> Cheese, stamped with the crest of Etruscan Luna, will afford your slaves a thousand lunches.

But the region, called Lunigiana, preserves this city's name. Most of it is subject to Genoa.

On the right-hand side of the Magra, above Luna, is Sarzana, whose citadel is called Sarzanello. I have mentioned that the famous Genoese Tommaso [301A] Campofregoso fortified it well, and finished inside the walls a glorious and splendid building program. On the same side of the river are also Castelnuovo di Garfagnano, Fosdinovo, Ortonovo, and Villafranca in Lunigiana; the stream Bagnone, with a town of the same name; Filattiera, and Malgrate. And at the foot of the Apennines is Pontremuli, a famous town of the region. In the interior from here are Fivizzano, Verrucola, and Gragnola. Then come Monzone, Carrara, Massa and some lesser fortified villages in the mountains once called the Ligustini, which formerly belonged to peoples long ago robbed of them, the Tiguli, Segauni, and Apuani. These mountains, from the Apennines to the shore of the Tyrrhenian Sea, extend-

verso, ab oriente ad meridiem tractu producti, Montana nunc Lunensis Carrariae dicuntur. De hisque sic habet in decimo Livius:

> Sempronius a Pisis in Apuanos Ligures, vastandoque vicos et castella eorum aperuit saltum usque ad Meram fluvium et Lunae portum. Hostes autem antiquam sedem maiorum suorum ceperunt. Et inde superata locorum iniquitate proelio deiecti sunt.

Ex ipsis montibus fodinas habentibus celeberrimas, magna vis marmorum Romam olim importata est, adeo ut usque in praesens tempus columnae ibi et alia marmorum **[301B]** ingentia cernantur frusta, quae post fractas Romani imperii vires derelicta nullus qui quaesiverit, aut potuerit, aut deterrente impendio asportare voluerit est inventus. Cum tamen minoris impendii et laboris marmora, Pisas olim et nuper Florentiam et quandoque Romam Genuamque importata sint. Unde Iuvenalis de marmoribus Ligustinis, quae Romam portabantur, sic habet,

> Nam si procubuit qui saxa Ligustica portat
> Axis. . . .

Dicitque Plinius albos Liguriae lapides serra faciliter secari.

Secundus in Etruria fluvius Auxeris a quibusdam vetustis, sed a Livio Mera, ut supra apparet appellatus, quem nunc Serclum dicunt, cui est remotius ad sinistram in maris litore Mutronum arx vetustissimo in monumento aedificata, quam a Florentinis, ad annum salutis sexagesimumquintum supra ducentesimum et millesimum, captam Carolus Siciliae rex Lucensibus reddidit. Et tamen eam aetate nostra receptam nunc populus obtinet Florentinus. Intus Petra Sancta, et ad Auxeris ipsius ostium est Virego.

Libet vero priusquam mediterranea, et ad dexteram Auxeris ripam sita attingam, ad certiorem locorum indaginem oram Etruriae maritimam usque ad Tiberim describere. Quae quidem sicut **[301C]** semper hactenus fuit, nunc

ing from the east to the south, are now called the mountains of Carrara Lunigiana. Livy writes about them in his tenth book:

> Sempronius went pillaging the villages and fortified towns from Pisa into the land of the Ligurian Apuani. He opened up the pass as far as the river Mera and the harbor of Luna. But the enemy captured the ancient home of their ancestors. From there, although they overcame the unfavorable terrain, the Romans drove them out in a battle.

Out of the famous mines in these very mountains, a large quantity of marble was in time past brought to Rome, so that even now one can see here columns and other huge pieces of **[301B]** marble. After the downfall of the Roman empire, these were left behind, and no one could be found willing or able to undertake the expense involved in carrying them off. But it was less expensive and less toilsome in earlier times to transport the marble to Pisa, and more recently to Florence and sometimes to Rome and Genoa. For this reason, Juvenal speaks of Ligurian marble's importation to Rome:

> For if that axle with its load of Ligurian marble breaks down...

And Pliny says that it is easy to cut with a saw the white stones from the land of Liguria.

The second river in Tuscany is the Auser, we are told by certain ancient writers. But as we see from the passage of Livy cited above, it appears to have been called the Mera, and is now called the Serchio. Farther away on its left bank along the coast is Motrone di Versilia, a fortress built on an ancient monument. In 1265, after its capture from the Florentines, king Charles of Sicily restored it to the people of Lucca. But in our times the Florentines have regained possession of it. Towards the interior is Pietrasanta, and right at the mouth of the Auser is Viareggio.

I prefer to describe the seacoast of Tuscany up to the Tiber before I touch upon the places on the right bank of the Auser, and those inland, in order to conduct a more reliable investigation. As it certainly **[301C]** always

maiori ex parte est silvosa. Nam Flavius Eutropius in Aureliani imperatoris vita sic habet:

> Statuerat vinum gratuitum populo Romano dare, ut, quemadmodum et panis et porcina gratuita praebentur, sic etiam vinum daretur, quod perpetuum hac ratione constituerat facere. Etruriae per Aureliam usque ad Alpes maritimas ingentes agri sunt, hicque fertiles et silvosi sunt. Statuerat itaque a dominis locorum incultorum, qui tamen vellent, gratis dare emere, atque ex eo vinum dare gratuitum.

Prima post Auxerim sunt Arni ostia, a quibus paulum recedit Liburnium Pisani portus munitissima arx, apud quam in scopulo passus mille a continenti recente fundata est turris Pharea, nocturnum Tyrrheno mari navigantibus lumen quam remotissime praebens, et Pisanum a longe ostendens portum. Arnumque recedentes tertio a mari miliario Pisae pontibus iungunt, superbisque aedificiis ornant. Eam urbem vetustam et gestarum rerum gloria claram, ab Alpheis originem habuisse dicit Virgilius. Et Plinius Pisas inter Auxerim et Arnum amnes a Pelope et Atintanis Graeca gente ortas asserit. Iustinus vero dicit Pisas in Liguribus Graecos auctores habere. Et Lucanus in primo,

> **[301D]** Hinc Tyrrhena vado frangentes aequora Pisae.

Livius XXI: "ea causa consuli fuit, cum Pisas navibus venisset ad Padum festinandi." Pisae tertio Eugenio pontifice Romano ornatae fuerunt.

Eam urbem florentibus Romanorum rebus nullum habuisse potentatum videmus. Postquam vero maritimae urbes Etruscae, hinc Luna inde Populonia deletae fuerunt, quiescentibus per Caroli Magni et filiorum tempora Italiae rebus, Pisae multos habuerunt praestantissimos maritimo bello viros,

was up to now, it is mostly forested. Flavius Eutropius, in his *Life of the Emperor Aurelian*, writes:

> He had decided to give free wine to the Roman people, so that wine too might be furnished them just as free bread and pork were. And on the following reasoning he decided to do this permanently: along the Via Aurelia up to the maritime Alps, Etruria had enormous fields, fertile and wooded; and so he had decided to buy land from the owners of the uncultivated places who nevertheless wanted to make the land a free gift, and to supply free wine from this land.

The first river mouth after the Serchio is that of the Arno, and a little ways into the interior from it is Livorno, the well-fortified citadel of the harbor of Pisa. A mile out from the mainland, on a ledge in the sea, a lighthouse has been built which shines its far-reaching light at night to help sailors on the Tyrrhenian Sea and makes visible the harbor of Pisa. Three miles from the sea, Pisa spans with its bridges, decorated with magnificent buildings, the Arno river. Virgil says that this ancient city, with its famous reputation for glorious exploits, traces its origins from the Alpheae. Pliny also places Pisa between the Auser and Arno rivers and says it originated from Pelops and the Atintani, a Greek race. But Justin says Pisa, among the Ligurians, was founded by Greeks. And Lucan, in his first book, says:

> **[301D]** On this side the waves of the Tyrrhenian sea break on the shallows at Pisa.

Livy, in book 21, says, "For this reason the consul had come to Pisa in ships, then hurried to the Po." Pisa was distinguished as the birthplace of Pope Eugenius III.

We see that during the height of the Roman Republic this city had no power. But after the Etruscan cities of the coast-to the north Luna, to the south Populonia-were destroyed, in the period of calm in Italy during the reign of Charlemagne and his sons, Pisa had many men eminent in naval

quorum gesta in nostris historiis celebrantur. Sed ab annis quadraginta, postquam ea civitas Florentinis subiecta fuit, infrequens populo opibusque exinanita penitus est reddita.

Liburno intus contigua sunt stagna, eius oppidi nomine appellata, deinceps est Mons Niger. Succedit eo in litore fluvius Cecinna, sicut nunc fit a Plinio appellatus, cui ad sinistram in ostio haerent vada Volaterrana a priscis appellata. Quod autem hic portus fuerit Volaterranorum et Volaterrani cognomine Volienses appellati sint, auctor est Plinius.

Magna dehinc ad Umbronem fluvium, quem Plinius navigiorum capacem fuisse scribit intercapedo habetur. In qua primum est in litore oppidum Sanctus Vincentius. Interius est Vibona, vetusti nominis oppidum. Superius est Subretum. Sinum deinceps efficit mare ad quem oppidum est portus Barattus. Supra est Campilia, maior deinde habetur sinus, ad quem est Plumbinum, novi **[302E]** nominis oppidum, quem locum Romanae ecclesias rerum scriptores anno nunc trecentesimo Plumbinariam dixerunt. Ad partem Plumbini sinus adversam est portus Foresius, in mediterraneis Scarlinum oppidum, deinceps in litore Castrum Trove, Castilionum, Piscariae. Dehinc habetur litoreum paene castellum, ad paludis olim caenosae emissorium. Inde progressi lacum inveniunt Orbitelli, olim Aprilem dictum; postea Umbronis sunt fluvii ostia, mediocres admittentia naves. Apud quae Populonia fuit vetustissima, de qua Livius libro XXX,

> Claudium cos. profectum ab urbe inter portus Consanum Laurentinumque atrox vis tempestatis adorta Populoniam impulit. Inde cum stetisset ibi dum reliquum aestatis exiret, Iluam insulam et ab Ilua Corsicam, a Corsica Sardiniam traiecit.

Et Virgilius, "... misit Populonia mater." Nicea patricius Constantinopolitanus dux navalis exercitus, regnante in Italia Bernardo Caroli Magni nepote, vi captam diripuit, et igni ferroque funditus evertit, ut parva ipsius urbis vestigia nunc appareant.

warfare, whose exploits are commemorated in my *Histories*. But now in the fortieth year after its subjection to the Florentines, this city has been rendered almost uninhabited and utterly stripped of its resources.

Farther inland next to Livorno are swamps, named after this town. Then comes Montenero. There follows it, on the shore, the Cecinna river, as Pliny calls it, and at its mouth on the left is a ford called by the ancients Volaterrana. This, moreover, was the harbor for the Volaterrani, called by the cognomen Volienses, as Pliny tells us.

There is a great interval from here to the Ombrone river, which Pliny writes was spacious enough for navigation. In this space, on the shore, the first town is San Vincenzo. Farther inland is Vibona, a town with an ancient name. Above it is Suvereto. Next following that, the sea creates a bay on which is located the town Porto Baratti. Above that is Campiglia Marittima. Then there is a greater bay, on which is located a town with the new name of Piombino. The *History of the Roman* **[302E]** *Church* 300 years ago called this place Plumbinaria. In the opposite direction to Piombino there is a bay, the harbor Portoferraio, and inland is the town of Scarlino; then, on the shore, *Castrum Trove*. From here is Castiglione della Pescaia, a fortified town on the shore, at the outlet of what was once a muddy swamp. If you go on from here, you find the Laguna di Orbetello, formerly called Aprilis. After this is the mouth of the Ombrone river, which admits medium-sized ships; here was the site of ancient Populonia, about which Livy writes in book 30,

> The consul Claudius had left Rome and was assailed by a violent storm between the harbors of Cosa and Laurentinum, which drove him to Populonia where he lay at anchor until the rest of the storm let up, then moved on to the island of Elba; from Elba to Corsica, and from there to Sardinia.

And Virgil says, "Mother Populonia sent..." The patrician Nicetas, admiral of the Byzantines in Italy during the rule of Charlemagne's grandson Bernard, captured Populonia by force and plundered it, destroying it completely with fire and sword so that now little remains of the city.

Umbroni ad sinistram adiacet Grossetum civitas, ad dexteram vero Ischia, post Insula, superius Bonconventus. Et paulo infra eius fluvii fontem Assianum, deinceps maritimo in sinu Telamonis est portus Telamotosa a Plinio appellata, Senensi mercaturae **[302F]** satisfaciens. Inde Argentarius Mons in paene insulam mari immissus, in quo est vetusti nominis portus Herculis, quae loca nullae nunc inhabitant gentes, cum tamen eo in monte et circa portum, multa aedificiorum fundamenta cernantur. Post Montem Argentariam a mari paululum recedit Caput Alvei castellum, ad cuius fines Pissia labitur torrens mutilatae in patrimonium Sancti Petri Etruriae finium limes. Terra namque quam de Etruria Matildis certe gloriosa, ut scriptores appellant, comitissa anno nunc tricesimo supra trecentesimum septimo Gregorius pontifex Romanus in beati Petri patrimonium dono dedit, ad illum Pissiae torrentem hac in parte terminata fuit.

Sequitur fluvius Martha appellatus lacu Vulsinensium nunc Bolsenae effusus, super cuius ostia paulum a mari recedit Mons Altus castellum, vetusto in loco Graviscarum, ut appellat Virgilius intempestarum, quod amnis propinquitas indicat, situm. Scribit vero Plinius apud Graviscas corallum gigni solitum, prout nunc et gigni et expiscari constat. Minio inde habetur, cuius meminit Virgilius eo item nunc nomine appellatus.

Iuxta quem tertio a mari miliario Cornetum est civitas, quam turrium frequentia, moeniumque superbia **[302G]** vetustissimam esse ostendunt. Id vero esse crediderim, quod Ptolemaei Plinii Pomponii Melae descriptiones Castrum Novum appellant. Auctum vero traditur esse Tarquiniae, ibi proximae olim urbis vetustae, ruinis, qua ex Tarquinia postremi Romae reges Tarquinii Priscus et Superbus originem duxere. Magnum aetate nostra ornamentum habuit ea civitas malo terminatum fine, Ioannem Vitellensem Romanae ecclesiae cardinalem, qui in Hadriani mole (castello Sancti Angeli) captus interiit. Eius superest nepos litteris et prudentia ornatus Bartholomaeus Cornetanus, et Monteflasconensis episcopus.

Abest a Corneto passuum milia decem, portus celebris arcem habens munitissimam, cui Civitati veteri nunc est appellatio. Nec dubito quin is fuerit Centumcellensis portus, mentio cuius apud veteres saepe habetur. Parvo enim spatio inde abest Centumcellensis olim civitatis locus, quam Saraceni per tempora Italiae regis Bernardi, Caroli Magni nepotis, destruxerunt.

On the left bank of the Ombrone is the city of Grosseto, on the right bank, Istia d'Ombrone, and after that Isola, and higher up Buonconvento. And a little below is the source of the river at Asciano, and then on a bay the harbor of Talamone, which Pliny calls Telamatosa; the Sienese use it **[302F]** for commerce. From here, Monte Argentario lies on a peninsula where there is a harbor whose ancient name was Portus Herculis. Although it is now uninhabited by humans, you can see, on that mountain and around the harbor, many foundations of buildings. After Monte Argentario, a little way in from the sea is the fortified town of Capalbio. At its borders the stream Pescia flows; it constitutes the limits of the territory of Tuscany, fragmented into the Patrimony of St. Peter. The land in Etruria which the glorious countess Matilda, as writers call her, gave 337 years ago to Pope Gregory for the Patrimony of St. Peter was bounded in this direction at this stream Pescia.

There follows the river Marta, with its source in what was called Lacus Vulsinensium, and is now called Lago di Bolsena. Above its mouth, a short distance from the sea, lies the fortified town of Montalto di Castro, on the site of the ancient Graviscae, which Virgil calls "unhealthy." I have based this identification on the proximity of the river; indeed, Pliny writes that coral was produced at Graviscae, just as it is certain that coral is now both produced and farmed there. From there, you arrive at the Mignone, which has the same name as Virgil called it.

Next to it and three miles away is the city of Corneto, whose many towers and lofty walls give **[302G]** evidence of its antiquity. Indeed, I believe it is this city which Ptolemy, Pliny, and Pomponius Mela call Castrum Novum. It has been handed down that it was augmented by the nearby ruins of the ancient Tarquinia, the original home of the last of the Roman kings, Tarquinius Priscus and Tarquinius Superbus. In our times, this city was greatly distinguished by the ill-fated cardinal Giovanni Vitelleschi, who died a prisoner in the Castel Sant'Angelo. He was survived by his grandson, well-known for his literary learning and wisdom, Bartolomeo, bishop of Corneto and Montefiascone.

Ten miles from Corneto is the busy harbor, with its well-fortified citadel, now called Civitavecchia. I am certain that this is the ancient harbor of Centum Cellae often mentioned by ancient writers; for a short distance away from it is the site of the former city of Centum Cellae destroyed by the Saracens during the reign in Italy of Bernard, grandson of Charlemagne.

Et postea aedificatam, nos ultimo habitatoribus anno nunc undevigesimo destitui vidimus. Fuitque is locus in **[302H]** quo Plinius posterior in epistolis narrat, Hadrianum imperatorem centum aedificasse cellas, centum iudicibus audiendis se praesente causis publice institutis deputatis; et in quo beatum Aurelium Augustinum librum de Trinitate constat scripsisse.

Civitatis vero veteris portum praetergressi, magna inveniunt vetusti aedificii fundamenta, in quibus Pyrgo appellatis parvum est sacellum, eoque in loco Pyrgos fuisse veteres a Virgilio appellatos constat. Et proximo in litore monasterium est Severae virgini dicatum, quod in arcem portumque proximis temporibus communitum est.

Proximusque mari influit Caeretanus amnis, secus quem intus est Cervetere nunc, quod fuisse scimus Caere Servatorum, quo tempore Galli Senones urbem ceperunt, sacrorum memoria celebre oppidum, cuius facti exemplar caeremoniis vocabulum dedisse grammatici affirmant, de quo Livius in primo: "Inde Turnus Rutulique diffisi rebus ad florentes opes Etruscorum Mezentiumque eorum regem confugiunt, qui Caere opulento tunc oppido imperabat." Et Martialis poeta scribit pernam fieri optimam apud Caeretanos, sic:

> Caeretana mihi fiet vel massa licebit.

Et interius mille quadringentis passibus sicut vult Plinius, ab oppido Caere distat locus Agillinae, urbis vetustissimae, quam inter capita Etruriae diximus numeratam fuisse. Estque nunc saxoso in tumulo parvis aedificiorum reliquiis notus. Sequitur pertenuis **[303A]** locus in paludibus, cui Pergae olim appellato, nunc Palus dicitur, ab Ursinis possessus. Nec est quicquam aedificiorum aut ruinarum ultra quousque Romani portus a Claudio primum, post a Traiano aedificati reliquiae inveniuntur, certe maiores quam credere possit, qui illas non inspexerit, quorum partem in Roma instaurata diximus. Et tamen quod inadvertentia ibi est omissum addere hic volumus: Portuensem urbem genuisse Formosum pontificem Romanum, et omni ea in palustri litoreaque insula, quam scissus supra Ostiam urbem secundo miliario Tiberis efficit, marmorum frusta herbis rubisque et virgultis obsita, ac alluvionibus semisepulta passim paene contiguae videri, quae scabra et impolita a mercatoribus per felicia rei publicae et imperatorum tempora mari avecta quoscumque in aedificii usus poterant dedolari, et cum multitudo

Nineteen years ago I saw the city was deserted, although it was later rebuilt. This was the site, **[302H]** Pliny the Younger tells us in his *Letters*, where the emperor Hadrian built a hundred rooms with one hundred judges who heard cases in public in the emperor's presence. Here, it is believed, St. Augustine wrote his book *On the Trinity*.

If you go on beyond the harbor of Civitavecchia, you come to some great foundations of ancient buildings. Among them are some called Pyrgo, which contain a small chapel. It is clear that this is the site of what Virgil called ancient Pyrgi. The next place on the shoreline is the monastery dedicated to the virgin Santa Severa, in recent times fortified into a citadel and a harbor.

And next to it debouches the Ceretano river, near which, towards the interior, is the town now called Cerveteri, which I know used to be Caere Servatorum. In the time of the capture of the Rome by the Galli Senones, it was famous for its preservation of the religious objects. This is why the grammarians assert that it gave us the word "ceremonies." Livy mentioned it in his first book: "And from there Turnus and the Rutuli, who did not have confidence in their resources, took refuge with the wealthy Etruscans and their king Mezentius, who then ruled over the rich town of Caere." And the poet Martial writes that the best ham is found at Caere:

> Let me have ham from Caere, or it may be from Massa. . . .

Forty miles inland from Caere, according to Pliny's measurement, is the site of the ancient city of Agillina, numbered, as I have mentioned, among the capital cities of Etruria. It is known now as a collection of ruins of small buildings on a rocky mound. There follows a very small **[303A]** settlement in the swamps, which used to be called Perga but is now called Palus and held by the Orsini. The only buildings or ruins beyond this are those of a Roman harbor built first by Claudius, after that built by Trajan, greater than you could believe if you had not inspected them. I have mentioned part of them in my *Rome restored*. But I wish to add here something I forgot to mention in that work: the port city of Ostia gave us Pope Formosus; and in all this coastal swampland and the island where the Tiber branches two miles above Ostia, one can see here and there fragments of marble almost touching, overgrown with grass and brambles and thickets, half-buried in silt. In the prosperous days of the republic and empire, merchants brought there in rough and unpolished condition whatever pieces they could hew smooth to

sit maxima urbem, ut videtur aedificatura, cernere est eorum partem tantae molis, ut qui obeliscos ignoret Egypto advectos illa non credat potuisse navibus comportari. Litteras unumquodque frustum numerales duobus in lateribus est inscriptum. Quarum unis docente Plinio pondus lapidis, alteris missorum a mercatore frustorum ordinem significari novimus.

Ut autem **[303B]** unde supra digressi sumus revertamur, Auxeris fluvius, quem nunc Serclum vocant, primum habet ad dexteram oppidum Librafactam; ad ortum suum in Apennino habet Grignanum, ignobile castellum; et ad perpetuum fluvii alveum, quosque ad mediterranea sit descensum, vallis est Carfagnana, castellis villisque plurimis habitata, maiorem cuius partem nunc obtinet marchio Ferrariensis. Eorum vero oppidorum quae Auxeri descendendo ad dexteram adiacent notiora sunt Castrum Novum et Barcha; Serclusque in mediterraneis Lucae, urbis Romanae coloniae, latera abluit, de qua Livius XXI: "Hannibal in Ligures, Sempronius Lucam concessit."

Ostendimus vero in Historiis Narsetem eunuchum Lucam a Gothis possessam septem mensibus oppugnasse, priusquam ea potiri potuerit. Ea urbs tertium Lucium pontificem Romanum atque etiam Alexandrum secundum, adversus quem Lombardi Cardolum Parmensem erexerant in idolum, genuit, quam ad annum quinquagesimum malo suo sibi subegit Paulus, gente Lucensi Guinisia nobili genitus. Cumulaverat is triginta in annis ingentem vim pecuniarum et filios procreaverat. Sed cum magno in fastu ipse et filii adolescentes degunt, beatique sibi et suis esse videntur, **[303C]** fortuna derepente mutata exemplar facti sunt multis, quia nihil in rebus humanis solidum, nihil est firmum. Capti enim et patria violenter abacti divitias diu accumulatas, postea vitam in carceribus amisere.

Luca autem post Guinisiorum eiectionem variis et multiplicibus agitata bellorum motibus, intra XX annos magnas est passa calamitates, quae tamen Florentinum populum eius ambientem dominium pariter afflixerunt. Nam praeter alias ibi acceptas clades eorum exercitus, cui Guidantonius praeerat Urbini comes, sicut in Historiis diffuse ostendimus, a Nicolao Piccinino superatus fususque est, quo in proelio quattuor equitum, tria peditum milia, et ingentem machinarum bellicarum vim Florentinus amisit. Lucaque dudum

use for building. From their great number they seem intended for the building of a city; part of them are of such a great bulk that someone unaware that obelisks were brought to Italy from Egypt would not believe that ships could carry them. Each has been inscribed on two sides with numeral letters. From Pliny's evidence we know that some of the numbers indicate the weight of the stone, while others indicate the order in which the pieces were sent by the merchant.

But **[303B]** let me return to the point at which I digressed, the river Auser, which is now called the Serchio. The first town on the right is Ripafratta. At its source in the Apennines is the undistinguished fortified town of Gragnana, and near the bed of the river as it continues as far as you can descend towards the interior, is a valley named Garfagnana, the site of many fortified villages and farmsteads, most of them now in the possession of the Marquis of Ferrara. The most famous towns on the right as the Serchio flows downwards are Castelnuovo and Barga; in the interior the Serchio flows past the former Roman colony of Lucca, about which city Livy writes in book 21: "Hannibal withdrew into Liguria, Sempronius to Luca."

Indeed, I have written in my *Histories* that, when Lucca was held by the Goths, the eunuch Narses besieged it for seven months before he could capture it. This city was the birthplace of Pope Lucius III, and also Pope Alexander II, against whom the Lombards set up as antipope Cadalus of Parma. In about the fiftieth year Paolo, of the noble Lucchese Guinigi family, subdued it, to his detriment. Within thirty years he had acquired enormous reserves of money and begotten sons. But although he and his young sons led their lives in arrogance and seemed fortunate to themselves and their relatives, **[303C]** their fortune suddenly reversed itself and made them an example to many others, that nothing in human affairs is substantial or stable. For they were captured, driven violently from their country, lost their long-amassed fortune, and died in prison.

But in the space of twenty years after the expulsion of the Guinigi, Lucca was troubled by many different wars, and suffered great disasters. The kingdom which surrounded them, the Florentine Republic, nevertheless suffered the same disasters. For in addition to the other slaughters which took place there, their army, led by Guidantonio count of Urbino (I have treated this here and there in my *Histories*), was routed and defeated by Niccolò Piccinino; and in this battle the Florentines lost 4,000 cavalry, 3,000 infantry, and the greatest part of their war machines. For a long time now,

honestis mercatoribus frequentata Ianipetro ornata est Graece et Latine eruditissimo, et Victorini Feltrensis, sui praeceptoris, mores redolente.

Habet item ad dexteram Luca colles, in quibus est castellum Verucula, inde Altus Passus, supra Lumenicus, et ad fluvium Colorum eiusdem nominis oppidum. Cui fluvio item adiacet Pisa oppidum, quod ad annum salutis LXX supra ducentesimum et millesimum Florentini Lucensesque, sicut scribit Leonardus Arretinus, **[303D]** destruxerunt. Et paulo inde abest Bugianum, superiusque est Ugianum. Qua vero Lucensis ager vergit in Florentinum palus, est Bentina, in lacu a Florentinis conclusa, cui supereminet Mons Carolus oppidum. Et ubi is lacus in Arnum exoneratur, Bientina est castellum.

Supremo autem in sinu amplae, quam habet primum Etruria, planitiei, Pistoria est civitas, in cuius agro Catilinae exercitum fuisse superatum, multi ex vetustis scripsere. Ea, sicut Arretino placet, prima fuit Etruriae urbium, quas populus Florentinus tunc primum liber, ad annum salutis duodecies centenum et quinquagesimum, in potestatem redegit. Circumstantque Pistoriam Summanum, Seravalle, Victolinum, et superius Mons Catinus. Circumdant Pistoriam parvo distantes spatio amnes duo, Stella et Umbro, qui secus Carmagnanum delapsi apud monte Lupum oppidum in Arnum exonerantur. Visentiusque amnis deinceps ex Apennino defluens Prati oppidum omnium Etruriae opulentissimi moenia praeterfluit. Supra Pratum est Murlus oppidum, et Marina torrens Calencranum oppidum praeterlabitur.

Ultimusque ad Florentiae moenia Munio habetur amnis. Florentiae urbis inclutae originem gestasque res abunde complexus est in Historia clarissimus Leonardus Arretinus. Quod autem ad nos attinet eius urbis origo refertur in Sullanorum militum, quibus is ager a Sulla assignatus fuit, adventum. **[304E]** Et quia primas illi sedes ad Arni fluenta ceperint, Fluentiam inde primo dictum volunt. Et quidem Plinius, apud quem primum eius loci mentio facta est, Fluentinos dicit profluenti Arno appositos. Venerunt vero hi milites ad annum conditae urbis Romae sexcentesimum et septimum supra sexagesimum, unde initium Florentia habuisse videtur ante Christi dei nostri adventum, annos circiter octogintatres.

Multis ea civitas per Gothorum tempora incommodis agitata est. Nec tamen a Totila aut alio quopiam tunc aut alias umquam destructa fuit. Idque quod de reaedificatione a Carolo Magno facta aliqui sentiunt non probamus,

honorable businessmen have filled Lucca; and it is distinguished by Gian Pietro, a man learned in both Greek and Latin, and imbued with the noble character of his teacher, Vittorino da Feltre.

On the right of Lucca are hills which contain the fortified town of Verrucola, and then Altopascio; above this is Lumenico, and at the river Collodi a town of the same name. Also next to this river lies the town of Pescia, which, according to Leonardo Bruni, the people of Florence and Lucca **[303D]** destroyed in 1270. A little ways from that is Buggiano, and above it is Uzzano. Where the territory of Lucca borders on that of Florence is a swamp, Bientina, in a lake which has been dammed by the Florentines. Above this towers the town of Montecarlo. And where this lake discharges into the Arno river, there is a fortified town, Bientina.

The city of Pistoia lies in the high bend of a wide plain, which is the main one in Tuscany. The army of Catiline was defeated in this territory; many of the ancients have written about it. According to Leonardo Bruni, Pistoia was the foremost of the cities of Tuscany which the Florentine republic, free then for the first time, subjected in about 1250. Encircling Pistoia are Monsummano, Seravalle, Montevettolini, and, higher up, Montecatini. Two rivers flow around Pistoia, not far from each other: the Stella and the Ombrone. They flow down near Carmagnano and debouche into the Arno at the town of Montelupo Fiorentino. Next, the river Bisenzio flows down from the Apennines and past the walls of the town of Prato, wealthiest of all towns in Tuscany. Above Prato is the town of Montemurlo, and the stream Marina flows by the town of Calenzano.

And the final river, the Mugnone, flows near the walls of Florence. The illustrious Leonardo Bruni has written at length in his *Histories* about the origin and achievements of the famous city of Florence. But as far as concerns us: Sulla allocated its territory to his soldiers and its beginnings are traced to their settlement there; **[304E]** and since they first settled at the Arno river, they first named it Fluentia (from the river). Pliny is first to mention Florence; he calls its people Fluentini because they live beside the running water of the Arno. These soldiers came in about the 667th year after the founding of the city of Rome; so Florence appears to have been founded about eighty-three years before the birth of Christ.

This city-state was disturbed by many troubles in the times of the Goths; yet it was not destroyed, not by Totila, nor by anyone else then, nor at any other time. And so I do not agree with the opinion of some writers

cum gesta Caroli ab Alcuino eius praeceptore scripta, tantummodo dicant illum Romam euntem, bis in Florentia dominicum pascha celebrasse. Servata vero est ab ingenti desolationis, quod incurrerat periculo unius civis Farinatae Ubertini virtute, cum Pisanis Senensibusque et aliis Etruscis in conventu apud Emporium habito, Florentiam esse destruendam censentibus, Farinata licet longo postliminio in ipsam patriam reversus, eam se dixit, quam non aedificasset, se vivo ab illis destrui non passurum. Itaque Florentia, acceptis vi et in se populariter traductis Faesulanis, **[304F]** ad annum salutis quartum et vigesimum supra millesimum, plurimum opibus et gloria est aucta. Quo item anno, Henricus primus imperator ecclesiam Sancti Miniatis ad muros Florentiae aedificavit.

Arsit vero Florentia duobus incendiis, parvo in temporis spatio, ad annum salutis sextum et septuagesimum supra undecies centenum. Ex eo fere tempore primum per priores artium et vexilliferum iustitiae, sicut nunc fit gubernari coepit, fuitque inter primos vexilliferos ex nobili gente Strozza unus. Basilica insignis, quae per nostram aetatem curante Philippo Brunalicio nobilissimi ingenii Florentino stupendi operis fornice est ornata, gloriosaeque virgini dicata, anno salutis duodecies centeno et nonagesimoquarto inchoata est, et quarto abinde anno palatium item superbissimum, quod inhabitant priores, aedificari coepit.

Quintoque postmodum anno productum est pomoerium, et moenibus quae nunc exstant urbs est ampliata. Turris vero marmorea inter ceteras orbis campanarias speciosa ad annum inde primum et tricesimum excitata, per quae tempora civitas Florentina duobus ornata est poetis Dante Aldegherio, et Francisco Petrarcha, quorum hic patre Florentino, sed **[304G]** exule apud Arretium natus, et Arquadae inter colles Euganeos mortuus ac sepultus est. Ille Florentinis parentibus Florentiae natus obiit Ravennae patri exul.

Paulo post Florentia Iotum habuit pictorem celeberrimum Apelli aequiparandum. Habuit quoque Accursium iureconsultorum principem, qui ius civile nunc exstans egregie interpretatus est. Famaque est nullo nobis con-

who mentioned its rebuilding by Charlemagne, since in his teacher Alcuin's *Deeds of Charlemagne* it is written only that Charlemagne celebrated Easter Sunday twice in Florence on his way to Rome. The courage of one Florentine citizen, Farinata degli Uberti, saved the city from an enormous risk of devastation. When the peoples of Pisa, Siena, and other Tuscan cities had assembled at Empoli and entered into an agreement to destroy Florence, Farinata returned to his country after a long exile, and said that he would not allow those who had not built the city, to destroy it while he lived. And so, after the people of Fiesole had been taken forcefully and led over to Florence in a popular uprising, **[304F]** in the year 1024, Florence was enhanced by great wealth and glory. In the same year, Emperor Henry I built the church of San Miniato next to the walls of Florence.

But Florence was burned in two fires close together in time in 1176. From about that time, it began to be governed by the Priors of the Guilds and the Standard-Bearer of Justice, as it is now governed. Among the first Standard-Bearers was a man from the noble family of the Strozza. A famous basilica was begun in 1294: dedicated to the glorious Virgin, it was embellished in my times by a dome, a stupendous work overseen by Filippo Brunelleschi, a Florentine of noble talent. Four years later, construction began on a very splendid palace for the Priors.

Five years later the city limits were enlarged, and the city was expanded by the walls which now exist. A marble bell-tower was raised, about thirty-one years after this, which is most beautiful among all the world's bell-towers. And in these times the Florentine Republic has been distinguished by two poets, Dante Alighieri and Francis Petrarch. The latter had a Florentine father, but **[304G]** was born in exile in Arezzo; he died and is buried in Arquà in the Euganean Hills. The former was born in Florence of Florentine parents, but died an exile in Ravenna.

A little after these men, Florence boasted the very famous painter Giotto, who is to be compared with Apelles. She also produced Accursius, the foremost jurisconsult, who is still alive and has contributed outstanding interpretations of civil law. And there is no corroboration of this in any

firmata auctore Claudianum poetam fuisse Florentia oriundum. Colutius vero Salutatus et si prius didicerit, quam Ciceronianae imitatio eloquentiae sui saeculi adolescentibus nota esse coepisset, et eloquens est habitus, et multa scripsit prudentiam magis et doctrinam, quam eloquentiam redolentia. Nicolaus Nicoli per aetatem nostram, et si nihil scripserit et doctus fuit et multis adolescentibus, ut litteris operam darent opem attulit.

Ab his vero plus minus centum annis, qui Francisci Petrarchae mortem, et haec tempora intercedunt mirabili felicitate Florentia opes auxit. Cuius imperio per aetatem nostram Castrum Carum, Mutiliana, Donadula, Cassianum, Porticus, et alia castella in Romandiola et Pisae ac Cortona urbes vetustae ac Burgum ad Sepulcrum, et regio Casentina **[304H]**, in Etruria sunt subactae. Ab ipsis vero centum annis superavit omnia Florentia ornamenta concilium in ea celebratum, in quo quartus Eugenius, pontifex gloriosissimus, orientalis ecclesiae cum occidentali unionem, maximo diu quaesitam impendio celebravit, Ioanne Paleologo imperatori Constantinopolitano et patriarchis, archiepiscopis, episcopisque, ac ingenti doctissimorum nobiliumque totius Graeciae virorum qui interfuerant multitudine Romanae ecclesiae sumptibus in patriam reportatis. Armenii etiam, Aethiopes, Georgiani, et Iacobitae, Libyam, Asiamque incolentes catholicae fidei documenta, in eodem concilio a praedicto pontifice Eugenio acceperunt. Viris etiam nunc Florentia, sicut antea consuevit, omni virtutum laude praestantissimis ornatur, Cosmo imprimis Mediceo, quem omnes totius Europae cives opum effluentia superantem prudentia, humanitas, liberalitas. Et quod nos maxime ad eius laudes incitat, bonarum artium, praesertim historiarum peritia, celebrem reddunt. Cumulantque eius felicitatem Petrus, Ioannes, et Carolus, nati paternae virtutis imitatores. Nec supprimenda sunt maxima, quae Cosmus Florentiae urbi addidit ornamenta. Monasterium celebre Sancti Marci, in quo cum superbae sunt, et ut aiunt insanae exstructiones ceterae; tum maxime bibliotheca alias superat omnes quas nunc habet Italia. Et ad Sancti Laurentii fornices **[305A]** marmoreae columnae, et opus totum summi viri magnificentiam ostendunt. Quid, quod privatae aedes suae recens in Via Lata exstructae, Romanorum olim principum et quidem primariorum operibus comparandae sunt, quin ego ipse, qui Romam meis instauravi scriptis, affirmare non dubito nullius exstare privati aedificii principum in urbe Romana reliquias, quae maiorem illis aedibus prae se ferant operis magnificentiam.

author, but the poet Claudian is supposed to have been born at Florence. Coluccio Salutati, even if he was taught before imitation of Cicero's eloquence had begun to be known to the youth of his times, was also considered eloquent, and wrote many things imbued more with wisdom and learning than with eloquence. Niccolò Niccoli our contemporary, even if he wrote nothing, was learned and helped many young people to give attention to literature.

For the approximately 100 years between Francis Petrarch's death and our times, Florence has increased in wealth and enjoyed marvelous good fortune. In our age she has subjected to her rule: Castrocaro, Modigliana, Dovadola, Casciana, Portici; other fortified towns in the Romagna; and in Tuscany the ancient cities of Pisa and Cortona, and Borgo Sansepolcro, and the region of Casentino **[304H]**. But the council celebrated at Florence surpassed all the city's distinctions of the past hundred years. Here the most glorious Pope Eugenius IV celebrated the long- and dearly-sought union of the western with the eastern church. In addition to the enormous crowd of the most learned and noble men of all Greece, Ioannes Paleologus, the emperor of Constantinople, the patriarchs, archbishops, and bishops were taken back into their country at the church's expense. Also the Armenians, Ethiopians, Georgians and Jacobites, Libyans, and Asians, received from Pope Eugenius at this council lessons of the Catholic faith. Even now, as was her custom in times past, Florence is distinguished by men outstanding in the glory of their virtues: among the first, Cosimo de'Medici, surpassing all the citizens of Europe in the abundance of his wealth; his wisdom, humanity, and generosity make him famous, and his experience in the liberal arts, particularly history (which especially inspires me to sing his praises). Emulating their father's virtue, his sons Piero, Giovanni, and Carlo heap up his happiness. I must not pass over the architectural ornaments which Cosimo has added to the city of Florence: the famous Monastery of St. Mark, with its buildings, splendid and as they say extravagant; then, particularly, the Library, which surpasses all others now standing in Italy. And at the arches of S. Lorenzo **[305A]** marble columns, in fact the entire work, display the magnificence of this very great man. His private residence, recently built on the Via Larga, can be compared with the architectural works of the Roman princes of old, indeed the foremost men among them. In my *Rome restored* I have treated the remains of Roman monuments, and can affirm that none of the remains of the private residences of the princes in the city of Rome display a greater magnificence than that building.

Palla Strozza, clarissimus equestris ordinis Florentinus, opera, studiis philosophiae assidue Patavii impensa exilii incommoda prudentissime consolatur. Angelus Acciaiolus equestris ordinis, non minus clarae gentis suae nobilitatem prudentia, ingenuis moribus et litterarum studiis ornat, quam ab illa decoratur. Andreas Floccus, apostolicus secretarius canonicusque Florentinus, vir optimus eloquentia et edito De Magistratibus opere, ac Ianectus Manectus, litterarum Graecarum Latinarumque peritia atque eloquentia, et Baptista Albertus, nobili et ad multas artes bonas versatili ingenio, patriam exornant. Decorat etiam urbem Florentiam ingenio veterum laudibus respondente Donatellus, Heracleotae Zeusi aequiparandus, ut "vivos," iuxta Virgilii **[305B]** verba, ducat "de marmore vultus."

Secus Florentiam Faesulana urbs vetusta, et multorum scriptis praesertim Sallustii in bello Catilinario et Livii illud idem scribentis bellum libro centesimosecundo celebrata interiit, vel quod supra diximus in Florentiae populum opesque mutavit. Oritur ex montibus Faesulanis, qui ad orientem vergunt solem, Munio torrens, Florentina abluens moenia, secundum cuius alveum sexto ab urbe miliario sacellum est, cui ea ratione inditum Ad Cruces opinor, quod eo in loco sepulta fuerit moles illa cadaverum, quae facta fuit in stupenda strage illa magnae partis ducentorum paene milium ex Radagasii Gothorum regis exercitu apud Faesulas, sicut in Historiis ostendimus interfectorum.

Interque eos montes et Apenninum vallis est amoenissima, et vicis villisque praesertim Mediceorum speciosissimis frequentata, Mugellum sicut consueverat appellata, quae Dinum habuit Mugellanum iureconsultorum superioris saeculi celeberrimum. Eam illabitur dividitque mediam Seva fluvius ex Apennino oriundus. Primumque regionis Mugellanae oppidum est via Bononiensi Scarparia, Iacobo ornata Angeli filio, cuius Graece Latinaeque doctissimi **[305C]** exstat M. Tullii Ciceronis vita ex Plutarcho in Latinitatem luculenter traducta. Deinceps habetur Nicolaium dura Piccinini obsidione cui fortiter restitit nostris in Historiis clarum.

In Sevam defluit Ronta torrens, ad quem Via Faventina, eiusdem nominis est vicus, et sub eo Sancti Laurentii burgus. Quinto ab inde miliario Sevam pariter illabitur Ducaria, a cuius torrente apud Gaudentium Apennini vicum oriundo quicquid magno sinu complectitur Arnus amnis usque ad agri Arretini fines dicitur Casentinum, quam regionem montuosam populo

Palla Strozzi the famous Florentine knight consoles himself wisely in his unfortunate exile in Padua with continual study in philosophy. Agnolo Acciaiuoli, a knight, distinguishes with his upright character and literary studies the nobility of the famous family which gives him distinction. Andrea Fiocchi, the apostolic secretary and canon of Florence, a man of eloquence who published the work *On Magistracies*; Giannozzo Manetti, skilled and eloquent in Greek and Latin literature; Leon Battista Alberti, nobly talented in a variety of liberal arts; all these men adorn their native city. The city of Florence is also graced by Donatello whose talent proves a match for the glory of the ancients, and can be compared with Zeuxis of Heraclea, "drawing," in Virgil's words **[305B]**, "living features out of marble."

Next to Florence is Fiesole, the ancient city of Faesulae, famous from the writings of many authors, especially Sallust in his *War with Catiline*, and Livy, in his hundred and second book. This city perished, or as I said earlier, it transferred to Florence its population and wealth. In the mountains of Fiesole, which face the east, is the source of the stream Mugnone, which flows past the walls of Florence. If you follow its course you come upon a chapel, six miles from the city, called "The Crosses," because, I believe, it holds buried the mass of corpses from the spectacular slaughter near Fiesole of nearly 200,000 men, a great part of the Gothic king Radagasius's army. I have written about it in my *Histories*.

Between these mountains and the Apennines is a very pleasant valley, planted with villages and splendid estates, notably those of the Medici. The valley is called Mugello, and boasts Dino da Mugello, the most famous jurisconsult of the previous century. The river Sieve arises from a source in the Apennines and flows through it, dividing it in two. The first town in the region of Mugello on the road to Bologna is Scarperia, distinguished by Jacopo Angeli da Scarperia, a man very learned in Greek and Latin **[305C]** who translated into excellent Latin Plutarch's *Life of Cicero*. Next comes *Nicolaium*, a town famous in my *Histories* for its brave resistance to the harsh siege of Piccinino.

The stream Ronta flows down into the Sieve, and at this stream is the Via Faventina with a village named after it, and below that Borgo San Lorenzo. Five miles from there, the stream Ducaria flows into the Sieve; it has its source at the village of San Godenzo in the Apennines and from this stream, whatever the Arno river embraces in a great bend right up to the territory of Arezzo is called the Casentino. I have described how this

Florentino proximis temporibus quaesitam fuisse ostendimus. Ubi vero Sena fluvius Arnum illabitur, est castellum moenibus munitum, Pons Ad Sevam dictus.

Florentinam urbem dividit Arnus amnis, pontibus in ea quattuor magni operis iunctus. Sed quantum ad inchoatam attinet Florentini agri descriptionem, secundum Arni fluenta sub Florentia sunt castella, Mons Lupus et Signia quousque navigia admittit Arnus.

Supra Florentiam ad quintumdecimum lapidem, primum est ad Arni fluenta oppidum Incisa cuius oppidi nomen originem habuisse coniector, ab succiso obiice saxeo cursum Arni solito remorari. Indicant **[305D]** namque quernarum trabium stipites maximi, quos defodientes inveniunt agricolae, vallem Arni superiorem, qua nullam habet nunc ager Florentinus vini optimi feraciorem, quantum profluenti Arno apposita planities ambit fuisse palustrem. Et qui XXII Historiarum Livii Patavini in principio attente leget, paludem illam in qua

> Hannibal aeger oculis et verna primum intemperie variante calores frigoraque elephanto, qui unicus superfuerat quo altius ab aqua exstaret, vectus vigiliis, tum et nocturno umore palustrique coeno gravante caput, altero captus est oculo,

hanc fuisse vallem Arni pervidebit. Nam "cum fama esset Flaminium consulem Arretium cum exercitu praevenisse," Hannibal ex hibernis movens, quae in Liguribus habuerat, Arretium contendebat. Sunt autem Livii hac in parte verba, "Cum aliud longius ceterum commodius ostenderetur iter, propiorem viam per paludem petiit, qua fluvius Arnus per eos dies solito magis inundaverat." Et paulo infra, exercitus incommoda et iumentorum hominumque stragem, quae fiebat describens, per praealtas dicit "fluvii et profundas voragines haustos paene duces." Et maxime omnium confecisse vigilias per quattriduum iam et tres noctes tolerata, "cum omnia obtinentibus aquis, nil ubi in sicco fessa sternerent corpora, inveniri posset."

mountainous region was obtained by the Florentine Republic in the most recent times. But where the Sieve river flows into the Arno, there is a town fortified with walls called Pontassieve.

The Arno river divides the city of Florence; and four bridges, of great workmanship, span the Arno here. But to return to the description of Florentine territory which I had begun: following the course of the Arno, below Florence are the fortified towns of Montelupo Fiorentino and Signa. Up to this point, the Arno is navigable.

Above Florence, fifteen miles up the Arno, the first town is Incisa in Val d'Arno. I guess the origin of its name is the fact that rocky obstacles were cut to obstruct the course of the Arno. Large trunks of oak trees which farmers find when they dig deeply **[305D]** indicate that the upper valley of the Arno, as much of the level ground which borders on and surrounds the Arno, used to be a swamp; Florentine territory now has no more fertile vineyard, nor any more productive of the best wines. If you look carefully at the beginning of the twenty-second book of Livy's *Histories*, you will see that he is talking about this valley of the Arno when he writes,

> Hannibal caught some eye infection, the result of the dangerous alternations of heat and cold in the early spring weather; he rode the one surviving elephant, to keep himself as far above the water as he could, but in the end lack of sleep combined with the marsh climate and its nocturnal fog affected his head . . . he lost the sight of one eye.

For "when Hannibal learned of the consul Flaminius' arrival with his army at Arretium," he moved out of his winter camp, which was in Liguria, and hastened to Arretium. These are Livy's words about this episode: "Although he had been informed of a longer but more comfortable route for his march, he decided not to take it; instead, he took the shorter route through country which the Arno had recently flooded to a greater extent than usual." And a little farther on, Livy describes the hardships the army encountered, and the slaughter of pack animals and men which followed: "The leaders were half drowned by the soft mud as they went through deep pits and holes filled by swirling eddies from the river." And they were done in most of all by sleeplessness which they endured for four days and three nights, "when the water overwhelmed everything, and no dry land was to be found where they could lay down their tired bodies."

Iter igitur quod "longius" **[306E]** Arretium ab Liguribus ducturo offendebatur per Lucensem, Pisanum, Volaterranum, et eius quae nunc est Sena agros esse oportuisset, quod certe nullus regionis peritus dubitat fuisse "commodius," quam cum propiorem ingressus ad Arni fluenta, ubi nunc est Florentia venit. Et inde amnis Arni alveum apud nunc Incisam, vel paulo supra est ingressus, tamdiuquam per paludem, qua fluvius Arnus per eos dies solito magis inundaverat est profectus, quousque siccum ubi consisteret primum in Arretino inveniret.

Eam vero inundationem, easque paludes non fuisse, sicut aliqui volunt in ea planitie, quam Pratum Signiamque et Florentiam intercedere videmus. Ea constat ratione quod regionem illam dicit Livius, in qua Hannibal primum in sicco constiterit, imprimis Italiae fertilem tunc fuisse Etrusci campi, qui Faesulas inter Arretiumque iaceret. Subiungitque Livius:

> Quoque pronior esset in vitia sua consul irritare eum atque agitare Poenus coepit, et laeva relicto hoste Faesulas petens, Etruriae agros praedatum profectus, quantum maximam vastationem potest caedibus incendiisque consuli procul ostendit.

Qui itaque "relicto hoste" apud Arretium agente ad laevam Faesulas petiit vallem **[306F]** Arni superiorem profecto attigerat, atque ut in sicco consisteret, ea post tergum relicta ulterius processerat.

Sed palus illa quo obduruerit modo, ut aratrum pateretur, cum aliquando scire cupiverimus, confragosas saxis apud Incisam oppidum Arni ripas et saxorum fragmenta medio adhuc alveo haerentia cernentes, adapertum fuisse tenemus humano ingenio tumentem saxo, et repagulum aquae facientem fluminis fundum, labentibusque postea pro iusto amnis cursu aquis, quae residere et superiori in parte quaqua versum stagnare fuerant consuetae, exsiccatum limi umorem, quod alibi saepe contingit campos feracissimos reliquisse.

Habet ea vallis ad dexteram Arni post Incisam Fichinum, quod oppidum Arretinus scribit a comite Guidone Novello exulibusque Florentinis occu-

The "longer route" through the territory of Luca, Pisa, Volaterrae, and what is now Siena, which **[306E]** presented itself to him as he prepared to lead his army from Liguria to Arretium, ought to have been more comfortable, which no one acquainted with that region would dispute, than the shorter route by which he advanced to the Arno river and came to where Florence now is. And from there he progressed along the channel of the river Arno where the town of Incisa now lies, or a little above it. And he set forth through the swamp "which the Arno had recently flooded to a greater extent than usual" until he first found dry land where he could take a stand, in the Arretine territory.

But it is clear to me that this flooding and those swamps were not, as some assert, on that level ground which lies between Prato and Signa and Florence. I say this because Livy says that the region where Hannibal first set foot on dry land was "among the most productive in Italy, the Etruscan plain lying at that time between Faesulae and Arretium." And Livy adds,

> In order to make Flaminius more inclined to display his natural defects of character, Hannibal prepared to provoke him and rouse him to action; leaving the Roman camp on his left he made for Faesulae, harrying and devastating Etruscan territory with the intention of showing to Flaminius from a distance how much damage fire and sword could inflict.

And so he left the enemy behind at Arretium and made for Faesulae on the left and in this way quickly reached the upper valley **[306F]** of the Arno. And in order to reach dry land, he turned his back on Faesulae and proceeded farther.

I once wanted to know how the swampland there had hardened into arable land. I saw that the banks of the Arno at Incisa in Val d'Arno were rough with boulders, and I saw that pieces of rock are to this day stuck in the middle of the river bed. I conclude that it was swollen with rock and opened up by human ingenuity, a restraint acting to create a new bottom for the river. The water flowed along there instead of in the true course of the river. The water had become accustomed to settle and overflow on the upper level, and the moisture in the mud had dried up. In other places this process has often produced very fertile fields.

After Incisa, on the right bank of the Arno in this valley lies the town of Figline. Leonardo Bruni writes that Count Guido Novello and the Florentine

patum pace, per quam exules in Florentiam reducti sunt, facta, fuisse a populo Florentino destructum. Habet quoque ea vallis Sanctum Ioannem Monte Vargum et Quaratam. Ad sinistram vero Castrum Franchum, Terram Novam, Laterinam, Pontenanam, quorum Sanctum Ioannem et Castrum Franchum populus Florentinus ducentesimo et nonagesimosexto supra **[306G]** millesimum salutis anno aedificavit; et Terram Novam, Poggi viri eloquentissimi et aliquot editis operibus clari, patriam, Guido Petramalensis, Arretinus episcopus, muro quem nunc habet, cinxit.

In montibusque altissimis, qui ad sinistram Arnum intercedunt, est Vallis Umbrosae monasterium. Sunt etiam aliquot regionis de qua diximus Casentinae oppida, quorum primaria habentur Romena burgus et Puppium a comitibus dudum habitata cognomine Guidis, quos proximis temporibus pepulit populus Florentinus. Ad alteram vero Arni ripam et sub ipsius fonte est Porclanum, inferius Stia, post Pratum vetus, infra quod oppidum Arnus Corsolana augetur torrente secus Bibienam oppidum, ut in montibus, nobile delabente. Augetur etiam Larchiano torrente, qui ad dexteram habet Gellum et Choretium, parva oppida. Qua etiam Arnus se Arretium versus incurvat est Castrum Novum.

Si agrum Florentinum Arretino Senensi, ac Pisano et Volaterrano conterminum describere volumus, ad proximam vallem versus meridionalem plagam transeundum est a Pesa fluvio appellatam, cui fluvio ad sinistram proxima sunt ad ostium, quo exoneratur in **[306H]** Arnum Mons Lupus, supra Colina. Supra ipso sub fonte Sambuca, ad dexteram Mons Iustus, Linarium, Sanctus Donatus. Aliusque sequitur fluvius Elsa appellatus, cui sunt ad sinistram Emporium, Mons Rapolus, Mons Partolus, Barberinum, Castellina, et ad dexteram Saminiatum, Cambassium, Florentinum, Certaldum, Ioannis Boccatii, vulgaris potius quam Latinae eloquentiae fama clari, patria, et ad fontem Casulum. Augetur vero Elsa amnis torrente uno, qui apud Staggiam oppidum delapsus, fertur ad Bonicium, nobile oppidum. Et in ea insula, quam Elsa fluvius torrensque praedictus efficiunt, Collis et Geminianum sunt oppida, paucis Etruriae oppidis secunda. Est etiam Elsam inter et proximum, qui Arnum illabitur torrentem, Mons Topulus oppidum.

Sequiturque Era fluvius, cui hinc est Pons ad Eram, oppidum proelio clarum, in quo cum Pisani Lucenses Florentinorum socios fudissent, super-

exiles occupied it. After the conclusion of the peace which enabled the exiles to return to Florence, it was destroyed by the people of Florence. This valley also contains S. Giovanni, Montevarchi, and Quarata. On the left are Castelfranco di Sopra, Terranuova, Laterina, and Pontignana. Among these towns, S. Giovanni and Castelfranco were built by the people of Florence **[306G]** in 1296. As for Terranuova, it is the birthplace of Poggio Bracciolini, a very eloquent speaker, famous for several works. Bishop Guido Tarlati di Pietramala gave it the walls which still gird it.

In the high mountains which border on the left bank of the Arno is the monastery of Vallombrosa. There are also in the region of Casentino some towns I have already mentioned; and considered the foremost are the town of Castel di Romena, Borgo, and Poppi; a short time ago the counts named Guidi lived here. In the ensuing times, the people of Florence drove them out. But on the Arno's other bank and below its source is Porciano; below this is Stia, and then Pratovecchio. Below this town, the stream Corsolona flows into the Arno beside the noble town of Bibbiena as it flows down in the mountains. The stream Larchiano also flows into it. On the right of this stream are the small towns Gello Biscardo and Cerreto. Following the curve of the Arno towards Arezzo we find Castelnuovo.

If I wish to describe the Florentine land bordering upon Arezzo, Siena, Pisa, and Volterra, I must cross over to the next valley, its southern zone, which is named after the Pesa river. On the left bank of this river, at its mouth where it debouches into **[306H]** the Arno, the nearest towns are Montelupo and, above that, Collina. Above this, below the river's source, is Sambuca; on the right are Monte San Giusto, Linari, and San Donato. There follows another river named the Elsa. On its left are Empoli, Monterappoli, Montespertoli, Barberino Val d'Elsa, Castellina; and, on the right, San Miniato, Gambassi, Castel Fiorentino, and Certaldo; this latter is the birthplace of Giovanni Boccaccio, famous for his eloquence in the vernacular tongue rather than in Latin. At the river's source is Casole d'Elsa. One stream flows into the Elsa; this stream glides down at the town of Staggia, and descends to the noble town of Poggibonsi. On an island created by the river Elsa and the stream I mentioned, are the towns of Colle di Val d'Elsa and San Gimignano, second to few in Tuscany. The town of Montopoli also lies between the Elsa and the next stream to flow into the Arno.

There follows the river Era; the town of Pontedera, next to it on this side, is famous for the battle in which the people of Pisa routed those of

veniens Florentinorum exercitus fortuna proelii conversa Pisanos fudit, ex quibus ad tria milia sunt caesi; et superius est Petriolum. Inde Calcinaria, proximoque torrenti in Arnum defluenti, hinc Pons Sachi oppidulum, inde est Balneum Aquarum, in quibus solis calentibus a sulphure aquis ranas gigni Plinius dicit. Ea in regione Pisani agri castella sunt alia Volaterranis contermina.

Superiusque arduis in **[307A]** montibus Volaterra, de qua Livius in decimo: "Scipioni hostes Etrusci ad Volaterras structo agmine occurrunt. Pugnatum maiore parte diei, magna utrimque caede, nox incertis qua data victoria esset, intervenit." Fuit Volaterra Persio satirico cive ornata, nunc Casparis nostri patria qui, Graecas Latinasque litteras edoctus, celeberrimi Graecorum cardinalis Niceni Bissarionis epistolarum est scriba. Vetusta est haec civitas, quam simul cum Arretio et Clusio a Tyrrhenis ante bellum Troianum fuisse conditam, Leonardus Arretinus in Polybio edoctus affirmat. Nosque supra docuimus inter capita Etruriae numeratum fuisse. Livius bellum civile Marii et Sullae describens libro LXXXVIII dicit, "Volaterras quod oppidum adhuc in armis erat, in deditionem accepit." Auctorque est Plinius in calidis Volaterranorum aquis haud procul a mari sitis pisces gigni.

Ea urbe in hunc maxime modum potiti sunt Florentini, ad annum salutis quinquagesimum et ducentesimum supra millesimum. Cum Volaterrani a Florentinis proelio, quod ad montis, in quo sita est urbs, radices committebatur, superati in urbem confugere eniterentur, insecutus eos miles Florentinus **[307B]** victor pari impetu cum victo ingressus urbem cepit.

Ab agri Volaterrani finibus regio incipit maritimae orae Etrusci pelagi, quam descripsimus, adiacens, quae vastissima et populis pro ambitu infrequens Senensi populo subdita est. In qua sunt praeter superius enumerata, Massa civitas, Mallianum, Paganicum. Post, ad sinistram, Campagnaticum, arduo in colle situm, vinis ceterisque frugibus feracissimum, Petrioli, et alia

Lucca, allies of the Florentines, and the army of the Florentines came and reversed the battle's fortune by routing the Pisans, slaughtering close to 3,000 of them. Above this is Peccioli, and then Calcinaia. On this side of the next stream which flows into the Arno is the little town of Ponsacco. After that comes Casciana Terme, the only waters, Pliny says, which produce frogs due to their heating by the sun. In this region of Pisan territory are other fortified towns bordering on the territory of Volterra.

And higher up, in **[307A]** steep mountains, is Volaterrae itself. Livy writes about it in his tenth book: "The Etruscan enemy drew up their line of battle and came to meet Scipio at Volterra. They fought for the greater part of the day, and there was great slaughter on each side. When night put an end to the fighting, it was not clear which side had won." Volterra is distinguished as the birthplace of Persius the satirist, and now as the home town of my friend Gaspare, learned in Greek and Latin literature, the secretary of the famous Greek cardinal of Nicaea, Bessarion. This city is ancient; Leonardo Bruni, an expert on Polybius, corroborates the story of its foundation by the Tyrrheni before the Trojan War, at the same time as Arretium and Clusium. And I have previously shown that it was numbered among the capital cities of Etruria. Livy, describing the civil war of Marius and Sulla, says in book 88 "Volaterrae was still in arms and he accepted its surrender." And Pliny asserts that fish are born in the warm waters of Volaterrae, not far from the sea.

The Florentines gained possession of Volterra in the following way in the year 1250: the Volterrans had been conquered by the Florentines in a battle at the foot of the mountain where the city is located, and were struggling to take refuge in their city. The victorious Florentine soldiers **[307B]** pursued them and gained entrance to the city in the same movement as the vanquished and captured it.

At the borders of Volterran land begins the area adjacent to the seashore of the Tyrrhenian Sea which I have already described. This land is very vast and relatively sparsely inhabited, and has been subdued by the people of Siena. Here are located, in addition to the towns I have mentioned above, the city of Massa Marittima; Magliano; and Paganico. After them on the left comes Campagnatico, on a high hill, very fertile in vines and other crops; and Petrioli and other bathing places. I note that many of the baths in Sie-

balnea. Nam multa quae nunc etiam frequentantur agri Senensis balnea olim fuisse grata videmus. Martialis coquus poeta ad Oppianum:

> Etruscis nisi tremulus laveris,
> illotus morieris, Oppiane.

Et ad dexteram in montibus Mons Altinus.

Ea regio maritima superiori in parte vestigia habet urbis Rusellanae, quam diximus inter capita Etruriae numeratam esse, de qua Livius in decimo:

> M. Valerius Maximus dictator castra in agrum Rusellanum promovit. Eo et Etrusci hostes secuti, ubi cum forte quodam loco male densatus agger, pondere superstantium in fossam procubuisset, atque eo cum deos pandere viam fugae conclamassent, plures inermes quam armati evasere. Hoc proelio fractae iterum **[307C]** Etruscorum vires, et pacto annuo stipendio et duum mensium frumento indutiae biennii datae.

Et infra: "In Rusellanum agrum exercitus ductus. Ibi non agri tantum vastati, sed oppidum etiam oppugnatum, capta amplius duo milia hominum, minus duum milium circa muros caesa." Et inferius: "Tres validissimae urbes Etruriae, Rusellae, Perusia, Arretium pacem petiere." Adiacetque Rusellarum loco balneum cognomine Rusellarum.

Sena est interius urbium Etruriae viribus opibusque nunc secunda, quae et ipsa inter novas numerari potest, cum nullis in veterum monumentis reperiatur. Suntque qui affirmant Carolum, cui Malleo fuit cognomentum, eam condidisse. Et Caroli aetatem plus minus sexcentesimo et septuagesimo ab hinc anno abfuisse constat. Sed nuper Venetiis in Sancti Georgii de Alga celebri monasterio, quod gloriosus pontifex Eugenius relicto primum saeculo propria aedificavit paternae hereditatis pecunia, invenimus in libro litteris scripto pervetustis Ioannem Romanum pontificem nominis ordine duodevicesimum acceptis de **[307D]** Perusina, Clusiensi, Arretina, Faesulana, Florentina, et Volaterrana dioecesibus sex plebatibus civitatem hanc aedificasse, quae ab ipso sex plebatuum numero Sena fuerit appellata.

nese territory which are crowded even now were popular also with the ancients. For example, the poet Martial the cook wrote to Oppianus,

> If you do not bathe in the warm baths of Etruria,
> you will die unbathed, Oppianus.

And on the right in the mountains is Montalcino.

This area on the coast contains, in its higher part, the traces of the city of Rusellae; I mentioned this as one of the capital cities of Etruria. Livy writes of it in book 10,

> The dictator M. Valerius Maximus moved his camp into the territory of Rusellae. And there the Etruscan enemy followed him. As it happened, in one place the rampart had not been sufficiently pressed down, so that the weight of those standing on it caused it to collapse into the ditch. They shouted that the gods had, by this accident, opened up a way of flight for them. But more unarmed men escaped than those with arms. In this battle **[307C]** the power of the Etruscans was broken for the second time. After they agreed to supply a year's pay for the army and a two months' supply of grain, they were given a two-years' peace.

And below, "The army moved on to the territory of Rusellae, where not only were the fields laid waste but the town attacked as well. More than 2,000 were taken prisoner, but fewer than that number were killed fighting around the walls." And later, "Three very powerful cities, the principal ones in Etruria-Rusellae, Perusia and Arretium-asked for peace." Next to the site of Rusellae is the site of Balneum Rusellarum.

Siena is farther inland. It is now inferior in strength and wealth to the cities of Etruria and can be counted among the new ones, since one can find no mention of it in the ancient records. There are writers who assert that it was founded by Charles Martel, and it is established that he lived 670 years ago, more or less. But recently I found in Venice, in the famous monastery of S. Giorgio in Alga (which the glorious Pope Eugenius built with inherited money, upon first leaving secular life behind), a book written in ancient letters saying that Pope John XVIII built this city, when the six diocesan parishes had contributed revenues: **[307D]** Perugia, Chiusi, Arezzo, Fiesole, Florence, and Volterra; and it was called Sena after the number six, the number of parishes.

Habuit ea civitas tertium Alexandrum pontificem Romanum, qui a Federico Barbarosso agitatus, quattuor adversa se erectos in idola adulterinos pontifices superavit. Magno autem decori Senarum urbi fuit celebratum in ea concilium, in quo Gerardus Florentinus episcopus in secundum Nicolaum pontificem Romanum creatus, constitutionem fecit, quae in Decretis patrum exstat, distinctione tertia et vigesima, pontifices Romanos eligendi cardinalium collegio, et nemini ulterius ius esse. Cui concilio centum et triginta episcopi interfuere.

Proelio etiam felicissime gesto, ornati fuerunt Senenses. Nam cum Florentini Altinatibus foederatis opem laturi ad Arbiam fluvium, quarto a Senis miliario Via Arretina distantem consedissent, Senenses auxiliaribus copiis Manfredi regis exulibusque Florentinis immixti, facta eruptione Florentinum exercitum fuderunt. Occisique sunt Florentini tres mille, capti milia quattuor, et curru qui ex more vexilla deferebat cum ipsis vexillis Senas relato, tantus Florentinos pavor incessit, ut urbe propemodum deserta meliores quique pars Bononiam, pars Lucam commigrarint, exulesque in patriam sunt reversi.

Obiit proximo tempore Ugo Senensis, medicus et philosophus, **[308E]** ceteris sui saeculi post functum vita Iacobum Forliviensem doctior clariorque habitus. Habuit etiam nuperrime Sena illustrans sidus Sanctum Bernardinum, cuius reliquiae apud Aquilam urbem miraculis per singulas dies multiplicatis coruscant. Quamquam nescio quae maiora viri unius dici aut scribi possint miracula operibus, quae per triginta annos in religione fecit, qui eloquentissimus tam vehemens, tamque efficax divinorum eloquiorum suasor fuit, ut omni in Italia mirabilem fecerit animorum a vitiis ad virtutes commutationem. Primusque omnium ordinem beati Francisci ad eam, quae nunc tantopere viget observantiam regulae perduxerit. Quo in divino opere eum summis adiuvit conatibus, quartus Eugenius pontifex omni in gerendo pontificatus munere, sed imprimis augenda conservandaque religione praestantissimus. Nuncque Sena Silvio Aenea poesis primum laurea, post episcopali mitra redimito Franciscoque Patricio studiis et eloquentiae deditissimo, viris quoque plurimis iurium et philosophiae doctrina excultis ornatur.

This city gave birth to Pope Alexander III, who was harassed by Frederick Barbarossa and defeated four antipopes who had been raised against him into idolatry. Moreover, Siena gained great distinction because of a famous council held there, in which Gerard, bishop of Florence, elected pope with the name of Nicholas II, promulgated a decree which exists in the twenty-third distinction in the decrees of the church: that election of the popes would be by the college of cardinals and no one else had the right. 130 bishops took part in this council.

Siena was also distinguished by a battle conducted with great fortune. For when the Florentines were preparing to bring aid to their allies, the people of Montalcino, and had taken a stand at the river Arbia, four miles from Siena on the Via Arretina, the Sienese forces, aided by the combined forces of King Manfred and Florentine exiles, burst forth and routed the Florentine army. 3,000 Florentines were killed, and 4,000 captured. The *carroccio*, which used to carry the standards, along with the standards themselves, was taken back to Siena. A great fear seized the Florentines, and the better people migrated from the nearly deserted city, some to Bologna, some to Lucca. The exiled Florentines returned to their city.

In recent times, the doctor and philosopher Ugo of Siena has died. **[308E]** After the death of Giacomo della Torre da Forlì, he was considered more learned and more famous than other men of his age. Still more recently, Siena was illuminated by the star of San Bernardino; his remains cast on their resting-place, the city of Aquila, the glittering light of miracles compounded daily. I do not know, however, what greater miracles can be attributed to one man than the works which he performed through the thirty years of his religious life. So vigorous and powerful an advocate of divine eloquence was he, that throughout Italy he miraculously converted souls from vice to virtue. He first led the order of St. Francis to the observance of that Rule which now flourishes so vigorously. In this divine work he was helped with the greatest efforts of Pope Eugenius IV, most outstanding in managing every duty of his pontificate, but particularly in advancing and preserving the Christian faith. And now Siena is further distinguished by two men: Aeneas Silvius Piccolomini, who was first wreathed in triumph for poetry and later with the bishop's mitre; and Francesco Patrizi, dedicated to intellectual and rhetorical pursuits; as well as many men also cultivated in law and philosophy.

Umbronem Senensis agri fluvium inter et paludem Clanam, sive fluvium Paliam, quae ea palus efficit, multa **[308F]** sunt montana ac campestria oppida, quae nullo, ut in superioribus factum est, ordine describi possunt. Inestque Clusium, vetustissima urbs, quam Plinius Carmon olim nominatam fuisse dicit. Fuit vero inter capita Etruriae primaria olim nominata, quam Gallorum Senonum bella et Porsennae regis sui historia imprimis claram reddunt. Ea paene derelicta nunc urbi Senae subiecta est. Nec aliqualiter dubitamus, quin populorum ceterarumque rerum reliquis interiturae, olim Clusium et Rusellae urbem Senam a principio dum conderetur, auxerint. Refert ex M. Varrone Plinius Porsennam regem exstruxisse sibi apud Clusium monumentum, in quo mirabili opere labyrinthus fuit, cuius nullae Plinii temporibus exstabant reliquiae. Adiacent vero civitatis ipsis ruinae episcopo etiam nunc ornata palustri fluvio Clanae a Plinio, sicut etiam nunc fit, dicto.

Ad superioremque eius partem Senas versus Politianum est, nobile oppidum Florentinis subditum, amoenis in collibus situm. Post Turria, dehinc Lucinianum. Interius sunt Sanctus Quiricus, Corsignanum, Chiancanum, et, arduo in monte, Radicofanum. Estque ultimum ea in parte patrimonii beato Petro et Romanae ecclesiae **[308G]** a Mathildi comitissa dati castellum. Deinceps ultra Clusium Sarthianum est oppidum, Alberto Minorita divinorum dogmatum praedicatore insigni ornatissimum, et post Cetona.

Fecit agrorum Florentini et Senensis describendorum necessitas, ut illis conterminam urbem Arretium distulerimus. Ea civitas vetustissima inter primaria Etruriae capita annumerata est. Nam Livius libro X dicit legatos ad consulem venisse ex Arretio, Cortona, et Perusia, quae tunc principes civitatum Etruriae erant. Innuit vero Plinius Arretium in duas urbes fuisse divisam. Nam scribit "Arretini veteres, Arretini novi." Causam huius eam videmus fuisse, de qua principio "Etruriae" diximus: cum Hannibale Italiam premente Etrusci ducibus Arretinis in rebellionem proclives viderentur, sicut in Livio habetur XVII, "C. Terentius Varro obsides ab Arretinis senatorum filios accepit CXX. Romani enim tumultum in Etruria ab ipsis oriri verebantur. Et cum claves ac seras novas portis imposuisset in Apuliam rediit."

Between the Ombrone, the river in the Sienese territory, and the swamp Chiana or the river Paglia which this swamp creates, there are many towns, **[308F]** in the mountains or in the plains, which I cannot describe in any order as I have described the towns I previously mentioned. In this area is the very ancient city of Chiusi, which according to Pliny was formerly named Carmon. In fact, it was once numbered among the most important capitals of Etruria, which I named above; and was particularly famous in history for the wars with the Galli Senones and with its king Porsenna. The city is now almost abandoned and has been made subject to Siena. Nor do I have any doubt that formerly Chiusi and Rusellae, which were going to perish, increased the population of Siena with their people and other things, while Siena was being founded. Pliny, drawing on Varro, relates that King Porsenna had built for himself at Clusium a monument which included a marvelous labyrinth. In Pliny's time, nothing remained of it. The ruins of the city itself, even now distinguished by a bishop, lie near the swampy river Chiana, so called by Pliny just as it is now.

On the Chiana's upper reaches, towards Siena, is located the noble town Montepulciano, subject to Florence. After it comes Torrita da Siena, and from there Lucignano. Farther inland are S. Quirico, Corsignano, Chianciano, and, on a lofty mountain, Radicofani, the last fortified town in that part of the patrimony of St. Peter given to the Church **[308G]** by Countess Matilda. Then beyond Chiusi is the town of Sarteano, most illustrious because of Alberto Minorita, the famous preacher of divine teachings. After this comes Cetona.

The task of describing the territories of Florence and Siena has made it necessary for me to put off my description of the neighboring city of Arezzo. This very ancient city was numbered among the principal Etruscan capitals. For, as Livy tells us in book 10, envoys came to the consul from Arretium, Cortona, and Perusia, which were at that time the principal cities of Etruria. In fact, Pliny hints that Arretium had been divided into two cities, for he writes "the ancient Arretines" and "the modern Arretines." I see that the reason for this was, as I stated at the beginning of my chapter on Tuscany, that when Hannibal was threatening Italy the Etruscans seemed ready to revolt, and the ringleaders were from Arretium. Livy says in book 17, "C. Terentius Varro took as hostages 120 children of the senatorial class from Arretium. For the Romans were afraid that they were stirring an uprising in Etruria. And after he had placed new keys and bars on the gates, he returned

Postmodum bello Marsico sive sociali, cum Etrusci sese Marsis et Picentibus furoris socios adiunxisset, L. Sulla, qui ei bello finem imposuit, in Faesulanos Arretinosque desaevit, adeo **[308H]** ut Arretio civibus proscriptis exinanito, novam postea coloniam superinduxerit, unde novi et veteres fuerunt Arretini.

Dicere enim solitus fuit Leonardus Arretinus se vidisse Arretii in ecclesia Sanctae Mariae ad Gradum lapidem litteras incisum vetustissimas, inscriptumque decretum Arretinorum veterum. Aucti tamen postea sunt opibus Arretini, quos Livius in bello secundo Punico dicit iuvisse classem mirabili illa celeritate ab Africano paratam, multis variisque rebus construendis navibus, et alendo milite opportunis.

Viros Arretium habuit praestantissimos. Exstat namque in Macrobii Saturnalibus divi Augusti epistola, per quam affirmat Maecenatem suum fuisse Arretii oriundum. Et Horatium videmus dicere Maecenatem ipsum genus ab Etruscis regibus duxisse. Cornelius vero Nepos in Attici Pomponii vita, quod ad Arretii dignitatem facit, Atticum ipsum dicit praedium in Arretino possedisse, quod Caecilianum sit appellatum. Remotioribus postea temporibus, Arretium ad annos salutis millesimum et decimumoctavum Guidone ornatum fuit celebri musico, et anno inde ducentesimo alterum Guidonem, episcopum ex Petramalensi familia habuit civem et dominum, qui urbem ipsam muro cinxit, quem nunc habet. Burgum quoque Sancti Sepulcri, Civitatem Castelli, Castilionem, Arretium, Terram Novam vallis Arni, et Civitellam **[309A]** nunc ea de causa episcopi appellatam moenibus cingi communirique curavit. Insuper vias, quae ad omnes portarum Arretii exitus nunc cernuntur dirigi, dilatari, et ubi oportere visum est sterni, aut pontibus iungi fecit. Quin etiam eius fuit opus recta et spatiosa via, in qua ab Angulario ad Burgum Ad Sepulcrum ducente Nicolaum Piccininum ab ecclesiae copiis superatum videmus.

Per aetatem quoque nostram eloquentissimo ac clarissimo Leonardo Arretino Caroloque Graecis et Latinis litteris eruditissimo, nunc populi Florentini cancellario, et Benedicto ac Francisco fratribus iureconsultissimis cognomine Accoltis, quorum Franciscus non minus bonas artes, et oratoriam ac omnem historiam, quam leges excellenter edoctus est; et Ioanne Tortel-

to Apulia." Later, in the Marsic or Social War, when the Etruscans had attached to themselves as allies the Marsi and Picenes, Lucius Sulla, who brought this war to a close, exacted such a toll on the people of Faesulae and Arretium that **[308H]** he emptied Arretium of its citizens by his proscriptions, and later imposed on the city a new colony. And so we can speak of "new" and "old" Arretines.

Leonardo Bruni used to say that he had seen at Arezzo in the church of S. Maria in Gradi a stone inscribed with very old letters, and the inscription was a decree of the ancient Arretines. But afterwards the Arretines' wealth increased, and Livy, in his narration of the Second Punic War, says that they helped Scipio when he was preparing his fleet with amazing speed for Africa. According to Livy, the Arretines provided many different materials for the ships' construction, and for the support of the soldiers.

Arezzo has produced outstanding men. For example, there exists in Macrobius' *Saturnalia* a letter of the deified Augustus, asserting that his friend Maecenas was born in Arretium. And we see that Horace says that Maecenas himself was even descended from Etruscan kings. In Cornelius Nepos' *Life of Atticus* there is a statement which adds honor to Arretium, namely that Atticus himself owned an estate which was called Caecilianum in Arretine territory. A long time after that, Arezzo was distinguished around 1018 by the famous musician Guido. And two hundred years later, another Guido, the bishop, of the Pietramala family, was citizen and lord of Arezzo: he surrounded the city with its present wall. He also provided for the fortified walls of Borgo Sansepolcro, Città di Castello, Castiglion Aretino, Terranuova Valdarno, and Civitella del Vescovo **[309A]** (named after him for this reason). In addition, he caused the roads to be widened, which are now seen leading to all the gates of Arezzo; and where it seemed necessary he had roads paved, or extended with bridges. He even made the straight and spacious road where, on its way from Anghiari to Borgo San Sepolcro, we see Niccolò Piccinino was defeated by the papal troops.

And in our times, too, the city of Arezzo has been distinguished by the eloquent and famous Leonardo Bruni; and by Carlo Marsuppini, learned in Greek and Latin literature, who is now the chancellor of Florence; and by the Accolti brothers, Benedetto and Francesco, legal experts, Francesco no less learned in the liberal arts and rhetoric and all of history. Arezzo also

lio Romani pontificis subdiacono et cubiculario Graecis ac Latinis litteris, ac singulari humanitate praedito, cuius praeclarum De Orthographia opus verba edocet selecta, quibus e Graecia sumptis Latine utimur, Arretina urbs decorata est. Nec indignum ducent, quod referemus tam multi praestantes Arretini, Plinium scripsisse Arretinos in Italia fictilium vasorum nobilitatem obtinuisse, quod quidem Martialis affirmat **[309B]** libro primo:

> Sic Arretinae violant cristallina testae.

Cortona sequitur, urbium Etruriae vetustissima, quam Pelasgi condidere, hisque pulsis possedere Tyrrheni. Expugnaverunt vero eam ac moenibus privaverunt Arretini, a quibus diu possessa fuit. Per aetatem vero nostram Ladislaus rex Neapolitanus ipsam vendidit Florentinis, in quorum subiectione perseverat. Quam Iacobus Perusinus episcopus civis suus nunc plurimum exornat. Ad eius urbis agri proximos fines lacus est Trasumenus, qui dicitur Perusinus acceptae per Flaminium consulem ab Hannibale cladis memoria notissimus. Isque lacus in circuitu oppidis ornatur, et castellis Malborghetto ad eam partem, quae in Cortonam vergit, Castilione, Clusino, et Panicali Cla*n*as versus. Deinceps Monte Pontighino, et qua Perusium a Florentina petitur, Passignano. Trasumenumque et Cla*n*as inter oppidum est castellum Plebis. Sunt etiam in lacu tres insulae habitatae.

Succedit ordine Perusia urbs vetustissima capitum et ipsa Etruriae, sicut saepe supra diximus, olim primaria, quam Iustinus ab Achaeis conditam fuisse dicit. Estque haec sola inter omnes Italiae urbes felicitatem nacta penitus inauditam, quod eandem **[309C]** paene status, et rerum conditionem, quam ante conditam urbem Romam, et postmodum Roma sub regibus, consulibus, et imperatoribus, et tyrannis agente habuit, nunc retinet. Passa est tamen varias, sed tolerandas agitationes. Nam Livius in nono:

> Eodem anno cum reliquiis Etruscorum ad Perusiam, quae et ipsa indutiarum fidem ruperat Fabius consul nec dubia, nec difficili victoria dimicans ipsum oppidum, cum ad moenia accessit, cepisset, ni legati dedentes urbem exissent.

boasts Giovanni Tortelli, subdeacon and chamberlain of the pope, learned in Greek and Latin literature, and an extraordinarily humane man. His famous work *De Orthographia* explains which words we use in Latin which come from the Greek. These many outstanding citizens of Arezzo will not find it inappropriate if I mention that Pliny wrote that the Arretines held the primacy in Italy for pottery vases; in fact Martial corroborates **[309B]** this in his first book:

> In the same way Arretine vases degrade crystal ones.

Next is Cortona, oldest of the cities of Etruria, founded by the Pelasgians. When the Tyrrhenians drove them out, they took possession of it. But the Arretines attacked the city and destroyed its walls, and have held it for a long time. In fact, in my time King Ladislaus of Naples sold Cortona to the Florentines, and it remains in their possession. Now its citizen the bishop Jacopo greatly honors the city. At the border of the territory of Cortona lies Lake Trasimene, called Lago di Perugia, most famous for Hannibal's slaughter of the consul Flaminius' army. And this lake is encircled by towns and fortified villages, by Borghetto on the side towards Cortona, by Castiglione del Lago, and Panicale on the side towards the Chiana. Then comes *Mt. Pontighinus*, and, on the way from Florence to Perugia, Passignano sul Trasimeno. Between Lake Trasimene and the Chiana is the town Città della Pieve. Also in this lake are three inhabited islands.

There follows the city of Perugia, the most ancient of the capitals and, as I have reiterated above, the foremost city of Etruria. Justin says that it was founded by the Achaeans. It is the only city among all of Italy to have found the unheard-of happiness of now possessing nearly **[309C]** the same status, and terms, which it had before the foundation of Rome, and afterwards when Rome was governed by kings, consuls, emperors, and tyrants. But it has endured various, although bearable, troubles. Indeed, Livy says in book 9:

> In the same year, the consul Fabius fought a battle with the remnants of the Etruscan armies near Perusia, one of the cities which had broken the terms of the peace. From the beginning the battle went his way and he had an easy victory with little trouble. He approached the walls and would have captured the town itself, if envoys had not come out to surrender it.

Et libro decimo:

> Nec in Etruria pax erat, nam et Perusinis auctoribus post deductum a consule exercitum rebellatum fuerat. Fabius quattuor milia quingentos Perusinorum occidit. Cepit ad mille septingentos quadraginta, qui redempti sunt singuli aeris CCCX, praeda alia omnis militi concessa.

Et inferius, "Tres validissimae Etruriae urbes Rusellana, Perusia, et Arretium pacem petiere."

Etsi vero per infaustissimi triumviratus tempora L. Antonium, M. Antonii fratrem, Octavius Caesar in Perusia obsedit, famemque raro alias similem auditam Antonii exercitus in ea clausus, et Perusinus populus sustinuere, et capta urbs diruptaque est. Eam tamen brevi instauratam moenibus, **[309D]** portisque nunc exstantibus communivit, idem Octavianus Augustus, quam a suo cognomine Perusiam Augustam, sicut litterae cubitales portis incisae ostendunt, voluit appellari. De causis autem diruptionis sic habet Livius, libro CXXV:

> L. Antonius consul M. Antonii frater Fulvia consulente, bellum Caesari Octavio intulit. Et receptis in partes suas populis, quorum agri veteranis Caesarianarum olim partium assignati erant, inter quos Perusinus erat, et M. Lepido qui custodiae urbis Romae cum exercitu praeerat, fuso hostiliter in urbem irruit.

Libro autem CXXVI Livius sic sequitur: "Caesar annorum XXIIII obsessum in oppido Perusia L. Antonium conatum aliquando erumpere, et repulsum fame coegit in deditionem venire. Ipsique et omnibus militibus ignovit, Perusiam diruit."

Baldus patruum nostrorum memoria in ea claruit, prout magis magisque eius nomen in dies claret, qui cum Bartolo Saxoferratensi iurium civilis et pontificii obtinuit principatum. Viris vero pacis et belli artibus, sed imprimis

And in book 10,

> . . . there was no peace either in Etruria; for war had broken out again at the prompting of the Perusini, after the consul had withdrawn his army . . . Fabius killed 4,500 of the Perusini taking 1,740 prisoners; these were ransomed for 310 *asses* each. All the other spoils were handed over to the soldiers.

And later, "Three highly powerful cities, the principal ones in Etruria-Rusellae, Perusia and Arretium-sought peace."

In the times of the cursed triumvirate, Caesar Octavian besieged in Perusia L. Antonius, M. Antonius' brother. And Antonius' army, shut in the city, and the people of Perusia survived a hunger whose like has rarely been heard of in other times, and the city was captured and destroyed. But in a short time it was rebuilt and it was fortified by the walls and gates **[309D]** which are still standing. It was Octavian too who had inscribed on the gate, in letters a cubit high, "Perusia Augusta," in accordance with his wish that the city take his cognomen. Livy speaks of the reasons for the city's demolition in book 125:

> The consul L. Antony, brother of M. Antony, with Fulvia's advice, made war on Octavius Caesar. And he got the support of the people whose land had once been assigned to the veterans of the Caesarian faction; included in this land was part of the territory of Perusia. He attacked the city and routed M. Lepidus, who with his army had been put in charge of protecting the city of Rome.

Moreover, in book 126, Livy goes on as follows:

> In 23 B.C., L. Antonius tried to break out of the town of Perusia, where he had been besieged. Then, after enduring a long famine, Antonius was forced to surrender. Octavian pardoned Antonius and all the soldiers, but demolished Perusia.

In the memory of our fathers' generation, Baldo degli Ubaldi was a famous citizen of Perugia. Accordingly, his name grows more and more famous, as he shared the preeminence in the study of civil and canon law with Bartolo of Sassoferrato. In fact, Perugia is now blessed with many men outstanding

docendo et dicendi iure praestantissimis, ea nunc abundat, inter quos Ivonem, Sallustium, Ioannem Petrucium, et Benedictum Bargium primarios novimus. Ex his vero qui rei bellicae operam dedere, Biordus et Ceccolinus Michelotti primum, post eos Nicolaus, Franciscus, et Iacobus Piccinini, de quibus in Montono oppido simul **[310E]** cum Braccio dicemus, fuere clarissimo. Nuncque Braccius Balionus incipit esse clarus.

Supra Perusiam a Tiberis ripa paulisper recedunt, Cisterna primum, post Anglarium, quod e regione Burgi Ad Sepulcrum regionis Umbriae situm viam habet ad illud rectissimam, in qua Nicolai Piccinini copias a quarti Eugenii gloriosissimi copiis fusas fuisse in Historiis ostendimus. Distatque ab Anglario Tiberis ea via passuum tria milia, et superius ad Tiberis fontem est Cotulum arx aerea.

Restat in Etruriae partibus regio, quam beati Petri patrimonium diximus appellari. Supra Pissiam torrentem, ad quem eam in maritimis inchoare diximus, est Soana oppidum septimo Gregorio pontifice Romano certe praestantissimo cive ornatum. Superiusque est oppidum Sancta Flora, interiusque medium id quod hinc Soanam inde montem Alcinum et Radicofanum interiacet spatium, montes complent altissimi Apennino paene, a quo plurimum distant celsitudine comparandi, Monsamita appellati. In quibus diversa regione aliquot sunt castella, sed praestantius est Sancti Philippi balneum, et proxime illis montibus Vulsinensium inter lacum et Paliam amnem sunt Porcenum, **[310F]** Aquapendens, Griptae, Sanctus Laurentius, Romanae ecclesiae oppida. Vulsinensium vero lacui adiacet oppidum Bolsena dictum, in ruinis aedificatum urbis Vulsinensium inter capita Etruriae olim numeratae, de qua Livius in decimo: "Consul alter Postumius in Etruriam traducto exercitu, primum pervastaverat Vulsinensium agros. Deinde cum egressis ad tuendos fines, haud procul moenibus eorum depugnat. Duo milia trecenti Etruscorum caesi." Et infra idem Livius undecimo libro eam dicit totius Etruriae potentissimam a servis occupatam, qui dominos ceperant, Romanis

in the arts of war and peace, but most of all in teaching and practicing law. Among the foremost of these men I know of Ivone, Sallustio, Giovanni Petruccio, and Benedetto Bargio. Indeed, I also include Biordo and Ceccolino Michelotti first among those who gave their attention to military matters, and then after them Niccolò, Francesco, and Jacopo Piccinino. The latter were famous along with **[310E]** Braccio da Montone and I will deal with them under the town of Montone. And now Braccio Baglioni is beginning to be famous.

Above Perugia, set back a little from the bank of the Tiber, there is first Cisterna; then Anghiari, the latter accessible by a very direct route from the area of Borgo Sansepolcro in the region of Umbria. On this road Niccolò Piccinino met the troops of the glorious pope Eugenius IV and was defeated; so I have related in my *Histories*. The Tiber is three miles from Anghiari on this road. Higher up, at the Tiber's source, is the high citadel of Cotulo.

There remains a region, in parts of Etruria, which I have said is called the patrimony of St. Peter. Above the stream Pescia, which I designated as the beginning of this region in the coastal areas, is the town of Soana, distinguished as the native town of the most eminent pope Gregory VII. And above this is the town of S. Fiora. Farther inland, very high mountains occupy the middle ground which lies between Soana on the one side and Montalcino and Radicofani on the other; they are called Monte Amiata and are almost comparable in height to the far-away Apennines. In a different region among these mountains are some fortified towns, but Bagni S. Filippo is the most eminent. And next to those mountains, between Lago di Bolsena and the river Paglia, are the papal towns Proceno, **[310F]** Acquapendente, Grotte, and S. Lorenzo Nuovo. The town called Bolsena lies next to Lago di Bolsena, built in the ruins of the city of Volsinii, once included among the capitals of Etruria. About it Livy writes in book 10,

> The other consul, Postumius, had taken his army into Etruria . . . began by destroying the countryside around Volsinii. Then, when the people came out to defend their territory, he defeated them in a battle not far from their town walls. 2,800 Etruscans were killed. . . .

And Livy continues a little later, in book 11, saying that the same city, the most powerful in all Etruria, was occupied by slaves, who had taken their

permittentibus populo in libertatum restituto subactam fuisse. Scribitque Plinius nullum esse in Italia agrum feraciorem ole quam Vulsinensem, in quo sata primo anno fructificet.

Ad dexteram haud longe absunt castella: Caput Montis lacui imminens, cui propinqua est insula nunc a fratribus Sancti Francisci habitata, et in qua rex secundus Ostrogothorum Almaricus Amalasuntham genitricem suam praestantissimam mulierem occidi est passus. Et post Martha ad lacus emissorium, ubi fluvius eiusdem nominis incipit. Deinceps in mediterraneis Castrensis civitas, cavis rupibus **[310G]** adeo circumdata, ut speluncam potius ingredientes, quam civitatem adire suspicientur. Obiitque nuper clarus civitatis ipsius civis Paulus iureconsultorum sui saeculi saule princeps.

Et proxime est Tuscanella, oppidum ecclesiae opulentissimum. Demum arduo in colle Mons Faliscorum corrupte dictus Mons Flasconus. Interiusque arduis item in collibus Paliae amni vicinis civitates sunt: hinc Balneumregium, inde Urbsvetus, nomina quarum ante millesimum annum nullus ponit scriptor. Sed in Historiis asserit Aretinus Urbevetanos a Florentinis originem habuisse. Fuit vero Urbsvetus per hanc aetatem infelicitate par Bononiae et Narniae civitatibus, quod in hac sicut et in illis inter cives Malcorinae et Beffatae, ut appellant, factionum maxima ac crudelissima sanguinis effusio est commissa. Eaque civitas ornata est ecclesia et palatio magnifici operis, quod Urbanus V pontifex Romanus ad annum salutis sexagesimumseptimum supra millesimum exstrui curavit. Eam urbem praeterlabitur Pallia fluvius, qui a Cla*n*is paludibus, ut diximus, ortum ducens inter Ameriam et Ortam, cadit in Tiberim.

Estque Orta ad Tiberis fluenta civitas vetusta, cuius nomen prior habet inter veteres scriptores **[310H]** Plinius, nisi forte eam esse velimus, de qua Virgilius, "Ortanae classes." Post eam secundum Tiberis ripam, in Via Flaminia, pons invenitur, olim Tiberi ad Viam Flaminiam a Caesare Augusto impositus, nuncque castello superimposito dirutus. Continebant vero stante Romana re ad eum pontem hincinde maxima aedificia, quae ab Ocriculo ad ipsam urbem Romam ita continuabantur, ut non vicus unus neque plures villae viderentur esse, sed ipsam urbem usque ad Ocriculum protendi appareret. Siquidem Ammianus Marcellinus Constantii Caesaris Constantino primo nati adventum a Constantinopoli Romam libro sextodecimo describens,

masters captive; and that the Romans allowed this; the city was subjected to Rome and its people restored to freedom. And Pliny writes that there is no territory in Italy more fertile in olives than that of Volsinii, where they bear fruit the first year after being planted.

On the right, now far off, are several fortified towns. Overhanging the lake is Capodimonte, and next to it is an island now inhabited by the monks of St. Francis. On this island Almaricus, the second king of the Ostrogoths, allowed his mother, the outstanding woman Amalasuntha, to be killed. After that comes Marta, at the outlet of the lake, where the river of the same name begins. Inland from there lies the city of Castro, surrounded **[310G]** by hollow cliffs, so that people who enter it suppose they are going into a cave rather than a city. A famous man of this city, Paolo di Castro, recently died; he was the foremost jurist of his age.

And next is Tuscania, a very wealthy papal town. Finally, on a high hill, is Mons Faliscorum, a name which has been corrupted to Montefiascone. Farther inland, also on high hills, are the cities around the Paglia river: on this side Bagnoreggio, on that side Orvieto. No writer before the year 1000 records their names. But in his *Histories,* Leonardo Bruni says that the citizens of Orvieto trace their origin from the people of Florence. Orvieto truly suffered as great misfortunes in these present times as did the cities of Bologna and Narni; here as well as in those cities there was great and cruel bloodletting as a result of strife between the citizens of the Merculina and Beffata factions, as they are called. This city is graced by a church and a magnificent palace which Pope Urban V had built in 1067. The river Paglia flows past this city; it has its source in the swamps of the Chiana, as I have said, and begins its course between Amelia and Orte, and is a tributary of the Tiber.

Orte is an ancient city on the Tiber; among ancient authors, **[310H]** Pliny is first to mention its name (unless we identify it with the city mentioned by Virgil in the phrase "the troops from Orta"). After this town, as you follow the Tiber on the Via Flaminia, you find a bridge, which in time past Augustus built over the Tiber. It has now been destroyed, and a castle placed on its site. But in the time of the Roman Republic, on both sides of this bridge there were enormous buildings which continued in uninterrupted succession from Ocriculum to the city of Rome itself, so that it appeared that there was not only one village, or many estates, but rather that the city itself extended all the way to Ocriculum. Proof of this is Ammianus Marcellinus' description in book 16 of Constantine's eldest son Constantius' first arrival in

dicit ipsum duxisse in comitatu Ormisdam Persarum gentis architecturae peritissimum, iussisseque illi ut primaria quaeque dignioraque urbis Romae aedificia diligenter inspecta, ordine sibi ostenderet. Et cum Ocriculum de itinere esset ventum, Persam, imperatore iubente omnium colloqui destitutum, ab Ocriculo Romam prius ingressum fuisse quam quo in loco urbs inchoasset discernere ac intellegere noverit.

Post Tiberis pontem, ut diximus, dirutum prius in Via Flaminia burghettus est Vicus Sancti Leonardi appellatus. Octavoque inde miliario eadem via est civitas Castellana altissimis insuperabilibusque rupibus adeo circumdata, ut ad inexpugnabilem munitionem nullo indigeat muro. Eam vero nonnulli ex doctioribus aetatis nostrae opinantur **[311A]** praedicantque fuisse locum Veientanae urbis, decennio a Romanis obsessae, et postea a Camillo felici in relegatione sua habitatae. Sed Tiberis remotior primum, post Plinius eos redarguunt erroris. Dicit namque Tiberim intra sextumdecimum lapidem dividere Veientem agrum a Crustumino, et post a Fidenate, deinceps Latium a Vaticano, et Crustumium fuisse ubi nunc Mons Rotundus, Fidenasque prope Romam secus Anienem in Umbriae descriptione ostendimus. Quod quidem Francisci Fiani poetae Romanarum historiarum peritissimi auctoritas confirmat. Is enim Fiano oriundus propinquo Tiberi castello, certissimis docuit coniecturis Veios fuisse apud Pontianum castellum Tiberi item, et Fiano propinquum.

Veiorum urbis loco situque ostenso, rerum quas cum populo Romano gesserunt breviarium conficere libet. Fidena Veientium Etruscorum colonia trans Tiberim fuit inter Crustumium Romanumque agrum. Fidenates itaque praeda onustos in Romano agro facta, Romulus tanto impetu est insecutus, ut fugientes insecutique Fidenas simul sint ingressi. Veii ut Fidenates ulciscerentur, agrum populati sunt Romanum, in quos Romulus legiones eduxit. **[311B]** Paxque inter utrosque composita. Postmodum rege Tullo Hostilio regnante Fidenates Romanis per Romuli pacem subditi rebellarunt, Veientesque opem tulerunt, Mettio Fufetio rege Albano in id bellum advocato, qui cum

Rome from Constantinople. He writes that Constantius had brought in his retinue Ormisda, the most skilled architect among the Persians. He ordered this man to point out to him, after careful inspection and in order, the principal buildings worth mentioning in the city of Rome. And when they had reached Ocriculum, at the emperor's command, everyone left off conversation with the Persian, and they had left Ocriculum and entered Rome before he could distinguish where the city began.

After the site of the destroyed bridge over the Tiber which I mentioned, the first place you come to on the Via Flaminia is a small town, called Vico S. Leonardo. Eight miles from there on the same road is Civita Castellana, so surrounded by insurmountable and lofty rocks that it needs no walls to be impregnable. Indeed, some of our modern scholars declare the opinion **[311A]** that this was the site of the city of Veii, besieged for ten years by the Romans, and after that the home of Camillus in his untroubled exile. But, first of all, the Tiber is more distant; and then Pliny refutes these errors; for he says that the Tiber demarcates, within sixteen miles, the Veientine territory from that of Crustumerium, and after that from Fidenae, and then Latium from the Vatican territory. I have shown in my description of Umbria that Crustumium was where Monterotondo now is, and Fidenae is near Rome along the Aniene river. This is confirmed by the authority of Francesco da Fiano, a poet well-versed in Roman history, who comes from the fortified town of Fiano near the Tiber, and asserts with convincing opinions that Veii was at Ponzano Romano, a fortified town close to both the Tiber and Fiano.

Now that I have revealed the location of the ancient city of Veii, I may summarize the city's dealings with the Roman people. Fidenae was a colony of the Etruscans from Veii, across the Tiber between the territories of Crustumium and Rome. When the Fidenates were loaded down with booty from Roman territory, the Romans in hot pursuit burst into town close on their heels, before the gates could be shut against them. To avenge the Fidenates, the Veientes sent a raiding force into Roman territory. Romulus led his legions out of Fidenae into Roman territory **[311B]** and a peace was concluded on both sides. Afterwards, during the reign of king Tullus Hostilius, the Fidenates, whom the terms of the peace with Romulus had made subject to the Romans, rebelled against them. The Veientes brought aid to them. Mettius Fufetius, the king of Alba, was summoned to this war; when he betrayed

neutris fidem servasset, a Tullo in quattuor frusta corporis laceratus est. Tullusque victor Fidenas recepit, Albam evertit.

Tertium regibus ex actis cum populo Romano Veientibus bellum fuit, in quo prima pugna Romani fuerunt inferiores. Secunda vero omnium atrocissima superati milites iurare coegerunt, se nisi victores numquam redituros. Qua religione obstrictis animis, obstinatius quam ante pugnatum est, non sine utrorumque maxima occisione. Cecideruntque Cn. Manlius consul et Q. Fabius alterius consulis frater. Capta Romana castra, sed mox fortuna mutata, sunt recuperata, victique tunc Romani vicerunt. Quartum exinde fuit bellum, in quo trecentos Fabios cum quinque milibus servorum clientumque Veientes ad Cremeram interfecerunt. Quinto bello Veientes L. Memmium consulem non procul item a Cremera castra habentem, magno aggressi impetu repulsum fugatumque castris exuerunt. Moxque fugientes Romanos insecuti Ianiculum [311C] ceperunt, urbemque Romanam aliquot mensibus obsessam tenuerunt. Sexto demum bello urbs Veientana decem annis a Romanis obsessa, a Camilloque capta est. Ubi tantum praedae fuit, quantum Romani ante per annos quinquaginta et trecentos ex omnibus aliis victoriis habuerant. Universusque populus Romanus tunc ad praedam in castra vocatus est. Fuitque tam gratus Romanis situs, ut de Roma relinquenda Veiosque transferenda aliquando sit cogitatum, et inter patres actum. Hinc est versus:

Roma domus fiet Veios migrate Quirites.

Sequitur ad Tiberim Mons Soracte, a priscis dictus, de quo Virgilius, "Hi Soractis arces habent. . ." et Plinius, "Ad Soractem Varro asserit fontem esse, cuius sit latitudo quattuor pedum, soleque oriente eum exundare ferventi similem. Avesque quae gustaverint iuxta mortuas iacere." Quod quidem nos certius ea ratione credimus, quia cum vir summus Prosper cardinalis Columna Romanus nosque simul Antiatis urbis ruinas perlustraremus, silvas ibi vicinas, in quibus maxime sunt ruinae, ingressi fonticulum offendimus, in cuius labris aviculae duae post gustatam, ut apparebat, aquam occubuerant. Soracte autem monti nomen mutatum est novum [311D] Sancti Silvestri, ab eius sancti pontificis Romani sacello, quod summo in cacumine aedificatum habet. Idemque obtinet silvestri vocabulum ad radices eius

both sides, Tullus had him drawn and quartered. The victorious Tullus recaptured Fidenae and destroyed Alba.

After the expulsion of the kings, there was a third war against Veii, in which the Romans were beaten in the first battle. But in the second battle, the fiercest of all, the Roman soldiers were forced to swear that if they did not win they would never return. As their spirits were stringently bound by this oath, they fought more stubbornly than before, and both sides suffered from great slaughter. The consul Cn. Manlius and Q. Fabius, brother of the other consul, fell, and the Roman camp was captured. Still, their fortunes soon changed for the better, and the conquered Romans became conquerors. After this, there was a fourth war, in which three hundred Fabians with five thousand clients and slaves were killed by the Veientes at the river Cremera. In the fifth war, the Veientes made a violent attack on the consul L. Memmius, who had a camp again not far from the Cremera, and routed him and deprived him of the camp. Soon, in their pursuit, they captured **[311C]** the Janiculum and for a few months besieged the city of Rome. Finally, in the sixth war, the Romans besieged the city of the Veientes for ten years, and Camillus captured it. The Romans took from there as much booty as they had taken in all their other victories in the preceding three hundred and fifty years. The entire population was summoned to the camp to take part in the plundering. The location of Veii was so attractive to the Romans that at one time the senate considered and voted on a resolution that Rome should be abandoned and moved to Veii. This episode is the source of the line of verse

Rome will become one house. Romans, move to Veii.

There follows next to the Tiber the mountain called by the ancients Soracte, about which Virgil writes, "These men possess the citadels of Soracte." And Pliny says, "Varro asserts the existence of a spring, four feet wide, which at sunrise pours forth steam as if it is boiling. And birds which have drunk from it lie dead next to it." I believe this all the more since I investigated the ruins of the city of Antium with the excellent Prospero cardinal Colonna. When we had entered the woods there, we came upon a small spring and on its edges two little birds lay dead, apparently from drinking the water. The name of Mt. Soracte has undergone a change to **[311D]** S. Silvestro, after the name of the chapel of Pope Sylvester, which was built on

montis Tiberi imminens oppidulum. Soracte autem per hiemem esse nivosum sic ostendit Horatius carminum primo:

Vides ut alta stet nive candidum
Soracte nec iam sustineant onus
Silvae laborantes, geluque
Flumina constiterint acuto.

Ulterius Via Flaminia est Arianum oppidum, quod ab ara Iani olim dictum in Theodorae nobilis Romanae mulieris praedio, per tempora beati Gregorii aedificatum fuisse legimus. Ultra Arianum eadem Flaminia est Castrum novum, et nil ultra usque ad portam olim Fluentanam post Flaminiam nunc populi dictam, habet Via Flaminia communitum. At post Ortam civitatem intus sunt hinc Galliensium oppidum Romano urbis Romanae pontifice ornatum. Inde Nepesum civitas in Romanorum historiis crebro inventa, quam Livius XXVII dicit fuisse unam ex duodecim coloniis, quae difficillimis rei publicae temporibus Hannibale in Italia agente militiam detractavere; et libro XXVIII scribit eam cum aliis post sextum annum dedisse duplum.

Lacum Vulsinensium praetergressos campi excipiunt amplissimi, in quibus est Viterbium, civitas parum vetusta, cuius primum nomen parvo in castello ad annum nunc sexcentesimum erat Viturvium. Et e regione illius ad sextum lapidem, ruinae exstant **[312E]** ingentes Faleriae urbis, quam diximus inter capita Etruriae numeratum fuisse. Eius a Camillo captae celebris est memoria, qui perfidum ille grammaticum vinctum verberatumque in urbem reduci curavit a pueris, quos hosti prodere quaesivisset. Scribitque Plinius in Falisco agro, amnis aquam potatam candidas boves facere. Et alibi, haud procul urbe Roma in Faliscorum agro familiae sunt paucae, quae vocitantur Hirpiae, quae sacrificio annuo quod fit ad Montem Soracte Apollini, super ambustam ligni struem ambulantes non amburuntur. Et ob id perpetuo senatus consulto militiae omniumque aliorum munerum vacationem habent.

Adiacet Viterbium monti quem Ciminum fuisse appellatum constat, quod etiam nomen olim fuit subiecto ad alteram montis partem lacui nunc

its peak. And the same name, Silvestro, is applied to the little town perched over the Tiber which is at the base of this mountain. But that Soracte is covered with snow in the winter, Horace indicates in the first book of his *Odes*:

> See how Soracte stands
> white with deep snow, and the woods cannot
> withstand the burden of ice,
> and the rivers are frozen. . .

Farther on along the Via Flaminia is the town of Riano Flaminio, named after the altar of Janus which I have read was built in St. Gregory's time, formerly said to be on the estate of Theodora, a Roman noblewoman. Beyond Riano on the same road, the Flaminia, is Castelnuovo di Porto; and beyond this, up to the gate at the end of the Via Flaminia once called Porta Fluentana, now Porta del Populo, there is no fortified dwelling on the Via Flaminia. But after the city of Orte, towards the interior, on this side, there is Gallese, a town distinguished by the Roman pope Romanus; and then the city of Nepi, frequently mentioned in histories of the Romans. Livy, for example, says in book 27 that Nepesum was one of the twelve colonies which, during the troubled times of Hannibal's activities in Italy, refused military service. And in book 28 he writes that Nepesum, along with other cities, had given double the number of soldiers after the sixth year.

Passing beyond Lago di Bolsena, you enter spacious fields which contain Viterbo, not a very ancient city, whose original name was Viturvium; it is in a small fortified town where it has been for 600 years now. And leaving that region, at the sixth milestone, there stand forth the huge **[312E]** ruins of the city of Falerii, which, as I mentioned, was counted among the capitals of Etruria. Falerii is famous for being captured by Camillus after a schoolmaster had tried to hand over to the Romans the boys in his charge. Camillus had him bound and whipped, and then led back to the city by his boys. And Pliny writes that in the Faliscan territory the cattle are white because of the water they drink from the river. And elsewhere he says that in Faliscan territory, not far from the city of Rome, there are a few families called Hirpiae who hold an annual sacrifice to Apollo near Mt. Soracte, during which they walk on a pile of burning wood and are not burned. For this reason, by a decree of the Senate, they enjoy perpetual exemption from military service and all other duties.

Lying next to Viterbo is the mountain which was called Ciminus. This was formerly also the name of the lake lying beneath it, on the other side of

Vici dicto. Quorum utriusque Virgilius sic meminit, "Et Cimini cum monte lacus," de quo monte et rebus apud eum, apudque Sutrium, gestis, sic habet Livius in nono:

> Sutrium ab Etruscis obsidebatur; flectit consul Fabius in clivos agmen. Aspreta erant strata saxis, non tulerunt impetum Etrusci, versisque signis fuga effusi castra repetunt. Sed equites Romani provecti per obliqua campi, cum **[312F]** se fugientibus obtulissent in silvam Ciminam penetratum est. Romanus multis militibus Etruscorum caesis duodequadraginta signis militaribus captis, castris etiam hostium cum praeda ingenti potitur. Silva erat Cimina magis tum invia atque horrenda, quam nuper fuere Germanici saltus. Nullus ad eam diem nec mercatorum quidem, abdita ea intrare aut ferre quicquam praeter ducem ipsum audebat. Tum ex ducibus qui aderant, M. Fabius vel Caeso. . . .

Caesa aut capta eo die hostium milia ad quadraginta.

Eodemque in monte, qua Via olim fuit Cassia, castellum est Surianum arcem habens omnium Italiae munitissimam, quem diu a Britonibus etiam postea quam eos Albricus Cunii comes Italiae expulerat possessa fuit, nullaque itinera Romam perducentia per aetatem nostram aliquamdiu tuta esse permiserunt, quousque Martini V pontificis Romani opera operibusque in potestatem ecclesiae arx ipsa pervenit.

Euntibusque ea via Romam obvium est oppidum, nunc Vetralla, olim Forum Cassii dictum, quod indicat Sanctae Mariae ecclesia Vetrallae contigua, quae in Foro Cassii appellatur. Adiacent ad sinistram Sutrium versus colles castigatioresque monticuli, quibus dicitur **[312G]** Montaniola, quae est aliquot oppidulis habitata, in quibus duo sunt, quae Romanae ecclesiae integerrimam fidem Longobardorum temporibus servaverunt, Polimartium et Bleda, duobus Romanis pontificibus suis civibus Sabiniano, cuius temporibus fames horrenda Italiam et urbem Romam vexavit; et Pascali primo ornata.

the mountain; it is now called Lago di Vico. Virgil mentions both of them: "Mt. Ciminus and its lake." Livy, in book 9, speaks of this mountain and the events which took place around it and Sutrium:

> The consul Fabius turned his line of troops into the hills. The rough places were strewn with rocks. The Etruscans could not withstand their attack, turned their standards around, were routed, and made for their camp. But the Roman cavalry advanced sideways and met [312F] the fleeing Etruscans, who made for the Ciminian Forest. The Romans killed many thousand Etruscans, captured thirty-eight military standards, and also took possession of the enemy's camp with a vast amount of plunder.... At this time the Ciminian Forest was more impenetrable and fearful than the wooded ravines of Germany were in recent times. Hardly anyone, even a trader, was bold enough to set foot in it at that time, except the commander himself. Among the leaders who were present, M. Fabius or Caeso....

On that day about 40,000 of the enemy were killed or captured.

On the same mountain, on the road which was formerly the Via Cassia, is a fortified town, Suriano del Cimino, which has the best-defended citadel in all Italy. For a long time the Bretons held it, even after Alberic, count of Cunio, had driven them out of Italy. They prevented any roads leading to Rome being safe for a while through our times, until Pope Martin V, through his efforts, brought the citadel into the control of the church.

As you go along the Via Cassia towards Rome, you come to a town now called Vetralla, but formerly Forum Cassii, which identification is proved by the church of S. Maria of Vetralla nearby, called S. Maria di Foro Cassio. Lying next to this on the left towards Sutri are hills and well-defined small mountains which give rise to the collective name [312G] Montaniola, which contains some small towns. Two of these, Polimarzo and Blera, kept the Christian faith in the times of the Lombards. They were distinguished as the birthplaces of two Roman popes: Sabinian, in whose times a terrible famine afflicted Italy and the city of Rome; and Paschal I.

Deinde Sutrium civitas vetustissima, apud quam proelium illud ingens superius sumptum ex Livio commissum fuit, cui urbi in montibus adiacet hinc Roncilionum, inde Crapalica. Et in Via Cassia duodecimo a Sutrio absunt Bachanae vetusti nominis locus, qui sicut nunc est semper antea tabernis hospitatoriis deputatus fuit.

Ex parvoque lacu Bachanas attingente, parvus oritur fluvius apud Valcham in Tiberim cadens, qui licet aquis sit tenuis ac exilis celebratum in historiis habet nomen. Est namque Cremera, apud quem trecenti Fabii cum quinque milibus servis a Veientibus, sicut supra diximus, ad internecionem caesi fuerunt. Bachanisque secundo miliario adiacet Campagnanum Ursinorum oppidum. Supra Sutrium ad dexteram quintodecimo miliario est lacus Tarquiniae, nunc Anguillariae, ab oppido quod illi imminet dictus, **[312H]** ex quo familia fluxit, ut in Romanis nostrae aetatis vetusta, comitum Anguillariae appellata, quorum Ursus urbis senator Franciscum Petrarcham laurea insignivit.

Adiacetque lacui huic Barbatanum populi praesentis Romani peculiare oppidum. Inde Vicarellum, et Romam versus, Galeria Ursinorum. Sunt quoque plurima Sutrium, Ameriam Nepesumque inter et Romam castella in villis olim civium Romanorum aedificata, quae et alia loca nihil vetustatis, aut alicuius memorandae dignitatis habentia duximus omittenda; praeter unum fama celeberrimum, et aspectu penitus neglegendum. Nam ad montem Rosulum, qui quattuor passus milia a Sutrio Nepesoque paene pariter abest, lacus est altam quidem aquarum profunditatem habens, circuitu vero brevis, quem inspecta Livii descriptione lacum esse coniicimus Vadimonis, apud quem superati a Romanis Etrusci ad annum urbis conditae septuagesimum supra quadringentesimum manum dedere. Et sese Romano populo publice permiserunt, sicut in Livii nono his verbis habetur:

> Interea res in Etruria gestae ad Vadimonis lacum, Etrusci lege sacrata coacto exercitu, cum vir virum legisset, tandem superati sunt. Illeque primum dies fortuna vetere abundantes Etruscorum opes fregit, caesum in acie quod roboris fuit, castra eodum impetu capta direptaque.

Then there is the city of Sutri, very ancient, where an enormous battle was joined (cited above from Livy); and next to it in the mountains on this side lies Ronciglione, on that side Capranica. And on the Via Cassia, twelve miles from Sutri, lies Baccano, a place with an ancient name which is now, as it was before, a lodging for guests.

A small river has its source in the little lake bordering Baccano; it flows into the Tiber at Valca. Although a slender stream, it has a famous history. For this is the Cremera, at which 300 of the Fabii with 5,000 slaves were killed by the Veientes, as I mentioned above. At the second milestone from Baccano is Campagnano di Roma, a town of the Orsini. Fifteen miles away, above Sutri on the right, is Lacus Tarquiniae, now called Lago di Anguillara from the town which hangs over it. **[312H]** From this town comes the very old, by contemporary Roman standards, family of counts named Anguillara. One of these was the senator Orso, who decorated Francis Petrarch with the crown of laurel.

Lying next to this lake is Barbarano Romano, a town belonging to the modern people of Rome. Then comes Vicarello, and, towards Rome, Galeria degli Orsini. And between Sutri, Amelia, Nepi, and Rome, there are also more fortified towns, built on the former estates of Roman citizens. These I have decided to omit, along with other places of no great age or other quality to make them worth of commemoration. But I except one, because it is so famous, although very unimportant in appearance. For at Monterosi, which is four miles from Sutri and Nepi, and about equidistant, is a lake which has very deep waters but a small circumference. After reading Livy, I conclude that this is Lake Vadimonis, where the Romans defeated the Etruscans in the year 310 B.C. They allowed them to surrender publicly to the Roman people. This is in Livy's book 9, in the following words:

> Meanwhile events were taking place in Etruria near Lake Vadimonis. The Etruscans had raised an army under a sacred law, in which each man had selected the next.... Finally they were defeated. That was the first day of the destruction of Etruscan power, which had long flourished in good fortune. Their strongest soldiers were killed in battle; in the same attack, their camp was captured and plundered.

Regio Tertia
Latina

[313A]

Finis Etruriae ad Tiberim nos perducens Romam ordine describendam offerebat. Sed cum id anno ante quarto tribus libris IIII Eugenio Romano pontifici celeberrimo inscriptis, sub Romae Instauratae titulo effecerimus, urbem ipsam relinquentes, regionem in qua est Latinam, novo volumine describemus. Huius regionis vocabuli causam Virgilius in VIII ponit his versibus:

> Primus ab aethereo venit Saturnus Olympo
> Armi Iovis fugiens, et regnis exul ademptis.
> Is genus indocile ac dispersum montibus altis,
> Composuit legesque dedit, Latiumque vocari
> Maluit, is quoniam latuisset tutus in oris.

Servius autem grammaticus Virgilium in VII exponens populos proprie Latinos appellatos, dicit eos qui intererant Albani montis viscerationi, quos quidem Latinos tanto amore Romanam gentem prosecutos fuisse videmus, ut Livius libro LXXII, enumeratis Italiae populis, qui bello sociali defecerunt **[313B]** a Romanis, dicat auxilia Latini nominis, et exterarum gentium missa populo Romano.

Hanc autem regionem aetatis nostrae ac superiorum aliquot saeculorum morem licet absurdum secuti, Campaniam et Maritimam appellabimus, et quidem Campaniam scimus dictam fuisse a priscis regionem, quae est circa Capuam. Scimusque Latii appellationem a principio angustiora complexam fuisse, quam quae nunc Campaniae et Maritimae vocabulo comprehenduntur. Sed contra videmus Strabonem Cretensem, qui per tempora Tiberii Augusti floruit, ponere in Geographia fines Latinorum, maritima regione ab ostiis Tiberinis ad Sitanum sinum, in quo fuit Sinuessa urbs maritima, et in mediterraneis Aborigines, Rutulos, Volscos, Hernicos, Aequicolos, Marsos,

Third Region
Lazio

[313A]

The border of Tuscany at the Tiber is drawing me to Rome, and the logic of my plan dictates that I should now describe it. But four years ago I described Rome in three books with the title *Rome restored*, which I dedicated to his glorious holiness Pope Eugenius IV; so I shall now pass by the city itself, and describe in this new book the region, Lazio, where it is located. Virgil gives the etymology of the region's name in book 8 (of the *Aeneid*), in the following verses:

> Saturn first came down from heaven, trying to escape the weapons of Jupiter, an exile, stripped of his kingdom. He collected this uncivilized race, scattered among the high mountains, and gave them laws. He preferred to call the place Latium, since in this region he had *lain hidden*.

But the grammarian Servius, explicating the seventh book of the *Aeneid*, says that the people properly called Latins are those who participated in the sacrifice on the Alban Mount. We see that these Latins indeed associated themselves with the Roman race with such affection, that Livy, enumerating in book 72 the peoples of Italy who rebelled [313B] in the Social War, relates the troops sent to aid the Roman people by the peoples of the Latin name and foreign nations.

This region, however, I shall call by the absurd custom of our times and some earlier ages, Campania and Marittima. I know, in fact, that Campania was named by the earlier inhabitants for the region around Capua. And I know that the name of Latium was more restrictive in its scope from the beginning, than what is now understood by the name Campania and Marittima. I see, however, that the Cretan Strabo, who was active in the time of Tiberius, in his *Geography* placed the territory of the Latins in the coastal region from Ostia to the gulf of Sitano, where the coastal city of Sinuessa was; and he puts in the inland area the Aborigines, Rutuli, Volsci, Hernici,

et eos qui proximum Marsis incolunt Apenninum usque ad veteris Campaniae terminos.

Unde peritissimum hunc vetustatis scriptorem, et simul Plinium, qui ab eo sumpsit, secuturi eam Latinorum regionem, nostrae nunc Campaniae et maritimae cogimur applicare. Nec satis scio si in ipsa praesentis temporis Latina regione satis potero facere, sicut Livius Patavinus, [313C] divus Augustus, Virgilius, Strabo, et Plinius, ut vetustissimis satisfaciam adiuvabunt, quamquam non est in eo flore nunc, quem priscis habuit temporibus, adeo ut per eius oppida Hadrianum imperatorem gloriosissimum dictatorem, aedilem et duumvirum fuisse scribat Aelius Spartianus.

Ut ergo a maritimis incipiamus: Ostiam urbem condidit mare inter et Tiberim Ancus Marcius, quamquam Servius grammaticus in Virgilii VII dicit exitum Tiberis naturalem non esse, nisi circa Ostiam, ubi primum Aeneas nostra constitui, cum postea in agro Lavino castra fecerit ingentia, quorum vestigia suis temporibus videbantur. Describit vero eam Strabo importuosam propter alluviones Tiberis, oportuisseque dicit tunc adhiberi scapharum copiam, quae ministeriis servirent, et onera exciperent, ac rursus onerarent, ut levatae naves facilius flumen attingerent. Per ea enim tempora portus non erat Romanus, quem postea Claudius fecit; et Tiberius Strabonis temporibus Antii portum inchoabat.

Unde haec legens scribensque in eam venio considerationem, quae prudentes quosque debet attentos vigilesque, ut rebus humanis parum [313D] confidant reddere: non potuisse imperatorum Romanorum, et quidem potentissimorum profusionem opum, et adhibitam diligentiam efficere, quin Ostiae civitatis Antiatisque et urbis et portus, ac Romani item portus opera paucioribus annis mille, integra permanserint, et eadem quae prius fuerat Ostiae, annis iam quingentis manserit importuositas. Primam calamitatem passa est Ostia Cinnae et Marii temporibus, cum scribat Livius libro LXXIX, Cinnam et Marium quattuor exercitibus, ex quibus duo Q. Sertorio et duo Carboni dati sunt, urbem circumsedisse; Ostiam coloniam expugnasse, ac crudeliter diripuisse.

Habuitque aliquando Ostia ingentia aedificia, quorum nullum nunc exstat vestigium. Flavius Eutropius scribit Aurelianum Augustum coepisse fundare Ostiae forum nominis sui ad mare, in quo postea praetorium publicum fuit constitutum. Nec omittendum duximus eam optimos habuisse melones, quorum decem Claudium Albinum imperatorem unica cibatione inter multa alia comedisse scribit Iulius Capitolinus. Et quia aerem semper

Aequicoli, Marsi, and those who live next to the Marsi, inhabiting the Apennines all the way to the borders of ancient Campania.

For this reason, I am compelled to use the name which this most knowledgeable ancient writer used, and also Pliny who followed Strabo, and have Latium include Campania and Marittima. And I am unsure as to whether I can do justice to this modern region of Lazio. Livy **[313C]** of Padua, the divine Augustus, Virgil, Strabo, and Pliny will help me to treat adequately the ancient times, although the region is not now in the flourishing state it enjoyed in those days. For example, the most glorious of the emperors, Hadrian, was dictator, aedile, and duumvir in the towns of Latium, according to Aelius Spartianus.

To begin, then, with the coast: Ancus Marcius founded the city of Ostia between the sea and the Tiber. However, Servius the grammarian, commenting on Virgil's seventh book (of the *Aeneid*), says that the Tiber does not have a natural mouth, unless it is around Ostia, where Aeneas first established a camp; afterwards he built an enormous camp in the territory of Lavinium, and one could still see the remains of it in Servius' time. Strabo, however, describes the Tiber as lacking a harbor on account of its deposits of silt, and he says that it was necessary then to use a lot of light boats to assist the labor by taking off the cargo, and loading the large ships back up again, so that the ships, sufficiently lightened, could enter the river easily. Indeed, in those times the harbor was not the Roman one, which Claudius later built; and Tiberius, in Strabo's time, was beginning to build the port at Antium.

As I read this, and write this, I am struck by the thought that one should exercise prudence and vigilance, and **[313D]** not trust in human affairs; as the Roman emperors, even with their most powerful and abundant wealth, could not with all their effort create a permanent port at Ostia and Antium, which ports stayed open only for somewhat less than a thousand years. And the one that existed 500 years before at Ostia has remained unusable. The first disaster that happened at Ostia was in the times of Cinna and Marius, as Livy writes in book 78: Cinna and Marius surrounded the city with four armies, of which two were assigned to Q. Sertorius and two to Carbo; they besieged the colony of Ostia, and cruelly devastated it.

Ostia had at one time enormous buildings, but no trace of them now exists. Flavius Eutropius writes that the emperor Aurelian had built at Ostia a Forum by the sea, named after him, and afterwards the praetor's residence was installed there. It is also worth mentioning that Ostia had the best melons, and the emperor Clodius Albinus, writes Julius Capitolinus, consumed

habuit, ut in maritimis habitatoribus gravem, sacrosancta lege populi Romani vacationem militiae et publicorum munerum habuit, quam vacationem Livius XXVII scribit sub adventum Hasdrubalis in Italiam fuisse ad dies XXX suspensam, ut plures milites res publica haberet.

Urbem Ostiam, cum a Saracenis fuisset destructa, Leo IV pontifex **[314E]** Romanus instauratam Corsis replevit. Et tam diu destructa ac derelicta mansit, ut nil sit reliquiarum, praeter turrim, qua celebris famae pontifex Romanus Martinus V in urbis Romae potiusquam in ostiorum Tiberis et portus custodiam aedificare curavit.

Deinceps Antium est Romana colonia, de qua Livius in VIII, "Antium nova colonia missa, naves inde longe abductae, interductumque mare." Et infra, "Naves Antiatum partim in navalia Romae subductae, partim incensae, rostrisque earum suggestum in foro exstructum adornari placuit, rostraque id templum appellatum."

Eam urbem Strabo dicit ab Ostia distantem stadiis ducentis sexaginta fuisse temporibus suis aedificatam super saxo, ab imperatoribus Tiberio, Druso, et Germanico ad otium relaxationemque laborum civilium, et additas fuisse aedes multas magnificentissimi operis, cum antea Antiates praedae studium cum Tyrrhenis commune haberent, quamvis Romanis subiecti essent. Unde Alexander Epirota, et postea Demetrius successor captivos praedones remittentes Romanis dixerunt dono eis dare corpora propter illam, quam cum Graecis haberent cognationem: indignum tamen ducere, viros ipsos, et **[314F]** simul Italiae imperare, et myoparones ad piraticam emittere.

Fuit autem in Antiatum foro Castoris et Pollucis templum, quos servatores suos nominabant: haec a Strabone. Sed Horatius voluisse videtur Fortunam ab Antiatibus in primis fuisse cultam, his versibus ad Fortunam scriptis,

O diva gratum quae regis Antium,
Potens vel imo tollere de gradu
Mortale corpus, vel superbos
Vertere funeribus triumphos. . .

ten of them at one meal, among many other dishes. And because Ostia has always had unhealthy air, as is the case in coastal towns, it was declared by a law of the Roman people exempt and immune from the draft and from taxes. About this exemption, Livy writes in book 27 that Hasdrubal's invasion of Italy caused the Romans temporarily to suspend it for thirty days, so that more soldiers could be drafted for the Republic.

The city of Ostia was destroyed by the Arabs, and Pope Leo IV rebuilt it and filled it with Corsicans. It remained destroyed and abandoned for so long [314E] that there is none of its remains to be seen, except for the famous tower which Pope Martin V had built to guard the city of Rome rather than the mouth of the Tiber and its harbor.

Then comes Anzio, originally a Roman colony. Livy writes about it in book 8, "Antium was established, a new colony. Their ships were confiscated, and they were forbidden to go to sea." And a little later he writes,

> Of the ships taken from Antium, some were put into the Roman dockyards, and some were burned, and it was decided to decorate with their beaks a raised platform built in the Forum; and that public place was called the Rostra.

Strabo says that Antium was 260 stades from Ostia and was built in his own time on rock by the emperors Tiberius, Drusus, and Germanicus, for leisure and rest from their public duties, and many houses of splendid workmanship were built. In times before the citizens of Antium used to cultivate, in common with the Etruscans, the habit of piracy, despite their being subjugated by the Romans. For this reason Alexander of Epirus, and later his successor Demetrius, would give captive pirates to the Romans saying that they were giving their bodies as a gift on account of the relationship the Romans had with the Greeks; but, they added, it is poor behavior for them both to rule over Italy and, at the same time, send vessels out to commit piracy.

There was in the Forum at Antium [314F] a temple of Castor and Pollux, and according to Strabo they called them the Saviors. But Horace asserts that the goddess Fortuna was the deity most worshipped by the people of Antium; he wrote the following verses to this goddess:

> O goddess, you who rule over pleasant Antium,
> Powerful enough to elevate mortal flesh from the lowest rung of the ladder,
> Or to overthrow, in turn, with death, the triumphs of the arrogant. . . .

Livius autem libro LXXX scribit Cinnam et Marium expugnasse Antium. Et videmus Suetonium ad alios scribere Neronem postea tam insanis molibus exstruxisse et portum et urbem Antiatum, ut non modo aerarium, sed Romanum quoque imperium pecuniis exhauserit, effodiendisque postea thesauris ita applicuisse animum, ut mentitos per singula mathematicos hariolosque nihilominus sectaretur. Habuitque Antium, sicut supra de Ostia diximus, sacrosanctam a publicis muneribus vacationem, quae pariter eodem tempore est suspensa. Urbem vero Antiatum nunc esse nullam, sed in mari, in litore, in nemoribus mirandas exstare ruinas vidimus.

Neptunnium autem, oppidum in Antii vestigiorum angulo aedificatum, novam et iucundam in re parva **[314G]** considerationem effecit; mirarique soleo nullam eius rei, quam cum orbe condito originem habuisse oportuit, fieri a Plinio mentionem. Alitur eius oppidi populus non exiguus piscatione, aucupio, et venatu. Qui Antiatum olim ager, ut Strabo innuit, tunc segetis vinique feracissimus, nunc a Lavinio oppido in maris litora duodeviginti milia passuum latitudine silvis obtegitur.

Estque haec non Lavinia, sicut multi opinantur, prima Aeneae urbs, cuius incolis postea ob Aeneae memoriam bello Latino Romani pepercerunt, sicut Livius VIII libro sic scribit, "Laviniis civitas data sacraque sua reddita, cum eo ut aedes lucusque sospitae Iunonis communis Laviniis cum populo Romano esset." Quin potius Lanuvium, cardinalis Columnae Prosperi oppidum, a quo Murenarum genus Romae praeclara fuit, quodque omnibus paene in vetustis Romanorum monumentis celebre habetur.

Sed ad Neptunnium: pisces quidem saxosum, vel potius glareosum mare multos ac optimos habet. Venationem, sicut alibi, amplissimae silvae apris capreisque abundantem praebent. Aucupium vero est duplex, cuius tempora sunt diversa. Nam cum ad prima veris signa hirundines et simul cum ipsis **[314H]** coturnices nunc dictae a sono vocis qualeae, transmisso mari infero in Italiam redeunt, omnia Antiatum quondam litorum supercilia, passuum

Livy also writes in book 80 that Cinna and Marius besieged Antium. And we see Suetonius write to others that Nero, after he had built his extravagant structures in both the harbor and the city of the citizens of Antium, exhausting not only the treasury but also the Roman Empire, afterwards was so intent upon digging for treasure that he questioned in detail those passing as astrologers and soothsayers. Antium also enjoyed, as I mentioned above about Ostia, a legal exemption from taxes, and this was also suspended in the same time of trouble as was Ostia's. But now there is no city at the site of Antium; however, we have seen marvelous ruins in the sea, on the shore, and in the woods.

Nettuno, a new town built in a corner of the ruins of Antium, although slight, gives occasion for a recent and pleasing comment: I am always amazed that no mention of it is made by Pliny, although it must have originated with the existence **[314G]** of the world. Its population is rather numerous and subsists on fishing, bird-catching, and hunting. The former territory of Antium, according to Strabo, was very fertile with crops and vineyards; but now, an area eighteen miles in width from the town of Lavinium towards the coast is covered by woods.

This is not, by the way, the Lavinium that was the first city of Aeneas, as many people think. The Romans spared its inhabitants afterwards, in the war with the Latins, in memory of Aeneas. Livy writes about this in book 8:

> The people of Lavinium were given citizenship, and their religious rites were restored to them, on the condition that the temple and the grove of Juno Sospita should be held in common between the townspeople of Lavinium and the Roman people.

But it is rather the Lanuvium of Prospero cardinal Colonna, the town which was the birthplace of the famous Murena family of Rome; and is considered famous in almost all the ancient records of the Romans.

To return to Nettuno: it has excellent fishing, with lots of good fish, although the ocean there is rocky, or rather gravelly. As for hunting, just as is the case elsewhere, its great forests contain an abundance of wild boars and goats. But for birdcatching, there are two distinct seasons. At the first signs of spring, swallows and thrushes, now called quail (from the sound of their voices) both return to Italy from across the Tyrrhenian Sea. The citi-

quinque milia Neptunienses contiguis retibus complent, sedensque unusquisque in fundi proprii, et magno pretio comparati loco ad particulam retium propriam, venientes noctu coturnices fistula illectat. Et cum turmatim illae retibus intricentur, si aliqua de longissimo volatu fessa extra rete in sabulum ceciderit, eam auceps manu percipit. Fuisseque audivimus intra mensem unum, quo id continuatur aucupium dies aliquot, in quorum singulo centies huiusmodi avicularum mille sit captum.

De ipsis vero coturnicibus sic habet Plinius:

> Coturnices ante semper adveniunt quam grues. Parva avis et cum ad nos pervenit, terrestris potius quam sublimis. Advolat non sine periculo navigantium, cum appropinquavere terris, quippe velis saepe incidunt, et hoc semper noctu, merguntque navigia. Austro non volant, humido scilicet et graviore vento, aura tamen vehi volunt propter pondus corporeum viresque parvas.

Et infra, "In Campania primum veris principio multiplicare conspiciuntur, priusquam venisse sciantur."

Aliud item in Antiate agro est aucupium per autumnum. Palumbae cum mari transvolato Italiam relicturae sunt aliquamdiu in nemoribus Antiatum commorantur. Quare peritissimi Neptunienses retia **[315A]** quam maxima, in id aucupii magno parata impendio suspendunt. Exinde palumbes quascumque longo tractu viderint congregatas in arboribus considere, iactu lapidis et clamore territas in aera volare compellunt. Dumque aves in magnum coactas numerum advolando, tensis retium insidiis viderint supereminere, contorta funda parvum lapidem vel naturaliter album, vel gypso delinitum maximo emittunt crepitu, quo territae bombo palumbes, ut accipitres chiluones a Plinio appellatos, quibus nunc falconibus est nomen, quas in lapide bomboque fundae timent, declinando serventur, terrae quam possunt volatu rapidius appropinquant, sicque amentes in retia se praecipitant.

izens of Nettuno place nets side-by-side throughout all **[314H]** the five miles of shore that was once the territory of Antium. Each man sits in his own place (for which he has paid a high price) at the part of the net that belongs to him. They catch with birdcalls the thrushes which come at night. And when the birds are caught in the net, if any of them are so tired from their long migration that they fall out of the net onto the sand, the birdcatcher catches it by hand. I have heard it said that in one month during which this birdcatching goes on for some days, in a representative day they catch a hundred thousand of this type of little bird.

Pliny has this to say about the thrushes:

> The thrushes always come before the cranes. They are small birds, and, what is especially relevant to our purposes, they remain on the ground rather than the air. When they are reaching land, they present a danger to sailors, because they often fly into the sails and cause ships to sink. They do not fly in a south wind, because it is humid and weighs them down. But they prefer to be carried by the breeze, on account of the light weight of their bodies and their lack of strength.

And further on he says, "They are seen breeding in Campania first, in the beginning of springtime, before they are known to have arrived."

There is, too, another birdcatching season in the territory of Anzio, in the autumn. This time it is doves, who have flown across the sea and are preparing to leave Italy; they linger for a while in the woods at Anzio. Consequently, the most skilled of the birdcatchers from Nettuno hang the largest nets **[315A]** they can find. The nets have been prepared at great expense for this hunt. When they see the doves which have settled in the trees over a long expanse of the forest, they drive them by throwing stones and shouting at them. Terrified, the birds fly up into the air, and when they see the birds flying up massed together in a great bunch, right over the treacherous nets, they draw them tight. They then whirl a slingshot and throw over the flock of birds a small stone or a white stone smeared with gypsum. They make a loud noise. The doves are terrified by this loud humming noise, thinking that it is made by the hawks Pliny calls *chiluones*, for which the modern name is falcons. These doves are frightened by the stone and by the humming noise of the slingshot, thinking that falcons are making it, and to save themselves they swerve downwards in their flight. They fly to earth as swiftly as they can and, panicked, fly into the nets.

De palumbis Plinius dicit eas quot annis advolare mari in Veliternum agrum, qui quidem ager Antiati continet. Et alibi scribit, "Post hirundines, sturnos, turdos, abeunt palumbes, sed quonam incertum. Hirundines vero in propinqua Africos montes petunt." Ex aucupio palumbarum Romanus nostri temporis populus nuptias et convivia maiori ex parte parat. Meliores namque saporis et nutrimenti hae parvae quam aliae sunt palumbes.

In medio duarum, quas descripsimus maritimarum **[315B]** urbium, Ardeam ponit Strabo Rutulorum olim habitationem, stadiis circiter septem a mari recedentem, et dicit prope eam fuisse Aphrodisium, ubi panagyrim Latini agerent. Idque Plinius appellat lucum Iovis Indigetis, cui propinquus est amnis Numicus. Virgilius autem libro septimo sic habet:

> Audacis Turni ad muros quam dicitur urbem
> Ausoniis demum fundasse colonis
> Praecipiti delata Noto. Locus Ardea quondam
> Dictus avis, et nunc magnum manet Ardea nomen.

Et infra,

> Quinque adeo magnis positis incudibus urbes
> Tela novant, Atina potens, Tiburque superbum,
> Ardea Crustumeri et turrigerae Amiternae.

Et Servius Virgilii septimo dicit, "Iginius ab augurio avium Ardeam. Et Ovidius improprie ac fabulose incensam ab Hannibale Ardeam, et in hanc avem esse conversam." Item Servius eodem libro verbum exponens "Sacranae acies,"

> Dicunt quendam Coribantem venisse ad Italiam, et tenuisse loca, quae nunc urbi vicina sunt; et ideo populos Sacranos appellatos, nam sacrati sunt matri deorum Coribanti. Alii Sacranas acies Ardeatum volunt, qui aliquando cum pestilentia laborarent, ver sacrum voverunt, unde Sacrani sunt dicti.

About the doves, Pliny says they fly every year over the sea into the territory of Velletri, a territory which borders that of Anzio. And elsewhere he writes, "After the swallows, starlings, and thrushes, the doves migrate. But it is not clear where they go. The swallows make for the nearby mountains of Africa." The yield of the dove hunt provides modern Romans food for weddings and feasts. These small doves have a better taste and nutritional value than others.

In the middle of the two coastal **[315B]** cities I have just described, Strabo places Ardea, once the home of the Rutuli, at about seven stades from the sea. He says that near Ardea there was a temple of Aphrodite, where the Latins held a common festival. And this is the place Pliny calls the grove of Juppiter Indiges. Near it is the Numicus river. Virgil in the seventh book (of the *Aeneid*) writes the following about it:

> . . . to the walls of bold Turnus, the city which is said
> to have been built for Ausonian colonists,
> Allecto came, carried there by the south wind.
> This place was once called Ardea by our ancestors, and now the
> great name of Ardea remains.

And farther along he says,

> On five great anvils they had set out,
> Five cities forged new weapons: powerful Atina; and proud Tibur;
> Ardea, Crustumium, and turreted Amiternae.

And Servius comments on book 7 of the *Aeneid*,

> Hyginus says that Ardea was named after the practice of augury from the flight of birds. And Ovid fantastically and incorrectly says that Ardea was burned by Hannibal and was turned into this bird.

Servius also says, explicating the word "Sacranae acies" in the same book,

> a Corybant came to Italy and took possession of the places which are now near Rome, and for that reason the people were called "Sacrani," for the Corybantes are sacred to the Great Mother of the gods. But other sources say that the "battle line of the Sacrani" (in Virgil) belongs to the people of Ardea because the people from time to time when suffering from a plague vowed a "sacred spring," and for this reason were called "Sacrani."

Dicit Plinius Ardeam fuisse [315C] conditam a Danae Persei matre. Fuitque Ardea una ex duodecim coloniis, quae dum Hannibal magis urgeret Romanos, militiam et collationem tributorum detractaverunt.

Id vero oppidum raro habitatum colono, nunc Iacobus Columna possidet, quod Leone Romano pontifice, sicut coniicio, nominis ordine secundo ornatum fuit. Numicus vero fluvius, quem Strabo dicit propinquum esse Ardeae a Virgilio sic celebratur in septimo: "et fontis vada sacra Numici." Et infra, "ac fontis stagna Numici." Super quo Servius,

> Ista iam ab incolis discuntur, quod ait stagna verum est. Nam Numicus ante ingens fluvius fuit, in quo repertum est cadaver Aeneae et consecratum. Post paulatim decrescens, in fontem redactus est, qui et ipse sacratus est. Vestae enim libari non nisi de hoc fluvio licebat.

Post Antium est quinto miliario Asturae Antonii Columnae arx mari circumdata, prope quam Astures fuere vetustissimi, de quibus Virgilius, "Astur, equo fidens." Ad quam parum feliciter divertit M. Cicero, Antonii gladios fugiens, evasurus tamen, si coeptam ibi navigationem continuasset. Pari item infelicitate ad eandem Asturam se de fuga contulit Conradinus Henrici [315D] filius, quem genitor Federicus secundus imperator Siciliae rex in carcere mori coegit. Namque rex Petrus Arago insulam Trinacriam Constantiae uxori suae, hereditario iure avi sui Federici superius dicti debitam, armis ceperat. Conradinusque Carolum primum Andegavensem sic posse Neapolitano regno pellere confisus, sicut illum Arago Trinacria expulerat, apud Beneventum infauste conflixerat. Qui unico sociatus comite fugiens Asturae interceptus, ad Carlumque perductus, tam detestando, quam

Pliny says that Ardea was **[315C]** founded by Danae, the mother of Perseus. And Ardea was one of the eighteen colonies which refused to contribute levy and tribute when Hannibal was pressing the Romans hard.

But now this town has few inhabitants, and is a possession of Jacopo Colonna. It is famous as the birthplace of Pope Leo, who I speculate was the second of that name. The Numicus river, which Strabo places near Ardea, is celebrated by Virgil in book 7: "And the sacred shallows of the source of the Numicus." And later he says of it, "And the shallows of the source of the Numicus." Servius, explicating this line, says,

> That those waters are shallow is a fact that has been learned from the inhabitants, that what he says is truly the case. For the Numicus was formerly an enormous river, in which the body of Aeneas was found and he was consecrated there. Afterwards, it got smaller little by little, and was reduced to a spring, which was also consecrated. Libations to Vesta were allowed to be made only from this river.

After Anzio, five miles away, is Torre d'Astura, a fortress belonging to Antonio Colonna, surrounded by the sea. Near this place were located the Astures, a very ancient people. Virgil says about them, "Astyr, trusting in his horse." And M. Cicero, fleeing from the henchmen of Antony who had been sent to kill him, unfortunately turned aside to Astur; he would have escaped if he had only continued by boat the journey which he had begun there. Conradin, the son **[315D]** of Henry, whose father, the emperor Frederick the second, king of Sicily, forced him to die in prison, also went to Torre d'Astura in flight; it was a disastrous decision for him too. For King Peter of Aragon, by force of arms, took possession of the island of Sicily, which he claimed was his wife Constance's by right of inheritance from her grandfather Frederick, of whom I spoke above. Conradin, trusting that he could drive Charles of Anjou out of the Kingdom of Naples, just as Aragon had driven him out of Sicily, clashed with him in an ill-omened battle at Beneventum. As Conradin was fleeing with a single companion, he was caught at Torre d'Astura and brought to Charles, who had him publicly beheaded,

semper alias regibus et praestantibus insueto principibus more exemploque, securi publice est percussus.

Deinceps Circeius mons magna parte mari circumdatus, in quo Circen fabulae perhibent habitasse. Habuit vero is mons Strabonis aetate urbem, ut dicit, parvam, et Circes templum ac Minervae antra, dicitque monstrari consuevisse quandam Ulyssis fialam. Servius, in Virgilii septimo, "super Circeae raduntur litora terra," "Mons est, ante insula fuit. Paludibus enim a continenti separabatur, quas exclusit fluvius de Albanis montibus fluens." Et dicebatur Circeis ab errore transeuntium, quia homines mutabat in feras; de qua re beatus Aurelius Augustinus, dum Dei civitatem aedificat, sic habet: "Varro astruit Circen socios Ulyssis mutasse in bestias." Et infra,

> Nam de mulieribus malis artibus imbutis, et nos dum essemus in Italia **[316E]** audiebamus talia, de quadam regione illarum partium, mulieres imbutas his malis artibus in caseo dare solere, quibus possent sive vellent viatoribus, unde in iumenta verterentur, necessariaque comportarent. Post quae perfuncta opera iterum ad se redirent. Nec tamen in eis mentem fieri bestialem, sed rationalem humanamque servari.

In hoc monte oppidum fuit, quod et Circeum dictum est. Liviusque utrumque Circeos appellat. Sed nos in Romanae ecclesiae gestis rebus, praesertim Gelasii secundi temporibus, ad annum salutis centesimum vigesimum et millesimum saepe legimus, in Circeo monte fuisse arcem Circeam, omnium quas Romana ecclesia ubique haberet munitissimam, quae afflictis Romanae ecclesiae rebus, auxilio saepe fuit. Nunc ad eius montis radices oppidum est Sanctae Felicitatis.

an example as hateful as it has been unaccustomed for kings and princes in other times.

Next comes Monte Circeo, for the most part surrounded by the sea. Here, in myths, Circe is said to live. But in Strabo's time it had a city, small, according to him, and a temple of Circe and a cave of Minerva. Strabo says that inhabitants used to show people a cup which was supposed to have belonged to Ulysses. Servius, commenting on the seventh book of Virgil, "The land extends above the shore of Circe," says:

> It is a mountain; it was formerly an island. For it was separated from the mainland by swamps, which were cut off by the river flowing down from the Alban Mount.

And it was called "Circean" through the error of people who passed through there, because she used to change men into beasts. St. Augustine says this about the matter, in *The City of God*: "Varro adds that Circe changed the companions of Ulysses into animals." And further,

> While I was in Italy, **[316E]** I heard such stories, about women skilled in the evil arts, concerning a certain region in that area. The women skilled in these evil arts are accustomed to give drugs in cheese to whatever travellers they could or wanted to; as a result they were changed into pack animals and carried the necessary things. After they performed their work, they were changed back into themselves. But their minds did not become those of animals; they preserved their human capacity for reasoning.

On this mountain there was a town, which was also called Circeium. And Livy also calls both mountain and town Circeii. But I have often read in the histories of the church, especially in the time of Pope Gelasius the second, in the year 1020, that on Monte Circeo there was a fortress called Circeian, the most heavily fortified of all the fortresses the Roman church had anywhere. And it was often a help to the church in troubled circumstances. Now, at the foot of this mountain, there is a town, S. Felice Circeo.

Fluvium qui proxime illabitur Storacem Strabo, Plinius Numpheum vocat, super quo hi Formium fuisse dicunt oppidum. Deinceps perpetuum mare. Et in mediterranea regione porrigitur campus Pontinus, quam regionem totam vetustissimis et multis ante conditam urbem temporibus Ausones habitarunt, qui etiam Campanum habebant [316F] agrum, unde Italiam Ausoniam, et Ausonium pelagus vocitatum fuisse Strabo asserit. Post Ausones fuerunt Osci, quibus etiam Campania erat communis, et postmodum omnia fuerunt Latinorum usque ad Sinuessam. Sed quicquid Strabo hic habeat, Plinius sic dicit:

> Mirum est quod de hac re tradere hominum notitiae possumus. Theophrastus qui primus externorum aliqua de Romanis diligentius scripsit; nam Theopompus ante quam nemo mentionem habuit, urbem tantummodo a Gallis captam dixit. Dithargus ab eo proximus, legationem tantum ad Alexandrum missam, hic iam et plusquam fama Circeiorum insulae mensuram posuit stadia octuaginta milia eo volumine, quod scribit Nicodoro Atheniensium magistratui, qui fuit urbis nostrae quadringentesimo quadragesimo anno. Quicquid vero terrarum est, praeter decem milia passuum ambitus, annexum insulae, post eum annum accessit Italiae. Aliud miraculum a Circeis palus Pontina est, quem locum XXIIII urbium fuisse Mucianus ter cos. prodidit.

Deinde flumen Aufentum, supra quod Terracina oppidum, Volscorum lingua Anxur dictum, ubi fuerunt [316G] Amyclae a serpentibus deleti. Repetii a Strabone Plinioque vetustissima, quae et ipsi a vetustissimis acceperunt. Livius vero XLVI scribit Pontinas paludes a Cornelio Cethego consule cui ea provincia obvenerat siccatas. Agrumque ex his factum a campis Pontinis ad Terracinensem agrum stadia fuisse tradit Strabo, cum nostri octo milia nunc computent.

The river that flows into the sea next to it is called the Storax by Strabo, but the Nymphaeus by Pliny, and above it the town of Formiae is said to have been located. After this, there is uninterrupted sea. And in the inland region extend the Pomptine Marshes, and the entire region was built in very ancient times, long before the founding of Rome. The Ausones lived here and possessed even the territory of Campania, and for that reason, **[316F]** Strabo claims, Italy was called Ausonia, and the gulf was called the Ausonian Sea. After the Ausones came the Osci, who also possessed Campania with the Ausones. Afterwards, all the area down to Sinuessa belonged to the Latins. But whatever Strabo says about this area, Pliny says the following:

> It is amazing what we can hand down to public knowledge about this subject. Theophrastus was the first foreigner to write about the Romans with any accuracy; since Theopompus, the first to make any mention of Rome, says only that the city was captured by the Gauls. And the next writer immediately after him, [Clitarchus], says only that an embassy was sent to Alexander. This writer [Theophrastus] relied on authorities better than hearsay evidence, and established the exact measurement of the island of Circei at eighty stades, in the volume which he wrote in the archonship of Nicodorus at Athens, which was in the 440th year after the founding of Rome. Accordingly, all the land which was added to the island above and beyond a circumference of ten miles, was added to Italy after that year. Another amazing fact: going on from Circeii, the Pomptine Marshes extend, where there were twenty-four cities; so reported Mucianus, who was three times consul.

Next comes the Uffente river, and above it is the town of Terracina, called Anxur in the language of the Volscians. Here is the site of **[316G]** Amyclae, which was destroyed by serpents. (I am taking from Strabo and Pliny these very ancient notices, which they themselves took from very ancient sources.) But Livy says in book 46 that the Pomptine Marshes were drained by the consul Cornelius Cethegus when he obtained this province. Strabo provides in stades the extent of the land reclaimed from these marshes, from the Pomptine fields to the territory of Terracina, a distance our contemporaries calculate at eight miles.

Terracinae etiam nunc adiacet paludis Pontinae pars, quam paludem faciunt amnes duo, eorumque maior Aufens appellatus, apudque Terracinam via Appia primum mare inferum attingebat. Terracinam dicit Livius, cum fuisset a Romanis direpta, causam dedisse solutioni stipendii militaris.

> Fabius, quod maxime petebatur, ad Anxur oppugnandum sine ulla populatione accessit. Anxur fuit, quae Terracinae nunc sunt, urbs prona in paludes, et ab ea parte oppugnationem ostendit. Circummissae quattuor cohortes cum C. Servilio [A]Hala, cum imminentem urbi collem cepissent, loco altiore, qua nullum erat praesidium, ingenti clamore ac tumultu moenia invasere. Pronuntiatum, ne quis praeter armatos violaretur, reliquam omnem multitudinem voluntariam exuit armis, quorum **[316H]** ad duo milia quingenti vivi capiuntur, a cetera praeda Fabius militem abstinuit. Postea ubi venerunt tribuni, oppidum vetere fortuna opulentum tres exercitus diripuere, cuius praedae gratia factum est, ut stipendium miles tunc primum acciperet, cum ante id tempus de suo quisque munere eo functus esset.

Octavo autem libro Livius habet, "Cohors una, cum haud procul Anxur esset, ad Lautulas saltu angusto inter mare et montes consedit."

Et Servius septimo Virgilii super verbo "Circeiumque iugum," dicit, "Circa hunc tractum Campaniae colebatur puer Iuppiter, qui Anxurus dicebatur a verbo Graeco, quod sine novacula interpretatur, quia non barbam rasisset." Est autem fons circa Terracinam, qui aliquando dictus est Anxur. Et infra Servius, "Haud longe a Terracina oppidum est Satura, et eius cognomine fluvius Ufens, quem Virgilius significat angustum esse, qui inter valles serpens mare petat."

Part of the Pomptine Marshes even now lies next to Terracina. A swamp is created there from two rivers; the greater of these is called the Uffente, and at Terracina the Via Appia first touched the Tyrrhenian Sea. Livy says that the plundering of Terracina was the first cause of military pay:

> Fabius approached Anxur, the Romans' principal goal, to attack it without sacking it. Anxur was then what is now Terracina, a city falling into the marshes, and in this direction Fabius directed the attack. Four cohorts were sent around the city in the other direction under the command of C. Servilius Ahala, and captured the hill overhanging the city, in a rather high place where there was no garrison. The cohorts invaded the walls with an enormous noise of shouting and uproar. It was announced that only those bearing arms would be attacked; the rest of the crowd voluntarily put down their weapons. **[316H]** About two thousand five hundred of these men were taken alive, and Fabius held back his soldiers from any other plundering. Afterwards the tribunes came, and three armies plundered this town which was wealthy as a result of its ancient good fortune. As a result of that plunder, it happened that the soldiers were then for the first time paid a salary; before that time, each man had done his military duty relying on his own funds.

And Livy, again, in book eight, writes, "One cohort, since it was not far from Anxur, took up a position between the sea and the mountains, in a narrow pass at Lautulae."

And Servius, commenting on the seventh book of Virgil, on the word "Circe's ridge," says:

> Around this area of Campania Jupiter was worshipped as a young boy, and he was called "Anxurus" from the Greek for "without a razor," because he had not yet shaved his beard. There is, in addition, a spring around Terracina, which at some times in the past has been called Anxur.

And after this Servius writes,

> The town of Satura is not far from Terracina, and the river Ufens has this as an epithet, which Virgil interprets as meaning "narrow," as the river creeps towards the sea between valleys.

Suetonius Tranquillus in vita Tiberii imperatoris scribit, "Iuxta Terracinam in loco, cui praetorio nomen est, cenante eo complura et ingentia saxa fortuitu superne delapsa sunt, multisque amicorum et ministrorum elisis, praeter spem evasit." Aelius Spartianus in vita Hadriani dicit Palmam consularem virum Hadriani insidiatorem Terracinae interfectum fuisse. Idemque Aelius Spartianus scribit Antoninum Pium [317A] instaurasse Tarracinensem portum. Et Livius libro XXVI dicit Ansurinam coloniam habuisse sacrosanctam vacationem, quae adventu Hasdrubalis sit suspensa. Libro autem XXI dicit Minucium a Fabio Maximo dictatore missum ad firmandum saltum, qui sub Terracina imminent mari, ne Hannibal per viam Appiam in agrum Romanum iret praedatum. Lucanus autem accessum Caesaris primum post leges ad Rubiconem transgressas describens sic dicit,

Iamque praecipites superaverat Ansuris arces
Et qua Pontinas via dividit uda paludes.

De Ansure sic habet Martialis coquus poeta ad Faustinum:

O nemus, O fontes, solidumque madentis arenae
Litus, et aequoreis splendidus Ansur aquis.

Et ad Frontinum:

Ansuris aequorei placidos, Frontine, recessus.

Suetonius Tranquillus, in his *Life of Tiberius*, writes:

> As he was dining near Terracina in the place called "Praetorium," there was an accident, a rockslide of many huge stones, which fell down from above, and many of his friends and attendants were killed, but he escaped-contrary to all hope.

Aelius Spartianus, in his *Life of Hadrian*, says that the consular Palma, who had conspired against Hadrian, was killed at Terracina. And the same author writes that Antoninus Pius [317A] began work on a harbor at Terracina. And Livy, in book 26, says the the colony of Anxur had an exemption, which was temporarily removed when Hasdrubal approached. Moreover, in book 21, he says that the dictator Fabius Maximus sent Minucius to strengthen the forces at the pass which overhangs the sea below Terracina, so that Hannibal would not go along the Via Appia to plunder the territory of Rome. And Lucan, describing Caesar's initial approach after he had illegally crossed the Rubicon, says the following:

> And now he had passed beyond the high citadel of Anxur,
> and where the road, covered with water, cuts through the Pomptine marshes.

The poet Martial the cook writes to Faustinus about Anxur,

> O grove, o shore of wet sand,
> And Anxur shining with its sea-waters.

And to Frontinus he writes,

> Frontinus, you have retreated to the calm of seaside Anxur.

Servius grammaticus Virgilii versum libri IX Aeneidos, "Tacitis regnavit Amyclis" exponens, sic habet:

> Inter Caietam et Terracinam, oppidum est constitutum a Laconibus, qui comites Castoris et Pollucis fuerunt, ab Amyclis provinciae Laconiae civitate. Hi secundum sectam Pythagoream a caede omnium animalium abstinuerunt, adeo ut natos in vicinis paludibus serpentes occidere nollent, a quibus interempti sunt.

Aliter:

> Cum frequenter **[317B]** nuntiaretur hostes affuturos, et inani terrore civitas quassaretur, lege caverunt, ne quis hostes nuntiaret affuturos. Postea cum vere venirent hostes, nullo nuntiante deleti sunt, et sic Amyclae silentio periere, unde Lucilius satiricus, "Mihi necesse est loqui, nam scio Amyclas tacendo periisse."

Solum Terracinum dicit Strabo intus attingere Formias, Minturnam, et Sinuessam; additque venientes a Brundusio Romam, prope Terracinam attingere fossam plenam in multis locis palustribus et fluvialibus aquis, propinquam viae Appiae; et navigari nocte maxime, quandoque interdiu, eosque qui ad vesperam intrant, mane egredi.

Deinceps haberi Formias Laconicum aedificium, quod antea Hormiae dicebatur, a bono portu, quem Lacones Euormon dicunt. Eam urbem amoenissimi situs, in qua Cicero Formianum habuit villam, Saraceni ad annum salutis octingentesimum quinquagesimum sextum destruxerunt, et tunc Erasmi martyris reliquiis Caietam translatis, datus est Caietanae ecclesiae

The grammarian Servius comments on a verse from Virgil, *Aeneid* 9, "he reigned at quiet Amyclae,"

> Between Caieta and Terracina there is a town built by the Laconians, who were companions of Castor and Pollux, and they were from Amyclae, a city in the province of Laconia. They followed the teachings of the Pythagorean school, to abstain from killing any living thing, to such a point that they were unwilling to kill the snakes which were born in the swamps. And they were killed by the snakes.

Another thing about them:

> Since it frequently happened that the enemy **[317B]** was reported to be approaching, and the citizens were shaken with useless fear, they passed a law that no one should announce that the enemy was at hand. After this, when the enemy was in fact approaching, no one reported it, and they were destroyed. And in this way Amyclae perished on account of silence, which caused the satirist Lucilius to write, "It is necessary for me to speak, for I know that Amyclae perished through silence."

Strabo says that the territory of Terracina, extending inland, touches Formiae, Minturnae, and Sinuessa, and adds that people traveling from Brundisium to Rome reach near Terracina a ditch full in many places with stagnant waters and river water, next to the Via Appia, and people travel on it especially at night, and sometimes in the daytime. And people who get on it at evening, come out in the morning.

Next comes Formia, founded by the Laconians, and previously called Hormiae from its good port, which the Laconians call "Euormon." This city is in a very pleasant spot, where Cicero had his villa, Formiana; but the Saracens destroyed the place in the year 856. And then the remains of the martyr Erasmus were moved to Gaeta. Its first bishop was given to Gaeta by

Gregorio IIII Romano pontifice primus episcopus. Et tamen Strabo consentit Caietam scribere quosdam a nutrice Aeneae fuisse dictam, sicut Virgilius sexti principio,

> Tu quoque litoribus nostris Aeneia [317C] nutrix,
> Aeternam moriens famam Caieta dedisti.

Sed licet Caietae sinus arxque celebris et pervetustae fuerint famae, ea tamen non fuit civitas priusquam Formias, ut supra ostendimus, destruxerunt Saraceni. Distat vero a Terracina arx, ut Strabo, et ut nunc est civitas Caieta stadiis centum, quae nunc viginti milia computantur. Portum Caieta eo in sinu habuit semper optimum, quem tamen Aelius Spartianus ab Antonino Pio magnis exstructionibus instauratum scribit. Et Faustinam eius uxorem scribit idem Aelius conditiones sibi et nauticas et gladiatorias Caietae elegisse.

Primaque est in via civitas Fundana decimo a Terracina miliario, de qua Livius libro VIII, "Fundanisque per fines eorum tuta parataque semper fuisset via, civitas sine suffragio data." Et infra,

> Fundanus Vitruvius Vaccus Privernis se ducem rebellionis exhibens Romanos compulit, ut Lu. Papirium consulem in eos mitterent. Fusi Privernates. Plautius alter cos. in Fundanos ducebat, ingredienti fines senatus Fundanus occurrit, negare se pro Vitruvio sectamque eius secutis precatum venisse, sed pro Fundano populo, quem extra culpam belli esse, ipse Vitruvius indicasset, cum receptaculum fugae Privernum [317D] habuit non patriam Fundos. Consul collaudatis Fundanis eis pepercit.

Fundanorum vina Martialis Cocus innuit non esse talia, quae inveteranda sint:

> Haec Fundana tulit felix autumnus Opima.
> Expressit mustum consul, et ipse bibet.

Pope Gregory IV. And yet Strabo agrees that some people write "Caieta," because it was also said to have named after Aeneas' nurse, for example Virgil in the beginning of his sixth book,

> You also, O Caieta, nurse **[317C]** of Aeneas,
> With your death gave renown to our shores.

But although the Gulf of Gaeta and the citadel are of ancient fame, it was not a city until the Arabs, as I noted above, destroyed Formiae. The distance between Terracina and the citadel of Caieta, according to Strabo, and this is now also the case, was a hundred stades, which is now calculated to be twenty miles. Gaeta has always had an excellent harbor in the gulf, but Aelius Spartianus writes that it was restored by an enormous construction project of Antoninus Pius. He also says that Faustina, his wife, chose sex partners for herself from the naval battles and gladiatorial shows at Caieta.

The first city on this road is Fondi, ten miles from Terracina. Livy, book 8, writes about it, "Because the road had always been safe and well-maintained through their territory they were given the status of city without voting privileges." And later on,

> The Fundanian Vitruvius [Bacchus] was leader of the rebellion at Privernum and forced the Romans to send the consul Lucius Papirius against them. The Privernates were routed. The other consul, Plautius, was leading his army against the people of Fundi, when the senate of the Fundanians said that they had come, not to plead for Vitruvius, but for the people of Fundi, from whom Vitruvius had removed any blame for the war when he made Privernum his refuge, **[317D]** not their own city. The consul praised the people of Fundi and spared them.

Martial the cook indicates that Fundanian wine was not the type to age:

> This Fundanian wine was produced in the rich autumn of Opimius' year. The consul squeezed out the must, and he himself will drink the wine.

Euntibus a Fundis Formias sinistrorsum est Villa oppidum, a quo Galba imperator originem duxit. Dextrorsumque est lacus Fundanus. Inde Itrum quinto, quae civitas Lemurnarum fuit, de qua Horatius,

> Tandem defessi Lemurnarum venimus urbem.

Et altero item quinto, sed extra viam Appiam est Caieta, ea autem decem milia passuum viam habent, silicibus Romano veteri modo stratam, inter arduos celsosque montes, sed viti olea arborumque consitionibus amoenissimos.

Et secundum litus marisque undas a Terracina petitur Turris S. Anastasii, deinde oppidum Spelunca appellatum, ubi dicit Strabo speluncas patere ingentes, quae habitationes magnas speciosasque exciperent. Post Speluncas in litore est Caieta, a qua nunc urbe ad Traiectum sive Lirim fluvium nunc Gaurianum appellatum, milibus decem terra est omnium, nedum Italiae, sed orbis totius amoenissima, quod fontibus ibi scatentibus, aquae passim lucidissimae citrangulis arantiisque consita interfluunt, irrigantque loca. Praecipuusque fons decimo post primam scaturiginem passu, molas versat plurimas, vico celebri pulcherrimoque circumdatas, per quae loca **[318E]** Scipionem Laeliumque conchas et umbilicos legisse Cicero indicat in secundo De oratore. Laelius et Scipio semper adinvicem rusticari, tuncque mirabiliter repuerascere erant soliti, cum rus ex urbe tamquam e vinculis evolassent. Et ad Caietam Laurentumque conchas et umbilicos legere consuevissent, et ad omnem animi remissionem ludumque descendebant.

Quo quidem in decem milium spatio Herculanea fuit via, omnium quas Romanum ubique habuit imperium amoenissima, de qua Cicero oratione in legem agrariam Rulli secunda sic habet, "Accedent sileta ad Minturnas, adiungitur et illa via vendibilis Herculanea multarum deliciarum et magnae pecuniae."

Suntque deinceps Castellonum et Honoratum villa, quam Honoratus Fundorum comes speciosissimam aedificavit. In conspectu autem Speluncarum, quas ad Caietae sinum esse diximus, sunt propositae in pelago insulae duae, Pandana et Pontia, colonia, sicut Livius IX libro dicit, a Romanis deducta. Easque dicit Strabo parvas, sed pulchre habitatas inter se parum, sed a continenti ducentis quinquaginta stadiis distare. Fuerunt vero hae insulae post Strabonis tempora multorum martyrum et Christi confessorum exsilio decoratae.

As you go on from Fondi, on the left is the town of Villa, where the emperor Galba was born. And on the right is Lago di Fondi. Then five miles farther is Itri, the city of the Lemurnae, about which Horace wrote,

> Finally, exhausted, we come to the city of the Lemurnae.

And another five miles along, but not on the Via Appia, is Gaeta; those ten miles, however, have a road paved with stones in the ancient Roman style, and it winds between steep high mountains which are nevertheless very pleasantly planted with vines and olive trees.

And following the coastline and the waves of the sea from Terracina, we come to Torre Anastasia, and then the town called Sperlonga, where according to Strabo there are enormous caves, which shelter grand and splendid dwellings. After Sperlonga on the shore is Gaeta. Now from this city it is ten miles to the Traetto, or the ancient Liris river, now called the Garigliano. The land here is the pleasantest in all the world, let alone in Italy. Here are fountains gushing everywhere with clear water, irrigating places planted with citrus, orange trees, and the chief spring, ten paces beyond its first outlet, turns many mills surrounded by a famous and beautiful district. In this place **[318E]** Scipio and Laelius, according to Cicero in his second book *de oratore*, collected shells and small pebbles. Laelius and Scipio always vacationed in the country and were miraculously rejuvenated when they escaped, as if from chains, from the city, and at Caieta and Laurentum they used to gather shells and sea-cockles. They resorted to every type of enjoyment for relieving the mind of cares.

The Via Herculanea was ten miles away, the pleasantest of all that the Roman Empire possessed. Cicero mentions it in the following selection from his speech against Rullus' agrarian law: "They will add the willow thickets at Minturnae, there will be added too that valuable Herculanean road, which includes many delights and is worth a great deal of money."

And then there are the town of Castellone and the splendid villa called Castellonorato which Count Onorato I Caetani of Fondi built. Within sight of Sperlonga, which I mentioned on the bay of Gaeta, are two islands exposed to view in the sea: Ventotene, and Ponza, a colony established by the Romans (so Livy says in book 9). And Strabo says they were small but well-inhabited; that there was little distance between them, but they were 250 stades from the mainland. After Strabo's time, they were distinguished by the exiles of many martyrs and confessed Christians.

Sinum Caietanum [318F] Caecubus mons, vini praestantia celeber, tangit, et Caecubum civitas Fundorum in via Appia, haecque omnia loca boni vini copiam habere dicit Strabo. Utraque autem civitas vetusta singulo ornata fuit Romano pontifice: Caieta secundo Gelasio, Funda Sotere, patre Concordio.

Sed iam limites attingimus nostrae huius Latinae regionis Sinuessam, et Liris, sive Gauriani ostia, et maritimam absolvimus oram. Et tamen priusquam ad mediterraneam redeamus, ea docebimus, quae Liris ad sinistram in regione Latina habet. Supra Traiectum oppidum tria milia passuum a mari distans, est Liri contiguum Speninum castellum, a quo distant octo milia passuum Fractae oppidum totidem a Pontecorvo semotum, quod oppidum Fregellas fuisse ostendimus. Superius aliis item octo milibus abest Ceparanum nobile oppidum, reliqua ad fontem Liris proximius accedentia in Vestinorum Samnitiumque partibus dicentur. In mediterraneo autem Latinorum solo frequentes fuere urbes, infinitaque paene oppida et castella, ex quibus auctor est Plinius quinquaginta tres populos sine vestigiis interiisse.

Hac autem describenda mediterranea regione modum hactenus in aliis servatum a fluviorum ostiis fontibusque et discursu servare nequibimus. Sed alium [318G] certius facturum satis, qui in nulla reperiatur alia Italiae regione, tenebimus: Viis incedendo tribus Appia, Latina, et Tiburtina, quae inter se diversae ad Lirim amnem et Sinuessam Caietamque perducunt. Nec tamen certiore gradu ita per singulas pedem figere poterimus, quin delabi et aberrare videamur, quod quidem necessitas faciet, cum viae alicubi dirutis pontibus aversae, alicubi ut penitus ignorentur, omnino sint perditae.

Igitur Roma nunc petentibus Terracinam, iter est primum duodecimo miliario Marinum, quod non absurde Marianam villam fuisse, ut credam facit proxima L. Murenae villa semi etiam integra, et praedium Portium vulgo notum. Eademque Lucii Murenae villa, priscum etiam retinens nomen, nos hactenus fecit credere, aut Marinum, si non fuit ut diximus, Mariana villa aut Zagarolum novi nominis oppidum, sed ut indicant ruinae, vetustae fuisse Lanuvium, ex quo vetustissimo et celebratissimi nominis municipio

Adjacent to the bay of Gaeta is **[318F]** the Caecuban Mount, famous for the excellence of its wine, and the city of Caecubum of the Fundani on the Via Appia. All these places have good wine in abundance, as Strabo says, and each of these ancient cities is distinguished as the birthplace of a pope: Gaeta of Gelasius the second, Fondi of Soter, whose father was Concordius.

But now we are reaching the limits of this region of Lazio, Sinuessa and the mouth of the Liri, or Garigliano, river. I have put the finishing touches on the description of the seacoast, but before returning to the inland areas I shall describe the places in Lazio to the left of the Liri. Above the town of Traetto, three miles from the sea, next to the Liri river is the fortified town of Spigno Saturnia. Eight miles from it is the town Fratta, as many miles distant from Pontecorvo, which was the town of Fregellae, as I noted. Above the other towns likewise, and eight miles away, is the important town of Ceprano. The rest of the places which approach closer to the source of the Liri, I shall describe in the sections on the Vestini and the Samnites. In the inland areas in the land of the Latins, there were cities closely crowded together, and an enormous number of towns and fortified settlements, of which Pliny reports fifty-three peoples have perished without a trace.

In describing this inland region, I shall depart from my method: up to now I have observed a method of following rivers from their mouths and sources. Now my account will not be able to continue observing this method: in this area alone, and in no other region of Italy, I shall follow another, **[318G]** sufficiently informative, method: that of proceeding along the three roads, the Via Appia, Via Latina, and Via Tiburtina, which by different routes lead to the Liri river and Sinuessa and Gaeta. And I shall not be able to advance with steady progress step by step without necessarily appearing to go astray, because the roads have deviated from their route, sometimes because their bridges have been ruined, sometimes because the roads have been completely destroyed, with the result that they are completely unknown.

So, as you leave Rome and travel towards Terracina, the first town, at the twelfth milestone, is Marino. It is likely that this was the villa called Marianum, so that the next villa, still half standing, is that of L. Murena, and the estate commonly known as Porzio. This same villa of L. Murena still retains its ancient name. Up to this point I am induced to believe that either Marino, if it was not, as I said, the villa called Marianum, or Zagarolo, a town with a new name, was, as the ancient ruins indicate, Lanuvium.

urbi propinquo, Murenas patricios et consulares viros originem duxisse Cicero in oratione pro L. Murena affirmat. Nuper autem in oppido, quod corrupte Civita Indivina appellant, a Prospero cardinale Columna possesso, lapis repertus est litteras inscriptus maiusculas, **[318H]** quae Lanuvium illud oppidum esse ostendunt.

A Marino autem octavo distant Velitrae, civitas vetusta, de qua Livius in octavo,

> In Veliternos veteres cives quod toties rebellassent graviter saevitum: et muri deiecti, et senatus inde abductus, iussique Transtiberim habitare. In agrum senatorum coloni missi, quibus a[d]scriptis speciem antiquae frequentiae Velitrae receperunt.

Easque ea civitas tum aliter vetustate sua, tum ea ratione notissima, quod Octavii Caesaris Augusti progenitores inde originem habuere. Quintoque ab ea miliario ad sinistram distat vetustissimi nominis oppidum Bora, ab uno trium fratrum condita, quorum alius Tibur aedificavit, alius monti proximo Catillo cognomen dedit, de quo Virgilius in VII:

> Tum gemini fratres Tiburtia moenia linquunt,
> Fratris Tiburti dictam cognomine gentem,
> Catillusque acerque Corax, Argiva iuventus.

Deinceps a Velitris recto itinere instituto distat XIIII oppidum Sarmineta, et tertio absunt Aquae Foetidae, ad quas palus incipit Terracinam usque non minus nunc, quam Strabonis aetate consueverit, navigabilis, quam locorum vicinitatem Martialis cocus poeta indicat his versibus:

> O nemus, O fontes, solidumque madentis arenae
> Litus, et aequoreis splendidus Anxur aquis,
> Et non unius spectator lectulus undae,
> Qui videt hinc puppes fluminis inde maris.

From this very ancient and famous town near Rome came the Murenae, patricians and consulars, as Cicero asserts in his speech *For Murena.* But in recent times in the town which people incorrectly call Civita Indivina, a property of Cardinal Prospero Colonna, a stone has been found containing an inscription in capital letters **[318H]** which shows that that town is Lanuvium.

But eight miles from Marino is Velletri, an ancient city which Livy mentions in the following terms in book 8:

> They took out their anger on the people of Velitrae, who had been Roman citizens for a long time, but had rebelled so many times. They tore down their walls, and forced their senate to leave town, and ordered the senators to live across the Tiber. They sent colonists to occupy the senators' land, and when they had been enrolled Velitrae regained its old densely-populated appearance.

This city is well-known not only for its antiquity but also because the ancestors of Augustus were born there. And five miles from Velletri, on the left, is Cora, a town with a very ancient name. It was built by one of three brothers, another of whom built Tibur and yet another gave his surname to the nearby mountain, Catillus. Virgil wrote about them in his seventh book:

> Then the twin brothers leave the walls of Tibur,
> (The race was named after the surname of their brother Tiburtus)
> Catillus and fierce Corax, the Argive youth.

After this, in a direct line from Velletri and fourteen miles away, is the town of Sarmineta; and three miles from it is Aquae Foetidae, where the marsh begins which extends right up to Terracina. It is as navigable now as in Strabo's time. The poet Martial the cook mentions the neighborhood in the following lines of verse:

> O grove, O springs, and shore of hard wet sand,
> and Anxur shining in the ocean waters.
> And a couch that looks upon two bodies of waters,
> which can see on this side ships in the river, on that side those on the sea.

Ab hisque aquis quinto distant Setia vetusti **[319A]** nominis oppidum, arduo in colle situm, vini ut refert Plinius optimi ferax. Et Martialis poeta,

> Pendula Pontinos quae spectat Setia campos,
> Exigua vetulos misit ab urbe cados.

Et alibi,

> Setinum dominaeque nives densique trientes,
> Quando ego te medico non prohibente bibam.

Privernumque item vetustum quinto a Setia distans, non ut olim campestre est, sed arduum in collem mutatum, postque Theotonica simul et Britonum rabie fuit destructum; cuius alumna fuit Camilla, quam virginem Virgilius miris effert laudibus: "Volsca de gente Camilla." Super quo verbo Servius exponit eam fuisse Privernatem, solidior vero et certior Privernatium laus fuit illa argutissima oratoris eorum ad senatum Romanum responsio, cum interrogatus qualis esset pax, quam Privernates tantopere peterent, respondit perpetuam si bona daretur futuram. Fluviusque ipsum praeterfluens oppidum, dictus est olim Amasenus, de quo Virgilius in VII "Amasene pater."

Circumstantque Privernum oppidula, Maientia, Arx Gorga, et Arx Sicca. Somninum hinc quinto abest oppidum, quod sit arduo in colle situm pro Summino dictum, a quo abest item quinto Terracina. Hanc inter ubique montuosam, et eam viam, quae primo **[319B]** secundum litus est descripta, habetur Appia, eiusque vitae prima urbs Alba XVI ab urbe distat. Qua quidem in via multo maiora sunt aedificiorum monumentorumque et iactarum molium vestigia, quam quisque possit credere, qui omnia attente non viderit. Estque haec Alba cuius meminit Virgilius in primo, "Albanique patres." Nam tredecim fuerunt Albani reges de Aeneae et Laviniae gente. Et Livius scribit Albam a Romanis destructam Albanos in urbem receptos Caelium montem incoluisse, de cuius origine Virgilius in VIII, "Ascanius clari condet cognominis Albam."

Five miles from these waters is Sezze, a town which retains its ancient [319A] name, located high on a hill; it produces, as Pliny tells us, wine of the best quality. And Martial writes,

> Setia, a small city which looks down from a height
> on the Pomptine fields, has sent little old casks of wine.

And in another poem, he writes,

> When shall I drink you with my doctor's permission,
> You Setine wine strained in lordly snow and filling the cups?

Priverno, an old town five miles from Sezze, is likewise not situated in a plain, as it formerly was; but it changed location to a high hill after it suffered destruction from the furious attacks of the Germans and the Bretons. It was the home of Camilla, the maiden Virgil praises so effusively with "Camilla from the race of the Volsci." Commenting on this line, Servius explains that she was from Privernum. But a more substantial and unambiguous praise of the people of Privernum occurs in the most eloquent reply of their orator to the Roman senate, on being asked what kind of peace it was that the people of Privernum were so anxiously seeking. He replied, "It will be a perpetual peace, if a good one is given them." The river which flows by the town was formerly called Amasenus; Virgil in his seventh book writes, "Father Amasenus."

Around Priverno are the small towns of Maenza, Roccagorga, and Roccasecca dei Volsci. Five miles from here is the town of Sonnino, located on a high hill; which derives its name from the town, which is also five miles from Terracina. Along this mountainous route, [319B] following the shoreline, the Via Appia was first marked out, and the first city along this road is Alba, sixteen miles from the city. The ruins of buildings and monuments, and the remains of massive piled-up structures on the road, are much larger than anyone could believe if he had not looked carefully at all of them. It is this town, Alba Longa, which Virgil mentions in his first book with the phrase "The Alban fathers." For thirteen Alban kings were descended from the race of Aeneas and Lavinia. And Livy writes that Alba Longa was destroyed by the Romans and its inhabitants came to live in Rome on the Caelian Hill; and Virgil wrote about its origin in his eighth book, "Ascanius will found a city with a famous name."

Eam urbem trecentis ante Romam annis conditam, ultimo imminutam reddidit Henricus III rex Germanicus. In parvo cuius angulo oppidulum nunc exstat a Sabellis civibus Romanis possessum, sicut et possident Sabellum vetustissimi nominis nunc oppidum, a quo familiae hinc Romanae nobili nomen fluxit, Ludovicusque cardinalis Aquileiensis Romani pontificis camerarius, monasterium quod Henricus III de gente Sabella ibi aedificavit paene funditus dirutum magna instauravit impensa, adeo ut sive monasterii, sive villae inter ceteras Italiae amoenissimae rusticanas inibi habitationes habeat, ductus aquarum instauraverit, **[319C]** et demortuae urbi aliquam oppidi faciem reddiderit.

Eademque in via Appia est proxima Albae sexto miliario Aritia olim civitas vetusta, de qua Livius in VIII, "Aritini eodem iure quo Lavinii in civitatem accepti." Nunc vero penitus est derelicta, cuius marmora et cetera ornamenta Marini oppidi ecclesias decorarunt. Estque Aritia una ex urbibus quinque quas facit Virgilius in VII ministrasse tela Aeneae. Quo in loco appellat eam potentem, quia fuit praestans in regione civitas. Eam dicit Servius nactam esse nomen a morbis, quos gigneret, quia vicina esset Pontinae paludi. Et alio loco dicit Aritiam a Virgilio appellari matrem, ut plauderet adulareturque Augusto, cuius mater fuerit Aricina. Nam Iulia Caesaris soror genuit Actiam ex Balbo in Aritia, et Actia ex Octavio genuit Octavianum.

Sic enim habet Virgilius,

> Ibat et Hippolyti proles pulcherrima bello,
> Virbius insignem quem mater Aritia misit.

Est vero haec Hippolyti fabula ab Ovidio scripta. Nam Diana Hippolytum ab inferis revocatum misit Aritiam, quem nutriri curavit ab Egeria nympha Numae Pompilii amica, cuius monitis et consilio rem publicam administrare simulabat. Appellat itaque Virgilius **[319D]** Hippolytum Virbium, id est, bis virum.

Nota est vetus historia: Etruscos, qui cum Arrunte regis Porsennae filio adoppugnandum Aritiam iverant, amisso duce redeuntes Romam amice et

The German king Henry III deprived Albano of its defenses; now, in a corner of it, there is a small town which is the possession of the Roman family of the Savelli. They also possess Castel Savelli, a modern town with a very ancient name from which this noble Roman family derives its name. Ludovico cardinal Scarampi of Aquileia, chamberlain of the pope, restored there at great expense a monastery which Henry III had built, and which had been almost completely torn down. As a result, he has in that place dwellings, among the pleasantest country dwellings in Italy, whether monastery or villa; he restored the aqueducts **[319C]** and gave back to a nearly dead city some appearance of a town.

And next along the same road, the Via Appia, at the sixth milestone, is Ariccia, formerly an ancient city; Livy in his eighth book states that the people of Aritia were received as Roman citizens under the same conditions as the people of Lavinium. But now Ariccia is completely abandoned: its marbles and remaining architectural ornaments decorate the churches of the town of Marino. Aritia is one of the five cities which Virgil in his seventh book mentions as furnishing weapons to Aeneas. In this passage he calls Aritia powerful because it was a city of outstanding importance in the region. Servius says that it obtained this name from the diseases which arose due to its proximity to the Pomptine marshes. And in another passage he says that Virgil called Aritia "mother" in order to praise and flatter Augustus, whose mother was from Aritia. For Julia, the sister of Caesar, bore Actia to Balbus in Aritia, and Actia bore Octavianus to Octavius.

And Virgil says,

> Handsome Virbius, the fairest son of Hippolytus,
> also went forth to war, whom mother Aritia sent to gain glory.

Indeed, this is the story about Hippolytus, which Ovid tells; Diana sent Hippolytus, after he had been raised from the dead, to Aritia to be cared for by the nymph Egeria, lover of Numa Pompilius (it was by her advice that he claimed to manage the government). And so Virgil calls **[319D]** Hippolytus Virbius, that is, *bis virum* or "twice a man."

And there is a famous old story that the Etruscans went to attack Aritia with Arruns, son of king Porsenna. They lost their leader and returned to

hospitaliter fuisse acceptos, quibus fuit datus ad inhabitandum in urbe celeberrimo loco vicus, semper postea Tuscus appellatus. Quam ob rem Porsenna obsides in foedere habitos benigne remisit. Livius libro LXXX scribit Cinnam et C. Marium expugnasse Aritiam coloniam. Plinius vero dicit brassicam Aricinam altitudine non excelsam reputari utilissimam, quia sub omnibus paene foliis fructificat cauliculis peculiaribus, cum Sabellanae brassicae folia dicat fuisse in admiratione crispa, eorumque crassitudinem extenuare caulem, sed dulcissimum ex omnibus perhiberi. Et Martialis poeta Aritinos porros sic laudat, "Mittit praecipuos nemoralis Aritia porros."

Deinceps eadem via secus Storacem, sive Nymphaeum amnem, ubi olim fuit Forum Appii, vetus oppidum, nunc est monasterium Fossa Nova appellatum, quod centum olim pluribusque monachis habitari solitum, postquam multis annis manserat derelictum, quarti Eugenii pontificis religiosissimi opera adiumentoque Cistertiensium abbas anno ante quinto decem duodecimve monachis habitari curavit. Fundique civitas postmodum habetur, quae superius descripta ab Honorato Caietano principe humanissimo possidetur.

[320E] Alia quae nos ad Latinorum limites ducit, via est Latina, in qua primum decimo ab urbe miliario cernuntur vestigia Columnae oppidi, a quo clara Columnensium familia multis ante saeculis originem habuit et cognomen. Ibique Algidum incipit vetusti, et in historiis celebrati nominis silva, in cuius medio bifurcatum est iter hoc nostrum: et hinc ad dexteram XIII a Columna distat Valmontonum, ubi Lavicos fuisse ad finem huius regionis ostendemus; inde ad sinistram minore spatio abest Gallicanum, quem locum Gabios fuisse coniicimus.

Eo autem itinere in ipso Algidi silvae ingressu Regillus est lacus, apud quem Aulus Postumius dictator prospere adversus Tarquinium Superbum patria eiectum, et Latinorum exercitum Romanis bellum inferentes pugnavit, a Gallicano autem sive Gabiis tertio distat Praeneste civitas, de qua inferius copiose dicemus. Et inde secundo absunt Cavae Odoardi Columnae oppidum, et pariter secundo item miliario abest Zinzanum, quod oppidum civitatulae cuipiam aedium ornatu, populi frequentia, et opum affluentia comparandum, a Martino quinto pontifice gloriosissimo, multisque

Rome and were received amicably and hospitably. They were given a place to live in the city, in a famous district which was forever after called "Tuscan." For this reason, Porsenna kindly sent back the hostages who had been held under the terms of a treaty. Livy writes in book 80 that Cinna and Marius attacked the colony of Aritia. But Pliny says that the cabbage of Aritia, due to the altitude, is not tall, and is considered very useful, because under almost every leaf it produces florets; while he says that the leaves of the Sabellian cabbage were amazingly crisp and their thickness weakens the stalk, but they are said to be the sweetest of all. The poet Martial praises the leeks of Aritia in the following line of verse: "Wooded Aritia sends the most excellent leeks."

Next, following the same road, beside the Storax or Nymphaeus river, where the ancient town of Forum Appii formerly stood, there is now a monastery called Fossa Nova, which in the past used to shelter a hundred or more monks, but now has been deserted for many years. Through the efforts and help of the very devout pope Eugenius IV, the abbot of the Cistercians five years before saw to it that ten or twelve monks lived there. And the city of Fondi comes next, which I described above; it is the possession of Onorato I Caetani, a most civilized prince.

[320E] Another road which leads us to the boundaries of Lazio is the Via Latina. The first place on it, at the tenth milestone from Rome, is the ruins of the town of Colonna, from which the famous family of the Colonna originated many centuries ago and took its name. And at this point begins the forest called Algidus, an ancient name well-attested in history. Our road comes to a fork in the middle of it. On this side, to the right, fourteen miles from Colonna, is Valmontone, where I shall show Labici was, at the border of this region. On that side, to the left, a shorter distance away, is Gallicano nel Lazio, which I have concluded was the location of ancient Gabii.

Along that route, at the entrance to the forest of Monte Compatri, is Lago Regillo, where the dictator Aulus Postumus fought successfully against the exiled Tarquinius Superbus and his allies, the army of the Latins, both of whom were the aggressors in war against the Romans. Three miles from Gallicano or Gabii is Palestrina, a city I shall say much about later on. And two miles from there is the town Cave, owned by Odoardo Colonna; and equidistant at the second milestone is Zinzano, a town comparable to any small city in the embellishment of its buildings, the density of its population, and its wealth. Here the illustrious Pope Martin V, along

Romanae ecclesiae **[320F]** cardinalibus, et simul a Romanae curiae viris, per aestatis caumata saepenumero inhabitatum est.

Abest a Zinzano decem milibus Anagnina civitas in Hernicis vetustissima, de qua Virgilius, "Hernica saxa colunt, quos dives Anagnia pascit." Servius vero exponit Virgilium allusisse ad historiam. Nam Antonius, Fulvia Augusti sorore contempta, postquam duxit Cleopatram Aegypti reginam, eius monetam in Anagnia cudi iussit, unde dives est a Virgilio appellata. Hernicos autem Servius Sabina lingua a saxosa patria dictos vult, quia "herne" Sabini saxum dicerent. Livius in IX,

> P. Cornelius Arvina M. Tremulus cos., concilium populorum omnium habentibus Anagninis in circo, quam maritimum vocant, praeter Alatrinatem et Verulanum omnes Hernici bellum Romnis indixerunt.

Et infra, "Marcius consul omnem gentem Hernicam in deditionem accepit." Et inferius, "Anagninis, quia arma Romanis intulerant, civitas sine suffragii latione data, concilia conubiaque adempta, et magistratibus praeterquam sacrorum curatione interdictum fuit."

Anagnia civitas duobus Romanis pontificibus, tertio Innocentio et octavo Bonifacio, civibus decorata. Bonifaciusque vel ea ratione **[320G]** gloriosus pontifex fuit, quod annum Iubilaeum primus Romanorum pontificum Romae instituit. Isque qui quartum praesenti anno celebratur Iubilaeus maiorem multo ceteris hucusque habuit populorum multitudinem, melius in dies ut videbatur processurus, nisi exardescere incipiens praesenti Iunio pestilentia et multos assumpsisset, et curiam abire suasisset, et populos ab adventu deterruisset. Inde vero fuit Bonifacius infelix, quod Sarram Columnensem capitali persecutus odio Praeneste vetustissimam urbem, quam is Sarra paterna possederat successione solo aequavit, et duos ex hac familia cardinales dignitate privavit, quos Clemens V illico restituit. Et postmodum regem Franciae Bonifacius adeo irritavit, ut immissus adiutusque ab eo

with many **[320F]** cardinals and foremost men of the Curia, lived on many occasions in summer to escape the heat.

Ten miles from Zinzano is the city of Anagni, most ancient among the cities of the Hernici, about which Virgil wrote, "inhabitants of rocky Hernici, fed by rich Anagnia." In fact, Servius explains that Virgil was alluding here to actual history, for Antonius, after rejecting Fulvia, the sister of Augustus, married Cleopatra, queen of Egypt, and ordered coins commemorating her to be struck in Anagnia; for this reason Virgil calls it "wealthy." And indeed Servius maintains that the Hernici were so named on account of their rocky country, because "herne" in the language of Gabii means "rock." In his ninth book Livy says:

> In the consulship of P. Cornelius Arvina and Q. Marcius Tremulus, the inhabitants of Anagnia held a council of all the people in the Circus which they call the Maritime Circus; except for the people of Aletrium and Verulae, all the Hernici declared war on the Romans.

And further on he says, "The consul Marcius received the surrender of the entire people of the Hernici." And below this,

> The people of Anagnia, because they had taken up arms against the Romans, received citizen status without the vote; the councils of their government and their right of intermarriage were taken away, and their magistrates were forbidden to perform any duties except those involving religious rites.

The city of Anagni has been distinguished by two popes, Innocent III and Boniface VIII. The latter is **[320G]** famous for being the first Roman pope to establish the practice of a Jubilee year. This Jubilee being celebrated in the present year is the fourth, and has been celebrated by a much greater crowd of participants than others, and seemed that it would enjoy increasing success, if the plague had not broken out in June and killed many men, caused the Curia to leave, and kept people away. But from then on Boniface was truly unfortunate, because he pursued Sciarra Colonna with implacable hatred, and so reduced to rubble the ancient city of Praeneste, which this Sciarra had owned as inherited property. Boniface stripped two Colonna cardinals of their rank, but Clement V restored them. Afterwards, Boniface so irritated the king of France that Sciarra with his help was em-

Sarra eundem pontificem in patria et domo paterna ceperit, Romamque captivum abduxerit, ubi nulla magis ratione alia, diem male obiisse creditus est, quam quia simplicem corde et sanctum virum Celestinum quintum, qui pontificatu, quo se per renuntiationem exuit, illum ornaverat, in Fumonis carcere mori coegerat.

Scribit Plinius Fucinum lacum, qui Marsorum appellatur, subterraneos habere cuniculos, quibus aqua certo [320H] effluens tempore amnem faciat. Et sive Plinii textus, ut saepe alibi eo in loco corruptus, sive aliter vitiatus et mutilatus est, non satis potuimus intellegere, quo in loco fluvium ille oriri affirmet. Sed fontem esse scimus Agnaniae Tophanum nomine, qui hieme quando Fucinus glacie astringitur, siccus; vere postmodum aestate ac autumno, ingentem evomit vim aquarum, quae Lirim amnem a Sancto Vito oriundum adaugent.

Distat quinto ab Anagnia Ferentinum, Romana colonia olim et ipsa Hernicorum, de qua Livius libro tertio, "Progressus Tullius ad caput Ferentinum." Et libro VII, "Ferentinum urbem Hernicorum vi cepit." Et libro IX, "Hernicorum tribus populis Alatrinati, Verulano, Ferentinati, suae leges quia maluerunt quam civitatem Romanam, redditae." Item inferius,

> Ferentinum inde quamquam nihil quietis dabatur, tamen summa alacritate ductum. Ceterum ibi plus laboris et periculi fuit, et defensa summa vi moenia, et locus erat munimento naturaque tutus. Sed evicit omnia assuetus praedae miles. Ad tria milia hominum caesa, praeda militum fuit.

Suetonius autem Tranquillus scribit Othonis imperatoris, qui Galbae successit, maiores ortos fuisse oppido Ferentino familia vetere honorata, atque ex principibus Etruria.

boldened to capture the pope in his own city, indeed in his family home, and led him as a captive to Rome. Here, it is believed, he met a bad end because he had forced to die in prison at Fumone a simplehearted and holy man, Celestine V, who had honored him with the papacy by renouncing it himself.

Pliny writes that the Fucine Lake, which is called "of the Marsi," has underground channels through which water **[320H]** flows at certain times and forms a river. And either the text of Pliny is corrupt at this point, as it often is elsewhere, or it has been in some other way flawed or damaged, with the result that I cannot understand sufficiently where that author states the river has its source. But I do know that there is a spring at Anagni called Tufano which is dried up in winter when the Fucine Lake is frozen, but afterwards in spring and fall spews out a huge torrent of water to join the Liri river, which has its source at S. Vito Romano.

Five miles from Anagni is Ferentino, once a Roman colony, and a possession of the Hernici, as we know from Livy, book 3, "Tullius rode on ahead to the source of the Ferentina." And in book 7, "He took by force Ferentinum, a city of the Hernici." And in book 9:

> To three peoples of the Hernici, the inhabitants of Aletrium, Verulae, and Ferentinum, the Romans restored their own government, because they preferred that to Roman citizenship.

Also, below this,

> Despite having no rest, they hurried from there to Ferentinum; there was more trouble and danger there, and the defenders of the walls called upon all of their energy. The place had both natural and man-made fortifications, but the soldiers' desire for booty overcame every obstacle. About 3,000 of the enemy were slain, and there was booty for the soldiers.

And in fact Suetonius writes that the emperor Galba's successor, Otho's ancestors were born at Ferentinum of an old and distinguished family, one of the royal families of Etruria.

Et ab eo totidem Frusinona, de qua Livius, "Frusinates tertia parte agri damnat, quod Hernicos ab eis sollicitatos compertum." **[321A]** Fuitque duobus olim ornata Romanis pontificibus, Hormisda patre Iusto per Symmachi et Boethii tempora consulatus, et Silverio eodem genito Hormisda, quem Iustiniano primo imperatore Theodatus rex Gothorum tertius per pecuniam ordinavit.

A Frusinonaque distat duodecimo Ceperanum, nostrae huius regionis alter limes. Sed propinquo huic itinere sunt ad Zinzani dexteram Pallianum, Serronum, Pillium, Acutum, Trivilianum, Collis Padi, Anticulum, Verulae vetus oppidum, de quo Livius in IX, "Verulanis suae leges, quia maluerunt quam civitatem Romanam, redditae; conubiumque inter suos quod aliquamdiu soli Hernicorum habuerant permissum." Fumone, Caelestini pontificis Romani carcere et morte clarum. Deinceps Alatrum, vetusti nominis civitas, cui simul cum Verulanis suae leges redditae a Romanis et conubium permissum, et Babucum, olim civitas apud Livium Bovillarum nomine nota. Turritium, Pofe, Vicus, Ripae, Porcilianum, Trevum, Felectinum.

Altera autem via, quam medio in Algido liquimus, primum est oppidum olim Lavicanum, de quo Livius libro IIII:

> Et renuntiatum est novos hostes Lavicanos consilia cum **[321B]** veteribus iungere. Lavicos legati missi, cum responsa inde retulissent dubia, quibus nec tum bellum quidem parari, nec diuturna pacem fore appareret, Tusculanis negotium datum adverterent animo, ne quid novi tumultus Lavici oriretur. Nuntiarunt legati Lavicanos arma cepisse, et cum equorum exercitu depopulatos agrum Tusculanum castra in Algido posuisse. Q. Sulpicius Priscus dictator, captis direptisque illorum castris, oppidum Lavicos corona circumdatum scalis diripuit, censuitque Senatus frequentem coloniam Lavicos deducendam. Coloni ab urbe mille quingenti missi bina iugera acceperunt.

The same distance away is Frosinone, about which Livy writes, "The people of Frusinum had to pay a fine amounting to a third of their land, because it was found that they had stirred up the Hernici." **[321A]** This town gave birth to two Roman popes: Hormisda, son of Justus, in the time of the consulships of Symmachus and Boethius; and Silverius, son of that same Hormisda, whom Theodatus, third king of the Goths, ordained for money in the time of the emperor Justinian I.

Twelve miles from Frosinone is Ceprano, the second boundary of our region of Lazio. And on the route near this town are, on the right of Zinzano, Paliano, Serrone, Piglio, Acuto, Trivigliano, Collepardo, Fiuggi, and Veroli, the latter an ancient town about which Livy in book 9 writes,

> To the inhabitants of Verulae, the Romans restored their own government, because they preferred that to Roman citizenship, and they were given the right of intermarriage, a right which they were for some time the only Hernici to possess.

Then comes Fumone, famous for the imprisonment and death of Pope Celestine V. Next is Alatri, a city with an ancient name, whose citizens along with the Verulani were given back their own laws by the Romans, and the right of intermarriage. Then there is Bauco, formerly a city known in Livy by the name Bovillae. Then come Torrice, Pofi, Vico, Ripi, Porciliano, Trevi nel Lazio, Filettino.

But along the second road which we left behind in the middle of the forest on Monte Compatri, the first town is Colonna, the site of the ancient Labici, about which Livy writes in book 4,

> It was announced at Rome that a new enemy, the inhabitants of the town of Labici, **[321B]** had joined the old ones. Envoys were sent to the Labicani, when they brought back ambiguous replies, indicating that war was not being prepared, but neither did peace appear likely to last long. The people of Tusculum were given the task of paying attention to any new uprising among the Labici. The envoys announced that the Labici had taken up arms, and together with the army of the Aequi had devastated the territory of Tusculum and had pitched camp on Mt. Algidus. Their camp was captured and sacked; the dictator Q. Sulpicius Priscus surrounded their town, Labici, besieged it successfully with scaling ladders, and plundered it. The Senate decreed that a large colony should be established at Labici. 1,500 colonists were sent out from Rome and received two *iugera* apiece.

Id oppidum nunc dicitur Valmontone, quod a nobili comitum familia cuius est possessum, nuper magno privatum est decore Lucido diacono cardinale studiorum humanitatis flagrantissimo. Sed eius frater Altus, vir doctus simul et prudens, Ioanne ornatus filio rei bellicae gloriae apud Venetos florente, oppidi illius aliorumque quibus praesunt decus conservat. Fuitque Lavicanum olim uvis copiosum optimis, ex quibus Clodium Albinum pondo viginti unica cibatione comedisse scribit Iulius Capitolinus.

Proximumque est Valmontoni **[321C]** Monsfortinus oppidum Stephani nostri familiae nobilis, quae oppidi cognomen habet, oriundi patria atque villa. Deinceps sunt Zanchatum, Gavignanum, et Signia, oppidum vetus; vinum, ut inquit Plinius, faciens Signinum, quod alvum maxime restringit. Et Martialis poeta,

> Potabis liquidum Signina morantia ventrem.
> Ne nimium sitias, sit tibi parca sitis.

Quae Signia Vitaliano pontifice Romano patre Anastasio ornata fuit. Ulteriusque sunt Scucula, Merulum, Supinum, Patrica, Cecanum, et Castrum; ibi alius est nostrae Latinae regionis nunc Campania limes.

Tertia restat nobis, per quam ad alios nostrae Latinae regionis limites itur, Tiburtina via. Eam civitatem sexto decimo ab urbe distantem, multo ante Romam originem a Graecis habuisse vult Strabo, et Virgilius eam a Tiburtio conditam facit, cuius frater Catillus nomen monti dederit propinquo. Fuitque Tibur ex quinque civitatibus, quas facit Virgilius Aeneae arma fabricasse, ubi Tibur appellat superbum. Et Servius exponit, "aut nobile, aut quia aliquando Tiburtini a senatu responsum acceperunt, quod essent superbi." Ubi etiam Virgilius in septimo dicit "sub Albunea," Servius exponit **[321D]** Albuneam altum esse fontem in Tiburtinis montibus ob aquae qualitatem, quae in ipso fonte est, sic dictum. Et Plinius Tiburtinum lapidem non

This town is now called Valmontone, from the noble family of counts who possess it. It has been recently bereaved by the loss of one of its distinguished citizens, Lucido de' Conti, the cardinal deacon, and a very enthusiastic student of the liberal arts. But his brother Alto, a learned and wise man, has been distinguished by his son Giovanni's glory in war among the Venetians. Together they preserve the honor of that town and others they rule. And Labici was known for its abundance of excellent grapes; Julius Capitolinus writes that Clodius Albinus consumed twenty pounds of them in a single meal.

Next to **[321C]** Valmontone is the town of Artena, the home of my friend Stefano, born on their estate to the noble family which takes its surname from the town, previously known as Montefortino. Then there are Zancato, Gavignano, and Segni, an ancient town. The latter produces, as Pliny notes, a wine called Signine, very constipating. And the poet Martial writes,

> Will you drink the wine of Segni which binds loosened bowels?
> Do not be too thirsty, so that you don't get constipated.

This town was distinguished as the birthplace of Pope Vitalianus. And farther on are Sgurgola, Morolo, Supino, Patrica, Ceccano, and Castro, where we now come to another of the boundaries of our region of Lazio, now known as Campania.

There remains the third road by which one can reach the other boundaries of our region of Lazio: that is the Via Tiburtina, named after the ancient city of Tibur, sixteen miles from Rome. Strabo says that it was founded by the Greeks long before Rome, and Virgil says it was founded by Tiburtus, whose brother Catillus gave his name to the nearby mountain. And Tibur was one of the five cities which Virgil has prepare arms for Aeneas, where he calls Tibur "proud." Servius explains, "either because Tibur was noble, or because at one time the inhabitants of Tibur received a reply from the Senate that they were 'arrogant.'" Also, where Virgil says in the seventh book "under Albunea," Servius explains **[321D]** that Albunea was a spring

magis ab ipso vocabulo Romae trito construenda, ornanda, conservandaque Roma iuvisse dicit constare, quam eum ad omnia fortem idoneumque fuisse. Sunt Tiburi propinquae ingentes admirandaeque ruinae, cum aliorum paene infinitorum magnificentissimi operis aedificiorum, tum villae quam Hadrianus imperator exstruxit, de qua sic scribit Aelius Spartianus, "Tiburtinam villam mire aedificavit, ita ut in ea et provinciarum et locorum celeberrima nomina poneret."

Cetera Strabonis verbis paulo post dicemus. Ea civitas Simplicium pontificem Romanum genuit, quam Federicus primus imperator Romanus Theotonicus, ab aliis Theotonicis aliquot annis prius spoliatam dirutamque, reaedificavit. Supra eam civitatem montes sunt ardui et late diffusi, in quibus fortissimi olim habitaverunt Aequicoli, de quibus Virgilius in septimo Aeneidos,

> Horrida praecipue cui gens assuetaque multo
> Venatu nemorum duris Aequicola glebis.
> Armati terram exercent, semperque recentes
> Convectare iuvat praedas et vivere rapto.

Fuerunt vero ex primis Latinorum populis, qui Romana re publica crescente deleti sunt. Nam Livius, libro nono, "Populus Romanus bellum fieri Aequis iussit. Ad XL oppida intra LX **[322E]** dies omnia oppugnando ceperunt, quorum pleraque diruta atque incensa sunt, nomenque Aequorum prope ad internecionem deletum."

Primum ipsis in montibus ad Anienis sinistram est oppidum, amoenis Ursinorum Taliacoccii comitum domibus ornatum, Vicus Varronis appellatum, superius Porcella et Cantalupum oppidula. Deinde arduo in monte Rivus Frigidus, quo superato alii item celsiores superandi sunt montes Apennini iugis quamtumlibet altissimis comparandi, in quorum summitate putei, ut fertur, plures; sed quos viderimus duo exstant tam alte excisi defossique, ut deiectum bilibre saxum non prius referat casus sui sonitum, quam duo Virgiliani versus debita sint pausa pronuntiati. Quae quidem perforatis succisisque et excavatis in imo montibus, sive a Martio aedile, sive a Claudio imperatore perducendis Romam a lacu Fucino aquis, ne conclusus aer cursum aquae moraretur, spiracula fuerunt adhibita. Suetonius namque

high up in the Tiburtine mountains, so called from the quality of the water in it. And Pliny says it is well-known that stone from Tibur was not fit for constructing and decorating and preserving Rome, in the formulaic phrase, but it was strong and suitable for all purposes. Near Tivoli are enormous and wondrous ruins, not only of other almost numberless buildings of magnificence, but also ruins of the estate which the emperor Hadrian built. Aelius Spartianus says "he built his estate at Tibur with wondrous skill, so that he named parts of it after the most famous names of provinces and places."

I shall mention a little later other notices in the words of Strabo. This city was the birthplace of Pope Simplicius, and the German emperor Frederick I rebuilt it after it had been despoiled and demolished some years before by other Germans. Above this city the mountains are steep and scattered; in them lived in ancient times the Aequicoli, a robust race, of whom Virgil says in the seventh book of the *Aeneid*,

> A rough tribe, who hunt all day in the woods and are used to a hard land. They work the land under arms, and enjoy driving off others' herds as prey and living on plunder.

Indeed, these were among the first Latin populations to be destroyed by the growth of the Roman Republic. For Livy, in book 9, writes:

> The Roman people declared war on the Aequi. They besieged **[322E]** and captured about forty towns within sixty days. Most of these they destroyed and burned, and the race of the Aequi was nearly destroyed.

In the Monti Tiburtini, on the left bank of the Aniene, the first town is called Vicovaro, and it is distinguished by the pleasant homes of the Orsini, counts of Tagliacozzo. Above are the hamlets of Percile and Cantalupo. Then, on a high hill, there is Riofreddo, and when you cross that hill you must also cross other even higher mountains, comparable in height to the loftiest mountains you please in the Apennine chain. At their summits are many wells, as they call them, but we saw only two of them still in existence. These were cut and dug out so deep into the earth that when we threw down a two-pound stone we did not hear the noise of its hitting the bottom until after we had finished reciting two verses of Virgil. The aedile Marcius or the emperor Claudius had cut through and hollowed out the depths of the

Tranquillus Claudium principem dicit triginta milia servorum undecim annis emittendo lacu Fucino, et aqua Romam perducenda tenuisse.

Supra Rivum Frigidum recta est Arceolum, secus quod planities incipit, ut in ea montium summitate **[322F]** gratissima. In qua vetustissimi fuerunt Carseoli, de qua Livius libro decimo scribit, "Eodem anno Carseolo colonia in agrum Aequicolorum deducta." Et libro XXVII dicit eam fuisse unam duodeviginti coloniarum quae, Hannibale in Italia agente, milites et pecuniam senatui dare recusaverunt.

Deinceps sunt Celae, Sculcula, et Peretum; unde in Taliacotium est descensus, quod novi nominis oppidum, sed populo divitiisque refertum nuper maximum amisit ornamentum, Ioannem cardinalem Tarentinum philosophiae litterarumque sacrarum dogmatibus clarissimum.

Iamque ad Marsorum regionem est perventum, quam Hannibal, sicut Livius vigesimo secundo scribit, devastavit; et iterum revertens ab urbe Roma, sicut Livii vigesimosexto habetur, per eius agrum iter fecit. Eaque in regione interiit Valeria civitas, Bonifacii quarti pontificis Romani (quo cohortante Focas imperator Pantheon Romae in omnium Christi martyrum basilicam permisit consecrari) patria. A qua civitate per Longobardorum tempora Marsorum nomen in Valeriam est conversum. Fuisse vero Marsos urbem, a qua nomen regio accepit, Plinius sic asserit, "Gellianus auctor est lacu Fucino **[322G]** haustum Marsorum oppidum conditum a Marsia duce Lydorum." Virgilius, libro VII, "Quin et Marubia venit de gente sacerdos," et Servius exponit Medeam, quando relictis Colchis Iasonem secuta est, ad Italiam pervenisse, et populos quosdam circa Fucinum ingentem lacum habitantes, propter paludis magnitudinem docuisse remedia contra serpentes. Quamquam alii Marubios a rege dictos volunt, hique populi Medeam Angitiam nominaverunt, eo quod serpentes suis carminibus angeret. Et Plinius:

mountain to conduct water from the Fucine Lake to Rome, and made air-holes so that trapped air would not block the flow of water. For indeed Suetonius Tranquillus tells us that Claudius employed 30,000 slaves for eleven years to drain the Fucine Lake and to bring the water to Rome.

Above Riofreddo, right ahead is Arsoli, and beside it begins the level ground so welcome in the high mountains. **[322F]** Here was the ancient Carseoli, about which Livy writes in book 10, "In the same year, the Romans established a colony at Carseoli in the territory of the Aequicoli"; and in book 27 he says that it was one of the eighteen colonies which, during Hannibal's actions in Italy, refused to contribute soldiers and money to the Roman Senate.

Next come Celle, Scurcola Marsicana, and Pereto, from where one can travel down to Tagliacozzo, a town with a new name but densely-populated and wealthy; it recently lost its eminent citizen Giovanni, cardinal of Taranto, famous for his learning in philosophy and sacred writings.

And at this point we come to the region of the Marsi: Hannibal, according to Livy, book 22, laid waste the area and in book 26 of the same author, he came back again from the city of Rome and made his way through this land. And in this region the city of Valeria has been lost; it was the birthplace of Pope Boniface IV, at whose urging the emperor Phocas allowed the Pantheon at Rome to be consecrated as a church to all the Christian martyrs. In the times of the Lombards, the city changed its name, Marsi, into Valeria. But that there was a city called Marsi, from which the region took its name, Pliny corroborates in the following words: "Gellianus affirms that the Fucine Lake submerged a town of the Marsi founded by Marsyas, leader of the Lydians." And Virgil, in the seventh book of the *Aeneid*, writes, "And there also came the priest sent from the Marruvian race. . . "; and Servius explains that when Medea left Colchis to follow Jason, she came to Italy and taught magic charms against snakes to the people living around the Fucine Lake, because of the size of the swamp. Other authorities, however, state that the Marruvians were named after their king. These people named Medea 'Angitia,' because she tortured snakes with her charms. And Pliny says,

> Simile et in Italia Marsorum genus durat, quos a Circae filio ortos tradunt, et inde inesse eis vim naturalem eam. Et tamen omnibus hominibus contra serpentes inest venenum. Ferunt ictas saliva, ut ferventis aquae contactu fugere, quod si in fauces penetraverit, etiam mori, idque maxime humani ieiuni oris.

Quam serpentum in ea regione frequentium, et peritiae incantationis Marsorum opinionem confirmat Iulius Capitolinus, ubi vitam scribens Heliogabali imperatoris, dicit serpentes eum per Marsicae gentis incantationem collegisse, eosque subito ante lucem, ut solet populus ad ludos celebres convenire effudisse, multosque afflictos morsu aut fuga allisos. Nec falsa **[322H]** aut fabulosa tenenda sunt ea, quae hic de serpentum incantatione sunt scripta. Propheta namque David in Psalmo LVII sic habet, "Furor illis secundum similitudinem serpentis, sicut aspidis surdae et obturantis aures suas, quae non exaudiet vocem incantantium et venefici incantationis sapienter." Et beatus Aurelius Augustinus in dicti psalmi expositione sic scribit:

> Attende quid ibi dicatur ad similitudinem, quid moneatur ad prohibitionem. Ita ergo et hic data est quaedam similitudo de Marso: qui incantat, ut educat aspidem de tenebrosa caverna utique in lucem vult educere. Illa autem amando tenebras suas, quibus se involutam occultat, dicitur quod cum exire noluerit, recusans tamen audire illas voces, quibus se cogi sentit, allidit unam aurem terrae et de cauda obturat alteram. Atque ita voces illas quantum potest evitans non exit ad incantantem.

Livius, bellum scribens Italicum libro LXXII, quod quia a Marsis inchoavit dictum est Marsicum, inter populos qui Romanis rebellarunt enumerat Marrucinos et Marsos. Et libro LXXVI dicit Marsos a [*C*]inna, et

> A similar race lingers on in Italy also, the Marsi, said to be descended from the son of Circe and to possess this natural property on that account. All men, however, contain a poison available as a protection against snakes: people say that snakes flee from contact with saliva as from the touch of boiling water, and that if it gets inside their throats they actually die; and that this is especially the case with the saliva of a person who is fasting.

Julius Capitolinus confirms this assertion that snakes are abundant in this region and the Marsi are skilled in charms against their bites. In his *Life of the Emperor Heliogabalus* he says that he collected snakes by a charm of the Marsic tribe, and before dawn when the people were accustomed to gather for the games he suddenly poured the snakes out and many people were bitten, or crushed while fleeing. Things which are written here about snake-charming should not be thought **[322H]** untrue or fantastic. For we find also in the writings of the prophet David, in Psalm 57:

> They have a madness like that of a serpent, they are like the deaf adder that stops its ear, so that it does not hear the voice of charmers, even one who charms wisely.

St. Augustine comments on this psalm:

> Pay attention to what is said here in regard to the simile, the warning it gives. So this is given as an allegory about the Marsian: he who chants magic charms, so that he may entice a viper out of the shadows of a cave, and by all means wishes to bring it forth into the light. But the snake loves the shadows where it hides curled up: it does not want to come out, and refuses to hear the voices which are compelling it. It puts one ear to the earth and stops up the other with its tail and avoids hearing the voices as much as it can, and does not come forth to the charmer.

Livy, narrating the story of the Italian War in book 72 (because it began with the Marsi it was called Marsic), names among the peoples who rebelled against Rome the Marrucini and the Marsi. And in book 76 he says that the Marsi were defeated by the legates Cinna and Caecilius Pius, and

Caecilio et Pinna legatis superatos pacem petiisse a Sulla. Bellumque hoc id felicitatis Romae urbi attulit, quod M. Cicero in eo militans abominatus est Romanorum civium crudelitates, et ad litterarum studia se contulit. Unde factum est, ut Roma ingenium haberet, **[323A]** quod suo magnitudine illi par esset.

Abest a Taliacoccio Fucinus Marsorum lacus decimo miliario, et edito in colle Apenninum versus est Alba Marsorum, Romana colonia, sicut Livium diximus libro X scripsisse, qui et libro XXVII eam fuisse dicit unam ex duodeviginti coloniis, quae Hannibalis temporum difficultate militiam detrectarunt. Eamque Strabo urbem, ut appellat, solam in Latina regione pro mediterranea scripsit, quam dicit excelso in monte sitam lacui Fucino imminere pelagi similitudinem magnitudine habenti, ex eo lacu ductos fuisse fontes aquae Marciae, qua potaretur Roma. Nosque in Roma instaurata ostendimus Marcium in sua aedilitate introduxisse aquam eius nomine appellatam, quae quidem aqua supra omnes alias introductas probabatur. Et Plinius dicit Iuvencum amnem supernatare Fucinum, qui Iuvencus Romam a Marcio sit perductus. Additque alibi Plinius in lacu Fucino piscem esse qui octonis natet pennis, cum ceteri omnes ubique quaternis tantummodo natent.

Alba vero dicit Strabo, quia esset natura loci et munimento arcis valida saepe Romanos praesidii loco servandis in custodia noxiis usos fuisse. Et nos in Livio invenimus libro **[323B]** XXII Q. Fabium Maximum consulem Paulli nepote adversus Allobrogas et Bituitum Arve[r]norum regem feliciter pugnasse, ex Bituitique exercitu occisa CXX milia, ipsumque cum ad satisfaciendum senatui Romam profectus esset Albam custodiendum fuisse missum. Circumstant lacum Sancti [Potiti] Sancti Ionae castella, Paternumque Transacum, Gaianum, Avecianum, Mallianum oppida. Et comitatus titulo ac opibus praecipuum est Celanum, nostrae hac parte Latinorum regionis limes.

sought peace from Sulla. And this war brought a measure of good to the city of Rome, in that when M. Cicero fought in it, he was so disgusted by the cruelty of Roman citizens that he turned to the study of literature. In this way, Rome gained a talent **[323A]** equal to her own greatness.

From Tagliacozzo, it is ten miles to Lago di Fucino of the Marsi; high up on a hill towards the Apennine range is Alba dei' Marsi, near the site of the Roman colony Alba Fucens, as I mentioned Livy attests in book 10. He also mentions, in book 27, that Alba was one of the eighteen colonies to refuse military support to Rome during the Hannibalic invasion. And Strabo refers to Alba as a city—the one in the region of Latium which is most inland—located on a lofty mountain hanging over the Fucine Lake which is like a sea in size. And from this lake flow springs whose water the Aqua Marcia carries to Rome. I have shown in my *Rome restored* that Marcius, when he was aedile, constructed the aqueduct named after him, and its water was judged the best, above that of all the other aqueducts which carried water to Rome. Pliny says that the Juvencus river floats on top of the Fucine Lake, and that Marcius brought this Juvencus to Rome. Elsewhere Pliny adds that in the Fucine Lake there is a fish which swims with eight fins, whereas all the rest everywhere swim with only four.

Indeed, Strabo says because Alba was a natural stronghold, and strongly fortified by a citadel, the Romans often used it as a garrison for detaining criminals in custody. And we find **[323B]** in Livy, book 62, that the consul Q. Fabius Maximus, grandson of Paulus, waged a successful war against the Allobroges and king Bituitus of the Arverni, in which one hundred twenty thousand of Bituitus' soldiers were killed. When he had set out for Rome to give satisfaction to the Senate, he was sent into custody at Alba. The fortified towns of S. Potito and Sta. Iona surround the lake; also the towns of Paterno, Trasacco, Gaiano, Avezzano, Magliano de' Marsi, and Celano, distinguished by the title of a count, the chief town in regard to reputation and wealth. This is the boundary of our region of Lazio in this area.

Omissa vero sunt a nobis superius nulli praedictarum trium viarum propinqua aliquot castella et oppida, una tamen eademque in montium regione Praeneste Tiburque inter et Vicum Varronis ac Zinatianum sita, Rocha Cavarum Capranica, quae praestantissimam Romae dedit familiam Capranicensem, in qua Paulus archiepiscopus gravissimo Martini quinti pontificis Romani testimonio maximae in suo saeculo prudentiae vir fuit. Et Dominicus cardinalis Sanctae Crucis frater suus multa civilis pontificiique iuris et studiorum humanitatis doctrina, multaque prudentia nunc claret, cum tamen Angelus Asculanus episcopus, et Nicolaus protonotarius nepos eisdem doctrinis **[323C]** virtutibusque ornentur.

Deinceps sunt oppida, Guadagnolum, Polium, Casa Corbola, S. Gregorius, Rocha Liricis dicta. Sunt etiam his proxima oppida Caecilianum, Sambuca, Sarracinescum, Rocha Mutiorum, Giranum, Ceretum, Anticulum, Rivate, Afile, Civitella, et Olibanum, clarissimae ac prudentissimae mulieris Suevae, Albae Marsorum comitissae, Prosperi cardinalis Columnae et fratrum genetricis, deliciae. Post Olibanum sunt Piscianum et Sanctus Vitus oppidum, fonte uno Liris sive Gauriani, quem propinquum habet clarum. Estque superius celsis in montibus Sublacum, vel uti Plinius appellat Sublaqueum nobile oppidum, lacui eiusdem, et tamen prisci nominis imminens. Redditque utrumque fama celebratum beati Benedicti, non magis diutina conversatio ibi habita, quam eius toto orbe notissimum ibi aedificatum magnifici operis monasterium. Cernitur vero in dextera Anienis ripa ab ipso Sublaci lacu ad Vicum usque Varronis incisus saxeo in monte ductus aquarum, quem formis partim eo incisis modo, partim altum defossis, partim sublimi fornice muroque excitatis Romam quadragesimo miliario veniebant.

Sed in hac eadem Latinorum regione ad praedictorum **[323D]** declarationem Romanis in conspectu esse dicit Strabo Tibur et Praeneste, et Tusculum et Tibur quidem qua est Heraclium habere cataractem, quem facit Anio decidens ex loco altissimo in profundam vallem, et per lucos iuxta ipsam urbem ubi incipiat esse navigabilis. Inde digredi ad metalla lapidis Tiburtini, et eius qui est in Gabiis, qui etiam dicitur rubeus, unde plurima Romae opera fabricata sunt.

But in the preceding material I have left out some fortified villages and towns which do not lie along any of the three roads I mentioned before. Still in the same single region of hills, between Palestrina and Tivoli, and Vicovaro and Genazzano, is located Rocca di Cava Capranica, which gave Rome a most distinguished family, the Capranica, among whom Archbishop Paolo was preeminent in wisdom in his time, according to the very weighty evidence of Pope Martin V. And his brother, Domenico, cardinal of Sta. Croce, is now famous for his great knowledge of civil and canon law and his learning in the liberal arts. Angelo Capranica, bishop of Ascoli, and their nephew Nicolò, a protonotary, are adorned with learning in the same areas, and with virtue. **[323C]**

Next are the towns of Guadagnolo, Poli, Casape, San Gregorio, Rocca Lerici, and next to these are the towns of Ciciliano, Sambuci, Saracinesco, *Rocha Mutiorum*, Gerano, Cerreto Laziale, Anticoli Corrado, Roiate, Affile, Civitella, and Olevano Romano, the favorite resort of Sveva, countess of Alba of the Marsi, and illustrious and wise mother of Prospero cardinal Colonna and of his brothers. After Olevano are *Piscianum* and S. Vito Romano, a town famous for its proximity to one source of the Liri or Garigliano River. And higher up, in the high mountains, is Subiaco, or as Pliny calls it Sublaqueum, a noble town overhanging a lake of the same name, which still keeps its former name. This town receives fame on both sides from S. Benedict, both for his long-time visit there, as well as for the splendid monastery, known throughout the whole world, which he built there. Indeed, on the right bank of the Aniene river, extending from Lake Subiaco as far as Vicovaro, you can see cut in the rocky mountainside an aqueduct which brought the water forty miles to Rome through pipes partly cut in this way, partly deeply buried, at some points raised up on a high arch and wall.

But in this same region of Lazio, just to clarify what I have said before, **[323D]** Strabo says that Tibur, Praeneste, and Tusculum are visible from Rome. In fact Tivoli, in the place where there is a temple of Heracles, has a waterfall made by the Aniene river as it falls from a very high point into a deep valley and flows through groves next to the city itself, where it begins to be navigable. From there it flows past the stone quarries of Tibur, and those of Gabii, the stone in the latter also called "red stone." From this stone are made very many of the sculptured works at Rome.

De Praeneste dicit Virgilius in septimo,

> Nec Praenestinae fundator defuit urbis Caeculus.

Et Plinius dicit Praeneste dici, quia arbor prinus multa sit eo in monte. Eam vero civitatem dicit Strabo habuisse insigne templum Fortunae a Sulla aedificatum, a quo putabatur oraculum. Additque Plinius simulacrum id Fortunae adeo fideliter fuisse inauratum, ut crassissimae inaurationes dicerentur Praenestinae. Et alio loco de pavimentis tractans, dicit lithostrata coeptavere iam sub Sulla parvulis certe crustis, quod in Fortunae delubro Praeneste coepit.

Et ambas urbes, Tibur et Praeneste, Strabo dicit, in eadem montana regione constitutas esse, sed distare invicem stadia centum. Et Praeneste distare ab urbe Roma etiam duplo, sed Tibur minus. Dicitque a quibusdam Graecas esse ambas, atque Praenestinam Polistephanum vocari prius. Qua in parte Strabonem crediderim divinasse, cum possit Praeneste nunc Polistephanum dici, **[324E]** qua civitas est Stephani Columnae. Additque Strabo, quamquam utraque munito sit loco positam, tamen munitiore Praenestum, quod urbis summitas montem habet excelsum, et retro quidem a continenti montana regione dorsum elatum, quem non dubito esse montem, in quo est munitissima arx Rocha Cavarum dicta. Dicit quoque idem praeter situs Praenesti munitionem occultas fossas undique foratas usque in campos esse, alias aquationis gratia, alias ob latentes invasiones, in quarum una obsessus Marius interiit.

Livius libro LXXXVII scribit, "Sulla C. Marium exercitu eius fuso deletoque ad Sacriportum in oppido Praeneste obsedit"; et libro LXXXVIII, "Praenestinos inermes occidi iussit." Qua crudelitatis maxime historiam Lucanus in II perstringit his verbis,

> Iam quot apud Sacri cecidere cadavera Portum,

et infra,

> . . . Vidit Fortuna colonos
> Praenestina suos cunctos simul ense receptos,
> unius populum pereuntis tempore mortis.

As for Praeneste, Virgil says in book 7,

> And the founder of the city of Praeneste, Caeculus, did not fail to report for duty.

And Pliny says that Praeneste is so called because there are many holm-oak trees on the mountain. Indeed, Strabo says that this city had a remarkable temple of Fortuna, built by Sulla, where people consulted an oracle. And Pliny adds that the statue of Fortuna here was so solidly gilded that the thickest gildings were called "Praenestine," and in another place, writing about floors, he says that mosaics had already begun to be made in Sulla's time, with small tiles, and this style started with the shrine of Fortuna at Praeneste.

And both cities, Tibur and Praeneste, according to Strabo, were built in the same hilly region but are 100 stades from each other, and Praeneste was twice as far from Rome (as it is from Tibur), but Tibur was closer to Rome. He also says that some people report that both cities are of Greek origin, and that Praeneste was formerly called Polystephanum. In this matter I tend to believe Strabo was prophetic, since Palestrina now can be called Polystephanum, because **[324E]** it is the city of Stefano Colonna. Strabo also says that although each city is located in a place naturally fortified on either side, still Praeneste is better fortified, because its highest point is on a high mountain, and on the back side has a ridge raised up and separate from the continuous chain of mountains. This ridge I do not doubt is the mountain in which is located the well-fortified citadel called Rocca di Cave. He also says that, in addition to its natural defenses, Praeneste has hidden subterranean tunnels hollowed out in all directions which reach to the fields, some made to provide water, some for secret invasions. In one of these, Marius the younger died while being besieged.

In book 77 Livy writes, "After Marius' army had been routed and destroyed at Sacriportus, Sulla besieged him in the town of Praeneste." And in book 88, "He ordered the deaths of the unarmed citizens of Praeneste." Lucan touches upon this history of extreme cruelty in his second book:

> Again, how many corpses fell at Sacriportus!

and further on,

> The Fortune of Praeneste saw all her colonists receive the deathblow at the same time, her population dying a single death.

Et item Livius infra, "C. Marius Praeneste obsessus a Lucretio Asella Sullanarum partium, cum per cuniculum caperet fugam, et sentiret se evadere non posse, cum Telesio fugae suae comite, utrimque gladio concurrerunt et occisi sunt."

Usi [324F] autem sunt libenter Romani principes eo secessu ad animi curarumque relaxationem, sed Aurelius Antoninus imperator optimus ibi parum fortunatus fuit. Nam scribit Iulius Capitolinus eum in secessu Praenestino agentem, filium nomine Verum Caesarem septennem amisisse, quem non plus diebus quinque luxerit. Et Plinius, de metallis tractans, sic habet,

> Anno urbis CCCCCCLXXI quod ex Capitolinae aedis incendio, ceterisque omnibus delubris Caius Marii filius Praeneste detulerat, tredecim milia pondo auri sub eo titulo in triumpho transtulit et argenti sex. Item ex reliqua omnia victoria pridie transtulerat auri pondo quindecim milia argenti pondo centum, quindecim milia.

Prosequitur vero Livius libro XXIII, Praenestinos milites miris laudibus, quod cum apud Cannas infelicissime pugnatum esse audiissent, apud Casilinum divertentes durissimam in oppido obsidionem, omnium memorabilem fortissime pertulerunt; unde senatusconsulto duplex stipendium et quinquennii vacationem militiae habuerunt.

Addit vero unum Strabo usu per aetatem nostram, et saepius ante actis temporibus compertum: munitionem scilicet, quae aliis civitatibus conducere consueverit, [324G] Praenestinis saepe calamitati fuisse ob Romanorum seditiones. Defugere enim illuc eos, qui tumultu sint usi, hisve expugnatis fieri, ut etiam Praenestini urbem deserant causa in eos translata. Quod enim supra est dictum, hac de qua Strabo dicit, ratione factum videtur, ut Sarrae Columnensis temporibus Praeneste fuerit desolatum. Et Poncelletti et Nicolai Fortebratii, aliorumque urbi infestorum receptione factum vidimus, ut urbs obsessa captaque solo aequarent.

Livy also relates later on,

> C. Marius, besieged at Praeneste by Lucretius Asella of the Sullan faction, fled through an underground passage; and when he realized he could not escape, he and Thelesius, his companion in flight, committed suicide by running onto each other's swords.

[324F] In addition, the Roman emperors enjoyed this place as a retreat for relaxation and release from care, but the excellent emperor Aurelius Antoninus had very bad fortune here. For Julius Capitolinus relates that at his retreat at Praeneste the emperor lost his son, Verus Caesar, age seven; he did not mourn for him more than five days. Pliny, in his discussion of metals, says:

> In the year 671 A.U.C., Marius the younger appropriated from the fire in the Capitoline temple and from all the other shrines and brought to Praeneste 13,000 pounds of gold. [Sulla] showed off this gold in his triumph with a placard and 6,000 pounds of silver. [Sulla] also had conveyed on the day before, from the rest of his victories, 15,000 pounds of gold and 115,000 pounds of silver.

But Livy goes on in book 23 to tell, with the highest praise, how the soldiers from Praeneste, when they heard they news of the disastrous battle at Cannae, turned aside to Casilinum and bravely endured in that town that harshest siege in anyone's memory. As a result, the Senate decreed for them a double wage and five years' exemption from military service.

Strabo adds one factor experienced in our age, and rather often in ancient times: a natural defense, which is generally an advantage for other cities, **[324G]** was often disastrous for Praeneste, because of the factional strife among the Romans, since those who were involved in uprisings took refuge there, and when they have been overcome, the citizens of Palestrina also lose their city because the blame for the insurrection is transferred to them. This very sequence of events I mentioned earlier, in conformity with Strabo's description: in the time of Sciarra Colonna, Palestrina was devastated. We have seen this happen in the case of the city's allowing in Poncelletto and

Fluvium eius regionis Verrestim Strabo appellat, et addit in ea montana regione ipsarum urbium aliud dorsum esse, quod inter tibias linquit Algidum. Et illud quidem dorsum esse excelsum usque ad montem Albanum. In quo dorso sit Tusculum sita, urbs non inepte fabricata. Romanae vero nascenti rei publicae haec urbs hinc infesta fuit, quod Manlius Tusculanus gener Tarquinio exsuli socero auxilium attulit, unde pugna ad Regillum originem habuit. Cui Romanus populus post rebelliones cum Latinis factas pepercit, sicut Livius in VIII scribit, "Tusculanis servata civitas quam habebant, crimenque rebellionis a publica fraude in paucos auctores versum." Et Plinius inter insignia fortunae variantis [324H] exempla ponit Lucium Furium Tusculanum. "Is Tusculanorum Romanis rebellantium consul eodem quoque honore transfuga exornatus est a populo Romano, qui solus eodem anno, quo fuerat hostis, Romae triumphavit ex his, quorum consul fuerat."

Livius libro XXVI, accessum Hannibalis ad urbem Romam describens, dicit, "Per Anagninum agrum venit in Lavicanum, inde Algido Tusculanum petit. Nec receptus moenibus infra Tusculum dextrorsum Gabios descendit." Continuat vero supradictis Strabo Tusculum ornari insitionibus circum atque aedificiis, et ad eam maxime partem quae est versus Romam. Tusculi namque collem dicit esse fecundam aquisque abundantem, et paulatim multis in locis in altum attolli, habereque regiam magnificentissimi apparatus, et continua esse loca, quae ad Albanum vergunt montem, eandem tum virtutem, tum apparatum habentia. Deinceps campos esse, quorum alii ad Romam attingunt eiusque suburbia, alii ad mare.

Nicolò Fortebraccio and other enemies of Rome: the city was besieged, captured, and leveled to the ground.

The river of this region, the Ninfa, Strabo calls the Verrestis, and adds that in that mountainous region where those cities are, there is another ridge, which leaves Mt. Algidus between the ridges. That ridge is high and extends all the way to the Alban Mount. On this ridge was Tusculum, a well-constructed city. In the early days of the Roman Republic, this city was hostile, because Manlius of Tusculum, the son-in-law of the exiled Tarquin, brought help to him. The result was a battle at Lake Regillus. The Roman people spared Tusculum after it had joined in rebellion with the Latins, so Livy writes in book 8: "The Tusculans were allowed to keep their government as they had before, and the charge of rebellion was turned from a public charge into one against a small number of instigators." Among outstanding examples of the vacillations of fortune **[324H]** Pliny cites that of Lucius Furius of Tusculum. "This man was a consul of the Tusculans when they rebelled against Rome; but he deserted to Rome. He was given the same office by the Roman people, and was the only man to triumph at Rome, in the same year in which he had been an enemy, over the people whose consul he had been."

Livy, in book 26, describes Hannibal's approach to Rome:

> He came through the territory of Anagnia into that of Labici, and from there he made for Tusculum over Mt. Algidus. But he was not allowed within the walls there, so he turned to the right below Tusculum and went down to Gabii.

Indeed, Strabo continues the description I cited from him above, saying that Tusculum is adorned with a ring of gardens and buildings, especially in the part of it that faces towards Rome, as Tusculum is on a hill that is fertile and well-watered, and in many parts rises gradually up high and has a splendidly-constructed palace. And nearby are also the lower slopes of the Alban Mount; they enjoy the same fertility and have the same type of building construction. Then come the plains: some of them reach to Rome and its suburbs, others extend to the sea.

Haec sumpsimus paene ad litteram ex Strabone, de hac regione Columnensi familiae ante quadringentos annos, sicut nunc est, maiori ex parte subiecta. Et quidem apud Praeneste montes peritissime sunt descripti, sed minora non ponit Strabo loca, qui illis in montibus sitam Horatii Flacci poetae villam omisit, ubi Sancti Ioannis in campo Horatii nunc appellant. Alia etiam a Strabone omittuntur, quae si **[325A]** tunc temporis non erant, scimus ante quingentos annos fuisse. Cavas enim a situ dictas, quem in cava fossa habent, nunc Odoardi Columnae oppidum, Petrus Columna per secundi Paschalis Romani pontificis tempora possedit paterna, sicut Pandulfus Hostiarius scriptor tradit, hereditate, sicut etiam tunc Praeneste, Pullum, et Pullanum, nunc dicta Pilium et Palianum possidebant.

Quae autem de Tusculanae olim urbis collibus dicit, vera esse ostendunt etiam nunc monasterium Sanctae Mariae de Griptaferrata in villa Ciceronis Tusculana aedificatum, et Marinum, ac superiori edito in colle Roccha Papae, Prosperi cardinalis Columnae oppida. Circa quae duobus aut tribus a Tusculo milibus distantia agri fertilitatem et aquarum abundantiam videmus esse maximam. Regiae autem magnificentissimi, ut Strabo dicit, apparatus fundamenta esse non dubitamus, quae proximis pariter Griptae et Marino locis fornices a manu factos, cavernasque habere videmus oppidi unius populum in habitationem et quidem commodam admissuras.

Est etiam Tusculo propinquum olim Lucullanum, Lucii Luculli villa, cui nunc dicitur Frascatum, ubi Aquam Virginem, quae nunc unica Romam perducitur, **[325B]** inventam esse constat. Tusculanique duce Rainone eorum tyranno Federici imperatoris Barbarossae appellati copiis coniuncti populum Romanum clade maxima affecerunt, quae Cannensi cladi prope similis numero caesorum fuisse dicitur, adeo ut Roma postmodum caput numquam attollere potuerit. Unde factum est ut anno inde septimo Romanus populus ipsam urbem tanta animorum ferocia demolitus sit, ut vix fundamentorum vestigia nunc appareant.

Ea vero vetus et praeclara olim urbs, nunc solo titulo civitas gentem Porciam inde oriundam, et quod est consequens illustrissimos Catones habuit cives, quae diu post pontificibus Romanis tribus, sexto Benedicto qui primum Henricum regem Theotonicum coronavit, decimononoque Ioanne illius germano, et septimo Benedicto utriusque nepote ornata fuit. Nec aliam habet aliquam pristinae felicitatis et gloriae partem, praeterquam quod eam titulo episcopatus gubernat vir summus Graece Latineque eruditissimus, et

I have taken almost *verbatim* from Strabo my description of this area, which belonged to the Colonna family 400 years before and is also now for the most part ruled by them. Strabo has certainly described accurately the mountains around Praeneste; but he omits some of the lesser places, including the farmhouse of the poet Horace, located in those mountains, in the place they now call S. Giovanni in Campo Orazio. Strabo also omits other places, which **[325A]** may not have been there at his time, but which we know were there 500 years ago. For example, the town of Cave, named after its location in a hollow where there is now a town belonging to Odoardo Colonna: it was a hereditary possession of Pietro Colonna in the time of pope Paschal II, so we are told by the writer Pandolfo Hostiario. The Colonna also possessed at that time Palestrina, and the former Pillum and Pullanum, now called Piglio and Paliano.

But the truth of what Strabo says about the hills of the former city of Tusculum is demonstrated by the survival, even now, of the monastery of S. Maria di Grottaferrata, which was built on the site of Cicero's Tusculan villa; and by Marino; and, higher up on a hill, Rocca di Papa. All these are towns possessed by Prospero cardinal Colonna. Around them, two or three miles from Tusculum, we see very fertile soil and abundant water. I am certain that what Strabo refers to as a splendid palace still exists in the form of the man-made vaults or grottoes we see near both Grottaferrata and Marino, which will easily allow the population of a town into their space.

Also near Tusculum is the villa of Lucius Lucullus, in ancient times called Lucullanum; now it is called Frascati. Here it is established that the Aqua Virgo **[325B]** originated, now the only acqueduct that conveys water to Rome. The Tusculans, under the leadership of their tyrant Rainone, allied with the troops of the emperor Frederick Barbarossa, inflicted a great slaughter on the Roman people, who are said to have sustained in this battle nearly as many casualties as in the battle of Cannae, so that Rome could never afterwards hold up her head. And so seven years afterwards the Roman people destroyed Tusculum with such ferocity that now one can hardly see traces of its foundations.

But that ancient and formerly famous town, now a town in title alone, gave rise to the family of the Porcii, and as a result had as citizens the very distinguished branch of that family known as the Catones. A long time afterwards, it was distinguished by three popes: Benedict VI (VIII), who crowned Henry (II) the first German emperor; his brother John XIX, and the

summa praeditus cum bonitate, tum etiam humanitate, Bissarion Graecorum cardinalis Nicenus, Bononiae nunc et exarchatus Ravennatis Apostolicae sedis legatus.

De campis quos **[325C]** Strabo dicit aut ad urbem, aut ad mare pertinere, nimis verum esse videmus, quod suburbiis tunc et villis habitatos nunc solis tectos ruinis et silvis proprie magis campos appellari posse constat. Cum autem Albam Strabo a principio nominaverit, proximam illi Aritiam omisit, quam nunc solo aequatam tunc urbem in via Appia fuisse supra ostendimus. Est Albae Marinoque proximus Albanus lacus, emissorio cuius mirabili opere facto licet tenues effluant aquae. Origo nunc habetur amnis, qui apud locum caedis apostoli Pauli labens paludem ad Aquas Salvias appellatam efficit. Estque is lacus de quo vates Etruscus, sicut Livius refert, praedixit futurum ut, si emitteretur inde aqua, Romani Veiis potirentur.

Distat ab Albano Aritiaque pariter passus circiter quattuor mille lacus, quem Suetonius Tranquillus Nemorensem appellat, ad quem dicit C. Caesarem villam inchoasse quam reliquerit imperfectam. Cuius quidem lacus aqua mirabilis operis emissorio educta Numicum amnem efficit, quem apud Ardeam in mare labi diximus. Ad eumque lacum est situm oppidum Nemus appellatum. Servius grammaticus in septimo Virgilii versus hos exponens, "Audiit et Triviae longe **[325D]** lacus," dicit Nemus appellari lucum haud longe ab Aritia, in quo lacus est ubi speculum Dianae dicitur. Et Nemorensi item oppidum proxime adiacet Cinthianum, quod a Cinthia quae et Trivia nomen licet nunc corruptum habuit. Hunc vero lacum Dianae speculum a maioribus appellatum Romana re florente, eo fuisse dignum nomine nullus mirabitur, qui praesentis temporis amoenitatem eius inspexerit. Vallem enim concavam duo in circuitu mille passus complexam hic lacus dimidiam obtinet. Pars reliqua ubi Caium Caesarem aedes diximus inchoasse, tunc, ut videtur, nemorosa fuit, a qua oppidum exstans Nemus appellatum est. Eaque nunc arboribus frugiferis adeo pulchre est consita, ut nulli in Italia quantumvis cultissimo consitionibus loco cedat.

nephew of these men, Benedict VII (IX). The sole remnant of Tusculum's former happiness and glory is the fact that it is governed by the Nicene Cardinal, Bessarion. A bishop in title, a man most learned in Greek and Latin, and endowed with the greatest goodness and refinement, he is now also legate of Bologna and the exarchate of Ravenna.

Of the fields which **[325C]** Strabo mentions as extending either to the city or to the sea, I observe that his comment is only too true: rather than being inhabited by suburbs and farmhouses, as formerly, it is now obviously more accurate to call these areas covered by ruins and woods, "fields." Although Strabo initially named Alba, he omitted the neighboring Aritia. Aritia is now leveled to the ground; it was, as I have shown above, a city on the Via Appia. Next to Alba and Marino is Lago di Albano. Although the lake's outlet has been marvelously constructed, only a small amount of water flows out. Now it is thought to be the source of the river which, flowing down in the place of the Apostle Paul's murder, creates a marsh called Ad Aquas Salvias. This lake, as Livy tells us, figured in an Etruscan soothsayer's prediction that if the Romans brought the water of the Alban Lake to Rome, they would become masters of Veii.

About four miles equidistant from Lago di Albano and Ariccia is the lake which Suetonius calls Nemorensis (Lago di Nemi), on whose shores he says Julius Caesar began to build a villa which he left unfinished. The drainage of this lake by a marvelous operation creates the Numicus River, which I said flows into the sea at Ardea. On this lake is the town called Nemi. Servius, commenting on the lines of verse in *Aeneid* 7, "And the lake **[325D]** of Diana, far away, listened...," says that not far from Aritia is a grove called Nemus, where there is a lake called the Mirror of Diana. And next to the lake, likewise called Nemi, is the town of Genzano di Roma, which takes it name, albeit now corrupted, from Cynthia (also known as Trivia). This lake was indeed called "Diana's Mirror" in the days of the Roman republic; and no one who has seen its present beauty will be surprised that it was thought worthy of this name. For this lake takes up half of a hollow two miles in circumference. The remaining part is where, as I mentioned, C. Caesar began to build a villa; then, as it appears, it was wooded, and as a result the town which stands above it was called Nemus. This area is now beautifully planted with fruit trees; no place in all of Italy, no matter how well planted, is superior to it.

Quantum autem lacus ipse maioribus fuerit gratus, magnum hoc tempore apparuit argumentum. Prosper Columna cardinalis, patriciusque Romanus, cum Nemorense illud Cynthianumque castellum paterna possideat hereditate aliquando audivit Nemorenses dicere, naves suo in lacu binas esse submersas, quae nec adeo putres sint, ut laceratae funiculos de industria alligatos, nec retia casu implicita tractae sequantur, nec integrae suis ipsorum omnium incolarum viribus queant extrahi. Quare vir ipse bonarum artium studiis et imprimis historiae deditissimus nec minus vetustatis indagator **[326E]** curiosissimus quod magnae naves parvo et altissimis undique circumdato montibus in lacu sibi voluerint nosse animum adiecit, nosterque Leo Baptista Albertus geometra nostri temporis egregius, qui De re aedificatoria elegantissimos composuit libros, ad id operis est vocatus.

Qui vasa vinaria multos colligata in ordines ea ratione in lacu disposuit, ut de ipsis tamquam pontibus hincinde penderent machinae, quibus harpagone ferreo densioribus appenso rudentibus, captam mordicus navem fabri peritiores lignarii attraherent. Et a Genua urbe maritima mercede conducti aderant, piscibus quam hominibus similiores nonnulli, quorum partes fuerunt in lacus profundiora natando descendere, et quanta esset navis quamque integra sentire, et demissos funibus harpagones in morsum capturamque applicare. Tandem capta ligataque ad proram navis, cum integra non sequeretur, fracta est, et eius particula trahentes harpagones est secuta. Spectaculo fuit omnibus Romanae curiae nobilioris ingenii viris, particula navis, quam hac ratione fabricatam fuisse apparet.

Navis tota larice ligno, asseribus trium digitorum crassitudine compacta, bitumine extrinsecus delibuta **[326F]** fuit, quod bitumen ut etiam nunc apparet croceum purpureumve contexuit continuitque velamen, et plumbeis desuper chartis superficies tota ab aquis imbribusque navem bitumenque defensura obtecta est, quas quidem chartas claviculi, non ut nunc assolet

A convincing piece of evidence from our times, moreover, has made clear how attractive to our ancestors was this very lake. Prospero Colonna, cardinal and Roman aristocrat, came into possession of Nemi and the fortified town of Genzano as a result of an inheritance from his father's family. He heard a report from the inhabitants around Nemi that two ships were submerged in the lake there. They had not decayed to such an extent that they would come apart when dragged up by ropes that were intentionally bound around them, nor would they come apart when they accidentally became entangled in nets. They could not be dragged entire to the surface even when all the inhabitants applied all their strength to the task. Prospero Colonna is dedicated to the study of the liberal arts and especially to history, and no less diligent in the investigation of antiquity, so he was **[326E]** very curious as to why these large ships were at the bottom of a small lake which was surrounded by very high mountains; and he applied his mind to investigating the question. He summoned to this task my friend Leon Battista Alberti, the outstanding mathematician of our time, who has written very fine books *On Architecture*.

Alberti collected wine barrels, and arranged them in lines on the lake in such a way that they formed a sort of pontoon bridge. From this he hung on either side machines with iron grappling hooks, suspended from thick ropes, so that workmen skilled in wood-working could take fast hold of the ship and could drag it up. And he had hired men from the seafaring city of Genoa, divers who were more like fish than like men. They were to dive into the depths of the lake to find out how large the ship was and how much of it remained preserved, and to catch hold of it by means of grappling hooks which had been lowered on ropes. They finally caught hold of the ship and attached its bow to the ropes, but it did not come up in one piece, and broke apart; the hooks brought up a small piece of it. This small part provided a sight of great interest to all the noble intellectuals of the Roman Curia who were watching. From the evidence of the piece, the ship seems to have been constructed in the following way.

The ship was made completely of larch-wood, joined together by beams three inches in thickness, with pitch smeared on the outside. As can be seen even now, this pitch was protected and connected **[326F]** by a yellow or red covering, and it was completely covered above with lead plates to protect the ship, and the layer of pitch, from water and rain. These lead plates had

ferrei, sed aenei, frequentes infixi, ita compresserunt ut omnis umor perpetuo arceretur.

Interior navis pars non ab imbribus magis et umore quam ab igne et ferro fortissimam habuit defensionem. Nam cum argilla et creta quicquid ligneae soliditatis navem intus compegerat, ad digiti unius crassitudinem tectum delibutumque esset, ferrum vehementi igne concoctu liquefactumque super infuderunt, quo ad digiti unius et alicubi duorum crassitudinem sensim dilatato, tantundem magnitudinis ferrea, ut ita dixerim, habuit navis, quantum laricea prius habuerat, et ferro insuper alia argillae ac cretae bitumatio, vel ut olim in aedificiis appellabatur complastratio super infusa est. Observatumque fuisse videmus, ut concocto liquefactoque ferro priusquam refrixisset argilla cretaque et ipsa eodem decoquenda calore superinducerentur, quo et substrata et superius deducta argilla, unum sicut etiam nunc sunt commixtum **[326G]** ex lateritio et ferro bitumen efficerentur. Dumque huic expiscandae navi omnis undique insudat multitudo, fistulae in fundo lacus inventae sunt plumbeae, bicubitales longitudine, firmissima crassitudine, quas mutuo morsu ac compagine combasiantes in quantumvis maximam longitudinem producere licuit. Earum vero singulis elegantes insculptae sunt litterae, auctorem, ut coniicimus, navis suum Tiberium Caesarem Augustum indicantes.

Censuitque Leo Baptista fontis copiosissimi lucidissimique ad Nemorense oppidum, scatentis aquas nunc molas convolventes multo ipsarum fistularum ordine ad medium usque lacum fuisse perductas, quae aedibus inservirent amplissimis latissimisque, quas navibus praedictis superimpositas fuisse tenemus. Pulchrum autem et paene mirum est videre clavos maiores aeneos, quibus cubitalibus navis constructa erat, ita integros, ita politos, ut nuper a fabri ferrarii incudibus exiisse videantur.

Lucanus in tertio viam, sicut supra diximus, describens qua C. Caesar primum post belli civilis initia Romam venit, infra scriptos ponit versus, qui ad Albani quoque montis descriptionem satisfacere poterunt. Constabitque Caesarem a Terracina **[326H]** supra Aritiam ad Cinthianum, inde ad montem Albanum, ubi nunc castrum est Gandulfum, pervenisse, quo de excelso monte Romam primum inspexit:

bolts fastened in them, not iron, as are usually made these days, but bronze, driven in at close intervals. They fastened it together so tightly as to keep any moisture out forever.

The ship's interior had just as strong a defense against fire and attack from iron as against rain and moisture. For inside, the ship had been joined together by solid wood covered and smeared with white clay and chalk one inch thick; then they poured over it iron melted in a very hot fire. This molten iron was one inch thick, and in some places two inches thick. As I have said, the ship had a layer of iron the size of the layer of larch-wood under it, and over the iron was another of clay and chalk, like the plaster (as it was called in the past) that used to be applied to houses. We see that it was their practice, when the iron had been heated and before it had grown cool, for the clay and chalk to be laid over it to be cooked in its heat. The lower and upper layers melted into one, a mixture just as even now is put together **[326G]** from brick and iron. And while a great number of men gathering from everywhere around were exercising themselves over the recovery of this ship, lead pipes were found at the bottom of the lake. They are two cubits long, and very solid in width with reciprocal catch and joint, to be combined in any length desired. The letters inscribed on each of them are elegant and inform us that the ship's proprietor was Tiberius Caesar Augustus.

Leon Battista Alberti's theory was that the spring at Nemi, which gushes forth with a great abundance of very clear water, and is now used to supply power to a mill, had been carried by these lead pipes to the middle of the lake, and provided water to the large and splendid structures that I believe were installed on the previously mentioned ships. It is beautiful, nearly miraculous, to see that the larger bronze nails a cubit long, from which the ship had been constructed, were so intact and so polished that they seem to have been just recently struck from the blacksmith's anvil.

Lucan, in book 3, describes the route we mentioned above, whereby C. Caesar first came to Rome after the beginning of the civil war, in the verses cited below, which will suffice as a description of the Alban Mount. It will be clear that Caesar came from Tarracina, **[326H]** above Aritia, to Cinthianum, and from there to the Alban Mount where Castelgandolfo is now. From this height he first contemplated Rome:

Iamque praecipites superaverat Anxuris arces
Et qua Pontinam via dividit uda paludem
Qua sublime Nemus Scythicae qua regna Dianae
Quaque iter est Latiis ad summam fascibus Albam.
Excelsa de rupe procul iam prospicit urbem.

Et dixit,

"Tene deum sedes non ullo Marte coacti
Deseruere viri, pro qua pugnabitur urbe?"

Ultima nunc reliqua est nobis in hac Latinorum regione pars urbi Romae Tibur Anienemque versus propinqua ostiis Tiberinis, unde incepimus e regione adversa. Et ut eo unde nuper digressi fuimus revertamur: Praenestini montis radicibus Algido proximum est Laurentii Columnae oppidum nunc Gallicanum, qui ut diximus olim Gabii fuerunt vetustissimi; quos Livius in primo dicit fraude Sexti Tarquinii captos a Tarquinio patre. Et Virgilius in VII, "Quique arva Gabinae Iunonis," ubi Servius exponit Gabios diu in agris moratos tandem Gabios condidisse, quam ob rem Virgilius dixit "arva," non "moenia." Alibi tamen Servius super verbo Nomentum et Gabios dicit ab Albanis regibus eas conditas fuisse.

Et paucis milibus inde abest Anio fluvius, quem Virgilius dicit "frigidumque Anienem." Habet originem a Sublaco, de quo scribit Plinius, "Anio in monte **[327A]** Trebanorum ortus lacus tris amoenitate nobiles, qui nomen dedere Sublaqueo, defert in Tiberim." Livius scribit Camillum apud Anienem Gallos Roma redempta exeuntes trucidasse, ubi Manlius, torque detracto Gallo, Torquatus est appellatus. Is in via Tiburtina ponte iungitur marmoreo maximis tamen, quae habere solitus fuit ornamentis paene spoliato, quem nunc Mamolum appellant. Hunc vero pontem Mammeam Alexandri Syri imperatoris Romani certe optimi genitricem Christianam mulierem aedificasse, in Gelasii secundi pontificis Romani rebus gestis invenimus.

> And now he had crossed over the heights of Anxur, and where the road soaked with water divides the Pomptine marshes, where the lofty grove ruled by Scythian Diana is, and where the Latins climb the Alban Mount for the Latin festival; now he looked out from a high cliff at Rome far away and said, "Abode of the gods, have your men deserted you, driven off without even a war? For what city, then, will war be fought?"

Now one part remains for me to treat in the region of Lazio, the part near the city of Rome, towards Tivoli and the Aniene river, in the area opposite the mouth of the Tiber, from where we began. So, to return to the place from which we recently went off on a digression: At the bottom of the hill of Palestrina, next to *Mt. Algidus*, is the town belonging to Lorenzo Colonna, now called Gallicano del Lazio, which I said was formerly ancient Gabii. This town, Livy says in book 1, was captured, through a trick of Sextus Tarquinius, by his father Tarquin. And Virgil, in book 7, writes, "... men who live in Juno's fields at Gabii...," to which Servius adds in explanation that Virgil says "fields," not "walls," because the inhabitants had stayed for a long time in fields before finally building Gabii. But elsewhere Servius, commenting on the word Nomentum, says that Gabii too was built by the Alban kings.

And a few miles from here is the river Aniene, which Virgil calls "the chilly Anio." It originates in Subiaco; as Pliny writes,

> On another side, the Anio has its origin on the mountain **[327A]** of the Trebani, and carries into the Tiber the water of three lakes which are famous for their loveliness; they have given its name to Sublaqueum.

Livy writes that Camillus killed the departing Gauls at the Anio after Rome had been ransomed and they were leaving; this is where Manlius received the *cognomen* Torquatus for pulling the necklace off the Gaul. This river is spanned by a marble bridge on the Via Tiburtina. The bridge used to have very impressive decorations, but has been stripped of almost all of them. It is now called Ponte Mammolo. Indeed, this bridge (so I have read in the records of Pope Gelasius II) was built by Mammea, a fine Christian woman and the mother of Alexander Severus (certainly the best Roman emperor). I

Sed quis proxime illi subiectum Numentanae viae pontem construxerit nobis incertum est, qui certiores sumus omnes tres Anieni superimpositos pontes a Romanis fuisse destructos quando, urbe a Belisario instaurata, Totilae adventum pavidi exspectabant. Secundusque est viae Nomentanae pons, et ipse licet integer ornamentis quae maxima habuit spoliatus. Demum tertius in via Salaria exstat a Narsete eunucho duce praestantissimo Ostrogothorum oppressore, sicut incisus illi marmore titulus indicat aedificatus.

Ad proximaque Anienis ostia quibus in Tiberim fertur, sed **[327B]** ultra ipsum Anienem in Umbria regione fuisse coniicimus Fidenas urbem vetustissimam, de qua Suetonius Tranquillus in vita Tiberii Caesaris, "Fidenis casu viginti hominum milia interierunt." Cui cladi similem Nero saevissimus imperator sui imperii temporibus optavit. Plinius etiam dicit "in Fidenate agro iuxta urbem ciconiae nec pullos nec nidum faciunt"; et alibi Romanos accepisse lapides ad structuram ex Fidenate agro circa urbem optimos.

Et supra diximus Tiberim dividere agrum Veientem a Fidenate, mox Latium a Vaticano. De hac Virgilius in VI, "urbem Fidenam." Et Livius libro IIII scribit, legatis Romanorum a Fidenatibus occisis, quia ob rem publicam occisi erant, statuae in rostris positae. Et post Fidenas in potestatem redactas, eoque colonos missos, quibus occisis Fidenates cum defecissent a M. Aemilio dictatore victi et Fidenae captae ac desolatae sunt.

Facta est alicubi superioribus in locis mentio accessus Hannibalis a Capua, tunc a Romanis obsessa et triplici vallo circumdata ad urbis Romae moenia. Quare libet ordine viam repetere qua is venit. Livius libro XXVI primum dicit, "Q. Fulvium Flaccum cos. iterum Romam Hannibalem **[327C]** secutum via Appia, et Setiam Lanuviumque praemisisse, qui commeatus in via pararent exercitui suo." Setiaque et Lanuvium notissimae sunt et supra a nobis descriptae. Hannibalem vero dicit praeter Cales in agrum Sidicinum, per Suessulam Alifanumque et Casinatem Interamniam ac Fregellas, ad

am uncertain as to the name of the builder of the bridge next to it, on the Via Nomentana, although I am more reliably informed that all three of the bridges over the Anio River were destroyed by the Romans in their fear at the coming of Totila, after the city had been restored by Belisarius. The second was the bridge on the Via Nomentana, which is itself whole, but despoiled of its many ornaments. Finally, the third, on the Via Salaria, still exists; it was built by the eunuch Narses, excellent general, suppressor of the Ostrogoths; an inscription on marble tells us this.

Next is the mouth of the Aniene, where it flows into the Tiber. But **[327B]** beyond the Aniene itself, in the region of Umbria, I have concluded is the site of the very ancient city Fidenae. Suetonius writes about it in the following words from his *Life of Tiberius Caesar*, "At Fidenae, 20,000 men died in the fall of the theatre." Nero, the cruelest emperor, wished for a similar slaughter in the time of his rule. Pliny too writes about Fidenae, saying "in the land next to the city, storks do not make nests or hatch their chicks," and elsewhere he says that the Romans took the best stones for construction from the territory around the city of Fidenae.

And I mentioned above that the Tiber divides the territory of Veii from that of Fidenae, and soon after that it divides Lazio from the Vatican territory. Virgil, book 6, writes about ". . . the city of Fidenae." And Livy in book 4 writes that Roman ambassadors had been killed by the inhabitants of Fidenae, and since they had been killed in the service of their country, their statues were placed on the Rostra. Afterwards Rome brought Fidenae back under her power, and sent out a colony to that place. But the Fidenates killed the colonists. After they had defected, M. Aemilius was named dictator and conquered them, and Fidenae was captured and laid waste.

Elsewhere (I have cited it earlier), Livy mentioned Hannibal's march from Capua to the walls of Rome. Capua was besieged at that time by the Romans, and surrounded by a triple rampart. It suits me to retrace the route by which he came to Rome. In book 26, Livy first says,

> The consul Q. Fulvius Flaccus was going to travel to Rome, **[327C]** following Hannibal, on the Via Appia; and he sent ahead to Setia and Lanuvium to prepare supplies for his army along the way.

Setia and Lanuvium are very famous; I described them above. But, Livy says, Hannibal passed by Cales into the territory of the Sidicini, through

Lirim venisse. Quae loca partim in veteri Campania, nunc Terra Laboris dicta, partim in Samnitibus a nobis infra sunt indicata.

Hannibal postea, Liri transmisso, agrum praesentis Latinae regionis attigit. Primo Fregellanum, qui locus licet fuerit in Samnitibus, tamen habuit agrum suum in regione Latina, et nunc dicitur Pons Corvus. De quo Livius in VI, "Hannibal infestius perpopulato Fregellano agro propter incisos pontes." Et in octavo, "P. Plautio Proculo P. Cornelio Scapula coss. Fregellas colonia deducta." Et infra,

> C. P[o]et*e*lius dictator, cum audiisset arcem Fregellanam ab Samnitibus captam, omisso Boviano, ad Fregellas pergit. Unde nocturna Samnitum fuga sine certamine receptis Fregellis, praesidioque valido imposito in Campaniam rediit.

Ornataque fuit Fregellana colonia M. Sextilio, quem Livius dicit respondisse pro duodeviginti coloniis, **[327D]** quae milites prius denegatos et tributa dare promiserunt.

Sequiturque Livius in Hannibalis itinere. Post Frusinatem Ferentinatem et Anagninum, quae loca nunc parva nominis mutatione facta sunt notissima, ex Anagnino autem in Lavicanum venit, quem locum maxima nominis mutatione facta diximus Valmontonem nunc appellari. Dicit enim Livius peritissime, Hannibalem qui esset in Lavicano agro movisse Algido, quia oppidum illud, sicut nunc est, tunc etiam Algido proximum ac prope contiguum erat. Et pervenisse Tusculum ea scilicet via, qua nunc a Valmontono Marinum silvis petitur, et quia sequitur Livius Hannibalem cum non esset Tusculi moenibus receptus, dextrorsum descendisse Gabios, certissimum nobis facit quod superiore diximus loco, Gabios fuisse, quod nunc est oppidum Gallicanum. Quae autem fuerit Pupina quam post Gabios accesserit ignoramus, quod plurimas ea regio habet oppidorum villarumque ruinas a nemine habitatas, prisca quarum nomina nullus novit.

Suessula, Allifae, and Casinum, Interamna and Fregellae, to arrive at the Liris river. Of these places, some are located in ancient Campania, now called Terra di Lavoro; some are in Samnite country, as I have indicated below.

After crossing the Liris, Hannibal reached the land which is now in the region of Lazio. First Fregellae, although it was in Samnium, still had its territory in Latium, and is now called Pontecorvo. Livy, book 6, says "Hannibal laid waste all the more belligerently to the territory of Fregellae because its inhabitants had destroyed the bridges." And in book 8, "in the consulship of P. Plautius Proculus and P. Cornelius Scapula, Rome sent a colony to Fregellae." And further on he says,

> The dictator C. P[o]et*e*lius learned that the citadel of Fregellae had been captured by the Samnites. Having given up Bovianum, he hastened on to Fregellae. From there, the Samnites fled in the night, and he regained it without a battle. He left a strong garrison there, then returned to Campania.

The colony of Fregellae was distinguished by M. Sextilius, who Livy says replied on behalf of eighteen of the colonies **[327D]** which promised to send soldiers, which they had reneged on before, and to pay tribute.

Livy then continues to follow Hannibal's itinerary. After he had passed Frusinum, Ferentinum, and Anagnia, places which are now famous with slightly changed names, from the territory of Anagnia he arrived at that of Labici, a place whose name has undergone a great change, as I mentioned, being now called Valmontone. Livy says with accuracy that Hannibal moved from the territory of the Labicani to Mt. Algidus, as that town now is, and was then, very close to, in fact nearly contiguous with, Mt. Algidus. He arrived at Tusculum by the road which now leads from Valmontone through the woods to Marino. And since Livy is following Hannibal, and "Hannibal was not received within the walls of Tusculum," he informs us that Hannibal "went down on the right-hand side, to Gabii." This corroborates what I mentioned earlier, that Gabii used to be where the town of Gallicano del Lazio is now. What Pupinia was, where he arrived after he left Gabii, I do not know. This region has many towns and estates now in ruins and uninhabited, whose former names no one knows.

REGIO TERTIA, LATINA

Sed iam magno circuitu ab ostiis Tiberinis secundum maris inferi litus ad Lirim sive Gaurianum, et inde per Marsos et mediterranea ad Anienem facto ad Tiberim est reditum. Quo in circuitu omnis regio olim Latina, sive ut nunc dicitur Latium, Campania et Maritima, est conclusa.

But now we have completed a big circle, from Ostia, following the shoreline of the Tyrrhenian Sea to the Liri or the Garigliano river, and from there through the Marsi and inland to the Aniene, returning to the Tiber. With this circle we have taken in all of the region of the former Latium or, as it is now called, Lazio, Campania and Marittima.

Regio Quarta
Umbria Sive Ducatus Spoletanus

[328E]

Prolixiores fuisse videmur tertia describenda Latina regione quam aliarum habenda ratio postulabat. Et tamen multo pauciora, quam oportuit, certe quam voluissemus, in illa diximus, quae plura habeat loca a Livio Virgilio et a vetustissimis scriptoribus frequentata ceteris Italiae regionibus. Sed cum plus iacturae in ea quam in ceterarum aliqua sit factum, adeo ut nulla incultior populisque infrequentior manserit, brevitatem nostram ab inveniendi ea quae non exstent impossibilitate consolemur.

Ad quartamque regionem transeamus, eam prisci dixere Umbriam, nostri ducatum appellant Spoletanum. Idque ducatus nomen primo ab exarchis Italiae sedem Ravennae tenentibus, sicut in Historiis ostendimus inditum, eam habuit vim ut a militari consuetudine tractum dignitatem nunc referat, quae post regiam est suprema. Quantis vero olim **[328F]** polluerint viribus Umbri, hinc maxime apparet, quod Livius in IX scribit: Umbri se urbem Romam oppugnaturos minati fuerunt. Quam latos autem fines haec regio olim habuit, hinc maxime constat, quod Plinius dicit sextam regionem Umbriam complexam agrumque Gallicum circa Ariminum. Et eam Galliae Umbrorum gentem Italiae antiquissimam existimari, trecentaque eorum oppida a Tuscis quando Etruriam ceperunt debellata fuisse. Sabinos etiam videmus fuisse in Umbris comprehensos, et Umbriam ad superum usque nunc Adriaticum mare pertinuisse hinc constat, quod Trogus et magis aperte Plinius dicunt interiisse in Umbris Spinam urbem Delphicis thesauris claram, a Diomede aedificatam, quae ostio Padi sibi proximo dedit Spineticum nomen,

Fourth Region
Umbria or The Duchy of Spoleto

[328E]

I seem to have gone on at too great length in my description of the third region, Lazio, given the length of my treatment of other regions. Still, I included in that description many fewer mentions of toponyms than was fitting, and certainly fewer than I wished to include, because Lazio contains more places which are familiar from Livy, Virgil, and ancient writers in general, than the other regions of Italy. But since there has been a greater loss of place-names in Lazio than in the other regions, to the point that no region has remained less cultivated or more sparsely-inhabited, let us console ourselves for this brevity with the knowledge that it is impossible to discover places which no longer exist.

Let us pass over, then, to the fourth region, the one the ancients called Umbria, and our contemporaries call the Duchy of Spoleto. The Byzantine exarchs who occupied the capital of Italy at Ravenna first gave this name "Duchy" to the region (and I have shown this in my *Histories*). The force of the term comes from its use of rank in a military context; now, it describes a rank next highest in power after the kingdom. But how **[328F]** powerful the ancient Umbri were is very clear from the statement of Livy in book 9: the Umbrians threatened to attack the city of Rome. This region's territory was formerly quite extensive; this is shown especially in Pliny, who says that the sixth region, Umbria, encompassed also the territory of Gaul around Ariminum. He also says that this tribe, the Umbri of Gaul, was considered the most ancient tribe in Italy; and that the Etruscans had subdued thirty of their towns when they took Etruria. We see that the Sabines also were included among the Umbri. It is established that Umbria extended to the "Upper" Sea, now called the Adriatic, as Trogus, and, more explicitly, Pliny, say that the city of Spina perished among the Umbri; it was famous for its treasures deposited in the Delphic treasury, had been built by Diomedes, and gave the name to the mouth of the Po nearest to it ("Spineticum"). That Spina was

et Ravennam cui proxima fuerit Spina, cuiusque ruinis ea sit aedificata, Sabinorum oppidum fuisse Valerius Martialis poeta sic docet,

> Mollis in aequorea quae crevit Spina Ravenna.

Nos itaque, cum Umbriae fines Latio finitimi fuerint, huius nostrae regionis quam consuetudinis [328G] inveteratae necessitas ducatum Spoletanum appellare coegit, fines constituemus: Apenninum a Tiberis fonte superius in Etruria indicato usque ad Anienis fluvii etiam apud urbem notissimi sinistram ripam, et Tiberim quousque eum Anio illabitur.

Prima ex Apennino ad sinistram Tiberis partem descendentibus, obvia sunt oppida Pratolinum et Mons Dolius. Exinde unico a Tiberi miliario abest oppidum Sancti Sepulcri Burgus appellatum, moenibus arcibusque quattuor munitissimum, quas Guido de Petramala episcopus et dominus Aretinus superiori saeculo exstruxit. Nullum vetustatis signum eo in loco esse inspeximus; et tamen C. Plinii nepotis epistolam legentes, in qua villam suam ad radices Apennini et prope Tiberim amnem describit, theatralem sicut ipse dicit montium in circuitu positorum aspectum, hoc in loco esse deprehendimus, ut in eius villae ruinis prima dicti oppidi fundamenta fuisse iacta credamus. Ornatur autem nunc id oppidum Malatesta Cataneo, iureconsultissimo, quem non magis Camertinorum, cui praeest ecclesia, quam vitae integritas sanctimoniaque conspicuum reddunt.

Infra ad Tiberim est Tifernum, Civitas Castelli dicta, quae nunc cive ornatur praestantissimo Nicolao [328H] Vitellio equestris ordinis, quem studia humanitatis et mores ingenui apud quartum Eugenium pontificem praestantissimum imbibiti clarum reddunt. Ab eaque urbe Plinius maior in Naturali Historia dicit Tiberim ratibus Romam usque navigabilem fuisse. Incipit eo in loco Tiberis quam longe ab Apennino recedere, ut quanto magis urbi Romae appropinquamus, eo magis nostrae regionis distantia amnem ipsum montemque intercedat.

Distatque a Tiferno viginti milia passus Eugubium civitas, ad Apennini radices sita, quae vetusta Romanae ecclesiae iuris a Federico gubernatur comite montis Feretri, quem rei militari cum gloria deditum litterae et prudentia plurimum ornant.

Supra Eugubium castella sunt: Brancha, deinde Schigia, quo tramite facillimus est per viam olim Flaminiam Apennini in Romandiolam transitus.

near Ravenna, and built on its ruins; and that Ravenna was a town of the Sabines, the poet Valerius Martial informs us:

> The soft stalk that has grown in watery Ravenna.

Since the territory of Umbria borders on Lazio, I will set the boundaries for this region of ours **[328G]** (which I am compelled by established usage to call the duchy of Spoleto) in the following way: the Apennines from the source of the Tiber (which I identified above in the chapter on Tuscany), to the left bank of the Aniene river which is very well-known also near the city, and the Tiber up to the point where the Aniene flows into it.

As you go down from the Apennines on the left-hand side of the Tiber, the first towns you come across are Pratolino and Montedoglio. From there, one mile from the Tiber, is Borgo Sansepolcro, well-fortified with walls and four towers, built by the bishop Guido Tarlati di Pietramala, who was lord of Arezzo in the previous century. I have not seen any indication of anything ancient in that place; but Pliny the Elder's nephew in a letter describes his villa as being at the base of the Apennines and next to the Tiber river. I caught the shape of a theatre in the mountains which lie around it in a circle, just as he describes it. From this I deduce that his villa was in this place, and I believe that the foundations of the town I mentioned were laid among its ruins. But now Borgo Sansepolcro is distinguished by Malatesta Cataneo, a great legal expert, who is famous for the purity of his life and for his presiding over the church of Camerino.

Farther down on the Tiber is the ancient Tifernum, now called Città di Castello and distinguished by its eminent citizen **[328H]** Nicolò Vitelli, a knight famous on account of the liberal arts and noble character he absorbed in the entourage of the excellent pope Eugenius IV. Pliny the Elder says that the Tiber is navigable from this city as far as Rome. At this point in the Tiber's course, it begins to draw away from the Apennines, so that the closer we get to the city of Rome, the greater the distance in our region between the Tiber river itself and the mountain range.

And twenty miles from Città di Castello is the city of Gubbio, located at the foot of the Apennines. Long a subject of the church, it is governed by Federigo, count of Montefeltro, a man gloriously dedicated to military pursuits, but most distinguished with learning and wisdom.

Above Gubbio are fortified towns: Branca, then Scheggia, through which it is easy to cross the Apennines into the Romagna by way of what

Et a Schigia secundum Apennini latera hanc ingredienti provinciam obvium fit Costaciarium Eugubini agri oppidum; deinceps est Sigillum Perusinorum; inter quae duo oppida fluvius oritur Chiesius, qui inter Eugubinos Assisinatesque montes delapsus fertur sub Cannaria oppido in proximum amnem Tinium, sive ut nunc dicitur Topinum. Post Signum est Fossatum, arduo in Apennini colle castellum.

Et quarto inde miliario abest Vallidum, cui Gualdum **[329A]** dicunt, quod oppidum in civitatis a Longobardis subiecto in campo excisae locum fuit aedificatum. Parvusque torrens a Vallido brevi cursu labitur in Chiesium, per cuius amnis alveum venientibus Ancona Picenique regione per Fossatum Vallidumque qui ex Fabriano traiecerunt Apenninum iter est Perusiam. Et medio itinere Casa Castalda oppidum, arduo in colle, Chiasio imminet. Deinceps in Planellum, vicum campis adiacentem, via continuatur quousque ad Patullorum sive Vallis Cippi sive Sancti Ioannis vicum pontibus Tiberis transmittitur.

Post Vallidum recedere ab Apennino oppida incipiunt, primaque est Nuceria civitas cognomine Alphatenia vetusti nominis, de qua Livius, "Consul profectus ad Nuceriam Alphateniam oppugnando ad deditionem subegit." Estque ad Tenium amnem, nunc Topinum, posita, secundum cuius alveum ingentes cernuntur moles, sternenda via olim Flaminia iactae. Iturque illac duodecimo miliario Fulgineum, per quam is amnis defluit civitatem, quae suffecta fuit Foro Flaminii, vetustae urbi a Longobardis propinquo in loco ad annum nunc septingentesimum funditus excisae. Fuisse tamen legimus vetustis temporibus **[329B]** alios in Umbris Fulginates ab hoc loco remotissimos, qui apud Tudertinos habitasse videntur, eosque crediderim ad hanc inhabitandam urbem novam populariter commigrasse. Ornata vero fuit Fulginei civitas, patrum nostrorum memoria, Gentili medico sui saeculi celeberrimo. Est apud Fulgineum planities totius Umbriae amplissima pariter et amoenissima, in qua sunt quinto ad Fulginei dexteram miliario Pellium, ut appellat Plinius, et ut nunc dicitur Spelium, vetusti nominis oppidum.

Deinde pari paene spatio Assisia, arduo in colle sita, civitas vetustissima passuum tria milia a Chiesio recedens. Seraphicoque Francisco cuius servat reliquias eius et eius templo omnium Italiae aedificii magnifi-

was formerly the Via Flaminia. And if you enter Umbria from Scheggia following the slopes of the Apennines, you come to Costacciaro, a town in the territory of Gubbio. Then comes Sigillo; and between these two towns begins the river Chiascio, which flows down among the mountains of Gubbio and Assisi, until it reaches the next river, formerly the Tinius but now called the Topino, below the town of Cannara. After Sigillo comes Fossato di Vico, a fortified town on a high hill in the Apennines.

And four miles from there is the town now called **[329A]** Gualdo Tadino, because it was built in place of a town in a plain below, which was destroyed by the Lombards. A small stream flows for a short stretch from Gualdo, then into the Chiascio, and along this river travellers who have crossed the Apennines from Fabriano by way of Fossato and Gualdo can get to Perugia after coming from Ancona and the region of its March. In the middle of this route you come across the town of Casa Castalda, on a high hill, overhanging the Chiascio. Then the road proceeds towards Pianello, a village in the plains, all the way to Ponte Patulli or Ponte Valleceppi or Ponte S. Giovanni, where it crosses the Tiber on bridges.

After Gualdo, the towns begin to draw away from the Apennines. The first is the city of Nocera Umbra, in antiquity Nuceria, with the additional name of Alphatenia. About it Livy writes, "The consul set out to Nuceria Alphatenia, and by besieging it brought it to the point of surrender." And at the Tenius (now Topino) river, following its course you can see huge masses of materials, deposited as foundations for the road which was once the Flaminia. If you proceed by that way, twelve miles along is Foligno, and through this city the river flows. It was a replacement for Forum Flaminii, an ancient city located nearby which was completely destroyed by the Lombards 700 years ago. But I have read that in ancient times there were other **[329B]** inhabitants of Fulginia among the Umbrians, far removed from this place, who seem to have lived among the people of Tuder. I believe that they migrated as a people to settle this new city. The city of Foligno has been distinguished by a man of our fathers' generation, Gentile da Foligno, the most famous physician of his generation. Around Foligno there is a plain that is at once the broadest and pleasantest in all Umbria; on it, five miles from Foligno on the right, is a town with an ancient name: Pellium as Pliny calls it, and Spello as it is now called.

Then, about equidistant, is Assisi, a very ancient city located on a high hill and set back three miles from the Chiascio. The relics of the blessed Francis are kept here, and his church, the most magnificent of any building

centia celeberrimo ornatissima, quam Propertius poeta Axim appellat, innuitque construendo eius urbis muro consilium attulisse his verbis:

Scandentisque axis consurgit vertice muros,
Muros ab ingenio notior ille tuo.

Tennius sive Topinus amnis cum ad Cannariam oppidum Chiesio iunctus est, suum amittit nomen, et deinceps Chiesius appellatus Bettonio oppido a libertate diu servata insigni ad sinistram relicto apud Torsanum oppidum labitur **[329C]** in Tiberim, nec ullo Tiberis praeter Narem Anienemque maiore augetur fluvio. Ad alteram vero Chiesii partem multa sunt Perusini agri oppida, quorum Fracta Tiberi est contigua, et interius est Montonium, Braccio rei bellicae praestantissimo duce illustratum, a quo Braccianorum sectam factionemque habuimus, in qua magnae per aetatem nostram celebritatis fuerunt Nicolaus Piccininus, et postea Franciscus filius, fuitque pariter Nicolaus Braccio ex Stella sorore nepos. Supersunt etiam Carolus Braccii et Iacobus, Nicolai Piccinini filii, quorum ille aliquas, hic magnas in Venetorum exercitu copias ducunt, maximo exinde pressi onere, quod paternae virtutis et potentiae eorum uterque exemplar ad imitationem propositum habeat.

Supra Fulgineum ad sinistram arduo in colle, qui tamen longe Apennino abest, Trivium est, cuius oppidi et situs et nomen faciunt ut credam hunc esse locum, de quo scribit Servius in expositione Virgilii super verbo, "oliviferaeque Mitustae." Dicit enim, "haec Trevia postea dicta est, quam modo Trebulam dicunt," de qua Martialis:

Humida qua gelidas submittit Trebula valles,
Et viridis cancri mensibus alget ager.

Et quidem **[329D]** hoc Trivium est nunc valde oliviferum, et in Sabinorum vetustis finibus situm, sicut Mitustas fuisse scribit Virgilius.

E regione autem Trivii amoeno in colle Falcum est oppidum, haudquaquam vetusti nominis, sed populo frequentatum. Ad collisque illius radices in via olim Flaminia est Mevania, de qua Livius in IX, "Decius consul magnis itineribus ad Mevaniam ubi tum copiae Umbrorum erant perrexit." Fuitque id oppidum cive ornatum Propertio Aurelio, qui de se ipso scribit ad Tullum libro Monobiblo vel, ut Nonio Marcello placet, libro Elegiarum, scribit:

in Italy. The poet Propertius calls this town Axis, and he alludes in the following lines to the planning he contributed to the construction of the walls:

> The wall of Axis climbs, sloping upwards to the hill,
> that wall more famous as a result of your genius.

The Tennius or Topino river loses its name when it joins the Chiascio at the town of Cannara. From then on, it is called the Chiascio and, leaving on its left the town of Bettona famous for its long-preserved freedom, it flows **[329C]** into the Tiber at the town of Torgiano; the Tiber has no larger tributary, besides the Nera and the Aniene. But on the other side of the Chiascio are the numerous towns of the territory of Perugia; Fratta is next to the Tiber, and towards the interior is Montone, distinguished by Braccio, eminent leader in war. From him comes the company of Braccioni, among whom the most famous in our age were Niccolò Piccinino and after him his son Francesco, and equally famous was his nephew Niccolò Braccio, son of his sister Stella. Still living are Carlo and Jacopo, the sons of Braccio and Niccolò Piccinino. The former leads some Venetian troops; the latter is a leader of a great number of troops in the army of the Venetians. Both are purposeful in emulating their fathers' virtue and ability.

Above Foligno on the left, on a high hill, but still far from the Apennines, is Trevi. This town's location and name make me believe that this is the place Servius refers to when he explains Virgil's phrase "olive-bearing Mitustae." For he says "this place was afterwards called Trevia, and now they call it Trebula." Martial says about Trebula:

> where moist Trebula lowers cold valleys,
> and the green land is cold in the summer months.

And indeed **[329D]** this Trevi is now an abundant producer of olives, and in the ancient territory of the Sabines, just as Virgil writes Mutusca was.

In the region of Trevi, Montefalco is the next town, located on a pleasant hill. Its name is not an old one; but it is densely inhabited. And at the foot of that hill, on what was the ancient Via Flaminia, is Bevagna, about which Livy writes in book 9, "The consul Decius reached Mevania by forced marches, where troops of the Umbrians were then positioned." It was this town that was the birthplace of Propertius, who writes about himself in his single volume to Tullus or, as Nonius Marcellus has it, his book of *Elegies*:

Proxima suppositos, contingens Umbria campos
Me genuit terris fertilis uberibus.

Idemque in Elegiarum quarto,

Umbria te notis antiqua Penatibus edit,
Mentior, an patriae tangitur ora tuae,
Qua nebulosa cavo irrorat Mevania campo,
Et lacus aestivis intepet Umber aquis.
Scandentisque axis. . .

et cetera. Postquam vero Propertii testimonium de se ipso attulimus, alium Umbriae poetam dare volumus ignotae nobis sicut et ipsi Propertio fuit patriae. Nam in eodem Elegiarum IIII sic dicit,

Ut nostris tumefacta superbiat Umbria libris,
Umbria Romani patria Callimachi.

Et Lucanus in primo:

Est qui tauriferis qua se Mevania campis
Explicat, audaces ruere in certamina turmas.

Planitiei item quam hoc in loco amplissimam esse diximus post Trivium imminet **[330E]** Spoletum, quam civitatem Livius libro vigesimo coloniam a Romanis deductam fuisse scribit, et libro XXII Hannibalem dicit post Trasumeni pugnam recto itinere per Umbriam usque ad Spoletum pervenisse. Inde cum depopulato agro urbem adorsus esset expugnare cum magna caede suorum repulsum, coniectantem ex unius coloniae haud prospere tentatae viribus, quanta moles Romanae urbis esset, in agrum Picenum convertisse exercitum. Et libro XXIIII idem Livius prodigia unius tempestatis enumerans, narrat Spoleti nunc ex muliere virum factum. Eusebius autem dicit Melissum Spoletanum grammaticum insignem Spoleti natum fuisse. Martialisque poeta vinum laudans Spoletinum sic dicit:

De Spoletinis quae sunt cariosa lacunis
Malueris quam si musta Falerna bibas.

Et nos historiarum XII ostendimus Theodericum regem primum Gothorum Spoleti amplissimas aedificasse aedes, et alios qui successerunt Gothos destruxisse Spoletum moenibus eversis, quam Narses eunuchus refici

Umbria, rich in fertile lands, bore me,
Where it is closest [to Perugia] on the plains lying below.

Propertius also wrote in his fourth book of *Elegies*,

Ancient Umbria, with its household gods, brought you forth
—Do I lie, or do I touch on your native land?
Where misty Mevania sheds dew on the field,
And the waters of the Umbrian lake are warm in summer,
The wall of Assisi sloping upwards. . .

and so forth. But after recording Propertius' testimony about himself, I want to attribute to Umbria another poet, to a fatherland unknown to me just as it was to Propertius himself. For in the same book, the fourth of his *Elegies*, he says the following:

. . . so that Umbria may swell with pride because of my books,
Umbria, fatherland of the Roman Callimachus.

And Lucan says in his first book,

A messenger reports that, where Mevania spreads out in bull-producing fields, troops of cavalry are boldly rushing into battle.

After Trevi comes **[330E]** Spoleto, also hanging over the plain which I said was most spacious in this place. Livy writes in his twentieth book that the Romans established this city as a colony; and in book 22, he says that after the battle of Lake Trasimene Hannibal made a straight path through Umbria and arrived at Spoletium. From there, after he laid waste to its territory, he attacked the city. After a great loss of life among his soldiers, he was driven off, and he concluded, on the basis of the strength of one colony which he had failed to take, that attacking the city of Rome would be an enormous undertaking; and he turned aside into the territory of Picenum. And in book 24 Livy recounts the prodigies of one season, and tells that at Spoletium a woman turned into a man. But Eusebius says that Melissus, a famous grammarian, was born at Spoletium. And the poet Martial praises the wine of Spoletium in this way:

From the flasks of Spoletium you would prefer
Flat wine to drinking Falernian.

And in the twelfth book of my *Histories*, I told how Theoderic, the first king of the Goths, built a spacious palace in Spoletium, and other Goths who succeeded him destroyed Spoletium and tore down its walls; Narses

curavit. Ea civitas, ubi stante Romanae rei publicae felicitate theatrum fuit, arcem habet omnium Italiae munitissimam, et quae [330F] aedificiorum pulchritudine nuperrime ornatissima est reddita.

Nuceriae civitati, et praeterlabenti Tennio sive Topino amni, ac Fulgineo Trevio et Spoleto adiacent atque imminent colles montesque altissimi, pluribus tamen vallibus torrentibusque inter se divisi, ut ab amplissima quam descripsimus planitie Spoletana valle appellata ad Apenninum magna sit distantia, castellis, oppidis, civitatibus vicis et villis etiam vetusti nominis habitata, quae altera paene regio, sed montosissima possit appellari. Primum his in montibus supra Fulgineum est Caput Aquae castellum, a scaturiente ibi celeberrimo fonte dictum, qui fons amnem efficit brevi cursu Tennium adaugentem. Supra est collis Floridus, item castellum lacui adiacens parum amplo, et castelli ipsius nomine appellato, quem parvulus rivulus prope Fulgineum exonerat in Topinum.

Imminentque undique lacui montes altissimi, in quibus Sanctae Notoriae notius est, oppidum Camertinis subiectum. Et per Collem Floridum itur ad arctissima Apennini claustra, per quae Seravallis appellata Camerinum petitur, civitas vetustissima in Piceno a nobis post hac describenda. Quamquam Seravallis prima [330G] domus tectum habet, cuius anterior pars in Umbros, in Picentes posterior aquam pluviam dimittit. Subest colli in quo Trivium esse diximus perlucidus fons, tantam subito evomens aquam, ut intra stadii unius cursum efficiat fluvium, qui infra Fulgineum labitur in Topinum. Est vero is amnis Clitumnus, de quo Virgilius in Georgicis:

Hinc albi Clitumne greges et maxima tauri
Victima saepe tuo perfusi flumine sacro,
Romanos ad templa deum duxere triumphos.

Quod vero Virgilius supradictis in versibus innuit, Plinius diffuse scribit, eam oram tauros gignere omnium Italiae maximos, in quis plurimi sint albi; unde Lucanus supra ostendit Mevaniam secus quam Clitumnus labitur

the eunuch saw to their rebuilding. When the Roman republic was flourishing, there was a theatre here; and on its site is the best-fortified citadel in all Italy, and [330F] most recently it has been decorated with beautiful buildings.

Some very high mountains and hills tower over and lie next to the city of Nocera Umbra, the river Tennius or Topino which flows past it, and Foligno, Trevi, and Spoleto. They are, however, separated by many valleys and streams, with the result that there is a great distance between what I have described as the spacious plain called "the valley of Spoleto" and the Apennines. This plain is settled by fortified settlements, towns, cities, villages, and estates, some even with ancient names; it can almost be called another region, but it a very mountainous one. In these mountains, the first castle above Foligno is Capodacqua, named after the famous spring which gushes forth there; from it arises a tributary of the Topino which has a short course. And above that is Colfiorito, also a fortified village which lies next to a small lake, and the lake takes its name from it, and a small stream issues from it and discharges into the Topino near Foligno.

On every side of the lake there are overhanging mountains; among them the best-known town is S. Notoria, a possession of the Camertini. If you go to Camerino, the way leads through Colfiorito to the narrowest passes in the Apennines, called Seravalle di Chienti. Camerino is very ancient, located in the March of Ancona, which is the next region for me to describe. However, the first house in Seravalle [330G] has a roof off whose front part the rain slopes into Umbria, and whose back part sheds rainwater into the March of Ancona. At the foot of the hill where I said Trevi is located there is a very clear spring, which sends forth a great amount of water with much force, and in the length of a stade it creates a river, which flows into the Topino below Foligno. This is the Clitunno/LaVene river, which Virgil describes in the *Georgics*:

> From here come your white herds, Clitumnus, and the bulls,
> Magnificent victims, bathed often in your sacred stream,
> Which have led Roman triumphal processions to the temples of
> the gods.

What Virgil hints at in these lines, Pliny writes about extensively: that is, that this place produces the largest bulls in all Italy, and many of them are white. From this fact the verses of Lucan cited above demonstrate that Mevania, where the Clitunno flows into the Topino, was located in "bull-

in Topinum esse in campis tauriferis. Et Propertius item post superius ab eo scripta de Mevania addit,

> Et pecus et niveos abluit unda boves.

Trivium inter et Spoletum multa sunt Spoletinorum castella, quousque montes arduos penetrantes Ceretum et subiectum illi Pontem oppida inveniunt. Quorum primum infamis quaestus populo frequentatur, quod omnem paene Europam illi peragrantes, diversis ad fallendos homines suae miseriae famique religiosi alicuius **[330H]** instituti praetensis coloribus, stipem mendicando petunt, et divitias inde multas accumulant. Et eo usque gentis illius cessit infamia, ut quemadmodum a Gnatone adulatore Gnatonici, sic ab hac gente importuni inverecundique petitores Ceretani ubique per Italiam vocitentur. Quae ignominia per Italos paene omnes ne Europam et alios ducatus Spoletani incolas per Italiam inquinet, publico Romani pontificis edicto inhibitum est Ceretanis, ne ultra mensem iniussu praetorum domo absint.

Pontani vero licet a Cereto originem ducant, aliquot viros per aetatem nostram doctissimos habuerunt, inter quos Ludovicus iureconsultorum consultissimus fuit; et ex eadem cognatione ac professione Paulus Romae consistorialis advocatus celeber habetur. Magnae etiam indolis praedictae succrescit Pontanae genti adolescens Iovianus, qui iambico versu et scribendis elegiis assiduo deditus studio Propertii et Callimachi contribulium, aut vici in Ovidii, aut quem magis imitatur Catulli Veronensis laudibus responsurus videtur.

Pontem, oppidum a ponte dictum Narem ibi prope fluvium iungente praetergressi ad sextum miliarium inveniunt Cassiam novi nominis oppidum, sed populo frequens ac libertate conspicuum, quod fluvius attingit Corvus, apud **[331A]** altissimum regionis montem, qui et ipso Corvus appellatur oriundus, et in Narem fluvium apud Tripontium castellum defluens. Cuius castelli iurisdictionis possessionisque causa Nursini Spoletinique crudelissima inter se proximis temporibus proelia commiserunt, in quibus capti superatique concertatoris sanguini et vitae nullus pepercit.

Septimo a Cassia miliario arduos inter montes, vallibus tamen cum amplis tum etiam amoenis distinctos, est Nursia urbs vetusta, quam Livius libro XXX dicit dedisse milites Publio Scipioni armanda classe quam in Africam duxit. Parvusque illius moenia attingens torrentulus medio inter

producing fields." And Propertius also, after the lines cited above, adds about Mevania,

> And its waters wash the flock and the white cattle.

Between Trevi and Spoleto are the numerous fortified towns of the territory of the Spoletans. Travellers who penetrate the high mountains in the interior come upon the towns of Cerreto di Spoleto and its possession Ponte. The first of these towns, Cerreto, is home to a crowd of hypocrites dressed in various religious garb, who make money in a shameful way. These men go begging through almost all of Europe, deceiving people with their **[330H]** claims of misery and hunger. From this begging they acquire a heap of wealth. Just as the Gnathonici are named from the parasite Gnatho, in the same way shameless beggars throughout Italy who will stop at nothing in their disgraceful behavior are called "Cerretani" after them. And in order that this disgrace may not pollute Italians throughout Europe, or the other inhabitants in the duchy of Spoleto, the pope has pronounced a prohibition upon the Cerretani, that they not be away from home for more than a month without leave from the magistrates.

Although the inhabitants of Ponte originally came from Cerreto, they still include some very learned men among those of our generation, for example Lodovico, most expert in the law; and in the same family and profession, Paolo Pontano is considered famous as a consistorial advocate at Rome. The young Gioviano Pontano has grown into the great talent among the Pontani, because he has dedicated himself to writing iambic and elegiac poetry, and to studying the work of his countrymen Propertius and Callimachus, and it seems he will receive praise comparable to that given to his neighbor Ovid, or—the poet he most resembles—Catullus of Verona.

Ponte gets its name from the bridge which spans the river Nera nearby. If you go past it, at the sixth milestone you find Cassia, a town with a new name, but densely inhabited and famous for its freedom. The river Corno, which flows past it, and has its source in the **[331A]** highest mountain in the region (also called Corno), flows into the Nera at the fortified town of Triponzo. The people of Norcia and Spoleto fought bloody battles for the possession and rights over this fortress in the last generation, and those enemies who were defeated and captured found no mercy for their blood or their lives.

Seven miles from Cassia, among the high mountains, but where there are valleys not only spacious but also pleasant, is the city of Norcia, the an-

Cassiam et Narem tractu illabitur Corvum amnem. Vetustum vero a scriptoribus celebratum est Nursiae nomen, quod quidem oppidum libertate, sed imprimis beato Benedicto monachorum patre alumno clarissimum, priorem tempore Benedicto summum genuit virum Quintum Sertorium, nulli Romanorum ducum virtute secundum. Servius grammaticus in Virgilii expositione ubi verba sunt, "quos frigida misit Nursia," sic dicit: "Civitas frigida re vera, aut certe venenosa nocens, nam ubique in contionibus suis Gracchi Nursinos sceleratos appellaverunt." Servius vero videtur situm eius oppidi ignorasse, namque poeta excellentissimus qui **[331B]** omnia et in primis historiam ac Italiae regiones peritius nosset quam Servius, frigidam dixit Nursiam, non quia sceleratos scelerati Gracchi Nursinos iudicaverint esse, sed quia altissimis frigidissimisque Nursia montibus cingeretur. Quod enim ipse docet effectus, Nursia gignit viros, quorum qui inferioris videntur esse conditionis, non magis perite et industrie aratrum et ligones sive fibulam et forfices quam rei publicae ad quem sedent clavum tractare noverunt.

Et digniori in civium coetu multos vidimus, plures audivimus litteris ornatissimos, qualem habet aetas nostra Benedictum Reguardatum, qui originem sicut et nomen referens in beati Benedicti progeniem, vir est non magis philosophiae et physicae quibus claret artibus, quam prudentia et consilio excellens. Nursinum multas gignere rapas Martialis sic indicat:

> Nursinas poteris parcius esse rapas.

Est supra Cassiam decimo miliario Conissa, novi nominis oppidum, sed populo ut in montosissimis frequentissimum. Et haec quidem in ea montium parte, quae Spoletum e regione respicit. Citra Narem Vissium est, vetusti nominis oppidum, viginti passuum **[331C]** milibus a Cereto, et sub ipsis paene Apennini iugis remotum. Vissii moenia abluit Nar fluvius, de quo Virgilius, "Sulphurea Nar albus aqua," ortum suum superiori in Apennini iugo habens. Est amnis ipsius origo ea ratione memorabilis, quam sicut a maioribus tradi videmus et vis ipsa verbi significat, fons geminus fluvium inchoans ex duobus manat orificiis, narium animalis cuiuspiam speciem in saxosi montis capite imitantibus.

cient Nursia. Livy says in book thirty that it provided soldiers for Scipio's fleet which he had to prepare for the campaign in Africa. And a small stream flows next to its walls; in the middle of its course, between Cassia and the Nera, it flows into the river Corvo. Indeed, the name "Nursia" is ancient, and famous due to the ancient writers, and the town is famous for its freedom, but mostly because it gave birth to S. Benedict, the father of monasticism. Before Benedict, this town produced the great Quintus Sertorius, second to none of the Roman leaders in courage. The grammarian Servius, explaining Virgil's words "men whom the chilly climate of Nursia sent," says the following: "The city is 'chilly' either actually, or harmful because poisonous, for throughout their speeches the Gracchi call the men of Nursia 'criminal.'" But Servius seems not to know the location of this town, for the excellent poet who **[331B]** knew everything, especially the history and regions of Italy, more expertly than did Servius, said "chilly Nursia," not because the criminal Gracchi judged the men of Nursia to be criminals, but because Nursia was surrounded by very high mountains with a cold climate. And the reality proves this judgment: Norcia produces men who may seem to be of inferior status, but know how to steer the state they govern as skilfully and diligently as they know how to wield the plow and mattock, or the bolt and shears.

And in the worthier group of citizens I have seen many, and heard of more, men distinguished in letters, for example in our generation Benedetto Reguardati, who recalls the family of S. Benedict in his place of origin just as in his name, a man excelling in the arts of philosophy and natural science, for which he is famous, and also in wisdom and discernment. Martial, in the following verse, shows that Nursia produces many turnips:

> You will be able to eat more cheaply the turnips of Nursia.

Ten miles beyond Cassia is Conissa, a town with a modern name, but densely inhabited for a town in mountainous parts. It is in the part of the mountains which faces Spoleto, away from Umbria. On this side of the Nera is Visso, a town with an ancient name, twenty **[331C]** miles from Cerreto, and secreted almost under the very ridges of the Apennines. The Nera river flows past the walls of Visso; about it Virgil wrote, "The Nar, its water white with sulphur." It has its source on the topmost ridge of the Apennines. The source of the river is worth mentioning in itself, as (just as we see transmitted in the ancient authors) the very meaning of its name, Nar, indi-

Ad hanc Naris ripam descendentes cum Ceretum Pontumque oppida praetergressi sunt, Schizinum inveniunt oppidum, sex a Spoleto milibus semotum, ubi sublicius pons Narem iungens iter Spoleto ad montem Leonem oppidum Cassiamque et Leonessam ac ad castella circiter octo monasterii Ferentili praebet. Et inferius Narem pariter iungit pons lapideus ad oppidum Haronem, infra quod oppidum fluvius Nar Velini amnis lacusque casu mirabili adaugetur. Is amnis Velinus in Apennino binos habet fontes. Primum remotioremque apud oppidum civitatem Regalem appellatum, et alterum apud Interdochum oppidum. Delapsusque ad civitatem Reatinam Velinus intersecat paene mediam. De qua Livius libro XXVI, adventum Hannibalis ad urbem Romam describens, **[331D]** Caelium dicit scriptorem iter ab Reate et Cutiliis ordiri. Ea civitas, sicut recte opinari videor, Vespasianum genuit, et Titum ac Domitianum, filios imperatores Romanos quandoquidem vicus Phenne, a quo ipsi duxere originem, non solum in Reatino agro sed Reati propinquum est. Dicit tamen Suetonius, a quo haec sumpsimus, Phenne vicum modicum in Samnio esse, sicut iure optimo Reatina civitas est ponenda, quae Thomam nunc habet Morronum eloquentia et singulari memoria praeditum.

Progressus parvo ab Reate spatio Velinus amnis e multis rivulis et fontibus, quorum unum Neptunini appellatum dicit Plinius, alio atque alio exoriri Velinum facit lacum, nunc a Pede Luci propinquo oppido vocitatum. Prius vero quam in lacum tot colligantur aquae paludes efficiunt, in quibus tantummodo scripsit in Admirandis Cicero ungulas iumentorum indurari. In eo autem lacu Italiae umbilicum esse, M. Varronem scripsisse refert Plinius.

Decidit autem eo ex lacu in Narem idem fluvius alta rupe, in quo exitu saxum crescere dicit Plinius. Sonitumque facit is fluvii in Narem amnem casus, qui decimo exauditur miliario, cum tamen eundem ob casum fumus ascendat perpetuus, aerem in sublime obnubilans. Et spumans cum in fundum cadit aqua scintillas exsilire facit, quae apud Interamniam sexto distantem miliario conspiciuntur. Virgilius in septimo:

Est locus **[332E]** Hesperiae medio sub montibus altis
Nobilis, et fama multis memoratus in oris,
Ansancti valles, densis hunc frondibus atrum
Urget utrumque latus nemoris, medioque fragosis

cates that it springs from a double fountain which flows out of two holes, like the nostrils of an animal on the top of the rocky mountain.

Travellers who go down this bank of the Nera and pass beyond the towns of Cerreto and Ponte, find the town of Scheggino, six miles from Spoleto, where a wooden bridge spans the Nera and provides a way from Spoleto to the town of Monte Leone, and Cassia and Leonessa and to the approximately eight fortresses of the monastery of Ferentillo. And farther downstream another bridge, this one of stone, crosses the Nera at the town of Arrone, and below Arrone the river Nera is joined by the amazing waterfall of the Velino river and lake. This river, the Velino, has two sources in the Apennines: the first is farther away, at the town called Cittareale, and the second one is at the town of Antrodoco. The Velino flows down to the city of Rieti and cuts through it in almost the exact middle. About this city Livy wrote in book 26, describing Hannibal's approach to the city of Rome: he says that the historian Caelius had his route start from Reate and Cutilia. **[331D]** In my opinion, Rieti is the birthplace of Vespasian, and of his sons Titus and Domitian, Roman emperors. I say this because the village of Phenne, where they came from, is not only in the territory of Rieti, but near the city itself. But Suetonius, my source for these matters, says that the modest village of Phenne is in Samnium, just where the city of Reate ought to be located. Rieti boasts as its citizen Tommaso Morroni, endowed with eloquence and extraordinary powers of memory.

The Velino river goes on a little way from Rieti, and issues from many little streams and springs (one of which, according to Pliny, is called Neptuninus), and creates the Veline lake, which is now called after the nearby town of Piediluco. But before these many waters are brought together into the lake, they create marshes, in which alone, Cicero wrote in his *Book of Marvels*, the hooves of animals are hardened. And Pliny reports that M. Varro wrote that the navel of Italy is in this lake.

This river falls from the lake into the Nera from a high cliff, and Pliny says that rock grows in this outlet. As this river falls into the Nera, it makes a sound that is heard ten miles away; yet from the same waterfall a continuous plume of steam rises, which creates a cloud high in the air, and as the foaming water falls to the bottom, it sends forth sparks which can be seen at Terni six miles away. Virgil, in *Aeneid* 7, writes:

> There is a renowned place **[332E]** in the center of Italy, at the foot of high mountains, mentioned in the myths of many lands, the valley of Ampsanctus. A grove of trees dark with dense leaves hems

> Dat sonitum saxis et toto vertice torrens.
> Hic specus horrendum, et saevi spiracula ditis
> Monstrantur, ruptoque ingens Acheronte vorago
> Pestiferas aperit fauces. . .

Et cetera. Servius sic exponit:

> Hunc medium Italiae cosmographi dicunt. Est autem in latere Campaniae et Apuliae iuxta Venusium ubi Hirpini sunt, et habet aquas sulphureas. Ideo graviores quia ambitur silvis; ideo ibi dicitur aditus inferorum, qui gravis odor iuxta accedentes necat, adeo ut victimae circa hunc locum non immolarentur, sed odore perirent ad aquam applicatae. Hoc erat genus litationis. Sciendum est, tamen, Varronem enumerare, quot loca in Italia sunt eiusmodi, unde Donatus dicit, Lucaniae esse qui describitur locus a poeta, fluvium qui Calor vocant. Quod adeo non procedit, quia cum Italiae medio sub montibus altis hoc nisi ad totam Italiam referas non procedit, et si non est in valle Italiae montosa. Nam in hoc loco montes penitus non sunt.

Servius autem, cuius sunt praedicta verba, non minus a me quam Donatus ab eo reprehendi potest, **[332F]** quia iuxta Venusium non est Italiae medium, sed in hoc lacu Velino, sicut a Marco Varrone habetur. Et licet Venusii locus nobilis sit, et habeat circa valles sanctas, si fertiles, tamen non habet mirabilem fertilitatem, quam hic habuit Velinus quando a principio fuit exsiccatus. Nam ipse idem Servius verba Virgilii alio in loco exponens, "Rosea rura Velini," dicit,

> Lacus iuxta agrum qui Rosulanus vocatur. Varro tamen dicit lacum hunc a quodam consule in Nare fluvio derivatum, post quod tanta est consecuta fertilitas, ut perticae longitudinem altitudo superaret herbarum; quin etiam per diem quantum demptum esset tantum per noctem crescebat.

Unde Plinius liber VIII, "Caesar Vopiscus cum causam apud censores ageret, campos Rosiae dixit Italiae sumen esse, in quibus perticas pridie defectum gramen operiret."

> it in on either side. A rapid stream runs down the middle of it, crashing on the broken rocks with its swirling eddies. Here is shown a frightful cave, and the air-holes for the fierce god of the underworld, and a deep chasm, where Acheron bursts forth, opens its noxious jaws. . .

And so on. Servius explains this in the following way:

> The geographers say that this is the center of Italy. And it is on the border between Campania and Apulia, next to Venusia where the Hirpini live, and it has mephitic waters. They are heavier on account of being enclosed in woods; for this reason people say the entrance to the underworld is there, because a heavy smell kills those who come near to it, so that victims were not slaughtered around this place, but died from the exhalations after coming close to the waters. This was a method of obtaining omens. But one must keep in mind that Varro was listing the places of this type in Italy; as a result, Donatus says that the place Virgil describes is in Lucania, around the river which they call Calore. What he says is not valid, because it says "in the middle of Italy." "At the foot of high mountains": this does not apply, unless you understand it to refer to all of Italy. And if the place is "in the valleys of mountainous Italy," in this place there are not mountains.

But I find fault with Servius, whose words I have cited, just as he criticizes Donatus; **[332F]** for the area around Venosa is not the middle of Italy. It is rather in this lake, Velinus or Lago di Piediluco, just as Varro says. And although Venosa is a "famous" place, and has around it "sacred" valleys, even if that means "fertile" they still do not have the marvelous fertility which this Velinus had since it was from the first reclaimed land. For Servius himself also says, in his explanation of Virgil's words elsewhere, "the Rosean district near the Veline lake":

> The lake is near the territory which is called Rosulanus. But Varro says that some consul diverted this lake into the Nar river, and as a result the land in this place became very fertile, so the grass grew higher than ten feet; indeed it even grew back at night what had been cut during the day.

This is why Pliny says in book eight, "Caesar Vopiscus, pleading his case before the censors, said that the fields of Rosia were the sow's udder of Italy, where the grass that had been cut the day before would cover a ten-foot measuring rod."

Dicitur ergo notanter Virgilium significasse hanc soli fertilitatem per verbum "ansancti," quod ipse Servius exponit omni ex parte sancti. Et cum cetera congruant, medium Italiae, altitudo montium, casus fluvii et lacus qui speciem prae se ferat "spiraculorum saevi Ditis," esse hunc Velini casum in Narem locum Italiae medio a Virgilio descriptum ostendunt.

[332G] Interamnia est prima in ordine superiore post Spoletum, civitas vetusta, quam Livius libro vigesimoseptimo dicit unam fuisse ex coloniis Romanis duodeviginti, quae difficillimis per Hannibalis praesentiam Romani populi rebus militiam et collationem tributorum detractaverunt. Cuius prata dicit Plinius quater in anno irrigua secari et non irrigua ter. Quod Naris illam circumeuntis vicinitas efficere videtur. Ornatur ea civitas Ioanne Macincollo, camerae Apostolicae auditore, legum ac bonarum artium studiis decorato.

Prius vero quam ad Naris fluenta ulterius prosequamur, omissa secundum Tiberim repetamus. Postquam amnis Chiesius in Tiberim est delapsus, primum adiacet haud procul Tiberi oppidum Diruta, populo frequentatum. Deinceps Ameria, civitas vetustissima. Nam Marcus Cicero, sicut refert Plinius, eam ante Persei bellum annis nongentis LXXIIII conditam prodidit. Virgilius in Bucolicis, "Amerina retinacula"; et Servius exponit, "Virgas quibus vites ligantur, quae virgae abundant circa Ameriam." Fuitque Roscio olim ornata cive, quem Marcus Cicero parricidii accusatum contra Sullae dominantis potentiam defendit. Patrem **[332H]** enim Roscii hominem locupletem et bonum, sed magis quam par esset erga filium inclementem clam occiderunt quidam. Filiusque per occasionem discordiarum quasi paternae caedis auctor ab hisdem interfectoribus accusabatur. Praed[*i*]a ad Chrysogonum quendam Lucii Sullae satellitem redibat. Nemine itaque ob Sullae metum audente defensionem suscipere, innocentem bonumque adolescentem defendit Cicero, qui in Sullano exercitu militaverat. Fuitque postea Roscius tantae in histrionia excellentiae, ut Cicero et ceteri florentissimae illius aetatis viri recitantem sedulo audirent, qui adeo doctus fuit, ut librum scripserit, in quo histrioniam eloquentiae comparavit.

Interius est Tudertum, civitas vetusta, sive ut Plinius appellat, Tuder, tertio Martino pontifice Romano cive ornata. Cui multa subsunt oppida et

So that Virgil means, by the word Ansancti, to refer to the fertility of the soil; which Servius explains as "holy in every part." All the rest of its aspects agree with the idea that this waterfall that the Velino makes into the Nera was the place Virgil described as "in the middle of Italy": its position in the middle of Italy, the high mountains, the river's waterfall, and the lake which corresponds to the image of the "breathing-holes of the fierce god of the underworld."

Terni is the first city as you travel up from Spoleto according to the order I used before: an ancient city, which Livy says in book **[332G]** 27 was one of the eighteen Roman colonies which refused Rome military and financial contributions in the evil times of Hannibal's invasion. The meadows here that are irrigated, Pliny says, are mowed four times a year; those not irrigated are mowed three times. This seems to be the result of being surrounded by the Nera. This city is distinguished by Giovanni Mazzancolli, auditor of the Apostolic chamber, made glorious by his studies in the law and the liberal arts.

But before we follow the Nera river farther, let us go back to the places we passed over as we were following the Tiber. After the Chiascio river flows into the Tiber, there is first, lying near the Tiber, the densely-inhabited town of Deruta. Then comes Amelia, a very ancient city. For Cicero asserted (so Pliny tells us) that it was founded 974 years before the war with Perses. Virgil in the *Georgics* has the line "ties from Ameria," which Servius explains as follows: "Twigs which are used to hold vines; they are abundant around Ameria." Ameria was in ancient times honored by having as its citizen Roscius, defended by Cicero against a charge of parricide which was supported by the dominant tyranny of Sulla. For Roscius' father was a wealthy and good man, but undeservedly **[332H]** nasty towards his son. Certain persons killed him in secret. The son was accused of killing his father by the murderers, who were taking advantage of the history of unpleasantness between father and son. The estate was going to go to Chrysogonus, a henchman of Lucius Sulla. Because of the widespread fear of Sulla, no one dared to undertake a defence of the innocent and worthy son, but Cicero did; he had served in Sulla's army. Afterwards, Roscius became such a great actor that Cicero, and other men of that period so rich in culture, would listen attentively to his performances; and he was learned enough to write a book comparing acting to eloquence.

Towards the interior is Todi, the ancient city of Tudertum or, as Pliny calls it, Tuder, distinguished as the birthplace of Pope Martin III. Below it

castella Tiberis ripas et colles montesque adiacentes complentia, sed minime digna quae describendo singulariter prosequamur. Proxime vero illis, atque etiam Interamniae nisi medius interesset Nar, est S. Geminus, praestans in regione oppidum. Abest Interamnia sexto miliario a Narnia, arduo in colle sita, a profluenti Nare dicta, quam Livius et Plinius Nequinum fuisse dictam affirmant. Una coloniarum quae Hannibale Italiam premente, militiam et collationem tributorum detrectaverunt, in cuius agro dicit Plinius **[333A]** scripsisse in Admirandis Ciceronem terram esse, ex qua siccitate lutum fiat, imbre pulvis. De qua Martialis sic dicit,

> Narnia sulphureo quam gurgita candidus amnis
> Circuit, ancipiti vix adeunda iugo.

Quae pontem habuit superbissimi operis nunc dirutum, de quo Martialis:

> Sed iam parce mihi nec abutere Narnia Quinto,
> Perpetuo liceat sic tibi ponte frui.

Ea civitas vetustissima, civili divisione alias per aetatem nostram, sed magis magisque proximo tempore lacerata, horrendas suorum mortes vidit, quae Gattamelatam genuit clarissimum belli ductorem. Et nunc Berrardum habet, Spoletinum episcopum, civilis et pontificii iuris excellentia celeberrimum.

Septimo inde abest miliario in via item Flaminia Ocriculum, vetusti nominis oppidum, ultra quod Sabinae fines Tiberim attingunt. Livius in nono: "Ocriculani sponsione in amicitiam accepti"; et in XXII dicit Fabium dictatorem via Flaminia profectum obviam consuli exercituique cum ad Tiberim circa Ocriculum conspexisset agmen, viatorem misisse, qui nuntiaret ut sine lictoribus ad dictatorem veniret. Igitur a Velino lacu repetentes omnem ex veteri Umbria nobis reliquam regionem, ea quae ipsum Velinum **[333B]** et Reatinam urbem, Tiberim Anienem flumina ad lacum Marsorum interiacent explicemus.

Maximus autem is est montium et camporum globus, et quem nec incolae satis norunt, in quo multa fuerunt prisci vocabuli loca, quae praesentibus conferri nequeunt, tum quia interierunt quaedam, tum quia incompre-

are many towns and fortified villages which throng the banks of the Tiber and nearby hills and mountains; but they are not important enough to describe individually. Next to them, and next to Terni too, if the Nera did not intervene, is Sangemini, an important town in the region. Terni is six miles from Narni, which is located on a high hill, and named after the Nera river, which flows past it. Livy and Pliny corroborate that it was called Nequinum. It was one of the colonies which, during the threat of Hannibal in Italy, withdrew from the Romans its military and financial contributions. In its territory, Pliny says, Cicero **[333A]** wrote in his *Book of Marvels* about how in drought conditions the earth produced mud, and dust was produced when it rained. About this city Martial says the following:

> The river Nar, colored white by sulphur in its eddying waters,
> encircles Narnia, approachable with difficulty over two mountain ridges.

This city had a splendid bridge, but it is now destroyed; Martial wrote about it,

> But now, Narnia, let me have Quintus; do not monopolize him.
> Thus may you always enjoy your bridge.

This very ancient city has suffered from internal conflicts in our age, but torn apart in more and more recent times has seen its citizens meet frightful deaths. It produced the famous condottiere Gattamelata; and now boasts Berardo, the bishop of Spoleto, renowned for his expertise in civil and pontifical law.

Seven miles from Narni, also on the Via Flaminia, is Otricoli, a town with an ancient name, the last place before the edge of Sabine territory reaches the Tiber. Livy writes in book 9, "The Ocriculani were taken into a treaty of friendship with Rome"; and in book 22 he says that the dictator Fabius went out along the Via Flaminia to meet the consul and his army; and that when he looked around Ocriculum near the Tiber, he saw the line of soldiers and sent an officer to summon the consul to approach the dictator without lictors. And so let me go back from the Veline lake to give an account of the entire region that remains of ancient Umbria, the places that I omitted which lie between the lake itself **[333B]** and the city of Rieti, and the Tiber and Aniene rivers to the lake of the Marsi.

Even the natives do not have adequate knowledge of the great mass of mountains and plains here. Many ancient toponyms among them cannot be identified with contemporary names, both because some of them have perished, and because others have suffered an indecipherable change of name.

hensibilis mutatio in aliis est facta. Erant autem olim haec omnia Sabinae loca regionis omnium Italiae vetustissimae. Nam videmus Virgilium dicere ante inditum nomen Italiae Oenotros illam coluisse. Et Oenotriam fuisse constat Sabinorum tractum, quod docet Servius in VII super verbo "Oenotria tellus." Romanos etiam originem habuisse a Sabinis per raptum mulierum constat; unde est quod dicit Virgilius, "in parte est data Roma Sabinis," et factum inter Romulum et Titum Tatium foedus, per quod recepti sunt in urbem Sabini, ea lege ut in omnibus essent cives Romani, nisi in ferendis suffragiis. Nam magistratus non creabant.

Dicimus ergo fuisse in Sabinorum montibus, qui nunc Reate et inter Sabinam praesentis temporis regionem altissimi cernuntur, "Tetricem horrentis rupes montemque Severum" et Casperiam ac Forulos civitates. Fuerunt etiam "Arcades genus **[333C]** a Palante profectum, qui regem Evandrum comites sunt secuti," et Imela fluvius. His generatim dictis notiora particulariter explicemus.

Primum est a Velini in Narem casu Sabinos nostri temporis petentibus colles Scipionis oppidum populo frequentatum. Post Mons Bonus et Teranum castella fluviolo propinqua, qui nunc nomine carens Imela fuit ex montibus oriundus, quos Virgilius supra docuit casui Velini in Narem imminere, et inter Ocriculum ac Malianum cadens in Tiberim. Ab ipso autem Imelae ortu apud Pedelucum montes incipiunt, qui sinistra civitate Reatina perpetuo in meridiem cursu continuati semperque crescentes, et quam longe ab Apennino recedens Aequicolorum olim nunc Taliacotii montibus proxime adhaerent, Tiburque feruntur. Quos quidem montes si vetustiora quaerimus Arcades incoluerunt, et Tetricae horrentis rupes monsque olim Severus, Mons S. Ioannis nunc et Mons Niger dicuntur.

Supraque eos dextrorsum est oppidulum Caputfarfari dictum, quod eo in loco Farfarus amnis habet originem, qui fama notissimus Sabinam regionem praesentis temporis mediam dividit. Imelae autem sinistrorsum est propinquum villae, nunc oppidum **[333D]** Vacunna appellatum, cuius meminit Horatius ad Aristium,

All these places were also, in ancient times, located in the very oldest region of all Italy, the Sabine territory. For we see that Virgil says that, before Italy received its name, the Oenotri settled it. And it is well-known that Oenotria was an area belonging to the Sabines, as Servius informs us in his comment on the phrase "the land of Oenotria" in book 7 of the *Aeneid*. It is also established that the Romans traced their descent from the Sabines as a result of the rape of their women; this is the reason Virgil says, "the Sabines were given a share in Rome"; and a treaty was struck between Romulus and Titus Tatius ensuring that the Sabines were received into the city under the same conditions that governed Roman citizens except that they did not obtain voting privileges. For they did not participate in the election of the magistrates.

I therefore assert that it was in the Sabine mountains, which are very high and can now be seen between Rieti and the present Sabine region, that the "rough cliffs of Tetrica and Mt. Severus" and Casperia and Foruli were located. For there were also "the race of Arcadians who descended **[333C]** from Pallas, the companions who were followers of King Evander," and the river Imela. Now that I have spoken of these places in general terms, let me give an individual account of the more famous of these places.

The first place after the waterfall the Velino makes as it plunges into the Nera, as you make for what our age refers to as the Sabine area, is the densely-inhabited town of Collescipoli. Then come Montebuono and Tarano, fortified towns beside a small river, which now has no name, but was the Imelle, and has its source in the mountains which Virgil informs us (cited above) overlook the waterfall of the Velino into the Nera. Between Otricoli and Magliano Sabina it flows into the Tiber. From exactly this point, the source of the Imelle at Piediluco, begin the mountains which leave Rieti on the left and extend continuously to the south, getting higher as they go along; and receding from the Apennines, but staying close to the mountains formerly assigned to the Aequicoli, but now to Tagliacozzo. The mountain range extends to Tivoli. Indeed, if we look for more ancient names, these mountains were inhabited by the Arcadians, and were the "rough cliffs of Tetrica and Mt. Severus"; but now they are called Mte. S. Giovanni and Mte. Nero.

Above these on the right is the little town called Castelnuovo di Farfa, because the source of the river Farfa is in that place. This river is very famous, and cuts through the middle of the Sabine region of today. And on the left next to the Imelle is a town now called Vacone **[333D]** which Horace mentioned to Aristius,

Haec tibi dictabam post fanum putre Vacunnae.

Acronque exponit Vacunnam apud Sabinos plurimum cultam. Quidam Minervam, alii Dianam putaverunt; nonnulli Venerem. Sed Varro rerum divinarum primo victoriam esse ait, quod ea maxime hi gaudent qui sapientiae vacant.

Imelae vero dextrorsum imminet Mallianum civili cultu habitatum et primarium hoc tempore regionis Sabinae oppidum. Post arduum montem in quo Mallianum est descendentes in Sabinae mediterranea vallem inveniunt, ut in montosa regione amplam, in qua Imelae fluvio proxima est S. Mariae sanctique Eutimi ecclesia Sabinae regionis episcopi. Cui dextrorsum adiacet oppidum Turres pro Curibus vetustissimis Numae Pompilii patria appellatum. Beatus enim Gregorius in Registro scribit Gratioso episcopo Nomentano, "Curam gubernationemque S. Eutimi ecclesiae Curium in Sabinorum territorio constitutae tibi providimus committendam." Nomentum namque regioni Sabinae ad hanc urbi Romae conterminam partem continet.

Quam urbem Seneca epistola quinta supra centesimam dicit aerem habere insalubrem, unde nunc penitus derelicta est. Martialis autem cocus poeta, cum villam ibi possederit, eam saepenumero laudat.

Nomentana meum tibi dat vindemia Bacchum.
Si te Quintus emat **[334E]** commodiora bibas.

Et de rosa tractans sic habet:

Seu tu Paestanis genita es, seu Tiburis arvis
Seu rubuit tellus Tuscula flore tuo
Seu Praenestino te vilica legit in horto,
Seu modo Campani gloria ruris eris,
Pulchrior ut nostro videare corona Sabino,
De Nomentano te putet esse meo.

Nomentumque cive ornatum fuit praestanti Crescentio, qui dignitatem consularem Eugenii III et quintidecimi Ioannis pontificum Romanorum temporibus, omnium ultimus resumere, ac aliquamdiu retinere est ausus. Habuitque pro arce Hadriani molem ab ipso postea castrum Crescentii appellatam.

> I was writing this to you right behind the decaying shrine of Vacuna.

Acron explains that Vacuna was faithfully worshipped among the Sabines; and that some think she corresponds to Minerva, some to Diana; some to Venus. But Varro, in his first book *On Divine Antiquities* says that she was a goddess of victory, the name derived from the fact that those who rejoice most in her are those who have time free for wisdom.

On the right, overlooking the Imelle, is Magliano Sabina, a town whose citizens enjoy a refined standard of living, and the chief town of the modern Sabine region. After the high hill where Magliano is located, travellers going down into the inland valley of Sabine territory will find a valley, a spacious one for a mountainous area. In it, next to the Imelle river, is the church of S. Maria and S. Eutimo, belonging to the see of the Sabine region. Next to it on the right is the town of Torri, named for ancient Cures, the home of Numa Pompilius. Accordingly, we find in the *Register* of St. Gregory the Great's letters, he writes to Bishop Gratiosus of Nomentum, "I am entrusting to you the care and governance of the church of St. Euthymius which has been established at Cures in the Sabine territory." For Mentana borders on the Sabine region, the edge of it which is next to the city of Rome.

Seneca says in *Letter* 105 that this city has unhealthy air, and for this reason it is now completely abandoned. But the poet Martial the cook often praises it, as he had a villa there:

> My vineyard at Nomentum gives you this wine.
> If Quintus should buy you, **[334E]** you would drink more desirable wine.

And he writes in the following way about the rose:

> Whether you were born in the fields of Paestum or of Tibur,
> or whether the earth of Tusculum grew red from your flower,
> or a farm-steward's wife picked you in a garden at Praeneste,
> or you were just now the glory of the Campanian countryside,
> let my friend Sabinus think you are from my villa at Nomentum,
> so that you may seem to make a more beautiful garland.

And Mentana was distinguished by its outstanding citizen Crescentius, who was the last to attain, and to keep for some time, consular rank in the times of popes Eugenius III and John XV. He had a massive fortress in front of the Castel Sant'Angelo which was afterwards called Castro Crescenzio after him.

Supra Cures sinistrorsum in montibus sunt castella: Stronconum, Mons Calvus, et S. Petrus; inferius ad dexteram Cotanellum, Rocha Antiqua, et aspera, secus quam torrens labitur Calentinus brevi cursu in Tiberim cadens. Cotanellum etiam et Rocham Antiquam supereminent colles ardui, ultra quos Buccinianum est, oppidum S. Petri. Inter Calentinum etiam et Mallianum oppidum sunt castella, Collis Vetus, Stemiliana, Furanum, Cabinianum; transmissoque Calentino castellum est in colle Poggium Mirtetum, cui torrentulus adiacet Rivus Solis dictus. Videturque is esse quem Horatius in primo epistolarum sic describit **[334F]**:

> Me quotiens reficit gelidus Digentia rivus,
> Quem Mandela bibit, rugosus frigore pagus,
> Quid sentire putas, quid credis amice precari?

Et Acron exponit, "Mandela pagus in Sabinis ubi rivus Digentia."

Supraque eius rivi fontem dextrorsum est Montopolis oppidum, publicam cuius aream innatum ferrei coloris obdurum sternit saxum. Dedit vero Montopolis magnum huius saeculi Sabinis ornamentum Petrum Odum, qui grammaticus Romae celeber Nasonianam Flaccianamque simul in omni carminum genere facultatem facilitatemque est nactus.

Sequitur ad Tiberim Farfari amnis ostium, fuitque is fluvius priscis temporibus Farfar et Fabaris appellatus. Nam Servius dicit Fabarim esse fluvium, qui per Sabinos transiens et Farfarus dicitur; unde Plautus, "Dissipabo te tamquam folia Farfari." Ovidius vero, "Et amoenae Farfaris undae," prout certe nunc etiam sunt amoenissimae. Longissimo enim tractu postquam Farfarus montes reliquit per plana labitur culta opacis undique tectus arboribus. Qua quidem in amoenissima planitie, monasterium, ipsi fluvio dextrorsum imminet amplissimum Farfense appellatum, castella ad decem possidens, quorum primum Fara dictum colli impositum est monasterio imminenti.

[334G] Et illi dextrorsum adiacet oppidum Poggium Curtesii, a Curtesio amne subtus delabente vocatum. Quem quidem fluvium Alliam prisco nomine dictum fuisse constat. Farfensi etiam monasterio dextrorsum imminet Nerula oppidum nobile. Superius sunt Scandrilia, Tophia, Mons S.

Above Cures in the mountains on the left are the following fortified towns: Stroncone, Calvi, and S. Pietro; lower, on the right side, are Cottanello, and Roccantica, a rough place. Next to Roccantica a stream, the Calentino, flows a short distance before it goes into the Tiber. High hills overhang Cottanello and Roccantica, and beyond them is Bocchignano, a town, S. Pietro. Also between the Calentino and the town of Magliano Sabina there are fortified towns: Collevecchio, Stimigliano, Forano, Gavignano; and after you cross the Calentino there is a fortified town on the hill, Poggio Mirteto, and next to it flows a small stream called Rio Sole. This seems to be the one Horace [334F] describes in his first book of *Epistles*:

> As many times as I have been refreshed by the stream of the Digentia,
> from which the inhabitants of Mandela draw their water, a village
> shriveled with cold, what do you think I feel, my friend,
> what do you believe I pray for?

And Acron explains, "Mandela is a village among the Sabines where the stream Digentia is."

Above this stream's source, on the right-hand side, is the town of Montopoli di Sabina; its public square has a pavement of hard native stone the color of iron. Montopoli has greatly enhanced this century by giving it Pietro Oddo, a famous grammarian at Rome, the equal of Ovid and Horace in his expertise in writing poems of every genre.

There follows at the Tiber the mouth of the Farfa river, and this river was called in ancient times Farfar and Fabaris. Indeed, Servius says that the Fabaris is the river which crosses the Sabine territory and is called Farfarus. From this name comes the line of Plautus, "I shall scatter you like leaves of the Farfar." And Ovid writes, "And the pleasant waves of the Farfar," inasmuch as they are definitely, even now, very pleasant. For the Farfa goes in a long course, after it leaves the mountains and flows across the cultivated flatlands, and is shaded everywhere by trees with dense foliage. And in this pleasant plain, a great monastery called Farfa overlooks this same river on its right-hand side. It possesses ten castles, and the first of these, called Fara, is located on a hill hanging over the monastery.

[334G] And on the right-hand side, next to that place, is the town of Passo Corese, named after the Corese river which flows beneath it. It is certain that this is the river which was called by the ancient name of Allia. Also overlooking the monastery of Farfa on the right is the well-known town of Nerola. And above it are: Scandrilia, Toffia, Mte. S. Maria, Frasso

Mariae, Fraxum, Poggium, Donadeum, Salixanum, Poggium Maiani. Haec vero vallis quam Farfarus efficit tam multis habitatam castellis illa esse videtur, in qua Horatius villam habuit. Montes enim quos a Pedeluco Tibur usque continuari ostendimus, hac sola valle interrumpuntur. Horatius ad Quintum:

> Scribetur tibi forma loquaciter et situs agri,
> Continui montes ni dissocientur opaca
> Valle, sed ut veniens dextrum latus aspiciat sol,
> Laevum discedens curru fugiente vaporet.
> Temperiem laudes, quid si rubicunda benigni
> Corna vepres, et pruna ferant, et quercus et ilex
> Multa fruge pecus, multa dominum iuvet umbra.

Scribit etiam Horatius in primo carminum de eodem sic:

> Velox amoenum saepe Lucretilem
> Mutat Lycaeo Faunus et igneam
> Defendit aestatem capellis
> Usque meis pluviosque ventos.

Et Acron exponit Lucretilem esse montem in Sabinis. Ex eaque villa vinum fuit vile, sicut in frigidis locis nasci **[334H]** videmus. Quod Horatius Maecenati misit cum his versibus:

> Vile potabis modicis Sabinum
> Cantaris Graeca quod ego ipse testa
> Conditum levi, datus in theatro
> Cum tibi plausus.

Erat etiam in huius villae agro silva, de qua Horatius carminum item primo sic scribit:

> Namque me silva lupus in Sabina,
> Dum meam canto Lalagen et ultra
> Terminum curis vagor expeditus
> Fugit inermem.

Sabino, Poggio, *Donadeum*, Salisano, Poggio Moiano. Truly, this valley which the Farfa creates, so crowded with fortified towns, appears to be the one in which Horace had his villa. For as I have demonstrated, this is the only valley which breaks the continuous range of mountains extending from Piediluco to Tivoli. As Horace wrote to Quin[*c*]t[*i*]us:

> About the appearance and location of my farm, I will speak to you at length.
> The mountains stretch unbroken, except where a shady valley separates them;
> It allows the morning sun to shine on the right slope,
> And when it sets it warms their left slope.
> You would praise its moderate climate. What would you say about the generous thorn-bushes which bear red berries and wild plums?
> The oaks which provide acorns in plenty for the herds, and abundant shade for their master?

And Horace also writes about the same place in the following words from his first book of *Odes*:

> Faunus often quickly journeys to
> Pleasant Lucretilis from Lycaeus and wards
> Off from my flocks both the summer heat
> And winter's rain-bringing winds.

And Acron explains that Lucretilis is a mountain in the Sabine region. Also, the wine produced from Horace's villa was cheap, as we see is the case in cold climates. [334H] Horace sent some to Maecenas accompanied by these verses:

> You will drink a cheap Sabine wine from modest
> Cups which I myself bottled in a Greek jar
> Sealed with pitch, in the year when you
> Were applauded on appearing in the theatre.

There was also in the territory of this farm a wood, about which Horace writes in his first book of *Odes*:

> For a wolf fled from me in the Sabine wood,
> Although I was unarmed,
> While I composed a poem about my Lalage,
> Wandering carefree off my property.

Fuitque Horatio tam grata haec villa ut carminum tertio scribat,

Cur valle permutem Sabina
divitias operosiores.

Et infra eiusdem villae fontem sic laudat:

O fons Blandusiae splendidior vitro,
Dulci digne mero non sine floribus
Cras donaberis haedo.

Et infra,

Te flagrans atrox hora caniculae
Nescit tangere, tu frigus amabile
Fessis vomere tauris
Praebes et pecori vago.

Fies nobilium tu quoque fontium,
Me dicente cavis impositam ilicem
Saxis, unde loquaces
Lymphae desiliunt tuae.

Ut non sit mirandum si Horatius ad hanc veniens villam, fidem amico fefellit sicut his versibus:

Quinque dies tibi pollicitus me rure futurum,
Sextilem totum mendax desideror.

Sequuntur ad Tiberim fluvii Curtesii sive Alliae ostia, ubi Sabinae regionis olim finis erat et Crustumii incipiebant, quorum populorum locorumque appellationem Plinius scribit XVI ab urbe Roma miliario post Sabinos inchoasse. Et Veientes ab ipsis Crustuminis e regione positis ibi fuisse divisos. Unde [335A] Mons Rotundus Ursinae, Palumbaria Sabellae familiarum urbis Romae patriciarum oppida ut in regione opulentissima in Crustumeriis annumeranda erunt.

Allia vero fluvius est, de quo Virgilius, "Quosque secans infaustum interfluit Allia nomen." Et Servius exponit, "Allia fluvius haud longe ab urbe est, iuxta quem Galli Brenno duce XV Calen. Augusti deleto Romanorum exercitu, postridie deleverunt urbem." Quam historiam Livius in sexto

And this farm was so pleasing to Horace that, in his third book of *Odes*, he writes,

> Why would I exchange my Sabine valley
> for wealth, which would be more burdensome?

And further on he praises the spring on his property:

> O fountain of Bandusia, more sparkling than any glass,
> You deserve a libation of sweet pure wine and the gift of a garland;
> Tomorrow I shall sacrifice a kid to you.

And after this he continues,

> The cruelly burning heat of the Dogstar cannot spoil you
> You offer your welcome coolness to the bulls worn out from the plough,
> And to the wandering herds.
>
> You will be numbered among famous fountains,
> As I sing of the oak growing from your hollow rocks,
> And your murmuring waters flowing down from it.

So it is not surprising if Horace came to this villa and betrayed his promise to his friend, as he describes in the following verses:

> Five days I promised you I would be in the country.
> I lied; you have missed me the entire month of August.

There follows at the Tiber the mouth of the river Corese, or the ancient Allia, where the boundary of the Sabine region used to be, and the territory of Crustumium began. Pliny writes that the use of Crustumium, as the name of these people and places, started sixteen miles from the city of Rome after the Sabines; and that the people of Veii were separated off from those of Crustumium located beyond the region there. For this reason, towns which are possessions of aristocratic Roman families—**[335A]** Monterotondo, belonging to the Orsini; Palombara Sabina, belonging to the Savelli—very wealthy for the region, have to be classified as located among the people of Crustumium.

The Allia river was here, about which Virgil writes, "Those whose land is divided by the Allia of ill-omened name." And Servius explains, "The Allia is a river not far from Rome, beside which the Gauls under Brennus destroyed the Roman army on July 18, and on the next day they destroyed the city." Livy relates this episode at length in his sixth book. For this rea-

diffuse narrat. Unde dies illa Alliensis dicta prae ceteris omnibus nefasta semper est habita.

Fidenae dehinc describendae inter Montem Rotundum Anienemque et Tiberim fuerunt. De quibus in Latina regione, et in Etruria Veos describentes, quorum coloniae erant abunde diximus. Ornata fuit Sabina regio Landone Romano pontifice, cuius patriam ignoramus. Postquam ager Sabinus Crustumenusque cum fluvio Allia Monteque Rotundo post tergum est relictus, Anio fluvius tertio a Roma miliario fertur in Tiberim.

son, that day was forever called *Dies Alliensis*; it was considered ill-omened before all other days.

From here, Fidenae remains to be described; it is located between Monterotondo and the Aniene and the Tiber. I have written a great deal about Fidenae in my chapter "Lazio," and in "Tuscany" in my description of Veii, which sent out Fidenae as a colony. The Sabine region has been distinguished by the pope Lando, but I cannot identify his native town. When you leave behind you the country of the Sabines and of Crustumium and the river Allia and Monterotondo, the Aniene river flows into the Tiber three miles from Rome.

Regio Quinta, Picenum
Sive Marchia Anconitana

[335B]

Sed iam perventum est ad fines omnes ducatus Spoletini, Anioque fluvius nos traxerat ad loca in Latinorum partibus a Strabone Plinioque enumerata. Quare pedem referentes ad propinquam conterminamque regionem transeamus, quae olim Picenum dicta; nunc est Marchia Anconitana, cum tamen aliquando prius fuerit appellata Marchia Firmana. Nam in gestis rebus septimi Gregorii pontificis Romani in concilio Lateranensi legimus Robertum Guiscardum quia Marchiam occupasset Firmanam fuisse excommunicatum.

Piceni fines sunt: a septentrione, Apenninus eum a ducatu Spoletano, ut ostendimus, dividens; et ab oriente praesertim hiemali fluvius, olim Isaurus, nunc Folia dictus; a meridie superum mare; post fluvius Troentus Asculum praeterlabens. Livius libro XXII, Hannibalis progressus describens post inflictam ad lacum Transumenum populo Romano cladem, dicit eum venisse in agrum Picenum, non copia solum omnis generis **[335C]** frugum abundantem, sed refertum praeda. Et Plinius scribit Picentes quondam uberrimae multitudinis trecenta sexaginta milia in rei publicae deditionem venere, a Sabinis orti. Cum vero socialis belli incentores aut primi Marsis incentoribus socii fuissent in eos a Romanis crudeliter est saevitum.

Livius libro XXIII, "C. Terentio procos. negotium datum ut in Piceno agro conquisitionem militum haberet." Et libro vigesimo septimo Claudii Neronis cos. ad Livium Salinatorem cos. adversus Hasdrubalem ituri describens iter, eum dicit flexisse in Picenum.

Martialis cocus poeta attribuit rerum trium proprietatem Piceno his versibus,

> Haec quae Picenis venit subducta trapetis:
> inchoat atque eadem fuit oliva dapes.

Et alibi,

Fifth Region
March of Ancona

[335B]

Now we have surveyed all the borders of the Duchy of Spoleto; and the Aniene river had drawn us before to the places Strabo and Pliny included in Latium. So let us retrace our steps and cross over to the adjacent region, which was in antiquity called Picenum, but is now called the March of Ancona. In the past, however, it was sometimes called the March of Fermo: for in the records of Pope Gregory VII's actions in the Lateran Council, we read that he excommunicated Robert Guiscard because he had seized the March of Fermo.

These are the boundaries of the March of Ancona: in the north, the Apennines, dividing this region, as I have shown, from the Duchy of Spoleto; in the east, specifically the northeast, the river formerly called Isaurus, now the Foglia; in the south, the Adriatic Sea, and after that the river Tronto which flows past Ascoli. Livy, book 22, describes Hannibal's march after his slaughter of the Romans at Lake Trasimene, saying that he came into the Picene territory, which was not only [335C] abundant in every type of crop, but teeming with opportunities for plunder. And Pliny writes that the Picenes traced their origin to the Sabines; "from this formerly very densely-populated region, 360,000" came to surrender to the Romans. But the Romans treated them with savage cruelty because they had either incited the Social War or had been the first allies of the Marsi who had incited it.

Livy writes in book 23: "To the proconsul C. Terentius was assigned the recruiting of soldiers in the territory of Picenum." And in book 27: describing the route of the consul Claudius Nero to reach the consul Livius Salinator and to move against Hasdrubal, that he deviated into Picenum.

The poet Martial the cook credited Picenum in these lines with three native delicacies:

> These olives have come to you, rescued from the mills of Picenum;
> they begin and end banquets.

In another poem he says,

Picentina ceres niveo sic nectare crescit
ut levis arrepta spongia turget aqua.

Item alibi,

Filia Picenae venio laucanica porcae
pultibus hinc niveis grata corona datur.

Libet vero ab orientali parte Piceni, sive Marchiae Anconitanae, descriptionem incipere. Isaurus amnis Folia nunc dictus ex Apennino ad Cotulum arcem ortum habens Pisauri civitatis vetustae moenia attingit ubi portum, sed tenuem raro maioribus navigiis apertum, facit. Eam civitatem quam penes **[335D]** Isaurum fit nomen nactam a Romanis conditam fuisse constat. Livius etiam libro XXXIX eam a Romanis simul cum Mutina et Parma coloniam deductam scribit. Scribit Eusebius, de temporibus, Accium tragoediarum scriptorem natum parentibus libertinis Pisaurum inter colonos fuisse deductum, et fundum Accianum fuisse iuxta Pisaurum. Credimusque fuisse ubi nunc corrupte dicitur Farnazanum.

Pisaurum urbem nos a Totila destructam a Belisauroque instauratam in Historiis ostendimus. Quae superiori saeculo principem nacta est praestantem Malatestam Pandulfi filium litteris moribusque ornatissimum, qui natos tres et unicam inter rarissimas clarissimasque numerandam mulierem genuit Paulam, Mantuanorum praesentis temporis principum genitricem. Primum supra Pisaurum ad Isauri sive Foliae sinistram ripam oppidum est Mons Abbatis, e regione cuius oppidi Idaspis torrens Isauro iungitur. Quod poeta Lucanus novit ubi dicit, "et iunctus Idaspis Isauro."

Suntque multa inter Idaspim et Isaurum Pisaurensis et Urbinatis agrorum oppida, quorum Mons Fabrorum notius habetur. Editissimo autem inter flumina ipsa monte Urbinum est, vetusti nominis civitas, cuius inter veteres primum meminit Cornelius Tacitus Vitelliensi bello; et Plinius dicit, "Urbinates cognomine Methaurenses." Nosque in quinto Historiarum ostendimus Belisarium, quia fons in civitate per **[336E]** aestatis caumata arruerat, civitate ipsa per incolarum deditionem fuisse potitum. Fuit ea urbs diu a Montis Feretri comitibus pro Romana ecclesia gubernata prout etiam nunc

The bread of Picenum swells from soaking in its white nectar,
as a sponge swells up from taking on water.

And in still another poem,

Daughter of a sow from Picenum I come, a Lucanian sausage;
I provide a welcome crown around snowy porridge.

I prefer to begin my description of Piceno (or the March of Ancona) from the eastern side. The Isaurus river, now called the Foglia, has its origin in the Apennines at the fortress of Cotulo. It flows past the walls of Pesaro, an ancient city, where it creates a harbor, but one which is too narrow for the regular use of large ships. **[335D]** This city took its name from its location *penes Isaurum*, or "beside the Isaurus." Livy in book 39 writes that Pisaurum was, together with Mutina and Parma, a colony established by the Romans, and Eusebius in his *Chronicle* writes that the tragic poet Accius, born of freedman parents, was among the colonists sent to Pisaurum. I believe that the estate of Accius was near Pisaurum, where now is the corruptly named Farnazzano.

The city of Pisaurum was destroyed by Totila and rebuilt by Belisarius; I have written about this in my *Histories*. It acquired in the previous century an outstanding prince, Malatesta the son of Pandolfo, distinguished in letters as well as character. He produced three sons and a single daughter Paola, mother of the present princes of Mantua, who must be numbered among the most exceptional and famous women of her time. Beside the left bank of the Isaurus or Foglia, the first town above Pesaro is Montelabbate, in the area where the stream Apsa joins the Foglia. The poet Lucan was aware of this confluence when he wrote, "And the Idaspis joined to the Isaurus."

There are many towns between the Apsa and Foglia in the territories of Pesaro and Urbino; Montefabbri is the best-known of these. And indeed, between the rivers on a high hill is the city of Urbino, which has kept its ancient name. It is first mentioned among the ancient writers by Tacitus in his account of the war of Vitellius, and Pliny mentions "the people of Urbino with the cognomen *Metaurenses*." And in the fifth book of my *Histories* I told how Belisarius **[336E]** took possession of this city when the inhabitants surrendered, because the source of water inside the city walls had dried up in the summer heat. Urbino has been long governed by the counts of Montefeltro as vicars of the church, and in this capacity Federigo now

gubernat idem Federicus, cui supra diximus Eugubium esse subditum. Habet vero nunc ipsa civitas Saraphinum iuris et bonarum artium doctrina ornatissimum consistorialem in Romana curia advocatum.

Supra Pisaurum ad sinistrum oppida sunt quam plura; sed notiora mons Barocius, et Nuvolaria, inter quae torrens labitur Argilla, nomen a limo quem altum et tenacem habet nacta, Fani Fortunae moenia attingens, quae maritima civitas et ipsa Romanos habuit conditores. A Totilaque sicut Pisaurum destructa fuit et a Belisauro instaurata. Absunt tertio a Fano Fortunae miliario Methauri fluvius ostia. Ad dexteram cuius partem intus est Forum Sempronii civitas vetusta viae imminens Flamineae, quam Federicus idem Feretranus pro Romana ecclesia nunc gubernat. Est vero is Methaurus amnis velox a Lucano appellatus, clade Hasdrubalis per Livii Salinatoris Claudiique Neronis cos. Romanorum victoriam libro Livii XXVII copiose narratam clarus.

Quem ad sinistram [336F] tertio supra Forum Sempronii miliario fluvius illabitur Candianus sinistra in cuius ripa viae Flamineae, quam Augustus Octavianus ab urbe Roma Ariminum usque stravit, pars visitur mirabili et sumptuosissimo opere facta, quam durissimi saxi mons quingentis excisus in longitudinem passibus iter praebuit curribus. Et ne subiectus amnis rapidum currens viae corroderet fundamenta, murus ab aquis in summam viam quadrato lapide pluribus locis in sublime excitatus illam sustentat. Sed maiori opera impensaque saxum siliceam habens duritiem ducentis ut teneo passibus longitudine et octo altitudine perforatum: curribus item factum est pervium cui a forma actuque Forulo est appellatio. Docetque titulus litteris cubitalibus in fronte excisus, T. Vespasianum et non Octavianum Augustum, qui viam straverat Flaminiam, id Foruli opus fieri curasse.

Is Candianus torrente auctus uno ad dexteram habet Aqualeneam vicum tabernis hospitatoriis frequentatum. Et paulo supra habet Montem Falconem. Supra vero ad sinistram Callii civitatis moenia abluit Candianus. Et superius est Candianum, oppidum ab eo fluvio appellatum, quod tamen ex Luceolis oppidi vetusti [336G] propinquo loco, qua est via Flaminia Eugubium est iter a Longobardis excisi, ruinis aedificatum fuisse, non dubito. Estque Luceolis locus ad quem libro Historiam septimo ostendimus Narsetem eunuchum castra habuisse quando mors Totilae sibi fuit nuntiata. Et libro nono diximus Eleuterium Italiae exarchum ab Eraclio imperatore con-

governs it, the ruler, as I mentioned, of Gubbio. Urbino now boasts as its citizen Serafino, a consistorial advocate distinguished in his learning in the law and in the liberal arts.

Above Pesaro on the left are numerous towns, the best-known among them Mombaroccio and Novilara. Between them the stream Arzilla flows, named for its deep and thick mud. It grazes the walls of Fano, a sea-coast city also founded by the Romans. Like Pesaro, it was destroyed by Totila, then rebuilt by Belisarius. Three miles from Fano is the mouth of the Metauro river. On its right bank towards the interior is Fossombrone, an ancient city which overhangs the Via Flaminia, now ruled by the previously mentioned Federigo da Montefeltro as vicar of the church. This is the ancient Metaurus river which Lucan called "swift," and which is famous from Livy's extensive account, in book 27, of the disaster the victorious consuls Livius Salinator and Claudius Nero inflicted on Hasdrubal.

The Candigliano river flows into the Metauro on the left three miles **[336F]** above Fossombrone; on its left bank one can see part of the Via Flaminia, which Augustus laid from Rome to Ariminum. It is a marvelous piece of work involving a great outlay of money: cut a half-mile into a mountain of the hardest stone, it provides a way wide enough for vehicles. And so that the river rushing rapidly below would not rot away the foundations, a wall was built of square blocks of stone, on the surface of the road, which holds it up. It is, in many places, raised on high all the way from the water to the surface of the road. But a tunnel for vehicles which I estimate to be two hundred feet long, cut into the stone a depth of eight feet, has been created with even greater effort and expense. It is called Gola del Furlo from its function and shape. The inscription carved on its face in letters a cubit high shows that Titus Vespasian, and not Augustus, who built the Via Flaminia, caused this passageway to be built at Furlo.

A small tributary flows into the Candigliano, and here on its right bank is Acqualagna, a village well-supplied with inns for travellers. And a little above it is Montefalcone; higher up on the left the Candigliano skirts the walls of the city of Cagli, and above this is the town Cantiano, named after the river. I am certain that it was built from the ruins of the ancient town **[336G]** of Luceoli, its neighbor, which was destroyed by the Lombards and was located where the road to Gubbio splits off from the Via Flaminia. And at Luceoli, as I showed in the seventh book of my *Histories*, Narses the eunuch was in camp when he got news of the death of Totila. And in book 9 I wrote that Eleutherius, who had been named exarch of Italy by the emperor

stitutum; quia usus perfidia ad imperium aspiraret ab exercitu Ravennate apud Luceolum interfectum.

Supra forum Sempronii plus minus octavo passuum miliario Methaurus amnis Firmiani moenia abluit oppidi Urbinatium, iuxta quod mons est Hasdrubalis nomen habens, quod eum ducem ibi superatum fuisse et constans in regione fama est; et nos Livii Patavini libris attente lectis certissima deprehendimus coniectura. Interius vero ad Methauri superiora progredientes planitiem inveniunt speciosissimam, in qua primum est oppidum a Methauro paene in insulam circumdatum, quod Guilielmus Durandi Carnotensis decanus pontificii iuris consultissimus speculi eius doctrinae libri auctor, cum Martini quarti pontificis Romani nuntius et Romandiolae thesaurarius esset a fundamentis aedificavit, et a suo nomine Castrum Durantis **[336H]** appellavit.

Quinto inde miliario abest sancti Angeli in vado, oppidum mercatoribus frequentatum. Et proxime Apennino Mercatellum, superiusque Amola castellum ad Apennini tramitem positum qua in Etruriam a Romandiola difficili ascensu itur. Eam vero regionem a Federico Feretano possessam quae Massa Trabaria appellatur: Romanam ecclesiam cuius iurium est sic vocasse constat, quia ex ipsis Apennini iugis immensae magnitudinis abiegnae trabes Romam in aedium basilicarumque structuram portari consueverint, prout etiam nunc portantur. Unde videtur hac ratione Plinium non absurde scripsisse quod supra rettulimus, Tiberim amnem a Tiferno hinc Apennino appropinquante fuisse Romam ratibus navigabilem, prout certe nunc est quando imbribus adeo intumuit ut clausurae eius cogendis ad molendina aquis ubique in alveo iactae omnino prohibere nequeant.

Sunt etiam in montibus qui Methaurum inter et Isaurum ac Apenninum Massae imminent Trabariae Carola oppidum, et minora aliquot castella: Raspagatta, Miraldella, Forbedulum, Sanctus Martinus, Brasticaria, Belforte Campus, Turris Fossati, Paganicum, Perlum, potentis olim Ubaldinorum dominii reliquiae quas Octavianus possidet Ubaldinus patre genitus Bernardino, cuius adolescentis egregie docti humanitatis modestia gravitate condiuntur **[337A]** prudentiaque senili, ut alterum in ipso expectemus Ioannem Accionis proavum, qui patrum nostrorum memoria, virorum sui saeculi

Heraclius, was put to death at Luceoli by the army of Ravenna because he was engaged in treachery in order to seize the throne.

About eight miles above Fossombrone, the Metauro river flows past the town of Fermignano, which belongs to Urbino. Next to it is the mountain called Monte Asdrubaldo after Hasdrubal, because this general was conquered there; and this legend persists in this region, and I know this also because I have diligently perused the work of Livy of Padua and from it made a very sure deduction. But farther inland, as you go up the Metauro, you find a very beautiful plain, where the first town is on a peninsula in the middle of the Metauro. This town (Urbania) was built from the ground up by Guillaume Durand, dean of Chartres, most expert in canon law and author of a learned book entitled *Speculum iudiciale*. At the time he was papal nuncio for Pope Martin IV and treasurer of the Romagna, and he named the town after himself, Castel Durante **[336H]**.

Five miles from here is the town of S. Angelo in Vado, a popular marketplace. And next to the Apennines is Mercatello sul Metauro, and higher up the fortified town Lamoli on the path up into the Apennines, where the journey uphill from the Romagna to Tuscany is very difficult. This region, called Massa Trabaria, is held by Federigo da Montefeltro. It is thought that it was so named by the church, which has jurisdiction over it, because enormous beams of fir-wood used to be transported from the ridges of the Apennines to Rome, where they were used to build palaces and churches, as indeed they are today. For this reason, it is plausible what Pliny says, as I related above, that the Tiber was navigable from Tifernum, close to the foothills of the Apennines, to Rome; as it is in these days, when it is swollen with rain. This is why in some places dams have been constructed in the riverbed to stop its flow and direct it to the mills, but they are not sufficient to hold it back.

There are also, in the mountains between the Metauro, the Foglia, and the Apennines, above Massa Trabaria, the town of Carola, and some small fortified villages: Raspagatti, Miraldella, Sorbetolo, Santo Martino, *Brasticaria*, Belforte all' Isauro, Torre di Fossato, Paganico, and Pirlo. They are the remains of the former powerful dominion of the Ubaldini, now possessed by Ottaviano Ubaldino, son of Bernardino. With his outstanding learning in the liberal arts and his seriousness and modesty, **[337A]** and wisdom beyond his years, this young man makes us hope that he will be another Giovanni Azzo, similar to his great-grandfather, who was considered

arma tractantium facile princeps, et tamen prudentissimus gravissimusque est habitus.

Post Methaurum fluvium in Hadriatici litore sequitur Cesanus torrens, ad cuius sinistram intus est Mondosum, et inde Mondavium, et supra Sanctus Laurentius oppidum Ugone ornatum domino familiae Montis Vetuli, qui vita et moribus dignitatem magis decorat abbatialem quam ab ea decus accipiant. Et interius ad Cesani fontem Pergula oppidum quod nuper habuit Angelum rei bellicae gloria clarum. Misa fluvius post torrentem Cesanum primus mare illabitur ad Senae, nunc Senogalliae, moenia, urbis vetustissimae a Gallis quondam Senonibus habitatae; qui urbe capta, dirempta, incensa ac auro redempta, postmodum a Romanis duce Camillo ad internecionem fuerunt caesi. Et nunc solo aequata in cuius superborum olim moenium partis ambitu arces sunt pertenues duce a Sigismundo Malatesta cum Fano Fortunae ac Arimino pro Romana ecclesia gubernatur.

Sunt vero multa interius circa Misam amnem oppida et castella quorum [337B] notiora mons Boddii, Corinaltum, et Rocha, cuius nomen saepe in aetatis nostrae historiis invenitur. Et paulo superius augetur Misa Sentino amne ad Saxiferati moenia delabente. Cuius oppidi nomen saepe "per ora virum volitare" facit Bartolus iureconsultorum superioris saeculi excellentissimus. Habet vero nunc id oppidum Alexandrum theologia ac philosophia et Nicolaum Perottum eloquentia ornatissimos.

Sentinus amnis vetustum retinet nomen, secus quem secundo supra Saxumferratum stadio Sentina urbs fuit vetusta, in cuius agro Livius libro X proelium scribit praeclarum fuisse gestum, in quo Fabio Maximo Decio cos. ab Umbris, Etruscis, Gallis, et Samnitibus cum Romanis pugnatum est, et Decius filius genitoris Decii exemplo devotus hostium telis obrutus interiit, Romanique victoria potiti, peditum quadraginta milia trecentos triginta, equitum sex milia de hostibus interfecerunt. "Samnitiumque agmen," cum fuga prolapsi "per agrum Pelignum fugerent, circumventum a Pelignis est, ex milibus quinque ad mille caesi." Estque id proelium in quo

> cum structae acies undique starent, cerva fugiens lupum e montibus exacta per campum [337C] inter duas acies discurrit. Inde divisae ferae cerva ad Gallos, lupus ad Romanos cursum deflexit;

by our fathers' generation easily the greatest military leader of his age, and yet also the wisest and most influential.

After the Metauro, the next stream on the Adriatic coast is the Cesano, on whose left bank towards the interior is Mendoso, and then Mondavio, and higher up S. Lorenzo in Campo, a town distinguished by its citizen Ugone Montevecchio, an abbot whose pure character decorates his office, rather than receiving glory from it. And farther inland at the source of the Cesano is Pergola, a town which recently boasted Angelo della Pergola, famous in warfare. After the Cesano comes the Misa river, which flows into the sea at Senigallia, the ancient Sena, a very old city once inhabited by the Galli Senones. (They are the ones who captured Rome, plundered it and burned it; the city was ransomed for gold and later these Gauls were killed off by the Romans under Camillus.) Now Senigallia has been razed, and in the fragmentary circle of its once proud walls are two small fortresses, which are governed for the church by Sigismondo Malatesta, along with Fano and Rimini.

Towards the interior around the Misa river are many towns and fortified villages, but the **[337B]** better-known are Monte Bodio, Corinalto, and Rocca, a name which occurs frequently in the histories of our time. A little higher up the Misa is joined by the Sentino river, which flows past the walls of Sassoferrato. This town's name will always "flit about on the mouths of men" thanks to its native son Bartolo da Sassoferrato, the most renowned lawyer of the previous generation. But today this town boasts Alessandro da Sassoferrato, distinguished as theologian and philosopher, and the very eloquent Nicolò Perotti.

The Sentino river still keeps its ancient name, and along it, a quarter of a mile above Sassoferrato, is the site of ancient Sentinum. In its territory, Livy writes in book 10, a famous battle was fought between the Umbrians, Etruscans, Gauls, and Samnites, on the one hand, and the Romans on the other, during the consulship of Fabius Maximus and Decius. Decius, son of Decius, followed his father's example and went to his death, sacrificing his own life to the enemy forces. The Romans were victorious, killing 40,330 of the enemy footsoldiers, and 6,000 of the enemy cavalry. "The Samnite army" fled through the territory of Sulmo, and "were surrounded by the Peligni, and out of 5,000, up to 1,000 were killed." This was the was the battle in which

> . . . as the lines stood ready for combat, a deer ran down from the mountains fleeing from a wolf. The two animals arrived in the field **[337C]** between the two armies and separated from each other,

> lupo data est inter ordines via, cervam Galli confixere. Tum ex antesignanis Romanus miles, "Illac fuga," inquit, "hinc victor Martius lupus, integer et intactus, gentis nos Martiae et conditoris nostri admonuit."

Ex Sentinae urbis a Longobardis destructae ruinis Saxumferratum, et pariter sexto ab inde miliario Fabrianum oppida fuerunt a principio inchoata. Ortum vero habet Sentinus in Apennino ad tramitem, unde Fossatum Umbriae oppidum est accessus. Post Senogalliam prima inveniuntur in litore fluminis Esini ostia, ad quae arx est munitissima Anconitanorum praesidio custodita. Intus ad eundem fluvium sui nominis est civitas Esis et ipsa vetus, et interius ac sub primis Apennini collibus frequens opificibus Fabrianum, quod nobilissimum totius Piceni sive Marchiae oppidum, Sentinae urbis vetustae ibi ad sex mille passus vicinae excidio aedificatum per aetatem nostram Gentilem habuit pictorum sui saeculi celeberrimum.

In eoque familia nobilis Elavelensium viri simul pueri et infantes in quibus Baptista litteris ornabatur, civium conspiratione dum sacris in basilica **[337D]** interessent, ad internecionem sunt caesi. Fortunatum vero est praesenti anno sicut et proximo fuit Fabrianum Romanae curiae eo ductae praesentia, unde multas divitias maxima cum dignitate accumulat. Tulitque ipsius oppidi fors ut adulterini pontificis reliquiae pestiferi dogmatis in eo fuerunt punitae, quod quidem memorabile facinus non ab re censuimus referendum.

Cum Ioannes XXII pontifex Romanus Ludovici Bavari adulterini imperatoris importunitati ac insolentiae constanter resisteret, veniens Roma ipse Bavarus quendam Petrum Colutii de Corbario Reatinae dioecesis minorum ordinis in Antipapam profanari curavit. Qui miser factae de se electioni cum esset assensus anticardinales creavit, et complicibus in vesania impietateque sua coactis pro viribus est conatus scindere Dei ecclesiae unitatem. Et tamen interim Ioanna Mathei filia de Corbario repetiit in iudicio eundem maritum suum qui secum annis quinque priusquam ad fratres minores inhabilis confugisset, matrimonialiter fuerat copulatus, fuitque per episcopum servato iuris ordine in Petrum sententia redintegrandi matrimonii promul-

> the stag running to the lines of the Gauls, the wolf to those of the Romans, who made room for it between the ranks; but the Gauls killed the deer. Seeing this, one of the Romans in the front ranks said, "That way flight, this way Mars' wolf, unharmed and victorious, is a portent showing that we are the race of Mars and he the founder of our race."

Out of the ruins of the city of Sentinum, which was destroyed by the Lombards, Sassoferrato started to be built, and in the same way the town of Fabriano six miles away. The Sentino has its source in the Apennines at the path where you enter the Umbrian town of Fossato di Vico. After Senigallia, the first feature on the coast is the mouth of the river Esino, where there is a well-garrisoned fortress guarded by the men of Ancona. Inland, on the same river, is an ancient town, called Jesi after the river, and towards the interior at the foothills of the Apennines is Fabriano, a town full of artisans, the principal town of all Piceno or the March of Ancona, built from the ruins of the ancient Sentinum about six miles away. It has boasted as its citizen Gentile da Fabriano, the most famous painter of our generation.

The noble family of the Chiavelli-both adults and children, among whom was Battista, distinguished in literature-were all killed here. Through a conspiracy of their fellow-citizens, they were slaughtered while in church participating in divine offices **[337D]**. But Fabriano enjoyed the good fortune of hosting the papal Curia last year and this year, and as a result much wealth and great distinction accrued to the town. This town through the operations of Fate turned out to be the place of punishment of the remaining members of the evil sect of the "Spiritual Franciscans." Their crime was certainly memorable, and not irrelevant to my topic; thus I have considered it worth recounting here.

When Pope John XXII was refusing the title of Emperor to the arrogant imposter, the false emperor Louis the Bavarian, the latter came to Rome, where he sacrilegiously named as Antipope a certain Pietro da Coluccio of Corvara, who was a Franciscan, a member of the order of Minorites in Rieti. This wretch, acquiescing in his election, in turn elected anticardinals, and compelled his accomplices in insanity and sacrilege to bring about a schism within the Church. But meanwhile Giovanna, daughter of Matteo of Corvara, brought action in court against this Pietro, on the grounds that he had lived with her as her husband (although incompetent to do so), for five years before he had taken orders as a Franciscan. After observing the legal process, the bishop handed down the opinion that Pietro should return to his

gata. Sed cum Petrus ipse in idolum prophanatus a Bonifacio comite Pisano captus et ad Romanum pontificem Avinionem perductus esset diem in carceris paedore obiit.

Nec tamen semper postea defuerunt illius vesaniae sectatores, Fraticelli de **[338E]** opinione vulgariter appellati, asserentes nec Ioannem XXII nec quempiam illius successorem iure et ordine creatum esse pontificem quod malum adeo diffusum est ut in multis magnisque Italiae atque per oram Graeciae praesertim in Athenarum urbis reliquis multi hactenus sint inventi Romanis pontificibus eam ob fatuitatem animis et conventiculis clam initis adversantes. Quamquam magis luxus et libidinis sequi oblectamenta videntur quam iuris pontificii quaerere fundamenta. Nam praeter stupra et adulteria, quae passim unusquisque abditis in locis, et ad hoc occulte paratis committunt, aliud publicis eorum caerimoniis tale fit scelus vocatae et de industria seductae speciosiores quaeque vel viduae vel virgines vel matronae cum in antra noctu convenerint, sacerdotes et clerici eius sectae eodem in antro clausi, divinas quidem laudes ad fidem a simplicibus comparandam ex ritu Christiano legunt, cantitant, immurmurant, quibus nocte, ut aiunt, media finitis, sacerdos eorum maior alta admonet voce, binos debere masculum et feminam sancto spiritu invocato, in complexum carnalemque copulam commisceri. Inde luminibus illico extinctis quemque **[338F]** virum proximam, aut manu captam, aut etiam de industria observatam, mulierem sibi prosternere.

Si vero ex huiusmodi coitu conceperit mulier, infans genitus ad conventiculum illud in speluncam delatus, per singulorum manus traditur tamdiu totiensque baiulandus quousque animam exhalaverit. Isque in cuius manibus infans exspiravit maximus pontifex divino, ut aiunt, spiritu creatus habetur. Et cum alter item ex tam multis vitiatis mulieribus offertur fetus, eum sacerdotes collegialiter congregati prunis assant, collectumque inde pulverem in vasculum mittentes, vinum superfundunt, quo novitios et execrabilibus huiusmodi initiandos sacris potant. A quo combibendi modo crudelis haec superstitio vasculi quo fit vocabulo Barilotum appellata est.

Retulitque nobis religiosissimus et certe sanctus vir Ioannes Capistraneus, huic persequendae hominum sectae praefectus scelestissimam mulierculam sponte sibi fassam fuisse cum eo ex diabolico coitu peperisset infan-

wife for the purpose of restoring his marriage. But since Pietro had committed sacrilege by being established as Antipope, he was captured by Boniface Count of Pisa, and sent to the pope in Avignon, where he died in the filth of prison.

But this mad sect, the so-called "Spirituals," persisted afterwards. They denied that John XXII and his successor **[338E]** were duly elected popes. They spread their evil not only in many great Italian cities, but also into Greece, especially in the remains of the city of Athens, where up to recently there were found clandestine cells of these wretches, in their insanity and in their secret assemblies opposing the popes. They seem more interested, however, in pursuing the pleasures of luxury and lust than in investigating the foundations of canon law: for in addition to the illicit sex which each of them frequently commits here and there, in hideaways fitted out for this purpose, they are involved in another such crime, this committed in their public ceremonies. They call together and take aside the more beautiful women, widows, virgins, and wives, and when they have assembled at night in a cave, the priests and ministers of the sect, joining them in the cave, read, chant, and murmur religious hymns from Christian ritual to gain the trust of the simple-minded women. When they have finished, in the middle of the night, the chief priest announces in a loud voice that couples should invoke the holy spirit and pair off, one male and one female, to embrace and copulate. Then right away the lights are put out, and each **[338F]** man pushes to the ground the woman nearest him, whom he has either laid hands on or carefully marked out for himself.

But if a woman conceives as a result of this type of copulation, after the baby is born it is brought to the place of assembly in the cave, and passed from hand to hand among the members, for so long and so many times until it dies. The man who has it in his hands when it dies is named Chief Priest and, as they say, considered to have been chosen by the holy spirit. And when another infant is offered from so many corrupted women, the priests assemble for a meeting, and roast it on live coals, and collect the ashes and put them in a vessel, pour wine over the ashes, and make the novices and initiates into these detestable rites drink the mixture. This savage ritual is named after this practice of drinking "barilotto" (small cask), derived from the word for the sacrilegious vessel.

I learned from the very holy and religious Giovanni da Capestrano, who was in charge of persecuting this sect, that one of the perverted women had confessed to him that she had conceived a baby as a result of this diabolical

tem genitum laeto animo laetioreque fronte in cistellam de industria ornatissimam ad speluncam detulisse, praefatam se munus afferre pretiosissimum, eandemque parentem non modo siccis oculis sed [338G] hilari animo eiulantem miserandumque vociferantem affari filium inspexisse. Eam itaque crudelissimam haeresim cum Fabriani degentes accuratius prosequuntur, convicti ad duodecim et resipiscere pertinaciter recusantes igni, ut erant meriti, sunt consumpti.

Et vero ad Esis fluvii dexteram sub ipsis Apennini iugis qua Validum Umbriae oppidum petitur, locus fratrum Seraphici Francisci heremita dictus, quo viso, ut inquit poeta Ovidius, "potes dicere numen inest." Aedificiis certe quantum religiosis viris sat sit ea in locorum asperitate tam commode instructus, ut alia eiusdem ordinis Italiae urbium loca amoenitate superet. Servaturque picta in eo tabula Gentilis Fabrianensis, opus ceteris, quas viderimus praeferenda.

Habet Esis fluvius ad dexteram intus Serram oppidum Sancti Quirini appellatum quingentis passibus ab ipso amne et arduo in colle semotum ei aversa a Fabriano regione Mathelica oppidum non ignobile, cuius nomen in Picentibus ponit Plinius sexto abest miliario, iuxta quod labitur torrens brevi cursu in Esim et ipse cadens. Secundum litus post Esis ostia promontorium Cimera incipit, Mons Anconae dictus. Quod quidem promontorium tam propinquum [338H] est Apennino, ut aliqui montem ipsum ibi opinati sint scripserintque finiri. Unde ostendit Plinius eo in loco Italiam se flectere, et adversam huius cubiti partem concavum esse lunatum ac maximum, quod a Pistoria incipiens per Casentinum Burgumque ad Sepulchrum tamquam primo cornu procedens, centralem sinum apud Fossatum Validumque, et postea alterum cornu ad Nursiam Cassiamque habeat.

Sub promontorio qua vergit in mare est Ancona ab ipsa litoris et Italiae se flectentis curvitate dicta, cuius vetustae urbis et a Doricis Graecis ut Iuvenalis et ut Plinius a Siculis aedificatae portum Traianus imperator, quod exstantes tituli etiam nunc ostendunt, insigni opere et tutissimum navibus et ornatissimum exstruxit. Ostendimus historiarum quarto Anconam urbem dum Conon Iustiniani imperatoris partium dux male defensat, Gothos subur-

intercourse, and had given birth to the child and had carried it, with a happy heart and expression, into the cave inside an ornate small chest, notifying the congregation that she was bringing them a precious gift. As she watched them roast her crying, screaming child, she bore the sight not only with dry eyes but **[338G]** with a happy countenance. After this cruel heresy had been closely investigated at Fabriano by the inquisitors, about twelve were found guilty, but stubbornly persisted in their beliefs. They were burned alive, as they deserved.

But returning to the Esino river: on its right bank immediately under the Apennines themselves, where is the route to Gualdo in Umbria, there is a house belonging to the brothers of S. Francisco, called Valleromita; if you were to see it, you would say with the poet Ovid, "A divinity resides in the place." It has buildings sufficiently well-furnished for monks to stay in that rough place, and it is a more pleasant place than other Franciscan houses in the towns of Italy. Here is preserved a painting by Gentile da Fabriano which is preferable to any work I have seen.

The Esino river has on its right bank, towards the interior, the town of Serra S. Quirico, a half mile from the river on a high hill. Six miles away, in the opposite direction from Fabriano, is Matelica, a noble town which Pliny places among the Picentes. Next to it a stream with a short course flows into the Esino. After the mouth of the Esino on the coast is the beginning of the promontory of Cimera, in these days called Monte Conero. This promontory is so close **[338H]** to the Apennines that some have believed and written that the Apennines end here. For this reason Pliny indicates that Italy bends back on itself here, and that the part opposite this "elbow," or curvature of the shoreline, is a great crescent-shaped hollow. This bend begins at Pistoia, and goes on through the Casentino to Borgo Sansepolcro, where it has its first projection, then makes its central bend in the middle at Fossato and Gualdo. After that it makes a second projection extending as far as Norcia and Cascia.

At the foot of the promontory, where it juts into the sea, is Ancona, named after that same curve in the shoreline where Italy turns in on itself. This ancient city was built, according to Juvenal, by the Dorian Greeks or, as Pliny states, by the Sicilians. The emperor Trajan built an excellent port here, a safe harbor for ships and beautifully constructed. An inscription which survives even now bears witness to this construction. I have shown in the fourth book of my *Histories* that, while Conon the general of the emperor Justinian was mounting a poor defense, the Goths devastated that part

bium quod tunc mare inter et montem urbe inclusum est, igni ferroque vastasse; et libro septimo diximus Narsetis eunuchi duces cum triginta navibus quadragintaseptem Gothorum naves profligasse et Anconam obsidione durissima tunc levatam fuisse. Undecimoque docuimus libro Saracenos per tempora Lotharii imperatoris et Sergii papae, qui dictus fuerat Os Porci, Anserensi urbe in Dalmatis eversa, navibusque Venetorum ceteis tribus in Tergestino sinu captis incensisque Anconam quoque captam ac **[339A]** spoliatam incendisse. Qua expeditione Saraceni dissensionibus freti, quibus cum fratribus agitabatur Lotharius imperator, post incensam desolatamque Anconam quicquid urbium et locorum usque Idruntum ea habet ora maritima spoliarunt.

Civibus ea civitas moratis et imprimis mercaturae deditis sed maxime omnium servatae dudum libertatis gloria decoratur. Habetque nunc Franciscum Stalamontem et Nicolaum iureconsultos bonarum litterarum studiis ornatos, cum nuper amiserit Ciriacum, qui monumenta investigando vetustissima mortuos ut dicebat virorum memoriae restituebat.

Primus post Cimericum promontorium est amnis Musio, quem ad ostia Aspidum vocant. Tertioque ab eo amne miliario et paulo supra mare vetustissima interiit urbs Humana; et parvo ab inde spatio adhaeret mari ipso in promontorio Siriolum oppidum. Ad alteram vero promontorii partem in mediterranea versam primum est Castrum Ficarellum.

Interius decimo ab Ancona miliario est Auximum civitas vetustissima, cuius ardui montis in quo est sita radices Musio attingit. Ea urbs in multis locis praesertim in Belli Civilis C. Caesaris Commentariis et nostris Ostrogothorum **[339B]** historiis invenitur celebris, quam ostendimus duram pertulisse et longam obsidionem priusquam in Belisarii potestatem deveniret, ea maxime causa quia Gothi illam valido praesidio defensabant. Superius item duodecimo miliario sub Apennini collibus est Cimbulum oppidum a Labieno aedificatum, cuius item celsum sicut Ausimi montem Musio circuit, et paulo superius ortum habet.

Sed medio inter Auxinum Cimbulumque spatio est Staphilum haud ignobile Piceni oppidum, superiusque ad dexteram inter colles Apennino

of the suburbs of Ancona which was then inside the city between the sea and the mountain. And in my seventh book I wrote that the forces of Narses the eunuch, with thirty ships, defeated in battle forty-seven ships of the Goths, and thus the harsh siege of Ancona was raised. In the eleventh book I wrote that the Arabs had destroyed the city of Anser in Dalmatia in the time of the emperor Lothar and Pope Sergius (formerly known as Pig's Face); and had captured and burned three Venetian ships in the Gulf of Trieste; and that they also captured and **[339A]** sacked Ancona, then set it on fire. The Arabs on this expedition took advantage of the disagreements between the emperor Lothar and his brothers to sack all the cities on the coast all the way down to Otranto after they had burned and pillaged Ancona.

Ancona is distinguished by well-mannered citizens, who are particularly dedicated to sea-trade; and it is especially distinguished by the glory of its long-preserved freedom. It now boasts Francesco and Niccolò Scalamonti, experts in the law who are also enthusiasts of the liberal arts. Recently Ancona lost Ciriaco de' Pizzicolli who, through his research into the monuments of antiquity, was restoring the dead to human memory, as he used to say.

After Monte Conero, the first river is the Musone, which at its mouth has the name of Aspio. Three miles from this river, and a little above the sea, was located the ancient city of Humana (now called Numana). And a little way from Numana, next to the sea on the promontory itself is the town of Sirolo. On the other side of the cape, where it faces the interior, the first town is Castelfidardo.

Farther inland, ten miles from Ancona, is the site of the ancient city of Auximum, now called Osimo. It sits on a high mountain at whose foot flows the Musone. Auximum is famous from many passages in history: especially in the *Commentaries on the Civil War* of Julius Caesar, and in our history of the Ostrogoths **[339B]**, where its long and harsh siege by Belisarius is described; because it was strongly defended by a garrison of Goths, it held out for a long time before it fell into the power of Belisarius. And farther up, twelve miles above at the foot of the Apennines is the town of Cingoli, which was built by Labienus, also situated on a high hill whose foot is encircled by the Musone, like Osimo; and a little above this is the source of the Musone.

But between Osimo and Cingoli is Staffolo, a notable town in the March of Ancona, and higher up on the right-hand side between the foothills of the Apennines is Apiro, a fortified town with an ancient name.

proximos est Lapirus vetusti nominis castellum. Attingit vero in mediterraneis mari propinquioribus Musio Recanetum civitatem, quae Ricinetum principio appellata est, cum enim Gothi Eliam Tricinam civitatem campestrem ab Aelio Pertinace Romano imperatore aedificatam, cuius Maceratae propinquiora cernuntur fundamenta, demoliti essent. Eius incolae in oblongum istud dorsum demigrantes Recanetum civitatem sumpto nomine a prima parum mutato aedificarunt, idque decreta Ricinatum marmoribus incisa, quae apud Maceratam sunt ex parte ostendunt. Ea civitas magnum ex patria et affinitate nostra Forlivio habet ornamentum Nicolaum Asteum **[339C]** Recanatensem et Maceratensem episcopum sacris et philosophiae ac medicinae litteris quibus adolescens operam dedit egregie eruditum.

Recanetum inter et Adriaticum mare paululum a Musione recedit celeberrimum totius Italiae ut in aperto immunitoque vico sacellum gloriose virginis Mariae in Laureto appellatum quo in loco preces supplicantium a deo genitricis suae intercessione exaudiri illud maximum certissimumque et argumentum, quod eorum, qui votis emissis exauditi fuerunt, ex auro argento cera pannis veste linea laneaque appensa donaria, magno luenda pretio basilicamque omnem paene complentia, episcopus in dei virginisque gloriam intacta conservat.

Potentia amnis sequitur, ad cuius ostium vetusta interiit eiusdem nominis urbs inter primas Picentum aliquando numerata. Is amnis in Apennino supra Matelicam et quasi e regione Nuceriae Alphateniae oriundus habet intus ad dexteram et sub primis Apennini collibus ad duos mille passus distans Monticulum oppidum. Ad sinistram vero inferius Montem Sanctum, egregium in Picentibus oppidum. Superius vero et ad primos Apennini colles Potentia praeterlabitur Sanctum Severinum, nobile **[339D]** sed novum oppidum ad ruinas aedificatum Septempedae oppidi vetustissimi a Longobardis solo aequati.

Asinus inde torrens perexiguus mare illabitur cui superius adiacet Sancta Maria in Cassiano oppidum ad dexteram. Et intus ad sinistram paulum a mari recedit Civitas Nova nobile oppidum. Et sexto ab Asino torrente miliario absunt Chienti amnis ostia cui intus ad dexteram adiacet Mons Casuarius oppidum, pauloque remotius Morrum, et tertio ab inde miliario superius Macerata, civitas novi nominis; et ipsa Aeliae Ricinae, sicut Recanetum, excidio inchoavit. Quintoque inde miliario superius est Mons

Inland among the places the Musone river reaches, closer to the sea, is the city of Recanati, in its early days called Ricinetum, because the Goths had destroyed a city in the plain built by the Roman emperor Aelius Pertinax called Helvia Ricina. The ruins of this latter city can be seen near Macerata. Its inhabitants migrated to this elongated backbone of the mountain to build a new city; slightly changing the name of their former home, they called it Recanati. We can tell this from some marbles near Macerata that are inscribed with decrees of the people of Ricinetum. A great source of pride to this city is Nicolò dell'Asti of Forlì, my countryman and relative, **[339C]** and bishop of Recanati and Macerata, eminently learned in theology, philosophy, and medicine, which he studied as a young man.

Between Recanati and the Adriatic Sea, a little set back from the Musone river, is the very famous chapel of the glorious Virgin Mary of Loreto, the most famous in all of Italy, considering that it is in an open and unfortified village. Here the prayers of suppliants are answered by God through the intercession of his mother. And the proof of this is that those whose vows have been granted have given thank-offerings of gold, silver, wax, cloth, garments of linen and wool. They would bring a high price, and they fill nearly the entire church, whose bishop preserves them, untouched, to the glory of God and the Virgin.

The river Potenza is next; at its mouth was once a very ancient city with the same name of Potentia, formerly numbered among the most important in Picenum. This river has its source in the Apennines above Matelica, almost in the district of Nocera. It has, towards the interior, on its right bank, at the first foothills of the Apennines, about two miles away, the town of Montecchio. On the left side and lower down, it has Montesanto, an outstanding town in the March of Ancona. But higher up, where the foothills of the Apennines begin, the Potenza flows past S. Severino Marche, a **[339D]** noble town but without much history; it was near the ruins of Septempeda, an ancient town destroyed by the Lombards.

Next, a small stream, the Asola, flows into the sea, and next to it, going up from sea level, on the right side lies the town of S. Maria in Cassiano. And towards the interior on the left, not far from the sea, is Civitanova Alta, a well-known town. And six miles from the stream Asola is the mouth of the Chienti river. Going inland on its right side you come to Montecosaro, and a short distance from there is Morrovalle, and three miles from there, higher up is Macerata, a new city which, like Recanati, had its beginnings from the ruins of Helvia Recina. Five miles above that is Montolmo, a

Ulini, oppidum non ignobile, quod Franciscus Sfortia quo tempore primum Eugenio quarto pontifici Romano hostis esse coepit diripiendum militi concessit. Inde est Arantia Varanensium villa. Superius item ad Chientum amnem est Tollentinum, vetus oppidum quod populo frequens beato confessore Nicolao ornatur, cuius relationis in numerum sanctorum apostolicas litteras ego quarti Eugenii pontificis Romani secretarius confeci. Habuit vero Tollentinum per aetatem nostram Nicolaum Matrucium Tollentinatem inter primarios rei militaris duces annumeratum habetque nunc Franciscum Philelphum litterarum Graecarum Latinarumque excellentia ac editorum operum fama notissimum.

Supraque Tollentinum tertio miliario est Belforte oppidum. Ubi vero Chientus **[340E]** fontes in Apennino habet, Seravallis est, et castellum et vicus, quo tramite Camerinum ex Umbria adiri ostendimus. Est ad sinistram superius Camerinum, civitas vetustissima, ad quam Livius libro nono Fabii Maximi fratrem, quando motus Etruscorum iverat exploratum, pervenisse et multa exceptum comitate scribit; et libro decimo dicit Camertes dedisse P. Scipioni armanda classe quam duxit in Africam cohortem unam sexcentorum militum armatorum. Ea dudum fuit in Picentibus, sicut et nunc est, populi frequentia opibusque primaria, quae proximis annis similem vidit Fabrianensi nobilium Varanensium caedem sed nunc a duobus ex eadem Varanensium gente adolescentibus Rodulpho et Iulio litteris virtutibusque ornatis gubernata quiescit.

Influit Chientum amnem supra Tollentinum torrens Fiastra, in Apennino proxime fontibus Naris Umbrorum amnis oriundus. Cui in ipsis Apennini iugis adiacet Fiastrum inde appellatum castellum; et qua torrens ipse in Chientum labitur est Chaldarola, oppidum non exile. Ad Chienti sinistram intus est Sancti Elipidii oppidum. Superius Sancti Iusti castellum, quod torrens Laetus cognomine Vivus attingit, et in Chientum brevi cursu labitur. Itemque superius ad **[340F]** primos Apennini colles Sancti Genesii est oppidum haud ignobile cui interius Servana adhaeret. Interque ea duo oppida planities Plicae est, apud quam Laetusvivus torrens originem habet.

Ad eumque torrentem, quinto infra Servanum miliario, urbs est Salvia, vetus nomen et pariter multae vetustatis ingentes aedificiorum ruinas ha-

noteworthy town; in the period of Francesco Sforza's hostility to pope Eugenius IV, he allowed it to be sacked by his soldiers. After that comes Castello della Rancia, an estate of the da Varano. And also on the way up-river, beside the Chienti, is the historic and populous city of Tolentino. It is distinguished by the blessed confessor S. Nicola da Tolentino, who was ascribed into sainthood by Pope Eugenius IV; I prepared the documents for his elevation when I was secretary to this pope. But in our generation Tolentino boasts Niccolò Mauruzzi, also known as Niccolò da Tolentino, among the foremost military commanders; and it now claims Francesco Filelfo, very famous for his expertise in Greek and Latin literature and the works he has published.

And above Tolentino, three miles away, is the town of Belforte. Indeed, where the Chienti **[340E]** has its source in the Apennines is Seravalle di Chienti, both a castle and a village, and as I have pointed out, this is the route from Umbria to Camerino. Higher up on the left is Camerino, an ancient city, where, as Livy writes in book 9, the brother of Fabius Maximus, who went to investigate the uprising of the Etruscans, arrived and was received with great friendliness. And in book 10 Livy says that the Camerti contributed a contingent of 600 infantry to Scipio for the fleet he was assembling to take to Africa. For a long time this city was, as it is now, the most important in the region of the Picentes, and densely populated. In recent years the city witnessed a slaughter of the noble family of the da Varano, like the slaughter that happened at Fabriano; but now Rodolfo and Giulio Cesare of the same family rule over it in peace, young men endowed with literary learning and with virtue.

Above Tolentino the stream Fiastra flows into the Chienti river. It has its source in the Apennines, near the source of the Nera river of Umbria. Next to this stream, right on the peak of the Apennines, lies Fiastro, a fortified village named after it; and where the stream Fiastra itself flows into the Chienti is Caldarola, a good-sized town. On the left of the Chienti, towards the interior, is the town of S. Elpidio al Mare. Higher up is the fortified village of Monte S. Giusto, beside the stream Ete Vivo, which runs in a short course before discharging into the Chienti. And also higher up, in the foothills of the Apennines, is the noble town of S. Ginesio, and next to it, but farther inland, is Sarnano. **[340F]** Between the two towns is the plain of Pieca, where the Ete Vivo has its origin.

Beside this stream, five miles below Sarnano, is the site of an ancient city, Urbs Salvia; its name is ancient and all that remains of it are enormous

bens, inter quos certum est tria fuisse theatra nec satis invenimus quo tempore, aut a quo ea urbs fuerit condita. Paucis etiam in locis praeter quam in Plinio et nostra Gothorum Historia illius nomen apud vetustos invenitur, nunc quidem reliquiarum et quidem ingentium loco derelicto exstat in earum angulo oppidum, urbis aliae corruptum a vetusto tenens nomen.

Sunt etiam tertio infra Salviae vestigia miliario ad Laetivivi torrentis undas ingentis monasterii Claravallensis ruinae. At in litore prima sequuntur amnis nunc Tennae olim Tigniae ostia, cui amni haud longe ad dexteram adiacet oppidum, nunc S. Maria in Georgio appellatum, inter primaria Marchiae annumeratum. Quae urbs olim fuit Tignium, de qua in commentariis C. Caesaris sic habetur:

> Interea certio factus Tignium Thermum praetorem cohortibus quinque tenere, oppidum **[340G]** munire, omniumque esse Tigniorum optimam erga se voluntatem, Curionem cum tribus cohortibus, quas Pisauri et Arimini habebat mittit. Cuius adventu cognito diffisus civium voluntate Thermus cohortes ex urbe educit et profugit. Milites in itinere ab eo discedunt ac domum revertuntur. Curio summa omnium voluntate Tignium recepit.

Et citra ultraque Tennam multa sunt ibi propinqua agri Firmani oppida et castella. Sed primum superius ad Tennam est Mons S. Martini, et tertio supra abest miliario Penna. Post quarto miliario ad primos Apennini colles est Amondula, et ipsum inter primaria Piceni oppida numeratum. Ad sinistramque Tennae in Apennino est Mons Fortinus nobile oppidum, supra quod in Apennini iugo Tenna is fluvius fontem habet. Inferiusque ad ostia eadem sinistra castellum est portus Firmanus appellatum, cum tamen mare et fluvius nedum faciant ibi portum, sed vix tolerabilem navibus praebeant mansionem.

Intusque tertio miliario est civitas Firmana Romanorum colonia ex duodeviginti, quae difficillimis secundi belli Punici temporibus primo detrectarunt militiam et tributorum collationem, post in senatus et populi **[340H]** Romani potestatem se permiserunt. Et tamen haud quaquam in hoc murorum ambitu quem habet vetusta, quo illam circumdedit superiore saeculo Ioannes Avolius Vicecomes rei bellicae ductorum sui temporis praestantis-

ruins, also of great age. Among them are definitely the remains of three theatres. I cannot find out when, or by whom, this city was built. For its name is found in few passages among the ancients, except in Pliny and my *History of the Goths*. Indeed, in this deserted place now stands a town in a corner of these huge ruins, which keeps the name, Urbisaglia-a corrupt form of the other, ancient city's name.

Three miles below the ruins of Salvia, next to the Ete Vivo, are the ruins of the great monastery of Chiaravalle. Then, as you return to the coast, the first feature is the mouth of the river now named Tenna, in ancient times Tignia. Not far from this river on the right lies a town which is now called S. Maria in Giorgio, numbered among the most important towns in the March of Ancona. In ancient times this was the city of Tignium, and Julius Caesar mentions it in his *Commentaries*:

> Meanwhile Caesar had learned that the praetor Thermus was holding Tignium with five cohorts, and was **[340G]** fortifying the town; and that the citizens there had great good will towards Caesar. He sent Curio with three cohorts, which he had at Pisaurum and Ariminum. When Thermus learned that Curio was on his way, since he did not trust the citizens of Tignium, he led his cohorts out of the city and fled. His soldiers deserted him on the march and returned home. Curio recaptured Tignium with the agreement of all its citizens.

On this side and the other of the Tenna, and lying close to it, are many towns and fortified villages of the territory of Fermo. But first, higher up on the Tenna is Monte S. Martino, and three miles away is Penna. Four miles from there, at the foothills of the Apennines, is Amandola Salvi, one of the principal towns of the Marches. And on the left side of the Tenna in the Apennines is Montefortino, an impressive town, and above that on the upper slopes of the Apennines is this river's source. Below at the mouth of the Tenna, on the left, is a fortified town called Porto S. Giorgio; although the sea and the river, however, do not create there any good harbor, offering only barely sufficient mooring for ships.

Three miles inland from here is the city of Fermo, a Roman colony and one of the eighteen colonies which first, in the most troubled times of the second Punic War, denied military levies and money to the Romans, but then gave itself into the power of the senate and the Roman **[340H]** people. And this city is surrounded by walls which did not exist in antiquity, but they were built in the previous century by Giovanni Avello Visconti, the

simus, cum tamen saxeo in tumulo, qui moenibus includitur oppidum fuerit pervetustum, cui Castello Firmano erat appellatio. Cernunturque in saxo cubitales litterae, divi nescio cuius Augusti titulo incisae. Fuit pridem eo in tumulo arx munitione et ornatu inter primas Italiae numerata, quam deturbato ac per arma pulso pontificis Eugenii viribus Francisco Sfortia populus Firmanus muro et omni munitione simulque ornatu spoliavit.

Absunt a Firmano portu quinto miliario torrentis Laetimortui ostia, ad quae magni aedificii vestigia cernuntur. Estque fama nullius quod sciam vetusti litteris confirmata Picenum ibi fuisse urbem, a qua provinciam nomen autumant nactam esse. Isque torrens paulo supra Petriclum inter et Belmontem oppida ortum habet. Eundemque torrentem inter et proximum Asonem fluvium est Mons Rubianus oppidum, et superius ad Asonis dexteram intus sunt Servilianum, post Sancta Victoria, et superius Mons Falco oppida.

Et superius item summo in Apennino Mons Monachus, non ignobile oppidum, sub Asonis fluvii fonte situm. Ad Asonis sinistram litori fluvioque adhaeret Pedasum castellum. Supraque est Mons Florae, **[341A]** superius oppidum Mons Novem dictum, quod a novem nobilibus fuit aedificatum. Inde habetur Mons Altus et Forte et superius oppidum Communalia Asculana appellatum. Illabitur post haec mare torrens perexiguus, ad cuius ostia est Morcinum castellum, interius Ripa Trasonum, quod oppidum loci natura muroque munitissimum nulli Picentum populo divitiis concedit. Et tamen dum pellendo provincia Francisco Sfortia bellum geritur, id oppidum Sfortiani diripuere.

Supra est Cossignanum nobile oppidum; superius Castignanum. Superius his in mediterraneis abest tertio miliario a Cossignano Aufida, nobile munitissimumque natura loci oppidum. Altissimis vero in montibus qui praedictis oppidis e regione respondent. Summo in Apennino est Mons Sanctae Mariae in Gallo oppidum, cui ipso in Apennino propinqua est caverna ingens Sibyllae vulgo appellata. Et paulo superius est lacus ille in Nursinorum agri Apennino, quem vano ferunt mendacio piscium loco daemonibus scatere. Ea tamen duorum locorum fama multos diebus nostris et plures superioribus ut audivimus saeculis pellexit necromantia delectatos aut noscendarum **[341B]** rerum mirandarum avidos, ut arduos hos montes magno vanoque labore conscenderent.

foremost military captain of his age. But still there was a very ancient town, inside the walls, on a rocky hill, which used to be called Castellum Firmanum. One can see today, inscribed on the rock, great letters a cubit high, giving the title of some deified Augustus. In earlier days there was on this hill a citadel, one of the most impressive in Italy for its defenses and ornaments, which the people of Fermo tore up, along with its wall, after the forces of Pope Eugenius had ejected Francesco Sforza from it.

Five miles from Porto S. Giorgio is the mouth of a stream, called the Ete Morto, and beside it you can see the remains of some large buildings. They say that here was the city of Picenum (although I have not found confirmation of this in any ancient sources), which according to legend gave the region its name. And the source of this stream is a little higher up, between the towns of Petritoli Piceno and Belmonte. And between the same stream and the next river, the Aso, is the town of Monterubbiano, and higher up on the right bank of the Aso towards the interior are the towns of Servigliano, and then S. Vittoria in Matenano, and above them Montefalcone.

And also higher up, at the summit of the Apennines, is Montemonaco, a considerable town located beneath the source of the Aso river. On the left bank of the Aso, close to the shore and river, is the fortified town of Pedaso; above it is Montefiore, **[341A]** and above that the town called Montedinove, because it was built by nine noblemen. After this there is Montalto, and Force, and above them a town called Comunanza. After these places, there runs down to the sea a little stream at whose mouth is the fortified town of Morcino, and farther inland Ripatransone, a town wealthy as any in the March of Ancona, and well-fortified by its natural situation as well as its walls. And yet it was destroyed by the Sforza forces during the war to drive Francesco Sforza out of the province.

Above this is the noble town of Cossignano, higher up is Castignano, and above both of these towns towards the interior, three miles from Cossignano, is Offida, a distinguished town and naturally well-fortified. But in the highest part of the mountains opposite these latter towns, there is another town on the summit of the Apennines called Monte S. Maria in Gallo, and near it, right in the Apennines, is the huge cavern popularly called the Sibyl's Cave. And a little higher up is the famous lake in the territory of Norcia in the Apennines (Lago di Pilato), which people falsely claim to be full of demons instead of fish. But the reputation of the two places has attracted many men in our times, and more people in previous ages, so I have heard, fascinated by necromancy, or keen on knowing **[341B]** about magical phenomena, to climb these high mountains with great effort on a fool's errand.

Distant in litore ab Asonis fluvii ostio Griptae oppidum octo, a Griptisque Sanctus Benedictus item oppidum duo milia passuum. Quae maritima regio omnium Italiae praeter Surrentinam Caietanamque amoenissima mali quod arantium vocant feracissima, vitibus item arboribusque et oleis est consita, et tribus Sancto Benedicto milibus distat arx, Asculanus Portus appellata, quae ostiis Troenti fluminis ad custodiam est apposita, ubi fines sunt litorei nostrae regionis Piceni sive Marchiae Anconitanae.

Est primum intus ad Troenti dexteram oppidum Mons Brandonus, cive nunc uno felicissimum Fratre Iacobo ordinis Sancti Francisci de Marchia appellato, quem ardentissimum pariter et eloquentissimum verbi divini praeconem vitam ducere in terris angelicam constans fama consentit, adeo ut nullus dubitet quod multi vidisse affirmant eum, ut est vivum, miraculis coruscare.

Tribus ab hoc oppido et totidem milibus a Ripa Trasonum abest Aquaviva oppidum, ex quo duces Adriae provinciae Aprutinae originem duxere. Secundum hanc Troenti dexteram **[341C]** ipso in Apennino est Arquata oppidum nobile, quod Nursini pontificum Romanorum concessione in aliena obtinent regione. Superius quinto miliario pariter ad Troenti dexteram est Accumulum, nobile oppidum, et item superius sub Troenti fonte est Amatrix oppidum, ut in montanis egregium, quod fortassis propinqua in regione cum ultra fontem et ad Troenti sinistram sit annumerari debuit.

Difficilis vero est montium huiusmodi et sitorum in ipsis locorum descriptio, quam saltuosissima sunt et rivis altisque rupibus quandoque ita dividuntur, ut nec pictura sit nec elocutio, quae plenam illorum notitiam dare possit. Hinc unum dictis addere libet, quod suo loco commode nequivimus explicare. Ea in Apennini parte, in qua superius oppidum Arquatam esse diximus, ipse Apenninus se ipsum superans arduum facit grumum, qui Nursinos a Picentibus dirimit. Appellaturque Mons Victor quod ceteros regionis montes altitudine vincat. Ad cuius orientale lacus ille daemonibus infamis, ad aliudque latus in meridiem versum duo ipsius colles altissimi et paulisper in profundo inter se divisi furculas faciunt Prestae appellatas, **[341D]** inter

If you go along the coast, eight miles from the mouth of the Aso you come to a town called Grottammare, and two miles away from Grottammare is the town of S. Benedetto del Tronto. This coastal region is the pleasantest in all Italy, with the exception of the area around Sorrento or Gaeta. The area abounds in oranges, vineyards, and olive trees, and other types of fruit trees. Three miles from S. Benedetto is a fortress called Porto d'Ascoli, planted as a guardpost at the mouth of the river Tronto. Here is the border of the coast of our region of Piceno or the March of Ancona.

Going towards the interior, on the right side of the Tronto the first town is Monteprandone, distinguished by its native son fra Jacopo della Marca, of the Franciscan order, who preaches the word of God with passion and eloquence and has the reputation of living the life of an angel while on this earth. As a result no one questions, and many claim to have witnessed, the miracles that he shines with even now, in his lifetime.

Equidistant three miles from Monteprandone and Ripatransone is the town of Aquaviva Picena, from where the Dukes of Atri in Abruzzo originally come. On this right-hand side [341C] of the Tronto, actually in the Apennines, is the noble town of Arquata del Tronto, which the people of Norcia possess, after obtaining it by a papal concession, although it is in a region different to their own. And higher up, five miles away and also on the right side of the Tronto is Accumoli, a distinguished town, and even higher up, beneath the source of the Tronto, is the town of Amatrice, an important enough town, considering its location in the mountains. It would be perhaps more appropriate to include it among places in the adjacent region, because it is to the left of the Tronto and beyond its source.

It is truly difficult to describe this kind of mountainous terrain, and the places located within it, because it is so full of woods, divided by streams and high cliffs, that there is no map or verbal description which can give a complete account of them. I should like to add one point to what I have said, something which I was unable to explain conveniently in the appropriate place. That is that the Apennines, in the region where the town of Arquata del Tronto is located, project upward and create a high ridge which divides the territory of Norcia from that of the March of Ancona. This is called Mte. Vettore, because it "conquers" in height the other mountains in the region. On its eastern slope it has that lake which is notorious for harboring demons, and on its southern side there are two very high peaks, slightly separated by a deep gorge. This pass is called Forca di Presta, [341D] and at the

quas Troentus labitur, et mox ab ipsis furculis per arctam et tamquam manufactam decurrens fossam Arquatae moenia attingit.

Ultra atque etiam infra Amatricem medio in Apennino fluvius oritur nomine Castellanus, qui parvo cursu ad moenia Asculi defertur, et parvo inde spatio cadit in Troentum, ut hinc Castellanus iste Troentus inde Asculi moenia circumluant. Ea civitas vetustissima aliquando Picentum primaria fuit. Et Livius cum libro LXXII dixisset Italicos populos bello sociali defecisse, primos ponit Picentes. Postea libro LXXVI dicit Asculum a Pompeio Strabone captum quo in proelio cum terra tremuisset, Strabo Tellurem aede promissa placavit. Et tamen post caedem incendiaque commissa urbem evertit, quia Asculani initio belli missos ad se legatos interfecerunt.

Asculum viros saepe habuit praestantissimos, Titum Betutium Barrum oratorem, quem Cicero in Bruto ceteris suae aetatis oratoribus externis praefert; Ventidium Bassum ducem Romanum, qui primus Parthos attigit, in quem militare illud laedorium fuit dictum, "qui mulos fricabat factus est consul." Habuit etiam Nicolaum tertium pontificem Romanum Cicumque excellentiorem mathematicum quam vulgarem poetam.

bottom of this defile flows the Tronto river, which not long after runs down from Forca di Presta through a narrow ditch that looks almost man-made, and bathes the walls of Arquata del Tronto.

In the middle of the Apennines, beyond and also below Amatrice, there arises a river named the Castellano, which flows in a short course to the walls of Ascoli Piceno, and from there traverses a short distance before flowing into the Tronto; so that the Castellano flows around one side of Ascoli, and the Tronto flows around the other. This very ancient city was formerly the chief city in Picenum. Livy, when he named in book 72 the people among the Italians who defected from the Romans, put the Picentes in first place. Afterwards in book 76 he says that Asculum was captured by Pompeius Strabo; when during this battle there was an earthquake, Strabo placated the earth goddess Tellus by vowing a temple to her. And after slaughtering its citizens in battle, setting fire to the city, he still destroyed it, because the men of Asculum, at the beginning of the war, had killed the Roman ambassadors who had been sent to them.

Ascoli has always had many outstanding men: the orator Titus Betutius Barrus, whom Cicero in the *Brutus* places before all the other speakers of his age; Ventidius Bassus, the Roman general, who was first to attack the Parthians, and against whom the soldiers delivered that well-known insult, "the man who used to rub down the mules is now elected consul." Ascoli Piceno also boasts Pope Nicholas III, and Cecco d'Ascoli, a better astrologer than vernacular poet.

PART TWO

SOUTHERN ITALY

Regio Duodecima
Aprutium, Sive Samnium, Campania, Apulia, Lucania, Salentini, Calabria Et Brutii

[389A]

Absoluta Histria regionum Italiae ad Alpes Liburnicas ultima, brevis a F[*l*]anatico eius sinu promontorioque nunc Carnario, per Liburnicum mare in Troenti amnis ostia est traiectus, ut alias a nobis describendas septem regiones aggrediamur: Samnium, Campaniam, Apuliam, Lucaniam, Salentinos, Calabros, et Brutios. Licet vero mihi in hac parte, quod Livius Patavinus septimo libro habet usurpare: maius solito negotium meis impendere humeris, cui maiora deinceps sint pervestiganda, quod his in regionibus celebriora bella quam alibi in Italia fuere gesta, et viribus hostium et longinquitate temporum, quibus bellatum est. Facile tamen erit Alexander Epirota, Pyrrhus, Hannibal, Alaricus, Totila vetustiores earum regionum hostes, quas res et quibus in locis gesserint, a maiorum aut nostris Historiis sumere, et per singulas civitatum locorumque descriptiones, sicut supra **[389B]** fecimus, edocere.

Quae vero a quadringentis annis postquam septem hae regiones in unicam regni appellationem sunt confusae in eo acciderint, et qua ratione facta sit ipsa regni constitutio, videtur unico contextu diligentius enarrandum, ne singulis postea in locis cogamur saepe dicta identidem replicare.

Per Ludovici Francorum regis tempora, Tancredus miles Normannus generosi vir animi, quod liberorum duodecim ex duabus procreatorum uxoribus pondere premerent, novas quaerere sedes constituit, fortunam meliorem, et opes sub alio caelo viribus sibi et ingenio facere confisus. Qui cum in Italiam pervenisset, primum in Romandiola substitit. Pandulfus per id temporis Capuanus princeps, bello adversus Guaimarum Salernitanum prin-

Twelfth Region
Abruzzo or Sannio, Campania, Puglia, Lucania, Salentini, Basilicata Calabria and Bruttium

[389A]

I have now completed Istria, the last region of Italy before the Liburnian Alps. There is a short distance to cross from its bay of F[*l*]anaticum and the promontory of the same name, now called Carnaro, through the Liburnian Sea, over to the mouth of the Tronto. In this itinerary I can tackle the seven other regions which I need to describe: Sannio, Campania, Puglia, Lucania, Salentini, Basilicata Calabria, and Bruttium. But in describing this region I may repeat the observation of Livy of Padua in his seventh book: "a greater task than usual presses on my shoulders," because I must next investigate greater matters, as more famous wars were waged in these regions than anywhere else in Italy, in regard to both the enemies' strength, and the wars' duration. But it will be easy to take from my *Histories* or earlier generations' histories the deeds, and their locations, of Alexander of Epirus, Pyrrhus, Hannibal, Alaric, Totila, the older enemies of these regions; and to show in what cities, and in what places these things happened, as I have done in previous chapters. **[389B]**

These seven regions were combined into one and called by the single name of the Kingdom of Naples. The events that happened in four hundred years in this kingdom, and how the actual arrangement of the Kingdom was accomplished, is worth telling in detail in a single composition, so that I may not be compelled to repeat afterwards, in separate places, things I have already said.

In the time of Louis, King of the Franks, Tancred, a Norman soldier, a man of noble spirit who was burdened by his responsibility for twelve children born of two wives, decided to look for a new home and a better fortune, and to rely on his strength and intelligence to obtain wealth in another land. When he had arrived in Italy, he first settled in the Romagna. At that

cipem multum implicitus, qui cum auxilia undique conquireret, hanc gentem armis deditam promisso stipendio accessivit. Tantaque ilico et talia Normanni gessere facinora, ut viros fortes praestantissimosque eos suo malo senserint hostes.

Pandulfus vero hebetioris ingenii ingratusque ipsos spernebat. Unde factum est ut tempore stipendii de quo in Romandiola convenerat finito, transiverint ad Guaimarum, [389C] cuius principatum multis praeclare gestis brevi auxerunt. Premebat vero Normannos duces, ut assolet, aulicorum Guaimari invidia, cum peropportune accidit imperatoris Constantinopolitani in Calabris, Brutiis, Lucanis, et Neapolitana urbe magistratus petere Salernitanum illi subditum imperio auxilia, adversus Saracenos, Siciliam opprimentes, cuius insulae pars maxima, Graecis per id temporis erat subdita, Graecique forti ac fideli Normannorum opera usi, Saracenos omni paene Sicilia deturbarunt. Sed et ipsi Graeci Normannorum virtute per singulos dies cum admiratione considerata, in eorum invidiam suspicionemque, quam in accepti beneficii munerationem, procliviores esse coeperunt. Id cum Normanni qua erant prudentia pervidissent cupientibus Graecis faciliter persuaserunt dimittendum esse in pinguis uberrimaeque rerum omnium Apuliae hiberna victorem exercitum, qui exhaustam belli diuturnitate et barbarorum crudelitate Siciliam, instanti hieme consumpturus videbatur.

Traductis in Italiam copiis Normanni in Apuliam delati, magnam illius partem sibi subegerunt. Qui ut sedem haberent [389D] in qua mulieres pueros impedimentaque tuta conservarent, Melphim urbem arduo et natura communito loco aedificaverunt. Erat tunc temporis Constantinopoli imperator Michael Ethiriachis, qui magnis per legatos ex Graecia Siciliaque et Italiae sibi subditae regionibus comparatis exercitibus in Normannos duci curavit, commissumque est secus Aufidum Cannarium Apuliae amnem et Oliventum oppidum ingens proelium, in quo Normanni superiores victoresque evaserunt.

Multa hic de Normannorum successibus et gestis rebus dicenda omittimus, quae tertiodecimo Historiarum nostrarum libro continentur. Tancredo patre et post parum Drogone filio comite, ut tunc dicebant, Apuliae mortuis,

time the Capuan prince Pandulf, was much involved in leading a war against Guaimar of Salerno; this prince Pandulf was seeking aid everywhere and with the promise of pay called upon the family of Tancred which was devoted to the pursuits of war. The Normans performed so many great exploits in this conflict that their enemies realized to their chagrin that they were brave and outstanding men.

But Pandulf was made of duller stuff and ungrateful, and he looked down on them. As a result, when the time set for their pay had run out (this had been agreed upon in the Romagna), the Normans transferred their allegiance to **[389C]** Guaimar and in a short time increased his rule with many renowned deeds. As often happens, the Norman leaders were the object of the envy of the courtiers of Prince Guaimar. Now it happened that the magistrates of the emperor of Constantinople were in Calabria, Bruttium, Lucania, and the city of Naples, seeking aid from the prince of Salerno, then a subject of their empire, against the Arabs who were oppressing Sicily (a great part of Sicily was at this time subject to the Byzantine Greeks). The Greeks relied on the strong and loyal Normans to expel the Arabs from almost all of Sicily. But the Greeks also began to be more disposed to envy and suspect the Normans for the courage they had admired in them, than to reward them for their good deeds. When the Normans shrewdly perceived this, they easily obtained (something which pleased the Greeks) dismissal of their victorious army into winter quarters in the richest, most fertile of all the areas of Apulia; with winter coming on, they would have been the final ruin of Sicily, exhausted as the island was by the duration of the war and the barbarians' savagery.

The Normans brought their troops into Italy, and moved into Apulia, where they subjugated a great part of the region. As they wished to have a safe place **[389D]** to locate their woman and children and baggage, they built the city of Melfi in a high, naturally fortified place. At that time Michael Ethiriachis was emperor at Constantinople, and he had his legates raise great armies to lead against the Normans from Greece and Sicily and the regions of Italy which were subject to him. A great battle was fought near the river Ofanto, at Canne in Apulia, near the town of Olivento; and the Normans came out victorious.

I leave out many relevant details of the Normans' deeds and successes, because they can be found in the thirteenth book of my *Histories*. The father Tancred and, a little later, his son Drogo, who was Count of Apulia (as it

Hunfredus fratrum unus in eo comitatu successit. Hicque cum annis septem comitatum tenuisset moriens Gothfredum fratrem habuit successorem, per quod tempus, Leone quinto pontifice Romano, Guaimarus Salerni princeps a suis interfectus est. Gisulphusque Normannus Salernitanum obtinuit principatum, qui paulopost Beneventum Romanae ecclesiae urbem ut caperet est adnixus. Quod cum rescisset Henricus II imperator e Germania Romanus, Leoni pontifici per litteras et nuntios suasit ut Theotonicorum copiis, quas ipse Vercellis Italiae praesidio reliquerat acceptis, duceret in Normannos.

Id cum **[390E]** fecisset Leo pontifex, superatus proelio et cum aliquot cardinalibus captus fuit. Normanni tamen, sicut decuit principes Christianos, maxima usi erga pontificem reverentia, eum comitesque honore prosecuti ad urbem Romam qua venerat deduci curaverunt. Feliciorque fuit Normannis et melius in Romano pontifice, quam in ceteris quibus ad eam serviverant diem collocata liberalitas, quod Romanae ecclesiae et pontificis auctoritate ea permissi sunt gubernanda tenere, quaecumque de Italia tunc temporis obtinebant. Exinde Gothfredus fato functus, Bagelardum filium reliquit heredem, quod cum aegre tulisset Robertus cognomine Guiscardus filiorum Tancredi ordine sextus, vir ingentis animi, nepote deiecto gentis Normannae principatum assumpsit.

Erat tunc secundus Nicolaus pontifex Romanus. Is a capitaneis Romae, quos nunc barones appellant, agitatus, Guiscardum ad Aquilam urbem, parum ante conditam in colloquium accersivit, et cum Guiscardus Beneventum et cetera, quae iurium ecclesiae tenebat restituisset, papa illum terrae Apuliae et omnium quae in Italia obtinebat, sub ducatus Apuliae titulo legitimum instituit possessorem. Robertusque ligium se, quod arctissimum servitutis vocabulum est, pontifici et ecclesiae iureiurando **[390F]** addixit. Pauloque post in capitaneos ducens Romanos proceres, eos omnes edomitos pontifici parere fecit. Nec multo post auctus animis Guiscardus, Guillelmum fratrem Apuliae praefecit, et in Calabriam ducens sancti Marci urbem communire aggressus est. Inde progressus, et castra secus amnem Mocatum ad Aquas Calidas metatus, Consentinos, Martiranensesque subegit.

Secundum quam victoriam Sillaceum, sive ut appellant Squilaceum, accedens, per Ionii maris litora pervenit Rhegium, quam dum obsidet civitatem Leucastrum, Maiam, et Cannalem pactione recepit. Rogerius interim fratrum Guiscardi natu minimus, castris aliquamdiu in Viconensi monte habitis, vallem Salinarum et multa in circuitu Normannorum ditioni adiecit.

was then called), died; and one of the brothers, Humphrey, succeeded as Count. He held the title of Count for seven years until his death; his brother Godfrey succeeded him. At this time Leo V was pope. Guaimar of Salerno was killed by his own relatives. Gisulf took over the principate of Salerno and a little later tried to occupy Benevento, which belonged to the church. When the Holy Roman Emperor Henry II found this out from Germany, he ordered Pope Leo, through letters and messengers, to lead against the Normans the German troops which he had left at Vercelli as a garrison for Italy.

Pope Leo carried out the Emperor's orders **[390E]** and was defeated in battle and captured along with some of his cardinals. But the Normans showed the appropriate respect for the Pope and his comrades; they accompanied them to the city of Rome. The Normans' generosity was a happier choice in the case of this pope than in the case of the people they had served up to this time; for by authority of the church and the Pope, they were allowed to hold and to govern all the land in Italy of which they had gained possession at that time. Then Godfrey died and his son Bagelardus succeeded him. Robert Guiscard, the sixth son of Tancred, did not accept this decision happily; a man of enormous spirit, he expelled his nephew and usurped the Norman principate.

At this time Nicholas II was Pope. The Roman barons, who were then called Capitani, stirred Nicholas up to summon Guiscard to a talk at the newly-founded city of Aquila. When Guiscard had restored Benevento and the rest of the possessions he was holding, the Pope made him ruler of Apulia and all he held in Italy, conferring upon him the legitimate title of Duke of Calabria and Apulia. Robert declared himself liege, that is, bound by the closest tie of servitude to the Pope and to the church. **[390F]** Shortly afterwards, he brought the Roman barons into obedience to the Pope, by leading against them all their chiefs, whom he had conquered. Not long after this, Guiscard, strengthened in courage, put his brother William in charge of Apulia and, leading his forces into Calabria, began fortifying the city of San Marco Argentano. From there he marched on, laid out a camp at the hot springs on the Mucata river, and subdued Cosenza and Martirano.

After this victory, he approached Squillace by the shore of the Ionian Sea and arrived at Reggio and besieged it. During the siege, he took by an agreement Nicastro, Maida, and Cannale. Meanwhile Guiscard's youngest brother, Roger, who had for some time maintained a camp in Monte di Bibona, added to the Normans' agreement the Val di Saline and many areas

Nicepholam vero oppidum communiens proprio curavit praesidio conservari. Quo item tempore Guiscardus Ganfredo etiam fratri Guilliniacum et totam Teatinam in nunc Aprutii regione occupata attribuit gubernandam. Inde reversus ad Regii obsidionem Guiscardus Calabris Brutiisque omnibus et ipso regno in suam et fratrum potestatem redactis, tunc primum dux Calabriae et Apuliae fratrum consensu appellari coepit.

[390G] Forte per id temporis Bettieminus Bescavetti Maurorum principis Siciliam pro Saracenorum soldano administrantis admiratus, Rogerium Guiscardi fratrem in Brutiis agentem occultus adiit, et praemio proditionis impetrato, eum impulit, ut in Siciliam rebellare paratissimam duceret. Quem Guiscardus navigio est subsecutus, et prima de Siculis in Normannorum potestatem venit urbs Messana. Et ne plura hic quam tempus locusque postulet dicamus, omnis Sicilia in Guiscardi fratrisque Rogerii potestatem brevi est facta. Tuncque Rogerius Alexandro secundo pontifice Romano qui defuncto Nicolao suffectus erat, camelos quattuor praedae de Saracenis Sicilia pulsis factae partem dono misit.

Fuit vero mirabilis dicti Roberti et fratrum cursus victoriarum, quandoquidem intra decem et octo annos, quorum ultimus fuit septuagesimus post millesimum salutis annum, praedictis Italiae regionibus et Sicilia sunt potiti. Paulopost cum Henricus tertius imperator Germanus, Gregorium septimum pontificem Romanum acerrimo persequeretur bello, contulit se Aquinum dictus pontifex. Et eandem **[390H]** concessionem, quam secundus Nicolaus fecerat Roberto confirmavit; ea tamen adiecta condicione ut Marchiam Anconitanam, paulo ante Picenum appellari solitam, a suis Normannis occupatam dimitteret. Unde factum est ut cum Gregorius pontifex in mole Hadriani (castelli Sancti Angeli) ab Henrico obsideretur, accedens cum copiis Guiscardus et Romam per portam Flumentanam sive Flaminiam ceperit, et Henrico vi expulso pontificem obsidione liberatum deduxerit Salernum, ubi diem post parum obiit.

Tantis tamen multisque in Italia et Sicilia gestis rebus, pellendo Constantinopoli Alexio imperatore Graeco et quidem scelestissimo, quod Christianis inimicaretur, Guiscardus animum adiecit. Sed dum Dyrrachio plurimisque Epiri et Acarnaniae ac Graeciae oppidis, castellis, et insulis vi captis, maiora in dies molitur, apud Cassiopam insulam, febri per Iulium mensem ex caumate correptus, interiit.

around it; he fortified the town of Rocca Niceforo and took pains to keep it safe by putting over it a special garrison. At the same time Guiscard gave to his brother Geoffrey the government of Guilmi and all of Chieti, which he had seized, in the region now called Abruzzo. He returned to the siege of Reggio; he reduced Calabria, all of Bruttium, and the kingdom himself, and brought them into his and his brothers' power. His brothers then for the first time agreed to call him Duke of Calabria and Apulia.

It happened **[390G]** at that time that Guiscard's brother Roger, as he was conducting secret operations in Bruttium, was approached by Bettieminus, the admiral of Bescavettus, a Moorish prince who was managing Sicily for the Sultan of the Saracens. He persuaded him, with the promise of a reward for his treason, to lead troops into Sicily, which was ripe for rebellion; Guiscard followed through with a fleet. The first Sicilian city to come into the power of the Normans was Messina. To say no more than is required here, all of Sicily fell in a short time into the hands of Guiscard and his brother Roger. Then Roger sent four camels (part of the booty from the Saracens whom he had driven out of Sicily) as a gift to Pope Alexander II, Nicholas' successor.

The course of Robert's and his brothers' victories was truly miraculous, as in the eighteen years leading up to 1070 they had taken possession of Sicily and the previously-mentioned areas of Italy. A little while afterwards, when the German emperor Henry III was conducting a fierce war against Pope Gregory VII, the Pope went to Aquino and ratified the concession Nicholas II had made to Robert, **[390H]** but with one condition: that he should give up the March of Ancona, occupied by the Normans, which had a little before been called Picenum. Consequently, when Pope Gregory was besieged by Henry, shut up in the mausoleum of Hadrian (the Castel Sant'Angelo), Guiscard arrived with his troops through the Porta Flumenta or Porta Flaminia and took Rome, drove out Henry, freed the Pope, and took him to Salerno, where the Pope died a few days later.

After performing all these great exploits in Italy and Sicily, Guiscard turned his attention to expelling from Constantinople the Greek emperor Alexius, who was extremely wicked in his enmity to Christians. But after he had captured Durazzo and many towns, castles, and islands in Epirus and Acarnania and Greece, and was planning greater exploits on the island of Cassiopa, he was carried off in July by a fever caused by the heat.

Cuius filio natu minore Rogerio Urbanus secundus pontifex Romanus in Melphiensi concilio, paternum in Italia Apuliae et Calabriae ducatum concessit. Alter vero Roberti filius natu maior Boemundus, patris quem semper secutus fuerat dominii in transmarinis heres, et exercitus ductor relictus est. Qui cum in Rogerium fratrem dominio Italico eum excludere cupientem traduxisset exercitum, meliorem sibi a casu oblatam secutus est fortunam. Gallicos enim Germanos, Hispanos, et Anglicos **[391A]** proceres in Christianam expeditionem, ab Urbano secundo pontifice Romano apud Clarum montem Alverniae institutam, secutus, Antiochiam durissima obsidione cepit. Cuius ducatu et amplissimo principatu ab expeditionis magistratibus donatus fuit. Rogerio Normanno post quintum et vigesimum annum defuncto, Guillelmus filius successit. Qui Alexii imperatoris Constantinopolitani filiam in matrimonium promissam habere sperans, in Graeciam profecturus suos Apuliae et Calabriae ducatus, Calixto secundo pontifici Romano commendavit.

Sed Rogerius altero genitus Rogerio Normanno Guiscardi germano fratre, comes Siciliae, nihil pontificem veritus Calabriam invasit, et prius dimidiam cepit quam pontifex de ferenda ope potuerit cogitare. Misit tamen Ugonem cardinalem Calixtus, per quem sedis apostolicae legatum Nicephorim arcem, quam obsideret in Calabris Rogerius conservare, et ipsum verbis comminationibusque ab incepto deterrere speravit. Ipseque pontifex cardinalium collegio, et Romanorum copiis tumultuariae contractis sociatus, Beneventum usque se contulit. Qua infausta in expeditione multos sibi carissimos febribus correptos amisit. Et ipse mala pariter usus valitudine, lectica in urbem aeger maestusque relatus est. Qua fretus bene **[391B]** gerendae rei occasione Rogerius, Calabriam omnem Apuliamque subegit. Guillelmus vero uxoris spe fraudatus, cum ad affines Salernitanos in Italiam reversus confugisset, diem ibi nullis relictis filiis obiit. Ex eoque tempore Rogerius, tantarum rerum successu elatus, non se ultra Apuliae et Calabriae ducem, Siciliaeque comitem, sed Italiae regem appellare coepit. Secundus vero Honorius pontifex, Calixto defuncto suffectus, eam dissimulavit indignitatem, quam secundus Innocentius Honorii successor ferre non potuit, adeo ut iracundia magis ductus quam viribus ad tantam rem aggrediendam necessariis fretus, tumultuario contractum impetu exercitum in illum duxerit.

Tanta vero profectus est celeritate, ut Rogerium, qui nullos audiisset a pontifice factos apparatus, apud Sancti Germani oppidum, ex improviso adortus repulerit. Et eo oppido vi capto, tyrannum in castro Gallutio, in

At the council of Melfi, Pope Urban II conceded to his younger son Roger Guiscard's Italian dukedom of Apulia and Calabria. But Robert's other older son, Bohemond, who had always accompanied his father, was named heir to his foreign holdings and leader of the army. When his brother Roger tried to exclude him from the Italian dukedom, Bohemond led an army against him; but when a better opportunity for war arose, he took advantage of it. At the Council of Clermont, Urban II had organized a crusade of German, French, Spanish, and English **[391A]** princes; Bohemond accompanied them and took Antioch after a harsh siege.

The leaders of the crusade made a donation of the dukedom and extensive principate of this city. When Roger died after twenty-five years, his son William succeeded him. As he hoped to marry the daughter of Alexius, the emperor of Constantinople, who had been promised to him, he set out for Greece, entrusting to Pope Calixtus II his dukedoms of Apulia and Calabria.

But Roger, count of Sicily, a son of the other Roger the Norman, son of the brother of Guiscard, not at all deterred by fear of the Pope, invaded Calabria, and took half of it before the Pope could plan a defense. Calixtus, however, sent Cardinal Ugo, an envoy of the Apostolic See, to where Roger was besieging Rocca Niceforo in Calabria. Calixtus hoped Ugo would save Rocca Niceforo and deter Roger from his undertaking by threats. The Pope himself hastily allied himself with the college of cardinals and troops of the Romans and went to Benevento. On this ill-fated expedition, he lost many of the men dearest to him when they contracted fever. He himself was afflicted by disease and was carried back to Rome, ill and mournful, in a litter. Roger took advantage of this opportunity **[391B]** to conquer Calabria and all of Apulia. But William, cheated of his hope of marriage, returned to Italy, took refuge with his relatives in Salerno, and died there leaving no sons. From that time on, Roger, buoyed up by his considerable successes, began to call himself not Duke of Apulia and Calabria and count of Sicily, but King of Italy. But after Calixtus died, his successor Pope Honorius II claimed to have suffered such insult that his successor Innocent II could not bear it, with the result that he, motivated more by anger than by realistic assessment of his forces, levied an army in haste and attacked Roger.

Indeed, he moved so quickly that he suddenly engaged Roger (who had heard nothing of the Pope's preparation) at the town of S. Germano, and drove him back. When he had captured this town, he besieged the tyrant in

quod se de fuga receperat, obsederit. Sed Calabriae dux Rogerii filius cum exercitu veniens, et patrem obsidione liberavit, et pontificem cum cardinalibus, fusis eorum copiis, cepit. Usus tamen modestia Rogerius, **[391C]** pontifice cum suis omnibus liberato, quicquid voluit a*b* eo, praeter quam regni titulum, impetravit. Reversus Romam Innocentius, adulterinum pontificem novum sibi suffectum reperit Petrum Petrileonis filium, qui se Anacletum pontificem appellaret. Quare Pisanorum triremibus consensi in Franciam navigavit. Rogerius novo et adulterino Anacleto in pontificem adorato, regni titulum et coronam ab eo obtinuit. Primusque omnium Normannorum absurdum utriusque Siciliae regni titulum habuit.

Ad tertium inde annum Innocentius pontifex Pisanorum auxilio Romam reversus, Lotharium Theotonicum imperatorem Romanum declaravit, et in Lateranensi ecclesia coronavit. Amboque primarii Christianorum principes, adversus Rogerium cum exercitu profecti, omnibus eum spoliarunt, quae citra fretum Siculum occuparat. Nec multi intercesserunt anni, cum Rogerius Innocentii pontificis occasione mortis fretus secundo Celestino primum, post secundo Lucio, pontificibus Romanis rem suam frigide administrantibus, et demum Eugenio tertio praestanti Romano pontifice multis agitato difficultatibus, omnia de Italia receperit, quae Innocentius sibi Lothariusque abstulerant.

[391D] Is ad annum regni Siciliae assumpti quartum et vicesimum Panormi moriens, Guillelmum filium habuit successor, cui ab Hadriano quarto primum, post a tertio Alexandro, Romanis pontificibus regni Siciliae, et ducatus Calabriae, ac Apuliae titulis ornato, ad annum sui principatus quintumdecimum Panormi defuncto, alter Guillelmus filius heres successorque fuit.

Hic vero pacis quietisque amator, cum in multitudinem pontificum Romanorum intra annos XXV inciderit, tertium Lucium, tertium Urbanum, tertium Clementem, nulla ab eorum quoque molestia agitatus, Boni cognomine est ornatus. Tandem et ipse Panormi sine liberis est defunctus. Erat tunc Panormi Tancredus, quem Rogerio supradicto ex concubina genitum omnes ad eam diem spreverant. Sed regni Siciliae proceres, ne in Romani pontificis suum id regnum recipere adnitentis potestatem fierent, vel potius, ut hoc in regnum sublato et praetenso signum suam conservarent tyrannidem, huic regni titulum demandarunt.

Iamque Tancredus pro rege habitus, Siciliam retinebat, et Calabriae Apuliaeque manum inicere conabatur, cum Celestinus III, pontifex Roma-

Galluccio, where he had taken refuge. But Roger's son the duke of Calabria came with an army and freed his father from the siege. The papal troops were put to flight; and he captured the Pope and his cardinals. Roger behaved with moderation towards the Pope, **[391C]** freed him along with all his men, and obtained whatever he wished from him, except the title of king. When he returned to Rome, Innocent found he had been supplanted by a new anti-pope, Peter Petrileoni, who was calling himself Pope Anacletus. For this reason, he sailed to France with three triremes belonging to the people of Pisa. After paying honor to the new anti-pope Anacletus, Roger obtained from him the title and crown of King of Sicily. He was the first of all the Normans to hold the absurd title of King of both Sicilies.

Three years after this, Pope Innocent returned to Rome with the help of the Pisans and declared the German Lothar Roman emperor. He crowned him in the church of St. John Lateran, and both of them, and the Christian princes, set out with an army against Roger and stripped him of all his possessions up to the straits of Messina. Not many years later, Roger profited from the death of Pope Innocent, the feeble administrative skills of Celestine II and Lucius II, and the many difficulties which beset Eugenius III, an excellent Pope, to recapture all the holdings which had been taken from him by Innocent and Lothar.

[391D] In the twenty-fourth year after his assumption of the title of King of Sicily, Roger died at Palermo, and was succeeded by his son William. The popes—first Hadrian IV, and after him Alexander III—accorded him the title of King of Sicily and Duke of Calabria and Apulia. But in the fifteenth year of his reign he died at Palermo and was succeeded by his son and heir William.

This man was a lover of peace and quiet and lived in a time of many popes: within twenty-five years, Lucius III, Urban III, and Clement III; but was troubled by none of them and received the epithet of "the Good." Finally, he too died at Palermo, without heirs. At that time there lived in Palermo Tancred, son of the previously-mentioned Roger and a concubine. Up to that time everyone had looked down on him; but the barons of the kingdom of Sicily feared coming under the power of the Pope, who was struggling to regain his kingdom. They also thought that if Tancred were elevated to the kingship, if only as a figurehead, they would exercise a tyranny: so they demanded the title for him.

And now Tancred was considered King; and he held on to Sicily while attempting to gain power over Calabria and Apulia. Pope Celestine decided

nus, illi obsistere constituit. Sextum is Henricum Suevum tunc in imperatorem electum, ea confirmavit conditione, ut regno Siciliae propriis recuperato sumptibus, et censum solveret annuum, et terras iuris ecclesiastici sibi **[392E]** redderet. Idque quo facilius assequeretur, Constantiam Rogerii regis supradicti filiam virginem in monasterio Panormi agentem, natu grandiorem quam quae vix filios procreatura videretur, dispensatione apostolica ab eo uxorem traduci permisit. Ingressi cum exercitu rex et regina primo imperii vi anno Neapolim obsederunt, sed cum pestilentia exercitum invasisset, re infecta abeuntes, in Alemanniam se contulerunt. Quo anno inde quarto cum paratiore exercitu reversi, universo regno potiti sunt, Tancredo et Margarito Epirotarum rege, qui praesidio illi advenerat interceptis. Henrico ad octavum imperii annum mortuo, electores imperii dissidentes, pars Philippum Henrici defuncti germanum fratrem, pars Otonem Saxoniae ducem delegerunt. Quem Honorius III pontifex Romanus coronavit.

Et quia paulo post contra eius voluntatem regnum Siciliae hostiliter aggressus est, excommunicavit. Id enim regnum Federicus, Henrico sexto et Constantia monacha genitus, obtinebat; qui adolescens bonae, ut videbatur, indolis Saracenos omni Sicilia deturbaverat. Sed hic secundus Federicus ab Honorio praedicto pontifice, post Otonis excommunicationem in imperatorem declaratus, Federico primo Barbarossa immanior tamen multa in pontificem Honorium machinatus est, **[392F]** ut qui coronaverat eum, bonus pontifex, imperio ac regno privare atque excommunicare fuerit compulsus. Quem Gregorius IX pontifex Honorio suffectus, pariter privatum excommunicavit.

Isque scelestissimus Federicus pontifici Gregorio per annos XIIII, quibus vixit, a deo infestus molestusque fuit, ut diem ille maestitia confectus obiisse sit creditus. Ferunt Senebaldum de Fisco cardinalem Genuensem, per tempora Honorii et Gregorii pontificum supradictorum, non vulgari cum Federico amicitia usum esse, et cum is in Romanum pontificem Innocentium quartum Gregorio successisset. Dixisset Federicum malo eventu bonum se amicum cardinalem, in vehementem hostem Romanum pontificem permutatum habere.

Quod quidem ipse rerum successus verum fuisse ostendit. Namque Innocentius concilio apud Lugdunum congregato, his quae praedecessores sui

to resist him. Now at that time, Henry VI of Switzerland had been elected Emperor; Celestine gave his provisional ratification on the condition that Henry recapture at his own expense the kingdom of Sicily, pay the tax that was owed, and [392E] return to him the lands under jurisdiction of the church. And to enable Henry to achieve these ends, the Pope gave him a special dispensation allowing him to marry Constance, elder maiden daughter of the previously mentioned Roger; although she seemed past childbearing age and had to be dragged out of the Monastery of Palermo where she had been living. The King and Queen entered Naples with an army in the first year of their reign and besieged the city. But the plague attacked the army, and they left without achieving their purpose. They went to Germany for four years and prepared an army before returning to take possession of their kingdom. After Tancred and Margaritus, king of Epirus, who had come to support him, had been seized before they could get there, Henry died, in the eighth year of his reign. The imperial electors were in disagreement about a successor. Some favored Philip, brother of the deceased Henry, others Otto, Duke of Saxony. Pope Honorius III crowned the latter.

A little later, because Otto invaded the kingdom of Sicily against his will, Honorius excommunicated him. Frederick, the son of Henry VI and the nun Constance, took possession of this kingdom; a youth, apparently of good character, he expelled the Saracens from all of Sicily. But after Pope Honorius had excommunicated Otto and declared Frederick emperor, this Frederick II turned out crueler than Frederick I Barbarossa. He devised so many troubles for [392F] Pope Honorius that this good pope was forced to excommunicate the man he had crowned, and to deprive him of his kingdom. Pope Gregory IX succeeded him and he too excommunicated Frederick.

Frederick was very evil, and during his remaining fourteen years of life so hostile and troublesome to Pope Gregory that the latter is thought to have died from depression. It is said that Cardinal Sinibaldo Fieschi of Genoa, the papal treasurer during the times of popes Honorius and Gregory, enjoyed an unusual friendship with Frederick; and that Frederick said, when Fieschi had succeeded Gregory to become Pope Innocent IV, that an evil accident had changed his friend the cardinal into a fierce enemy, a Roman pope.

The resulting events showed the truth of his statement; for at a council at Lyons Innocent approved his predecessors' measures against Frederick

in Federicum gesserant approbatis, Langravium Hasiae illi in imperatorem primo, et paulopost eo defuncto, Guillelmum Hollandiae comitem subrogavit. Solemnique sancivit decreto, quod distinctione quarta et sexagesima exstat, nullum de cetero qui imperator sit Romanus regno Siciliae, quod peculiare est ecclesiae **[392G]** Romanae membrum, praefici posse.

Supervixit postea Federicus annis quinque, quo tempore multis agitatus est calamitatibus. Primo namque Henricum filium, quem sibi Constantia regis Aragonum filia uxor pepererat, ob ancillae zelotypiam in carcere necavit. Inde apud Parmam urbem proelio superatus, ditissima impedimenta, et decem milia militum ferro occisos amisit. Alterque filius legitimo matrimonio ex eadem uxore genitus nomine Enisius, a Bononiensibus, quorum infestaret agrum, occisus est. Tandem a Manfredo filio ex ancilla suscepto, quem Tarenti praefecerat, cum leviter aegrotaret, suffocatus interiit. Post cuius mortem electores illico Conradum dicti filium, quem ex filia Ioannis Hierosolymitani regis uxore susceperat, imperatorem declaraverunt, qui nullo deterritus paternae privationis exemplo, regnum Siciliae violenter ingressus est. Et Neapolim accedens, cum cives excommunicato deditionem facere obstinatius recusassent, urbe per obsidionem famemque potitus, moenia multis in locis aperuit, civesque praesertim primarios male habuit, subtractus tamen est paulopost morte, quam Manfredus frater dato veneno accelerasse dictus est. **[392H]**

At pontifex Innocentius quartus, qui sub ipsum necis Federici tempus exercitum parare coepisset, per opportune Conradi morte intellecta, Neapolim se contulit, quem apparuit etiam adversante magnis conatibus Manfredo potiturum regno, nisi eum mors brevi apud Neapolim subtraxisset, per cuius mortis occasionem Manfredus praetenso Conradini ex Henrico, quem patrem Federicum mori coegisse diximus, et Constantia Aragonensi nepotis tutelae titulo, regnum omne mirabili celeritate subegit, adeo ut prius rem confecerit quam Conradini pueri in Alemannia agentis tutores veri tantae victoriae certiores facti, aut venire potuerunt, aut oratores mittere principibus regni, ac populis factae celeriter deditionis gratiam a rege puero, sicut decuit relaturos. Quod quidem ne posset accidere, Manfredus dolo ex sua ingenii malignitate usus, nuntios de repente simulantes advenisse subornavit, a quibus in regno palam est factum, pueri regis Conradini interitum luctu omnia lacrimisque in Alemannia, ipsis praesentibus, replevisse. Moxque sub ipsum rumorem accurate disseminatum, Manfredus regio procedens

and elected first the Landgrave of Thuringia emperor and, upon his death a little later, chose in his place Count William of Holland. He ratified the election with a decree, in whose sixty-fourth distinction the following appears: **[392G]** Whoever was Roman emperor could not be King of Sicily because this kingdom was a private property of the church.

Frederick lived five years after this, during which he was afflicted by many disasters. First, on account of jealousy over a concubine, he killed in prison his son Henry, born to him by his wife Constance, daughter of the king of Aragon. Then he was defeated in battle at the city of Parma, and lost valuable baggage and 10,000 soldiers. His second son, Enzo, born from a legitimate union with the same wife, was killed while attacking the territory of Bologna. Finally, when he was mildly ill he died of suffocation at the hands of his son Manfred, born of a concubine, whom he had put in charge of Taranto. After his death, the imperial electors immediately declared emperor Conrad, the son born from his wife, the daughter of King John of Jerusalem. The example of his father's confiscation did not deter him from violent attack on the kingdom of Sicily. Marching on Naples, whose citizens had steadfastly refused to surrender to an excommunicate, he gained possession of the city by inflicting siege and famine, and breached the walls in a number of places. He treated the leading citizens with particular malice. But he was removed a little afterwards by death which, it is said, his brother Manfred hastened by the application of poison. **[392H]**

Up to the time of Frederick's death, Pope Innocent IV had begun to assemble an army; but when he heard of Conrad's timely death he hastened to Naples. Despite Manfred's strong resistance, Innocent appeared to have regained the kingdom; but his life was suddenly cut short at Naples, and Manfred took advantage of this death to subjugate the kingdom with amazing speed, holding out the title of guardian of his nephew Conradin, the son of Henry (who I mentioned forced the death of his father Frederick) and grandson of Constance of Aragon. So swift was his victory that he had accomplished this matter before the young Conradin's real guardians in Germany had been made aware of the victory or could come or send ambassadors to the princes and citizens of the kingdom to bring appropriate thanks from the boy king for the speedy surrender. To prevent this, Manfred, in accordance with his evil and deceitful character, corrupted the messengers who were suddenly pretending to have arrived. They openly filled all in Germany with grieving at the news of the boy Conradin's death. And soon after his careful dissemination of this rumor, Manfred came out of the pal-

apparatu, sese regem appellari salutarique curavit. Id cum rescisset quartus Alexander pontifex Romanus qui Innocentio successerat, et Manfredum de more excommunicavit, et paratissimum adversus eum duxit exercitum.

[393A] Manfredus vero pecunia abundans, quam in suorum caedibus, et regni direptione cumulaverat, et multos ex Africa Saracenos et Florentiae, aliarumque Lombardiae urbium extorres. Qui tunc multi erant, mercede conduxit; quo fretus exercitu Alexandrum papam cum ignominia repulit. Creatus post Alexandri mortem, quae tunc forte accidit, pontifex Urbanus IV ex Trecis Gallicus Saracenos a Manfredo in Italia Siciliamque perductos per crucesignatos undique ex Christiano orbe coactos primum repulit. Post Carolum Ludovici regis Francorum sancti fratrem germanum, Provinciae et Andegavorum comitem, regni Siciliae citra ultraque fretum regem declaravit. Carolus vero Romam veniens, senatoriam dignitatem tamdiu administravit, quousque suus ex Galliis venisset exercitus. Coronamque Carolus et Beatrix uxor regnorum Siciliae et Hierusalem accepturi, per solennem stipulationem annuos duodequinquaginta mille aureos pontifici, et eius successoribus spoponderunt.

Delatus ad Casinensem Saltum cum copiis rex Carolus eo vi superato, Manfredum quoque resistentem repulit, quem retrocedentem paribus castris usque Beneventum insecutus est; paresque animis et viribus praestantissimi [393B] duces ad diem quartum Kalendas Maii, anni sexti et sexagesimi supra duodecies centenum salutis conflixerunt. Manfredus vero quem aliquando variante proelio vicisse apparuit, superatus occisusque est, in cuius exercitu duo milia hominum ceciderunt.

Quarto Clemente paulo post in defuncti Urbani locum subrogato, cum Carolus adeptus, nullo post Manfredi mortem resistente, regnum quietissime possideret, Conradinus adolescens suis Alemannorum viribus, et quidem maximis fisus, ut avitum reciperet regnum adnixus est. Feruntque pontificem, qui habitus sit sanctus, cum Alemanno adolescenti ipse in Galliis oriundus, manifesti periculi audaciam dissuadere sit veritus, multis dixisse contraria in Romana curia et urbe sentientibus, puerum pro victima ductum ingredi regnum.

Sed erat tunc Romae senator Henricus Castellae regis frater, ex cuius sorore Constantia Conradini genitorem natum fuisse ostendimus, quo suadente, atque ex urbe Roma tunc sub banderesiis semilibera auxilium sub-

ace in royal dress and made sure that he was hailed as king. When he learned of this, Pope Alexander IV, who had succeeded Innocent, both excommunicated Manfred in the usual way, and led against him a well-trained army.

[393A] But Manfred had a great deal of money which he had accumulated from the slaughter of his own partisans and the plundering of the kingdom, and he had many allies among the Saracens from Africa and the exiles from Florence and other cities in Lombardy. With their aid, he handed Pope Alexander a shameful defeat. After Alexander's death, which came about at that time by accident, Pope Urban IV, a Frenchman from Troyes, for the first time drove back the Saracens whom Manfred had brought to Italy and Sicily. To do this, he had collected crusaders from everywhere in the Christian world. Afterwards he declared as king of both Sicilies Charles, brother of the French king Louis IX (later called St. Louis) and count of Provence and Anjou. When Charles came to Rome, he was given senatorial rank until his army had come from France. As Charles and his wife Beatrice were about to receive the crown of the two Sicilies and Jerusalem, they promised with a solemn pact to give forty-eight gold pieces a year to the pope and his successors.

King Charles arrived with his troops at the pass at Cassino. He defeated Manfred and drove him back, but he kept fighting, and when Manfred retreated Charles pursued him as far as Benevento. The two generals, well-matched in courage and strength, **[393B]** joined in a famous battle on February 26, 1266. The fortune of the battle was ambiguous for a while, and Manfred appeared to be victorious; but he was defeated and killed, and 2,000 men in his army fell with him.

A little later, when Urban died, Clement IV was chosen to replace him. After Manfred's death, Charles governed the kingdom peacefully and unopposed. The boy Conradin struggled to regain his grandfather's kingdom with the help of his considerable forces from Germany. The story is that the Pope, who was French-born and considered holy in the eyes of the German youth, was afraid to advise him against such a bold and clearly dangerous maneuver; and that the Pope contradicted many in the Curia and city of Rome who were expressing the opinion that the boy was being sacrificed in his attack on the kingdom.

Henry, brother of the King of Castile, was senator of Rome at this time; his sister Constance's son was the father of Conradin, as I have shown. At his instigation, and with his help from Rome, which was then half-free un-

ministrante, Alemanni furentes ingressi sunt regnum, commissoque in campis Palentinis proelio, cui Henricus ipse senator interfuit, Carolus superior evasit, cum caedes in Alemannis maxima **[393C]** committeretur, senator Romanis deducentibus in tuta evasit.

Conradinus et dux Austriae servorum habitu fugientes ad Asturam pervenerunt, ubi ad diem commissi proelii octavam recogniti sunt, ad Carolumque perducti, in quos Carolus publice animadverti iussit. Ad annum postea regnorum Caroli circiter octavum, Gallis suis in Sicilia pudicitiam mulierum lascive nimis et petulanter pertentantibus, Siculi omnium paene urbium, ac oppidorum populi coniurarunt, quam primum die constituta advesperascere Campanis significari coepisse, confodiendos esse a singulis Gallos intra moenia repertos. Quod cum esset non minus crudeliter quam constanter factum, dominio Gallis publice abrogato, Petrus Aragonum rex accersitus est, qui demandatum sibi Trinacriae regnum octogesimo secundo et duodecies centeno salutis anno, ea praetensa ratione audentius accepit, qui illud Constantiae uxori hereditario patris Manfredi iure diceret deberi.

Carolo ad duodevicenum quo regnare inceperat annum defuncto et Neapoli sepulto, successit alter Carolus, qui regni Italiae partem Siciliae regnum nihilominus appellatum quattuor et viginti annis obtinuit. Is nulla re alia notior quam quia proletarius in regno quievisse videtur, **[393D]** anno aetatis quadragesimo moriens quattuordecim filios ex Maria uxore regis Ungariae filia, novem mares, femellas quinque reliquit; quorum notiores fuere Carolus cognomento Martellus Ungariae regni titulo insignitus, Ludovicus qui ordinis minorum in sanctorum numerum translatus fuit. Et tertius Robertus, qui illi et patri in regna successor Francisci Petrarchae amicitia nobis est notus, huicque ad annum Christi tertium et quadragesimum supra tredecies centenum diem obeunti Ioanna, quae prima est dicta in regno successit. Ladislaus exinde diebus nostris, post secunda Ioanna, dehinc Ludovicus, demum Renatus extremi Galliarum ex Andegavis regum nostri huius regni gubernacula diversis rationibus successibusque usi, quod in nostris Historiis diffuse apparet obtinuerunt.

Et duodecimo iam anno quieta eius regni et Neapolitanae urbis possessione gaudet Alphonsus Aragonum rex inclutus, cui inter praedictos omnes soli contigit, ut de capto maximis XX annorum laboribus et periclis tanto

der the control of factions, the Germans violently invaded the kingdom. Battle **[393C]** was joined in the Campi Palentini, in which Henry the senator took part. Charles came out the winner, and the Germans were suffering a great slaughter, but the senator escaped thanks to Romans who led him to safety.

Conradin and the Duke of Austria disguised themselves as servants and fled to Astura. There, eight days after the battle, they were recognized. They were taken to Charles, who pronounced upon them a sentence of public execution. Afterwards, in about the eighth year of Charles' reign, after his French soldiers in Sicily had mistreated and assaulted Sicilian women, the Sicilians in almost every city and town conspired, as soon as the evening bell had begun to toll on a certain day, to stab to death all Frenchmen found within the walls. This was done cruelly and consistently: the reign of the French was publicly terminated; and Peter of Aragon was summoned as king. In 1282 he demanded the island kingdom of Sicily, taking over the kingdom on the basis of the technicality that it was the rightful inheritance of his wife Constance, who was Manfred's daughter.

Charles died in the eighteenth year of his reign and was buried at Naples; Charles II succeeded him. This king held on for twenty-four years to the part of Italy irrationally called the kingdom of Sicily. He was not famous for much, other than the common people remained peaceful in the kingdom. When he died **[393D]** at the age of forty, he left fourteen children he had sired with his wife Maria, daughter of the king of Hungary: nine boys and five girls; the most famous of whom were Charles Martel, who would become king of Hungary, and Louis, who was ordained a minor saint. The third son, Robert, who succeeded his father in the kingdom, is known as the friend of Francis Petrarch. When he died in 1343, he was succeeded by the queen known as Joanna I. Then came Ladislaus, in my time, and after him Joanna II. Then came Louis and finally René. These were the last governors of our kingdom among the Angevin kings. They enjoyed various methods, and various degrees, of success, which I have described in many places in my *Histories*.

Now in the twelfth year of peace in this kingdom, and in his city of Naples, the renowned king Alfonso of Aragon rules felicitously, who celebrated his triumph drawn through Naples in a golden chariot because he, alone of all the rest I have mentioned, succeeded in capturing the kingdom after twenty years of effort and danger. If I put this into numbers, as merchants do, the seven regions of Italy which I am about to describe, which

regno, curru aureo Neapolim invectus triumphaverit. Si vero, quod factitant mercatores calculum in summas redigere volumus, Normanni quinque et centum triginta, Germani sex et septuaginta, Galli octo et centum septuaginta, Alphonsus Aragonum XII annos quadringentos, et unum conficientes has, de quibus dicturi sumus, septem Italiae regiones sub unico regni quandoque Neapolitani **[394E]** quandoque Siciliae citra fretum dicti titulo tenuerunt.

Sed iam nostrum continuaturi ordinem ad Troentum amnem redeamus. Continet eius fluminis sinistrae Samnitium regio cum amplissima, tum etiam variis populis orisque distincta. Siquidem Praecutini, Pinnenses, Ferentani, Peligni, Marrucini, Furconenses, Amiternini, Vestini, plurima possidentes loca populi in Samnitibus annumerati sunt pertinuitque omnis ea regio (ut tandem nostrae aetatis nominibus utamur) ab hoc Troento amne ab Aquilaque Amiternensium, a Fregellis, ubi nunc dicitur Pons Corvus, ab Reate ab Suessaque Pometia Vestinorum nunc Sessa, hinc ad Beneventum, quam inclusit civitatem, inde ad Larinares Apulorum fines.

Mutatumque ex Samnio praesentis Aprutii nomen magnam illius partem complectitur. Absurda vero est haec facta mutatio, et propter quam multi ex doctioribus viris, sed regionum imperitis, credant Aprutium esse quod olim Brutii fuere, cum trecentis et alicubi pluribus passuum milibus Aprutium distet a Brutiis. Toleranda vero vel ea ratione videtur ipsa mutatio, quod ex particula licet tenui tam amplae Samnitium regionis, id Aprutii corpus sumpsit nominationem. Siquidem ubi Praecutinus dici fuit solitus ager, facta ab imperitissimis mutatione dici incepit Aprutinus. Et quod **[394F]** prima inchoavit Samnii ad Picentum fines particula, ceterae Samnitium particulae atque orae sunt complexae, ut omnis regio non Praecutium, sed corrupte Aprutium vocaretur. Nam Plinius ubi hanc describit regionem, a superioribus inchoans, ut ad Picenum veniat, sic habet:

> Ab Aterno amne, ubi nunc ager Praecutinus Pennensisque idem, Castrum Novum, flumen Iuvatinum, Truentum, cum amne quod solum Liburnorum in Italia reliquum est, flumen Albula Tessuinum, quo finitur Praecutiana regio, et Picenum incipit.

Est vero haec via, per quam duo omnium, qui arma tractarunt, exercitusque duxerunt praestantissimi duces Hannibal primum, et post C. Caesar

were made into one and ruled as one kingdom, called at times "Neapolitan" **[394E]** and at times "Sicily on this side of the straits,"—these regions were possessed by the Normans one hundred and thirty-five years; by the Germans seventy-six; by the French one hundred and seventy-eight; and by Alfonso of Aragon twelve years. This makes a total of four hundred years.

But now let me continue my arrangement by returning to the Tronto river. The region of the Samnites on the left-hand side of this river is not only very wide but also famous for diverse populations and areas, since indeed we number among the Samnites the Praetutians, Pinnenses, Ferentani, Peligni, Marrucini, Furconenses, Amiternini, Vestini, peoples who inhabit many places. Here is the extent of this entire region, expressed in the names of our times: from the Tronto river, from Aquila of the Amiternini, from Fregellae, now called Pontecorvo; from Reate and Suessa Pometia of the Vestini (now called Sessa); on this side, to and including the city of Benevento; on that side, to the Larinates, the boundary of Puglia.

The modern name of the former Samnium, Abruzzo, embraces a great part of that territory. This change of name is absurd; and because of it, many learned men unfamiliar with the regions believe that Abruzzo is what was formerly Bruttium, although Abruzzo is more than three hundred miles distant from Bruttium. But perhaps this change of name seems necessary because this body of Abruzzo has taken its name, from a part, although a slender one, of the nevertheless large region of the Samnites. This is true because where the Praetutian territory was customarily located, people unfamiliar with the area have, in accordance with this change in name, begun to call it Aprutinus, and because **[394F]** the first small part of Samnium began at the border with the territory of Picenum, other small parts of the Samnites and their area were included, so that the entire region was called not Praetutian but, mistakenly, Aprutium. When Pliny describes this region, working down from the upper parts to arrive at Picenum, he writes as follows:

> [The Picenes occupied the territory] from the Aternus river where now are ... the Praetutian and Pennensis [Palmensis] territory, Castrum Novum, the Iuvatinus [Batinus] river, Truentus, with its river which is all that remains of the Liburni in Italy, the rivers Albula, Tessuinus, ... where is the boundary of the territory of the Praetuti, and where that of the Picentines begins.

This is the route by which the two most outstanding leaders who have ever borne arms led their armies: first Hannibal and then Julius Caesar.

gerendis rebus maximis, in huius regni loca regionesque venerunt. Namque Livius libro XXII scribit, Hannibalem post cladem ad Trasumenum Romanis inflictam Spoleto nequicquam oppugnato duxisse in agro Picenum, et praeda omnifariam rerum per aliquot dies facta, profectum per Praecutinum et Adrianum agrum Marsos inde Marrucinosque et Pelignos devastasse. Gaius autem Caesar, sicut elegantissimis commentariis suis habetur,

> maximo progressu omnem agrum Picenum percurrit, cunctae earum regionum praefecturae libentissimis **[394G]** animis eum receperunt, exercitumque eius omnibus rebus iuverunt. Inde Caesar septem omnino dies ad Corfinium commoratus per fines Marrucinorum, Ferentanorum, et Larinatum, in Apuliam pervenit.

Sed iam urbes, oppida et flumina, quae Plinius hic in Praecutianis nunc Aprutii initio fuisse dicit, nostris nominibus declarare pergamus. Illudque imprimis non omittamus Truentum oppidum, quod Plinius a Liburnis Dalmatiae populis, secus Truenti amnis ostia aedificatum fuisse indicat non exstare, nec aliquod in eius vestigio parum apparente subrogatum esse vel oppidum, vel castellum.

Est vero primum ad dictam Troenti amnis sinistram oppidum Columella, deinde sequuntur Contraguerra, Ancaranum, Morrum, et Minotrassinium, quod vetus oppidum Plinius Tessuinum appellat, cui proximum est Castellani amnis Asculum ambientis ostium, quo se in Troentum exonerat. Et ad ipsius Castellani sinistram castella sunt Monssanctus, Macula, Buffarium, Sanctus Vitus; cui oppido haeret Vallis Castellana ab eius fluvii fonte, quem ibi habet, appellata, et aliquot viculis habitata. Ab eaque valle **[394H]** ad Amatricem nobile Praecutinorum oppidum Troento amni montes imminent altissimi, nullis castellis, aut oppidis habitati.

Secundus sequitur in Praecutinis fluvius Librata, quem ab aquarum colore Albulam maiores appellavere. Estque passuum quinque milia secundum litus a Troento semotus, cui dextrorsum ignobilia haerent oppida et castella Carapolis, Neretium, et ad sinistram Torturetum, Sanctomerus, et Sanctus Egidius, ad quod castellum Libratae sive Albulae amnis fontes origoque habentur.

They arrived in this kingdom and these regions to accomplish great deeds. Livy, book 22, writes that Hannibal, after inflicting great slaughter on the Romans at Lake Trasimene, and after unsuccessfully besieging Spoletium, led his army into the territory of Picenum. For some days he plundered the area on all sides, then set forth through Praetutian and Adriatic territory and went on to lay waste to the Marsi, Marrucini, and Peligni. But we read in Caesar's elegant commentaries,

> He went swiftly through the entire Picene territory. All the Italian cities of these regions which were governed by Roman authorities received him **[394G]** most willingly and gave their all in aid of his army. After Caesar had stayed at Corfinium seven days, he traveled through the territory of the Marrucini, Frentani, and Larinates, to arrive in Apulia.

But now let me list with their modern names the cities, towns, and rivers which Pliny says were here among the Praetutii (now the beginning of Abruzzo). In particular, let me remember to say that the town of Tronto, which Pliny says was built by the Liburnians of Dalmatia at the mouth of the Truentus river, does not exist now; there is not any town or fortified village which has grown up on the site of its barely visible remains.

On the previously mentioned left bank of the Tronto river is the town of Colonella. Then follow Controguerra, Ancarano, Morro d'Oro, and Tesino, an ancient town Pliny calls Tessuinum. Next to that is the mouth of the Castellano, a river which flows around Ascoli where it debouches into the Tronto. On the left bank of the Castellano are the fortresses of Montesanto, Macchia da Sole, Monte Bufario, and S. Vito. Next to this last town is Valle Castellana, named after the source of the river located there; the valley contains some small villages. In this valley, towering and uninhabited mountains hang over the noble Praetutian town **[394H]** of Amatrice.

The second river among the Praetutii follows, the Vibrata, which on account of the color of its waters the ancients called the Albula. It is five miles along the coast from the town of Tronto. On its right-hand bank are the undistinguished towns and fortified villages of Corropoli, Nereto, and, on the left bank, Tortureto, S. Omero, and S. Egidio. At the latter fortress we find the source of the Vibrata, or Albula, river.

Salinus deinceps est amnis ab Apennino defluens, a qua amne vix duo milia passuum a Librata recedente, remotiora sunt ad dexteram in mediterraneis montibus Rochetta castellum, et Civitella oppidum, arcem habens omnium eius orae, natura loci moenibusque munitam. Sinistrorsum vero castella illi adiacent Montorium, et superiore loco Poggium Morelli, superius Troia. Quinque dehinc milia passuum abest Tordinus amnis, quem Plinius Vivantium appellat, habetque in Apennino ad radices Corni montis originem. Haeret vero ei dextrorsum in maris litore oppidum Flavianeum olim nobile, nunc paucis habitatum colonis, quod Ptolemaeus Pliniusque Castrum Novum appellant. Supraque Flavianeum in mediterraneis Tordino dextrorsum proxima sunt oppida, Mosanum, Ripatoni et Villantum. Sinistrorsum vero eidem amni, et pariter litori proximum est castellum Mons Paganus.

[395A] Supraque XII a mari miliario Viciola fluvius in Apennino ad Cornum oriundus Tordinum auget. Ibique Teramum est nobilissimum regionis oppidum, quam Ptolemaeus Pliniusque Interamniam appellant. Paulo enim supra Teramum torrens nomine Flumicellus influit Tordinum, ut tot circumdatum amnibus oppidum Interamnia debuerit appellari. Genuit is locus magnum regioni ornamentum Simonem patrem et Theodorum filium iureconsultissimos gente progenitos Laelia, quorum ille in Pisana Constantiensi et Basiliensi synodis, pontificumque Romanorum curia causas egregie peroravit. Hic sacri palatii causarum auditor est, genitorque Venetiis natus Romam nunc incolunt.

Ad proximumque Flumicelli ortum, tria sunt proxima, et prope contigua, ut unicum oppidum solo Campli vocabulo nominentur. Supraque Viciolae ortum castella sunt Bisignum et Rugnanum. Tordinum autem sive Iuvantinum inter et proximum vetusti praesentisque nominis Vomanum amnem, sex in litore milia passuum intercedunt, oppidaque et castella inter utrumque sunt plurima, partim pariter ab utroque distantia, partim alterutris, pro montium in quibus sunt inaequalitate et alveorum utriusque amnis [395B] inflexu, proximiora, quae ab infimo ad supremum, quo sita sint ordine satis fuerit explicare, Morrum, Locharistum, Custodia Vomani, Castrum Vetus, Transmundum, Cantianum, Forcella, Mianum, Rapinum, Collis Vetus, Fornariolum, Montorium, Ripa Montorii, Poggium Umbrechi, et Rossenum.

The next river is the Saline. It flows down from the Apennines. As it flows away from the Vibrata, scarcely two miles from the Vibrata, on its right-hand side, the more remote settlements in the mountains in the interior are: the fortress of Rocchetta, the town of Civitella, with its citadel, most strongly fortified among all in that region with walls and by the nature of the place. On the left, next to Civitella, are fortified villages, Montone, and, higher up, Poggio Morelli and, higher than that, Troia. Five miles from here is the Tordino river, which Pliny calls Vivantium; it has its source in the Apennines, at the foot of the Corno Grande. Close to its right-hand bank, on the coast, is the town of Castel San Flaviano, formerly important, but now sparsely inhabited by colonists; Ptolemy and Pliny called it Castrum Novum. And above Castel San Flaviano in the interior, on the right-hand side next to the Tordino are the towns of Mosciano Sant'Angelo, Ripattoni, and Bellante. On the left bank of the same river, equidistant from the coast, is the fortified village of Montepagano.

[395A] Above this, twelve miles from the sea, is the river Vezzola, a tributary of the Tordino, which arises from a source at Mte. Corno in the Apennines. There is Teramo, the most distinguished town in the region, called by Ptolemy and Pliny Interamna. A little above Teramo a stream called the Fiumicino flows into the Tordino, giving the town the appropriate name Interamna, surrounded as it is by so many rivers. This place gave birth to a great source of pride for the region, the Lelli: Simon the father and Teodoro the son, both eminent jurists. The former was an outstanding orator at the synods of Basle, Pisa, and Constance, and in the Roman Curia. The latter is an apostolic auditor; the father, born at Venice, now lives in Rome.

And at the next source, that of the Fiumicino, there are three towns near each other, so close that they are called by one name, Campli. And above the Vezzola's source are the fortresses Bisegna and Rocciano. But it is six miles between the Tordino and the next river, whose ancient and modern name is Vomanus (Vomano). Between the two are many towns and fortified villages. Some are equidistant from the two. Some, in proportion to the unevenness of the mountains in which they are located and the curve in each river's beds, **[395B]** are closer to one than to the other. It will suffice for me to go through them from the ones at the bottom to the highest, in the order in which they come: Morro d'Oro, Notaresco, Guardia Vomano, Castelvecchio, Castiglione Messer Raimondo, Canzano, Forcella, Miano, Rapino, Collevecchio, Frondarola, Montorio al Vomano, Ripa, Poggio Umbricchio, and Roseto.

Ad Vomanique fontem vici sunt in Apennino populis frequentes, Campus Tostus, Poggium castellum, et Massionum. Habetque Vomanus sinistrorsum in mediterraneis castella Motullam, Montem Viridem, et Montem Gualchum. Hucusque fuerunt Praecutini, quandoquidem Plinius ad agrum Hadriae coloniae, et ad Aterni amnis fines agrum Praecutinum finiri dicit.

Deinceps versabimur in Marrucinis, quos Livius libro XXVIII dicit dedisse voluntaria nomina in classem, quam Scipio in Africam duxit. Et libro LXXII, bellum describens Italicum, dicit Marrucinos Marsis rebellibus consensisse. Et libro LXXVI scribit Sulpicium legatum Marrucinos cecidisse. Post Vomanum amnem fluvius Plumba sequitur, cui castellum haeret Hadriae Portus appellatum. Superius est Silva oppidum, et Troia, sicut Plinius, ut nunc autem quinque milia passuum a mari, et ab utroque fluvio pariter distat Hadria vetus, Romanorum colonia **[395C]** arduo in colle sita, quae cive ornatissima fuit Hadriano imperatore Romano, de quo Aelius Spartianus, "Hadrianus Hadria ortus maiores suos in Hispanis ortos, per tempora Scipionis in Italia resedisse in libro vitae suae scribit." Et infra, "Hadrianus apud Neapolim demarchus in patria sua Hadria quinquennalis fuit." Livius libro XXIIII, anno quinto belli Punici secundi "Hadriae aram in caelo, speciesque hominum circa eam candida veste visas esse."

Supra Hadriam Plumbae fluvio ad dexteram castellum haeret Celinum. Superiusque ad ipsius fluvii fontem oppidum est Schiranum. Eidem autem Plumbae fluvio secundo supra mare miliario sinistrorsum imminet oppidum nobile, civitas Sancti Angeli appellata, idque Plinius et Ptolemaeus Angolum dixere, quod enim in multis contigisse videmus tam facilis quam pia fuit Angoli ad Angelum Christianis temporibus facta mutatio. Et supra illud Plumbae amni Ilex oppidum pariter est propinquum.

Distant a Plumba fluvio secundum mare tria milia passuum amnis Salinus. Eique ad dexteram in litore haeret castellum, Portus Sancti Angeli dictum, supraque in mediterraneis Salinus fluvio augetur nomine Fino in Apennino ad Corni radices oriundo, **[395D]** cui dextrorsum octo imminent oppida et castella, quae satis fuerit ordine recensere: Cassilentum, Mons Siccus, Pignanum, Bisentum, Corvignanum, Serra, et Valuianum.

Paulo etiam supra Fini amnis ostium altero Salinus augetur flumine *T*avo, quod pariter in Apennino ad Cornum exoritur. Interque haec flumina pari paene distantia, et quarto a mari miliario oppidum est in regione

At the source of the Vomano, there are in the Apennines densely-inhabited villages: Campotosto, Poggio Cancelli, and Mascioni. On the left bank of the Vomano in the interior are the fortresses of Mottola, Monteverde, and Montegualtieri. Up to this point we are in the land of the Praetutii, seeing that Pliny says that the land of the Praetutii is bounded by the territory of the colony of Hadria and the borders of the Aternus River.

Next, we shall treat the Marrucini; Livy (book 28) says that they voluntarily enrolled in the fleet Scipio took to Africa. And in book 72, as he describes the Italian War, Livy writes that the Marrucini conspired with the Marsi to rebel; and in book 76 that the envoy Sulpicius killed the Marrucini. After the Vomano river comes the Piomba, close to whose banks lies the fortified village called Scerne. Above it is the town of Silva, and Troia. According to Pliny, Hadria, and as in Pliny's time, now also Atri, is five miles equidistant from the sea and from each of the two rivers. It is an ancient Roman **[395C]** colony located on a high hill, distinguished as the native city of the emperor Hadrian. In his biography, Aelius Spartianus says, "Hadrian was born at Hadria; his ancestors originated from Spain, but in the time of Scipio they emigrated to Italy." And, later on, "Hadrian, a demarch at Naples, was a quinquennal in his native land." Livy, in book 24, says in the fifth year of the second Punic War, "people saw at Hadria an altar in the sky and around it a vision of men in white clothing."

Above Atri on the right bank of the Piomba river lies the fortified village of Cellino Attanasio, and above it at the river's source is Scerne. Two miles above sea level, over the left bank of this same river hangs the noble town of Città S. Angelo, called Angolum by Pliny and Ptolemy. Many people seem to have found this accidental change of name as easy as it was devout, from Angolum to Angelus. Above it, equidistant from the Piomba river, is the town of Elice.

Following the coast, three miles from the Piomba river, is the Saline river. On the coast, on its right hand bank, is the fortified village called Porto Sant'Angelo. Above it, towards the interior, the Fino river flows into the Saline. It has its origin in the Apennines at the foot of the Corno Grande. **[395D]** Hanging over its right bank are eight towns and fortified villages which it will suffice to name in order: Castilenti, Monticchio, Appignano, Bisenti, Cermignano, Vaglio Serra.

Also a little farther up above the mouth of the Fino river is the a tributary of the Saline, the Tavo river, likewise in the Apennines at the foot of the Corno Grande. And almost equidistant between these rivers, four miles

primarium civitas Penne appellata, Pennensium nomine apud vetustissimos notissima. Sunt enim hi quos superius Plinium post Praecutinos Pennenses diximus posuisse. Eaque in fluviorum peninsula Tavo dextrorsum imminet collis Corvinus et Lauretum nobile oppidum. Sequitur in litore Aterni amnis in regione primarii ostium, quem amnem nunc Piscariam vocant. Is fluvius Nuria apud monasterium Casaenovae secus Apenninum oriundo dextrorsum augetur. Suntque ad Nuriae dexteram Mons Silvanus Castellum, Spoltorium oppidum, et Moscusum, Planellumque et Capagattum castella. Et sub ipso fonte abbatia, Casaenovae, aedificiis et cetero ornatu, ut in ea montium asperitate, conspicua.

Supra Nuriam fluvium Aterno sive Piscariae amni dextrorsum adiacent, Rosanum Alandum, Petranicum, turris Antonelli, et superius est Castilionum. Deinceps ascendenti obvius est fluvius Caput Aquae ductus uberrimo manans fonte, cui fluvio ad sinistram **[396E]** castella Buxum primo, et superius ad fontem Offenum adiacet. Interque ea Capistranum duo milia passuum ab eodem fluvio est semotum, quod oppidum viro nunc ornatur celeberrimo Ioanne Capistraneo seraphici Francisci ordinis, quem decorat, alumno, miraculis et quidem frequentibus, quod post Apostolorum tempora rarum ac prope inauditum fuit, in vita coruscante. Supraque Castranum in mediterraneis est oppidum Carapellum. Dehinc arduo ascensu Aterno amni adiacent Vetoritum et Raianum, et superius est Aquila, urbs praeclara.

Eius originem relaturi quaedam nostri huius operis intentioni accommodata altiuscule repetemus, ut minori sit miraculo nostris hominibus, tantam civitatem potuisse in ea montium asperitate, tam brevi tempore coalescere. Roma sub consulibus, atque etiam postea sub principibus florente, hi montes, in quibus Aquilam nunc esse videmus, duas habuere urbes, quarum unam nomine Amiternum populo, quam nunc sit Aquila frequentiorem fuisse constat. Livius enim libro X scribit Spurium Carvilium alterum consulem Amiternum oppugnatum de Samnitibus cepisse, caesaque oppidanorum duo milia octingenti, captos quater mille ducentos **[396F]** octuaginta. Et tamen postea idem Livius populos Italiae enumerans, qui Lucio Scipioni in Africam traducturo sponte auxilio fuere, dicit Amiterninos simul cum Umbris Nursinis et Reatinis milites illi dedisse.

from the sea, is the chief town of the region, a city called Penne, best known to the ancients as Pennensium. These are the people, as I have mentioned above, whom Pliny places after the Praetutii. Overhanging the right-hand bank of the Tavo, on the peninsula formed by the two rivers, are Collecorvino and the distinguished town of Loreto. There follows on the coast the mouth of the river Aterno, the chief river in the region, a river which is now called the Pescara. Its tributary the Nora river has its source at the monastery of Casanova beside the Apennines. On the right-hand bank of the Nora are Montesilvano, the town of Spoltore, and the fortified villages Moscufo, Pianello Cerratina, and Cepagatti. Below this river's source is the abbey of Casanova; with its buildings and other decoration, it stands out in the harshness of those mountains.

Above the river Nora, on the right-hand bank of the Aterno or Pescara river, lie Rosciano, Alanno, Pietranico, Torre Antonelli, and higher up is Castiglione. There, as you go up, you come to the Capo d'Acqua, flowing from an abundant spring. Next to this river, on its left bank, is first the **[396E]** castle Bussi, and above it, at the spring, Ofena. Between these two is Capestrano, two miles from the same river, a town which now boasts as its citizen the famous S. Giovanni da Capestrano of the Franciscan order. His life shone with frequent miracles, a thing which was rare, almost unheard of, after the time of the Apostles. And inland above Capestrano is the town of Carapelle Calvisio, and from there it is a steep climb to Vittorito and Raiano close beside the Pescara river. Farther up is the famous city of L'Aquila.

I shall narrate some details of its origins, making adjustments to the plan of my work, because I want to dispel my generation's considering a minor miracle the rise of so great a city in so short a time in so harsh a mountainous environment. In the time of the Roman Republic, and even afterwards during the principate, the mountains where L'Aquila is now contained two cities. One was called Amiternum, and it was fairly certainly more densely populated than L'Aquila is now. For Livy in his tenth book writes that the other consul, Sp. Cornelius, took the besieged city of Amiternum from the Samnites; and that 2,080 townsmen were killed, and he took 4,280 captive. Nevertheless, Livy **[396F]** later enumerates also the people of Italy who volunteered to cross to Africa in Lucius Scipio's fleet; and here he says soldiers were supplied from the men of Amiternum, together with those from Umbria, Nursia, and Reate.

Virgilius vero Amiternas appellat Turrigeras, fuitque situm Amiternum in continuato ac plano montis dorso quinque milia passuum ab Aquila distans, cuius theatri temporumque turrium ingentis, ut apparet, urbis reliquiae fundamenta cernuntur. Habuit vero ea urbs magni ornamenti civem Salustium Crispum nobilem historicum. Altera urbs in montibus Aquilae adiacentibus fuit Furconium appellata, quae et si Amiterno nominis vetustate populi frequentia, et opum magnitudine fuit impar, suam tamen temporibus Christiani habuit dignitatem, quod omnibus conciliis, quae ante annos sexcentos Romae, aut alibi per Italiam celebrata fuere, episcopum Furconensem adscriptum legimus. Eratque Furconium diversa ab Amiterno regione octo milia passuum ab Aquila distans in Aterni amnis fluenta, proclivior, ubi etiam nunc exstantia quadrati lapidis fundamenta Furconium appellant, videturque eius urbis agrum fuisse illum maiori ex parte, quem nunc possident Aquilani.

Itaque Amiternis ab ignoto nobis hoste, et Furconio quod **[396G]** scimus a Longobardis solo aequatis, ipsarum urbium et suorum agrorum populi, quos soli montuosissimi aerisque salubritas multos gigneret conservaretque, in grumosis arduisque ascensu montibus, communitis oppidis, et castellis sese continuerunt. Et cum dispersi ea in locorum asperitate ipsi populi nullam regiminis formam communem possent continere, in tyrannorum subiectionem potestatemque venerunt, a quibus diu multumque lacerati oppressique sunt, crediderimque quod tradita per quattuor, aut ad summum quinque aetatum successionem publica nunc fama Aquilani affirmant factum esse, ut cum diu invisum tyrannidis iugum excutere statuissent. Singuli castellorum populi, quod prius coniuratione unita se facturos spoponderant, suos quique tyrannos eadem trucidaverint hora. Quod autem magis constat liberati tot populi nihil duxere antiquius, quam hoc murorum orbe, quem nunc habet Aquila inchoato singulis castellorum populis, quos futura in urbe tenerent inhabitarentque vicos, qui hodie quoque internoscuntur distribuere, ut eo quisque ardentius operi intenderet, quo sese domui et rei suae familiari studium impendere intelligeret, operamque navare. **[396H]**

Nomen vero Aquilam non ab augurio, sicut gentiles olim, sed a similitudine indiderunt, qua speraverint eam urbem omnibus circa populis haud secus, quam aquila ceteris avibus potentiorem digniorem que futuram. Quo

Virgil calls Amiternum "turreted." Amiternum was located on an extensive level ridge of a mountain five miles from Aquila. What look like the remains of an enormous city, the ruins of the foundations of Amiternum's theatre and temples and towers, can be seen today. This city proudly boasted the noble historian Sallustius Crispus as its citizen. In the mountains next to Aquila was another city, called Furconium. This city was inferior to Amiternum in the number of its population and the antiquity of its name and the amount of its wealth. But in Christian times Furconium had its own distinction; we read that the diocese of Furconium was included in all the famous synods of six hundred years before, at Rome or anywhere else throughout Italy. Furconium was farther downhill towards the stream of the Pescara river in a different region from Amiternum, eight miles from L'Aquila. The extant foundations in *opus quadratum* are even now called Forcona. Apparently the territory of this city comprised the major part of the land now possessed by the citizens of L'Aquila.

Amiternum was destroyed by an enemy unknown to us, and Furconium **[396G]** by a known enemy, the Lombards. The mountainous soil and air of these cities and their territories are healthy, and gave birth to numerous peoples, who survived in their fortified towns and castles in the mountains, hilly and difficult of access. And as they were widely dispersed in those harsh places, the people could not maintain any common form of government, and came under the power of some very oppressive and abusive tyrants. I believe the common tradition—four, at the most five, generations old—asserted by the citizens of L'Aquila, says that when they had decided to free themselves from the long-resented tyranny, each people in its fortress fulfilled a previously-arranged plan, according to which they had conspired together to cut down their tyrants at the same time. It is more definitely established that when they had been freed, these numerous populations considered the most ancient settlement to be the walls which L'Aquila now possesses, marking the beginning for the individual peoples of the castles neighborhoods in the future city they would possess and inhabit, districts which also today are recognized as divided up, so that each man directed his energies more eagerly in proportion as he understood that his enthusiasm was expended on his house and his estate, and devoted his care accordingly.

[396H]

They took the name Aquila not, as foreigners formerly thought, from augury, but from an analogy, because they hoped that this city would be more powerful and virtuous than the other populations in the area, as an

autem anno Aquila urbs condi coeperit, incertum omnibus esse videmus. Sed eam scimus minus novam esse quam incolae opinentur et praedicent. Namque in secundi Nicolai pontificis Romani gestis rebus habetur, quod supra ostendimus, Robertum Guiscardum ad annum salutis decies centenum et sexagesimum, accepisse ab eo pontifice in Aquila civitate ducatus Apuliae concessionem. Coeperat vero eius urbis fortuna rei publicae proximis temporibus a civium discordia labare, adeo ut ad pristinam calamitatem reditura videretur, nisi maximo dei munere sanctum Bernardinum Senensem apud eos diem obire contigisset, tantus namque ex omni orbe Christiano populorum concursus ad sancti eius sepulcrum, miraculaque visenda est factus, ut cum urbs Aquila opibus sit aucta, tum maxime cives concordes unanimesque sint facti.

Supra Aquilam amnis Aterni sive Piscariae fonti subiacet in Apennino oppidum mons Regalis, cui oppido incolae affirmant, nobisque ostenderunt pirum esse proximam, colli innatam taliter fastigiato [397A] ut aqua in eam pluens arborem, triplici facta divisione in tres magnos amnes, diversas petentes regiones, Velinum, Troentum Aternumque, sive Piscariam dilabatur. Habet sinistrorsum Aternus ostio in maris litore proximum Piscariam oppidum, cuius nomen sicut fluvii est mutatum. Siquidem Aternum eam vetustissimam urbem Plinius Ptolemaeusque appellant.

Superiusque urbs Theatina Marrucinorum a Plinio dicta, septimo miliario a mari recedit, episcopo nunc et cive suo ex nobili Volognanorum familia oriundo ornata, quam Pipinus Caroli Magni filius, quod Longobardis obstinatiore favisset animo, demolitus est. Et tamen anno abinde paulo plus minus ducentesimo, Normanni eam duxerunt dignam, apud quam Aprutinorum gubernationis sedem tenerent. Nam quod supra ostendimus Gaufredus Roberti Guiscardi frater, per II Nicolai pontificis Romani tempora occupatae regionis caput hanc urbem Guillianicumque oppidum faciebat. Auget superiore loco Aternum Alba fluvius binis auctus torrentulis ex Maiella oriundus, inter quos oppidum est Manuplellum, Urso ornatum comite, ex patricia Ursinorum gente Romana oriundo, et litteris decorato. Et paulo [397B] superius Maiellae adiacet Rocha Morisii; inferius Cusanum, et ad Aterni ripam est oppidulum Turris dictum.

Lucus deinde oppidum Aterno est proximum ad fluvii unius ostium, quem hinc Rufeus inde Orta torrentes ex Maiella cadentes efficiunt. Interque eos torrentes Caramanicum est oppidum non exile. Cantalupum deinde

eagle is superior to other birds. Our sources are uncertain about the year in which Aquila was founded, but I know its foundation is less recent than its inhabitants believe and assert. For the records of Pope Nicholas II say, as I mentioned earlier, that Robert Guiscard in 1060 received from this pope in the city of Aquila the title of Duke of Apulia. In the times after the Republican era, the fortune of this city had begun to sink, so that it appeared to be reverting to its former misfortune. But by the greatest gift of God, S. Bernardino da Siena happened to die at Aquila; consequently there was such a gathering of people from all over the Christian world to see the holy man's tomb that not only was the city of Aquila enriched but its citizens became harmoniously reconciled.

Above L'Aquila, beneath the source of the Pescara river in the Apennines, lies the town of Montereale. Its inhabitants assert—and have shown to me—that on a hill close by this town grew a pear tree which sloped down in such a way **[397A]** that when it rains, the water which falls on this tree is split into three streams, which become the three great rivers flowing through the different regions: the Velino, the Tronto, and the Aterno or Pescara. On the left bank of the Pescara, on the coast next to its mouth, is the town of Pescara. Its name, like that of the river, has been changed, since Pliny and Ptolemy call this very ancient city Aternum.

And higher up, seven miles inland, is the city of Chieti, which Pliny says belongs to the Marrucini. It claims the distinction of native city of a bishop from the noble family of the Valignani. Pippin, son of Charlemagne, stubbornly favored the Lombards and destroyed Teate. But about two hundred years later the Normans decided it was worthy to be their seat of government over Abruzzo. As I mentioned earlier, in the time of Pope Nicholas II, Godfrey, brother of Robert Guiscard, made this city and the town of Guilmi the capital of the occupied territory. Higher up, the Alba river flows into the Pescara. The Alba itself has two small tributaries whose source is on the Maiella. Between them is the town of Manoppello, decorated by Count Orso of the Orsini family of Rome, a man distinguished for literary learning. And a little higher up, **[397B]** next to the Maiella, lies Roccamorice. Lower down is Cusano, and on the bank of the Pescara is a small town called Torre.

Then the town next to the Pescara is Luco, at the mouth of one river which is formed when the Rufento and the Orta rivers flow down from the Maiella. Between these rivers is the good-sized town of Caramanico Terme. Going away from the Pescara, next comes the small town of Cantalupo,

oppidulum ab Aterno recedens, monti haeret, sub quo fons olei Petronici perennis scatet, quod quidem oleum Theotonici Ungarique diligentius quam Italici et colligunt et asportant.

Proxime ad Aterni ripam Tochum est oppidum, et quattuor inde abest milia passuum Populium natura loci munitionibusque, et populi frequentia nobilissimum. Nam cum eo confluant Aternum conficientes fluvii hinc ab Aquila, sive a monte Regali, inde a Sulmone labentes, pons Aterno primum integro, et nusquam inferius vadoso apud Populium est impositus, et arces ductaque utrimque ad amnem murorum bracchia claustrum efficiunt, ut in regione montuosissima munitissimum. Hicque Peligni Marrucinis continere incipiunt, ad eam Aterni partem hinc inde appositi, quam labi diximus a Sulmone.

Primum vero ad hunc amnem oppidum fuit Corfinium, cuius diruti ruinis tertio miliario a **[397C]** Populio distantibus S. Pelini in Campis, et Pentinia est appellatio. Fuitque id Corfinium, in quo Domitius Ahenobarbus sese C. Caesari, ne Pompeium persequeretur, opposuit. Ostendit vero Lucanus pontem, qui eum iungeret fluvium fuisse prope Corfinium, ut non liceat suspicari eum fuisse, qui nunc est sublicius, ad Popilium:

> Ite simul pedites ruiturum ascendite pontem.

Pelignosque quod diximus continuisse Marrucinis, et his Ferentanos, postea Larinates, Hirtius in civilis belli commentariis sic ostendit, "Caesar septem omnino dies ad Corfinium commoratus per fines Marrucinorum et Ferentanorum et Larinatum in Apuliam pervenit." Sed Aterni amnis quod est reliquum, et illi adiacentes Pelignos, priusque Ferentanos describamus. Ea Aterni pars, quam diximus, ad Sulmonem labi, geminum habet fontem, unum apud Pacentrum, alterum apud Vallem Obscurum. Delabentesque inde fluvii apud Sulmonem coeunt, et Aternus a Populio Sulmonem usque integer planitiem XII milia passuum longitudine, et vix dimidio latitudine patentem intersecat, nec ipsi integro amni praeter Corfinii, ut diximus, diruti ruinas, aliud quam Pratula castellum adiacet.

Sulmoque proximum fluvio ad **[397D]** Vallem Obscuram oriundo oppidum est celebre, quod civibus opificibusque praestantibus, et populi multitudine frequentatur, eoque nos viso Nasoni Ovidio poetae excellentissimo

close to the mountain under which gushes a perpetual spring of petroleum. The Germans and the Hungarians are more diligent than the Italians about collecting and exporting this oil.

Next, on the bank of the Pescara, is the town of Tocco, and four miles away is Pópoli, excellent in its natural fortifications and dense population. When the confluence of the rivers, on one side from L'Aquila or Montereale, on the other side from Sulmona, produces the Pescara, there a bridge has been built over the Pescara, first where it is undivided and there is no bridge anywhere further down at Pópoli where it is shallow. And castles and walls constructed to the river on each side create a barrier which is an excellent fortification for such a mountainous place. And here the Peligni begin a common border with the Marrucini, located here and there on that part of the Pescara river which I said flows down from Sulmona.

The first town on this river was Corfinium. But it has been destroyed, and its ruins stand three miles from [397C] Pópoli, and the site is called S. Pelino in the Fields and Pentima. It was at Corfinium that Domitius Ahenobarbus resisted Julius Caesar when he was pursuing Pompey. Lucan demonstrates that the bridge, which used to span the river, was near Corfinium, which makes it credible that it was the one made of wooden piles which is now at Pópoli:

> Go, soldiers, mount the bridge which is about to fall.

As I said, the Peligni are bounded by the Marrucini, as are the Frentani and after them the Larinates; this is what Hirtius says in the *Commentaries on the Civil War*, "Caesar stayed at Corfinium the entire seven days before marching through the territory of the Marrucini, Frentani, and Larinates to arrive in Apulia." But before describing the Frentani, let me describe the remaining part of the Pescara river and the Peligni who live next to it. I noted that this part of the Pescara has a double source, one at Pacentro and the other at Valle Oscura; and the rivers flow down until they come together at Sulmo. The Pescara where it is undivided, from Pópoli to Sulmona, cuts across a plain that is twelve miles long and almost half that in width. The fortified town of Pratola is the only settlement to be found along the undivided Pescara (except for the ruins of Corfinium noted above).

The famous town of Sulmona lies next to the branch of the river which originates at [397D] Valle Oscura. It is densely populated with outstanding citizens and skilled workmen. When I visited Sulmona I rejoiced that the poet Ovid had distinguished a hometown completely worthy of him. Ovid

congratulati sumus, qui patriam se dignam tantopere exornaverit. Isque eam scribit aedificatam fuisse a quodam Solymo Aeneae comite, his versibus:

> Huius erat Solymus Phrygia comes unus ab Ida,
> A quo Sulmonis moenia nomen habent.

Erat vero Ovidius exul in Scythia, quando dictos et alios qui sequuntur versus in Fastis scripsit:

> Sulmonis gelidi patriae Germanice nostrae
> Me miserum Scythico quam procul ille solo est.
> Ergo ego tam longe, sed supprime, Musa, querellas.

Supra Sulmonem Pectoranum oppidum; superius est Vallis Obscura, vicus planitiei quinummilium, et in ea montium celsitudine tam mirabili, quam amplae adiacens. Fuit vero ea planities aliquot habitata vicis, quod exstantes ruinae ostendunt. Et Plinius eos populos Superaequanos Pelignorum appellat. Fluvius autem apud Pacentrum oriundus, cum Maiellam montem, a quo cadit linquere, et in campos Sulmonenses labi incipit, monasterium attingit aedificiis ornatissimum, quod frater Petrus de Morrono, quando in papam Celestinum electus fuit, inhabitabat. Hanc oram, et eam quae a Populio Sulmonem usque campestris est, et ipsam unde geminos diximus fluvios Aternum efficere, montes [398E] undique altissimi sinistrorsum Maiella Apenninus dextrorsum claudunt, adeo ut paucis, et quidem arduis praesidioque communitis aditibus in eam sit accessus. Unde factum est, ut ab octingentis annis citra antiquato Pelignorum nomine dicta sit Valuensis, qua ratione praepositum Sulmonensi ecclesiae, et omni olim Pelignorum orae episcopum Romana ecclesia Valuensem dicit. Sed haec iam de Aterno fluvio satis.

Alia quae de Pelignis Superaequanis reliqua nobis sunt ultra Maiellam ad dexteram Sari nunc Sangri amnis melius describentur. Aterno sive Piscariae amni proximus est ad mare Lentus fluvius, ex Maiella oriundus, Ferentanorum orae primus, cui dextrorsum et sub ipso monte Maiella adiacet monasterium Sancti Liberatoris, templo, aedificiis, et quod nos illuc traxit, multis et elegantibus libris vetustissimis Longobarda scriptis littera ornatissimum. Eiusque fluvii sinistrae in maris litore haeret nunc Franchavilla, quam prisci Frentanam appellavere urbem Frentanorum primariam, de qua Livius in IX, “Aulus consul Frentanos uno secundo proelio debellavit, ur-

writes in the following verses of Sulmo's foundation by a certain Solymus, comrade of Aeneas:

> Solymus was his comrade, from Phrygian Ida.
> From him the walls of Sulmo take their name.

Indeed, Ovid was an exile in Scythia when he wrote in the *Fasti* the following lines:

> . . . my chilly homeland, Sulmo—O Germanicus, miserable me!
> how far away that land is from Scythia. So I,
> so far away—but, Muse, check my complaints . . .

Above Sulmona is the town of Pettorano; and higher up is the village of Valle Oscura, a village lying next to the Piano delle Cinquemiglia, which is amazingly broad given the height of these mountains This plain was inhabited by some villages; their ruins can still be seen. Pliny calls these people the Superaequani of the Peligni. Moreover, a river has its source at Pacentro. When it flows down the Montagna della Maiella from that town, it begins a descent into the territory of Sulmona, and flows past a monastery distinguished with buildings. Brother Peter of Morrone, who was elected Pope Celestine, used to live in this place. From Pópoli to Sulmona is rural and the place from where I mentioned the two rivers come together to create the Pescara river, there are very high mountains **[398E]** all around which shut it in: on the left, the Maiella; on the right, the Apennines. They enclose it so that it can only be approached by a few very steep paths which are fortified by a garrison. For this reason, it was 800 years earlier called "of Valva" after the archaic name of the Peligni, so that the church gives the title "of Valva" to the bishop of the church at Sulmona and all the territory that was formerly the district of the Peligni. But now I have said enough about the Pescara river.

The areas of the Superaequani of the Peligni beyond the Maiella which remain for me to treat will be better described on the right-hand bank of the Saro, now Sangro, river. The Alento river is next to the Aterno or Pescara, at the sea. It has its source at the Montagna della Maiella and is the first river on the coast of the Frentani. On its right side, immediately beneath the Maiella, it flows past the monastery of S. Liberatore, which boasts a temple and buildings; and I myself have been drawn there to consult its many elegant books, written in Lombard script. And on the left side of this river, on the seacoast, is the modern Francavilla, which the ancients called Frentana, the chief city of the Frentani. Livy writes in book 9: "The consul Aulus de-

bemque ipsam quo se fusa contulerat acies obsidibus imperatis in deditionem accepit." Et infra, "de Aequis [398F] triumphatum, exemploque eorum fuit, ut Marsi, Marrucini, Frentani mitterent Romam oratores; his petentibus foedus datum est."

Frentanos vero omnium populorum solos fuisse fortissimos nonnulli opinantur, in eam adducti sententiam male consideratis verbis Plinii, hanc regionem quae sibi fuit quarta describentis. Ipse enim ordine procedens nostro huic contrario, et a superioribus inchoans dicit a Tiferno amne sequi regionem quartam gentium, vel fortissimarum Italiae in ora Frentanorum, ut intellegi velit et ipsos Frentanos, et qui sequerentur adiacerentque Marrucinos, Pelignos, et Praecutinos esse fortissimos. Notissimum vero est historias callentibus Romanas, cohortes Pelignas ceteris Latini nominis fuisse praelatas.

Lento amni in mediterraneis haeret Buchianicum, nobile ditissimumque olea oppidum. Superius item sub Maiella est Rocha Montisplani, et supra fontem Lenti est castrum Menale. Ad Lentum in litore sequitur Forus amnis Maiella pariter oriundus. Cui quinto a mari miliario proximum est dextrorsum Villa Maina oppidum, et superius sub Maiella Praetorium item oppidum, Foroque sinistrorsum est proximum Milianicum, et supra [398G] ad ipsum torrentem aliud oppidum Fara. Superius Rapinum castellum, et ad Maiellam Penna.

Recedit in litore a Foro Morus, alter fluvius octo milia passuum, et cum eo in spatio litori immineat, et Foro proximum sit castellum Tullum, Moro proxima est ad duos mille passus, marique contigua vetustissima urbs Ortona, quam Ptolemaeus simul cum Aterni amnis ostio in Pelignis enumerat. Sed Plinius, cui in rebus Italiae magis credimus, quicquid est ab Aterni amnis ostio in Larinates Frentanorum orae attribuit, quin ipse etiam Ptolemaeus sicut et Plinius Frentanam urbem Aterno sinistram, ubi nunc est Villafrancha, ponit, ut aut Ptolemaei picturam esse depravatam, quae contraria habeat, aut eos qui rettulerunt sibi errasse non dubitemus.

Inter urbem Ortonam et Forum amnem ad usque Maiellam montem multa sunt oppida et castella, quae ab infimis ad suprema, quo sint ordine sita,

feated the Frentani in one successful battle; their army fled into the city and he asked for hostages and received its surrender." And later on, Livy writes, "He **[398F]** triumphed over the Aequi, and this was an example and an admonition to the Marsi, Marrucini, and Frentani. They sent speakers to Rome to beg for a treaty, which they obtained."

Some men think that the Frentani were the bravest of all people, but they have arrived at that conclusion without considering well the words of Pliny, who describes this region, the fourth in his sequence. Pliny proceeded in the reverse order to mine, and began from the higher places. He says that the fourth region starts at the Tifernus river and is inhabited by peoples on the coast of the Frentani who are the bravest in Italy. What he means is that the Frentani themselves, and the peoples lying next to them, the Marrucini, Peligni, and Praetutii, are the bravest. But it is very well known to authorities on Roman history that the cohorts of the Peligni were preferred to others of the Latin name.

Next to the Alento river, and inland, lies Bucchianico, a noble town rich in olive oil. Also higher up beneath the Maiella is Roccamontepiano; and above the source of the Alento is Castel Menardo. Next after the Alento on the coast comes the Foro river, which also has its source at Mte. Maiella. And next to it, on the right bank, five miles from the sea, is the town of Villamagna. And higher up, also beneath Mte. Maiella, is the town of Pretoro, and the next town on the left bank of the Foro is Miglianico; and above it **[398G]** on the same river is another town, Fara. S. Martino Higher up is the fortified town of Rapino; and near the Maiella is Penna.

Another river, the Moro, is eight miles from the Foro on the shore. Since the fortified town of Tollo rises over the coast in that space, and is next to the Foro, the very ancient city of Ortona is next to the Moro, or two miles from it, and next to the sea. Ptolemy includes Ortona in the territory of the Peligni along with the mouth of the Pescara river. But I trust more in Pliny's authority for Italian places, and he allocates to the region of the Frentani whatever land extends from the mouth of the Pescara river to the Larinates. Indeed, even Ptolemy, along with Pliny, locates the city of Frentana on the left side of the Pescara, where Francavilla is today. I conclude that either Ptolemy's map was flawed, as it shows it on the opposite side, or the people who related the information to him were mistaken.

Between the city of Ortona and the Foro river up to Mte. Maiella, there are many towns and fortified villages. I shall go through them in the order in which they lie, from the lowest to the highest. Towering over Tollo is

docebimus. Tullo Iuvanum supereminet, et Ortonae ad dexteram Arum, Arovacrum, supraque ea oppida est Casa Candidella castellum. Superius Sanctus Martinus, et illi sinistrorsum est Flettum. Ortonam vero inter et Morum fluvium in mediterraneis est Crechium, superius **[398H]** sunt Ariellum atque Orsogna, Moroque fluvio ad sinistram haeret Sanctus Apollinaris. Supra est Frisium, et superius Castrum Novum Lanciani.

At supra eius fluvii fontem ad duos mille passus oppidum est Guardia Galli dictum. Parvus deinceps fluvius ad Morum sequitur Feltrinus, cui unicum haeret in litore castellum, Sanctus Vitus Lanciani dictum, et in eo quod quattuor milia passuum ad Sarum amnem intercedit spatio Lancianum oppidum praestantissimum quattuor item milibus a mari recedit, quod Anaxanum a maioribus appellatum magna populorum ad nundinas quotannis convenientium frequentia celebratur.

Lancianoque dextrorsum ad Maiellae radices Palumbarium procul abest, cui oppido Penna Castellum in montibus supereminet. Saro amni quem nunc corrupte Sangrum dicunt, dextrorsum in maritimis proximum est monasterium Sancti Ioannis, ubi celeberrimum fuit Veneris templum. Supra sunt castella, Fossa Caeca, et Rocha Sancti Ioannis Venere; superiusque Saro sunt proximae ingentes reliquiae urbis dirutae, quam Ptolemaeus et Plinius Bicam, nunc Secam incolae appellant. Auget dextrorsum amnem Sarum, sive Sangrum Aventinus fluvius, in Superequanis Pelignorum apud Furcam Palenae oriundus. In ipsumque Aventinum item dextrorsum se exonerat. Viridis torrens inter monasterium **[399A]** Sancti Martini, et Faram oppidum ex Maiella monte oriundus, et supra Sanctum Martinum Viridisque torrentis ortum Maiellae radicibus proxima sunt oppida, Civitella et Lama.

Aventino autem amni, postquam Viridi auctus est, dextrorsum proxima sunt oppida, Tarantum Lectumque Paleni, et Palenum pro Pelignum corrupte appellatum. Nam ea est Pelignorum altera pars, quos diximus Superaequanos a maioribus vocari, sicque paulo superius Furca oppidum, ubi Aventinus oritur, Palenae pro Peligna nunc dicitur, cui cernuntur proxima oppidi, ut apparet, vetustissimi fundamenta. Ornatum vero fuit Furca oppidum sancto et celebris famae anachorita Nicolao Furcensi, qui proximo anno apud urbem Romam centenarius est defunctus, miraculisque plurimis coruscavit.

Apud haec loca, ut in amplissimis montibus ampla et plana finit Mons Maiella, quem, ut diximus, superatum ab Apennino Samnitium olim, nunc Aprutii regio habet altissimum. Ad Furcam vero Palenae, sive Pelignam,

Iuvanum, and to the right of Ortona are Ari and Vacri, and above these towns is the fortified town of Casacanditella. Higher up is S. Martino, and to the left of it is Filetto. In the interior between Ortona and the Moro river is Crecchio. Higher up **[398H]** are Arielli and Orsogna, and on the left bank of the Moro is S. Apollinare. Above it is Frisa, and above that Castelnuovo.

But two miles above the source of this river is a town named Guardiagrele. Then a small river, the Feltrino, leads to the Moro. One fortified town clings to its bank, called S. Vito Chietino, and in the four-mile stretch between it and the Sangro river, and the same distance from the sea, is the outstanding town of Lanciano. It was called Anxanum by our ancestors, and is famous for the assembly every year of great crowd of people for a market.

The town of Palombaro is far off on the right of Lanciano at the foot of Mte. Maiella. In the mountains over this town hangs Pennapiedimonte. Next to the Saro river (which is now wrongly called the Sangro), on the right hand side on the coast is the monastery of S. Giovanni, where there was a famous temple of Venus. Above it are the fortified towns of Fossacesia, and Rocca S. Giovanni. Higher up next to the Sangro are the enormous ruins of a destroyed city, which Ptolemy and Pliny call Bica, but the inhabitants today call Seca. The Aventino river flows into the Saro (or Sangro) or the right-hand side; it has its source in the territory of the Superequani of the Peligni, at Furca Palenae. It empties into the same river, Aventino, on the right side. The stream called the Verde has its source on Mte. Maiella between the monastery **[399A]** of S. Martino and the town of Fara. S. Martino. And above S. Martino in valle and the source of the Verde, next to the foot of Mte. Maiella, are the towns Civitella and Lama dei Peligni.

After the Verde flows into the Aventino river, next to the Aventino on its right-hand side, are a number of towns: Taranta, and Lettopalena, and Palena, which is a name corrupted from Pelignum. For this is the other part of the Peligni, which I said our ancestors called the Superaequani; and so, a little higher up is the town of Furca Palenae, where the Aventino has its source, called by this name instead of Peligna. Next to it can be seen the foundations of a very old town. The town of Furca was distinguished by the famous and holy Anchorite Nicolò da Furca Palenae, who in the last year died in Rome at the age of a hundred, and shone with many miracles.

This region's highest mountain, surpassed by the Apennines of the former Samnium, now called Abruzzo, is the Montagna della Maiella. It borders these places, which are spacious and even, considering that they are in very great mountains. Bordering Furca Palenae (or Peligna), is a plain

planities sinistrorsum continet Furcae appellata, in qua sunt Peschum Constantium, et Rivus Sonulus oppida, populis frequentata, quae quidem loca brevibus, [399B] sed arctissimis, inter scabros montes semitis aditum habent ad planitiem quinummilium, quam supra in Superequanis Pelignorum primarium esse diximus.

Aventino amni sinistrorsum, qua eum influit torrens Viridis, proximum est Casale oppidum, superius collis Macinarum et Falascusium. Inde altissimi montes Piciorum Aventinum amnem usque ad fontem magnis et inaccessibilibus rupibus superincubant. Sed amni Saro sive Sangro supra Aventini amnis influxum item dextrorsum plurima adiacent oppida et castella, quae ascendendi ordo faciet notissima: Altinum, Rocha Scalogna, Gipsum, Turricella, Penna Hominis, Mons Niger, Bonanox, Villa, ubi ponte amnis est iunctus Mons Lapianus Fallum. Et paulo superius arduo inter montes altissimos aditu petitur Civitas Luparella oppidum, natura loci additis operibus, et populi frequentia munitissimum.

Supra sunt Quatrum, Misferatum, Gambatarum, Petra Ansuria, et secus Sari sive Sangri fluenta est oppidum Sancta Maria de quinque milibus, superius Rocha quinquemilium, deinde influit Sarum Rasinus torrens ad planitiem Furcae Pelignorum oriundus. Cui castellum haeret Rocha Rasini [399C] dictum. Superius ad Sarum sunt item dextrorsum Scontronum, post villa Vallis Regiae, Sari ipsius, sive Sangri, amnis fonti proxima.

At iuxta mare Saro amni sinistrorsum eiusdem nominis civitas vetusta erat apposita, cuius pridem destructae vestigia dinoscuntur. Superiusque Castrum Palietti proximis temporibus novum est suffectum a palearum copia dictum, quod in eum campestrem locum montanae adiacentis orae segetes demessae ad trituram a villicis congregantur. Prius vero quam adeatur proximus mons arduus Palani dictus, oppidum cui Archae appellatio est Saro proximum invenitur. In monte autem Palani oppida sunt, et castella, Bomia, Collis medius, et trans rivum Mons Ferrandus, inde Petra Ferracina.

Pertinet vero superius ad Sarum plurima item oppida et castella, quae ascendendo in fontem ordine describemus. Petrae Ferracinae supereminet Castrum Pili, et post est civitas Bucelli; deinde sunt Praesulum Pineatarii, Sanctus Angelus Pesculi, Castrum Iudicis clarum in regione memoria Iacobi Caudolae, magni per aetatem nostram exercituum ductoris, qui ex eo oppido duxit originem. Supraque est sinistrorsum, arduo in colle, oppidum Capra-

called *Furcae*. On this plain are heavily populated towns among which are Pescocostanzo and Rivisondoli. The approach to these towns is by short **[399B]** but narrow paths between rugged mountains to the Piano delle Cinquemiglia. As I mentioned, this is the chief plain among the Superaequani of the Peligni.

On the left of the Aventino river, where the stream Verde flows into it, is the town of Casale, then higher up are Colle di Macine and Fallascoso. From there, very high mountains of the Pici brood, with their great impassible cliffs, over the Aventino river right up to its source. But on the right-hand side of the Saro or Sangro river, above its juncture with the Aventino river, lie many towns and castelli; I shall note the best-known in ascending order: Altino, Roccascalegna, Gessopalena, Torricella Peligna, Pennadomo, Montenerodomo, Buonanotte, Villa S. Maria, where the river is spanned by a bridge; Montelapiano, Fallo, and a little higher up, you can reach by a difficult climb among high mountains the town of Civitaluparella. This town is well-fortified by the nature of the place, enhanced by manmade works, and by the density of its population.

Above this are Quadri, Pizzoferrato, Gamberale, Pietransieri, and next to the Saro or Sangro river and five miles away from it is the town of S. Maria, and Rocca is five miles higher up. Then the stream Rasino flows into the Sangro; it has its source on the plain of Furca Palenae. The fortified town called Roccaraso **[399C]** sits beside this river. Higher up on the Sangro are Scontrone on the right, and after that, next to the source of the Saro or Sangro river, the estate of *Vallis Regia*.

But next to the sea on the left-hand side of the Sangro river is an ancient city of the same name; you can see its ruins. Higher up is Paglieta, which has in recent times been given a new name after its abundant chaff, because the farm overseers gather the crops harvested from the nearby mountainous region at this level place for grinding. Before you get to the next high mountain, called Palani, you find next to the Sangro a town called Archi. On the mountain Palani are the towns and fortified villages of Bomba and Colle di Mezzo, and, across the stream, Monteferrante, and then Pietraferrazzana.

Higher up following the course of the Sangro are many towns, which I shall describe in order as they go up to the Sangro's source. Above Pietraferrazzana towers *Castrum Pili*, and after that is *Civitas Bucelli*; then come Pescopennataro, S. Angelo di Pesco, and Castel del Giudice. The latter is famous in local memory for Jacopo Caldora, a great military leader of our times who was born there. And above this, on the left, on a high hill, is the

cotta **[399D]**, et interius in depressa valle adiacet Maiellae Anglona, quod oppidum nunc in regione primarium prisci Aquiloniam appellavere. Inde Sanctus Petrus de Avelana, et postea ad Sari amnis fluenta oppidum est praestantissimum Castrum Sangri appellatum, opificibus variis, sed in primis fabris ferrariis frequentatum. Hi enim minima quaeque et maiuscula cuiusque usus instrumenta ex ferro tam fabre ducunt, ut paris ponderis ac mensurae argentea pulchritudine, ac pretio vel superent, vel aequent.

Supra Castrum Sangri eidem fluvio haeret oppidum Aufidena, de qua Livius in decimo, "Fulvii consulis clara pugna ad Bovianum fuit. Bovianum inde aggressus, nec multo post Aufidenam vi cepit."

Deinceps sunt castella, Vallis Regia, Civitella, Rocha; inter montes Opum et Pesculum Asserulum in Apennini iugo amnis Sarni fontibus subiectum. At in litore maris sequitur Sentus fluvius in monte Palario oriundus, cui in mediterraneis dextrorsum Atissa et Tornaticum oppida adiacent, et Sentum inter ac proximum Asinellam fluvium Sancti Stephani monasterium est in litore. Intus vero castella sunt et oppida: Turnium, Casale Burdinum, Polutrum, Sernium, Casalangra, Pilicornum. Ad Asinellaeque sinistram in litore est Penna castellum, superiusque Vastum Aimonis nobile et vetus oppidum, quod prisci dixere Histonium. **[400E]** Idque theatri vetustissimi vestigiis et palatio est ornatum quod Iacobus Caudola, ut in ea ora superbissimum, aedificavit.

Asinellaeque fluvio in mediterraneis dextrorsum adiacet Mons Dorisius oppidulum, comitatus ampli titulo insignitum, superiusque ad Asinellae fontem tendenti, castella sunt obvia, Gipsum, Carpinionum, Basilica, Gelinum, et Tripalum. Deinceps Asinellae proximus est in litore Trinius amnis Portuosus a Plinio appellatus. Sinistrorsum vero Trinius habet Montemnigrum oppidum quattuor milia passuum a mari, et totidem ad ipso fluvio semotum. Superiusque sunt Castellutium, Rochavivara, Triventum nobile oppidum, comitatus ampli titulum ditionemque habens, quod nunc Antonius Iacobus Caudola, et ipse fortissimus ductor possidet.

Inde sunt Salcitum, Fossa Caeca, Bagnodum, et Civitas Nova. Deinceps in ipsius Trivii amnis ortum, montes altissimi Apennino continuantur, quibus in montibus castella sunt rara, et ipsa populis infrequentia. Post Trivium

town Capracotta, **[399D]** and inland in a deep valley next to Mte. Maiella is Agnone, now the chief town in the region, called by the ancients Aquilonia. Next comes S. Pietro Avellana, and after that at the Sangro river is the outstanding town of Castel di Sangro, inhabited by many workmen in diverse trades, but especially by smiths. They forge very small and very large instruments, made out of iron so skillfully that they equal or surpass in beauty and value silver tools of the same weight and size.

Above Castel di Sangro, on the banks of the same river lies the town of Alfedena. Livy writes about it in book 10: "The consul C. Fulvius fought a famous battle at Bovianum, then attacked Bovianum, and soon after that took Aufidena."

Then come the fortified towns of *Vallis Regia*, Civitella, and Rocca; and in the mountains Opi and Pescasseroli on the Apennine ridge below the sources of the Sangro river. But the next river on the coast is the Osento, which has its source on Mte. Pallano. Next to it on the right towards the interior lie the towns Atessa and Tornareccio. On the coast between the Osento and the next river, the Sinello, is located the monastery of S. Stefano in Rivomare. Towards the interior are towns and fortified villages: Torre di Sangro, Casalbordino, Pollutri, Scerni, Casalanguida, Policorvo. On the left bank of the Sinello, on the coast, is the fortified town of Penna, and above it lies a noble and ancient town, Vasto, which the ancients called Histonium. **[400E]** And this town is distinguished by the traces of a very ancient theatre and a palace, the most splendid in that region, built by Jacopo Caldora.

On the right side of the Sinello river, towards the interior, lies the small town of Montedorisio, distinguished by the title of a full Count. And higher up, as you approach the source of the Sinello, you come across the fortified towns of Gissi, Carpineto Sinello, Basilica, Guilmi, and *Tripalum*. Then, next to the Sinello on the shore, is the Trigno river, called by Pliny "offering many harbors." On the left-hand bank of the Trigno is the town of Montenero, four miles from the sea, and equidistant from the same river, higher up, are Castelluccio, Roccavivara, and the noble town of Trivento, which possesses the title and terms of a full Count. Today it is the possession of Antonio, son of Jacopo Caldora, himself a very brave leader.

Next come Salcito, Fossalto, Bagnoli del Trigno, and Civitanova del Sannio. Then, towards the source of the Trigno river itself, very high mountains extend to the Apennines. In these mountains are few fortified villages, and the ones that are there are sparsely populated. After the Trigno river,

amnem Tifernus Samnitium in mare Adriaticum ultimus illabitur, qui fluvius apud Bovianum urbem vetustissimam in monte item Tiferno habet originem, de quo monte Livius in decimo, **[400F]** "Volumnius in Samnio interim res gerit. Samnitiumque exercitum in Tifernum montem compulsum, non deterritus iniquitate loci fundit fugatque."

Est in Tiferno amni ad dexteram oppidum Termole mari proximum, quam Guido Ravennas Interamniam vult fuisse dictam, ut locus videatur fuisse, in quo magnus philosophus Plato libros De ideis scripsit, quos in locis Italiae eius orae, et in urbe Interamnia illum scripsisse constant. Intus octavo a mari miliario amni Tiferno ad mille passus haeret Guillimacum oppidum nobile, et superius VII item miliario est Guardia Alferi dicta. Inde Luparia, Carchabotatium, Lucitum, Lumesanum, Castrum Pignani, Rochetta, Casale Riparandi, Lispinetum, Tornaquisium. Et supremo, ut diximus, loco, Bovianum, quae urbs ditissima, et paene omnium totius Samnii primaria aliquando fuit habita. Livius enim libro IX, "Consules egregia victoria parta protinus inde ad Bovianum oppugnandum legiones ducunt, ibique hiberna egerunt." Et infra,

> Inde victor exercitus Bovianum ductus. Captum hoc erat Pentheorum Samnitum longe ditissimum atque opulentissimum armis virisque. Spe praedae milites accensi, oppido potiuntur, praedae **[400G]** plus ibi, quam ex omni Samnio umquam est egestum, benigneque omnis militi concessa.

Et infra, cum Bovianum rebellasset, "C. Fulvii consulis clara pugna ad Bovianum fuit. Bovianum inde aggressus, nec ita multo post Aufidenam vi cepit."

Sed iam finis adest Samnitium regionis, quae a Troento ad Tifernum amnem Apulis continentem, Apennino et mari supero, sive Adriatico concluditur, quamquam nunc Aprutium, ut diximus, corrupto a Praecutinis verbo appellant. Ad aliam transeundum est partem Samnitum, qui Transapenninum incoluere. Difficiliorem vero habet haec regio ceteris omnibus descriptionem, non solum quod multis abundat rebus in ea gestis, verum quia haec sola Apenninum hincinde complexa est, ut flumina, quibus dividitur designaturque proxima regio Campania prius dimidiata in montibus huic ipsi Samnio, post in campos deducta Campaniae sint attribuenda. Habebit

the Biferno is the last river of the Samnites to flow into the Adriatic Sea. This river has its source at the very ancient city of Bojano, on the mountain also formerly called Tifernus, now Montagna del Matese. Livy writes about this mountain in his tenth book: **[400F]** "Volumnius meanwhile was conducting operations in Samnium. Undeterred by the uneven ground, he drove the Samnite army up onto Mt. Tifernus, and put them to flight."

On the Biferno river, on the right, is the town of Termoli, next to the sea. It is this town which Guido of Ravenna indicates was the ancient Interamna, in order to identify it as the place in which the great philosopher Plato wrote his *Republic*; it is well known that he wrote this in places on the Italian coast, and in a city called Interamna. Eight miles inland and a mile from the Biferno lies the noble town Guiglionesi; and seven miles above this is Guardialferia. From there: Lupara, Castelbottacio, Lucito, Limosano, Castropignano, Roccaspromonte, Casalciprano, Spinete, Colle d'Anchise. And in the highest place, as I said, is the very wealthy city Bojano, which was once considered the foremost city in almost all of Samnium. We know this from Livy, who writes in book 9, "The consuls won a great victory and immediately took their legions to besiege Bovianum. There they spent the winter." And later he writes,

> They led the victorious army to Bovianum. This is the capital of the Pentri, a Samnite people, and by far the wealthiest and most splendid in weapons and manpower. The soldiers' hope of booty was aroused. They gained possession of the town. **[400G]** More booty was taken from there than from all of Samnium. It all was conceded peacefully to the soldiers.

After this, Livy writes, when Bovianum had rebelled, "The consul Cornelius Fulvius fought a famous battle there. He attacked Bovianum and not long afterward took Aufidena."

But now we have come to the end of the Samnite region which is enclosed from the Tronto to the Biferno river, which bounds the region in Puglia, and by the Apennines and the upper, or Adriatic, Sea. Now, as I said, the name Abruzzo has been corrupted from Praecutini. My next task is to cross over to the other part of the Samnites who lived across the Apennines. The description of this region will be more difficult than all the rest, not only because it is rich in historical events, but because this region alone encloses the range of Apennines on either side. The result is that the rivers which delimit the next region, Campania, are first divided in the mountains into two equal parts and flow into this direction, Samnium; then, where they

tamen id commodi ipsa descriptio, qua faciliorem reddit Campaniae descriptionem, quia quae Samnium ad hanc partem in montibus terminant flumina, eadem quoque Campaniam in mediterraneis, et ad mare complectuntur.

Liris itaque nunc Gaurianus duos in Samnio habet **[400H]** fontes, unum ad Capistrellum, in Apennino castellum, et octavo supra Soram miliario; alterum ad postam castellum, quattuor ad Sora milibus distans; fonsque hic aquis copiosissimus esse videtur ille, quem Plinius asserit videri a lacu Fucino originem trahere. Duo hi rami, cum infra Soram coeant insulam efficiunt. In qua sunt castella Peschum, Posta, et Lobrottulum. Soram autem vetusti praesentisque nominis urbem Samnium primam hac in parte habet, de qua Livius in septimo, L. Genu*c*io, Sergio Cornelio consulibus Soram atque Albam coloniae deductae. Sora agri Vestini fuerat. Sed possederant Samnites. Eo quattuor milia hominum missa.

Quod autem Soram dicit Livius fuisse agri Vestini hac ratione certum est: quia cum Vestina urbs fuerit ad Lirim in campis, qui nunc Sessae dicuntur. Sicut in Campaniae descriptione dicemus, quicquid ab ostio Liris, quo in mare defluit, ad Soram usque ipsi adiacebat fluvio, Vestinorum vocabulo est comprensum. Unde Lucanus, Lirim describens, dicit, Vestinis impulsus aquis. Et Suessa Pometia, qua nunc est Sessa, Vestinorum appellata est. Cum vero Sorani ad suos Samnites defecissent, sic de eis dicit Livius,

> Mutata tamen belli sedes est ad Soram, et ex Samnio Apuliaque traductae legiones. Sora ad Samnites defecerat, interfectis colonis Romanorum, quo cum prior Romanus exercitus ad ulciscendum **[401A]** civium necem, recuperandamque coloniam magnis itineribus pervenisset, sparsi per vias speculatores sequi legiones Samnitium, nec iam procul abesse alii super alios nuntiant. Obviam itum hosti, atque ad Lausulas ancipiti proelio dimicatum est Soram inde reditum, novique consules M. Petilius, C. Sulpicius, quia per difficilem urbis situm Soranus transfuga decem Romanos in arcem duxit, et civibus per noctem refractis vi portis fugientibus ingres-

flow down into the plains, they should be assigned to Campania. The description of this region makes convenient, however, the description of Campania, because these same rivers bound Campania also, in the interior and on the coast.

And so the Liris, now called Garigliano, has in Abruzzo **[400H]** two sources: one, at Capistrello, a fortified town in the Apennines eight miles above Sora; the other, four miles from Sora at the fortified town of Posta Fibreno. This spring, with its abundantly flowing waters, seems to be the one which Pliny claims appears to have its source in the Fucine Lake. When these two branches come together below Sora, they create an island; and on it are the fortified towns of Pescosolido, Posta Fibreno, and Broccostella. Sora is both the ancient and modern name of the foremost city of the Samnites in this area. Livy writes about it in his seventh book:

> L. Genucius and Servilius Cornelius were the consuls. Colonies were sent to Sora and Alba. Sora had been part of the Vestine territory but the Samnites had taken possession of it. Four thousand men were sent there.

The fact that Livy says that Sora was part of Vestine territory is conclusive, for this reason: the city of Vestina was on the Liris river, in fields which are now called Sessae; so I will note in my description of Campania. The name of the Vestini comprises whatever land lies next to the river from the mouth of the Liri where it flows into the sea right up to Sora. Thus Lucan, in his description of the Liris river, says, "Driven by the waters of the Vestini." Also, the ancient Suessa Pometia, now Sessa, was called "of the Vestini." About the defection of the inhabitants of Sora to join their fellow Samnites, Livy wrote:

> The theatre of war changed to Sora, and the legions were transferred out of Samnium and Apulia. Sora had defected to the Samnites, and murdered its Roman colonists. The Roman army, after a long and difficult journey, arrived to avenge the slaughter **[401A]** of citizens and restore the colony. But one after another the scouts, dispersed throughout the roads, announced that the Samnite legions were in pursuit and not far away. The Romans went to meet the enemy, and fought a battle of ambiguous fortune near Lautulae.... Then the Romans returned to Sora, and the new consuls, M. Petilius and C. Sulpicius.... Because the city lay in a difficult position, a deserter from Sora led ten Romans into the citadel. The citizens broke down the gates at night in their haste to escape. The

> sus est Romanus exercitus, trecenti XXV qui omnium consensu designabantur nefandae colonorum caedis et defectionis auctores vincti, Romam ducti, et virgis in foro caesi, et securi percussi summo gaudio plebis, cuius maxime intererat tutam ubicumque in coloniis multitudinem esse.

Soram vero, cum post praedictam cladem deducta a Romanis fuisset nova colonia, et diu satis floruisset, Federicus secundus imperator Germanicus per tempora Gregorii IX pontificis Romani eam destruxit. Nihilominus ipsa nunc ducatus titulo et duce optimo litterisque decorato ornata mediocris oppidi populum divitiasque habet.

Insulae quam bifurcatus in Samnio Liris, sicut ostendimus, efficit. **[401B]** Montes supereminent altissimi ad Apennini iuga pertinentes, in quibus nulla est hominum habitatio. Eisque dextrorsum adiacet Plaga, ut in ea montium asperitate amoenissima, cui nunc Cominum est appellatio; montibus enim circumsaepta altissimis, castella habet ad octo populis frequentia Vicalium, Alvetum, Sanctum Donatum, Septem Fratres, Picinestum, Calinarium, et Casaliverum. Eam vero Plagam vetustissimi Comminium appellavere ab urbe eius nominis, cuius locum incolae nunc ignorant, de qua Livius in decimo. Inde Carvilius ad Comminium captum. Caesa quattuor milia octuaginta, accepta in fidem XV milia CCCC.

Sed hac eadem in ora montibus dextrorsum subiecta est Atina, urbs vetustissima, secus quam Melfa fluvius labitur, ex Apennino oriundus, et apud Fregellas in Lirim defluens. Estque Atina, quam Virgilius facit arma Aeneae fabricasse:

> Quinque adeo magnae positis incudibus urbes
> Tela novant Atina potens. . . .

Et Livius in nono,

> C. Petilius dictator, cum audiisset arcem Fregellanam ab Samnitibus captam, omisso Boviano, ad Fregellam pergit. Unde nocturna Samnitium fuga sine certamine receptis Fregellis, praesidioque **[401C]** valido imposito, in Campaniam reditum maxime ad Nolam armis repetendam. Quae capta est a C. Cassio consule, a quo etiam Atina et Calatia captae.

> Roman army entered the city. Three hundred and twenty-five men, who were by common consent identified as the instigators of the execrable slaughter of the colonists and of the defection, were led in chains to Rome and beaten in the Forum. They were executed with an axe to the great joy of the plebs, in whose interest it especially was that the great number of people sent out everywhere to colonies be safe.

After this slaughter, a new colony was sent out to Sora, which did well for a long time. The German emperor Frederick II destroyed it during the reign of Pope Gregory IX. Although it now has the distinction of the title of duchy and a great duke noted for his literary learning, its population and wealth are those of a middle-sized town.

I mentioned that the Liri river splits in two to create an island. **[401B]** There are very high mountains towering over it; uninhabited, they belong to the Apennine chain. And on the right-hand side, Plaga adjoins the mountains, a very pleasant break from their harshness. Its modern name is Comino; it is hedged around by very high mountains. It contains about eight densely inhabited fortified towns: Vicalvi, Alvito, S. Donato Val di Comino, Settefrati, Picinisco, Gallinaro, and Casalvieri. The ancients called this town Plaga Comminium from a city of that name; the modern inhabitants do not know its location. Livy writes about it in his tenth book: "Then Carvilius during the capture of Comminium killed about 4,800; 15,400 were received under terms."

But in the same area, lying under the right-hand side of the mountains, is the very ancient city of Atina. The river Melfa flows beside it; its source is in the Apennines and it debouches at Ceprano into the Liri. Virgil has the weapons of Aeneas manufactured at Atina:

> Five great cities, with anvils set up,
> renew his weapons: powerful Atina. . . .

And Livy, book 9, writes:

> The dictator C. P[o]et*e*lius, when he heard that the citadel of Fregellae had been captured by the Samnites and Bovianum had been lost, hastened to Fregellae. Without joining battle, the Samnites fled from there during the night. The people of Fregellae took them in, **[401C]** a strong garrison was put in place. They returned to Nola which they recaptured. The consul C. Cassius captured it and he also captured Atina and Collatia.

Descendendo ad infima praedictae regionis montanae, fluvio Melfae sub Casaliveri castello sinistrorsum haeret Schiavi oppidulum. Inferius celso item in loco est Arpinum, fama celeberrimum M. Tullii Ciceronis, et C. Marii, quos habuit gloriosissimos cives, de qua Livius in nono, "Eo anno Sora et Arpinum recepta a Samnitibus." Et libro decimo, "Arpinatibus et Trebulanis civitas data." Et sub Arpino Melfae fluvio sinistrorsum proxima sunt castella, Fontana et Arce. At sub Sora, ubi bina Liris capita coeunt, est Insula oppidum, ab ipsis duobus fluviis circumdatum, quod maiores Interamniam appellavere. Et secundum eius fluvii decursum castella, Turris, Campus Latus, et Insuletta inveniuntur. Est etiam nunc paulo superior parva nunc, sicut semper fuit insula magno eloquentibus gaudio invisenda, apud quam natus est et non Arpini M. Cicero. Sic enim ipse in suis Legibus scriptum reliquit:

> Sed ventum in insulam est. Hac vero nihil est amoenius. Ut enim hoc quasi rostro finditur Fibrenus, **[401D]** et divisus aequaliter in duas partes latera haec adluit, rapideque dilapsus, cito in unum confluit. Et tantum complectitur quod satis sit modicae palestrae loci, quo effecto tamquam id habuerit operis ac muneris, ut hanc nobis effecerit sedem ad disputandum statim praecipitat in Lirim. Et quasi in patriciam familiam venerit, amittit nomen obscurius, Liremque multo gelidiorem facit. Nec enim ullum hoc frigidius flumen attigi, cum ad multa accesserim, ut vix pede tentare id possim, quod in Phaedro Platonis facit Socrates.

Et infra, secundo libro,

> Quia si verum dicimus, haec est mea, et huius fratris mei germana patria, hic enim orti stirpe antiquissima sumus. Hic sacra, hic genus, hic maiorum multa vestigia. Quid plura? Hanc vides villam, ut nunc quidem est lautius aedificatam patris nostri studio, qui cum esset infirma valetudine, hic fere aetatem egit in litteris. Sed hoc ipso in loco, cum avus viveret, et antiquo more parva esset villa, ut illa Curiana in Sabinis, me scito esse natum. Quare id est nescio quid, quod latet in animo ac sensu meo, quo me plus hic locus fortasse delectet.

You will find the little town of Schiavi lying close by the left hand bank of the Melfa river, under the fortified town of Casalvieri, as it flows down to the lowest part of this region. And lower down is Arpino, famous as the birthplace and home of Cicero and Marius. Livy writes of it in book 9, "That year Sora and Arpinum were recaptured by the Samnites." And in book 10, "Citizenship was granted to the Arpinates and to the people of Trebula." Below Arpino, very close to the Melfa river on its left bank, are the fortified towns Fontana and Arce. But below Sora, where the two branches of the Liri come together, is the town of Isola di Liri. It is surrounded by the streams of these two branches of the river, so our ancestors called it Interamna. Following the descent of this river, we find the fortified towns of Torre, Colle Alto, and Isoletta. The latter is even now a little higher, and small, and now, as always, a pleasure for eloquent men to visit; it was actually at this island and not at Arpinum, that Cicero was born. He left the following evidence in his *Laws*:

> But we have come to the island. Truly nothing is pleasanter. It cuts the Fibrenus in two like the beak of a ship. **[401D]** The river flows past its sides, flows downwards swiftly, and comes back together into one stream. The island it makes is only about as large as a middle-sized palestra. Immediately after creating this island as if making a place for us to converse, it hurls itself into the Liris. And, as if it had entered a patrician family, it discards its less famous name, and makes the water of the Liris much colder. Although I have visited many rivers, I have never come upon one colder than this; so cold that I could hardly stand testing its waters with my foot, as Socrates does in Plato's *Phaedrus*.

And further on in the second book:

> This is my native place, and my brother's: for our family, a very ancient one, originated from this area; here are our sacred rites, here is the origin of our race; here are many traces of our ancestors. What more should I say? This is the farmhouse you see, with the painstaking renovations my father made to it. Since he was an invalid, he spent almost all of his time here among his books. I was born right here, while my grandfather was alive and while the property was small, in the old-fashioned way, like Curius's Sabine farm. So there is a certain feeling for the place deep in my soul that makes me take, perhaps, a greater pleasure in it.

Succedit ordine describendus a nobis fluvius apud pontem Corvum, ubi olim Fregellas fuisse diximus, cadens in Lirim, et apud montis Casini radices labens. Cui fluvio haud longe remotum, et Casino ad quinque milia proximum, est Campestre oppidum, **[402E]** gloria Arpino nullatenus cedens, Aquinum, Thoma primum sanctissimo atque doctissimo ecclesiae doctore, et Pescennino Nigro imperatore Romano, certe praestantissimo, ac Iuvenale poeta satirico civibus decoratum. Gregorius quoque VII pontifex Romanum, anno salutis tertio septuagesimo, supra millesimum, Roberto Guiscardo Apuliae et Calabriae ducatum in Aquino oppido solenniter concessit.

At ultra Aquinum hinc est sinistrorsum Rocha Sicca oppidum, inde celso in monte, ubi olim urbs fuit Casinensis, est monasterium Casinense a sancto celebrique monachorum patre Benedicto aedificatum, quamquam ea quae nunc exstant ipsius monasterii aedificia non sunt illa, quae bonus ipse pater Benedictus exstruxit, quod paulo post illius obitum Longobardi omnia funditus demoliti sunt. Contulit se ad id monasterium Totila rex Ostrogothorum fama ductus sanctimoniae tanti viri, et tentare volens, si quod sibi dictum erat, Benedictus spiritu prophetico occulta cognosceret. Sese famulum indumento mentitus alium praemisit, qui regio ornatu et apparatu regem Totilam simularet, quem recognitum sanctus abbas, cum placido vultu ad ceterum famulatum reiecisset, regem digito significatum, ut erat sordide indutus, ad se **[402F]** in monasterii vestibulum vocavit. Nec tamen haec et alia sanctitatis signa, quae Longobardi a Benedicto viderunt, adeo eos continere potuerunt, quin praescito, et per sanctum ipsum monachis praedicto Dei iudicio, crudelis et effera gens praedicta celebre id coenobium diruerit.

Ad Casini quoque montis radices novum est oppidum Sanctus Germanus, a sancti abbatis conditoris sui nomine appellatum, intra cuius moenia, et per circuitum scatentes uberrimi fontes, amnem augent quarto supra miliario apud oppidum Sanctum Eliam oriundum, qui tertius Lirim amnem in Samnitibus efficit. Isque amnis duodecim expletis passuum milibus, in maiorem Liris cursum apud castellum Pontem Corvum, sicut ostendimus, cadit. Urbs vero quam fuisse diximus in Casino monte republica florente, fuit Romana colonia, de qua Livius in nono, "Volsci Pontiam insulam sitam in conspectu litoris sui incoluerant, et vicerunt, ut Casinum deduceretur colonia, sicut factum est."

Traditque Plinius, Lucio Crasso, Caio Cassio Longino consulibus Casini puerum factum ex virgine **[402G]** sub parentibus, iussuque haruspicum

Following my regular arrangement, I must next describe the Melfa river at Pontecorvo (the location as I said, of ancient Fregellae), where it flows into the Liri, past the foot of Monte Cassino. Not far from this river, and about five miles from Cassino, is a town in the plains, **[402E]** Aquino, as famous as Arpino because it boasts as citizens Thomas Aquinas, the very holy and learned doctor of the church; the outstanding Roman emperor Pescennius Niger; and the poet and satirist Juvenal. It was at Aquino in 1370 that Pope Gregory VII formally conceded to Robert Guiscard the duchy of Apulia and Calabria.

But beyond Aquino on this side, on the left is the town of Roccasecca. On the far side, on a high mountain, where the city of Casinum used to stand, is the monastery of Cassino, which was built by the famous holy father of monks, Benedict. The buildings which stand there now are not those which the good father Benedict built, because a little after his death, the Lombards completely destroyed all of them. Totila, King of the Ostrogoths, went to that monastery, drawn by the report of the great man's holy nature. He wanted to test Benedict's famed powers of divination by seeing if Benedict would recognize him dressed as a slave. So he sent ahead of him someone disguised as him, in kingly dress with royal pomp. The holy abbot recognized this man and with a serene expression pushed him back to the rest of the slaves, and pointed with his finger to the king, who was dressed poorly, summoning him **[402F]** onto the front porch of the monastery. But although the Lombards saw this and other signs of holiness from Benedict, this cruel and savage race could not be restrained by these signs from destroying this famous monastery, a judgment of God foreknown and foretold by that holy monk.

Also at the foot of Monte Cassino there is a new town, called S. Germano after its founder, a holy abbot. Within its walls and around it are abundantly gushing fountains. Four miles above, at the town of S. Elia, they contribute to a river, which has its source here and is the third tributary of the Liri river in Abruzzo. Twelve miles along this river's course, it flows into the greater Liri river at the fortified town of Ponza, as I have shown. This city, which I said was located on Monte Cassino, was a Roman colony in Republican times. Livy wrote about it in book 9, "The Volscians had inhabited Pontiae, an island located in sight of their own coast. And they prevailed, and it happened that a colony was sent out to Casinum. . . ."

And Pliny tells us that in the consulship of L. Crassus and C. Cassius Longinus, at Casinum a girl turned into a boy **[402G]** before the parents'

deportatam in insulam desertam. Et Livius libro XXII, "imperat duci, ut se in agrum Casinatem ducat, edoctus a peritis regionis, si eum saltum occupasset exitum Romano ad opem ferendam sociis interclusurum." Livius quoque viam describens, qua Hannibal ex Campania Romam petiit, sic habet in XXVI:

> per Suessulam Alifanumque et Casinatem agrum in viam Latinam ducit, sub Casinum biduo stativa habita, et passim populationes actae, inde praeter Interamniam Aquinumque in Fregellanum agrum ad Lirim fluvium.

Interamniam vero fuisse credimus, ubi sub Sancto Germano ad duo milia passuum eidem fluvio magnae ingentesque vetustorum operum ruinae continent, et Fregellas fuisse, quem nunc Pontem Corvum dicimus, satis constat.

Ultimo supra dicti Liris fonte apud Sanctum Eliam oriundo, haud longe Vulturni amnis origo distat. Nam cum intra duodecim milia passuum Vallem Rotundam, et aquam fundatam oppidula ad Apenninum pergens, post tergum reliquerit, Sancti Vicentii oppidum reperit, quod monasterio eiusdem nominis, a quo id accepit nomen, ad mille passus est proximum. Idque monasterium olim **[402H]** frequentia monachorum opumque affluentia et magnificentia aedificii celeberrimum omnibus paene nunc temporum militia spoliatum est. Circumdatum vero est nascentis loco Vulturni fluviolo, qui brevi cursu maximum a scatentibus circumquaque fontibus accipit incrementum. Isque amnis superiore partem, sicut diximus, per Samnites delapsus Campaniam postea in mediterraneis et maritimis paene dimidiam dividit. Qua ratione cum ab ostiis, quibus in mare defluit, nunc ex more nostro non liceat descriptionem, econtra a fronte incipimus. Primum descendentes ad dexteram oppidum Vulturno adiacens Montaquillum inveniunt. Post Rocham Ravimolam, deinde Sanctam Mariam de Oliveto, deinceps obvium est Venafrum in Campaniae partibus describendum.

In montibus autem Apennino contiguis, qui Vulturni amnis fonti dextrorsum supereminent sunt castella, Mons Niger et Rivus Frigidus, et inferi-

eyes, and the soothsayers ordered her to be sent away to a deserted island. Livy writes in book 22,

> He ordered his guide to lead him into the territory of Casinum . . . having learned from those familiar with the area . . . if he had occupied the forest he would shut off an exit from the Romans bringing aid to their allies.

Livy also describes the road on which Hannibal left Campania and made for Rome. This is what he writes in book 26:

> . . . through Suessula and Alifanum and the territory of Casinum he led his army to the Via Latina . . . made camp for two days below Casinum, and then marched past Interamna and Aquinum into the territory of Fregellae to arrive at the Liris river.

I believe that Interamna is the city, two miles below S. Germano, whose enormous ruins of very ancient buildings lie beside this same river. It is securely established that ancient Fregellae was located where now is the place called Pontecorvo.

The source of the Volturno river is not far from the last source of the Liri I mentioned above, at S. Elia. When you go towards the Apennines, within twelve miles you pass the little towns of Vallerotonda and Acquafondata, and come upon the town of S. Vicenzo al Volturno. It takes its name from a nearby monastery about a mile away. Once this monastery was famous for **[402H]** its great numbers of monks, its wealth, and the splendor of its buildings. But now the evil of our times has almost ruined it. It is surrounded by the small stream of the Volturno as it rises from its source; in a short space it takes on greater size as a result of the tributary springs all around it. As I have mentioned, this river in its upper course falls through the territory of the Samnites into Campania, and then divides Campania almost in half, into inland and coastal areas. For this reason I cannot now follow my customary procedure and describe it starting from the mouths through which it flows into the sea. I begin my description on the contrary from its source. If you go down on the right hand side you find the town of Montaquila, lying next to the Volturno. After that come Roccaravindola, and then S. Maria de Oliveto. Then right on the way is Venafro, whose description belongs in the chapter on Campania.

Moreover, in the mountains adjoining the Apennine range which tower over the source of the river Volturno on the right-hand side, we find the fortified villages of Montenero and Riofreddo, and beneath them is the forti-

us est Forulum vetusti nominis castellum. Postea secundum Vulturni decursum descendentes Fornellum ipsi amni ad tria milia passuum proximum inveniunt, quod oppidum novi nominis populo opibusque plenum, vini praestantiam in regione habet. Vulturnoque e regione Fornelli continet vallis, quam Porcinam appellant, in qua vetusti, et ut apparet, magni olim oppidi ruinae conspiciuntur, pauloque inferius Vulturnum influit amnis ab **[403A]** Esernia delapsus vetusta olim Romana colonia, de qua Livius in belli Italici sive socialis LXXII, Esernia et Alba coloniae ab Italis obsessae.

Ad eum vero Eserniae fluvium paulo prius, quam in Vulturnum labatur, vestigia cernuntur ingentia urbis usque ad fundamenta dirutae. Quam fuisse constat Telesiam urbem Samnitium potentissimam, de qua Livius in XXII, "Hannibal ex Hirpinis in Samnium transit, Beneventanum depopulatur agrum, Telesiam urbem capit." Et in XXIIII, Fabius in Samnio oppida vi recepit Compulteriam Telesiamque.

Et Compulteria quidem Telesiae dextrorsum vicina fuit, in ea tamen proclivior loca, quae nunc Trapiatam et Pratum appellant ac Mastratum, deinceps Beneventana sequitur ora totius Samnii primaria, et ceteris de Italia rerum gestarum multitudine ac magnitudine copiosior, quae monte habet Apenninum sua celsitudine superantes, rivis alicubi, rupibusque omnino insuperabilibus separatos. Est tamen fluviis, torrentibus, lacu, fontibus quam irrigua, protenditur vero haec ipsa Samnii pars, si Apennini iugum sequimur milibus passuum octuaginta ab ipsis Vulturni fontibus ad Silaris Lucaniae fluvii ac limitis **[403B]** ortum. Et qui ipsi insunt orae fluvii praeter admodum paucos, unico amne Sabbato excepti, defluunt in Vulturnum, ut Sabbatum parte infima stipes ceteri amnes arboris rami esse videantur, unde cogimur ab ipso incipientes stipite ramos, qui ad dexteram ascendendo inveniuntur primum, postea eos, qui sinistrorsum Apennino dilabuntur ex superiore instituto nostro describere, intraque eam arboris amnium descriptionem, quicquid regionis Samnitium nobis est reliquum comprehendemus.

Attingamque prius eos amnes qui dextera Sabbati confluentia quam longe ab Apennino in mediterraneis oriuntur, primusque post Eserniensem Pratellus fluvius a proximo eius nominis oppido appellatus, ex infimis

fied town of Foruli, an ancient name. After that, if we follow the flow of the Volturno we find Fornelli, next to the river about three miles distant; a town with a new name, it has much population and wealth, and is considered to have the best wine in the region. There is bordering on the Volturno in the vicinity of Fornelli a valley called Porcina where one can see the ruins of an old and, as it seems, a formerly great town. And a little below, a river flows down from Isernia into the Volturno. **[403A]** Isernia is an old city, once a Roman colony. Livy writes about it in book 72, on the Italian or Social War: "The colonies of Aesernia and Alba were besieged by the Italians."

At this site, a little before the river Iserno flows into the Volturno, one can see the huge ruins of a city which was destroyed right to the foundations. It is fairly certain that this was Telesia, the most powerful city of the Samnites. Livy writes about it in book 22, "Hannibal crossed from the territory of the Hirpini into Samnium; he laid waste the territory of Beneventum, and captured the city of Telesia." And in book 24 he writes, "Fabius took back by force these cities in Samnium: Compulteria and Telesia."

And Compulteria was next to Telesia on the right-hand side, but more downhill towards the places which they now call Trapiata and Prato and Mastrata. Next comes Benevento, chief city of the entire Samnite coast; it is greater than the other Samnite cities, both in the importance of historical events there and in its size; and has mountains that surpass the Apennines in height. They are separated in places by completely impassable streams and rocks. It is well-watered, though, by torrents, a lake, springs. But this part of Samnium extends, if we follow the ridge of the Apennines, for 80 miles from the very sources of the Volturno to the source of the Sele, the river of Lucania and its border. And the rivers within the border **[403B]** except for a few, are received by the Calore river alone; and they all flow into the Volturno, with the result that the other rivers seem to be the branches of a tree which has as its trunk the Calore. Thus I must begin from the trunk of the tree and, according to my established method, describe first the branches which are found as you go up on the right-hand side, and then those which disperse from the Apennines on the left, beginning on the top according to my method. Within my description of this tree-like scheme of rivers, I shall include whatever part of Samnium I have omitted.

I shall first treat those rivers which have their source at the right-hand side of their confluence with the Sabato, before those which arise in the interior far from the Apennines. The first river after the one at Isernia is the Pratellus (Lete), which takes its name from the nearby town and has its

Mathesii montis radicibus ortum habet. Nam Mathesium Apennini promontorium et in sublime surgens, et longe in mediterranea lateque diffusum, sterile ut plurimum atque petrosum, unico ad hanc partem castello habitatum est Gallo Pratelli amnis fonti proximo. Fuitque mons in quo primarii Samnitium habitavere viri fortes, utpote montani, unde Montesii prius appellabantur, a quibus facta verbi corruptela Mathesium dicitur **[403C]** promontorium. Hi autem montes sunt, de quibus habet Livius IX,

> Samnites ea tempestate in montibus vicatim habitantes campestria et maritima loca contempto cultu molliore, atque, ut evenit, loci dissimilitudine ipsi montani atque agrestes depopulabantur. Quae regio si fida Samnitibus fuisset, haud pervenire Arpos Roman*us* quivisset exercitus.

Sub Mathesio lacus est decem milia passuum circuitu complexus, ad cuius inferiora parum a Vulturno distantia Aylonum est oppidum, inde Sancti Angeli castellum de Rupe Canina appellatum, a quo haud longe recedit pes montis oppidum colli superimpositum arduo, ex quo fluvius oritur brevi quattuor milium cursu secus Aliphas urbem decidens in Vulturnum, ut eum collem esse oporteat illum, in quo Fabius Maximus Hannibalem insecutus arduo consedit loco, sicut Livius in XXIII per haec verba habet,

> Hannibal transducto per saltum et quibusdam in ipso saltu hostibus oppressis in agro Aliphano posuit castra. Fabius quoque movit castra, transgressusque saltum super Aliphas loco alto ac communito consedit;

et de Aliphis in IX, "Dum haec in Etruria geruntur, consul alter C. Martius Rutilius **[403D]** Aliphas de Samnitibus vi cepit." Et infra,

> Fabius consul ad urbem Aliphas cum Samnitium exercitu signis collatis conflixit. Minime ambigua res fuit, fusi hostes, atque in castra compulsi, postera die deditio fieri coepta, et pacti qui Samnitium forent cum singulis vestimentis emitterentur; hi omnes sub iugum missi. Sociis Samnitium nihil cautum, ad septem milia

source at the bottom of Monte del Matese. This Matese is a promontory of the Apennines; it rises up to a great height. It spreads out far and wide in the interior and is for the most part dry and rocky. In this direction there is only one settlement, Gallo, next to the source of the Lete river. This was the mountain on which the Samnite chieftains lived, brave men, as one would expect with mountaineers. For this reason, they were first called "Montesii" (mountain men), then the word was corrupted and gave the name "Mathesium" to the **[403C]** promontory. Moreover, these are the mountains about which Livy writes in book 9:

> The Samnites were at that time living in villages in the mountains; they used to plunder the fields and places on the coast, wild mountain men who scorned their inhabitants' luxurious lifestyles which, as is often the case, reflected their soft environment. If this region had remained loyal to the Samnites, the Roman army could scarcely have gotten through to Arpi. . . .

At the foot of the Matese there is a lake ten miles in circumference. On its lower side, a short distance from the Volturno, is the town of Ailano. Then comes the fortified town of S. Angelo d'Alife, which is near the foot of the mountain. The town is perched on a high hill. Here is the source of a river which has a brief course, only four miles long. It flows into the Volturno beside the city of Alife, and this causes me to identify this hill with the one where Fabius Maximus, after pursuing Hannibal, "settled on a high place." Livy in book 23 says the following:

> . . . after leading his army through the pass and overcoming some of the enemy in the pass itself, Hannibal pitched camp in the territory of Allifae. . . . Fabius also changed his camp; crossing the glade, he took up a position in a high fortified place above Allifae.

Livy also writes about Allifae in book 9, "While these things were going on in Etruria, the other consul, C. Marcius Rutulus, took **[403D]** Allifae from the Samnites." And further on,

> the consul Fabius fought with the Samnite army at the city of Allifae. The outcome of the battle was not at all in doubt. The enemy were routed and driven into their camp, and on the next day they began to surrender. The arrangement was that the Samnites could be released with one garment each. They were all sent under the yoke. There was no provision made for the allies of the Samnites, so about seven thousand of them were captured and sold as slaves.

> sub corona venerunt, qui se civem Hernicum diceret in custodia habitus.

Fluvius inde sequitur supra Petram Roiam oppidum ex Mathesio oriundus Cusanum correctum habens oppositum, qui prope Puianellum oppidum labitur in Vulturnum, habetque sinistrorsum is fluvius oppidum Faviculum, et Loium in mediterraneis propinquum.

Sed iam ad Sabbati stipitem est perventum. Is amnis primo dextrorsum Seritella augetur ex Caudinis montibus oriundo, et in valle quam Seritella toto efficit cursu haec sunt oppida: Castrum Potonis, Pesolia, Mons Saticulus, de quo Virgilius in VII, "Saticulus asper," et Livius XXIII, Marcellus "a Casilino Calatiam petit. Inde Vulturno amne traiecto per agrum Saticulanum Trebulanumque super Suessulam pervenit Nolam."

Et superius vallis est Caudina, in qua apparent vetustae urbis Caudii fundamenta. Nec longe abest Harpadium nunc, quod prius Hirpinum dicebatur. In oppidum Furculis proximum est Caudinis clade Romanorum **[404E]** insignibus. De hisque duobus locis sic habet Livius in IX:

> Samnites eo anno consulem C. Pontium Herennii filium habuerunt. Exercitu educto circa Caudium quam potest occultissime ducit. Inde ad Callatium ubi iam consules Romanos castraque esse audiebat, milites decem pastorum habitu mittit, pecoraque diversos alium alibi haud procul Romanis pascere iubet, praecipiens ut ubi inciderint in praedatores, idem omnibus sermo constet: legiones Samnitium in Apulia esse; Luceriam omnibus copiis circumsedere, nec procul abesse, quin vi capiant. Saltus duo alti, angusti silvosique montibus circa perpetuis inter se iuncti; latet inter eos satis patens clausus in medio campus herbidus aquosusque, per quem medium iter est. Sed antea quam venias ad eum intrandae primo angustiae sunt, et aut eadem, qua te insinuaveris retro via repetenda, aut si ire porro pergas per alium saltum altiorem impeditioremque evadendum. T. Veturius Calvinus, Spurius Postumius consules erant.

> Anyone who admitted to being a citizen of the Hernici was kept in custody.

After this point, the river which has its source on the Matese proceeds from there to a point above the town of Petraroia. Cusano is directly opposite. It flows into the Volturno near the town of Puglianello. On the left-hand side of this river is the town of Faicchio; next to that, in the interior, is Gioia Sannitica.

Now we have arrived at the "trunk," the Sabato river. On the right-hand side of the Sabato, first the Seritella flows into it. It has its source in the Caudine mountains, and in the valley which it creates in its entire course there are the following towns: Castelpoto, Pesolia, S. Agata dei Goti (about which Virgil wrote in *Aeneid* 7, "harsh Saticulus"). Livy, too, in book 23, mentions Saticula: "Marcellus went to Calatia from Casilinum. From there, he crossed the Volturnus river. He arrived at Nola by going through the territory of Saticula and Trebula above Suessula."

And higher up is the Caudine Valley, where one can see the foundations of the ancient city of Caudium. Not far off is the modern Arpaia, formerly called Hirpinum. This town is next to the Caudine Forks, **[404E]** famous for the slaughter of the Romans. Livy writes of these two places in book 9:

> In that year the Samnites had as their general Gaius Pontius, the son of Herennius . . . he led his army out and, trying to conceal its actions, brought it to the area around Caudium. From there, he sent ten soldiers dressed as shepherds towards Calatia, where, he was informed, the Roman consuls were located with their camp. These men he ordered to pasture their flocks scattered in different places, but not far from the Romans. When they met with raiders, they were all to tell the same story: that the Samnite legions were in Apulia; that they were besieging Luceria with all their forces; and that they were close to taking it. Two narrow passes, deep and wooded, are joined by an unbroken chain of mountains all around. Enclosed between them there lies a fairly wide plain, grassy and well-watered, and the road goes through the middle of it. But before you come to it, you must first enter the first narrow passage, and then either go back the way you came, or—if you make your way forward—through another narrow pass which is deeper and more difficult. The consuls were T. Veturius Calvinus and Spurius Postumius.

Item Livius de Hirpino libro XXIII, "Hannibal post Cannensem pugnam ex Apulia in Samnium moverat, accitus in Hirpinos a Statio pollicente se Compsam traditurum." Item infra, [404F] "Eadem aestate Marcellus a Nola, quam praesidio obtinebat crebras excursiones in agrum Hirpinum et Samnites Caudinos fecit." Et infra, Hannibal "profectus Harpis ad Tiphata." Et Livius item in bello sociali libro XXV, Lucius Sulla Hirpinos domuit; Samnites fudit.

Absunt haec loca a Benevento fluviis, ubi expedit transmissis, decimo vallis Caudina miliario et Furculae quattuordecimo. Ad alteramque vallis Caudii partem oppida sunt Sanctus Martinus; Penna, Scurmina, et Sanctangelus ad Scalas. Fluvius deinde sequitur dexterum illabens Sabbatum ex monte virginis arduo quidem et late diffuso nascens. Ad cuius vallem Alta Villa primum est oppidum; post Mons Freddunus castellum, et in proxima valle Avelinum civitas vetusta, quam Ptolemaeus Abellam, Plinius Abelinum, vocat. Et tamen ab avelana nuce appellatum dicit, quae ibi plurima habebatur.

Superius est Mercuriale castellum, et longe supra virginis monasterium, quod ex magnae matris deum fano in gloriosae virginis Mariae Dei genitricis ecclesiam Christianis temporibus est mutatum. Nam Antoninus Pius in itinerario viam describens a Benevento ad Columnas, ad Mercurialem [404G] primum, post ad magnam partem posuit.

Altera iterum vallis superior torrenti apposita in Sabbatum defluenti, hinc Atram paludem, inde Serenum oppida habet. Deinceps sunt Apennini iuga, montes Tremuli appellata, a quibus Sabbatum habet ortum. Inferius ad Sabbati sinistram urbs est Beneventum, quam urbem Servius in Virgilii octavum super verbo Diomedis ad urbem, dicit a Diomede conditam fuisse, de qua Livius IX, ad Beneventum quod tunc Maleventum "triginta milia Samnitum caesa aut capta," Sulpicio et Petilio consulibus. Et libro decimoquarto scribit coloniam a Romanis cum Arimino fuisse deductam. Et libro XXII: Hannibal ex Hirpinis in Samnium transit, Beneventanum depopulatur agrum.

Et libro XXIIII, ubi et amnis proximi mentio est:

> et ad Beneventum, inquit, parte altera Hanno ex Brutiis cum magna peditum manu, altera Gracchus a Luceria accessit, qui prius

Livy also tells about Hirpinum in book 23: "After the battle of Cannae, Hannibal moved from Apulia into Samnium. Statius lured him into Hirpinum by promising to hand over Compsa." And further on **[404F]**, Livy says, "In the same summer, Marcellus made frequent attacks on the territory of Hirpinum and the Caudine Samnites, from a base at Nola." And he continues, "Hannibal set out from Arpi to Tifata." In the same vein, in his book (75) on the Social War, Livy says: "Lucius Sulla defeated the Hirpini and put the Samnites to flight."

If you travel by the easiest river crossings, you will find these places ten (Caudine Valley) and fourteen (Forchia) miles from Benevento. On the other side of the Caudine Valley are the towns of San Martino, Penna, Scurmina, and Sant'Angelo a Scala. After that, there is a river which joins the Calore on its right-hand side; this river has its source on Montevergine, a lofty and extensive mountain. In its valley, the first town is Altavilla. After that comes the fortified village of Montefredane, and in the next valley is the old city of Avellino, which Ptolemy calls Abella and Pliny Abelinum. But he remarks that it was named after the filbert, because that area contains many filbert trees.

Higher up, one finds the fortified town of Mercogliano, and far above the monastery of the Virgin. It was transformed in Christian times from a temple to the great Mother of the gods into a church dedicated to the glorious virgin Mary, Mother of God. I deduce this from the Antonine *Itinerarium*, in which Antoninus Pius, in describing the way from Beneventum to Columnae, locates **[404G]** first Mercuriale, and afterwards "great part."

Above this is another valley, beside a stream which flows down into the Sabato river. On one side of it is a dark swamp; on the other side, the town of *Serenum*. Then comes the ridge of the Apennines, called Mte. Terminio, where the Sabato has its source. Below, on the left bank of the Sabato, is the city of Benevento, a city Servius (in his commentary on Virgil's *Aeneid*, book 8, *s.v.* "Diomedes") says was founded by Diomedes. On this city Livy writes in book 9, "In the consulships of Sulpicius and Petilius, thirty thousand Samnites were killed or captured at Beneventum, whose ancient name was Maleventum. . . ." In book 14 he writes, "A colony was sent out by the Romans along with Ariminum." And in book 22, "Hannibal crossed from Hirpinum into Samnium and laid waste the territory of Beneventum."

And in book 24, where he also mentions the river nearby, he says,

> To Beneventum from one direction Hanno came from the region of the Bruttii with a great force of infantry. From the other direc-

> oppidum intravit. Inde ut Hannonem ad amnem Calorem tria milia passuum ipse egressus, mille ferme passus ab hoste castra locat. Nec hostes moram dimicandi fecerunt. Decem et septem milia peditum erant maxima ex parte Brutii **[404H]** et Lucani, equitum tria milia ducenti; pugnatum est quattuor horis. Volones facti sunt liberi, minus duo milia hominum ex tanto exercitu evasere, ex victoribus Romanis ferme duo milia ceciderunt, quam pugnam Gracchus Romae pingi fecit in atrio Libertatis in Aventino.

Et Livius vigesimoquinto:

> Hanno ex Brutiis cum Benevento appropinquasset ad tria miliaria castra communivit; quo Campani duo milia plaustrorum duxerunt, ut frumentum Capuam deferrent. Fulvius consul ex Boviano Beneventum cum venisset, castra vi cepit, caesa sex milia, capti septem milia.

Et libro XXVII, Benevantanos Livius ponit inter colonias ex rebellibus decem et octo, quae in potestatem senatus sunt factae.

Beneventanam urbem nos Historiarum sexto ostendimus a Totila Ostrogothorum rege destructam fuisse. Et libro XII scripsimus Saracenos montem Garganum tenentes Beneventum, quae pridem fuerat instaurata, et a Longobardis ducibus per annos supra ducentos possessa, iterum spoliatam dirutamque solo aequasse. Et infra diximus Gui*l*elmum Normannum Siciliae regem, ab Adriano tertio pontifice Romano in ecclesia Sancti Martini apud Beneventum, sese ligium hominem fecisse Romanae ecclesiae, et dimissa urbe ipsa pro peculari et propria Romanae ecclesiae in regno fuisse quod occupaverat confirmatum.

[405A] Est autem Beneventum in campestri solo, cui colles sunt proximi fertiles villis longe ac late frequentati. Hisque in collibus sexto a Benevento distat miliario Mons Fusculus oppidum, supra quod est turris et oppidum Mons Nitidum appellatum. Sabbati amnis vallis, quam sinistrorsum efficit, castella hoc ordine continet: Mons Falconus est primitus, Candida deinde et Serpitum. Superioribusque in montibus arduis Tremulis appellatis Vulturaria habetur oppidum. Calor fluvius tertio ferme supra Beneventum stadio Sabbatum influit, ad cuius dexteram in colles montesque vergentem, quos

> tion Gracchus approached from Luceria and entered the town first. Then, as Hanno had pitched his camp three miles from the city at the Calore river, Gracchus himself went out from the city and pitched his camp almost one mile from the enemy. The enemy did not hesitate to join battle. 17,000 of their infantry were for the most part Bruttians **[404H]** and Lucanians, and 2,300 cavalry. The battle took four hours. The slave volunteers were freed; fewer than 2,000 men escaped out of that enormous army. Of the victorious Romans, about 2,000 fell. Gracchus had this battle scene painted in the Atrium of Liberty on the Aventine.

And in book 25, Livy writes,

> Hanno had left Bruttium and drawn near to Beneventum and fortified a camp three miles away. The Campanians led 2,000 wagons there to bring grain from Capua. The consul Fulvius reached Beneventum from Bovianum. He took the city by siege: 6,000 were killed, 7,000 captured.

And in book 27 Livy names the citizens of Beneventum among the colonists who rebelled; eighteen of the rebel colonies were put under the power of the Senate.

In my *Histories* I told how the city of Beneventum was destroyed by Totila, king of the Ostrogoths. In book 12 I wrote that although Beneventum had been restored to its former condition and the Longobard rulers had held it for over two hundred years, when the Saracens, who at the time held Monte Gargano, plundered the new city of Benevento, they also destroyed and razed it. Then I told how William the Norman king of Sicily bound himself as liege to the Roman church through the agency of Pope Hadrian II in the church of S. Martino at Benevento. He gave up the city itself as property of the church, and was confirmed in the possession of the kingdom he had seized.

[405A] Benevento lies on a level plain; there are fertile mountains next to it and it is thickly settled with farms. In these hills, six miles from Benevento, is the town of Montefusco. Above it is Torre, and a town called *Mons Nitidum*. The valley which the Sabato river creates on its left side contains the following fortified villages: first comes Montefalcione, then Candida, and Sorbo Serpico. And in the lofty mountains higher up (Mte. Terminio), is the town of Vulturara. Almost three stades above Benevento flows the river Calore; on its right-hand side and bordering on the moun-

Benevento diximus supereminere castella et oppida inveniuntur: Iapygium, Cusanum, Castrum Vetus, et superius Montella oppidum nobile.

Calorique amni secundo supra Sabbatum miliario Valentinus pons fuit in Via Appia, positus a Valente imperatore appellatus, nunc dirutus. Et ipsi fluvio sinistrorsum adiacent oppida, primo Apicium, ubi alter dictae viae pons fuit eximius, post Mirabella, Taurasum, Cusanum, Balneolum, Cassianum, Nuscus, et superiori loco insurgit Apenninus, ubi dictus oritur Calor amnis. Quo item in loco alter **[405B]** fluvius habet originem, Aufidus, quem per Apuliam labi in mare Adriaticum ostendemus.

Tropoaltus inde fluvius Calorem dextrum influit, cui Tropoalto dextrorsum silva eiusdem nominis latissima continet, supra quam castella eidem fluvio haerent: Bonetium, Grypta Mamardi, Flomarlum, et Vicus civitas. Sinistrorsum vero castella habet is fluvius apposita Miletum, Amandum, Iunculum, et superius in Apennino Grumus est mons Crepacorius appellatus, ex quo is fluvius ortum ducit. Muscanus inde fluvius, a Crepacorio nascens, Calorem eodem loco quo et superior Tropoaltus influit. Cui dextrorsum adiacent Cursanum et Mons Calvus. Eoque quod praedictos Muscanum et Tropoaltum interiacet spatio, in colle est Arianum civitas, Ara Iani priscis temporibus appellata, et Muscani dexterae valli insunt oppida et castella: Mons Malus, Bonus Albergus, Casale Albulum, Castrum Franchum.

Sed et Calorem paulo priusquam ipse Sabbatum ingrediatur ad Valentini pontem Tamarus influit amnis, nulli praedictorum quos auget aquarum copia inferior. Ab ipsisque duobus fluviis pari paene spatio abest Padule oppidum, **[405C]** in regione primarium. Superiusque dextero haerent Tamaro oppida et castella: Sanctus Gregorius, Molinaria, Casale Ioannis, Reganum, Sancta Maria, Collis apud quem Iacobus Caudola apoplexi interiit; Carcellum, Coffianum, Sancta Crux, quo in loco silva incipit amplissima Apenninum hincinde complexa, ut pars in Fortorium Apuliae amnem, pars in hunc Tamarum se extendat; quae cum latitudine quattuor miliaria tum longitudine XX implet. Suntque illius quernae arbores sublimitate insignes,

tains which I said tower over Benevento, we find the following fortified villages and towns: Lapio, Chiusano di S. Domenico, and Castelvetere sul Calore; and higher up is the noble town of Montella.

Two miles above the Sabato, on the Calore, the Emperor Valentinus built on the Via Appia the Valentinian bridge, named after him and now destroyed. On the left-hand side of this river are located a number of towns. First comes Apice, where another excellent bridge lay on the same road. Then come Mirabella Eclano, Taurasi, Cusano, Bagnoli Irpino, Cassano Irpino, and Nuzzo. Higher up where the Apennines rise, as I noted, the Calore river has its source. In the same place, a second **[405B]** river, the Ofanto, has its source. I shall describe its course through Puglia to the Adriatic Sea.

Next, the Ufita river flows into the Calore on the right-hand side. A broad forest, also named Ufita, borders the Ufita river on its right bank. Above this forest next to this river are the fortified towns of Bonito, Grottaminarda, Flumeri, and Trevico. On the opposite bank of this river are the fortified towns of Melito, Torreamando, and Zungoli; and higher up in the Apennines is *Mons Grumus*, called *Crepacorius*. Here the river has its source. From here, the river Miscano, which has its source on Crepacorius, flows into the Calore at the same point where the Ufita higher up also enters it. On its right-hand side lie Corsano and Montecalvo. And in the same space which lies, as I noted, between the Miscano and the Ufita, the city of Ariano Irpino sits on a hill; in ancient times it was called Ara Iani. In the right-hand valley of the Miscano river we find the following towns and fortified villages: Montemalo; Buonalbergo; Casalbore, and Castelfranco in Miscano.

At the Valentinian bridge, the Tammaro river flows into the Calore a little before the Calore flows into the Sabato. The flow of the Tammaro is as abundant as the previously mentioned rivers to which it contributes. Almost equidistant from these two rivers is the town of Padule, **[405C]** the chief town of the region. Higher up on the right bank of the Tammaro are the following towns and fortified villages: S. Gregorio, Molinara, Casal di Janni di Reino, Reino, Sta. Maria, and Colle Sannita, where Jacopo Caldora died of apoplexy. Then follow Circello, Coffiano, and Sta. Croce del Sannio, where a great forest begins, four miles wide and twenty miles long, which covers the Apennine ridge on either side and extends in one direction to the river Fortore in Puglia, and on the other side to the Tammaro river. It consists of oak trees of remarkable height, whose tops are completely bare

ramis omnino in vertice carentes. Tamaro sinistro haec adiacent loca: Petra Pulcina, Pavum, Pestulum, Farnetrum, Campus Lotarius, monasterium Guiletti, Marconum, Saxum Honorii, et in Apennino Sepinum, vetusti nominis oppidum, de quo Livius XXI, "Papirio ad Saepinum maior vis hostium obstitit; obsidendoque vi ac operibus urbem expugnat. Uno de quadringentis captis minus tria milia caesi." Et post sequitur Alta villa; et supra est Castrum Vetus in Grumo, ad quem Tamarus fontem habet.

Sed iam ad sinistram stipitis Sabbati amnis est redeundum. Telesia, urbs vetusta colli in planitie subiacet miliario **[405D]** uno a Sabbati stipite remota. Eaque in urbe fluvius oritur cadens in Sabbatum tantae frigiditatis, ut nullos gignat pisces; de qua Livius XXI, "Hannibal ex Arpinis in Samnium transit; Beneventanum depopulatur agrum; Telesiam urbem capit." Limataque oppidum proxime Sabbato haeret; quattuor dehinc torrentes ad Castrum Pontis oppidum unicis ostiis in Sabbatum cadunt, quorum torrentum fontibus ab Apennino remotissimis quattuor haerent castella: Sanctus Laurentius, Sanctus Lupus, Pons Landulphi, et Casaltonum. Sabbato amne cum suis fluviorum torrentumque ramis descripto, ad finem Samnitium regionis est perventum, ut Campaniam ab ipso Sabbato in Capuanam urbem verso, hac in parte inchoantem describendam aggredi possimus.

of branches. On the left bank of the Tammaro river these towns are located: Pietrelcina, Pago Veiano, Pesco Sannita, Fragneto l'Abate, Campolattaro, the monastery of Guiletti, Morcone, Sassinoro; and, in the Apennines, Sepino, a town with an ancient name (Saepinum). Livy writes about it in book 21: "Papirius was opposed at Saepinum by the enemy's greater strength. He besieged the city and used force and machines to capture it. Thirty-nine were captured, fewer than three thousand killed." After Sepino comes Altilia, and above it is Terravecchia, on the hill where the Tammaro has its source.

But now I must return to the left-hand side of the Sabato, our "trunk" of the tree of rivers. The ancient city of Telesia lies on a plain at the foot of a hill, one **[405D]** mile from the trunk of the Sabato. And at this city there flows into the Sabato a river too cold to support fish. Livy writes about it in book 21: "Hannibal crossed over from Arpini into Samnium, where he laid waste the territory of Beneventum and captured the city of Telesia." The town of Limatola lies next to the Sabato. From here, four rivers debouche through one mouth into the Sabato at the town of Ponte Biferchia. Four fortified towns are located at the site of the sources of these rivers, far from the Apennines: San Lorenzo Maggiore, San Lupo, Ponte Landolfo, and Casalduni. Since I have described the Sabato river, with its tributary branches, I have come to the end of the Samnite region. Now I shall embark on the description of Campania starting at the place where the Sabato turns towards the city of Capua.

Regio Tertiadecima
Campania

[406E]

Samnii regione ad utramque Appenini partem absoluta, ad proximam continentemque atque connexam illi in Cisappeninis Campaniam est transeundum vel ea maxime ratione ut inchoatos in Samnitium montibus fluviorum cursus qui Campaniam quoque intersecant expediamus. Cur autem eam felicem Campaniam, postea alii Terram Laboris appellaverint, suo tempore et loco dicemus. Licet vero tota haec regio vetustissimis celebrata sit omnium dignitatum monumentis, nullum tamen locum nec ipsa nec alia pars Italiae habet in qua maior quam in hoc Campaniae initio dignarum relatu rerum mutatio sit facta.

Inchoat Campania ad dexteram Liris fluvii, quem nunc Gaurianum diximus appellari, quem quidem Lirim Strabo dicit ferri desuper ex Apennino et a Vestinis labique in mare ad Freteala vicum, quae fuerit urbs praeclara. Cui concordat Lucanus,

> et umbrosae Liris per regna Maricae Vestinis
> impulsus aquis. . . .

Et cur "Maricae regna" Lucanus dicat, Servius in Virgilii septimo **[406F]** sic ostendit: "Marica fuit uxor Fauni quae est dea litoris Minturnensium iuxta Lirim fluvium."

De Vestinis et Minturnensibus, qui fuerint dicturi prius Ausones, docebimus a quibus Italia olim Ausonia fuit appellata et proximum mare Ausonium pelagus est dictum de his tribus populis. Livius sic habet in nono, "Consules ab Sora profecti Ausonibus bellum intulerunt," et infra,

> Ausonum gens proditione civium sicut Sora in potestatem venit. Ausonia et Vestina et Minturnae urbes erant ex quibus principes iuventutis duodecim numero in proditionem urbium coniurati ad consules venerunt. Quibus auctoribus mota propius castra missi-

Thirteenth Region
Campania

[406E]

Having described the Samnite region on both sides of the Apennines, let us pass to Campania, especially to follow the courses of the rivers which began in the Samnite mountains and also cut through Campania. Why this was first called Felix Campania, then Terra di Lavoro, I shall tell at the appropriate time and place. Although all this region has been celebrated in the most ancient records of all, this first part of Campania has seen greater changes due to noteworthy events than has any other part of Campania or of Italy.

Campania begins on the right bank of the river called Liris by the ancients, which we have said is now called Garigliano. Indeed, Strabo says the Liris flows down from the Apennines and from the Vestini and descends to the sea near the village of Freteale, which was a famous city. A passage from Lucan corroborates this:

> and the Liris, whose course begins among the waters belonging to the Vestini, and flows through the kingdom of Marica, full of shade. . . .

And Servius, commenting on the seventh book of the *Aeneid*, **[406F]** shows why Lucan says "the kingdom of Marica": "Marica, wife of Faunus, was the goddess of the shore of the inhabitants of Minturnae next to the Liris river."

I shall show that the Vestini and inhabitants of Minturnae were called Ausones; from their name, Italy was once called Ausonia. The sea next to it was called the Ausonian sea after these three peoples. Livy, book 9, writes, "the consuls set out from Sora and started war against the Ausones," and later on he says:

> The Ausonian people, just like Sora, came into the power [of Rome] through betrayal by its citizens. Ausonia and Vestina and Minturnae were cities from which came the twelve leaders of the youth to betray their cities to the consuls. On their authority the

> que milites, partim armati, partim inermes. Ita portae occupatae. Triaque oppida eadem hora eodemque consilio capta, sed quia absentibus ducibus impetus factus est, nullus modus caedibus. Fuit deleta Ausonum gens vix certo defectionis crimine.

Ausonibus et eodem impetu Vestina urbe deletis, Vestinum nihilominus nomen ab ipso Liris ostio usque Soram mansit regioni et Ausonum omnino interiit, Minturnaque quam Liris divideret fuit Romana colonia, de qua Livius in decimo: "Ita **[406G]** placuit ut duae coloniae circa Vestinum Falernumque agrum deducerentur una ad ostium Liris fluvii quae tunc Minturnae appellata."

Fuit Marcellini papae temporibus generali concilio ecclesiae decorata cuius ingentia nunc vestigia cernuntur ubi, ad turrim Scaphanique Gauriani prope Traiectum oppidum, exstat theatrum paene integrum et aquaeductus forma. Inchoavit vero pridem Minturnarum urbis desolatio. Nam in beati Gregorii registro epistola est quam scribit Becardae episcopo Formiensi in haec verba:

> Et ideo, quoniam Minturnensium ecclesiam funditus tam cleri quam plebis destitutam consolatione cognovimus, tuam pro eo petitionem quatenus Formianae ecclesiae in qua corpus beati Erasmi martyris quiescit, cuique fraternitas tua praesidet, adiungi debeat . . . exaudiri necessarium duximus.

Fuit Minturna una ex urbibus quae propter aeris gravitatem sacrosanctam vacationem a Romanis habuit. Estque locus apud quem C. Marius, sicut Valerius Maximus scribit, ". . . urbe profugus cum in palustri canna delitesceret viso asino aquas hilarius petente, bonum concepit omen; et inde transvectus mare copiis reparatis **[406H]** victor in patriam est reductus." De quo Livius septuagesimo sic dicit:

> C. Marius pater cum in palude Minturnensium lateret, extractus est ab oppidanis et cum missus ad occidendum servus natione Gallus maiestate tanti viri perterritus, recessisset, impositus publicae navi delatus est in Africam.

> camp was moved nearer and soldiers were sent, some armed, some unarmed. In this way the gates were seized and the three towns were captured in one hour by the same plan. But because the attack was made in the leaders' absence, the slaughter was uncontrolled. The Ausones were destroyed without a certain charge of desertion.

The Ausones and the city of Vestina were destroyed in the same attack. The name of Vestina persisted for the region from the actual harbor of the Liri up to Sora, and the name of the Ausones died out completely. And Minturnae, which the Liri divides in half, was a Roman colony. Livy, book 10, says about it: "And so **[406G]** it was decided that two colonies would be established around the territories of Vestina and Falernae, one at the mouth of the Liris river, which then was called Minturnae."

In the time of Pope Marcellinus, this town enjoyed the distinction of a general council of the church. The visitor can still see the huge remains: at the tower of *Scaphanum* and *Gaurianum* near the town of Minturno, a theatre, almost intact, and the traces of an aqueduct. But the desolation of the city of Minturnae began long ago; for the *Register* of St. Gregory includes a letter he writes to Bishop Becarda of Formiae, with these words:

> And so, since I know the church of Minturnae is completely bereft of the consolation of clergy as well as of laymen, as far as the church of Formiae where the body of the blessed martyr Erasmus rests, over which your brotherhood presides, I have considered it necessary that your petition be granted, and the church of Minturnae be joined to the church at Formiae.

Minturnae was one of the cities exempted by the Romans from military levy on account of its unhealthy air. It was also the place where, Valerius Maximus tells us, C. Marius, "when he was a fugitive from Rome, hid in a swamp of reeds and saw a donkey cheerfully going along looking for water; he interpreted it as a good omen and sailed from there across the sea, regrouped his forces, **[406H]** and returned victorious to his own country." Livy, book 77, tells us about this incident:

> After C. Marius the father hid in the swamp at Minturnae, the townspeople pulled him out and sent him to be killed. But the executioner, a slave from Gaul, was intimidated by the great man's authority, lost his nerve; and Marius was put on a state ship and taken to Africa.

Hunc eundem locum duodecimo Historiarum docuimus illustratum fuisse insigni proelio quod decimi Ioannis Romani pontificis temporibus gestum fuit in Saracenos maxima occidione ibi superatos et tunc Italia penitus exactos. Sicque videmus duas urbes olim praeclaras, primo Fretealas, post Minturnas, ad Liris ostia interiisse. Et pariter omnino deletam esse omnem memoriam Ausonum et Maricae.

Mons vero praedicto Liris ostio in Campaniae initio proximior varias et fama celebres habet nominationes, qui alicubi Gaurus, alicubi Massicus, alicubi Gallicanus est dictus. Primaque pars et eidem ostio proximior Gaurus dicta Gaurelianum, ut diximus, illum appellari facit. Quem quidem Gaurum montem, Plinius dicit, sicut et Vesevum Campaniae, item montem sulphura sudare, quod aquae ostendunt calidae paulo superius etiam nunc scatentes, ubi turrim balneorum et balnea nunc videmus. Ceterae montis nominationes cum adiacentibus locis et urbibus ostendentur.

Secundum adiacens Minturnis oppidum in Gauro **[407A]** et Campaniae initio fuit Trifanum, quem locum Livius in octavo dicit medium fuisse inter Minturnas et Sinuessam. Tertio loco fuit Sinuessa, stadiis quadraginta sicut Strabo, sed sicut nunc octuaginta a Minturnis semota, de qua habet Livius in octavo, quod supra de Minturnis diximus:

> Ita placuit ut duae coloniae circa Vestinum Falernumque agrum deducerentur, una ad ostium Liris quae nunc Minturnae, altera in saltu Vestino Falernum agrum contingente, ubi Sinope Graeca urbs dicitur fuisse. Sinuessa deinde a colonis Romanis appellata.

Huius vero civitatis ad caput nunc Montis Draconis deletae ingentes et late diffusae in continenti, sed maiores in mari quae portus moles fuerunt apparent nunc ruinae. Livius etiam XXII scribit Fabium Maximum per iuga Massici montis ducentem prohibuisse Hannibalem ad Romanae coloniae moenia tendentem, cum supra dixerit Hannibalis milites praedatum ivisse usque ad Aquas Sinuessanas, unde patet aliam montis partem quae a Suessa Pometia, vel Aurunca (nunc Sessa) ad Calenum oppidum (nunc Carinulam) protenditur fuisse Massicum, post cuius iuga Fabius tunc ducebat.

I wrote about this same place in book 12 of my *Histories*, how it is famous for the notorious battle waged against the Arabs in the reign of Pope John X; as a result of the great slaughter here, the Arabs were defeated and driven completely out of Italy. And so we see the deaths of two once famous cities—first Freteale, then Minturnae-at the mouth of the Garigliano river. At the same time, we see the complete destruction of any memory of the Ausones, and the nymph Marica.

But nearer to the mouth of the Liri, at the beginning of Campania, there is a mountain which has had various, and celebrated, names: in one place Gaurus, in another Massicus, in still another Gallicanus. The first part, nearer to the river's mouth, called Gaurus, causes the river, as I noted, to be called Garigliano. This mountain Gaurus (Monte Barbaro), Pliny tells us, just like the mountain Vesuvius in Campania, exudes sulphur; this is verified by the warm waters which bubble up even now a little above it, where we now see the tower of the baths and the baths themselves. The remaining mountains' names will be listed with the adjacent places and cities.

Lying next to Minturnae was the second town on Mt. Gaurus **[407A]** at the beginning of Campania, *Trifanum*. Livy, book 8, tells us that it was the midpoint between Minturnae and Sinuessa. In the third place was Sinuessa, according to Strabo forty stades from Minturnae, but actually then, as it is now, eighty stades distant. Livy, book 8, says (as I noted above in reference to Minturnae):

> They decided to establish two colonies around the territory of the Vestini and the Falernian district. One, at the mouth of the Liris, is what is now Minturnae. The other, in the pass of the Vestini bordering on the Falernian territory, where the Greek city of Sinope is said to have been located; the Roman colonists therefore called it Sinuessa.

Visible at the extremity of what is now Mondragone, this city's enormous ruins are dilapidated and widely scattered on the land, larger in the sea where they formed the breakwater in the harbor. Livy, again in book 22, writes that Fabius Maximus led his army over Mt. Massicus and turned Hannibal away as he was approaching the walls of the Roman colony. He mentioned earlier that Hannibal's soldiers had gone to pillage as far as Aquae Sinuessanae. Another part of the mountain over whose ridges Fabius was then leading his army stretches from Suessa Pometia or Aurunca (now Sessa) to the town of Calenum (now Carinola).

Supplet autem vices Sinuessae oppidum **[407B]** arx Mons Draconis dictum, vel potius eius suburbium mille passus a mari semotum. Et paulo inde absunt supradicta Gauri Balnea, quae Strabo dicit morbis quibusdam prodesse plurimum. Post Montis Draconis arcem in Massico monte vicis villisque plurimis frequentato, ad partem in mare versam nullum est etiam oppidum vel castellum. Ad eam vero partem, qua adverso Liri et dextro Massico itur, solum est octo milia passus quaqua versum inter mare, viam Appiam, Lirim et Massicum patens, nuncque cultissimum et vicis villisque frequentissimum, quae Suessae Casalia appellantur, quod quidem solum stante Romana re publica silis sive trifoliis herbis prata conficientibus optima abundavit, unde Valerius Martialis poeta:

> Caeruleus nos Liris amat quem silva Maricae
> Protegit hinc silae maxima turba sumus.

Et quidem etiam nunc ea regio maximum habet in foeno quaestum. M. Cicero in oratione contra legem agrariam Rulli secunda, cum vellet dissuaderi venditionem agri Campani, montis Gauri praedictique campestris soli in pratis tunc culti, et viae Herculaneae a Gaieta ad ipsa prata productae sic habet: "Hac lege tribunicia decemviri vendent agrum Campanum. Accedit et Mons Gaurus; accedent silleta ad Minturnas; **[407C]** adiungitur et illa via vendibilis Herculanea multarum divitiarum et magnae pecuniae."

In Via autem Appia, ubi ea primum attingit Massicum montem urbs est vetus, Suessa olim Pometia, et quandoque Auruncorum dicta, quae varias fecit regionum mutationes quae Auruncorum olim qui et Ausones Sidicinorumque et post Volscorum demum fuit Vestinorum prout ex sequentibus faciliter apparebit. Livius in primo, "Anci liberi Suessam Pometiam exulatum ierant," et infra, de Tarquinio Superbo, "Is primum Volscis bellum in ducentos amplius post suam aetatem annos movit Suessamque Pometiam ex his vi coepit." Et infra idem Livius eandem Suessam rebellem praedae militi Romano datam ostendit. Et in octavo, "Arunci metu oppidum deseruerunt, profugique cum coniugibus ac liberis Suessam commigrarunt, quae nunc Aurunca appellata. Moenia eorumque urbs ab Sidicinis deleta." Item in nono, "Suessam eodem anno colonia deducta; fuerat Aruncorum."

In the place of the town of Sinuessa is the citadel, **[407B]** or rather its village, called Rocca Mondragone, a mile from the ocean. A little farther from there are the previously mentioned baths of Gaurus, which Strabo says can cure many diseases. On Mte. Massico, which is crowded with small villages and estates, there is not after Mondragone even a town or fortress on the part facing the sea. But in the direction facing the Garigliano betwen the sea, the Via Appia, and, on the right, Mte Massico, there is no more than eight miles of land. The villages and estates are called Casali di Sessa. During the time of the Roman Republic, this land had an abundant meadow of hartwort or trefoil grass. For this reason, the poet Martial wrote,

> The blue Liris, protected by Marica's forest, likes us.
> From there we come, a great catch of crustaceans.

And even now this region is very useful for its hay. Cicero, in his second oration against the agrarian law of Rullus, intending to prevent the sale of the public land in Campania, said:

> These lands the decemvirs will sell by using the agrarian law. There will be added to them Mt. Gaurus, and the willow thickets at Minturnae; **[407C]** there is added also the road to Herculaneum, easy to sell, which is the source of many pleasures and much money.

But on the Via Appia today, where this road first meets Mte. Massico, is the historic city of Sessa, called in ancient times Suessa Pometia, and Aurunca. It underwent various changes of region, because it was formerly said to belong to the Aurunci and to the Ausones and to the Sidicini. Afterwards it was said to belong to the Volsci and finally to the Vestini. This will easily be made clear in what follows. Livy, in book one, says "The children of Ancus were banished to Suessa Pometia"; and later in a passage on Tarquinius Superbus says, "He first started a war against the Volsci, which lasted more than two hundred years after his own time, and took Suessa Pometia from them by force." And later on Livy reveals that this same city rebelled and was given as booty to the Roman army. And in book 8 he writes, "The Aurunci deserted the town in fear, and in exile with their wives and children migrated to Suessa Pometia, which is now called Aurunca. Their walls and city were destroyed by the Sidicini." On the same topic, in book 9 Livy notes, "A colony had been established at Suessa in the same year; it was settled by the Aurunci."

Progressi Suessa Pometia sive Aurunca per Appiam silicibus stratam et per cavas vias dextro Massico Calenum octavo miliario inveniunt vetustam urbem quae nunc Carinula dicitur. Estque hinc Falerno agro inde Massico monti contigua, **[407D]** quamquam vetusta Caleni oppidi vestigia aliquantulum a Carinula nunc sunt remota, de qua urbe Horatius, "molle Calenum."

Continet sinistrorsum Appiae viae, qua Calenum urbem a Suessa peti diximus, et ipsi pariter civitati mons item Massicus supra Teanum civitatem, ut diximus, Calesque usque ad Calatiam continuatus. Et licet mons ipse dorso uno a Calibus sinistrorsum ad Venafrum, et inde ad Vulturnum recto cursu protendatur, altera pars fracta alicubi viis cavis et silvosa ad Caliculam, sive nunc Caianellum, se dextrorsum flectit, et Vulturnum, sed inferiori loco petit, adeo ut inter praedictos montes et Vulturnum, sed superiorem Samnitibus continentem, campi relinquantur Venafrani, semper antea sicut et nunc a civitate illis contigua, appellati. Namque Plinius de olivis tractans Venafranos campos dicit glareosos sed pingues feracissimosque oleae esse.

Hisque campis adiacent hinc Mignanum, Pesantianum, Varianumque, inde Sextum et superius sic, ut diximus, ultra Vulturnum sunt Alifae. Sed alia parte Vulturnum inter interiorem contra Caianellum labentem quousque per Capuam et olim Casilinum fertur in mare, et omne superius dictum montis tractum, et alteram eiusdem Massici partem, quae a Carinula ad maris litora et Sinuessanum olim agrum nunc montis Draconis suburbium pertinet, campestre est solum totius Italiae amoenissimum, quem **[408E]** olim campum Stellatem appellavere. Eidemque campo partim imminent, partim insunt Calenum primo, sive Carinula, Turris Francolisii, Teanum Sidicinum, Cales sive Calvi, et Calicula sive Caianellum. Sed quod Massico monti contigisse diximus, ut ad Liris ostia pars eius appellaretur Gaurus, pariter ad aliam contigit partem, ut inter Carinulam turrimque Francolisii Gallicanus olim sit dictus, ubi Cascanum incolae nunc appellant.

De campo autem Stellate sic habet Livius in nono: "In campum Stellatem agri Campani Samnitium incursiones factae." Idem in decimo: "Samni-

If you go out from Suessa Pometia or Aurunca along the Appian Way, which is paved with stones, and along sunken roads, leaving Mte. Massico on the right, eight miles away you find Calenum, an ancient city which is now called Carinola. It is adjacent to the Falernian district on one side and Mte. Massico on the other. **[407D]** The ancient ruins of the town of Calenum are somewhat removed, however, from what is now Carinola. Horace wrote of Calenum, "mellow Calenian [wine]."

On the left of the Via Appia, on which I said one travels from Sessa towards what remains of the city of Cales, Mte. Massico stretches above the city of Teano as I said, and above Cales, extending all the way to Caiazzo. And although the mountain itself stretches on one ridge from Cales on the left to Venafro, and from there it extends in a straight line in the direction of the Volturno river, another part is broken up by sunken roads and turns to the right and, thickly forested, goes to Calicula or, as it is now called, Caianello. This part extends to the Volturno, but in a lower place, so that between the mountains I mentioned and the Volturno, but its higher course bordering the Samnites, are the fields of Venafro, still now, just as they were before, named after the city which borders them. For Pliny, in his work on olives, says that the fields of Venafrum are gravelly, but rich and very fertile in olives.

And here, next to these fields, lie Mignano Monte Lungo and Presenzano and Vairano on one side, and on the other side Sesto, as I mentioned, and higher up, beyond the Volturno, is Alife. But in the other direction, between the Volturno in the interior (where it flows in front of Caianello, as far as where it goes through Capua and what was formerly Casilinum and flows into the sea) and the entire tract of the mountain I mentioned above and the other side of Mte. Massico which goes from Carinula to the sea, this area belonged to the territory of what was formerly Sinuessa, but today belongs to the territory of the village of Mondragone. This area is all fields and its soil is the pleasantest in all Italy. It was **[408E]** formerly called the plain of Stella. And partly projecting over this land and partly on it are first Calenum or Carinola; Torre Francolise; Teano; Cales or Calvi; and Calicula or Caianello. But as in the case of the part of Mte. Massico which was near the mouth of the Garigliano and was called Gaurus, so the other part of it has acquired its name: that part of the mountain between Carinola and Torre Francolise was formerly called Gallicanus, and the inhabitants now call it Cascano.

Concerning the plain of Stella, Livy says in book nine: "Hostile inroads were made into the plain of Stella, the Samnites' part of the territory of

tium legiones, cum partem Appius Claudius praetor, partem L. Volumnius proconsul persequeretur, in agrum Stellatem convenerunt. Pugnatum infestis animis. Caesa Samnitum sexdecim milia trecenta."

Item XXII,

> Hannibalem Telesia potitum auditis Capuanis duobus, alternis fidentem ac diffidentem, ut Campaniam ex Samnio peteret, monuerunt. Ipse imperat duci, ut se in agrum Casinatem ducat, edoctus a peritis regionum, si eum saltum occupasset, exitum populo Romano ad opem ferendam sociis interclusurum. Sed Poenum abhorrens ab Latinorum prolatione, nomen Casilinum pro Casino ducem accipere fecit. Aversusque **[408F]** ab itinere per Alifanum, Calatinumque et Calenum agrum in campum Stellatem usque ad Casilinum descendit; ubi cum montibus fluminibusque clausam regionem circumspexisset, vocatum ducem virgis caesum in crucem sustulit. Castris ad Vulturnum amnem communitis, Maharbalem cum equitibus in agrum Falernum praedatum dimisit. Usque ad Aquas Sinuessanas ea populatio pervenit, ut vero ad Vulturnum amnem castra sunt posita, exurebatur amoenissimus Italiae ager. Villaeque passim incendiis fumabant, per iuga Massici montis Fabio ducente, ut vero in extrema iuga Massici montis ventum est, hostes sub oculis erant Falerni agri colonorumque Sinuessae tecta urentes.

Qui ergo a Telesia nunc etiam id retinente nomen, et a nobis in Samnio supra Vulturnum dextro Eserniensi amne descripta movebat Hannibal ut ad Casinum iret, per Alifanum quidem primo, sed inde dextrorsum ad Venafrum, ab eoque oppido Casinum fuit ducendus. Sed dux errore nominis, averso, sicut proprie dicit Livius, itinere sinistrorsum flexit in Calatinum, cuius urbem nunc Caiaciam pro Calatia dicunt, et transmissis, quod evitari non potuit, angustiis cannarum silvosarumque viarum, quae **[408G]** ad Caliculam (nunc Cavanellum) ducunt, pervenit ad Calenum agrum, eius scilicet

Campania." And also in book ten: "The praetor Appius Claudius was following some of the legions of the Samnites, the proconsul L. Volumnius following another part, and they came together in the plain of Stella. There was a fierce battle; and 16,300 Samnites were killed."

And also in book 22:

> Hannibal took possession of Telesia. Then two Capuans advised him to move from Samnium into Campania; he heard them with alternating feelings of trust and suspicion. He ordered a guide to lead him into the territory of Casinum, because he had been instructed by men knowledgeable about the region that if he occupied the pass, he would shut off the exit from the Romans trying to bring aid to their allies. But his Carthaginian speech did not agree with the pronunciation of Latin names, and he gave the guide to understand the name "Casilinum" instead of "Casinum." And he deviated **[408F]** from the route and went down past the territories of Allifae, Calatia, and Cales into the plain of Stella as far as Casilinum. When he saw all around him a region shut in by mountains and rivers, he called the guide to him and had him whipped and crucified. He fortified a camp at the Vulturnus river and sent Maharbal with cavalry to plunder the Falernian territory. The devastation extended as far as the baths of Sinuessa. But when he pitched camp at the Vulturnus river and the pleasantest district in Italy began to burn; when Fabius was marching his troops along the ridges of Mt. Massicus while smoke was rising all around from the burning farmhouses, they arrived at the farthest ridges of the mountain and saw the enemy below burning the houses of Falernian territory and the dwellings of colonists around Sinuessa.

He was therefore moving from Telesia (which even now has kept this name, and which I described in Samnium above the Volturno and on the right side of the river at Isernia), to go to Casinum, first by way of Allifae, but then on the right hand side towards Venafrum, and he had to have been led to Casinum from that town. But the guide deviated from the route because of a mistake in the name, as Livy accurately remarks, and Hannibal had to turn to the left towards the territory of Calatia, whose city is now called Caiazzo instead of Calatia. He could not have avoided crossing the places overgrown with reeds and roads crowded with forests which **[408G]** lead to Calicula (now called Caianello), and on this route he reached the territory

civitatis, quae pro Cales Sidicino dicta est Calvi. Et per ipsum Stellatem procedens campum, non prius viae intellexit errorem, quam ad propinquum Casilini, quod nunc Castellutium appellant, Vulturnum perductus, clausam montibus et fluminibus Vulturno ac Saono regionem maestus circumspexit.

Castris itaque ad Castellutium, vel ibi prope positis, facile fuit Maharbali usque ad Aquas Sinuessanas, ubi scilicet Saonus in stagnum effusus labi incipit in Vulturnum, praedatum ire. Ut vero ad praedictum Vulturnum castra sunt posita, exurebatur amoenissimus Italiae ager, is scilicet, qui Falernus tunc appellatus pertinebat a Carinula ad Castellutium, sive tunc Casilinum, quod Livius agrum Falernum a Campano divisisse asserit. "Per iuga Massici montis" ea videlicet, quae a Carinula ad maritimam oram protenduntur, "Fabio ducente." "Ut vero ad extrema" ipsius Massici montis pervenit Fabius, hostes sub oculis erant, quod ab ipso monte Massico vix quattuor milia passuum Castellutium et Vulturni fluenta distant.

Prius vero quam Hannibalis reditum in Samnites describam, aliqua referre libet, ex quibus **[408H]** campus Stellas qualis quantusque fuerit patebit. Marcus Cicero, legem dissuasurus agrariam, qua Rullus Cornelius decemvir et collegae agrum Campanum Stellatemque campum, et supradicta ad Gaurum Lirimque et sileta quoque, cum via Herculanea vendere intendebat, sic habet: "At enim ager Campanus hac lege amittitur orbis terrae pulcherrimus." Et infra:

> Adiungit Stellatem campum agro Campano et in eo duodena distribuit in singulos homines iugera, quasi vero paulum non differat ager Campanus a Stellate. Nam dixi antea lege permitti, ut quae velint municipia, quas velint veteres colonias, colonis suis occupent; Calenum municipium complebunt; Tranum oppriment et Atellam.

Ostendit vero praedictis in orationibus Cicero non solum viam Herculaneam Gaurumque et sileta ad Minturnas, sed campum quoque Stellatem

of Cales, meaning, of course, of the city which is called Calvi but was formerly of Cales of the Sidicini. And going on through the plain of Stella itself, he did not catch the error in the route before he had been led to the Vulturnus near Casilinum, which is now called Capua. At this point he looked around unhappily and noticed that the area was fenced in by mountains and rivers (the Vulturnus and the Saonus).

He therefore had pitched camp at *Castellutium* or near there, and it was easy for Maharbal to be sent to raid as far as Aquae Sinuessanae, where obviously the Savone has created stagnant pools and begins to flow into the Volturno. As his camp was pitched at the previously mentioned Vulturnus river, the phrase "the pleasantest land in Italy was burning" refers of course to the area then called "the territory of Falernus," which extends from Carinola to Castellutium (at that time called Casilinum). This is obvious from Livy's assertion that Casilinum divided the territory of Falernus from that of Campania. "Along the ridges of Mt. Massicus," in the description of Fabius leading his army, clearly means the stretch which extends from Carinola to the coast. And when Fabius got to "the farthest part of the mountain," and the enemy were right under their eyes, this is because scarcely four miles separate Mte. Massico itself from *Castellutium* and the flowing water of the Volturno.

But before I describe Hannibal's withdrawal among the Samnites, I should like to relate some other information which will tell us what **[408H]** the plain of Stella was like, and how large it was. Cicero, speaking against the proposed agrarian law, which Rullus Cornelius and his colleagues were trying to use to sell the public land of Campania and the plain of Stella, and also Gaurus and the aforementioned willow thickets near the Liris river, along with the Via Herculanea, said, "But this law causes the loss of the public land in Campania, the most beautiful land on earth." And later on in the same speech,

> He adds the plain of Stella to the territory around Campania and divides it into twelve-acre lots for each man, as if there were no difference between the public land of Campania and the plain of Stella. In fact, I said earlier that the law allowed them to occupy the free towns that they wished, and what old colonies they wished to occupy, with their own colonists. They will fill up the town of Cales; they will overwhelm Tranum and Atella.

Cicero shows in this oration that not only were the Via Herculanea, Mt. Gaurus, and the fields at Minturnae public lands, but also the plain of Stella.

peculiares fuisse populi Romani fundos, ex quibus alerentur exercitus. Quod quidem Suetonius Tranquillus innuere videtur, cum dicit C. Caesarem in consulatu suo, ad gratiam Romani populi comparandam, divisisse campum Stellatem viginti milibus civibus Romanis, quibus tres sive plures filii essent.

Ut autem ad Hannibalem redeamus, dicit Livius Fabium tamdiu extraxisse reliquum aestatis,

> ut Hannibal destitutus ab spe summa appetiti certaminis, iam hibernis locum circumspectaret, quia ea regio praesentis **[409A]** erat copiae, non perpetuae, arbusta vineaeque et consita omnia magis amoenis quam necessariis fructibus. Itaque cum sciret Hannibali per easdem angustias, quibus intraverat redeundum esse, Gallicanum montem et Casilinum occupat modicis praesidiis.

Et infra,

> Inclusus deinde videri Hannibal et ad Casilinum obsessus, cum Capua et Samnium et tantum a tergo divitum sociorum Romanis commeatum subveherent, Poenus tunc intra fortunae minas saxa ac Linterni arenas, stagna per horrida situ hibernaturus esset.

Itaque cum per Casilinum evadere non posset, et iugum Caliculae superandum esset, "ludibrium oculorum in speciem terribile ad frustrandum hostem commentus," duo milia boum cornua fascibus sarmentorum igni accensorum in montem Gallicanum, nunc Cascanum, turri sicut diximus Francolisii imminentem, a Fabio praeoccupatum egit. Et interea Romani,

> qui ad transitum saltus insidendum locati erant, ubi in summis montibus ac super se quosdam ignes conspexerunt, praesidio excessere. Interea toto agmine Hannibal transducto, in agro Alifano posuit castra. Fabius quoque movit castra, transgressusque saltum super Alifas loco alto consedit. Tum **[409B]** Hannibal simulans se per Samnium petere Romam, usque in Pelignos pervenit.

Fuitque via nunc etiam trita, et qua nuper Neapolim ivimus ipsi.

These lands supplied food for the armies. Indeed Suetonius appears to confirm this, when he says that during his consulship Julius Caesar, in order to ingratiate himself with the Roman people, divided the plain of Stella among twenty thousand Roman citizens who qualified for the distribution by having three or more children.

But to return to Hannibal: Livy says that Fabius dragged out the rest of the summer

> so that Hannibal was deprived of the longed-for battle, and started looking around for winter quarters, as the area where he then was **[409A]** offered fruit-trees, vineyards, and types of produce that were pleasant rather than necessary. And so when Fabius realized that Hannibal had to return via the same narrow passes by which he had entered the territory, he occupied Mt. Gallicanus and Casilinum with a garrison of moderate size.

And further on,

> Then Hannibal seemed to be shut in and besieged at Casilinum, since Capua and Samnium and the rich allies in the rear could bring up provisions to the Romans. Hannibal seemed condemned to spend the winter between the threats of Fortune, rocks, and the sandy, swampy land of Liternum, an inhospitable environment.

And so since he could not escape via Casilinum, and had to pass over the ridge of Mt. Callicula, he "devised a way of deceiving the enemy, a terrifying sight to trick their eyes." He fastened on the horns of two thousand cattle bundles of brushwood which were then set on fire, and drove them onto Mt. Gallicanus, which Fabius had taken possession of. (This is the mountain we now call Cascano which, as I mentioned, towers over Torre Francolise.) And in the meantime the Romans,

> who had been placed at the crossing of the pass, where on the heights of the mountains and above them they saw some fires, left their garrison. Meanwhile Hannibal led his entire line of troops across the pass, and pitched camp in the territory of Allifae. Fabius also broke up his camp and crossed the pass and took up a position in a high place above Allifae. Then **[409B]** Hannibal, pretending to be directing his course through Samnium towards Rome, reached the territory of the Peligni.

And this was the road which is in use even now; in fact I recently traveled to Naples by this way.

Ab Alifis traiecto amne Vulturno sub Formelo monasterii S. Vincentii sicut in Samnio ostendimus castello, ad Castrum Sarni, sive ut dicunt Sangri, eo exinde superato, qui adiacet colle profectus Hannibal, amnem Rasinum sinistrorsum relinquens ad Furculas Pelignorum (nunc Palenae dictas) pervenit, unde flexo itinere per Frentanos, Ortonenses, Aprutinos retro Apuliam repetiit.

Sed iam ad nostrum ordinem redeamus. Vulturni amnis ostio dextrorsum urbs olim adiacebat, ipsius nomine Vulturnum appellata. Livius vigesimosexto,

> Capua interim summa vi a consulibus obsideri coepta est, quaeque in eam rem opus erant comportabantur parabanturque; Casilinum frumentum convectum, ad Vulturni ostium, ubi nunc urbs est, Castellum communitum, ante Fabius Maximus communierat, praesidium impositum ut mare proximum et flumen in potestate esset.

Item Livius libro trigesimosecundo ostendit, coloniam Romanam fuisse deductam Vulturnum urbem ad ostia Vulturni amnis sitam, ubi nunc oppidum Castellum **[409C]** ad mare dictum, videmus.

Supraque Castellum ad mare Vulturno dextrorsum adiacet viculus Castellutium appellatus, ubi Casilinum fuisse non coniecturis modo, sed multis quoque ducimur argumentis, primumque nominis similitudo in ceterarum concursu rationum non parum valet, sed et cetera habet Castellutium, quae de Casilino apud Livium scripta videmus. Propinquitatem Castello quod Fabius ad Vulturni ostium communiverat, ut in his duobus maritimis oppidis, vix tertio invicem distantibus miliario, frumentum deponi potuerit Sardinia avectum, quod postea Capuam importaretur.

Castellutium quoque dividit supra descriptum Falernum agrum a Campano, et propinquum est Sinuessano olim nunc Montis Draconis agro. Nec moveat quemquam ruinarum veteris aedificii paucitas, quae nunc in Castellutio apparet. Casilinum enim parva urbs nequaquam moenium structurarumque munimento, sed Praenestinorum Perusinorumque qui forte praesidio inerant virtute, eam pertulit durissimam obsidionem. Si vero fuerint qui apud vicos superiore loco appositos Vulturno, Cancellum et Arnonum fuisse Casilinum, ideo opinentur, quod in praedictorum aliquo maiusculae **[409D]** cernantur vetustates, considerare debebunt, solam eorum a mari et a Vulturno castello distantiam, ne maritima appellari potuerint adversari, et praeter

From Allifae, he crossed the Vulturnus river beneath Formelo, a fortress, as I have shown in "Abruzzo," of the monastery of S. Vincenzo al Volturno. He set out for Castel di Sangro (as they call it now), which lies next to a hill, and after going over that, he left the *Rasinum* river on his left and reached Furculae Paelignorum, now called Furca Palenae. From there, he turned and went back through the Frentani, Ortonenses, and Aprutini to reach Apulia again.

But now let me return to the regular order of my work. There was in ancient times a city on the right side of the Vulturnus river, at its mouth, named Vulturnum after the river. Livy in book 26:

> Meanwhile the consuls had begun to besiege Capua with all their energy. Whatever was needed for that effort was being transported and provided. Grain was brought to Casilinum. At the mouth of the Vulturnus river, where there is now a city, a stronghold was fortified, Fabius had earlier fortified a post. A garrison was placed there, to maintain control of the sea nearby and the river.

In addition, Livy shows in his thirty-second book that the Romans established a colony, the city of Vulturnum, located at the mouth of the Vulturnus river, where now **[409C]** we see the town called Castel Volturno.

And above Castel Volturno, next to the Volturno on its right side, is a hamlet called *Castellutium*. I am persuaded that *Castellutium* occupies the site of the ancient Casilinum, for I have heard many proofs of this, and not just conjectures. First, there is the similarity between the names, which would not be conclusive in a contest with other evidence; but *Castellutium* possesses other qualities which we see Livy attribute to Casilinum. For example, its proximity to Castellum, which Fabius had fortified at the mouth of the Vulturnus, so that grain from Sardinia could be deposited in these two seacoast towns scarcely three miles apart, then transported to Capua.

Castellutium also is the dividing-line between the Falernian district, which I described above, and that of Campania; and it is close to the territory of the former Sinuessa, now called Mondragone. Nor should anyone be dissuaded from agreeing with me by the small size of the ruins of old buildings which can now be seen at *Castellutium*. For Casilinum was a small city, unimpressive in the fortifications of its walls and buildings, but it withstood that harsh siege through the courage of men of Praeneste and Perusia who were by chance in the garrison. If some people hold that, because **[409D]** they

id esse apud Castellutium non apud Cancellum aut Arnonum eam amnis Vulturni tortuositatem, quam Livius apud Casilinum fuisse dicit.

Arnonum etiam paululum a prisco mutatum est vetus Romanum nomen, quo et non Casilino Livius, si voluisset, uti potuisset. Nam Petrus noster Candidus in Parallelarum Plutarchi translatione, vitam Fabii Maximi et gesta Hannibalis ad Casilinum describens, sic habet: "In ultimas Campaniae oras Casilinum usque delatus est, qua Vulturnus fluvius, quem Natoronum Romani appellant, defluit. Ea regio, montibus undique obsessa, versus mare dumtaxat importuosum ac fluminis ostia aperitur."

Cetera de Casilini obsidione notiora sunt quam ut ea hic poni oportere iudicemus. Sed id unum in Casilini praeconium libet dicere: Casilini obsidione factum esse ut salva fuerit ab Hannibale res Romana, quandoquidem eius loci obsidionis causa Hannibalis animi ex recenti victoria Cannensi ardentes refrixerunt. Et inclusus Capuae exercitus ille ferocissimus Campanis deliciis enervatus est.

Ne etiam Arnonum post amissam Casilini nominis vetusti gloriam, qua a nonnullis ornari consuevit, suo etiam careat praeconio, rem novam ipsius vici occasione dicemus, **[410E]** falconis avis aereae et rapacissimae aucupium, quo inclutus rex Alphonsus Arago apud Arnonum plurimo utitur, ante ducentos annos omnino incognitum fuisse. Nam etsi Servius grammaticus Capuam dicit ab augurio falconis eo nomine appellatam, quod Etrusci eius urbis conditores Capim inaugurantes viderint, quo nomine falconem appellabant, tamen quis fuerit hominibus dictae avis usus non scribit. Pariter Plinius cum multa ponat rapacium avium nomina, accipitres scilicet maiores et minores ac chiluones, quos aliqui falcones fuisse volunt, tamen nullam aucupii usus earundem avium facit mentionem, ut etiam non sit dubitandum quin, si temporibus Virgilii eius aucupii usus fuisset, Aeneam facturus fuerit et Di-

can see more ancient ruins in the villages of Cancello ed Arnone, Casilinum was in a higher place opposite the Volturno, where those villages are now, they will have to consider the argument that their distance alone from the sea and the fort on the Volturno, prevents them from being called seacoast towns; and besides that it is at *Castellutium*, not at Cancello ed Arnone that the Volturno makes that sharp bend which Livy says was at Casilinum.

Arnone bears an ancient Roman name which has changed little from the former one of Arnonum. If he had wished to, Livy could have called it by its own name and not Casilinum. For my friend Pier Candido Decembrio, in his translation of Plutarch's *Parallel Lives*, writes the following in his life of Fabius Maximus and the exploits of Hannibal at Casilinum:

> He was brought to the farthest edge of the Campanian coast to Casilinum, where the Vulturnus river, which the Romans call the Natoronum, flows to the sea. This region is hemmed in on all sides by mountains, and is open towards the sea which at this point offers no harbor, and the mouth of the river.

The rest of the story of the siege of Casilinum is too well-known to deserve mention here. But this one commendation is worth mentioning: throughout the siege of Casilinum, Rome was safe from Hannibal, because the siege of Casilinum caused Hannibal's courage, although it had been kindled by his recent victory at Cannae, to grow cool; and his fierce army shut itself up at Capua, and was weakened by the luxuries of Campania.

The glory of the ancient name of Casilinum, which used to cause many men to celebrate the town, has been lost. But so that Arnone may not lack praise, I shall not pass over its fame. I shall take this opportunity to tell of an innovation associated with this village. This is bird-hunting with **[410E]** falcons, greedy birds of prey, enjoyed here at Arnone by King Alfonso of Aragon, although more than two hundred years ago it was unknown. For although the grammarian Servius says that Capua was named from augury with falcons, because the Etruscan founders of this city saw a falcon when they were taking the auspices (*Capim* was their word for falcon), Servius does not mention what use men made of this bird. Nor does Pliny make any mention of bird-hunting using them, although he gives many names for birds of prey, naturally naming hawks, large and small, and swallows, which some people identify with falcons. We must therefore conclude that, if bird-catching had been practiced in Virgil's time, Virgil would have made Ae-

donem eas quoque aves in venationem tulisse, ubi dixit, "Massilique ruunt equites et odora canum vis." Audemusque confidenti assertione dicere, ante ducentesimum, ut diximus, annum, nullam gentem aut nationem consuevisse, rapaci aliqua ave mansueta alias aves terrestres aut aquatiles aut aerias capere.

Super Castellutium sive Casilinum et duodecimo a mari miliario amni Vulturno adiacet urbs Capua novo quidem loco, qui duo milia **[410F]** passus a priori Capua est semotus. Nec id multis disseri oportet, quando vetustae urbis fundamenta, portae, theatra, templa, et cetera aedificia moles magnae apud S. Mariae basilicam, cui de Gratia est cognomen, internoscuntur. De Capuae autem origine et nomine sic habet Livius in quarto:

> Peregrina res, sed memoria digna traditur eo anno facta. Volturnum, Etruscorum urbem, quae nunc Capua est, ab Samnitibus captam Capuamque ab duce eorum Capuo vel, quod propius est vero, a campestri agro appellatam. Cepere autem prius bello fatigatis Etruscis in societatem urbis accepti, deinde festo die graves somno epulisque incolas veteres novi coloni nocturna caede adorti.

Notissima vero sunt et relatu longiuscula, quae Livius de Capua tradit, sed digniora summatim accipiemus. Libro XXIII dicit Hannibalem cum descendisset ad mare inferum "oppugnaturus Neapolim," flexisse iter in Capuam "luxuriantem longa felicitate ac indulgentia fortunae," eamque recepisse. Et infra, eundem Hannibalem castris apud Casilinum communitis, praesidioque modico imposito, in hiberna Capuam concessisse, ubi exercitus ille Campanis emarcuit deliciis.

Quem vero finem habuerit **[410G]** Capuanorum cum Hannibale amicitia, et si vulgo notissimum est, paucis dicemus. "Capua a Romanis capta," dicit Livius, quosdam ex Romanis censuisse delendum esse urbem praevalidam propinquam inimicam, ceterum praesens vicit utilitas. Nam propter agrum quem omnium fertilitate terrae, satis constabat in Italia primum esse, urbs servata est ut esset aliqua aratorum sedes. Urbis frequentandae multitudo incolarum libertinorumque et institorum, opificumque retenta. Ager omnis et tecta publica populi Romani facta. Ceterum habitari tantum urbem Capu-

neas and Dido take birds of prey on their hunt, when he says, "Moorish horsemen rushed out, with keen-nosed hounds." So I am confident that two hundred years ago, as I said, no tribe or nation was accustomed to capture other birds by using any tamed bird of prey, either those dwelling on land, or sea-birds, or birds of the air.

Above *Castellutium* or Casilinum, and twelve miles from the sea, on the Volturno river, lies the city of Capua. It is in a new place, two **[410F]** miles distant from its former site. Not much proof is needed for this identification, as one can distinguish the foundations of the ancient city, its gates, theatres, temples, and the rest of its buildings, huge structures near the church of Sta. Maria delle Grazie. About the origin of Capua and its name, Livy says the following in book 4:

> A foreign matter, but one worth recording, is transmitted for this year. Vulturnum, a city of the Etruscans, which is the present Capua, was captured by the Samnites and renamed Capua from the name of their leader Capys or, more likely, from its level ground. Now the Samnites captured it first when the Etruscans, tired out by war, took them into partnership in the city; then, on a holiday, when the old inhabitants were heavy with sleep and banqueting, the new settlers attacked them at night and killed them.

The best-known information from Livy about Capua, however, is rather a long story, but one I think worth summarizing. In book 23 he says that Hannibal had marched down to the Tyrrhenian Sea, "intending to attack Naples," but he turned aside to Capua, "which was revelling in its continued prosperity and the indulgence of Fortune." And later on he says that Hannibal, after fortifying his camp at Casilinum and posting a small garrison, retired into winter-quarters at Capua. And his army grew slack from the luxurious life of Campania.

Even though it is commonly known, I shall say a few words about the end of the alliance **[410G]** between Hannibal and the Capuans. "After the Romans had captured Capua," Livy says, some of the Romans thought it best that this very strong and hostile neighboring city be destroyed. However that may be, the city's immediate usefulness won out; because of its territory, known to have the most fertile soil in all Italy, "the city was saved, to be a dwelling-place for cultivators of the public lands." The Romans allowed to remain the city's great number of inhabitants, freedmen, salesmen, and artisans. The entire territory and public buildings became property of the Romans. For the rest, the Romans allowed the city of Capua only to be

am frequentarique placuit, corpus nullum civitatis, nec plebis consilium, nec senatus esse, sine consilio publico, sine imperio. Nec saevitum incendiis ruinisque in tecta innoxia murosque.

Marcus autem Cicero cum legem agrariam supradictam dissuaderet, qua Capuam deduci coloniam volebant, oratione prima habet aliqua, quae non dubitamus Titum Livium, quando supradicta scribebat, perlegisse:

> Capuam deduci coloniam volunt, illam urbem huic urbi rursus opponere. Qui locus propter ubertatem agrorum, abundantiamque rerum omnium superbiam et crudelitatem genuisse videtur. Maiores nostri **[410H]** Capuae magistratus, senatum, consilium commune, omnia denique insignia rei publicae sustulerunt, neque aliud quicquam, nisi inane nomen Capuae reliquerunt. Quod videbant, si quod rei publicae vestigium illis moenibus contineretur, urbem ipsam imperio domicilium praebere posse.

Et in oratione item in Rullum secunda, "At enim ager Campanus dividitur orbis terrae pulcherrimus, et Capua colonia deducitur urbem amplissimam atque ornatissimam." Et infra,

> Unumne fundum pulcherrimum populi Romani, caput vestrae pecuniae, pacis ornamentum, subsidium belli, fundamentum vectigalium, horreum legionum, solacium annonae disperire patiemini? At vero hoc agri Campani vectigal cum eius modi sit ut domi sit, et omnibus praesidiis oppidorum tegatur, neque bellis sit infestum, nec fructibus varium, nec caelo et loco calamitosum.

Et infra,

> Campani semper superbi bonitate agrorum et fructuum magnitudine, urbis salubritate ac pulchritudine. Ex hac copia et omnium rerum affluentia, primum illa nata est arrogantia, quae a maioribus nostris alterum consulem postulavit, deinde ea luxuries, quae ipsum Hannibalem, armis etiam tunc invictum, voluptate vicit.

lived in and filled with people: they did not allow it to have any citizen body, nor a council, nor a senate; it was left without its own government, without power. But they did not punish it with fire, nor pull down its buildings and walls, as they were innocent.

When Cicero was delivering his first speech against the aforementioned agrarian law, which its proponents intended to use to establish a colony at Capua, he has the following words; Livy's thorough familiarity (in his words, quoted above) is obvious from a comparison with Cicero's words:

> They wish to send colonists to Capua. They are thinking of once again opposing that city to this one. Through the fertility of its fields and the abundance of its produce, this place seems to have brought forth arrogance and cruelty. Our ancestors destroyed the magistracies **[410H]** of Capua, its senate, its popular assembly, and all the marks of its political existence, so that nothing was left except the empty name of Capua. They did this because they saw that if its walls held any trace of a political entity, the city itself might offer an abode for power.

Cicero also said, in the second oration against Rullus, "But the territory of Campania is being divided up, the most beautiful land in the world; and a colony is being established at Capua, that large and splendid city." And further on,

> Will you endure the disappearance of the single most beautiful estate belonging to the Roman people, the source of your wealth, the ornament of peace, your support in war, the basis of your revenues, the granary of your legions, relief in case of a shortage of grain? But in fact the revenues from Campanian territory are of just this kind: they are located in our country and are protected by all the garrisons of our towns, and are neither exposed to danger from wars, nor variable in their produce, which is also invulnerable to damage from the weather or from their surroundings.

And below this,

> The Campanians have always been proud, due to the fertility of their fields, the abundance of their crops, the healthiness and beauty of their city. It is this abundance, this affluence of everything, which gave rise to that arrogance which made them demand from our ancestors that one of the consuls should be elected from Capua, then to that luxury which overcame Hannibal with pleasure although he had up to that point been invincible in war.

Hanc ipsam urbem contra ac Cicero suaserat Iulius Caesar coloniam deduci voluit, de quo Suetonius,

> Cum in colonia Capua deducti lege Iulia coloni, ad exstruendas villas vetustissima **[411A]** sepulcra disiicerent idque eo studiosius facerent, quod aliquantum operis antiqui scrutantes reperiebant, tabula aenea in monumento, in quo dicebatur Capis conditor Capuae sepultus, inventa est.

Eandem vero Capuam urbem, quam Romanus populus in tam iusto odio servavit, et quam Cicero tantis extulit laudibus, rex Vandalorum Gensericus ad annum sexcentesimum postquam Romanis fuerat subdita, ferro ignique destructam reliquit habitatoribus destitutam. Et cum Ostrogothis a Narsete omni potentatu deiectis eodem loco, eosdemque inter parietes et muros Capua rehabitata esset. Ad annum inde circiter centesimum a Longobardis sub triginta ducibus tunc agentibus iterum destructa fuit. Quis autem et quo tempore postea eam ad hunc, in quo nunc est duos mille passus remotum transtulerit locum, nec alicubi legimus, nec ab his qui inhabitant civibus scire potuimus.

Plinius in Italiae descriptione, cum ad Capuam pervenit, campum illi adiacere dixit Leborinum totius Italiae amoenissimum, et libro septimodecimo, de terrarum diversitate tractans, Leborinum Capuae campum nobilem appellat. Eiusque solum dicit arduum opera et difficile cultu bonis **[411B]** quam vitiis uberius pascere. Est vero hoc totum campestre solum, quod a Tiphatis monte urbi imminente ad Neapolitanos Puteolanosque colles pertinens, Vulturno ab ipsa urbe Capua ad eius ostia quibus se in mare exonerat est clausum. Et periti regionis Capuani cives affirmant campos, qui Aversam urbem novam ad Atellae urbis vetustae ruinas aedificatam circumstant, in trecentorum annorum publicis privatisque monumentis dici Leborios; eam vero vim habuit Leborinae terrae appellatio, ut Campaniae nomen in suum mutari obtinuerit. Idque nos meliuscule quam a pravis chronicorum scriptoribus est traditum, referre confidimus.

Capua urbe vetusti in eam Romanorum odii et binae desolationis exsecrabili infamia laborante, vicini urbium oppidorumque populi Campanos se appellari ignominiosum periculosumque ducentes, id declinarunt patrium nomen, et sese Leborinos pro Campanis dixere, effecitque obstinata eorum

Contrary to Cicero's dissuasion, Julius Caesar wanted to establish a colony at the site of the city itself; about this Suetonius wrote,

> The colonists settled at Capua under the Julian Law were tearing down very ancient **[411A]** tombs for the purpose of building villas, and they did this all the more assiduously because, in their digging, they came across some ancient artefacts. A bronze tablet was found in a tomb, which said that Capys, founder of Capua, was buried there.

But this very city of Capua, which the Romans so justifiably persisted in hating for so long, and which Cicero praises so highly-Genseric, king of the Vandals, destroyed it six hundred years after its submission to Rome. He left it deserted, and after the Ostrogoths had been driven out from there by Narses, Capua was resettled within the same walls. But about a hundred years later the Lombards, under the thirty leaders then governing them, destroyed it a second time with fire and the sword, and left it deserted. I have not read anywhere, nor have I been able to find out from its present inhabitants, who transferred the city's location to where it is now, about two miles distant, and when this removal happened.

When Pliny in his description of Italy mentioned Capua, he said that the Leborini Campi lie next to the city, and that this is the most pleasant land in all Italy. And in his seventeenth book on diverse lands, when discussing Capua's Terra di Lavoro area, he calls it noble and says that its soil is hard to cultivate more fruitfully than **[411B]** with good vines. But this entire territory is flat, because it is closed in by Mte. Tifata extending to the Volturno from the city of Capua itself to the river's mouth, where it empties into the sea. And citizens of Capua who are familiar with the region say that the fields which surround the new city, Aversa, which was built near the ruins of the ancient city of Atella, these fields have been called "Leborini" for three hundred years in public and private records. The name Terra di Lavoro carried such weight that the name of Campania was irresistibly compelled to change to it. And I have more confidence to repeat this assertion than what has been handed down by the unreliable writers of chronicles.

The ancient city of Capua suffered from unspeakable disgrace as a result of the Romans' hatred, and the fact that it had twice been deserted. So the people of the neighboring cities and towns considered their ancestral name shameful and dangerous, and avoided using it. They called themselves Leborini instead of Campani, and stubbornly persisted in this until all the

perseverantia ut, quicquid urbium et locorum in Campania censeri solebat, de Terra Leboris diceretur. Sed corruptum nunc laboris verbum in eam partem ab ignorantibus accipitur, ut Laboris Terram, cui labor utiliter impendatur, **[411C]** dictam existiment; quamquam non desunt, qui magis absurde dicant, terram hanc a labore, quem illi capiendae et dominio subigendae impendi oporteat, sic a maioribus appellatam.

Atella vero urbs, cuius saepe meminit Livius, et quam Cicero supra de lege agraria cum Teano opprimi aegre ferundum ostendit, fuisse ubi nunc est nova urbs Adversa, praeter alias rationes hoc uno constat argumento, quod S. Mariae ecclesia haud longe ac Adversa cognomen "in Atella" vetustum retinet. Libetque utriusque urbis et veteris et novae dignitates referre. Primum Atella haud quamquam minora in re parva, quam Capua in magnis praebuit Campanae luxuriae documenta. Si quidem pro superbiae et crudelitatis origine, quam Cicero tribuit Capuae, haec Atellanarum carminum lasciviam modulationemque, quod nomen indicat, et Macrobius affirmat, invenit. Quid vero hae fuerint Atellanae, M. Varro, Aulus Gellius, Macrobiusque et Iuvenalis satiricus saepe indicant, earumque artis cum non expediat, nec sit huius temporis et loci inquirere documentum, satis supraque fuerit obscenam notare lasciviam. Pueri et puellae luxuriemque spumantes natu maiores, compositum metro ac **[411D]** musica, modulatione, lascivis et omnia dictu factuque pudenda exprimentibus verbis carmen, motu quoque corporis et gestu, quaqua versum etiam resupinato, ita in choreis, et ad impudicorum mensas pronuntiabant gesticulabanturque, ut nihil praeter ipsum coeundi exquisitissimum deesset effectum.

Meliora autem originis et disciplinae rudimenta habuit urbs Adversa. Robertus Guiscardus, vir gloria et laude dignissimus, magnam et praestantem eam Italiae partem, quae regnum Siciliae aut Neapolitanum est appellata, a Saracenis Graecisque laceratam, ad regni ipsius formam primus redegit, qui Neapolim Capuamque una eademque premens obsidione, castra apud Atellam habuit communita, in quibus cum aliquot perseverasset annis civitatem condidit, ab ipsoque adversandi praeclaris et potentibus urbibus affectu, Adversae illi nomen in rei gestae memoriam dedit.

Sed iam ad maris litus est redeundum. Post Vulturnum sequitur Clanius apud Suessulam oppidum, medio paene inter Capuam et Nolam urbes tractu,

cities and places that used to be considered as in Campania were said to belong to Terra di Lavoro. But the word *laboris* has undergone corruption and been accepted by ignorant people in the sense that they think Terra di Lavoro means that on which labor is profitably expended, **[411C]** although some say, less sensibly, that our ancestors named this land after the *labor* necessary to capture it and subdue it.

The city of Atella (so our ancestors called it) is frequently mentioned in Livy. Cicero, in the speech I mentioned on the agrarian law, shows that Atella, along with Teanum Sidicinum, was located where the new city, Aversa, is now. In addition to other arguments, the site of the ancient Atella is established by this argument alone: that the church of Sta. Maria, not far away from Aversa, has kept its old epithet "in Atella." I should like to relate the merits of each of the two cities, the old and the new. First, Atella offered on a small scale as much proof of Campanian luxury as did Campania on a large scale. Consistent with the role of founder of arrogance and cruelty which Cicero attributes to Capua, the smaller city (as the name indicates, and Macrobius supports it) was the inventor of the lewd measures of the Atellan farce. In fact Varro, Aulus Gellius, Macrobius, and the satirist Juvenal often reveal to us what these plays were like. I do not think it worthwhile to explain their techniques, nor is this the time and place to look for evidence; it is sufficient to note that they were obscene and lustful. Older boys and girls, foaming at the mouth with wantonness, would sing a song whose lewd words, meter, and **[411D]** tune expressed every shameful act and saying, with movement and gesture to all sides, even lying on their backs in their dances, performing to shameless people at banquets with the result that they left nothing to the imagination in their suggestions of the most advanced sexual activities.

The city of Aversa, however, boasted better principles, both in its origins and in its accomplishments. Robert Guiscard, a most praiseworthy man, organized into a kingdom this great and distinguished part of Italy, the so-called kingdom of Sicily or Naples, which the Arabs and Greeks had carved up. He besieged Naples and Capua together, at the same time, and had a fortified camp at Atella, where after some years' duration he built a city. In memory of this siege he named the city Adversa, from the state of mind produced by the opposition of the famous and powerful cities.

But now I must return to the coast. After the Volturno river follows the Clanio at the town of Castel di Sessola, almost in the middle of the tract of land between Capua and Nola; it has its source in the mountains. And it was

in montibus oriundus. Estque is fluvius, de quo Virgilius Clanius non aequus Acerris, quia Acerrarum urbis agrum sicut et Capuanum olim Atellanum nunc Adversanum, multis inundat in locis, adeo ut longiusculis pontibus eum Capuam inter et Adversam urbem oporteat iungi, ad quos pontes molas esse multas videmus.

[412E] Eidem Clanio haud longe a mari infero turris apposita est parum vetusta nunc Patriae appellata, et in ruinis Linterni Scipionis Africani villae aedificata. Namque Ptolemaeus, Pomponiusque Mela, Plinius, et Guido Ravennas Iginii imitator Linternum inter Vulturnum et Cumas ponunt. Livius autem uno in loco cum supradictis sentire, in alio discrepare videtur. Nam libro vigesimosecundo, cum difficultates afferret quibus Hannibal coactus videretur ex Falerno agro, qua venerat angusta via in Samnium rediturus, quod supra diximus sic habet, "Poenus tunc inter fortunae minas ac Linterni arenas per horrida situ hibernaturus esset." Cum ergo ad sinistram Vulturni tunc ageret Hannibal, nec ipsum amnem ibi praealtum vado, neque ponte ad Casilinum communito ac praesidiis firmato, transmissurus videretur, oportuit ad Falerni agri partem esse Linternum, ubi eum Livius, nisi angustias superasset, hiematurum fuisse dicit. Et libro vigesimotertio idem Livius, cum fraudem scribit qua Capuani Cumas suis partibus adiicere sint conati, sic habet, "Interim Titus Sempronius consul Sinuessae, quo ad conveniendum diem edixerat exercitu lustrato transgressus **[412F]** Vulturnum flumen circa Linternum posuit castra."

Ex quibus nulli dubium fuerit constare Linternum fuisse, sicut dicti asserunt cosmographi, ad eam Vulturni partem, quae spectat in Cumas. Necessariumque erit et dicere et tenere Livium, qui loca perambulaverit, et Linterni, sicut infra ostendimus, Scipionis statuam tempestate disiectam viderit, scivisse villam quidem ultra Vulturnum, sed eius agrum arenosum stagnosumque circa exstitisse. Est vero Linternum locus in quo P. Scipio Africanus voluntarium egit exsilium, quem fama est morientem sepulcro inscribi iussisse: "Ingrata patria, ne ossa quidem mea habes." Quae facta in monumento ingratitudinis patriae inscriptio effecit, ut locum nuper certius exploratiusque invenerimus. Namque ad dictum amnem Clanium paulo supra ostium, quod

this river (the ancient Clanius) about which Virgil wrote, "The Clanius, unjust to Acerrae," because it flooded in many places the territory of the city of Acerrae (just as it floods the territory of Capua which belonged formerly to Atella, but now belongs to Aversa). The floods even forced men to build over it long bridges between Capua and the city of Adversa, and today we see many piers for those bridges.

[412E] Near the Clanio, not far from the sea, there is a tower, not very old, now called Torre di Patria, built among the ruins of Scipio Africanus' villa at Liternum. For indeed Ptolemy, Pomponius Mela, Pliny, and Guido of Ravenna, the follower of Hyginus, locate Liternum between the Vulturnus and Cumae. But Livy seems in one passage to agree with these authors, in another to differ; for in book 22, relating the hardships which were driving Hannibal out of the Falernian district, as he was preparing to return to Samnium along the narrow road by which he had come, he writes (I cited this above), "At that time it appeared that Hannibal would have to spend the winter between the threats of fortune and the sands of Liternum, in a rough environment." As Hannibal was then deploying on the left side of the Vulturnus, therefore, and did not seem able to cross the river, which was very deep there, nor at Casilinum where the bridge was fortified and equipped with a garrison, Liternum must be in the area of the Falernian district, where Livy says Hannibal would have had to spend the winter unless he could have gotten over the passes. And in the same vein, in book 23, where Livy describes the deceit which the Capuans tried to use to take over Cumae, he writes: "Meanwhile the consul Titus Sempronius had ordered his army to assemble for review at Sinuessa and had crossed the **[412F]** Vulturnus river, and pitched camp around Liternum."

From these reports, there can be no doubt that Liternum was located, as the geographers say, on the side of the Volturno that faces Cuma. Anyone who walks through the site ought to take with him a copy of Livy, and if he views the storm-torn statue of Scipio at Torre di Patria he will have to admit that Livy knew the villa was beyond the Vulturnus, but that the land around it was sandy and swampy. In fact, Liternum is the place where P. Scipio Africanus lived out his voluntary exile, where his tomb is supposed to have been inscribed at his order "Ungrateful fatherland, you possess not even my bones." This inscription commemorating his fatherland's ingratitude verifies and confirms my recent identification of the site. For at the previously mentioned river Clanio, a little above its mouth, stands a tower built on top of the

habet in mare, turris est ruinis aedificiorum veterum superaedificata, quam ut diximus "Turrim Patriae" vocant, ubi id monumentum fuisse tenemus.

Et praeter id patriae vocabulum, praeterque supradicta Ptolemaei, Plinii, Livii, et aliorum testimonia, certitudinem quoque attulit nobis evidentiorem fons aquae acidulae, quem Plinius Linterni fuisse dicit, cuius **[412G]** aqua vini modo faciat temulentos. Scatet enim nunc etiam inter praedictas aedificiorum ruinas aqua, quam pastores affirmant epotam omnes capitis langores curare. Nos eaque accurate gustata, saporem quidem ut ceterarum, quae bibuntur, bonum esse cognovimus. Sed quamvis fumos ab ea in nares, sicut a vino consuevit, non ingratos olfecerimus, quos potatio habeat effectus, forte ob haustus moderationem intellegere nequivimus.

Seneca epistola LI, "Linterni honestius Scipio quam Baiis exsulabat." Sepulcri autem eiusque inscriptionis et monumenti ac statuae si nullum nunc exstat certum indicium minus miror, quod Livius Patavinus, qui minus centum annis ab illius aetate abfuit, quid ipse viderit libro XXVIIII scribit, "Scipionem alii Romae alii Linterni mortuum et sepultum ferunt, utrobique monumenta ostenduntur et statuae." Nam et Linterni monumentum, monumentoque statua superimposita fuit, quam tempestate disiectam nuper vidimus ipsi. Et Romae extra portam Capenam in Scipionum monumento tres statuae sunt, duae Publii et Lucii Scipionum dicuntur esse, tertia poetae Q. Ennii. Et Seneca epistolae LXXVII initio videtur **[412H]** id ignorasse sepulcrum. Nam dicit in ipsa, "Scipionis villa iacens, haec tibi scribo adoratis manibus eius et ara, quam sepulcrum esse tanti viri suspicor."

Linterno Cumae ad quintum adiacent miliare, interque utrumque locum qua in parte litus inter stagnum et mare incurvatur villa fuit Servilii Vatiae, quam Seneca epistola LV describit, dicitque praetorium hominem illum divitem, nulla alia re notum fuisse, quam eius villae otio, in quo consenuerit, ut occupati aliquando clamaverint, "O Vatia solus scis vivere," cum tamen ille, iudicio Senecae, sciret latere, non vivere. Unde dicit de se ipso Seneca solitum quoties illac transiret iocando dicere, non de vivo sed tamquam de mortuo, "hic situs est Vatia."

ruins of ancient buildings; the tower is called, as I noted, Torre di Patria, where I submit this tomb stood.

And besides the word "fatherland," besides the abovementioned attestations of Ptolemy, Pliny, Livy, and others, I am also brought to clearer certainty about this identification by a spring of acidic mineral water which Pliny says was at Liternum, whose **[412G]** water made people drunk as does wine. For its water flows forth even now among the ruins of buildings I mentioned, and the local shepherds claim that drinking it cures all illnesses of the head. And I tasted it carefully and know that it certainly has a good taste, like other drinks. But although its effect was a smoky bouquet, as with wine, I did not find this an unpleasant smell. Perhaps I was unable, however, to make a well-founded judgment because I drank only moderately from the spring.

Seneca wrote in *Epistle* 51, "Scipio chose the more decent exile of Liternum, instead of going to Baiae." But I am not surprised at the present lack of definite information about the tomb, the inscription, the monument and the statue, seeing that Livy of Padua, who lived less than a hundred years after Scipio's time, writes in book 29 about what he saw: "Some say Scipio died and was buried at Rome; some say at Liternum. In each place, people point out monuments and statues." On the other hand, I have myself recently seen the monument at Torre di Patria, and the statue placed on top of it, which has been torn apart by storms. And at Rome, outside of the Porta Capena, are three statues on a monument to the Scipios, two of which are said to be dedicated to Publius and Lucius Scipio, the third to the poet Quintus Ennius. And Seneca, in the beginning of *Epistle* 77, seems **[412H]** not to know about the tomb; for he says in that letter, "I write this to you while staying at the former villa of Scipio; I have paid reverence to his shade, and to the altar which I think is the tomb of the great man."

Cuma lies five miles from the site of Liternum, and between the two places, where the shore curves between the marsh and the sea, was the villa of Servilius Vatia. Seneca, *Epistle* 55, describes him, saying that he was a wealthy man of praetorian rank, but not known for anything other than the leisure of his villa. Here he grew old, and busy men now and then called upon him with "O Vatia, you alone know how to live." (In Seneca's opinion, he knew how to be obscure, not to live.) For this reason, Seneca had a habit of making a joke about him whenever he passed by there, and saying about him as if he were not alive but dead, "Here lies Vatia."

Cumanae urbis originem hanc tradit Livius in VIII,

> Cumani a Chalcide Euboica originem trahunt. Classe qua advecti domo fuerant, multum in ora maris eius quod incolunt potuere. Primo in insulam Aenariam et Pithecusas egressi, deinde in continentem ausi sedes transferre.

Virgilius:

> Et tandem Euboicis Cumarum illabitur oris.

Et,

> Hic ubi delatus Cumaeam accesseris urbem,

super quo Servius,

> Euboea insula est, de cuius civitate Chalcide profecti sunt ad novas sedes quaerendas, et haud longe a Baiis, qui loco a Baio Ulyssis filio hic sepulto nomen accepit, invenerunt vacuum litus, ubi visa muliere gravida civitatem condiderunt.

Livius **[413A]** in secundo, "Accersita deinde auxilia et a Latinis populis et a Cumis. Cumanae cohortes arte adversus vim usae declinavere paululum, effuseque palantes hostes conversis signis a tergo adortae sunt." Et infra, "Insignis hic annis nuntio Tarquinii mortis. Mortuus est Cumis quo se post fractas opes Latinorum ad Aristodemum tyrannum contulerat." Et libro quarto, "Eodem anno a Campanis Cumae quam Graeci tunc urbem tenebant capiuntur." Et octavo, "Cumanos Suessulanosque eiusdem iuris conditionisque, cuius Capua esse placuit."

Est vero celsus in urbe Cumana collis, in cuius cacumine fuit templum Apollinis, de quo Virgilius,

> Arces quibus altus Apollos praesidet.

Et quidem nunc ea in urbe, quam vidimus omni destitutam habitatore, praeter rupes saxo stupendas vivo, pinnae cernuntur murorum excelsae. Et ubi

The origins of the city of Cumae are recorded by Livy, book 8:

> The people of Cumae trace their origin to Chalcis in Euboea. With the fleet which they had used to migrate from their home, they had a great deal of power on the seacoast along which they lived. They had first disembarked on the island of Aenaria and on Pithecusae, and then had the courage to transfer their home to the mainland of Italy.

And Virgil has,

> And at last [the fleet] glides towards the Euboean shores of Cumae.

And,

> Here, when you have been conveyed over the sea and have reached the city of Cumae.

On this verse Servius comments,

> Euboea is an island. From one of its city-states, Chalcis, colonists set out looking for a new place to settle, and they found an uninhabited shore not far from Baiae, a place which took its name from the fact that Baios, Ulysses' son, was buried there. In this place they saw a pregnant woman, and founded their city.

Livy, **[413A]** in book 2, says, "Then they called for aid from both the native Latin population and from the people of Cumae. The forces from Cumae employed strategy against force, and turned aside a little, and attacked the enemy from the rear as they struggled, spread out with their standards turned around." And later on Livy writes, "This year was marked by the announcement of Tarquin's death. He died at Cumae, where he had taken refuge with the tyrant Aristodemus after the resources of the Latins had been broken." And in book 4, "In the same year Cumae, a city which Greeks then possessed, was captured by the Campanians." And in the eighth book, "the people of Cumae and Suessa, under the same dominion and law, which Capua had."

But there is a high hill in the city of Cuma, on whose peak there was a temple of Apollo. Virgil writes about it,

> The citadel over which lofty Apollo presides.

And indeed, in that city which we see utterly deserted by humans, we can see even now, besides the incredible cliffs cut in the living rock, the lofty

Apollinis arx fuit, sacellum est Christianum et ipsum vetustate consumptum, nihilque exstat integrum, nisi caverna frontispicio decorata manufacto, quam Sibyllae antrum fuisse socius itineris nostri Prosper Camuleius, vir doctus eam ingressus, quibusdam coniecturis affirmavit.

Fuit quoque Cumis propinquus ad tria milia passuum Hamarum locus sacer, **[413B]** de quo Livius vigesimotertio: "Campani adorti sunt rem Cumanam suae iurisdictionis facere, primo sollicitantes ut ab Romanis deficerent. Ubi id parum processit, dolum ad capiendum eos comparant." Sacrificium ad Hamas nocturnum erat. Huius vero olim celebris loci mons arduus, qui a balneis nunc Tripergulanis vix mille quingentos abest passus, ruinis ad verticem tegitur conspiciendis, et quibus nulla est propior Tripergulis hominum habitatio aut cultura. Ad partem vero, qua Cumae spectant in Avernum et Baias, distat pariter ab utrisque urbibus fornix lateritio opere sublimibus columnis sustentatus, cuicumque Romano operi comparandus.

Abest deinde quinto a Cumis Misenus mons, Virgilii carmine celebratus, "et nunc Misenus ab illo dicitur." Eidemque qua spectat in Cumas lacunae adiacent nunc Mare Mortuum appellatae, circa quas in continentis supercilio ruinae et fundamenta cernuntur eximia. Fuit namque locus in quo Suetonius Tranquillus scribit Octavianum Augustum classem apud Misenum instituisse ingentem, quae versas in Tyrrhenum mare imperii Romani provincias, hinc Galliam et utramque Hispaniam, inde Mauritaniam **[413C]** Africamque et interiectas insulas tutaretur. Eratque eius classis praefectus Plinius Veronensis quando apud Vesevum montem incendio est absumptus.

Distant a Miseni promontorio hinc Cumae sicut diximus, quinto inde Lucrinus Avernusque totidem mille passus. Et cum a Cumis vix quattuor milibus terrestri via absit Avernus, illa quinum undique milium maritima longitudo, terram ambit omnium olim Italiae pulcherrimam, in qua Baiae fuerunt civitas opulenta. Idque omne solum et si quinis, ut diximus, productum est milibus, latitudine tamen parum variata, duo alicubi et minus alibi milia explet, ut digiti unius speciem prae se ferat, quo in terrarum, ut ita dixerim, digito tam multa cernuntur, partim integra in subterraneis, partim

battlements of walls. And this is where the citadel of Apollo was. It is now a Christian chapel that is also worn away with age, and nothing whole remains there, except a cavern decorated with a man-made façade. This has been definitely identified from reasonable inferences as the cave of the Sibyl by my companion on an archaeological excursion, the learned Prospero Camogli, who actually entered the cave.

Also near Cuma, about three miles distant, is the sacred place of Hamae, now Torre San Severino, **[413B]** mentioned by Livy in book 23: "The Campanians tried to put Cumae under their power, first inciting them to desert from their alliance with the Romans.... The sacrifice (at Hamae) was held at night." The high mountain where this place, famous in ancient times, was located, is scarcely one and one-half miles from the modern baths of Tripergola, and you can see the ruins which cover its peak, and there is no inhabited or cultivated place nearer to Tripergola. But in the direction in which Cuma faces Averno and Baia, equidistant from each city there is a brick arch held up on high columns, comparable to any Roman structure.

Then comes Capo Miseno, five miles from Cuma. It is famed in Virgil's poem, "and it is now called Misenus, after his name."

Next to it, on the side of it that faces in the direction of Cuma, are small lakes now called Mare Morto; around them on the brow of the mainland one can see some remarkable ruins of walls and foundations. It was the place where, Suetonius tells us, Augustus established a huge fleet at Misenum. This fleet was to protect the provinces of the Roman Empire facing the Tyrrhenian Sea, on this side Gaul and the two Spains, on the other side Morocco and **[413C]** Africa and the islands in between. And Pliny of Verona was in charge of this fleet when he was killed in the eruption of Vesuvius.

On this side, as I mentioned, lies Cuma, five miles from the promontory of Miseno, and five miles from Cuma are Lago di Lucrino and Lago di Averno. Although Averno is scarcely four miles by land from Cuma by the straight overland route, that distance by sea is five miles. The coast road of ten miles, taking the long way around, encompasses land that was once the most beautiful in all Italy, where the wealthy city of Baiae was. If that entire piece of land is extended, as I said, five miles, but its width is not much changed, it occupies two miles in some places, less in others, with the result that it creates the appearance of a finger of land. On that finger of land, as I said, many things can be seen, some of them intact but underground, some

superius semiruta, partim in ruinas collapsa veterum operum monumenta, ut extra urbis Romae moenia, nihil illi toto in orbe terrarum aedificiorum magnitudine ac pulchritudine par credam existimemque fuisse, ut non iniuria dicat Horatius,

> Nullus in orbe locus Bais praelucet amoenis.

Cumque Misenus e regione Puteolos spectet, mare quo invicem dirimuntur, ex Suetonii Tranquilli in via Caii Caligulae sententia, vix tria milia **[413D]** passuum et sexcentos implet, unde sinus utrobique dictus olim Baianus, a Miseno in intimum Averni sinum quinis et totidem ab Averno in Puteolos milibus est productus. Fuerit vero operosum singula describere, quae aut digitus ille terrestris, aut sinus Baianus habet. Sed digniora quantum fieri poterit breviter attingemus.

Primum Misenus ipse mons, qua in promontorium coarctatur et si natura cavernosus fuerit, tamen tantis excavatus est operum laboribus, tantis vel marmoreis, vel lateritio et lapide quadrato compactis, in sublime ductis sustentatur columnis, ut ubique pensilis videatur. Erantque ut apparet intus balnea, erant natatoria, erant ad cenas luxumque triclinia. Superius vero in continenti, et qua vergit in praedictum Misenatium classis locum, fundamenta visuntur his, qui non viderint incredibilia, ubi Piscinam vulgo Mirabilem dicunt. Nam cum ea pulcherrime, ut constat aedis desuper destructae fundamenta fuerint, pars haec exstans subterranea, sublimibus sustentata lateritiis columnis, ducentos quinquaginta longitudine centumque et sexaginta latitudine passus patet. Et ita est integra, ut nova videatur, quam Lucii Luculli domum, quae illi erat in Baiano fuisse tenemus.

Et quia in loco omnium Italiae calido est sita, videtur esse illa de qua Plutarchus scribit Lucullum perbelle cum Cn. Pompeio ac Marco Cicerone **[414E]** et plerisque illius saeculi viris iocatum fuisse. Cum ipsis omnibus Romanis in Lucullano nunc Frascato apud Lucullum aestate cenantibus, Pompeio imperitiam aedificandi in Lucullo damnanti, quod domum pulcherrimam sumptuosissimamque nimis multis porticibus fenestrisque apertam, aestati quidem idoneam sed hiemi omnino inhabilem fecisset. Ille respondit, virtuti suae Pompeium detrahere, qui grues se prudentiores existimet, aestiva

of them on the surface and partially destroyed, some of them structures of ancient workmanship which have collapsed into ruin. I don't believe there is anything the equal of these ruins in size and beauty outside of the city of Rome, anywhere in the world, and I should think that Horace speaks accurately when he says,

> No place in the world outshines pleasant Baiae.

Miseno faces Pozzuoli, and they are in turn separated by the sea, the stretch of sea which separates them is, according to Suetonius in his *Life of Caligula*, scarcely three miles **[413D]**; on each side the bay was formerly called "of Baiae," and it extended five miles from Misenum to the middle of Avernus, and extended the same distance from Avernus to Puteoli. It would, however, be burdensome to describe individual details of the finger of land on the bay of Baia. But I shall touch as briefly as possible upon the features which are worthy of notice.

First, there is Mte. Miseno itself, squeezed into a promontory. By nature it is full of cavities, but it has been excavated with great effort, and columns of marble, or brick and blocks of stone seem to hold it up, so that it appears everywhere to be hanging. And it seems that inside there were baths, swimming-pools, banqueting places and areas for luxury. Higher up on the neighboring mainland, where it borders on the place where the fleet was kept, can be seen foundations, incredible to those who have not seen them, commonly called the Marvelous Pool. These foundations supported a very beautiful house that has been destroyed; part of it still exists underground, held up by tall brick columns, 250 paces long and 160 wide. It is intact and looks as good as new, and I identify this as the house of Lucius Lucullus, which he possessed in the territory of Baiae.

Because the ruins are located in a hot area of Italy, this too supports its identification as the villa of Lucullus, about which Plutarch wrote, describeing a charming joke of Lucullus **[414E]** on Pompey and Cicero and many other men of that age. When all of these Romans were dining in the summer with Lucullus at his villa, located in what is now Frascati, Pompey criticized Lucullus for his lack of experience in building, because he had built a very beautiful and splendid house which was very open, with many colonnades and windows, most appropriate for summer but completely uninhabitable in winter. Lucullus replied that Pompey was disparaging his competence, because he thought cranes were wiser than he, since they live alternately in summer homes and in winter ones. For the architect who built this villa suit-

loca hiemaliaque alternis inhabitantes. Sese enim dicit qui hanc in Lucullano aestati idoneam fabrefecerit, alteram in semper vernanti Baiano hiemalem pulcherrimamque exaedificasse. Sepulchra vero et villarum aliorumque monumentorum vestigia, partim omnino prostrata, partim semiintegra tam multa eo in quinum milium peninsulae et digiti territorio cernuntur, ut continuatam ibi urbem potiusquam dispersas per agrum villas fuisse appareat.

Sed iam sinum describamus Baianum, de quo nihil est quod admirabilius dicere possimus, quam quod omnia eius litora decem milia passuum a Miseno ad Puteolos in circuitu protensa, aedificiis et quidem omnium quae raro alibi viderimus maximis **[414F]** contecta ac continuata fuerunt, cum eorum pars collibus imposita celsissimis, et in apertum prominentibus pelagum bracchiis sustentata fuerit, insanarum molium opere in profundissimum mare iactis. Exstant tamen aliqua paene integra, thermae scilicet ad ipsum Baianum sinum intimum, qui unicus nunc locus priscam Baiani appellationem memoriamque conservat. Sunt et aliae paene similes thermae illis propinquae, quarum conditoris et nominis notitiam habere nequivimus. Sed balneum longe infra Avernum petentibus et Lucrinum est obvium, nedum aedificii structuram sed et picturam quoque aliqua ex parte integram conservans, in quo versuum pars pictorum exstat, ex quorum verbis carptim lectis coniicere licet, id fuisse Ciceronis balneum, cui id carmen libertum eius adscripsisse Plinius asserit.

Supraque illud idem Ciceronianum aliud est balneum, in longam tortuosamque fossam saxo excavatum, quod sine aliquo aquae calentis usu solo vapore sudores provocat copiosissimos et, sicut ferunt medici, saluberrimos. Fuit vero maioribus thermarum huiusmodi usus, quas ab actu fricandi tergendique necessario Frictolas **[414G]** appellarunt, easque aeque ac balneas viduis et virginibus Christianis evitandas esse, gloriosus ecclesiae doctor Hieronymus admonuit. Tritolam nunc corrupte appellant.

Incipitque ad eam sinus Baiani partem Lucrinus esse, de quo in Virgiliani versus expositione "An memorem portus Lucrinoque addita claustra," Servius sic habet:

> In Baiano sinu Campaniae contra Puteolam civitatem lacus sunt duo, Avernus et Lucrinus, qui olim propter copiam piscium vectigalia magna praestabant. Sed cum maris impetus plerumque perrumpens exinde pisces excluderet, et redemptores gravia damna paterentur, supplicaverunt senatui. Et profectus Caesar ductis bracchiis exclusit partem maris quae ante infesta esse consueverat,

able for summer on Lucullus' estate had built another, suitable for winter residence, in the always springlike region of Baiae. On this peninsula and its five-mile-long finger of land, you can see tombs and the remains of villas and other monuments, some completely collapsed, some partly intact, so many that there seems to have been a continuous city there, rather than villas scattered through the territory.

But now let me describe the bay of Baia: I can say nothing more amazing than that all its coastline extends in a circle for ten miles from Miseno to Pozzuoli and is covered by a continuous series of very great buildings, the likes of which I have indeed rarely seen elsewhere. Part of them is located on high hills, **[414F]** and juts into the open sea held up by breakwaters, enormous works cast into the deepest part of the ocean. But some ruins are scarcely intact, I mean of course the baths at the innermost point of the bay of Baia; this place alone now preserves the ancient name and the memory of Baiae. There are also other baths nearby, but in no way similar, whose builder's name and reputation I could not obtain. But far below, travelers who are looking for Averno and Lucrino will find a bath, which does not preserve the structure of a building but a fragment of a painting, on which part of a verse survives, and if you read the fragments of it, you can reasonably infer that this was the bath of Cicero, for Pliny says that Cicero's freedman inscribed on it this poem.

Above this bath of Cicero is another bath, dug out from the rock into a long and twisting ditch. It does not produce any hot water, but brings forth sweat by steam alone. The sweat it produces is very abundant and, as doctors say, very healthful. This was in fact our ancestors' custom in using hot springs, and they called them Frictolae after the necessary motion of rubbing and scraping. **[414G]** Jerome, the famous father of the church, urged that the hot springs, and the baths, be off limits to Christian widows and virgins. The baths are now called Tritoli by a corruption of the original name.

At this part of the bay of Baia is the beginning of Lago di Lucrino, about which Virgil wrote "Or should I recall the harbor he added to Lucrinus," and Servius commented on this line,

> In the bay of Baiae of Campania facing the city of Puteoli are two lakes, Avernus and Lucrinus, which in ancient times provided a great income due to their abundance of fish. But when the sea rushed in and swept the fish out of there, the fish farmers suffered a great loss, and so they begged the senate for help. And Caesar enclosed part of the sea with breakwaters and left a short expanse

> reliquitque breve spatium per Avernum, quo et copia piscium posset intrare, et fluctus non essent molesti, quod opus Iulium dictum est.

De eodem Suetonius, "Portum Iulium apud Baias immisso in Lucrinum et Avernum mari lacum effecit." Et Servius in Virgiliani versus expositione "Divinosque lacus":

> . . . sic dicit Avernus et Lucrinus lacus antea silvarum densitate sic ambiebantur, ut exhalans inde per **[414H]** angustias aquae sulphureae odor suavissimus supervolantes aves necaret, unde et Avernus dictus. Quam rem Caesar audiens deiectis silvis amoena reddidit loca.

Et infra in Virgilianum versum "Acheronte refuso," "Acheron fluvius dicitur infernorum."

Sed constat locum esse haud procul a Baiis undique montibus saeptum, adeo ut nec orientem solem possit aspicere, nec occidentem, sed tantum meridionalem. Baiani sinus latitudinem de qua diximus, Suetonius in Caligulae vita sic ostendit:

> Baianum medium intervallum et Puteolanas moles, trium milium et sexcentorum fere passuum ponte iunxit, contractis undique onerariis navibus, et ordine duplici ad ancoras collatis, superiecto aggere terreno ac directo in Appiae viae formam. Per hunc pontem ultro citroque commeavit biduo continenti. Primo die falerato equo, insignis quoque civica corona, et scutum tenens, et gladio aureaque chlamyde. Postridie quadrigario habitu, curriculoque biiugi famosorum equorum.

Sed et Nero illius successor maiores circa Baianum excogitavit insanias, de quo Suetonius:

> Inchoabat piscinam a Miseno ad Avernum lacum contectam porticibus quasi conclusam, quo quicquid totis Baiis calidarum aquarum esset converteretur. Fossam ab Averno Ostiam qua navibus necnon via iretur, longitudine **[415A]** centum sexaginta milium, latitudine qua contiguae quinqueremes commearent.

> through Lake Avernus, where the fish could enter in great numbers, and the waves were not rough. This is called the "Julian work."

And Suetonius writes about the same project, "He built the Julian harbor at Baiae, by allowing the sea to flow into Lucrinus and Avernus and create a lake." And Servius in his explanation of Virgil's line of verse "the divine lakes" offers the following:

> this is what he calls lake Avernus and Lucrinus, which had before been so surrounded by dense forests, that they emitted from **[414H]** the narrow spaces there a smell of sulphurous water which killed birds flying above; for this reason Avernus got its name. When Caesar heard of this problem, he cut down the forests and made the places pleasant again.

And after this, explaining the line in Virgil "Acheron flowed back," Servius says, "Acheron is called the river of the underworld."

The location of Lake Avernus has been established to be not far from Baia; it is closed in on all sides by mountains, so that it does not receive sun at dawn or at sunset, but only at noon. The width of the bay of Baia, as I mentioned above, is attested by Suetonius in his *Life of Caligula*:

> He joined the middle of the bay of Baiae and the jetties at Puteoli, about three and one-half miles, with a pontoon bridge consisting of transport ships. They were brought together at anchor in a double row and a heap of earth was put over them in the shape of the Appian Way. Caligula went across this bridge for two days, on the first riding a horse, wearing the civic crown of oak leaves, and holding a shield, with a sword and golden cape. On the following day he rode in a chariot drawn by famous horses.

Caligula's successor Nero also devised excessively grand projects around the bay of Baiae, as Suetonius tells us:

> He was beginning a pool which would go from Misenus to Lake Avernus, covered and almost enclosed by colonnades, and into it the hot water from all the springs in Baiae would be directed. Also a canal from Avernus to Ostia, so that people would travel by ship, but not have to travel by road, 160 miles **[415A]** long, wide enough for ships with five banks of oars to pass side by side.

De eodemque scelestissimo imperatore Suetonius: Agrippinam matrem "litteris Baias evocavit ad solennia quinquatrium simul celebranda, datoque negotio trierarchis qui Liburnicam qua advecta erat velut fortuito concursu confringerent, protraxit convivium." Sed cum nando evasisset iugulari fecit. Servius Virgilianum exponens versum, "Infernique lacus," dicit Lucrinum et Avernum significari, inter quos est spelunca, per quam ad inferos descendebatur.

Sed iam satis de vetustioribus; ad recentiora veniamus. Aelius Spartianus de Alexandro imperatore optimo Mammeae Christianae filio sic habet:

> In Baiano palatium fecit cum stagno Mammeae matri, quae Mammea tunc dictum hodieque vocatur. Fecit et alia opera in Baiano magnifica in honorem affinium suorum, et stagna stupenda admisso mari.

Fuit Baiano sinui propinquus Bauli locus Herculis, quem Servius dictum putat quasi bovali quod illic habuerit animalia. Haec sunt quae de Baiano sinu sive vetusta, sive recentiora duximus dicenda; restat ut ea praesentibus applicemus.

Ad Frictolas (nunc Tritollam) **[415B]** Lucrinus incipiebat; cernuntur enim regione illius in litore bracchia murorum, quae Caesar ut violentum excluderet mare iecit. Avernus vero a Lucrino nunc separatus est quod breve spatium a Caesare relictum, quo piscium copia posset intrare mare superinducta arena conclusit, quae quidem clausura diligentissime de industria conservatur, ne crescentes accedente mari aquae balneis officiant, quae vicus nunc Tripergula appellatus plurima et, ut medici perhibent, omnium Italiae saluberrima habet. Adiacent vero ea omnia Averno lacui salsum in aquis retinenti saporem, quas quidem aquas ita habet altas, ut nullis etiam longissimis funibus saxo aut plumbo magni ponderis ad perpendiculum colligato, eius profunditas tangi possit. Mirumque est cernere stupendi et insani operis aedificia, quae aut in circuitu Averni, aut in eius aquis ripae proximioribus fuerunt iacta; cum tamen viae silicibus in circuitum stratae, et aquarum formae dulcium superioribus in collibus paene sint integrae.

Suetonius says more about this criminal emperor: his mother Agrippina

> he summoned by letter to Baiae, to celebrate the rites of Minerva. He ordered his sailors to stage a collision with the Liburnian galley which brought her, and make it look like an accident. He drew out the banquet.

But when she escaped by swimming, he had her stabbed to death. Servius, in his explanation of the Virgilian verse "Infernique lacus," says that Virgil means Lucrinus and Avernus, because between them was a cave through which one went down to the underworld.

But enough now about ancient times; let me come to more recent times. Aelius Spartianus writes the following about the greatest emperor, Alexander Severus, son of the Christian woman Mammea:

> In his property at Baiae he built a palace with a pool for his mother Mammea, which was called then, and is now called, "Mammaean." He also built other magnificent projects at his villa at Baiae, in honor of his relatives, and created an amazing pool by letting in the ocean.

Bauli, the place of Hercules, was next to the bay of Baiae; Servius thought it was so named as if from the word for cattle, because Hercules kept animals there. These are all the passages I think worth citing about the bay of Baiae, ancient or modern. It remains for me to correlate them with places of the present time.

Lake Lucrinus began at Frictolae (now called Tritoli). **[415B]** In that region, one can see on the shore the side-works of jetties which Caesar erected against the rough sea. But Averno is now separated from Lucrino, because Caesar left a short passage through which many fish could pass to the sea, and by bringing in sand he closed the passage off, a blockage very carefully preserved so that the sea water would not rush in and block the baths. (There are many baths at the village now called Tripergola and, as the doctors say, they are the most healthful in all Italy.) All these places are located close to Lago di Averno, which has retained the salt flavor in its waters, and its waters are so deep that they cannot be plumbed by even the longest ropes with a rock or a heavy lead weight attached to the line. It is marvellous to see the buildings of astonishing and extravagant workmanship which were erected either around Averno or in the water next to the shore. In addition, roads paved with stone laid around the periphery of the lake, and aqueducts for fresh water on the higher hills, are nearly intact.

Egressi depressa haec Lucrini et Averni loca et Puteolos petituri via incedunt silicata, ad quam undique maiorum supradictis aedificiorum in Baianum **[415C]** superne despectantium ruinae cernuntur, quousque ad viam est ventum Atellanam, quae ab urbe Roma Atellas per Appiam, et post ab Atellis ducebat ad Baias, qua quidem in via haud longe a Puteolis et Baiano medioque ad nunc Adversam spatio. Tam integra adhuc sunt veterum operum monumenta, ut si ostia addantur et fenestrae, videantur habitationem non incommodam praestitura. Eademque via ad Baiani supercilium ubi sanctae Mariae sacellum est post tergum relicta, maiorum etiam omnium, quae hactenus circa Baianum descripsimus, aedificiorum ruinae in sublimi erectae cernuntur, quas incolae Belgermanum appellant. Fueruntque opera sicut litterae pila incisae marmorea ostendunt, quae Tiberius Caesar bello Germanico feliciter perfecto, unde Germanicus est appellatus, ad facti eius famam memoriamque exstruxit. Eique pulcherrimo etiam nunc operi proximum est paene integrum exstans theatrum, cuius occasione factum esse dicit Suetonius, ut cum celeberrimis ludis, quibus Caesar intererat Augustus senatorium virum frequenti consessu nemo recepisset, idem princeps spectandi modum correxerit.

Dehinc sunt **[415D]** Puteoli, de qua civitate vetusta sic habet Livius in quarto: "Exitu eius anni Q. Fabius ex auctoritate senatus Puteolos per bellum captum frequentari fecit, emporiumque communivit, atque praesidium imposuit." Et infra de Hannibale:

> Ad lacum Averni per speciem sacrificandi re ipsa ut tentaret Puteolos descendit. Sacro deinde perpetrato ad quod venerat, et dum ibi moratur pervastato agro Cumano usque ad Misenum promontorium, Puteolos repente agmen convertit ad opprimendum praesidium Romanum.

Et infra: "P. Cornelius Scipio Africanus et C. Aelius Paetus magna inter se concordia senatum sine ullius nota regebant, et portoria navalium Capuae Puteolisque instituerunt." Et infra: "Consul Atinius tulit, ut quinque colonae in oram maritimam deducerentur, quarum una fuit deducta Puteolos." Aelius Spartianus dicit Adrianum imperatorem cum mortuus esset apud Baias,

If you leave these low places where Averno and Lucrino are located, and go towards Pozzuoli on the paved road, you see on all sides of the road the ruins of the ancient buildings I mentioned, **[415C]** which look down onto the bay of Baia. Then you arrive at the road to Atella, which used to go from the city of Rome to Atella by the Appian Way, and after that from Atella to Baiae; on that road, it is not far from Pozzuoli and the territory of Baia, in the middle of the distance, to what is now Aversa. The ancient monuments are in such good shape that if you restored to them doors and windows, they would appear to offer comfortable living quarters. And when you leave behind the road to the projection of the coastline in the territory of Baia, where the chapel of Sta. Maria is located, you see on high also the ruins of all the greater structures I have described up to this point around the territory of Baia. The inhabitants call these ruins Belgermano. And there were things like a marble pillar with inscriptions which show that Tiberius Caesar had them built after the successful completion of the war in Germany, to glorify and memorialize his exploit. From this it was called "Germanicus"; it is even now a very beautiful structure. Next to it is a theatre which survives nearly intact. Suetonius says it was the setting for the episode which took place when Augustus was present at some well-attended games: since no one had given a seat, in the packed amphitheatre, to a man of senatorial rank, the emperor regulated the arrangements for seating.

Next comes Pozzuoli, an ancient city about which Livy says the following in book 4: "At the end of that year, Fabius, **[415D]** with a decree of the Senate, fortified a trading-post and put a garrison over Puteoli which had attracted great numbers of people for trading." And later on, he writes about Hannibal,

> He went down to Lake Avernus, supposedly to sacrifice, but really to attack Puteoli. When they had completed the sacrifice he had come for, while he lingered there, since the territory of Cumae had been pillaged as far as the promontory of Misenum, he suddenly turned his army towards Puteoli to attack the Roman garrison.

And further on, "P. Cornelius Scipio and P. Aelius Paetus were controlling the membership of the Senate in great agreement together, and without censuring anyone; and they established a tax at Capua and Puteoli." And later, "The consul Atinius got a law passed that established five colonies on the coast, one of which was established at Puteoli." Aelius Spartianus tells

sepultum fuisse Puteolis in villa Ciceroniana, ubi Antoninus successor templum pro sepulcro illi consecravit.

Puteolis nostro ordine transmissis, locus occurrit medio inter ipsam et urbem Neapolitanam spatio, fama apud veteres celebratus. Namque villa, quam Plutarchus tradit Lucium Lucullum habuisse prope Neapolim, et apud eam montem excidisse, atque ita excavasse, ut mare introduceret, unde **[416E]** Cn. Pompeius et M. Cicero illum appellare soliti fuerunt Xerxem togatum, ea est cuius ruinae ingentes balneo supereminent Agnani dicto. Quamquam non balnea loco sed alterae sunt Frictolae superioribus meliores, et qui rerum huiusmodi magnarum ingenio viribusque factarum peritiam habent, facillime scissuram praevident, intelleguntque manu factam unde defossus reiectusque mons viam praebuit, nunc etiam levi opera reparabilem, qua mari nunc Agnani lacum ita impleret, ut ad villae muros porticusque navigari posset.

Procedentesque eo itinere ad cavernam perveniunt Griptam nunc appellatam, ubi Pausilippus pulcherrimis, olim sicut Plinius tradit, villis habitatus ad sexcentos passus excavatus planum via Puteolana curribus iter praebet. Quis autem id memorabile opus fecit ignotum est nobis, qui tamen legimus factam apud Senecam Cordubensem ipsius loci mentionem epistola quinquagesimaseptima, ubi dicit:

> Excepit me Cripta Neapolitana, nihil illo carcere longius, nihil illius faucibus obscurius, quae nobis praestant, non ut per tenebras videamus, sed ut ipsas cernamus, si locus haberet lucem, pulvis auferret, in aperto quoque res gravis et molesta, quid illic [ubi] in se volutatur, et cum sine ullo **[416F]** inspiramento sit inclusus in ipsos, a quibus excitatus est, recidit?

Et Donatus in Virgilii expositione tradit, ipsum poetam sepultum fuisse Neapoli via Puteolana ad secundum lapidem, quod sepulcrum circa praedictam Criptam saepe quaesitum nequivimus invenire.

Sequitur Neapolis, urbs vetusta atque praeclara, cuius originem Livius in octavo refert in Cumanos his verbis: “Palaepolis fuit haud procul ubi nunc Neapolis est. Duabus urbibus idem populus habitabat, Cumis erant oriundi.”

us that after the emperor Hadrian died at Baiae, he was buried at Puteoli in the former villa of Cicero, and his successor Antoninus dedicated there a temple to Hadrian.

Following my usual scheme, I have treated Pozzuoli, and the next place comes in the middle of the area between Pozzuoli and the city of Naples; this place is famous among the ancients. Here was the villa which Plutarch says Lucius Lucullus had near Naples, where he cut into and dug out the mountain to let in the sea; as a consequence, **[416E]** Gnaeus Pompeius and Marcus Cicero used to call him the "toga'd Xerxes." The villa's enormous remains tower over the baths called Agnano. There are no baths in the place but the others, at Tritoli, are better than the ones higher up. People who have knowledge of great structures made by ingenuity and strength can easily foresee and understand that the man-made cut, where they dug into the mountain and opened up a passage, can now be easily repaired, where the sea flows in and fills up the lake of Agnano so that you could reach by boat the walls and colonnades.

Those who go along that route come to a cave, now called Grotta. This is the site of the ancient Pausilypon, where there were very beautiful villas, as Pliny tells us. It has been dug out to a depth of 600 paces, and provides a smooth surface for carriages along the Via Puteolana. I do not know who built this remarkable structure, but I have read a mention of this place in Seneca of Cordoba's fifty-seventh letter, where he says:

> I arrived in the Crypt at Naples. There is nothing as long as that prison, nothing as dark as the torches, with which we could see, not through the shadows, but just the shadows themselves. If any light penetrated to this place, the dust would absorb it; this is a serious problem even in the open air. How much worse it is there, where it swirls **[416F]** unmixed with any breath of air, and falls back again onto the very people who have stirred it up.

Donatus, in his commentary on Virgil, says that Virgil was buried at Naples at the second milestone on the Via Puteolana. People have often searched for his tomb in the area around the Grotta I mentioned earlier, but I have not been able to find it.

Next comes Naples, an ancient and renowned city. Livy, in book 8, informs us about the connection of its origins with Cumae: "Palaepolis was nearby, where Naples is now located. The two cities had their origins from Cumae and the same population lived in them." And Livy goes on to say that Palaepolis was held by the Greeks and had been captured by the consul

Palaepolimque, quam tenerent Graeci, dicit infra Livius a Publio Plautio consule captam fuisse. Et infra, "Iam Publius inter Palaepolim Neapolimque loco opportune capto diremerat hostibus societatem auxilii mutui." Et infra item dicit Neapolim auxilio Nolanorum Romanis deditam fuisse.

Usi vero sunt semper postea Neapolitani erga Romanos et alios dominos constantissima fide, primum Romana re publica Cannensi clade consternata, cum "ad Gerionem iam hieme impendente consisteret bellum, Neapolitani legati Romam venerunt, ab his quadraginta paterae **[416G]** aureae magni ponderis in curiam delatae," quas quidem senatus contra morem suum accepit, et Neapolitanis gratias egit.

Cumque Hannibal Neapoli summopere potiri quaesiverit, Neapolitani in Romanorum partibus perstiterunt. Livius in XXII de Hannibale: "Ipse per agrum Campanum mare inferum petit oppugnaturus Neapolim, ut urbem maritimam haberet." Et infra, "Hannibal Capua recepta, cum iterum Neapolitanorum animos partim spe, partim metu nequicquam tentasset, in agrum Nolanum exercitum duxit." Et infra, quarto: "Inde ad populandum agrum Neapolitanum magis ira quam spe potiundae urbis duxit."

Floruit autem semper postmodum Neapolitana urbs, Romana re sub consulibus et pariter sub principibus integra, adeo ut apud eam graves viri animorum a curis laxamentum quaererent, et discoli lasciviae diversorium. Suetonius de Nerone: "Reversus e Graecia Neapolim, quod in ea primum artem musicam protulerat, albis equis introiit disiecta parte muri." Et infra, Nero "de motu Galliarum Neapoli cognovit die ipso quo matrem occiderat."

Sed et viros videmus litteris celebratos, Virgilium diu, Titum Livium **[416H]** aliquando, et Horatium Neapoli moratos fuisse. Et Servius asserit Virgilium scripsisse Georgica Neapoli, quam Parthenopem appellavit, ac otii ignobilis notavit. Franciscus quoque Petrarcha praestanti vir ingenio, a Roberto rege Neapolitano Gallicana oriundo progenie, rogatus Neapolim bis se contulit, nulla quidem maioris lucri spe suasus, quam ut optimo atque humanissimo regi doctos et virtuosos viros unice amanti gratificaretur, eamque vim habuit inita inter divitem regem et doctum integrumque, sed rerum inopem virum, et tamen animo et virtute divitem poetam, ut per unicam eiusmodi amicitiam conservatus nunc vivat rex Robertus. Nam quod omnibus in

Publius Plautius. And after this, "Now Publius captured a strategic place between Palaepolis and Naples, and had forced the dissolution of the enemies' mutual aid society." Later he says Naples had been surrendered to the Romans with the help of the people of Nola.

But forever afterwards the people of Naples maintained the utmost fidelity to the Romans and other masters, first after the Romans had been slaughtered and thrown into confusion at the battle of Cannae, when "the war was halted at Gereonium as winter was already coming on, the Neapolitan ambassadors came to Rome. They brought into the Senate house forty **[416G]** golden platters of great weight." Contrary to custom, the Senate accepted them, and thanked the Neapolitans.

And when Hannibal was exerting all his effort to get Naples under his control, the Neapolitans kept faith with the Romans. Livy writes about Hannibal in book 22, "He made for the Tyrrhenian Sea by going through the territory of Campania, and aimed at besieging Naples in order to acquire a seaport." And farther on, "Hannibal had taken Capua, and he had tried in vain to bring the Neapolitans over to him, partly using promises, partly using intimidation. So he led his army into the territory of Nola." And below this, in the fourth book, "Then he led his army to devastate the territory of Naples, more out of anger than in hopes of gaining possession of the city."

But forever afterwards the city of Naples prospered under the Roman government. It remained unharmed both under the Republic and under the Empire, with the result that important men used to go there for relaxation from stress and the diversions of pleasure. So Suetonius writes about Nero: "He returned from Greece to Naples, and because he had first exhibited publicly his musical skill in Naples, he entered the city through a hole he had had made in the wall, drawn by white horses." And further on, Nero "learned of the revolt among the Gauls while he was at Naples, on the anniversary of the very day on which he had murdered his mother."

But we see that famous literary men also spent time at Naples: Virgil lived there for a long time; Livy did from time to time, **[416H]** as well as Horace. And Servius declares that Virgil wrote the *Georgics* at Naples, which he called Parthenope, and called attention to its decadent leisure. Petrarch also, a man of genius, went to Naples twice at the request of King Robert of Naples, a native Frenchman. Petrarch went there not in hopes of greater material reward, but to please a very good king who supported the liberal arts and had a unique appreciation for learned and virtuous men. The result was that King Robert is now remembered mainly for this unusual friendship

quorum manus haec venient faciliter ostendere, ac quoad vixerimus probare poterimus, extra urbem Neapolitanam paucissimi ac paene nulli sunt viri quantumvis docti, qui Robertus rex quis et unde aut quo tempore fuerit alia noverint ratione vel causa quam quod eum in amicissimi Francisci Petrarchae operibus sive Latinis sive vulgaribus legendo recognoverunt.

Servius in Virgiliani versus expositione, "Nec tu carminibus nostris indictus abibis Oebale," dicit, "Oebalus filius est Thelonis et nymphae Sebetridis. Hic autem est iuxta Neapolim. Sed Thelo regnavit Capreis, filiusque eius transiit ad Campaniam, et multis subigatis **[417A]** populis, suum dilatavit imperium." At postquam Romani imperii inclinatio coepit, crescentibus barbarorum insultibus, Neapolitani partes Romanorum pro posse, supraque secuti sunt. Et quod in Historiis copiose ostendimus, rex Vandalorum Gensericus classe ingenti ab Africa ducta, Romanam urbem captam spoliatamque, et omni humano habitatore destitutam reliquit, qui et Capuam quoque evertit. Ad Neapolim vero cum venisset, eam diu obsidione pressam capere nequivit. Paucis ab inde annis Belisario Iustiniani imperatoris duci adeo constanti animo restiterunt Neapolitani, ut cum postea per lapideum aquaeductus foramen scalpris dilatatum urbs in eius potestatem facta esset, Neapolitani sola principis humanitate ab excidio sint servati.

Multis postea interiectis annis, cum Saraceni omnem oram maritimam, quae a Caieta Rhegium usque protenditur per bellum obtinuissent, Neapoli quoque sunt potiti, quam ad annos triginta possederunt, quousque Ioannes decimus pontifex Romanus vir excellentissimus, pellendis Italia Saracenis animum adiecit. Quo hortante, et auxilia subministrante, Neapolitani omnium primi id diu invisum abiecerunt **[417B]** iugum, secutique eius urbis exemplum, ceteri Campaniae, Lucaniae, et Brutiorum populi eam scilicet incolentes oram, quae a Neapoli continet freto Siculo, dominio Saracenorum abiecto, sese in Christianam vindicarunt libertatem. Qua afflicti clade Saraceni auxiliaribus copiis ex Africa Mauritaniaque accersitis, oppida et urbes, quae sibi erant in Italia reliquae praesidiis confirmatas maioribus retinere conati sunt: Formias, Minturnas, Sinuessam, Vulturnum, Linternum, Cumas, atque Baianum, nam Puteolani Neapolitanis ab initio in rebellione consenserant.

Perstitit vero perseveravitque sanctissimus pontifex in sua expellendae barbariei aeternis digna laudibus voluntate, et Italos omnes quantumvis inter

between a rich king and a learned and honest man who was poor in material goods, but wealthy in spirit and virtue. I will easily demonstrate to anyone who reads this, and I will try to prove it all my life. There are few, or next to none (outside the city of Naples), who know who King Robert was, and where he came from, and when he lived for any other reason than because they came to know him in reading the works of his close friend Francis Petrarch, either in Latin or in the vernacular.

Servius says, commenting on Virgil's line "Nor will you escape notice in my poems, Oebale": "Oebale is the son of Thelo and the nymph Sebetris. This is near Naples. But Thelo ruled at Capri; his son moved to Campania, and overcame many [417A] peoples, and enlarged his kingdom." But after the decline of the Roman Empire set in and the barbarians began more frequently to invade Italy, the Neapolitans did all they could and more to support the Romans. I have shown extensively in my *Histories* that Genseric, king of the Vandals, brought a huge fleet from Africa and captured and plundered the city of Rome, leaving it without human inhabitants. He also moved down to Naples but was unable to capture it after a long siege. A few years after that, Naples put up stubborn resistance to Belisarius, the emperor Justinian's commander, who was finally able to gain possession of the city only through a drainpipe which his men hollowed out with knives. The Neapolitans were spared from extinction only by the emperor's mercy.

Many years after that, the Arabs had conquered the entire seacoast from Gaeta to Reggio, and took possession of Naples as well and held onto it for thirty years until the excellent Pope John X applied his mind to expelling them from Italy. At his urging and with his help, the Neapolitans first threw off the long-hated Arab [417B] domination and the rest of the people of Campania, Lucania, and Bruttium, those who lived on that seacoast which goes from Naples to the straits of Messina, followed their example. They rejected the Arab rule and claimed for themselves a free and Christian way of life. The Arabs, suffering from the slaughter, summoned forces to help them from Africa and Mauritania as they tried to hold on to the towns and cities which remained under their control by strengthening their garrisons in them. These towns were: Formia, Minturno, Mondragone, Volturno, Liternum, Cuma, and Baia, as Pozzuoli had from the beginning joined Naples in the rebellion.

The holy pope persevered in his intentions, worthy of eternal praise, to throw the barbarians out of Italy. He succeeded in getting all the Italians—no matter how great their disorganization and discord in other areas—to arm

se aliis rationibus laceros atque discordes, in fidei Christianae tutelam orando suadendoque magis quam qui nequisset iubendo, armari obtinuit. Quibus in magnum coactis exercitum, pontifice Ioanne duce, ventum est ad Minturnas. Et quod in eius urbis descriptione diximus, proelium apud eam gestum est, in quo Saraceni maxima clade superati sunt. Unde factum est, ut ea gens impia, et non magis Christiano quam Italico nomini inimica regionem praedictam a Formiis [417C] ad Baianum, et quicquid urbium, oppidorum, munitorum locorum in ea praesidiis obtinebant, incendiis et toto conatu reliquerint dirutum, adeo ut ea quam hucusque vix conando potuimus singulis in locis ad nominis antiqui notitiam perducere manserit solitudo.

Aucta vero est semper postea opibus urbs Neapolitana; et feliciter sub Ioanne decimo inchoatas in barbaros inimicitias felicissime retinuit. Namque cum Leonis quarti papae temporibus Saraceni sanctorum Petri et Pauli apostolorum utrasque urbis Romae basilicas vi captas incendio absumpsissent, urbemque Romam diu obsessam capturi viderentur, nullis maioribus ex omni Italia quam Neapolitanorum viribus, et servata est Roma, et barbari sunt expulsi. Nimis multa huic operi et loco essent illa, quae de Neapolitanorum variis casibus scribi possent, dum Guiscardis Germanisque et Gallicis regibus, qui Neapolim a trecentis annis regia ornarunt dignitate obedientissime parent.

Sed omnes eorum laudes accumulat gloriosa calamitas in magnam conversa felicitatem, dum pro servata Gallico Andegauensi principi Renato fide durissimam ab Alphonso Aragonum rege [417D] obsidionem pertulerunt, quousque pari cum Belisarii temporum eventu per aquaeductus cuniculum ab ipso rege capti, atque ad hanc, in qua nunc beati florent felicitatem eiusdem regis praesentia clementiaque servati sunt, ut non immerito is rex triumphi consuetudinem diutissime intermissam, longo tandem postliminio in Italiam revocaverit.

Habet urbs Neapolitana basilicas, moenia, et arces, et publicas privatasque aedes superbas, et ceteris Italiae maioribus comparandas, in queis praeclarum est virginis Clarae monasterium. Quod a Sancta Aragone regina Roberti regis incluti uxore aedificatum, facile omnia Italiae monasteria antecellit, eique proximum esse videtur S. Martini extra urbis moenia Cartusiense coenobium aedificii magnificentia pulcherrimum. Constat tamen arcem unam, Castellum Novum appellatum, mari imminentem Alphonsi regis laude et memoria dignum opus, ceteris quae in Italia nunc exstent veteribus, sive novis operibus monumentis et structuris praeferendum esse, sive turrim eius murorumque altitudinem et crassitudinem et pulchritudinem, sive

themselves for the preservation of the Christian faith. And he did this more by pleading and persuading them than by ordering them, which would have been useless. When the Italians had been brought together into a great army with pope John at its head, they came to Minturno. There they fought an important battle and defeated the Arabs, inflicting on them a severe slaughter. Afterwards these infidels, who had been hostile to Christians and Italians alike, burned and destroyed the entire region I mentioned, from Formia **[417C]** to Baia, with whatever cities, towns, and fortified places their garrisons had taken; the desolation they caused has persisted, with the result that I can scarcely, with great effort, restore knowledge of the ancient toponyms for individual settlements.

But forever afterwards the city of Naples increased in wealth. It has maintained the hostility towards the barbarians which began auspiciously under John X. For when Leo IV was pope, the Arabs captured and burned down both of the basilicas of Ss. Peter and Paul in Rome, and they besieged Rome for a long time and seemed on the point of capturing it. But the Neapolitans, who had the greatest forces in all of Italy, saved Rome and threw out the barbarians. There are too many things to record in this work and in this context, but which I could write, about the different misfortunes of the Neapolitans, while they were obedient subjects of the Norman Guiscards, and the German and French kings who ruled there.

But the praise of the people of Naples culminates in one glorious reversal of fate: they survived a harsh **[417D]** siege, brought upon them for their fidelity to the French king René of Anjou, and (just as in the time of Belisarius) the city was captured by someone crawling through an underground passage, and its citizens were saved by the merciful presence of King Alfonso to enjoy their present blessed state. This king deservedly resurrected in Italy, in a restoration long in coming, the custom of the triumph.

The city of Naples has magnificent churches, walls, citadels, and private and public buildings, all of them rivaling other larger ones in Italy. Among them is the renowned monastery of S. Chiara, which Queen Santa of Aragon built, wife of the famous King Robert. It easily surpasses all the monasteries in Italy. And next to it is the Carthusian cloister of S. Martino outside the walls, with a most beautiful and splendid building. But one fortress, called the Castel Nuovo, which overhangs the sea and is a work worthy of the distinguished memory of King Alfonso, is agreed to surpass all the rest of the ancient buildings now remaining in Italy, or any of the new monuments. Anyone knowledgeable about such architecture would think so, whether focusing on the

aularum cubiliumque et singularum eius partium amplitudinem, et ornamenta peritus eiusmodi rerum existimet.

Ornata fuit Neapolis patrum nostrorum aetate Bonifacio nono pontifice Romano ex Tomacella gente oriundo, qui primus non modo urbem Romam, sed et ipsum quoque pontificatum in dominii potestate continuit. Pauloque post alterum Neapolis pontificem Romanum habuit Ioannem XXIII ex gente Cossea, quem alioquin prudentem Sigismundus imperator in Germaniam seductum a concilio Constantiensi, pro ecclesiae facienda unione privari curavit. Magno item per id temporis ornamento Neapolitanae urbi fuit Ladislaus rex Galliae regum prosapia, Neapoli genitus et nutritus, qui militiae omnino deditus, praeter id Neapolitanum omne regnum armis quaesitum, urbem quoque Romam Perusiamque et Assisiam de iuribus ecclesiae et Cortonam de Etruria cepit, quam vendidit Florentinis. Constansque fuit omnium eius aetatis prudentium opinio, ipsum Italico regno, et quod postea facillimum erat imperio Romano, nisi florentem eum mors intercepisset brevi potiturum fuisse.

Neapolitanae urbi secundum litus Pompeii a vetustis scriptoribus proximi describuntur, qui vicus olim fuit amoenissimus, Romanisque gratissimus, adeo ut M. Cicero legem, de qua saepe diximus, dissuadens Rulli agrariam aegre ferendum ostendat Pompeios a decemviris venundari. Et quia doctos **[418F]** qui hoc tempore Neapoli apud regem in pretio habentur errare videmus, Pompeios et Herculaneum ubi nunc Turris est Octavii fuisse affirmantes, vetus testimonium ostendendo certius Pompeiorum loco afferemus. Primumque dicimus, ubi nunc Annuntiata et Castellum est ad mare Pompeios vicum oblongum villisque speciosissimis frequentissimum fuisse. Livius in nono, “Per idem tempus classis Romana a P. Cornelio, quem senatus maritimae orae praefecerat, in Campaniam acta, cum appulsa Pompeios esset socii navales ad populandum Nucerinum agrum profecti,” facta praeda exuti sunt. Qui ergo Nucerinum praedaturi fuerunt agrum, navales milites Sarni ostia potius ingredi oportuit, quam ad distantem sexto miliario turrim Octavii facere excensionem.

height, thickness, and beauty of its towers and walls, or the spaciousness of its halls, bedrooms, and single rooms, and decorations.

In our fathers' generation, Naples has been distinguished by Pope Boniface IX, of the Tomacelli family. He was the first to hold under his control not only the city of Rome itself, [418E] but also the papacy itself. And a little while after him, Naples produced a second pope, John XXIII, from the Cossa family. Although he showed wisdom in other matters, he allowed the emperor Sigismund to get him to go to Germany and to be dethroned by the Council of Constance which was meeting to put an end to the schism. In the same way, and in the same era, King Ladislaus, from the royal family of France, born and brought up at Naples, was a great distinction to the city. He was dedicated to military pursuits, and in addition to winning the entire kingdom of Naples by arms, he also captured the cities of Rome, Perugia, and Assisi from the papal state, and Cortona from Tuscany, which city he sold to the Florentines. All intelligent men of that time held steadfastly that Ladislaus would shortly have gained possession of the kingdom of Italy, and after that easily have obtained power over the Roman Empire, if death had not cut short his success.

According to ancient authors, Pompeii lay next to Naples on the coast. This town was at one time very pleasant and popular among the Romans: Cicero, in his speech against Rullus' agrarian measure (which I have often mentioned) shows that the sale of Pompeii by the decemvirs was intolerable. The scholars [418F] presently held in high esteem by the king at Naples are in error when they say that Pompeii and Herculaneum were located where Torre del Greco is now; so I shall adduce a piece of ancient evidence to indicate more accurately the site of Pompeii. First, I assert that the site of the town of Pompeii, a rectangular site which was thickly settled with beautiful villas, was at the location of the modern Torre Annunziata and Castellamare di Stabia. Livy says in book nine,

> At the same time, the Roman fleet was brought to Campania, under the command of P. Cornelius, who had been put in charge of the coast; when the fleet had made land at Pompeii, the sailors went out to plunder the territory of Nuceria. . . .

and they were stripped of the plunder they had gotten. Now the naval forces that would have been in a position to plunder the territory of Nuceria ought to have gone in to the mouth of the Sarno river, rather than make landfall at the site of Torre del Greco, six miles away.

Herculaneum vero alterius et multis distans milibus fuisse infra ostendemus. Et quidem turris Octavii nominis novi vicus, cui distantia ab urbe Neapolitana dederit appellationem, nullas habet vetustatis reliquias, praeter superioris Plinii mortis locum, quem ibi fuisse necessarium tenemus. Nulla enim in parte alia Vesevi montis incendia, quibus imprudenter inspiciendis Plinius est necatus, **[418G]** navi potuerunt adiri, et quidem ea omnis ora ubicumque saxa etiam in litoris supercilio terrae supereminent, incendii vestigia ostendit adeo certa, ut nihil praeter flammam fumumque desit, quo illa passim nunc etiam ardere advena suspicetur. Fuitque id incendium, de quo Suetonius Tranquillus in Titi Vespasiani vita sic dicit:

> Quaedam suo tempore tristia acciderunt, ut conflagratio Vesevi in Campania; curatores restituendae Campaniae consularium numero forte duxit. Bona oppressorum in Vesevo, quorum haeredes non exstabant, restitutioni afflictarum civitatum attribuit.

Vesevum vero montem vitium agrorumque cultura ditissimum nunc appellant Summum, qui in conspectu Neapolitanae urbi positus, et hinc campis, inde mari maiore parte circumdatus videtur esse summus. In mediterraneis campestribus, quae Adversam urbem Vesevumque montem interiacent, duo exstant loca, veterum memoria celebrata: Merelanium olim nunc Marlianum oppidum, et urbis Acerrae, de qua Livius XXIII, "Hannibal Acerras cepit vacuas, et incendit." Et libro XXVII, "Acerranis permissum est, ut aedificarent, quae incensa erant," ad quam historiam **[418H]** allusit Virgilius in Georgicis, ubi terras laudans culturae excellentioris dicit:

> Talem dives arat Capua, et vicina Vesevo
> Ora iugo, et vacuis Clanius non aequus Acerris.

Quo in loco Virgilius id quod supradiximus de terra Leboris innuit, omnem eam regionem, quae undique Clanio amni adiacet, Leborinam olim appellatam, feracissimi esse soli. Sicut de ea Plinium scripsisse ostendimus, qui tamen de terris tractans ad sationem vitium optimis, dicit Campaniam ubique optimam vitibus esse, quae tenues exhalat nebulas, et cretam in Pompeianorum agro, ac argillam cunctis ad vineas generibus anteponi, quoniam excipitur cum illis invicem sabulum album.

In fact, I shall prove later on that Herculaneum was many miles farther away. And indeed Torre del Greco, a village with a new name, was originally named "eighth" from its distance from Naples. It offers no ancient ruins, except for the place where Pliny the Elder died, which I think must have been there. For Pliny was killed when he recklessly went to observe the fires on Mt. Vesuvius, and there is only one direction from which **[418G]** ships can approach it. And indeed that entire coastline with rocky heights towering over it even on the shore, shows the certain traces of a fire. Even now, only flames and smoke are lacking to present a stranger with abundant evidence of burning. It was this fire about which Suetonius writes in the following passage from his *Life of Titus:*

> During his reign, certain tragic events occurred. One was the fire on Vesuvius in Campania: he chose by lot from the ex-consuls officials in charge of the restoration of Campania. He assigned the goods of the victims of Vesuvius who did not have living heirs to the efforts to restore the damaged cities.

Vesuvius is now called "Monte Somma"; in sight of the city of Naples, it is rich in cultivation of crops and vines. It is surrounded by fields on the side next to the city; on the other side, for the most part, by the sea. In the flat plains which lie between the city of Aversa and Mt. Vesuvius, there are two places famous among the ancients, the former Merelanium, now called Marigliano, and the city of Acerra. About the latter, Livy writes in book 23, "Hannibal took Acerrae, which was empty, and burned it." And in book 27, "The people of Acerrae were allowed to rebuild the places which had been burned." Virgil, in the *Georgics*, refers to this history **[418H]** when he praises the land for its fertility and says:

> Rich Capua ploughs such land, and the shore near the ridge of
> Vesuvius,
> And the Clanius river, hostile to deserted Acerrae.

In the same passage, Virgil alludes to the subject of "Terra Leborina," which I mentioned before, when he says that that entire region which lies on either side of the Clanio river, formerly called Leborina, has very fertile soil. I showed that Pliny wrote in the same vein about this region; but when he treats the soils best for growing vines, he says that everywhere in Campania the soil is best for vines, because it exudes a fine mist; and chalky soil in the territory of Pompeii, and clay for all kinds of vines, are preferred, since on the contrary a white sand is taken out with them.

Sed iam ventum est ad superiorem Clanii amnis partem, cum ab Acerris distet quattuor mille passus Suessula oppidum nunc vacuum, iuxta quod sicut a principio diximus, fontem is fluvius habet. Sarnusque post hac nobis describendus ordine videtur occurrere, cum cetera explicuerimus de Suessula, de qua Livius in septimo: "Tertia pugna ad Suessulam commissa est, qua fugatus a M. Valerio Samnitium exercitus." Et in octavo: "Cumanos Suessulanosque eiusdem iuris conditionisque, cuius Capuam esse placuit." Et infra, "Inter Capuam et Suessulam castra castris conferamus"; et libro XXIII, "Hannibal super Suessulam per montes Nolam pervenit"; et infra, "M. Claudius proconsul **[419A]** ad eum exercitum, qui supra Suessulam Nolae praesideret missus." Et inferius, "Claudiana castra" erant "supra Suessulam."

Sed iam aliqua de Campanis propter dimidiatum in Samnio sicut ostendimus, Vulturnum superius omissa repetenda sunt. Ea in parte ad quam Sabbati amnis stipite utrimque descripto, Samnium omne finitum esse ostendimus, Isclerus sequitur, omnium Campaniae hac in parte fluviorum primum in Vulturnum supra Capuam quinto ferme miliario cadens. Qui Isclerus ex montibus Caudinam vallem claudentibus ortum habet. Et inter Soritellam fluvium superius in Samnio descriptum, et ipsum Isclerum, sunt montes altissimi, in quibus primum est Gripta oppidum, cui supereminet mons nunc Tabor, olim Taburnus, quem Servius Virgilium in Georgicis exponens, Campaniae montem esse dicit, qui vites ab industria contra naturam alat. Et idem super versu item Virgilii Aeneidos XII, "Ac velut ingenti Sila summove Taburno," dicit, "Taburnus mons est Campaniae."

Valli autem ex monte Taburno in Isclerum vergenti imminet Collis Pacis, et vallis quam Isclerus efficit dextrorsum habet Lunatulam et Ducentium. Superiusque in monte est Airola, nobile oppidum, comitatus titulo insigne, duobus miliaribus a Furculis Caudinis distans. **[419B]** Pertinet in haec usque loca montes ardui, Capuae ad adversam regionem imminentes, qui et longiusculo tractu ad Nolam urbem feruntur, Triphata olim appellati, in quibus oppida sunt Meronida, Caserta comitatu insigne, Magdalonum, et superius Duraganum. In proximaque valle Furculis Caudinis superiore Ar-

But now I have come to the upper branch of the Clanio river. The town of Suessula, now uninhabited, lies four miles from Acerra. Next to Cancello, as I said before, is where the Clanio has its source. It seems I must treat next the Sarno river, if I am to follow my orderly method of proceeding, when I have finished explaining other things about ancient Suessula, or modern Cancello. Livy says about it in book 7, "A third battle was joined at Suessula, and M. Valerius put the army of the Samnites to flight." And in book 8 Livy writes, "It was decided that the people of Cumae and Suessula would be subject to the same law and terms as were the people of Capua." And below this he writes, "Let us set up camps facing each other between Capua and Suessula." And in book 23, "Hannibal came through the mountains and arrived at Nola above Suessula," and further on, "The proconsul M. Claudius **[419A]** was sent to head this army, which sat in front of Nola above Suessula." And after this, "The camp of Claudius" was "above Suessula."

But now I must go back and take up again some aspects of Campania which I left out earlier because, as I have shown, the Volturno is half in Abruzzo. In the direction where I showed all Abruzzo is bounded by the trunk, as it were, as I described it, of the Sabato river, the next river is the Isclero, first of all the rivers in this part of Campania to flow into the Volturno, almost five miles above Capua. This Isclero river has its source in the mountains which enclose the Caudine valley. And between the Soritella river (which I described earlier in the part on Abruzzo), and the Isclero, are very high mountains. The first town in these mountains is *Gripta*, at the foot of the mountain now called Monte Taburno, but in ancient times Taburnus. Servius, commenting on Virgil's *Georgics,* says this is a mountain in Campania where vines are grown not naturally but by artificial techniques. In the same vein, commenting on a verse in book XII of Virgil's *Aeneid*, "And just as on huge Sila or the peak of Taburnus," Servius says, "Taburnus is a mountain in Campania."

Collis Pacis hangs over the valley which turns from Monte Taburno towards the Isclero, and the valley made by the Isclero has on the right hand side *Lunatula* and Dugenta. Higher up on the mountain is the noble town of Airola, distinguished by the title of a count. It is two miles from the Caudine Forks. **[419B]** There are high mountains in these places which tower over Capua and face the region opposite. They extend in a rather long stretch to the city of Nola, which was in ancient times called Triphata. In these mountains are located the towns of Meronida; Caserta, distinguished as the residence of a count; Maddaloni; and, higher up, Durazzano. In the next valley

gentum est, et infra Marilianum vetusti, ut diximus, nominis oppidum. Proxime ad medium montem est Cancellum oppidum, superius Forinum. Sunt vero hi montes Tiphata, de quibus sic habet Livius in septimo:

> Nam Samnites omissis Sidicinis, ipsam arcem finitimorum Campanos adorti, unde aeque facilis victoria praedae atque gloriae plus esset, Tiphata imminentes Capuae colles cum praesidio firmo occupassent. Descendunt inde quadrato agmine in planitiem, quae inter Capuam Tiphataque interiacet.

Et idem infra: "Proelium ad Tiphata atrox, in quo oculos Romanis ardere dixerunt. Fusi caesique Samnites." Et libro XXIII, "Hannibal ad Tiphata castra habebat, qui raptim currens Gracchum non invenit." Et infra, "Inter Capuam castraque Hannibalis, quae in Tiphatis **[419C]** erant." Et inferius, "Hannibal praesidio medio relicto in Tiphatis, profectus cum exercitu toto." Et libro XXIIII, "Hannibal profectus Arpis, ad Tiphata in veteribus castris super Capuam resedit." Livius item libro XXXII, "Cornelius Scipio Africanus, C. Aelius Paetus sub Tiphatis Capuae agrum vendiderunt."

Ad eiusdem montis declivia, quae aversa a Capua regione in Caudinae vallis suprema desinere incipiunt, Sarnum est oppidum, a Sarno fluvio ibi fontes copiosissimos habente dictum, in quibus fontibus scribit Plinius ligna et folia cum ceciderint, in lapides durescere. Sed inter eos fontes et Vesevum montem longe supra a nobis descriptum, Nola est urbs vetustissima, et in historiis celebrata, quam Iustinus a Iapygis conditam fuisse asserit. Cuius agrum esse fertilissimum, Virgilius in Bucolicis sic scribit,

> Talem dives arat Capua, et vicina Vesevo
> Nola iugo. . . .

licet "ora" posuerit pro Nola, Nolanis, sicut Servius scribit, iratus, quia eum aut hospitio non acceperant, aut aquulam noluerant ei concedere in suum agellum Vesevi radicibus subiectum derivandam.

Livius in nono, "In Campaniam reditum maxime ad Nolam armis repetendam, quae capta est a C. Livio consule." **[419D]** Et libro XXIII, "Hannibal

above the Caudine Forks is Arienzo, and lower down is Marigliano, a town, as I noted, with an ancient name. Next, halfway up the mountain, is the town of Cancello, and above that is Forino. These are the Tifata mountains; Livy writes the following about them in book 7,

> For the Samnites forgot about the Sidicini and attacked their neighbors the Campanians, their citadel itself, in fact, thinking they would get an easy victory, and more booty and glory. The Tifata mountains tower over Capua; they had occupied them with a strong garrison. They marched down from there in regular order of battle into the plain which lies between Capua and Tifata.

And below this, on the same topic, "There was a horrible battle at Mt. Tifata, in which they said the Romans' eyes were literally blazing. The Samnites were put to flight and slaughtered." And in book 23, he writes that Hannibal had his camp at Mt. Tifata and he moved quickly but did not find Gracchus. And farther on, "between Capua and Hannibal's camp, which was **[419C]** on Mt. Tifata." And below that, "Hannibal left a moderate garrison on Mt. Tifata and set out with his entire army." And in book 24, "Hannibal set out from Arpi and settled above Capua in his old camp at Tifata." In the same vein in book 32, "Cornelius Scipio Africanus and C. Aelius Paetus put up for sale the territory of Capua at the foot of Mt. Tifata."

On the slopes of this mountain which face away from the area of Capua and begin to slope downward, is the town of Sarno, named after the Sarno river which issues from an abundant source there. Pliny writes that when wood and leaves fall into these springs, they harden into stone. But between those springs and Mt. Vesuvius (which I described much earlier in this chapter) is the very ancient city of Nola. Nola is famous in history; Justin states it was founded by the Iapygians. We know that its territory is very fertile; Virgil writes about it in the *Bucolics*,

> Rich Capua ploughs such land,
> And Nola next to the ridge of Vesuvius.

He wrote "shores" instead of "Nola" because, as Servius tells us, he was angry with the people of Nola because either they had not received him hospitably, or they did not allow him water rights over a small stream for his farm at the foot of Vesuvius.

Livy says in book nine, "[C. Poetelius] returned to Campania, mainly to take back Nola by force; afterwards it was captured by the consul C. Livius." **[419D]** And in book 23,

Capua recepta cum iterum Neapolitanorum animos partim spe, partim metu nequicquam tentasset. In agrum Nolanum exercitum duxit." Item infra, "M. Claudius proconsul ad eum exercitum, qui supra Suessulam Nolae praesideret missus." Item inferius, "Et Nolae sicut priore anno, senatus Romanorum, plebs Hannibalis erat." Item inferius, "Eadem aestate Marcellus ab Nola, quam praesidio obtinebat." Et inferius, "Hannibal praesidio modico relicto in Tiphatis profectus cum cetero exercitu ire Nolam pergit." Et libro XXIIII, "Adventu Hannibalis Nolana mota est plebs." Livius item libro IIII de nonagesimo, "Sulla Nolam in Samnio recepit, et agros eius legionibus divisit."

Si autem Livius hoc in loco Nolam in Samnitibus annumerat, minime mirandum, quod eo in sociali bello, quod tunc is scribebat, Nola vicinis Samnitibus ita obstinate consenserat, ut ex ea regione haberi potuerit. Suetonius Tranquillus mortem Octavii Caesaris Augusti describens eum dicit a Capreis Nolam delatum in eodem cubiculo, in quo pater Octavius obiisse; et centuriones eum a Nola Bovillas umeris detulisse.

Plinio vero Sarnus, descriptio cuius bis supra a nobis est inchoata, in mare inferum cadit ad loca Annuntiatae nunc proxima, ubi olim Pompeios fuisse ostendimus. Isque fluvius, de quo Virgilius in septimo, "et **[420E]** qua rigat oppida Sarnus," et "nocturnae aurae editor" a Lucano appellatus, nunc dicitur Scafati a scaphis, quae ibi tenentur viatoribus in agrum Nucerinum traiiciendis. Nam proxima ad quattuor mille passus est urbs Nuceria, quam M. Cicero legem dissuadens agrariam, Rullo Cornelio propositam, queritur in decem virorum libidinem perventuram, his verbis, "Neapolim Pompeios Nuceriam suis praesidiis devincient." Livius autem libro XXII sic habet, "Nucerini Atellam quia id maluerant, Atellani Calatiam migrare iussi."

Nuceriae dextrorsum montes imminent, in quorum medio oppidum est a situ nomen nactum. Intermontes enim appellatur, vallisque his montibus sinistrorsum proxima sanctum Severinum habet nobile oppidum, a quo clara

> After he had captured Capua, Hannibal tried a second time to gain power over the Neapolitans, but did not succeed by either persuasion or intimidation. So he transferred his army to the territory of Nola.

And later, on the same topic, "The proconsul M. Claudius was sent to the army which was above Suessula, guarding Nola." And again, below this, "And just as in the previous year at Nola, the senate was for the Romans, but the people for Hannibal." Again on the same topic, further on, "In the same summer, Marcellus from Nola, which he was holding with a garrison." And below this, "He left a medium-sized garrison at Tifata and set out with the rest of his army and hastened to Nola." And in book 24, "At Hannibal's arrival, the common people of Nola rose up." And again, in book 86, Livy writes, "Sulla retired to Nola in Samnium, and divided the territory among his soldiers."

If, however, Livy counted Nola in this location in Samnite territory, it is no wonder that in the Social War about which he was then writing, Nola stubbornly made common cause with her neighbors the Samnites, as she could be considered part of that region. Suetonius, in his description of the death of Augustus, says that he was brought from Capri to Nola, in the same bedchamber in which his father Octavius had died; and centurions carried him on their shoulders from Nola to Bovillae.

But the Sarno river, which I twice began to describe in an earlier part of this chapter, according to Pliny debouches into the Tyrrhenian Sea at a place near what is now Torre Annunziata, where I demonstrated Pompeii was located in ancient times. Virgil writes about this river in book 7, **[420E]** "and where the Sarnus waters the towns," and Lucan calls it "producer of a breeze at night." It is now called the Scafati on account of the small boats which are moored there to transfer travellers to the territory of Nocera. In fact the city of Nocera lies next to it, only four miles away. Cicero, in his speech against Rullus' agrarian law, laments that Nuceria would fall prey to the greed of the decemvirs, saying "They will enslave, through their garrisons, Naples, Pompeii, and Nuceria." But Livy says in book 22, "The Nucerini were transferred to Atella because they preferred it; the people of Atella were ordered to migrate to Calatia."

On the right-hand side, mountains tower over Nocera, and in their midst is a town whose name was derived from the topography; for it is called Tramonti, and the valley on the left-hand side next to these mountains contains

eius cognominis familia originem habet, eaque vallis omnigenum fertilis frugum, vinis praesertim vermiculis abundat. Ad infimam vero eius vallis partem apud oppidum, quod Aqua Malorum appellatur, fluvius est, qui paucis delapsus passuum milibus hiatu terrae absorbetur, et post centesimi ferme passus spatium integer, et quantus fuerat in amplam scaturiginem evomitur. Cavaque urbs a situ appellata **[420F]** valli et fluvio dextrorsum in monte imminet.

Sed a Nuceria urbe ad praedictas cavas progressi, montes dextrorsum linquimus celsos amplissimosque in mare inferum excurrentes, et promontorium facientes, quod Minervae cognomen priscis temporibus habuit. Nunc ab Amalphi oppido appellatum, cuius oppidi nomen nullo in veteri loco invenimus. Primaque eius loci mentio nobis occurrit, ubi in Historiis ostendimus, ad annum salutis quintum vigesimum undeciesque centenum Othonem imperatorem Theotonicum ab Innocentio secundo pontifice Romano, contra Rogerium Siciliae comitem fuisse vocatum Rogerioque Italiae continenti pulso, Amalphim civitatem, et Rivellum cum castellis circumvicinis spoliatum fuisse.

Sed fama est qua Amalphitanos audivimus gloriari, magnetis usum, cuius adminiculo navigantes ad arcton diriguntur, Amalphi fuisse inventum, quicquid vero habeat in ea re veritas, certum est id noctu navigandi auxilium priscis omnino fuisse incognitum. Nam licet legamus Hispanos ad hesperi sideris **[420G]** directionem navigasse in Italiam, unde sicut operis principio diximus, Italia Hesperiae appellationem habuit, nullum tamen ad eam rem caelo nubibus obscurato a magnete, aut ab alio instrumento petebatur auxilium. Ipsis vero in montibus Amalphitanis vini oleique feracissimis, qua in mare inferum desinunt, et meridianum excipiunt solem, regio est omnium Italiae amoenissima cedri malique, quod arantium vocitamus, et Punicorum ceterorumque malorum ferax, quibus Neapolitana urbs imprimis gaudet.

Suntque hoc in promontorio praeter Amalphim oppida in mare pariter versa, Maius et Minus nomine appellata, inde Caput Ursi, et ulterius Veterum, vicus villis amoenissimus habitatus. Post promontorium est Salernum urbs ad Silerim fluvium, oriturque is fluvius in Apennino, qua in parte Drumentum, in mare superum currens, suos habet fontes.

the noble town of Mercato S. Severino. There is a famous family of that name that traces its roots to the town. This valley is fertile with all kinds of crops and produces wines, especially the red type. But on the lowest level of this valley, at the town called Acquamela, there is a river which flows for a few miles and then disappears into a chasm in the ground. Then after nearly a hundred paces it comes up again undiminished and gushes forth abundantly. The city of Cava, named after this feature of the landscape, perches over the valley and the river.

But if you go out from the city of Nocera on the right-hand side of the mountain to these caves I mentioned earlier, you leave the high mountains on the right-hand side and they extend downwards to the Tyrrhenian Sea, and create a promontory, which was in ancient times given the name of Minerva. Now it is named after the town of Amalfi; a name I have not found in any ancient source. The first mention of this name I found was (as I stated in my *Histories*) in the year 1125 A.D., when the German emperor Otto was summoned by Pope Innocent II to fight against Count Roger of Sicily. After driving Roger out of the Italian mainland, he plundered the city of Amalfi and Ravello with its neighboring fortresses.

But the greatest feature of their reputation is their claim to have invented the magnet, an instrument which they use to navigate, orienting themselves to the north pole. However much truth there is in this claim, it is certain that this aid to navigation at night was completely unknown to the ancients. Although I have read that the Spaniards sailed to Italy by orienting themselves to the evening star (and for this reason, as I mentioned at the beginning of this book, Italy had the name **[420G]** Hesperia), the Spaniards did not rely for help in this endeavor on the magnet—or on any other instrument—when the sky was covered by clouds. In the mountains at Amalfi, where they end at the Tyrrhenian Sea, abundant crops of grapes and olives are grown, because they receive the midday sun. This, the pleasantest of all the regions of Italy, produces cedars and the fruits which we call oranges. It is also fertile in pomegranates and the other kinds of soft-skinned fruits which are enjoyed especially at Naples.

Also on this promontory, past Amalfi, there are two towns which face the sea together, called Maiori and Minori. Then come Capo d'Orso, and beyond that Vietri, a village settled with very pleasant villas. After the promontory comes the city of Salerno, on the river Sele. This river has its source in the Apennines, where the *Drumentum*, which debouches into the Adriatic, has its source.

Vallem nunc describi oportuit, quam Siler amnis sinistrorsum a mari ad Apenninum oppidis alicubi castellis et vicis habitatam habet. Sed eam dexteramque simul Lucaniae regionis contiguae descriptionem aggressuri describemus, ut montes Lucaniae excelsos, et pleraque [420H] insuperabiles melius ostendamus. Sunt enim illi, de quibus dicit Livius in nono, cum difficultates enumerans, quas inventurus fuisset Alexander Magnus, si in Italiam traiecisset, interrogat, quis illi habitus fuisset Lucanos montes et saltus Apuliae cernenti. Sed iam Apuliae manu apponamus.

Now I must describe the valley on the left-hand side of the Sele river, which is inhabited in places by towns, fortified villages, and hamlets. But I shall describe at the same time the Sele valley and the valley on the right of the bordering region of Lucania, in order better to show the high and for the most part impassable mountains of Lucania. These are the mountains which Livy mentions, in book 9, as he enumerates **[420H]** the hardships Alexander the Great would have encountered had he crossed over into Italy. He asks what attitude Alexander would have experienced looking upon the mountains of Lucania and the forests of Apulia. But let me now take on the description of Apulia.

Regio Quartadecima
Apulia

[421A]

Oportuit supra Samnitium regione ad Tiferni amnis dexteram a nobis expedita, ad eiusdem fluvii sinistram transire, et ibi inchoantem Apuliam exordiri. Sed connexam, sicut ostensum est, Samnio Campaniam prius describere coacti fuimus. Itaque ad Apuliam finita Campania redeundum est.

Eam regionem a duce eiusdem nominis sic appellatam Ptolemaeus bifariam dividit, ut Apulos, Daunos, et Tifernos ad Barium urbem, Peucetios inde usque ad Salentinos esse velit. Servius vero in octavo Virgilii verba exponens Diomedis ad urbem, sic habet,

> Diomedes tenuit partes Apuliae. Et edomita omni Gargani montis multitudine, in eodem tractu multas condidit civitates, Beneventum, Equitucium, et Arpos, quae et Argyripa est dicta. Pars vero ad quam Virgilius facit missum fuisse Mesappum Mesappia, et Peucetia a fratre. Item Daunia a Dauno rege.

Gesta in Apulis referre operosum esset, sed aliqua ex more nostro summatim attingemus. Apuli prius **[421B]** bello quam amicitia Romanis noti fuerunt. Nam Livius libro octavo dicit C. Sulpicio Q. Emilio consulibus, ad defectionem Samnitium accessisse novum Apuliae bellum, cuius tunc ager sit vastatus. Et libro nono Publium consulem in Apuliam profectum, aliquot expeditionibus populos aut vi subegisse, aut condicionibus in societatem accepisse. Et infra,

> Inclinatis semel in Apulia rebus Teatini quoque Apuli ad novos consules, Q. Iunium Bubulcum, Q. Emilium Barbulam foedus pe-

Fourteenth Region
Puglia

[421A]

After concluding my description of the Samnite region on the right bank of the Biferno river, it would have been appropriate for me to cross over to the left bank of this same river and to set forth my description of Puglia, which begins at that point. But I have been forced first to describe Campania, as it is contiguous with Abruzzo. And so, now that I have finished with Campania, I must return to Puglia.

This region was named for a leader of the same name. Ptolemy divides it into two parts, with the result that he puts Apulians, Daunians, and Tiferni in the area that extends to the city of Bari, and the Peuceti from there all the way to the Salentini. Servius, commenting on Virgil's words "the city of Diomedes" in the eighth book of the Aeneid, says,

> Diomedes held parts of Apulia and, after he had conquered the entire population of Mt. Garganus, founded in the same area many cities: Beneventum, Quintucium, and Arpi, which is also called Argyripa. But the part where Virgil has Messapus settle was Messapia, and Peucetia is named after his brother. In the same way, Daunia is named for King Daunus.

It would be laborious indeed to narrate the history of Puglia; but, according to my custom, I shall touch cursorily on some of the events. The Apuli were known to the Romans more through **[421B]** war than through friendship; so Livy tells us in book 8, where he says that in the year C. Sulpicius and Q. Aemilius were consuls, the Romans had to face, in addition to the desertion of the Samnites, a new war in Apulia, and they then laid waste the territory of Apulia. And in book nine, Livy says that the consul Publ[*li*]lius set forth for Apulia and in some expeditions either overcame its people by force or took them into alliance by offering them terms. And below that,

> Once the situation in Apulia had taken this turn, the people of Teate in Apulia also came to the new consuls, C. Junius Bubulcus

> titum venerunt, pacis per omnem Apuliam praestandae populo Romano auctores. Id audacter spondendo impetravere ut foedus daretur, neque ut aequo tum foedere, sed ut in ditione populi Romani essent.

Sicque Apulia est perdomita. Libro autem decimo,

> Magnus motus servilis eo anno in Apulia fuit. Tarentum provinciam L. Postumius praetor habebat. Is de pastorum coniuratione, qui vias latrociniis pascuaque publica infesta habuerant, quaestionem severe exercuit. Ad septem milia hominum condemnavit, multi inde fugerunt, de multis sumptum enim supplicium.

Sunt prima Apulorum ad Tiferni sinistram oppida Campus Marinus in litore; et intus decimo miliario Larinum novum oppidum alteri suffectum, vetustissimo eiusdem [421C] nominis proxime ad duos mille passus demolito, de quo Livius libro viginti duo post descriptam Hannibalis fugam ab agro Falerno sic habet, "Hannibal ex Pelignis flexit iter, retroque Apuliam repetens Galeranum pervenit; ad urbem dictator in Larinate agro castra communivit." C. Caesar in Commentariis, "Inde Caesar septem omnino dies ad Corfinium commoratus, per fines Marrucinorum, Frentanorum, et Larinatum in Apuliam pervenit."

Quarto supra Larini veteris ruinas miliario est Casacalenda oppidum, cui ad duos mille passus proximae sunt ruinae Gerionis oppidi vetustissimi, de quo Livius libro XXII, "Cum ad Gerionem iam hieme impendente consisteret bellum, Neapolitani oratores venerunt Romam." Et infra, "Quam diu pro Gerionis Apuliae castelli inopis, tamquam pro Carthaginis moenibus pugnavit."

Superius sunt Ioveniscum, Morronum, Castellum Lineum, Petrella, Mons Saganus, Iacobi copiarum ductoris egregii patria, a qua cognomen habet. Inde coacta Rochetta, Ratinum, Bussum, Baranellum, Vinculatorium, quod a Boviano et Tiferni amnis origine quinque milia passuum abest. Medioque

> and Q. Aemilius Barbula, to ask for a treaty, as persons responsible for producing peace for the Roman people through all of Apulia. They gained what they were asking for by boldly promising this, but were given a treaty not on equal terms but one which made them subjects of the Roman people.

And in this way Apulia was conquered. Also in book 10,

> That year there was a great slave uprising in Apulia. The praetor L. Postumius had gotten Tarentum as his province. There was a plot hatched among the shepherds, who had made the roads and public pastures unsafe through their robberies. Postumius punished them severely with trials in which he condemned seven thousand men, many of whom escaped, but many of whom suffered the punishment decreed.

The first towns of the Apuli are on the left bank of the Biferno river, on the shore: Campo Marino, and ten miles inland, Larino, a new town which has taken the place of the other very ancient one of the same name **[421C]** which is about two miles from it, and has been destroyed. About the earlier settlement Livy says, in book 22, after describing Hannibal's withdrawal from Falernian territory, "Hannibal turned aside from the territory of the Peligni, went back to Apulia, and arrived at Galeranum. At the city the dictator fortified a camp in the territory of Larinum." C. Caesar in his *Commentaries on the Civil War* writes, "From there, Caesar stayed for seven days at Corfinium, and arrived in Apulia after traversing the territory of the Marrucini, Frentani, and Larinates."

Four miles above the ruins of ancient Larinum is the town of Casacalenda, and near it, two miles away, are the ruins of the very ancient town of Gereonium. About this town Livy writes in book 22, "When the fighting at Gereonium had come to a half, as winter was now coming on, speakers came to Rome from Naples." Also, later on, "How long has he been before the walls of Gereonium, a poorly-supplied fort in Apulia, as if he were fighting for the walls of Carthage."

Above Gereonium are the towns of *Ioveniscum*, Morrone del Sannio, Castellino del Biferno, Petrella Tifernina, and Montagano, the home of the outstanding military commander Jacopo who takes his last name from that town. Then come bunched together Rocchetta, *Ratinum,* Busso, Baranello, and Vinchiaturo, which is five miles from Bojano and the source of the Biferno river. In the area of mountains, midway between the sea and Bo-

in montium a mari ad Bovianum tractu Monti Sagano ad sinistram quarto proximum est miliario Campus **[421D]** Bassus, a quo oppido patriam quoque et cognomen habent comites Campi Bassi, quorum Carolus copias cum prudentiae et fortitudinis laude ducit.

A Tiferno autem fluvius nunc Fortorius viginti milia passus in litore distat. Qui quidem fluvius in mare se exonerat prope lacum Lesinae appellatum, passuum quadraginta milia in circuitu complexum. Lesinaque oppidum quattuor a mari milibus distans lacui cui dat nomen, mille passibus est propinquum. Intus autem quarto supra Lesinam miliario proximum est ad mille passus amni Fortorio, et arduo in colle oppidum, in regione egregium, Serra Capriolla appellatum. Superius sunt oppida et castella: Sanctus Iulianus, Collis Tortus, Machia, Petra Cratelli, Campus Petrae, Geldonum, et in summo Circus Maior, cui proximum Fortorius amnis habet ortum.

Ad sinistram vero Fortorii Sanctus Nicander oppidum quinque milia passuum a mari distans lacui Lesinae imminet ad eam partem, quae monti Gargano est proxima. Interiusque Porcina oppidum quindecim a Fortorio, duo a Gargani montis radicibus milia passus abest. Sextoque supra Forcinam miliario oppidum Sanctus Severus, sexdecim a Fortorio, et sex a Gargano milibus, recedit.

Priusquam ultra procedamus, Garganum prisci praesentisque nominis montem fama notissimum describamus. Is ad infimas radices in planitiem desinentes, ducentorum milium circuitu patet. **[422E]** Qua vero in parte ad occidentem solem versa, Fortorium amnem, et maris Adriatici sinum spectat, lacum habet Varrani appellatum, triginta milia passus in circuitu complexum, cui quidem lacui castella circumimminent, Caprinum, Cognatum, et Sitella. Et qua mons ipse in mare prominet Rodium, ut nunc appellant, oppidum inferiora obtinet. Quod quidem promontorium et oppidum Ptolemaeus Pliniusque et ceteri omnis prisci Tirium appellarunt.

Supra est oppidum Vicus dictum; et superius montis summitatem obtinet, praeclarum Sancti Angeli oppidum, a quo mons ipse praesentis temporis, ut plurimum nominationem habet. Ornaturque templo cum aedificiis, ceteroque apparatu, tum maxime ipsa religiositate conspicuo, quod archangeli Michaelis patrocinium apud deum nostrum imploraturi totius Christiani orbis populi, maximo per universa anni tempora concursu frequentant.

Qua vero Garganus spectat in orientem solem oppidum est portuosum, nunc Bestia, olim Vestice, appellatum. Unde ostendimus in Historiis, Alexandrum tertium pontificem Romanum a Guillelmo secundo Normannorum

jano, on the left next to Montagano, four miles away is **[421D]** Campobasso. From this town, the Counts of Campobasso have their origin and name. Charles commanded their troops with praise for their common sense and courage.

Twenty miles from the Biferno, nearby on the coast, is the river now called Fortore. This river debouches into the sea near Lago di Lésina, which is forty miles in circumference. The town Lésina is four miles from the sea and takes its name from this lake one mile away. Moving inland, four miles above Lésina and a mile from the Fortore river, on a high hill, lies the most important town in the region, called Serracapriola. Higher up are the following towns and castles: S. Giuliano di Puglia, Colletorto, Macchia, Pietracatella, Campodipietra, Gildone. At the summit is Cercemaggiore; next to it the Fortore river has its source.

On the left bank of the Fortore is the town of Sannicandro Garganico, five miles from the sea, overlooking Lago di Lésina on the side next to Monte Gargano. And towards the interior is the town of Apricena, fifteen miles from the Fortore, two miles from the base of Mte. Gargano. And six miles above Apricena is the town of S. Severo, sixteen miles from the Fortore and six miles from Mte. Gargano.

Before I proceed farther, let me describe Gargano (the mountain's ancient and modern name), because it is very famous. At its base it measures two hundred miles in circumference. The part of it turned eastward looks towards the Fortore river and the bay of the Adriatic Sea. It contains a lake, called Lago di Varano, which measures thirty miles in circumference. **[422E]** Overhanging this lake are the fortified villages of Carpino, Cagnano, and Ischitella. Where Mte. Gargano itself protrudes into the sea, the town called by the modern name Rodi occupies its lower part. Ptolemy, Pliny, and all the rest of the ancient writers called this promontory and town Tirium.

Above it is a town called Vico, and higher up the noble town of Monte Sant'Angelo occupies the top of the mountain. Many people of our time call the mountain itself by the name of the town. It boasts a church, with buildings and all the decorations, especially noteworthy for its holiness because the protection of the archangel Michael pleads with God on behalf of the people of the entire Christian world. In great throngs they flock here at all times of year.

On the eastern side of Gargano is the harbor town now called Vieste, in ancient times called Vestice. I recounted in my *Histories* that it was this place that Pope Alexander III, with the help of William the second,

gentis rege adiutum soluisse cum tredecim triremibus, ut pacem cum Federico primo imperatore pessimo compositurus Venetias navigaret. **[422F]** Eoque in loco cum sit secundum Gargani promontorium, Ptolemaeus Adriatici maris sinum finire, ac Ionium mare asserit inchoare. Qui etiam dicit Diomedis insulam Garganeo ad triginta milia passuum e regione proximam esse. Estque haec insula, de qua beatus Aurelius Augustinus de Civitate Dei scribens aliqua dicit, quibus ab ipso transcriptis unusquisque pro auctoris gravitate fidem, quam volet, poterit adhibere.

Diomedum ferunt deificatum, et socios suos in aves esse conversos, non fabuloso poeticoque mendacio sed historica attestatione, quin etiam templum eius esse aiunt in insula Diomedica, non longe a Monte Gargano; et hoc templum circumvolare atque incolere has alites tam mirabili obsequio, ut aquam impleant et aspergant. Et eo si Graeci venerint, aut Graecorum stirpe progeniti, non solum quietas esse, verum et insuper advolare. Si autem alienigenas viderint, subvolare ad capita cum gravibus ictibus, ut etiam perhibeant vulnerare. Nam duris et grandibus rostris satis ad haec proelia perhibentur armatae.

Eam vero insulam Tremiti appellatam, et Diomedis, ut videtur, templum illud nunc inhabitant religiosi Canonici regulares appellati, quos non minus hoc in loco **[422G]** quam Venetiis, sicut ostendimus, et fovit et auxit gloriosus pontifex quartus Eugenius. Quorum vitae austeritas, et sanctimonia adeo cunctis est admirabilis, ut cum advenis omnibus sint hospitales ac munifici, a nullis vel perditissimis quarumcumque gentium et nationum piratis ullam hactenus acceperint laesionem. Eorum nos quosdam narrare audivimus, has aves Diomedis nomen retinentes, magnitudine anseris insulam habere multas. Sed omnino omnibus innocuas, nec aliquod eius aut templo praestantes obsequium.

De Gargano monte habent aliqua Virgilius et Servius, quae ad universae Apuliae notionem plurimum faciunt. Nam cum Virgilius in nono dicat, "Garganii condebat Iapygis arces," exponit Servius, "Iapygia est pars Apuliae, in qua est mons Garganus, qui usque in Adriaticum protenditur pelagus." Lucanus etiam dicit, "Apulus Adriacas Garganus exit in undas."

Garganum montem adiacentiaque oppida Saraceni per Grimoaldi Longobardorum regis tempora, ad annum salutis paulo plus septingentesimum ceperunt. Quos idem rex expulit populis Christianis ubique conservatis, ut nullam gens Longobarda in ducentis **[422H]** regnorum suorum annis talem

king of the Normans, set sail for Venice with **[422F]** thirteen triremes to make peace with the evil emperor Frederick I. And in this place, the second promontory of Garganus, Ptolemy asserts that the gulf of the Adriatic ends and the Ionian Sea begins. Ptolemy also says that the island of Diomedes is opposite Garganus, thirty miles out to sea from the region. It is this island about which the blessed Augustine wrote in his *City of God*, saying some things which I have transcribed from Augustine himself, and to which each man will be able to apply the faith he wishes as befits the gravity of their author.

The legend is that Diomedes was deified and his companions turned into birds, and this has historical support and is not mere poetic fable and falsehood. They say that his temple is on the island of S. Domino not far from Mte. Gargano and the birds fly around and inhabit this temple with such devotion that they fill their beaks with water and sprinkle it on the temple. If Greeks come there, or descendants of Greeks, not only do they stay quiet, they fly over to them. But if they see foreigners they fly at their heads with fierce blows, so that they even wound them. For they are armed with great hard beaks, which they use in these attacks.

But this island, called S. Domino, and the famous **[422G]** temple of Diomedes, are now inhabited by a male religious order called regular Canonics and, as I have mentioned, the glorious pope Eugenius the fourth supported them and increased their number, not only in this place but also in Venice. The austerity and purity of their life is so admired by all that, as they are hospitable to all who come there, they have up to now not been harmed by any pirates of any nationality. I have heard some men say that this island has many of these birds of Diomedes; that they have kept their name, and are the size of geese; but that they are completely harmless to everyone but show no devotion to him or to the temple.

Virgil and Servius have something to say about Mte. Gargano which is very relevant to the general topic of Apulia. For when Virgil in book nine says, "His town, Argyripa (named for his father's people) he is building on land he won in Apulia," Servius explains that Iapygia is the part of Apulia where Mt. Garganus is, which extends into the Adriatic Sea. Lucan, too, says "Apulian Garganus debouches into the Adriatic waves."

In the times of Grimoald the Lombard king, a little later than the year seven hundred, the Arabs seized Mte. Gargano and the neighboring towns, but this king drove them out and **[422H]** Christian people everywhere were

praestiterint Italiae operam. Ad annum exinde paulo plus minus centesimum Carolus Magnus imperator et Francorum rex Saracenos Garganum opprimentes, cum expulisset, omnia pacifice possedit, quae ab ipso Gargano ad Cordubam Hispaniae urbem intercedunt.

Prius autem quam exposita mari post Garganum montem prosequar, alia describam, quae ad amnem Fortorium inchoavi. Supra Sancti Severi oppidum quarto miliario est Turris Maior castellum duodecim milibus e Fortorio recedens. Et supra totidem milibus a Turri Maiore abest Castellutium oppidum, unde parvo distat spatio mons Rotanus. Et supra est Cellentia, post oppidum Sanctus Marcus, inde Vulturaria, et proxime Sancti oppidum quod dicitur Gaudii. Supraque id est Rossenum, superius Fortori amnis fonti mons Falco castellum est proximum.

Blondi Forliviensis Italiae illustratae Finis.

saved. This was the greatest aid given by the Lombard race to Italy in their two hundred years of rule. About one hundred years from then, the emperor Charlemagne, king of the Franks, drove out the Arabs who were oppressing the promontory. He took peaceful possession of all the land which now extends from Mte. Gargano to Cordova in Spain.

But before I continue to describe the places after Mte. Gargano on the coast, I shall describe the other places on the Fortore river which I began to treat. Above the town of S. Severo and four miles from it, and twelve miles from the Fortore, is the castle Torremaggiore. And the same distance above Torremaggiore is the town of Castelluccio. A little way from this is Mte. Toro; above that is Celenza, and after that, the town of S. Marco. Then comes Volturara, and very near that the town called *St. Gaudius*. Above it is Roseto, and the fortified village of Montefalcone is higher up, next to the source of the Fortore river.

Here ends the "Italia illustrata" of Biondo of Forlì.

Second Region, Tuscany
Commentary

Biondo sets the boundaries of ancient Etruria as the Magra and Tiber rivers, the Apennines, and the Tyrrhenian Sea. At many points in the description of ancient Etruria and the location of Etruscan cities, he follows Pliny's account of the Augustan Regio VII, which included Etruria. How faulty his manuscript of Pliny was, can be seen from the number of his errors in comparison with *NH* 3.50, 3.52, and 3.80.

Biondo envisioned dedicating "Tuscany" to Piero de' Medici. Although the printed version of 1559 does not contain this portion, White (*Italy illuminated* 2.1) provides the dedicatory passage from the earliest redaction requesting Piero to obtain his father Cosimo's help with additions and corrections. This earliest redaction was published separately; see White, *Italy illuminated*, xx–xxi; 392 n. 74. The chapter is surprisingly brief, considering the region's antiquity, frequency of mention in ancient authors, and archaeological wealth. But we must remember that the region's archaeological remains were not as visible and accessible to Biondo and his fellow antiquarian humanists as they have been to modern scholars. The Etruscan tombs would not be excavated for a few centuries; and the region did not present the monumental ruins comparable to those visible in the first half of the fifteenth century around Rome and the Campi Flegrei.

Biondo concentrates his attention in "Tuscany," as we might expect, on cities and towns treated by his friend, mentor, and influence in the field of historiography, Leonardo Bruni, on whose *Historiarum Florentini populi libri XII* he draws frequently in this chapter. Thus the city of Arezzo receives detailed treatment, including a fairly extensive history, a description of the city-building activities of its fourteenth-century lord, Guido Tarlati di Pietramala, and discussion of a local inscription. The description of Florence is enhanced by numerous biographical comments on her famous men, including the architect Brunelleschi and several of his buildings and flattering mentions of Cosimo de' Medici's private dwellings as well as the standard praise of humanists and men of letters. The pride of place we would

expect to be occupied, however, by Florence, a city so central to the development of humanistic culture, has been claimed by the Romagna (see Biondo's praise of this region, vol. 1, pp. 44–51), where he mentions a number of Florentine humanists in connection with the seminal Romagnol figure Giovanni da Ravenna. This usurpation, perhaps surprising in view of the importance of Florence in B.'s intellectual development in the 1430s, is explained by Biondo's patriotic feelings for his native region.

[300F] *Duodecim autem urbes* ... The twelve Etruscan capital cities were probably Veii, Caere, Tarquinia, Rusellae, Vetulonia, Populonia, Clusium, Volsinii, Perusia, Vulci, Volaterrae, and Arretium.

quae Livius tradit ... *additque Livius* ... In 310 B.C., during the battle of Romans and Etruscans at Sutrium, the consul's brother, who had been educated at Caere, and thus knew Etruscan, volunteered to explore the Ciminian Forest, where the Etruscans had fled for salvation.

B. does not mention Cicero's comments at *Div*. 1.41 and 9.36 that the sons of the leading Roman families were sent to Caere for their education.

[300H] *Berengariusque Italicensis imperator et Lotharius eius filius rex* ... Berengar II reigned in Italy 950–961. He was a rival of Hugh of Arles, who was king of Italy from 936–947, but from 945 resided in Provence; Hugh's son, Lothar, was joint ruler with him. Hugh died in 947 and Lothar in 950. B. has confused Berengar II and Hugh; see Wickham, *Early Medieval Italy*, 177–183.

Luna inter capita Etruriae numerata ... B. erroneously cites Lucan 1.584–586, which refer to the abandoned city of Lucca. Lucan's context is the description of the apparition on earth, in the heavens, and on the sea, of portents related to Caesar's approach towards, and Pompey's flight from, Rome:

> Haec propter placuit Tuscos de more vetusto
> Acciri vates. Quorum qui maximus aevo
> Arruns incoluit desertae moenia Lucae...

> And so it was resolved to summon Etruscan seers, in accordance with the ancient custom. The oldest of them was Arruns, who lived in the abandoned city of Lucca.

Referring correctly to Martial 13.30, B. intends here to indicate the deserted city of Luni, abandoned finally around 1200. For its archaeology see

B. Ward-Perkins, "Luni: the decline and abandonment of a Roman town," in H. M. Blake, T. W. Potter, D. N. Whitehouse, edd., *Papers in Italian Archaeology* 1 pt. 2 (London: 1978) 313–321.

[301A–D] Pisa.

Thomas Fregosus Genuensis ... Tommaso Campofregoso; see vol. 1, p. 241.

De hisque sic habet in decimo Livius ... B. erroneously refers to Livy book 10, whereas this passage describes events of 185 B.C., in book 39.32.1–4.

[301C] *A Pelope et Atintanis* An example of the defects in B.'s manuscript of Pliny. *NH* 3.52 lists the peoples of region VII: ... *propiorque Pisae inter amnes Auserem et Arnum, ortae a Pelopi[d]is sive a Teutanis, Graeca gente.*

[301C–D] *Et Lucanus in primo* ... B. erroneously attributes this line to book 1; it is 2.401.

[302D] *Plinius navigiorum capacem fuisse scribit intercapedo habetur* ... *Intercapedo*, "an interruption in space," is noted as rare by Lewis and Short, *s.v.*

[302G] *iuxta quem tertio a mari miliario Corneto* ... B. comes close to the correct identification of Corneto with ancient Tarquinia (indeed, as White, *Italy illuminated*, 389 n. 44 notes, Corneto was renamed Tarquinia in 1922). Instead, B. identifies Corneto with Castrum Novum, as described by Ptolemy, Pliny, and Mela. Tarquinia was in fact the leader of the Etruscan League of twelve cities; but B. does not include it in the twelve. The ancient city's inhabitants and diocese were transferred to a nearby village with better natural defenses, and its name changed to Corneto.

[302G] ... *qua ex Tarquinia* ... *Tarquinii Priscus et Superbus originem duxere.* The Tarquins of Rome actually came from Caere.

Iohannes Vitellensis Giovanni Vitelleschi (c. 1400–1440), whom B. served as secretary when he was governor of the March of Ancona in 1432. A military commander, he was made a cardinal, bishop of Recanati, and archbishop of Florence under Eugenius IV; he suppressed the rebellion at Rome which had caused Eugenius' flight to Florence in 1434. One of the first palaces of the Renaissance to be built with a view in mind, Vitelleschi's handsome palace in Corneto now serves as the town's Etruscan museum.

[302G–H] *Nec dubito quin is fuerit Centumcellae* ... B.'s identification of Civitavecchia as ancient Centum Cellae is correct. Trajan was responsible for the construction here of an artificial harbor. The place was unknown to the elder Pliny (*NH* 3.51), as also to Strabo. Its name was evidently unfamiliar to the younger Pliny's audience. The site must have lain in the territory of Castrum Novum, 7 kilometers to the south, and replaced Pyrgi, which in Strabo's day was the harbour of Caere (Strabo, V [Sbordone E 5.2.8, p. 212]). See A. N. Sherwin-White, *The Letters of Pliny: A Historical and Social Commentary* (Oxford: Oxford University Press, 1966; repr. 1985) 391. The comment of Pliny to which B. refers is at 6.31, *Evocatus in consilium a Caesare nostro ad Centum Cellas* (*hoc loco nomen*), *magnam cepi voluntatem*. (I was very much gratified to be called to consult with the emperor at Centum Cellae [this is the name of the place]).

[302H] *Martialis* ... *scribit pernam fieri optimam* ... B. cites the first line of Martial 13.54,

> Cerretana mihi fiat vel missa licebit
> de Menapis: lauti de petasone vorent.

But modern editions write *Cerretana*: while B.'s reading, *Caeretana*, suggests to him the Etruscan city of Caere, most modern translations give "Cerretanian," from a Spanish people famous for producing good bacon. In addition, B. omits the second line of the epigram and writes *massa* while most modern editions have *missa*, "sent (from the Menapians)," another people who were a source of excellent bacon. B.'s version makes little sense, reinforcing the impression that he took many of these citations from a book of commonplaces.

Locus Agillinae ... *quam inter capita Etruriae diximus numeratam fuisse.* Agillina is not traditionally included in the twelve capital cities of Etruria.

Romani portus a Claudio primum, post a Traiano aedificati. This is the "new" harbor at Ostia.

[303B] *beatique sibi et suis esse videntur* ... Perhaps an intentional reminiscence of the story of the sword of Damocles in Cicero (*Disp. Tusc*. 5.20.57–62). B. had been imbued with enthusiasm for Cicero at an early stage in his intellectual formation and when in Milan in 1422 was first to transcribe the *Brutus*. His copy is still in the Vatican Library.

[303C] *Ianipetro ornata est* Gian Pietro da Lucca, d. 1457; this student of Vittorino da Feltre translated works of Plutarch and Isocrates into Latin, and was a professor of literature at Venice.

[303D] *Supremo ... in sinu amplae quam habet primum Etruria planitiei Pistoria ...* Pistoria, the city in whose territory in 63 B.C. Catiline was defeated and killed. Among the *multi ex vetustis* would be of course Sallust, *Cat.* 57.1, and Pliny, *NH* 3.52.

[304E] *initium Florentia ...* Florentine legend during the Renaissance attributed the founding of the city to either Caesar or Augustus; an alternative etymology for Florence is "city of flowers."

Farinatae Ubertini virtute White, *Italy illuminated* 391, notes that this story comes from Bruni (*History of the Florentine People* 2.69–71) who is "in effect commenting on Dante's description of Farinata in *Inferno* X."

[304F–G] **Famous men of Florence**. White's comment on this section (*Italy illuminated*, 391) is just: "Biondo's perfunctory treatment of Florence's cultural giants Brunelleschi ..., Dante ..., Petrarch ..., and Giotto may be compared with his more enthusiastic reaction to Gentile da Fabriano. ..." ([338G]).

Philippus Brunalicius Filippo Brunelleschi, 1377–1446, generally considered one of the initiators of the Renaissance, an architect who developed the law of perspective and whose constructions were much influenced by ancient Roman techniques of building. B. mentions here as *fornix* the cupola for the cathedral of S. Maria del Fiore, a structure begun in 1296, completed in 1434 and consecrated in 1436. B. seems here to confuse Brunelleschi with the medieval architect of the Duomo, Arnolfo di Cambio. The erection of its dome was not possible until Brunelleschi solved architectonic problems associated with its unprecedented size. The cathedral's consecration by Eugenius IV is probably one reason B. mentions it here. *Palatium* refers to the Palazzo di Parte Guelfa. See I. Hyman, "Brunelleschi, Filippo," *DBI* 14 (1972), 534–545.

Turris vero marmorea ... B. indicates the bell tower of the Duomo, the campanile begun by Giotto.

[304G] *Iotum* Giotto di Bondone, c. 1266–1337, considered the father of modern painting. Although attribution of surviving works is uncertain, this fundamentally important figure in Renaissance art was famous already in

the time of Dante and Petrarch; among his most famous works are the frescoes in the Arena Chapel at Padua and the altarpiece of Virgin and Child Enthroned from the Church of Ognissanti in Florence (now in the Uffizi). See M. Boskovits, "Giotto di Bondone," *DBI* 55 (2000), 401–423.

Accursium iureconsultorum principem ... Francesco Accorso, b. between 1181 and 1185; d. between 1259 and 1263. After studying law at Bologna, he taught there until near the end of his life. Despite this long residency at Bologna, he was commonly referred to as "Florentinus"; but although after his death Florence requested his body be moved there, he was buried at Bologna. His fame as a jurist stems from his selective compilation of glosses on the *Corpus iuris civilis* and incorporation of them into a new work which became official and authoritative (called simply *Glossa*), and was printed in the margins of the *Corpus iuris civilis* in all its editions from the oldest (the first edition dated to 1468). See P. Fiorelli, "Accorso," *DBI* 1 (1960), 116–121.

Claudianus poeta Although Claudian (c. 370–404) lived in Rome and Milan, he was born at Alexandria in Egypt. B. here participates in a tradition assigning Florence as his birthplace, probably following the example of Petrarch, who boldly claimed him as a Florentine-on no firmer evidence, apparently, than the dedication of *De Raptu Proserpinae* ii to a "Florentinus" (as can be inferred from the annotation to his own manuscript of Claudian, now in Paris). Despite rival claims for the honour of his birthplace, Petrarch was followed by Boccaccio, Coluccio Salutati, and many others. See Alan Cameron, *Claudian: Poetry and propaganda at the Court of Honorius* (Oxford: Clarendon, 1970), 425–426.

Colutius vero Salutatus ... Coluccio Salutati (1331–1406), chancellor of Florence for more than thirty years, was as important in the development of humanism as in the political sphere. It is largely to his credit that Florence became the center of humanism. He was instrumental in the creation of the Florentine humanist circle and the transplantation of Greek studies to the West when he persuaded Chrysoloras to come to Florence in 1397. Discoverer of the manuscript of Cicero's *Ad familiares*, his emphasis on Cicero's example in combining academic interests with a political career was influential. He wrote treatises himself, but was more appreciated as mentor to Poggio Bracciolini and Leonardo Bruni.

Nicolaus Nicoli Niccolò Niccoli (1364–1437), humanist scholar best known for establishing a splendid personal library which became the basis of the public library Cosimo de'Medici founded at S. Marco. He copied manuscripts and contributed to the development of humanist script.

[304H] *concilium . . . orientalis ecclesiae cum occidentali unionem* The Council of Ferrara- Florence, intended to end the schism by negotiating a reconciliation of the Greek and Roman churches. It began in 1438 and moved from Ferrara to Florence. Despite the ultimate futility of the council's agreement, B. must glorify it, as it was the initiative of Eugenius IV. One of its more lasting benefits was the permanent migration to Italy of cardinal Bessarion, who not only became important and influential in ecclesiastical affairs, but furthered the study of Greek among Italian humanists.

Cosmus . . . Mediceus Cosimo de'Medici (1389–1464), founder of the dynasty of the same name, which ruled Florence and directed foreign policy into the next century. Cosimo supported the arts (patronizing scholars and artists, e.g., the sculptor Donatello), collected manuscripts and encouraged and subsidized collecting by others, and founded the library known today as the Laurenziana. His building activity was famous for its grand scale, hence B.'s *ut aiunt, insanae exstructiones*.

Palla Strozza Palla Strozzi (1372–1462), important in Florentine politics in the 1420s and 1430s; the exile B. refers to began in 1434. He studied Greek with Chrysoloras in Florence, and became a translator of Greek into Latin.

Angelus Acciaiolus Agnolo Acciaiuoli (1397–c. 1468). Brother-in-law of Giannozzo Manetti, politically active as a supporter of Cosimo de'Medici, he undertook various diplomatic missions in Italy and abroad, and held important public offices. See A. D'Addario, "Acciaiuoli, Agnolo," *DBI* 1 (1960), 77.

Andreas Floccus Andrea Fiocchi (1401–1452), secretary, apostolic scriptor, and abbreviator. Fiocchi accompanied Eugenius IV to Florence in 1434 when the latter was forced to leave Rome; and to the Council of Ferrara in 1438. The work to which B. refers, *De magistratibus sacerdotiisque Romanorum*, a treatise on ancient Roman political and religious offices, was falsely promulgated as a work of Tiberius' time. Fiocchi's associations with B. through Eugenius IV led B. to name him also in *De verbis Romanae locutionis*, mentioning him as one of the discussants in the famous dispute about whether the vernacular was derived from Latin, or whether the an-

cient Romans had common and formal languages; Fiocchi upheld the former theory. See F. Pignatti, "Fiocchi, Andrea," *DBI* 48 (1997), 80–81.

Ianectus Manectus Giannozzo Manetti, 1396–1459. Very active in Florence as politician and statesman, he held many posts in the Republic's government. As a scholar, he was expert in Greek, Latin, and Hebrew; he was briefly employed as an apostolic secretary and wrote a *Life* of Nicholas V, who had been his patron and friend.

Baptista Albertus Leon Battista Alberti (1404–1472) mathematician, architect, theoretician of art and architecture and prolific writer of treatises in Latin and the vernacular on the subjects of painting, sculpture, and architecture; among the most famous are *Della famiglia* and *De re aedificatoria.* B.'s notice here is an early appreciation of Alberti. Thoroughly grounded in literature and humanist culture, Alberti was concerned to investigate and restore ancient architectural forms, and was involved in the papal renovations of Rome. Like B., he held a post in the Curia; and accompanied Eugenius in his exile in Florence in the 1430s, where he was prominent in the intellectual and aesthetic movements of the day. Through B.'s eyes we see him engaged in a project to reclaim one of the imperial ships from the bottom of Lago di Nemi (in "Lazio," **[326E–G]**).

Donatellus Again, an early appraisal of an important figure, the sculptor Donatello (1386–1466); by paying him tribute with this Virgilian phrase (*Aen.* 6.848), B. shares the contemporary acknowledgment of the sculptor's genius in depicting the human form. See P. Pontari, "Gli Artisti nel *Catalogus Virorum Illustrium* dell'*Italia illustrata* di Biondo Flavio," *Letteratura e Arte* 1 (2003): 80–110; 87–88.

[305B] *Mugellum . . . quae Dinum habuit Mugellanum iureconsultorum superioris saeculi celeberrimum . . .* Dino Rossoni (d.1298), alumnus of the University of Bologna, taught civil law at Pistoia, then at Bologna. He was one of the first jurists independent enough to depart from the tradition of following the rules of the glossators of legal texts (*e.g.*, Accursius, cf. above on **[304G]**). Many of his works are extant, including an apparatus to Sextus' *De regulis iuris* (Rome 1472), for the compilation of which Pope Boniface VIII summoned him to Rome.

[305B–C] *Scarperia Iacobo ornata Angeli filio . . .* Jacopo Angeli da Scarperia translated from the Greek into Latin Plutarch's *Life of Cicero* and other works (see v. 1, pp. 48–49).

[305C] *Incisa, cuius oppidi nomen originem habuisse coniector ab succiso obiice saxeo cursum Arni solito remorari.* B., and Leandro Alberti after him, are responsible for the perpetuation of two legends about Incisa in Val D'Arno: that the deep ravine was made by human labor (see below, **[306F]**); and that Hannibal's march through the swamps here resulted both in his losing an eye, and later in the foundation of Incisa by remnants of his army (cf. the similar myth about Hercules' companions stopping during their crossing of the Alps, vol. 1, pp. 304–305).

Today it is generally accepted that the Arno carved the deep gully at Incisa through a process of erosion, and that the toponym (originally "ad Incisa saxa" or "Petra Incisa") is derived from this natural "cut." But in medieval times local legend attributed the opening of the defile to human operation. One legend has it that when Hannibal camped in the area around Incisa between his victories at the Trebia (218 B.C.) and Lake Trasimene (217 B.C.), he had his soldiers remove the boulders which were obstructing the lake then in existence. When a plague afflicted his men, the majority of Carthaginians abandoned their camp, but the survivors stayed and founded Incisa. These and many other details of local history are found in Massimo Tarassi, *Incisa in Val d'Arno: Storia di una società e di un territorio nella campagna fiorentina.* (Florence: Salimbeni, 1985); see especially 4–10.

[305D] *Et qui XXII historiarum Livii Patavini in principio attente leget* . . . Hannibal's march after the battle of the Trebia and before that of Lake Trasimene. Livy's description cannot be taken as reliable topographical information, and it is not possible to know in detail the route Hannibal took. B. paraphrases 22.2.10–11 (as he admits, *Sunt autem Livii haec in parte verba*), differing to modern editions' readings of:

> Ipse Hannibal aeger oculis ex verna primum intemperie variante calores frigoraque, elephanto, qui unus superfuerat, quo altius ab aqua exstaret, vectus, vigiliis tamen et nocturno umore palustrique caelo gravante caput et quia medendi nec locus nec tempus erat altero oculo capitur.

The following citation must be a paraphrase as well; cf. Conway and Walters' text (22.2.2):

> Dum consul placandis Romae dis habendoque dilectu dat operam, Hannibal profectus ex hibernis, quia iam Flaminium consulem Arretium pervenisse fama erat, eum aliud longius, ceterum commo-

> dius ostenderetur iter propiorem viam per paludes petit, qua fluvius Arnus per eos dies solito magis inundaverat.

[306F] *adapertum fuisse tenemus humano ingenio* Clearly B. inspected this site himself, as he says out of curiosity as to when the swamp here dried up. His conclusion, that human labor had unblocked the course of the river, is not in accord with what most scholars today believe about the riverbed; see above on **[305C]**.

Habet quoque ea vallis ... The following names were among the fortified "new towns" laid out like Roman *castra* to secure conquered territory.

[306G] *Guido Petramalensis* Guido Tarlati di Pietramala, bishop and lord of Arezzo; see comments below on **[308H]–[309A]**.

[306H] *Balneum Aquarum* ... Casciana Terme (Bagno a Acqua), discussed in C. R. Mack, "The Renaissance Spa: Testing the Architectural Waters," in *Southeastern College Art Conference Review* XI 3 (1988), 196–197.

[307A] *Nunc Gasparis nostri patria* ... Gaspare Zacchi, 1425–1484, who was also bishop of Osimo.

[307B] *Petrioli et alia balnea* Petrioli and other central Italian thermal baths used during the Renaissance are discussed in C. R. Mack, "The Wanton Habits of Venus: Pleasure and Pain at the Renaissance Spa," *Explorations in Renaissance Culture* 26 No. 2 (2000): 257–276.

Martialis cocus ... At several places in *It. ill.,* B. modifies *Martialis* with this epithet. As Sullivan (261) notes,

> Little is heard of Martial in the tenth and early eleventh century, although at this time he picked up the name "Coquus," a title perhaps prompted by the list of comestibles in book XIII, if not due to a scribal error.

[308E] *Francescus Patricius* Francesco Patrizi (1413–1492), Sienese literary and political figure and friend of Aeneas Silvius Piccolomini, was widely read in Greek and Latin. His disgrace and exile from Siena and election as bishop of Gaeta occur after the publication of *It. ill.* He left poetry and orations in Latin, as well as two influential political treatises. His inclusion here in close conjunction with Piccolomini's name may indicate a desire on B.'s part to compliment the latter.

[308F] *Corsignanum* Corsignano was the small native town of Pope Pius II (Aeneas Silvius Piccolomini), who rebuilt it and renamed it Pienza after its transformation into a Renaissance city under the direction of the architect Bernardo Rossellino (see Charles R. Mack, *Pienza: The Creation of a Renaissance City* [Ithaca and London: Cornell University Press, 1987], esp. 31–42). In 1462 B. dedicated to Pius II the *Additiones correctionesque Italiae illustratae* which include an extensive recollection (in Nogara, *Scritti Inediti*, 236–238) of Pius' inspiration for the building projects at Corsignano when he traveled through it with his entourage on the way to Mantua for an ecclesiastical conference.

[308G] Arezzo.

B. obviously visited Arezzo; he acknowledges, of nearby Sansepolcro, *nullum vetustatis signum eo in loco esse inspeximus* (**[328G]**, p. 141). And it is extremely unlikely that he would not have directly observed Leonardo Bruni's native town, or would have relied solely on written sources to describe the walls and streets built by Guido Tarlati di Pietramala.

Innuit vero Plinius urbem in duas urbes fuisse divisam . . . Cf. Pliny, *NH* 3.52: *De cetero Arretini Veteres, Arretini Fidentiores, Arretini Iulienses* . . . Zehnacker, *ad loc.*, comments "le comparatif est éloquent!" and explains that the city took the side of Marius in the Civil War, and accordingly was punished by Sulla by the establishment of a colony there. The *Arretini Veteres* were the ancient inhabitants; the *Arretini Fidentiores* the Sullan colonists, and the *Arretini Iulienses* represented the veterans settled there by Augustus. B. takes the date of Sulla's establishment of a colony at Arezzo as the point of division between "old" and "new" populations. This inscription is today visible in the Museo Archeologico Nazionale G. C. Mecenate, Arezzo (inventory #69):

QUINQU
DECURIONES
ARRETINORUM VETER

It is the honorary inscription of a *quinquennalis*, a magistrate charged with celebrating every five years the ritual purification of the colony. The stone to which Leonardo Bruni called B.'s attention came from the church of Sta. Maria in Gradi; passed to a pilaster of the loggia of the Piazza Grande; then was transferred to the Palazzo del Comune in 1769, and finally to the Museum. White, *Italy illuminated*, 395 n. 126, rightly identifies it with *CIL*

11.1849. As Cherici notes, inscriptions were often found in churches, which were repositories for valued building material, and considered appropriate to decorate with *mirabilia*. They were also among the few cultural entities operating in a territory. And so a small museum complex seems to have formed in the church and convent of S. Maria in Gradi (see A. Cherici, "Arretium," *JAT* 7 [1997] 77–128; 121).

[308H] Horace *Odes* 1.1, the dedication of the first book of Odes to Maecenas, who claimed to be descended from Etruscan kings of Arretium:

> Maecenas atavis edite regibus. . . .
> (Maecenas, born from royal ancestors. . . .)

[308H]–[309A] *Guidonem episcopum ex Petramalensi familia* . . . The information about Bishop Tarlati (elected bishop in 1312, and *signore* for life in 1321; died 1327 or 1328), from the powerful Arretine family of the Pietramala, is B.'s most extensive piece of information on Arezzo. The cenotaph of Tarlati, an important work of Trecento Gothic sculpture, is visible today in the left front side of the Duomo at Arezzo and shows the principal works of Tarlati (see Plate I). Carved in 1330 by the Sienese Agostino di Giovanni and Agnolo di Ventura, the cenotaph was damaged in a rebellion against the Tarlati in 1341. In 1783 bishop Niccolò Marcacci had the monument transferred to the Duomo in Arezzo, and entrusted Angelo Bini di Prato with the work of restoring and refashioning the heads of the figures which had been damaged. B.'s description, a written version of selected cenotaph panels, exemplifies the concept of *illustrare* prominent in *It. ill.*, from B.'s title to his claim to have brought Italy to light (*noverimus illustrare*, vol. 1 pp. 64–65) by shedding light on its history. Indeed, the cenotaph "reads" like the page of a history book, depicting the scenes in chronological order from left to right and top to bottom, as if a page of history intended to be read. Although his brief treatment of Tarlati's works resembles a narrative of much of the cenotaph, B.'s narrative emphasizes Tarlati's "city-building" activities, in keeping with his customary portrayal of signori as city-builders and patrons of the arts and literature. Comparison with *Annali Aretini* shows agreement with the cenotaph: both emphasize military victories, including Tarlati's capturing of neighboring towns, whereas B. concentrates on Tarlati's urban development, omitting the subjects of a number of panels representing military exploits. Panel no. 5 depicts the building of the walls, which began in 1319. Of Tarlati's efforts at widening the roads we have no report other than B.'s mention.

The cenotaph shows sixteen panels narrating the chief events of the bishop's life. Above or below each scene is its title: 1. Made bishop by Clement IV; 2. voted Lord of Arezzo; 3. The comune "peeled" or "stripped," that is, of its authority; 4. The comune in power; 5. Making the walls (1319); 6. Submission of Lucignano of Valdichiana; 7. Submission of Chiusci [Chiusi della Verna]; 8. Fronzòla (fortress) conquered; 9. Castel Focognano surrenders; 10. Conquest of Rondine; 11. Occupation of Bucine; 12. Conquest of Caprese; 13. Capture and destruction of Laterina; 14. Capture and demolition of Monte San Savino; 15. Coronation of Louis the Bavarian (by Tarlati); 16. Death of Tarlati. See V. Franchetti Pardo, *Arezzo*. Le città nella storia d'Italia. (Rome and Bari: Laterza, 1986) 63–69; and Enzo Droandi, *Guido Tarlati di Pietramala Ultimo Principe di Arezzo* (Cortona: Calosci, 1967).

[309A] *Nicolaum Piccininum* ... The reference is probably to the battle of Anghiari, in 1440, which was the subject of a *cartone* by Leonardo, now lost, but visible in extant copies made by Rubens.

Famous men of Arezzo.

Leonardo Arretino The Florentine humanist and mentor of B. (see vol. 1, p. 47) known as "Aretino" from his native city.

Benedicto ac Francisco fratribus Accoltis The family of the Accolti were originally from Arezzo, but from the fourteenth century established residency in Florence. Benedetto Accolti (1415–1464) held a doctorate in civil and canon law, and was professor at Bologna and Florence. He practiced law and served Florence as chancellor, but was more famous for his interest in classical literature and culture. He wrote a dialogue, history, orations, and poetry in Latin; see A. Petrucci, "Accolti, Benedetto," *DBI* 1 (1960), 99–101. Francesco (1416–1488) also became famous as a jurist and man of letters. He taught civil and canon law at Ferrara, Siena, and Pisa; and was counselor to d'Este and Sforza dukes; see L. Mantovani, "Accolti, Francesco," *DBI* 1 (1960), 104–105.

Ioannes Tortellius Giovanni Tortelli, famous for his treatise *De Orthographia*. O. Besomi connects Tortelli with B. in their debate over the appropriateness of Latin neologisms (O. Besomi and Mariangela Regoliosi, "Valla e Tortelli I," *IMU* 9 [1966] 75–189). This mention is context for one of B.'s excisions of the name of Pope Nicholas V in ms. Ottob. lat 2369: fol 17v shows that originally B. had written "Et Ioanne Tortellio Nicolai V

pontificis subdiacono." The name of Nicholas has been partially erased, but remains clearly visible, and is substituted by "Romani" in the left margin.

[309A–B] *Plinius* ... *NH* 35.160. In a discussion of burial customs, Pliny cites Varro's mention of the Pythagorean custom of burial of the dead in leaves, then states that most people use earthenware. He proceeds to a discussion of well-known types of earthenware: *Samia etiam nunc in esculentis laudantur. Retinent hanc nobilitatem et Arretium in Italia* ... (Samian ware is praised even now among eating-vessels. And the Samian ware of Arretium holds pride of place in Italy . . .)

Martialis affirmat libro primo ... Not the only instance in *It. ill.* of B.'s misinterpreting the point of a poem by Martial (here 1.53). 14.98 corroborates Martial's bias; in the latter poem he again assumes a general contempt for Arretine ware:

> Arretina nimis ne spernas vasa monemus:
> lautus erat Tuscis Porsena fictilibus.
>
> [the vases speak] We caution you against too much disparagement of Arretine vases:
> Porsenna was resplendent by virtue of Tuscan pots.

I give the text and translation of the first eight lines of Martial 1.53 here, to make clear that the poem is a series of invidious comparisons intended to disparage the poetry of the addressee:

> Una est in nostris tua, Fidentine, libellis
> pagina, sed certa domini signata figura,
> quae tua traducit manifesto carmina furto.
> Sic interpositus villo contaminat uncto
> urbica Lingonicus Tyrianthina bardocucullus,
> sic Arretinae violant crystallina testae,
> sic niger in ripis errat cum forte Caystri,
> inter Ledaeos ridetur corvus olores. . . .
>
> Fidentinus, there is one page of yours in a book of mine
> (but stamped with the sure likeness of its author)
> which openly betrays your poems' acts of theft.
> In the same way that a hooded cloak from the Lingones contaminates
> with its greasy wool the purple garments of the city;
> so earthenware vessels from Arretium cheapen those of crystal glass;

Plate I. Cenotaph of Bishop Guido Tarlati di Pietramala (1330), Duomo di Arezzo. (Photograph by the author)

> so a black crow which happens to wander on the banks of the Cayster
> comes in for derision among the swans of Leda. . . .

Clavuot (*Biondo's »Italia illustrata«* 112 and n. 292), identifies the passages in Pliny and Martial, adducing them as evidence of B.'s attachment to places of a wide range of cultural-historical details; but does not mention the uncomplimentary nature of Martial's reference to Arretine ware, which B. neglects to acknowledge, saying simply that Martial's poem corroborates Pliny's attribution to Arezzo of primacy in this product.

[309B] *Perusia* . . . It is obvious to even the modern visitor that the city (today in the province of Umbria), naturally defended by its position on the top of a high hill, was well-equipped naturally to withstand a long siege. Modern scholars think that the ancient city, like the modern Perugia, was limited to the summit of the hill. Augustus rebuilt the city of Perusia after it had been nearly destroyed in consequence of the defeat of L. Antonius. The rebuilt city, stocked with a new citizen body, took the name Augusta Perusia. The walls B. mentions may belong to the Etruscan period, or may be Roman. The two ancient gates are probably Roman. The Arco Augusto bears the inscription "Augusta Perusia," probably dating from Augustus' rebuilding of the city.

[310G] *Paulus* Paolo di Castro (1360/62–1441), eminent jurist who remained attached to his hometown all his life despite a peripatetic career teaching law at such universities as Siena, Florence, and Padua. His writings include commentaries on Justinian. He was highly esteemed by his contemporaries because of his vast culture and the independence of his judgment. See G. D'Amelio, "Castro, Paolo di," *DBI* 22 (1979): 227–233.

[311A] *Veii* Veii is actually near the medieval hamlet of Isola Farnese, just off the Via Cassia. It is on the Cremera river.

[311C] *vir summus Prosper cardinalis Columna Romanus* Prospero Colonna, patron of B., was elected cardinal and was three times spoken of as a candidate for Pope (at the deaths of Eugenius IV, Nicholas V, and Calixtus III). He was involved not only in politics but in the circle of literary men around the Curia; was intensely interested in the rediscovery of Roman antiquities, and owned an important library. See F. Petrucci, "Colonna, Prospero," *DBI* 27 (1982): 416–418.

[311D–312E] *Viterbium* B. does not mention the extensive thermal baths near Viterbo, especially the Bagno del Papa rebuilt by Pope Nicholas V. This omission is perhaps due to his desire to suppress earlier laudatory mentions of this pope. See C. R. Mack, "The Bath Palace of Pope Nicholas V at Viterbo," in H. Millon and S. Munshower, edd., *An Architectural Progress in the Renaissance and Baroque*. Papers in Art History VIII. (University Park: The Pennsylvania State University, 1992): 100–119.

[312H] *Ursus urbis senator* . . . In 1341, Petrarch was crowned with the laurel at Rome by the senator Orso dell'Anguillara. Although Petrarch had requested King Robert of Sicily to crown him, in the end Robert could not leave Naples. He had, however, examined Petrarch before his coronation. Although B. does not state the connection explicitly here, the mention of Orso may be indirect flattery of his patron, Prospero Colonna, the intended dedicatee of the chapter "Lazio." The Anguillara and Colonna families were closely connected through marriage.

Third Region, Lazio
Commentary

There are indications that Biondo intended this chapter to stand alone as a tribute to the patron, Prospero cardinal Colonna, associated with this region. The Colonna were a family of nobles of Tuscany who also held possessions in Lazio, and the cardinal was a prominent figure in the rediscovery of Roman antiquities. But no independent copy of "Lazio" has been found corresponding to the ms. of "Romagna," dedicated separately to Malatesta Novello, lord of Cesena ("Whether or not this . . . region was to be dedicated to Colonna we cannot tell . . ." [White, "Towards a Critical Edition," 277]). Nevertheless, the humanist's additions and corrections to a ms. in the Vatican library (Ottob. Lat. 2369) contain flattering references to towns associated with the cardinal and his family. The cardinal and his family are mentioned frequently in this chapter (seven times; see Clavuot, *Biondos »Italia illustrata«*, 48 n. 53, who notes that Malatesta Novello is mentioned only six times in "Romagna"). B. also mentions a great number of small towns and castles in this region; in this attention to detail, "Lazio" is comparable to "Romagna." The expanded description of the Roman ships in Lago di Nemi and the attempt to raise them is surely inspired in part by B.'s desire to please this patron, the underwriter of the enterprise (see Clavuot, *Biondos »Italia illustrata«*, 112; F. Petrucci, "Colonna, Prospero," *DBI* 27 [1982]: 416–418).

B. avoids in "Lazio" the troubled history underlying the Colonna's possession of many towns and castles of the Roman Campagna, specifically their conflicts with the papacy over these possessions. Pope Martin V (Oddo Colonna), for whom the term "nepotism" might have been invented, gave many towns and fortresses to his nephews Prospero, Antonio, and Odoardo. After Martin's death Eugenius IV, most favorable of popes to B., demanded back the pontifical castles which the Colonna pope had given his nephews. Eugenius also refused to recognize the legitimacy of some of Martin V's concessions to his nephews, a conflict which led to his excommuni-

cation of Prospero Colonna. Civil strife involving supporters of the Colonna caused Eugenius IV to flee from Rome to Florence in 1434.

Biondo wrote most of this chapter while living either in Milan (spring 1450) or near Ferrara (autumn and winter 1450). The chapter "Lazio" includes comments connected with these places (on the Jubilee year, see Clavuot, *Biondos »Italia illustrata«*, 46–47); but also shows deep familiarity with and direct observation of the region of Lazio itself, both as a result of B.'s residence in Rome and as homage to cardinal Colonna, with whom he had undertaken antiquarian excursions in the Campagna less orchestrated than the recovery of the ships of Lago di Nemi (see Biondo's letter to Leonello d'Este in Nogara, *Scritti inediti*, 154–159, on which material B. presumably drew for the very similar descriptions here of Ariccia, Marino, the site of ancient Tusculum, and Nemi).

"Lazio" is unique in its reliance on Strabo to the neglect of Pliny, on whose demarcations of the other regions Biondo customarily depends. He relies particularly on the Greek geographer's description of Sabine territory between the Tiber and Mentana, and of Lazio and Rome and notes distances after Strabo in stades (1 stade equals 606 ft. 9 in., or 25 paces, or 625 Roman feet). For example, B. takes the eastern boundary of Lazio from Strabo, and counts the Fucine Lake in Lazio (**[322F]**, **[323A]**), whereas Pliny included it in Samnium (cf. Clavuot, *Biondos »Italia illustrata«* 57 n. 112). As Clavuot (*ibid.* 25) notes, Biondo's failure to make detailed use of Strabo, E.3.9–10, is surprising in view of B.'s imitation of the procedure Strabo outlines in these chapters. Despite Biondo's many references to the Greek geographer in this chapter, Clavuot (*ibid.* 252) persuasively concludes that Strabo must be considered only among his numerous secondary sources; for an extensive consideration of B.'s use of Strabo in "Lazio," see Clavuot (*ibid.* 249–252).

Biondo's reliance on Strabo in this chapter brings up the matter of his proficiency in Greek. He had acknowledged in *Historiarum Decades* (I, book 4) that he was not expert in the language (*Nos itaque cum perdiscendis litteris Graecis parum felices fuerimus* [cited in Nogara, *Scritti inediti*, XXXI]). White (*Italy Illuminated*, 400, n. 4) states "Biondo probably knew Strabo in the Latin translation of Guarino Veronese." Although Guarino's translation of Strabo was published too late (1455) for B. to have employed it in writing the 1453 edition of *It. ill.*, he could have had access to prepublication drafts of it, or informal aid from another source (as Clavuot,

ibid. suggests, 241–242 and n. 127). At one point ([324G]) I believe we can detect Biondo's unmediated attempt to translate Strabo's Greek.

[313C] *Ostiam urbem condidit mare inter et Tiberim Ancus Martius* Ostia is 25 km. west of Rome. Excavations at Ostia Antica began in 1909, with the most intense excavation activity taking place under Mussolini (in 1938–1942, by Calza and Gismondi). What we see today are the remains of the Hadrianic city. R. Meiggs, *Roman Ostia* (2nd ed. [Oxford: Clarendon, 1973], 98), cites the opinion of Rutilius, the last pagan poet, writing in 414 A.D. that no glory remains to Ostia except that of Aeneas. Although building continued at Ostia as late as the 4th c. A.D., Ostia was deserted and uninhabited by medieval times (for its decline in medieval times, see Meiggs, 89–101).

[314E] *Deinceps Antium est, Romana colonia* ... Modern Anzio, visited today not only for the conspicuous ruins of the villa of Nero, but as the landing site of Allied forces in January 1944, hence now the location of large military cemeteries. B.'s treatment of Anzio exemplifies his tendency to error when relying on ancient authors whose texts he did not possess in accurate form; and his direct observation of ancient sites through antiquarian investigation, especially in the company of patrons.

The history of Antium comprises a primitive Volscian period, its time as a Roman colony, and its second rebirth under the emperors. Although he could not possess the data yielded by modern archaeology about Antium's early existence as a Volscian city, B.'s description is historically organized, beginning with Livy's testimony (8.14.8) about the establishment of a Roman colony (338 B.C.) and the explanation of the name of the Rostra (8.14.12). He relies on Strabo for the following information, from Hellenistic and imperial times. Continued dependence on Strabo, however, leads him into error in his contrast of Strabo's mention of a temple of Castor and Pollux with Horace's testimony that Fortuna was the presiding deity at Antium. Strabo had recounted Alexander's and Demetrius' reproaches to the Romans for having a temple of Castor and Pollux in the Forum (at Rome), which B. interprets as a reference to a temple at Antium; and yet supporting piracy against Greeks. The anecdote, as Strabo tells it, has a point: the Romans should not, as worshippers of the Dioscuri, support piracy against Greece, the native country of the Dioscuri.

[314F] *Urbem vero Antiatum nunc esse nullam, sed in mari, in litore, in nemoribus mirandas exstare ruinas videmus.* After the barbarian infiltrations of the fifth and sixth centuries, followed by Arab incursions, the site of Antium was abandoned, not to be repopulated until the eighteenth century. Ruins from the imperial period are visitable today: they include, in addition to the imperial villa, a theatre and acqueduct. That B. had explored the ruins of Antium with Prospero cardinal Colonna he observes in a marginal note (in ms. Vat. ottob. Lat. 2369, fol 20r) to his discussion of the possibility of a lethal spring on Mt. Soracte (reported by Pliny, *NH* 31.27, ultimately derived from Varro). This addition to an early edition of *It. ill.* was incorporated into successive versions and appears in "Tuscany" (**[311C–D]**; see White, *Italy illuminated*, 2.57). Although B. uses his observation of a sulphurous spring at Anzio to corroborate Pliny's account, the marginal form indicates that B. was adding (between 1453 and 1455) flattering mentions of Colonna to this early version of the text, just as he later excised flattering mentions of Nicholas V after this pope's death (in 1455). See C. J. Castner, "Direct Observation and Biondo Flavio's Additions to *Italia illustrata:* The Case of Ocriculum," *Medievalia et Humanistica* N.S. n. 25 (1998), 93–108.

[314G] *Laviniis* B. reproduces for Livy's *Lanuviis*. As White, *Italy illuminated*, 405 n. 101, notes, B. will at **[318–319]** correct this mistake and assert on the basis of inscriptional evidence that Civita Indivina is the ancient Lanuvium. For Prospero Colonna, see "Tuscany" **[311C]**.

[315B] *Strabo ... stadiis circiter septem ... Aphrodisium, ubi panagyrim ...* Again, either B.'s weakness in Greek or a mistake in a Latin translation of Strabo causes an error. Strabo E. 3, 5, locates Ardea 70, not 7, stades from the sea: "Beyond Laurentum there is Ardea, abode of the Rutuli, 70 stades from the sea (ἐν ἑβδομήκοντα σταδίοις ἀπὸ τῆς θαλάττης); near it is the sanctuary of Aphrodite, where the Latins hold a common festival."

[315C] *Antonii Columnae arx* Nephew of the Colonna pope Martin V and brother of B.'s patron, Prospero cardinal Colonna.

[316E] *Fluvium qui proxime illabitur Storacem ...* Indeed, the map shows that the next river going south down the coast is, as Clavuot (*Biondos »Italia illustrata«*, 83) suggests, the modern Sisto. The name Στόρας, however, seems closer to that of the modern Astura, which flows into the sea just below Torre d'Astura.

[316F] *Plinius sic dicit* . . . There follows a long citation from Pliny *NH* 3.57, which according to Zehnacker (166–167) derived from Pliny's extensive reading, perhaps in Cornelius Nepos or Varro. Zehnacker (167) identifies the consul as C. Licinius Mucianus (*RE* s.v. Licinius 116a), and comments that the number of twenty-four cities seems excessive.

[317A–B] *Tacitis regnavit Amyclis* B. errs in his attribution of this phrase to *Aen.* 9—it is 10.654. He characteristically abridges Servius' commentary, omitting parts not strictly relevant to the toponym Amyclae but also omitting even a section integral to the explanation of the epithet *tacitis*. Servius provides two explanations of *tacitae* after *interempti sunt*: the first, that the inhabitants of Amyclae followed the Pythagorean doctrine of abstention from killing any living thing, and were consequently killed by the snakes which were born in neighboring swamps. The second of Servius' explanations of *tacitae* derives from Cicero, that the inhabitants of Amyclae were killed due to their reticence, as they received injury from their neighbors but kept silent about it.

[317B] *Solum Terracinum* . . . *intus* It is difficult to see through B.'s error to what he intends to say here. His model is Strabo E. 3, 6: ἐνταῦθα δὲ συνάπτει τῇ θαλάττῃ πρῶτον ἡ Αππία ὁδός, . . . τῶν δ'ἐπὶ θαλάττῃ πόλεων τούτων ἐφαπτομένη μόνον, τῆς τε Ταρρακίνης καὶ τῶν ἐφεξῆς Φορμιῶν τε καὶ Μιντούρνης καὶ Σινοέσσης, καὶ τῶν ἐσχάτων Τάραντός τε καὶ Βρεντεσίου. Although Strabo says here that among the coastal cities the Via Appia touches only Terracina and the others mentioned, B. takes as subject Terracina, and understandably mistakes ἐνταῦθα ("here") for the equivalent of the Latin *intus*, "inland" or "towards the interior."

[317D] *Horatius: tandem defessi Lemurnarum venimus urbem* . . . B. may be thinking of *Serm.* 1.5.94, *Inde Rubos fessi pervenimus*.

[319C] *Aritia olim civitas vetusta* . . . B.'s repeated observation on sites of ancient cities, *Nunc vero penitus est derelicta*, reflects not only the medieval *topos* of the fragility of good fortune, but also a common sequence of events (the process of *incastellamento*). Like so many settlements which had been continuously occupied since early Roman times, after the defeat of the last Roman emperor and successive barbarian incursions, the inhabitants of Aritia on the Via Appia had to abandon the city and flee to the nearby hill where its acropolis afforded walled protection (see **[319A]** for a similar description of ancient Privernum). Buildings on this hill were later de-

stroyed by Arab incursions. A new fortified center developed around 1000. As Clavuot (*Biondos »Italia illustrata«*, 195) observes, in B.'s comment that marbles and other *spolia* from ancient Aritia were used to decorate the church of Marino, we can see the humanist investigating the ancient structural elements in medieval building material and connecting them with historical topography. See Nogara, *Scritti inediti*, 158, B.'s letter of 1444 to Leonello d'Este: *Ariciam ex cuius marmorum reliquiis Mariana villa et nunc Marinum, cardinalis nostri oppidum, est ornatum...*

[318F] *modum hactenus in aliis servatum a fluviorum ostiis fontibusque ... servare nequibimus.* An important programmatic statement marks B.'s departure from his method in other chapters: he will now follow the consular and local roads Appia, Latina, and Tiburtina, which he acknowledges have suffered such change and destruction that he will not be able to follow their original routes.

[318G] ... *oppido, quod corrupte Civita Indivina appellant, a Prospero cardinale Columna possesso* ... B.'s identification of the site of ancient Lanuvium, which he had thought to be at the modern Zagarolo. White, *Italy illuminated*, 405 n. 101 (citing M. Filetico, *In corruptores latinitatis*, ed. Maria Agata Pincelli [Roma 2000], 48–50), shows that B. here corrects his earlier mistake **[314G]** on the basis of inscriptional evidence provided by his patron Prospero Colonna.

[320E] *Gallicanum, quem locum Gabios fuisse coniicimus.* Gallicano nel Lazio is B.'s nearly-accurate identification of the contemporary site of ancient Gabii. It is not much farther on the Via Prenestina from where the ruins of ancient Gabii are visible near the "conca di Castiglione," a dried-up lake bed now reclaimed for agriculture.

[320G] *Anagnia civitas duobus Romanis pontificibus ... civibus decorata.* B.'s narrative of Boniface VIII's stormy pontificate (1294–1303) provides a rare acknowledgment of the violent conflicts between the Popes and the Colonna. B.'s words, *Sarra eundem pontificem in patria et domo paterna ceperit*, refer to Sciarra Colonna's and a French minister's assault of Boniface in Anagni in 1303; he died in Rome the next month.

[320H] *Ferentinum* B. conflates the two Italian towns with this ancient name: the modern Ferentino in Lazio (between Anagni and Frosinone), and Ferento in Tuscany. B. intends to indicate the former by the three citations from Livy. But the report of Suetonius presents B. with evidence that Otho's fam-

ily was from Tuscany. This type of error supports Clavuot's general thesis that B. worked from collections of excerpts.

[321B] *Lucido ... Altus ... Ioanne*. The leading noble family of Valmontone. Lucido de'Conti, Lord of Valmontone and Berarda, cardinal deacon of Sta. Maria in Cosmedin, was involved in the conclaves to elect Martin V and Eugenius IV and the Council of Constance; became governor of Bologna in 1429; d. 1437. He and his brothers received many benefices from Eugenius IV; see M. Dykmans, "Conti, Lucido," *DBI* 28 (1983): 449–451. His brother Alto had the son Giovanni who was a condottiere in the service of Venice; see M. E. Mallett, "Conti, Giovanni," *DBI* 28 (1983): 415–417.

[321C] *Servius exponit ... quod essent superbi* ... B. drastically abbreviates Servius (*ad Aen.* 7.630), leaving out the Tiburtines' reminders of past benefits to the Roman people. But R. D. Williams comments on *Aen.* 7.629f.: "Tibur is the modern Tivoli (probably called 'proud' because of its high position)."

[322F] Pope Boniface IV (r. 608–615) received the Pantheon from the emperor Phocas; it was converted into a church and Boniface IV consecrated it as Sta. Maria ad Martyres.

[323B] *Sancti Apetiti* I have adopted White's reading (3.38) Sancti Potiti, as the various editions have the senseless *Apetiti* (mss) or *apetitus* (r); see White, *Italy Illuminated*, 371 n. 75.

Praestantissimam ... familiam Capranicensem ... Born at Capranica Prenestina, Domenico Capranica (1400–1457) and his brothers Paolo and Angelo all rose rapidly in the ecclesiastical hierarchy under Pope Martin V, as the Capranica family was connected as clients to the Colonna of Genazzano. Domenico occupied the positions of pontifical secretary; administrator of the diocese of Fermo in the March of Ancona; and rector of Forlì, Imola, and Cervia. Biondo's relations with him began with service to Capranica in 1427 when the latter was ecclesiastical governor of Forlì. In 1428 he became governor of Bologna, and in 1430 governor of Perugia. Domenico Capranica was a major figure in ecclesiastical politics in B.'s time in the Curia: despite being removed from his position as cardinal by Eugenius IV in 1431, Capranica was restored, reconciled with Eugenius, and served as chamberlain of the College of Cardinals and played an important role in preparation for the Council of Ferrara-Florence. At Eugenius's death (1437) Capranica was even considered "papabile."

Domenico Capranica's eldest brother Paolo was pontifical secretary under Martin V, from 1420 bishop of Evreux, and from 1427 archbishop of Benevento. He died in 1428. See A. A. Strnad, "Capranica, Domenico," *DBI* 19 (1976): 147–153. Domenico's younger brother Angelo Capranica (1410–1478) was made bishop of Ascoli by Nicholas V in 1447. However, his career took off only in the pontificate of Pius II, thus mostly after B. had published *It. ill.* He was governor of Bologna from 1458 to 1467, and was made cardinal in 1460. He enjoyed renewed prominence under Sixtus IV, won fame as a preacher, and contributed greatly to the renewal of Italian religious life. See A. A. Strnad, "Capranica, Angelo," *DBI* 19 (1976): 143–146.

[324G] *quod inter tibias linquit Algidum* Comparison of this passage with Strabo's text (E.3.12) indicates that B. (or the translation he used), in translating μεταξὺ αὐλῶνα καταλείπουσα, "separated (from Praeneste) by a valley," confused αὐλών, "hollow, glen" with αὐλός, "a flute," and translated the latter with the Latin *tibia.* This probably indicates B.'s own translation, as it is more likely that he, whose Greek was admittedly deficient, would make such an error, than that the more expert Guarino Veronese would have supplied him with an erroneous translation.

[324H–325A] *Tusculi collem . . . habere regiam magnificentissimi apparatus . . . et continua esse loca . . . apparatum habentia . . . regiae autem magnificentissimi.* Strabo's description of Tusculum (E.3.12) states that Tusculum is situated on the Alban Mount (the modern Monte Cavo); has magnificent royal palaces; and that the peaks of the Alban Mount, too, are continuous with it and have the same type of construction. The site of Tusculum is actually farther from Monte Cavo than B. (and Strabo) indicate. Strabo's information:

> Tusculum is situated on Monte Albano [by which Strabo means the modern Monte Cavo] . . . [Tusculum] has magnificent royal palaces. The peaks of the Alban Mount, too, are continuous with it, and they enjoy the same fertile status and have the same type of construction. Then come the plains . . .

To someone who knows Greek, it is clear that Strabo identifies these constructions as on the site of Tusculum. But for B., who admitted to imperfect knowledge of ancient Greek, it would be natural to fail to attribute the present participle δεχόμενος to the subject Τούσκουλον and predicate λόφος.

B.'s *videmus* indicates direct observation, and so does the greater specificity of his description when compared to Strabo's. B.'s *fundamenta* are Strabo's βασιλείων κατασκευὰς ἐκπρεπεστάτας. B. does not locate precisely the foundations of the *regia* near the Alban Mount. But it is clear from his text that he identifies these *fundamenta* with some he had directly observed in the vicinity of three Colonna towns (Rocca di Papa, Marino, and Frascati) which were part of a larger concession made to Prospero Colonna and his brothers by their uncle, Pope Martin V. B. locates the ruins in the places closest to and equidistant from Grottaferrata and Marino. He was familiar with the monastery at Grottaferrata (**[325A]** *monasterium Sanctae Mariae de Griptaferrara in villa Ciceronis Tusculana aedificatum*; founded by S. Nile in 1004, and now the Abbazia di Grottaferrata). It was indeed built upon the foundations of a Roman villa, whose arched portico is extant, although B.'s identification of this villa as Cicero's is no longer accepted. But because the ancient structure was built over in the 1000s by the abbey, B. may not have seen any more than we do today of the arches, in fact he may have seen less, and probably did not see what looked like ruins.

Corresponding to B.'s description of the great ruins near the Alban Mount are the ruins at Palazzolo (at the former abbey of Palazzolo, now owned as a summer retreat by a British college) near modern Rocca di Papa, on the lower part, but not on the very summit of Monte Cavo, where was the acropolis of Cabum (the *arx Albana* of Livy 7.24). Monte Cavo rises above the town of Rocca di Papa (its topmost area today occuped by the antennas of RAI [the national broadcasting corporation]). For the identification of the Alban Mount, which was the center of the Latin League and site of their celebration of the *feriae Latinae*, see G. Tomassetti, *La Campagna Romana*. 2nd ed. edited by Luisa Ciumenti and Fernando Bilancia. 7 vols. (Florence: Olschki 1979), v. 4, *Via Latina*, 42 ff.

The grottoes at Palazzolo were dug out of the mountain probably between the 11th and 13th centuries in an attempt to harvest valuable building material, and to create a protected space for human use. They still present today the same appearance as when they were drawn in the second half of the seventeenth century; see Plate II (illustration in Luigi Devoti, *Splendore dei castelli Romani: Espressioni artistiche dal secolo XVII al secolo XX* [Velletri: Edizioni tra 8 e 9, 1992], 129). They also answer to Pius II's description, cited below, of the ruins as *fornicibus innixa quam plurimis*. Pius, writing his *Commentaries* after B.'s death and therefore at least ten years

after B. wrote "Lazio," takes B.'s report, which B. himself took from Strabo (E.3.12), as a description of ruins at Tusculum. Using the passage in *It. ill.* as a source at this point in his *Commentaries*, Pius described an excursion in the Alban Hills and, apropos of his visit to Rocca di Papa, identifies these ruins with Tusculum (Enea Silvio Piccolomini, *I Commentarii*, ed. Luigi Totaro. 2 vols. [Milan: Adelphi, 1984]) 2:2252:

> Tusculi quoque in conspectu fuere. Romam urbem delevere post acceptam cladem sub Federico primo, quam ferunt fuisse maximam. Regiam ibi magnificentissimi apparatus fuisse Strabo commemorat, cuius adhuc fundamenta visuntur fornicibus innixa quam plurimis; sub quibus non procul Molara deserta iacet.

For Poggio Bracciolini's earlier assessment of this question of identification, see Letter LXXXV in Phyllis Goodhart Gordan, *Two Renaissance Book Hunters: The Letters of Poggius Bracciolini to Nicolaus de Niccolis* (New York: Columbia University Press, 1991), and Gordan's comment (343), "This description fits the caves of Marino, like Tusculum about 6 kilometers from Grottaferrata. . . ."

[325A] . . . *Rocchae Papa Prosperi cardinalis Columnae oppida* Important for the question whether Rocca di Papa can be identified as the site of the Alban Mount is Tomassetti, *La Campagna Romana.* These are in modern Rocca di Papa-but not on the very summit of Monte Cavo, elevation 760 m., where was the acropolis of Cabum (the *arx Albana* of Livy 7.24).

[325B] *Romanus populus ipsam urbem . . . demolitus sit.* The final destruction of Tusculum took place in 1191; the survivors then migrated to five new villages, one of which is the modern Frascati.

[325D–326G] The Roman ships of Lago di Nemi.

Prosper Columna cardinalis . . . audivit Nemorenses dicere naves . . . Cardinal Colonna was patron of the attempt (1446) to raise the Roman ships from the bottom of Lago di Nemi. He chose Leon Battista Alberti, scientist and artist, to carry out this enterprise. B.'s description of the undertaking is the third of three substantial notes added by B. himself to ms. Vat. ottob. Lat. 2369 (fol. 34v). As with B.'s addition to the same ms. relating a sulphurous spring on Mt. Soracte to one he and Colonna observed on an antiquarian excursion at the site of ancient Antium (**[311C]**), the marginal form indicates an afterthought intended to please the cardinal.

Plate II. Wall painting from second half of the seventeenth century depicting the grotto at the convent of Palazzolo near Rocca di Papa. From L. Devoti, *Splendori dei Castelli Romani: Espressioni artistiche dal secolo XVII al secolo XX* (Rome and Velletri: Edizioni tra 8 e 9, 1992). Reprinted by permission of Dott. Luigi Devoti.

Alberti attributed to Trajan, B. to Tiberius, the inscribed lead pipes found with the ships. Today they are thought to date to Caligula's reign (an identification Pirro Ligorio had already proposed in the sixteenth century). Suetonius, *Caligula* 37, describes boats similar to those from Lago di Nemi, fitted out with *magna thermarum et porticuum et tricliniorum laxitate.* Since Alberti's unfinished treatise *Navis*, which discussed this undertaking at Nemi as well as the construction of ancient ships, has been lost, B. is the most important source of information on the enterprise besides Alberti's own *De Re Aedificatoria.* See G. Uccelli, *Le Navi di Nemi* (Rome, 1927); and the comments of Anthony Grafton, *Leon Battista Alberti: Master Builder of the Italian Renaissance* (New York: Hill and Wang, 2000), 248–252. The ships were finally recovered in 1928 when Mussolini arranged for the partial draining of the lake. But in 1944, a fire set by Germans occupying the area destroyed them, although some of the mosaics, lead pipes, and bronze objects recovered with them have been preserved. Grafton, *Alberti*, 84, 91, recognizes B.'s analysis here as the impetus for his shipwreck metaphor in the *Preface* to *It. ill.* (vol. 1, pp. 2–3).

[326G] *fontis ... scatentis aquas nunc molas convolventes* B.'s letter to Leonello d'Este ([Nogara, *Scritti inediti* 157] written in 1444, two years before the attempt to raise the ships) describes this spring (*scaturit autem sub Nemo fons perennis ...*) and *in lacu demersa navis ingens.*

Fourth Region, Umbria
Commentary

The brevity of the chapter on the region of Umbria reflects the infrequency of B.'s visits to the area, the region's sparse population and lack of great cities; and the absence of a patron to whom B. might have dedicated the chapter or filled it with flattering references, as "Romandiola" and "Lazio" were connected with Malatesta Novello and Prospero cardinal Colonna. The most prominent person mentioned in "Umbria" (at **[328H]**) is Federigo da Montefeltro, whose name appears also in "Piceno" (**[336E]**).

Biondo takes the boundaries of Umbria to be the Apennines at the source of the Tiber to the left bank of the Aniene; and the Tiber down to the point where the Aniene joins it (**[328G]**). The name Umbria was not used in B.'s time; as he notes, with disdain at the Lombard provenance (**[328G]**), he is forced by *consuetudinis inveteratae necessitas* to use the name "duchy of Spoleto." In Biondo's lifetime Umbria was the object of campaigns to subdue it as part of the Papal state, so the chapter refers at times to the sporadic warfare waged in the region for this purpose. In comparison with the Augustan region, Biondo's Umbria appears as a smaller landlocked region sandwiched between the larger Tuscany and March of Ancona. Ancient authors attribute to Picenum a number of towns and cities which appear in Biondo's "Umbria," e.g., Nursia (Norcia).

[328E] *impossibilitas*: One of B.'s rare lapses into a post-classical vocabulary.

[328F] B. must be summarizing and paraphrasing this passage from Livy (9.41.8–9, italics mine):

> Tranquillas res iam in Etruscis turbavit repentina defectio Umbrorum, gentis integrae a cladibus belli, nisi quod transitum exercitus ager senserat. Ii concitata omni iuventute sua et magna parte Etruscorum ad rebellionem compulsa tantum exercitum fecerant ut relicto post se in Etruria Decio *ad oppugnandam inde Romam*

> *ituros*, magnifice de se ac contemptim de Romanis loquentes, iactarent.

Ravennam . . . . . Sabinorum oppidum . . . Martialis poeta Drawing on Pliny, *NH* 3.115, *Ravenna Sabinorum oppidum*, B. reports that Ravenna was a town of the Sabines. But in citing Martial, he mistakes the Latin word in Martial, *spina*, a stalk (of asparagus), for a toponym, thus concluding that the city of Spina grew on the site of Ravenna. The entire couplet:

> Mollis in aequorea quae crevit spina Ravenna
> non erit incultis gratior asparagis.

[328G] *Plinii . . . villam suam . . . theatralem aspectum* B. is nearly accurate in his identification of Sansepolcro with the site of Pliny's villa, which was at nearby Tifernum Tiberinum (so named by the Romans to distinguish it from a second Tifernum, also in Umbria on the Metaurus river, whose citizens were called Tifernates Metaurenses). See White, *Italy Illuminated*, 415: the villa of Pliny is "now believed to have been at a place called Colle Plinio, between Sansepolcro and Città di Castello." See also S. Mazzarino, "La regione umbra nella cultura romana," *Problemi di Storia e Archeologia dell'Umbria*. Atti del I convegno di studi Umbri (Gubbio 1964) 227–247, esp. 235–238, on the geographical attribution of Tifernum to Umbria or Etruria.

Eugubium civitas Federigo da Montefeltre (1422–1488), successful condottiere, was papal vicar of Gubbio; B. maintained connections with him (cf. Nogara, *Scritti Inediti*, 175, B.'s letter to Galeazzo Sforza in 1458 lamenting the loss of Federigo's son whom B. had helped with Latin). Not Gubbio, but Urbino, was the court which developed under Federigo into a center of wealth, learning and culture.

[328H] *Vallidum-Gualdum-Gualdo Tadino Gualdum* means ford, from *vadum*; after the destruction of Tadinum towards the end of the tenth century, Gualdo grew up in its place towards the end of the twelfth century.

[329A] *Nuceria*. The modern Nocera; site of Q. Fabius' defeat of a Samnite army at the beginning of the Samnite Wars. B.'s epithet Alphatenia, rightly Alfaterna, belongs to the Campanian city of Nuceria, to which city Livy actually applies it in 9.41.3, the passage B.cites here.

[329B] *Gentili medico sui saeculi celeberrimo* Gentile da Foligno (b. last quarter of 13th c., d. 1348). Profoundly influential on the development of

medicine and pharmacy, a practicing physician as well as a teacher and writer, he taught at Siena, Perugia, and Padua (as physician to Ubertino da Carrara). He left recipes for prescriptions, treatises, and a commentary to the *Canon* of Avicenna.

Assisia The name Asisium was never attested; we derive it from Pliny's mention, *NH* 3.113, of the ethnic Asisinates. On the basis of his reading of a passage of Propertius, B. erroneously concludes that Assisi was in antiquity called Axis. Following the discussion of Mevania, B. proceeds **[329D]** to misinterpret Propertius' claim to be the Roman Callimachus (*Eleg*. 4.1.125–126); apparently unaware of Callimachus' identity as a Greek poet and model of Propertius, he attributes Callimachus as well to Umbria, clearly an example of B.'s. confessed deficiency in Greek.

Montonium: B. mentions Braccio da Montone (Andrea Fortebraccio, 1368–1424) and Muzio Attendolo Sforza as commanders who learned the art of war from Alberico da Barbiano; see **[350F]**, vol. 1, p. 62, for an appreciation of this condottiere tradition.

oliviferaeque Mutuscae Virg. *Aen*. 7.711. Trebula Mutusca is now Monteleone.

Mevania: B. characteristically uses the poets Lucan and Propertius as testimony for the location of the Clitumnus river. In the second Samnite War (326–304 B.C.), the Umbrians rebelled, threatening to attack Rome. The consul Fabius was ordered, if there should be any relief in the Samnite War, to lead his army into Umbria. B. here cites Livy, 9.41.13; but it is the consul Fabius who is referred to here, not Decius, who had rushed to Pupinia to defend Rome from possible Umbrian attack (*Dicto paruit consul magnisque itineribus ad Mevaniam, ubi tum copiae Umbrorum erant, perrexit*).

Spoletum Clavuot (*Biondo's »Italia illustrata«* 104) notes Spoleto's exemplification of several typical patterns in *It. ill.*: the destruction of settlements in the early middle ages; and B.'s belief that ancient or great architecture was supposed to magnify a place's reputation (114) .

[330G] *Seravallis prima domum tecta habet* . . . As Clavuot (*Biondo's »Italia illustrata«* 73 and n. 177) notes, B.'s description of the important pass over the Apennines between Foligno and Camerino presents the opportunity for the "ridge of a roof" analogy for the Apennine watershed. In using this comparison B. follows Dante in *de vulgari eloquentia* 1.10.6, and ultimately

Lucan 2.396, the beginning of the description of the rivers of Italy (cf. my comments on **[299C]**, vol. 1, p. 244).

amnis Clitumnus Virgil *Geo.* 2.146; the modern Clitunno or LaVene river, this small river in Umbria was celebrated by ancient writers and its source worshipped as Juppiter Clitumnus. It was believed to turn white the cattle that drank from it.

Plinius diffuse scribit White, *Italy illuminated* 417, notes, "This is not a quotation of Pliny but derives from Servius on the above passage of the *Georgics*, where Servius wrongly says that Pliny places the white oxen at Clitumnus, whereas Pliny (*NH* 2.230) has them in Faliscan territory . . ."

[330G–H] *Cerretum . . . Pons* The Cerretani performed magic and sold medicines; B. likens them to charlatans named Gnathonici, from Gnatho (Γνάθων), a parasite in Terence's comedy *Eunuchus*. The Gnathonici were "disciples of Gnatho" or parasites. The poet Giovanni Gioviano Pontano (1426–1503) was active at the court of Alfonso V of Aragon (I of Naples); Lodovico Pontano, whose relationship to the poet is unknown, was a lawyer and teacher of the law in Florence and Siena, and an apostolic protonotary under Eugenius IV, which would partially account for B.'s mention of him here. See Carol Kidwell, *Pontano: Poet and Prime Minister* (London: Duckworth 1991), 38–40 and 356 n. 16.

contribulium is a rare and post-classical word, a strange choice.

[331A] *Nursia* (Norcia) The location of Nursia remains somewhat vague. B. here appears unaware that Norcia lay on the small river Sordo, although he mentioned its source, the Corno, only recently (Clavuot, *Biondos »Italia illustrata«* 89). Virgil. *Aen.* 7.715, *frigida Nursia*, gives rise to B.'s criticism of Servius' explanation of *frigida* in its extended sense of noxious, pernicious, or unfortunate, based on a mention of the inhabitants of Nursia as *sceleratos* in the speeches of the Gracchi. B. then criticizes Servius' ignorance of the location of Nursia, pressing the literal interpretation that Virgil called Nursia "frigid" because it is surrounded by high mountains, with a cold climate, and rejecting Servius' claim that Virgil here as often intends a metaphorical application of an epithet. B. implies here that he supports the ancient argument for the effect of climate on the character of a place's inhabitants. With the phrase *rei publicae ad quem sedent clavum tractare* B. borrows the common image of the ship of state, reminiscent of Cicero's description of Gabinius in *Pro Sestio* 9.20: *Quis enim clavum tanti*

imperii tenere et gubernacula rei publicae tractare in maximo cursu ac fluctibus posse arbitraretur hominem . . .

[331B] *Conissa* The same town appears below at **[331C]** as Leonessa. White, *Italy illuminated*, 418 n. 54, notes that this town is now called Leonessa: "The original name Gonessa (Connexa) is attested alongside the newer name of Leonessa . . . both names are found in B.'s mss."

[331C] *Nar fluvius*: the modern river Nera. It is an open question whether B. directly used Boccaccio's lexicon *De montibus, sylvis, fontibus, lacubus, fluminibus, stagnis seu paludibus, de nominibus maris* (Clavuot, *Biondo Flavio's »Italia illustrata«*, 145). The precursor of this view of the Nar is in Ennius: *sulphureas posuit spiramina Naris ad undas* (260 Vahlen), "he set blow-holes by the sulphurous waters of the river Nar," with a play on the synonymity of *nares*, "nostrils," and *spiramina*, "air-holes"; whether B. here imitates Ennius, or whether Ennius reflected local tradition, we cannot be sure; but *It. ill.* contains other evidence of B.'s familiarity with Ennius.

[331D] *Phenne* See White, *Italy illuminated*, 418 n. 59, "In Suetonius' text, the village is Falacrina (or, a variant, Pherine), perhaps near the modern Cittareale, and *in Samnio* is a variant of *in Sabinis*."

Thomas Morronus Tommaso Morroni da Rieti (1408–1476). A disciple of Guarino Veronese at Ferrara, he became a soldier, teacher, diplomat, poet, and orator, and wrote philosophical treatises; he and Poggio engaged in polemics against each other.

[332E] *Ampsanctus*: Virg. *Aen.* 7.565–572. Amsanctus was a lake in Samnium, considered dangerous because of mephitic exhalations, the modern Le Mofete or Lago d'Ansante. The ancients considered it an entrance to the underworld: cf. Cic. *Div.* 1.36; Pliny *NH* 2. 208.

[332F] *Caesar Vopiscus* Pliny *NH* 7.47.

[332G–H] *Ameria*: B. cites as from the *Bucolics* this phrase from the *Georgics* (1.265, *Amerina retinacula* with Servius's explanation); as Clavuot (*Biondos »Italia illustrata«*, 233) notes, he did not look at Virgil in the original, but relied on a secondhand transmission. B. conflates the biography of the Roscius Amerinus whose case he first describes here with that of the actor whom Cicero defended in *Pro Roscio Comoedo*.

Narnia ... quam Livius et Plinius Nequinum fuisse dictam affirmant: After the defeat of Nequinum by the Romans in 299 B.C. the colony Narnia afterwards stood on its site. B.'s treatment of Narnia shows, as Clavuot (*Biondos »Italia illustrata«*, 214) notes, B.'s mainly antiquarian, and not historical, interest. B. cites here Martial 7.93.7–8.

[333A] *Gattamelata* Erasmo da Narni, condottiere and disciple of Braccio da Montone, is best-known as a commander of the Venetian army. Donatello sculpted a bronze statue of him which was set up in Padua in 1453.

Ocriculum Surprisingly, B.'s bare mention here of Ocriculum, seven miles from Narnia and forty-three miles from Rome on the Via Flaminia, indicates no direct observation of the site. However, marginalia in his own hand in ms. Vat. ottob. lat. 2369, fol 19v (cf. **[310H]**) add an important notice on Ocriculum: B.'s discovery of a ms. of Ammianus Marcellinus, from which he cites an anecdote about Constantius' entry into Rome indicating that in the fourth century A.D. large buildings lined the Via Flaminia from Ocriculum to Rome, so that a stranger could not tell where Ocriculum ended and Rome began. In one of the typical transfers of population from the vulnerable plain to a more defensible hilltop, in the middle ages the site of the Roman city was abandoned and the dwelling-places were moved again onto the hill where the Umbrian center had stood. After belonging to the Roman duchy, Ocriculum passed to the rule of the Church; in 1433 it was occupied by Francesco Sforza. B. surprisingly apparently neglected to observe a site so promising for antiquarian investigation. The remains of the Roman settlement would have been visible to a visitor in B.'s day (see Castner, "Direct Observation").

Today in the valley of Otricoli one can see important ruins of the Roman city, most to be dated to the Augustan period: theatre, amphitheatre, a great construction with arches, and the baths of L. Iulius Iulianus from the second century A.D., from which came the mosaic of the Rotonda Vaticana. Between 1776 and 1786 Pope Pius VI patronized systematic excavations there, and there came to light many works of art which are now in the Vatican museum, among them a famous bust of Juppiter.

[333B] *Oenotria tellus* Virgil *Aen.* 7.85; *in partem data Roma Sabinis*, 7.709.

[333D] *Vacuna*: Roman goddess of rural leisure (connected with *vacuus*), a favorite deity of the Sabines. The work B. cites here as *rerum divinarum* is Varro, *Antiquitates Rerum Divinarum*.

[333D–334E] *Nomentana*: the modern Mentana, a little over 23 km. northeast of Rome. B. here cites Martial 9.60 and 13.119 as a basis for his statement that Martial frequently praises Nomentana (e.g., in 9.60). However, Martial's attitude towards his property there is actually more ambivalent; at 7.31.8, *nil nostri, nisi me, ferunt agelli*, he evaluates his land as unproductive.

[334E] *Crescentius* In the tenth century, on the site of the Castel Sant'Angelo, ". . . the Crescenzi family had taken possession of the site and constructed a tower on the summit, converting the monument into a fortress." (L. Richardson jr., *A New Topographical Dictionary of Ancient Rome* (Baltimore and London: Johns Hopkins University Press, 1992) *s.v.* Mausoleum Hadriani.

Sabine territory.

[334F] *Pietro Oddo da Montopoli.* A poet who taught in the studio at Rome; his pupils included Pomponio Leto. B. cited lines of his poetry in *Roma instaurata.*

Sequitur ad Tiberim Farfari amnis ostium. The Fabaris was a small river in Sabine territory, now the Farfa. B. cites Plautus, *fr. inc.* 171 *Dissipabo te tamquam folia Farfari*; and Ovid, *Met.* 14.330. But in his citation from Plautus, he mistakes the genitive of *farfarum* (which is the plant colt's foot, taken by most editors of Plautus as what the playwright intended in this line) for that of the toponym, which occurs both as Farfarus and Fabaris.

B.'s error in locating the villa of Horace in the Farfa valley has influenced scholars up to modern times. The site is now, however, generally agreed to be near Licenza (see Plates III and IV) and the river of the same name (the ancient Digentia); and the shrine of Vacuna can be identified with remains of a temple at modern Roccagiovine. B. relies on Horace's mentions of the Digentia river in evaluating the evidence for the villa's location, but was misled by the correspondence of the topography of the Farfa valley with Horace's description of the location of his farm: namely, a continuous range of mountains interrupted by only one valley, with a forest on the property. In support of his identification B. copiously cites Horace: *Odes* 1.17, 1.20, 1.22; *Epistles* 1.7. But see G. Lugli, "La Villa Sabina di Orazio," *Monumenti Antichi* 31 (1926) 458–598; and Clavuot, *Biondos »Italia illustrata«*, 175; this deduction is another example of B.'s arriving at an erroneous identification through his habit of taking as factual topographical data the literary uses of toponyms.

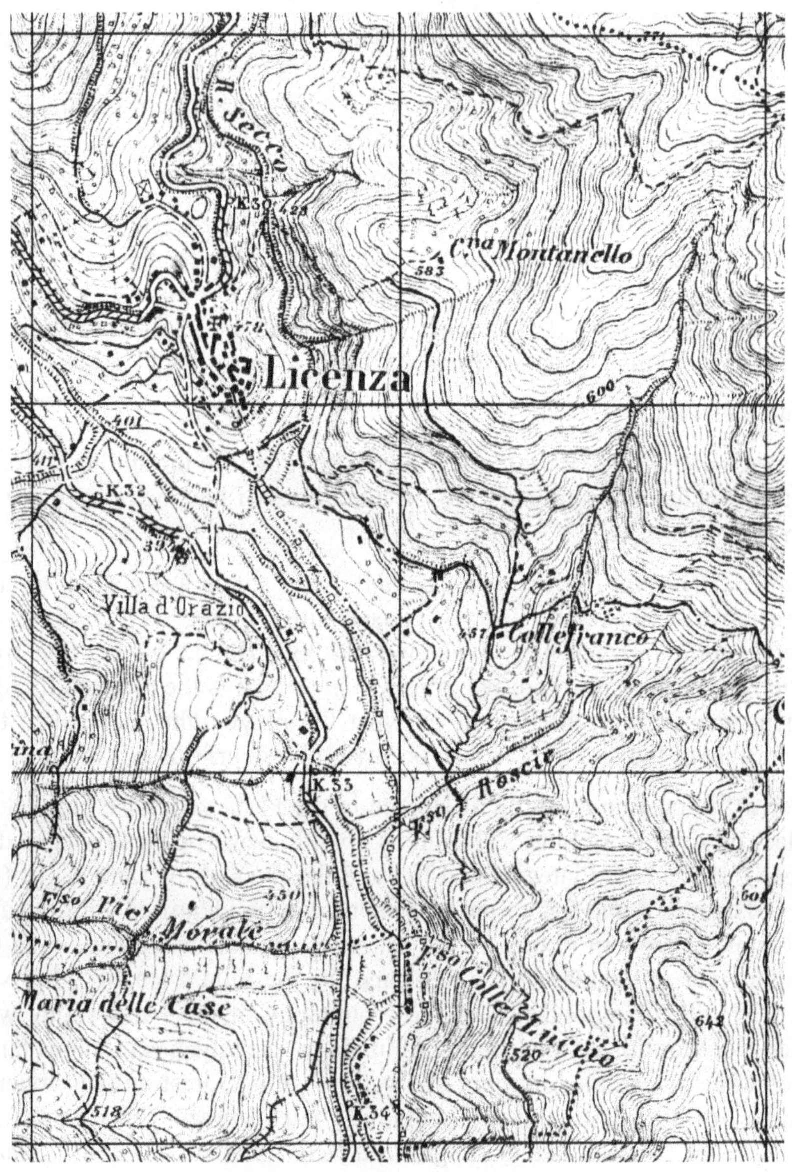

Plate III. Licenza in Sabine territory. Istituto Geografico Militare, map 144-II-SE. Dai tipi dell'ISTITUTO GEOGRAFICO MILITARE-Autorizzazione n. 6454 in data 03.12.2008.

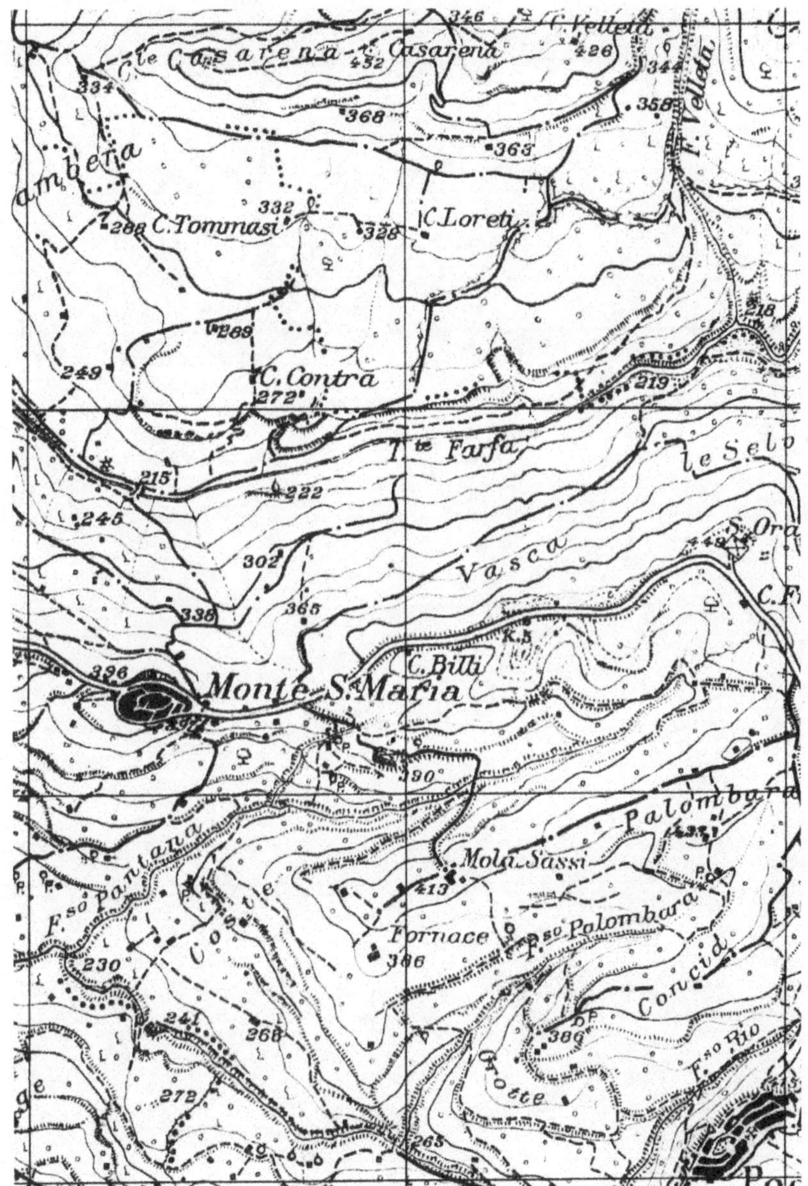

Plate IV. The valley of the Farfa river. Istituto Geografico Militare map 144-II-SE. Dai tipi dell'ISTITUTO GEOGRAFICO MILITARE – Autorizzazione n. 6454 in data 03.12.2008.

Fifth Region, March of Ancona Commentary

The fifth region also in the Augustan division of Italy, Picenum was known in medieval times as Marchia Anconitana or Marchia Firmana. Its borders according to Biondo are: to the north, the Apennines; to the northeast, the Foglia river; and to the south the Adriatic Sea and Tronto river at Ascoli Piceno. At the beginning of the chapter, Biondo gives the borders of the region with "compass points . . . more or less 90 degrees different from ours" (White, *Italy illuminated*, 422).

Biondo wrote the chapter in Milan in the summer of 1450. Despite having lived at Montescudo, in the Romagna but close to the March of Ancona, while composing part of *It. ill.*, he betrays less familiarity with this region than with Tuscany or Lazio, not to mention his native Romagna. Some evidence of familiarity with the region comes from direct observation, e.g., of inscriptions *in situ*. Some familiarity is due to circumstances unconnected with residency: his service in 1432 to Giovanni Vitelleschi who was governor of the March of Ancona; and his own role in arranging treaties to address the complex intrigues around the provisions for keeping papal territorial possessions secure. As Nogara (*Scritti Inediti,* CVII) notes, during Eugenius IV's exile in Florence, Biondo was instrumental in treaties with condottieri (*e.g.,* Francesco Sforza) rewarding them for military service to the church and its lands. These rewards took the form of titles and power over cities in the March of Ancona. Biondo had written about these missions also in *Historiarum Decades*. Their mention in *It. ill.* takes the form of expansion or embellishment in the notices of specific cities and towns.

The chapter is relatively brief and sparse in terms of prosopographical information, as it was out of the central path of humanist intellectual development. Its historical information is substantial, however, as the region was the site of campaigns of condottieri in the service of Filippo Maria Visconti, who attempted to take from the Papacy a great part of the March of Ancona. As with Biondo's diplomatic missions, he includes references to episodes

recounted in *Historiarum Decades*, *e.g.*, conflicts in the first half of the fifteenth century between Francesco Sforza and the papal forces.

Although he progresses through the regions of the Adriatic coast from south to north, Biondo describes the region of the March of Ancona from north to south. Following his customary procedure, he describes valleys of the larger rivers between the Foglia and Tronto: that is, inhabited and fortified settlements in the area of the Arzilla, Metauro, Cesano, Misa, Esino, Musone, Potenza, Chienti, Tenna, and Aso (Clavuot, *Biondos »Italia illustrata«* 77; 79).

[335D] *Livius . . . libro XXXIX* B. cites Livy 39.44.10 as his source, but obviously draws his information from the *Periocha* for 39: *Colonia Potentia et Pisaurum et Mutina et Parma deductae sunt.*

Farnazanum A corruption presumably resulting from running together in pronunciation *fundum Accianum.*

[336E] *Metaurus . . . clade Hasdrubalis . . . clarus* B.'s location of the battle site is corroborated by N. Alfieri, "La battaglia del Metauro (207 a.C.)," *Picus* 8 (1988): 7–35, who considers (8, n.3) the proposed identifications of historians and scholars in light of popular tradition, toponomastics, morphology, and archaeological finds. Apropos of B.'s comments here, Alfieri remarks (27, n. 56), "È degno di nota questo approfondimento da parte del Biondo, il fondatore della topografia storica."

[336F] *Forulus* The famous tunnel of the Gola del Furlo. That B. had seen the gorge Clavuot, *Biondos »Italia illustrata«* 77 n. 194, concludes on the basis of the precision and vividness of his description. The inscription B. mentions is *CIL* XI, 2.1, 6106, cf. 6107. On the word *forulus,* cf. *TLL* 6.1.1197.

[336G] *mons . . . Hasdrubalis nomen habens* Monte Sdrovaldo or Asdrubaldo.

Guilielmus Durante Carnotensis Guillaume Durand (1230/1231–1296), bishop of Chartres, was employed in the Roman Curia on legal work. B. refers here to his chief legal work, *Speculum iudiciale* or *Speculum iuris.* Named vicar of the Romagna by Martin IV, he founded Castrum Durantis, or Castel Durante, in 1284 on the banks of the Metauro, as a refuge for inhabitants of Castrum Reparum, which had been destroyed by Ghibellines. The name was changed to Urbania after pope Urban VIII in 1635. Clavuot

(92) notes that B. neglects to mention the destruction in 1227 of the previous settlement at this site, Castel delle Ripe.

[336H] *Massa Trabaria* Named after the Latin *trabs*, "beam."

[336H–337A] *Octavianus Ubaldinus . . . Ioannem Accionis* The Ubaldini were a famous Ghibelline family from Tuscany who attained great power in the thirteenth century. The cardinal Ottaviano (1210–1272) was one of the most important political figures of his age; B. hopes for this descendant Ottaviano a glory like that won by another ancestor, Giovanni Azzo.

[337B] *Bartolus de Saxoferrato* Bartolo da Sassoferrato (1314–1357), one of the great figures of the thirteenth century and the most renowned early Italian jurist, taught civil law at Bologna, Pisa, and, most famously, at the University of Perugia. He is best known as an exponent of the dialectical school, for his treatises on procedure and evidence, and his commentary on the Code of Justinian. See F. Calasso, "Bartolo da Sassoferrato," *DBI* 6 (1964): 640–669. A thinker beyond the field of law, his works on other topics include a treatise on topography, *Tractatus de fluminibus seu Tyberiadis*, which B. seems not to have consulted. In his application here to Bartolo of the Ennian *Volito vivus per ora virum* (*var.* 18 Vahlen), B. uncharacteristically cites Latin poetry for aesthetic effect, not for topographical information. For B.'s appreciation of the roughness of another Ennian line, see *De verbis Romanae locutionis* X.9–10 (Nogara, *Scritti Inediti*, 115–130; 122).

Alexandrum . . . Nicolaus Perottus Niccolò Perotti (1429/30–1480), a pupil of Vittorino da Feltre and Guarino Veronese, was employed in the Curia as apostolic secretary, taught at the University of Bologna and, a Latinist, translated from the Greek Polybius, Plutarch, Aristides, and Libanius. He became archbishop of Siponto and fulfilled diplomatic and political charges for the papacy, but was less successful as politician and administrator than as a humanist. He wrote the first humanistic comprehensive grammar; see Paul F. Grendler, *Schooling in Renaissance Italy: Literacy and Learning, 1300–1600.* (Baltimore and London: Johns Hopkins University Press, 1989), 173. White, *Italy illuminated*, 424 n. 38, identifies the *Alexandrum* here: "Alessandro Oliva da Sassoferrato (d. 1463), Augustinian, taught at Perugia for twenty years, rising to become Prior General of his order and in 1460 Cardinal of S. Susanna."

[337C] *Fabriano.* Although B. acknowledges (*frequens opificibus*) the significance of Fabriano in the development of art in this region, the compara-

tively extensive treatment he accords the town in the context of this briefly-described region is surely explicable in terms of its connections with the Curia. Pope Nicholas V and the Curia sojourned in Fabriano in 1449 and 1450, ostensibly to flee the plague, which was devastating Tuscany and had spread to Rome. Prospero cardinal Colonna was one of the churchmen who stayed there with Nicholas. The sect of the Fraticelli were especially numerous in the area and constituted a significant threat to the church. See Romualdo Sassi, *Documenti sul soggiorno a Fabriano di Nicolò V e della sua corte nel 1449 e nel 1450* (Ancona: Deputazione di Storia Patria per le Marche, 1955).

[337D–338E] *adulterini pontificis reliquiae pestiferi dogmatis in eo fuerunt punitae*

The Fraticelli. The Minorite Pietro di Corvaro was named Antipope (taking the name Nicholas V) by the emperor Louis the Bavarian in 1328 (see Clavuot, *Biondos »Italia illustrata«* 122 n. 291). Although the name "Fraticelli" (from the Italian *fraticelli de paupere vita*, "little brothers of the poor life") was used generally of friars who renounced material comforts, the more specific "Fraticelli de opinione" named a Christian heresy which grew out of the conflict between the Franciscan order and Pope John XXII over the issue of apostolic poverty. The latter also rejected the authority of the church and the Pope, after the papacy in 1322–1323 ruled that the Franciscans owned property. I have cited below an excellent description of the Fraticelli and the *barilotto* from John Monfasani, "The Fraticelli and Clerical Wealth in Quattrocento Rome," in *Renaissance Society and Culture: Essays in Honor of Eugene F. Rice, Jr.*, ed. John Monfasani and Ronald G. Musto, (New York: Italica Press, 1991), 177–195; 180–184.

> The Fraticelli arose from the conflict between the Franciscan Order and Pope John XXII more than a century earlier. In 1322, with the bull *Ad conditorem canonum*, John XXII forced the Franciscans to accept ownership of the property and goods they used, and thereby destroyed the Franciscans' special claim to evangelical poverty. The next year John XXII went further and outlawed their notion of evangelical poverty *tout court*. In the bull *Cum inter nonnullos*, he asserted that Christ and the apostles had indeed owned property. Nonetheless, from 1323 on, it was heresy to deny that Christ and the apostles held property. The doctrine of evangelical poverty that had inspired St. Francis of Assisi was now officially dead. One of the groups that took life out of the ashes were

> the Fraticelli. The name "Fraticelli" did not itself necessarily imply heresy. Through the 14th and 15th centuries, it also meant Franciscans and their lay followers who accepted church authority, but rejected the material comforts of the Franciscan Order and the rest of the clergy. . . . The unorthodox Fraticelli, on the other hand, who by the late 14th c. had received the distinguishing epithet *de opinione*, never accepted John XXII's settlement of the poverty issue . . . [According to B., who follows Giovanni da Capestrano,] the *barilotto* consisted of communal sex after a night mass. A child born of this fornication would be ritually murdered, its corpse burned, and the ashes mixed with wine to be drunk by the community (the rite of *pulveres*). But this description of *barilotto*, even in its language, duplicates a practice long ascribed to the sect of the Free Spirit and other medieval heretics. . . . By the fifteenth century, the Fraticelli *de opinione* were exclusively an Italian phenomenon found in Tuscany, Umbria, the Marches, Lazio, and Italian communities in Greece. The post-schism papacy vigorously persecuted them. In 1418, even while on his way to Rome from his election at the council of Constance, Pope Martin V ordered all bishops to suppress the Fraticelli in their dioceses. Once in Rome he ordered further measures against the sect, including the preaching campaigns of John Capistrano and Iacopo della Marca, both of whom continued in this task for thirty years. Martin's successors kept up the persecutions. The policy worked-the Roman *processus* of 1466 was the last trial on record against the Fraticelli.

[338F] *servaturque picta in eo tabula Gentilis fabrianensis opus caeteris quas viderimus praeferenda.* Gentile da Fabriano (c. 1372–1427), the dominant figure in the history of art in the Marches in the first part of the Renaissance, was one of the most significant Italian representatives of the Gothic style, and influential in the spread of naturalism in Italy. Among his pupils was Jacopo Bellini; perhaps his most famous work is the *Adoration of the Magi* now in the Uffizi. B.'s admiration of Gentile da Fabriano is compatible with modern aesthetics, although art historians now classify Gentile as late Gothic, a category unknown to Biondo. The altarpiece B. refers to is the "polittico di Valleromita," now in Milan, Pinacoteca di Brera. Its patron was Chiavello Chiavelli. For details from this painting, see A. DeMarchi, *Gentile da Fabriano: Un viaggio nella pittura italiana alla fine del gotico.* (Milan: Federico Motta Editore, 1992) plates 16–19; 31.

[338G] *Ancona ab … curvitate dicta* B. relates one of the popular derivations of the name Ancona from the Greek word for elbow because the coastline there makes a bend resembling a bent elbow.

[339A] *Franciscum Scalamontem et Nicolaum … Ciriacus.* Francesco Scalamonti was a friend of Ciriaco de' Pizzicolli (Cyriac of Ancona) and wrote a biography of him. Niccolò Scalamonti was a contemporary of Francesco, praised by many authors for his profound learning, especially in jurisprudence. Ciriaco de'Pizzicolli (1391–1452), merchant, then voyager and explorer, traveled and explored widely around the Mediterranean, including Greece and Egypt, as well as the Orient. On his trips he collected ancient artefacts, manuscripts, and inscriptions; the latter he published in a work, *Commentaries*, which was destroyed in a fire in the 16th century. Only some of his minor works remain. See *Cyriac of Ancona: Later Travels*, ed. and tr. E. Bodnar with Clive Foss (Cambridge, MA: Harvard University Press, 2003).

[339D] *Nicolaus Matrucius* The military captain Niccolò Mauruzzi (Niccolò da Tolentino, 1350–c. 1435). B. mentions him here perhaps because pope Eugenius IV presided at his funeral in Florence.

[340E] *Camerinum civitas vetustissima …* In the same location as the ancient city, notices of which go back to 309 B.C. (the second Samnite War). B. mentions here the slaughter in 1434 of the da Varano by a group of conspirators. One of the survivors, Giulio Cesare, whom B. mentions here, ruled until the beginning of the sixteenth century.

Ad Chienti sinistram intus est Sancti Elpidii oppidum White, *Italy illuminated*, 427, notes the abruptness of B.'s move "from Caldarola in the middle of Piceno to two towns near the mouth of the Chiento …" and his error in confusing the Ete Vivo with the Ete Morto, an impression borne out by his repetition of the error at **[340H]**.

[340F] *Salvia, vetus nomen et pariter multae vetustis ingentes aedificiorum ruinas … urbis aliae corruptum a vetusto tenens nomen.* B., still following the ancient custom of attributing a specific founder to any important city, despite admitting perplexity as to the date of foundation of the ancient site (the TCI volume *Marche*, 541, gives it as around the first century B.C.), locates correctly the ruins of the Roman Urbs Salvia and what would be, when the process of "corruption" of the name was completed, the modern Urbisaglia. The Roman city was destroyed by Alaric in 409–410. Its amphi-

theatre, which B. mentions as one of *tria theatra*, was built in the second half of the second century A.D., exists in a well-preserved state, and can still be visited. A theatre also visitable, from the end of the first century A.D., must be another of the three B. mentions.

Monasterii Claravallensis ruinae The ruins of the monastery of Chiaravalle are occupied today by the Abbey of Chiaravalle di Fiastra; what B. would have seen was the abbey finished towards the end of the twelfth c. Its destruction was accomplished in 1422 by Braccio da Montone.

[340G] *Firmanus . . . civitas Firmana Romanorum colonia . . .* Fermo was the Roman colony Firmum Picenum, established in 264 B.C.

[341D] *Iacobo ordinis sancti Francesci de Marchia appellata* Jacopo della Marca, a persecutor of the Fraticelli *de opinione*.

Ventidius Bassus . . . Asculum was besieged in 89 B.C. by Gnaeus Pompeius Strabo who captured it. P. Ventidius Bassus (*RE* 5), a Caesarean and Antonine commander mentioned in Cicero's correspondence, rose from servile origins to consul (43 B.C.) and *triumphator*. He became, in writers after Cicero, an example of the mutability of fortune. The modern Ascoli Piceno has a piazza named after him (Piazza Ventidio Basso).

Cicum poetam Francesco Stabili (1269–1327), born Giuseppe Revere, named Cecco d'Ascoli, was physician, philosopher, poet, and astrologer. He produced a number of works in both Latin and the vernacular. Perhaps the most famous was an allegorical didactic poem entitled *L'Acerba etas*, a poem on nature which featured a female figure symbolizing wisdom; the exact meaning of the title is uncertain, but the work conferred upon its author an aura of mystical magic. He is also an important source for the thirteenth- and fourteenth-century status of the baths of Agnano, which B. describes (erroneously identifying them with the villa of Lucullus) at **[415D–416E]**. Suspected of heresy, primarily for denying free will to man, Cecco was tried and burned alive at Florence in 1327.

Twelfth Region, Abruzzo Commentary

Biondo's treatment of the twelfth region opens the second part of *Italia illustrata*, which the humanist conceived as a description of the seven regions combined in the Regno. The enforced premature publication of the work, however, prevented his completing the description of the southern regions: the work breaks off abruptly and, despite Biondo's later composition of additions and corrections to *Italia illustrata*, the chapters he envisioned on Lucania, Salentini, Basilicata Calabria, and Bruttium never appeared.

As Clavuot (*Biondos »Italia illustrata«*, 80) has noted, description of the Abruzzo region presented a problem for Biondo's method, a journey following the hydrographic net: the region stretches from the Adriatic Sea across the Apennines all the way to the Beneventana, and of the rivers that debouche into the Tyrrhenian Sea, their upper courses belong to Abruzzo, their lower courses to Campania. For a systematic analysis of Biondo's approach to the description of this extensive and topographically difficult region, see Clavuot, *Biondo's »Italia illustrata«*, 80–81. In correlating Biondo's Latin toponyms in this region with their modern Italian equivalents, I have profited greatly from A. di Lorenzo, B. Figliuolo, and P. Pontari, edd., *Pietro Ranzano Descriptio totius Italiae* (*Annales XIV–XV*) (Florence: Sismel, 2007).

The structure of the entire chapter "Abruzzo" differs to that of the other thirteen chapters of *Italia illustrata* in that its first half (**[389B–393D]**) is a concentrated history of the last four hundred years of the Kingdom of Naples, starting from the migration of Tancred d'Hauteville, who founded the Norman dynasty in Italy, and culminating in the praise of the Regno's contemporary ruler, Alfonso I of Naples, V of Aragon ("il Magnanimo"). The Augustan division of Italy created the fourth region, "Sabina et Samnium," in what is now Abruzzo e Molise. Biondo does not demarcate the region until **[394E]**, at which point he describes a large irregular rectangular shape roughly comparable to Pliny's fourth region (*NH* 3.106), from the Tronto river to the Biferno river, between the Apennines and the Adriatic

Sea. Parts which Biondo includes in "Abruzzo," such as the territories of Teramo, Venafro, and Larino, belonged in the Augustan division to, respectively, Picenum, Campania, and Apulia. Towards the end of the Roman empire, this region was divided into two districts, "Valeria" and "Samnium." In the era of the Lombards, the names Aprutium and Comitatus Aprutinus began to be used.

The ancient encyclopedist did not give the region a name or delineate its borders, but described it in terms of the peoples who inhabited it. B. divides his actual treatment of the region of Abruzzo into two parts: the first comprises what was ancient Samnium from the Tronto river to the Biferno river (**[394E–400G]**), that is, the eastern slope of the Apennines and the area from the Apennines to the Adriatic Sea. The second part (**[400G–405D]**) comprises the western slope of the Apennines, the land of the Samnites living across the Apennines to the West. The chapter attests to direct observation at a number of points: for example, Biondo testifies **[397D]** to visiting Sulmona, Ovid's birthplace; and he had obviously observed the northern part of the region as a result of travel to the monastery of S. Liberatore a Maiella, where he investigated its "many elegant books written in Lombard script" **[398E]**.

In his treatment of other regions, Biondo introduces historical details in passing, as they relate to the towns, cities, and famous men whose description shapes the structure of other chapters. The unique structure of "Abruzzo" probably arose naturally, due to the larger geographical and political units which form the medieval history of southern Italy. The political organization and movement of the entire southern part of Italy happened in large outline, rather than in many separate directions as in the Lombard north or Tuscany. Independent city-states following their own political allegiances were not the rule in the south; as Biondo himself states (**[389B]**), the seven regions of the south (the last four of which he ultimately omits) were combined into one and called by the single name of the Regno, or Kingdom of Naples.

This unusual continuous historical narrative, as opposed to Biondo's standard descriptions of towns and cities organized as an itinerary along the hydrographic net, indicates that the humanist envisioned this chapter, if not as an independent work to be dedicated to Alfonso of Aragon, then certainly as connected to that ruler as "Lazio" is to Prospero cardinal Colonna, and "Romagna" (the only chapter actually realized as an independent work) to its dedicatee Malatesta Novello. It is in part to Biondo's desire to gratify

Alfonso that we must attribute the length of the historical section, although Clavuot (*Biondos »Italia illustrata«* 68) points out that Biondo intended the historical excursus on southern Italy here to obviate repetitions later, and as an introduction to, and unifying frame for, the southern regions combined in the Regno.

Despite Biondo's disappointment at Alfonso's failure to send him the requested materials on the Regno, for much of this historical background he was able to quarry primarily the thirteenth book of *Historiarum Decades* (*res . . . a maiorum aut nostris Historiis sumere*), his massive work, simultaneously composed but previously published, on the medieval history of Italy. Alfonso was, after all, the impetus for the composition of the entire *Italia illustrata*: to his request for an account of the famous men of the time, Biondo had responded in summer 1451 by giving Alfonso's ambassadors the part of the treatise he had completed. (As Fubini [*DBI* 548] noted, *Italia illustrata* began as a commissioned work but developed into Biondo's most personal creation.) Nogara (*Scritti inediti*, 165–166) gives the text of a letter from Biondo (1451, from Venice) to Bartolomeo Facio, in which Biondo asks Facio to give a part of the *Italia illustrata* to King Alfonso, whom Biondo terms expert in the area of history, especially that of the Regno, precisely the part of the treatise still unwritten. Biondo asks Facio to ensure that men at the Neapolitan court who are expert in local history correct and augment the work. (Cf. his letter to Prospero Colonna [Nogara, *Scritti Inediti*, 163] explaining that he could not begin the description of the regions of Italy most celebrated in ancient authors until cardinal Colonna provided assistance; the regions Biondo then lists include Abruzzo, *huius temporis locorum nomina situmque nec satis perlustravi nec alias plene novi*.) Biondo had approached Malatesta Novello with a request for information and corrections about places in the Romagna, and Prospero Colonna had apparently cooperated with his request for assistance in the composition of "Lazio." In the dedication which Francesco Barbaro composed to the manuscript intended for Alfonso containing the chapters of *Italia illustrata* completed up to 1451, Biondo alludes to Alfonso's request (see my comments on the Preface, vol. 1, p. 231):

> Et licet iam duos annos id cupiverim, postquam tuis verbis Reverendissime Pater, Iacobus Mutinensis Episcopus a me magno studio contenderit, tamen nec morem gerere potui voluntati tuae, nec immenso huic et difficili operi manum prius apposui, quam pestilentia me cum familia ab urbe Roma fugere coegit. . . .

> Although it is already two years since I have been longing to fulfill your request, which the bishop Giacomo delle Torre hastily and urgently communicated to me, I have not been able to do so. I did not start writing this enormous and difficult work until I along with my family was forced out of Rome by an outbreak of the plague. . . .

(A. Quirini, ed., *Diatriba praeliminaris in duas partes divisa ad Francisci Barbari et aliorum ad ipsum*, CLXXIII, and Clavuot, *Biondos »Italia illustrata«*, 23 n. 8.) It is all the more surprising to note with Clavuot (49 n. 84) that in *Italia illustrata* Alfonso is named only twice (at **[393D]** and **[410E]**). Biondo had in 1443 sent eight books of the first Decade to Alfonso, in hopes of obtaining from the king chronicles and documents necessary for further research on the historical work (cf. Nogara, *Scritti inediti*, XVII–XVIII). But in October 1452, having visited the area around Naples, Biondo managed to complete the chapters on Campania and Abruzzo.

For the historical sources for the coming of the Normans to southern Italy and Sicily, see G. A. Loud, *The Age of Robert Guiscard: Southern Italy and the Norman Conquest* (Essex, UK: Pearson Education Ltd., 2000), ch. II, "The Coming of the Normans." Biondo states that his main source here is the thirteenth book of his *Decades*, which we would expect to rely in turn on the Latin chronicle of the near-contemporary Ademar of Chabannes because, as Clavuot has demonstrated (253–254), Biondo's frequent marginalia appear in ms. Vat. Lat. 1795 of Ademar's work. Unlike his ancient sources, which he clearly viewed as conferring prestige on his work, Biondo seldom names his medieval sources, and never mentions Ademar by name. Two of the three major sources survive in Latin: *Gesta Roberti Wiscardi* of William of Apulia (c. 1096–99); and Geoffrey Malaterra's *Historia Sicula* or *De rebus gestis Rogerii* (c. 1098–1101). Biondo's account comports with that of Geoffrey Malaterra. The earliest contemporary account (1078–1086), followed by modern historians, is that of the chronicler Amatus of Montecassino, whose original work is lost, a translation of which survives, however, in French from the fourteenth century (*Storia de' Normanni di Amato di Montecassino*, ed. Vincenzo de Bartholomaeis, Fonti per la storia d'Italia. Scrittori. Secolo 11, No. 76 [Rome: Istituto storico italiano per il Medio Evo, 1935]). A recent English translation is *The History of the Normans by Amatus of Montecassino*, transl. Prescott N. Dunbar, revised with introduction and notes by Graham A. Loud (Woodbridge, UK: The Boydell Press, 2004).

At a number of points, Biondo's account conflicts with more recent histories of the deeds of the Normans in southern Italy. He begins his account with the arrival of Tancred d'Hauteville. In the traditional account, the beginnings of Norman lordship in Italy can be traced earlier than the arrival of the Hauteville clan, to Melo's (1016 or 1018) employment of Norman mercenaries in his defeat at the hands of the Byzantine Greeks (in William of Apulia and Amatus of Montecassino; see below on **[389B]**); and to Rainulf Drengot's establishment as lord of the town and territory of Aversa, the first Norman in Italy to thus establish himself. For reconciliation of different versions of the story of the Normans' arrival, see Loud, *Age of Robert Guiscard*, 63–66.

Unlike modern historians, Biondo does not draw general conclusions about the impact of the Normans on Italy and the repercussions of their influence on larger issues such as the unity of southern Italy, schism between Latin and Greek churches, Western confrontation with Islam, etc. His concern is to sketch quickly the 400 years which led up to the felicitous rule of Alfonso. In doing this, he cannot escape incidentally providing a brief history of the papacy. Although Biondo does not mention them, events in the history of the Normans' establishment in southern Italy were entangled with the disputes between the Byzantine and Roman churches (the two most important were marriage among clergy, a Byzantine practice, and simony). As we might expect from a member of the Curia, Biondo's bias is pro-papal when discussing, *e.g.*, the incursions of the Hohenstaufen into southern Italy.

[389B] *Pandulfus, Capuanus princeps . . . hanc gentem accessivit.* In making the first contact of the Normans with southern Italy their intervention between the warring Lombard princes of Capua and Salerno, B. seems to follow a variant to the traditional account of the meeting, usually dated to 1017, between the newly-arrived Normans and the Lombard Melo who asked them to aid him against the Byzantine Greeks (cf. Loud, *Age of Robert Guiscard*, 61).

[389D] *Melphim urbem . . . aedificaverunt.* Melfi was established by the Byzantine Greeks; see Loud, *Age of Robert Guiscard*, 68 n. 28.

Leone quinto pontifice Romano . . . As often, B. here confuses the numbers of popes and emperors. Leo IX was Pope; the Roman Emperor at the time was Henry III (not II as B. has it). B. must mean Leo IX, the pope ruling from 1049–1054, who in 1053 undertook an unsuccessful expedition against

the Normans of southern Italy who had been plundering lands belonging to the Church. In 1053 Pope Leo IX was defeated by the Normans at a plain on the Fortore river near Civitate. In defeat, the pope had to allow the Normans the continued possession of territory they had occupied.

[390E] Council of Melfi. This meeting did not take place at Aquila, as B. reports. Nicholas II, pope from 1059–1061, a German but an interruption in the line of pro-imperial popes, took the opportunity of the council of Melfi (1059) to ally himself with the Normans of southern Italy, welcoming the alliance Leo had refused. (The emperor Henry III declared the pope's rule illegitimate and his decrees nullified.) He made Robert Guiscard Duke of Puglia and Calabria, and accepted feudal loyalty from the Normans, an offer which his predecessors had rejected.

[390F] . . . *reversus ad Reggii obsidionem* . . . Robert Guiscard's capture of Reggio (1060) marked the end of Byzantine rule in Calabria.

[390G] *Rogerium . . . impulit ut in Siciliam . . . duceret.* A new chapter begins in the story of Norman conquests, with a new target (Sicily) and leader, Robert Guiscard's brother Roger, later called the "Great Count." Conflicts between Moslem emirs provided the weakness which allowed the Norman conquest of Sicily; it began in 1060 (fall of Messina) and took 30 years, although the ineluctability of Norman success perhaps occasioned B.'s *brevi* (**[390F]**). Palermo fell in 1071, and in 1091 the fall of Noto completed the process of Norman domination over the island. As Denis Mack Smith (*Medieval Sicily 800–1713* [London: Chatto and Windus, 1968], 14–15) summarizes the Norman penetration of Sicily,

> By agreement with Guiscard, the conquest of Sicily fell mainly to Roger de Hauteville. After defeating the Greeks of Calabria, he first crossed the straits with only some 60 knights, perhaps intending just to spy out the land and practise the technique of transporting horses by sea. Once he had tested Arab resistance, another larger expedition captured Messina. Making occasional forays, setting up a few small garrisons, by 1064 Roger became master of the northeast . . . Guiscard, as Duke of Apulia, received Palermo as his share, but . . . left Roger, as count of Sicily and Calabria, to complete the conquest and set up a government.

[390H] *Marchiam Anconitanam* . . . Cf. **[335B]**, where B. is more specific about the Pope's insistence; and see Clavuot, *Biondos »Italia illustrata«*, 43 n. 62.

[391C] *Rogerius . . . regni titulum . . . obtinuit.* Roger II, king of Sicily 1130–1154; succeeded by his son William, who was in turn succeeded by his son William II "the Good," who reigned 1166–1189.

[392E] *Constantiam Rogerii regis supradicti filiam* . . . After the emperor Henry VI had married Constance, he marched south to claim his wife's inheritance and was crowned king of Sicily in Palermo in 1194. Henry died in 1197.

[392F] *scelestissimus* Innocent IV was elected Pope in 1243. In 1245 at the Council of Lyons he deposed Frederick II; his encyclical *aeger cui levia* asserted the church's power over heaven and earthly territory. B. does not care to enlarge upon the cultural richness of Frederick II's kingdom, a center of philosophy, science, law, and art. Frederick II chartered the University of Naples and built beautiful castles in Puglia, but for B., apologist for the papacy, he is irredeemable.

[392G] *Supervixit postea Federicus* . . . Frederick died in 1250; the illegitimate Manfred continued the Staufen rule of Sicily and the anti-papal cause elsewhere in Italy, but was killed in 1266 at the battle of Benevento (cf. **[393B]**).

[393B] *Banderesi* Banderesi was the name given to the chiefs of the regions (and the principal political faction) of Rome at this time, named after the banners they carried in war.

[393B–C] *Alemanni ingressi sunt regnum* . . . *Carolus superior evasit* . . . *Conradinus et dux Austriae fugientes* 1265 is the correct date of Manfred's death and Pope Clement IV's election. In 1268, at the Battle of Tagliacozzo, near Scurcola, Charles d'Anjou decisively defeated Conradin of Swabia and established securely the Angevin monarchy.

[393C] *quam primum die constituta advesperascere* . . . In 1282, the beginning of the rebellion of the Sicilian Vespers was signaled by the tolling of the evensong bell.

successit alter Carolus . . . In 1289 Pope Nicholas IV, supporter of the Angevins, despite the revolt of the Vespers, crowned Charles II d'Anjou in

the Kingdom of Sicily and upheld the claims of his son Charles Martel to the throne of Hungary, which had been vacant following the death without sons of King Ladislaus, whose relative Charles Martel was.

[393D] *Neapolim invectus triumphaverit* . . . The triumph of Alfonso V of Aragon in Naples took place in 1443, a topic celebrated by humanists connected with Alfonso's court in the mid-fifteenth century: Porcellio Pandoni wrote a poem in praise of Alfonso's victory, and Panormita composed the inscription for the triumphal arch on the Castelnuovo. Panormita and Bartolomeo Facio described the triumphal procession, patterned after ancient Roman triumphs. For the sincere cultural and intellectual interests and erudition of Alfonso, who drew to his court some of the most prominent humanists of mid-fifteenth century Italy, including B., see Jerry H. Bentley, *Politics and Culture in Renaissance Naples* (Princeton: Princeton University Press 1987), 54–62. Bentley identifies among Alfonso's motives for this patronage (which earned him the epithet "Il Magnanimo") a desire for status and legitimation: he was a foreigner who had won his power by arms. Clavuot further develops this consideration of Alfonso's concern in "Flavio Biondo's »Italia illustrata«: Porträt und historisch-geographische Legitimation der humanistischen Elite Italiens," 55–75 in *Diffusion des Humanismus: Studien zur nationalen Geschichtsschreibung europäischer Humanisten*, edd. J. Helmrath et al. (Göttingen: Wallstein Verlag, 2002). B. expresses here the newly-emerging view of southern Italy as a national entity (see Clavuot, *Biondos »Italia illustrata«*, 69, n. 157).

[394E–F] The beginning of the second part of "Abruzzo." Here B. claims to know the authentic derivation of the name *Aprutium*, in scornful contrast to some unnamed learned men who, unfamiliar with the two geographically distant regions, derived the name *Aprutium* from Bruttium. B. himself in an unlikely etymology traces the name to the ancient *ager Precutinus*; cf. Clavuot, *Biondos »Italia illustrata«*, 43.

[394F] *Namque Livius libro xxii* . . . B. paraphrases and summarizes Livy 22.9.1–5. It is clear from comparison with the Livian passage, which I have reproduced in its entirety and translated below, that B. omits Livy's editorializing comments; changes the text from *oratio recta* to *oratio obliqua*; and keeps the importance of the time sequence, but leaves out some of the names of territories. He displaces slightly from its Livian context the phrase *per aliquot dies*.

Hannibal recto itinere per Umbriam usque ad Spoletium venit. Inde cum perpopulato agro urbem oppugnare adortus esset, cum magna caede suorum repulsus, coniectans ex unius coloniae haud prospere temptatae viribus quanta moles Romanae urbis esset, in agrum Picenum avertit iter non copia solum omnis generis frugum abundantem, sed refertum praeda, quam effuse avidi atque egentes rapiebant. Ibi *per dies aliquot* stativa habita refectusque miles hibernis itineribus ac palustri via proelioque magis ad eventum secundo quam levi aut facili adfectus.

Ubi satis quietis datum praeda ac populationibus magis quam otio aut requie gaudentibus, profectus Praetutianum Hadrianumque agrum, Marsos inde Marrucinosque et Paelignos devastat circaque Arpos et Lucinam proximam Apuliae regionem.

Hannibal came to Spoletium by a direct route through Umbria. Then he devastated the country and attempted to take the town of Spoletium by siege. But he was driven back, losing many of his men, and deducing from the example of one single colony's strength in successfully resisting him how great a challenge besieging the city of Rome would be, he changed course and deviated into the Picentine territory, which was not only rich in all types of grain, but also full of potential plunder. Here his needy men greedily and quite unrestrainedly seized whatever they could. The army *for some days* camped there, and the soldiers recovered their strength after their exhaustion from traveling in winter, through swamps, and from a battle which had been successful in its outcome rather than insignificant and easy to fight.

When Hannibal had allowed his soldiers enough rest (and they enjoyed plunder and looting more than quiet and rest), he set out for the territory of the Praetutii and the city of Hadria, devastating the area and then plundering the territories of the Marsi, the Marrucini, and the Peligni, and the area around Arpi and Luceria, and the neighboring region of Apulia.

[394G] Pliny *NH* 3.110 includes these places in *Quinta regio Piceni*.

[395A] *Simonem ... Theodorum ... gente progenitos Laelia* ... Teodoro de'Lelli (d. 1446) was *auditor causarum sacri palatii*, or judge.

[395D] ... *apud monasterium Casae Novae* ... The famous Cistercian abbey of Sta. Maria Casanova, founded in 1191; its ruins are visitable today just south of the modern Villa Celiera.

[396E] *Capistranum* Birthplace of the Franciscan S. Giovanni da Capestrano (1386–1456), whose strenuous opposition to heretics B. praised at **[337D]**.

[396E–H] *Aquila, urbs praeclara* The date of this city's foundation has been a topic of debate. In the thirteenth century the inhabitants of scattered fortified villages combined at L'Aquila. B. does not mention recent history involving the famous condottieri (Braccio da Montone, Muzio Attendolo Sforza) he has praised earlier in *It. ill.*

[396E] *Livius enim libro X* B. paraphrases in indirect statement, with some inaccuracy, the following sentences from Livy 10.39.2–4:

> Cum eius in Samnium profectus, dum hostes operati superstitionibus concilia secreta agunt, Amiternum oppidum de Samnitibus ui cepit. Caesa ibi milia hominum duo ferme atque octingenti, capta quattuor milia ducenti septuaginta.

[396G–H] *tyrannos . . . trucidaverint* Clavuot (*Biondos »Italia illustrata«*, 94 n. 246) surmises that this legend was a survival in the memory of Abruzzo's mountain-dwelling population of their ancestors' resistance against the lordship of the Hohenstaufen and the Normans.

[397A] *Maiella* The Maiella is the second-highest range of the central Apennines, and the highest part of the region of Abruzzo; it is located between the valley of the Pescara river and that of the Sangro.

[397B] *Cantalupum* The *oleus Petronicus* is petroleum. There is a general seeping of petroleum from the earth in the environs of the Biferno river. J. C. Husslein (*Flavio Biondo als Geograph des Frühhumanismus* [Würzburg 1901], 49), likens this phenomenon to a similar flow near the Tegernsee in Germany.

[397D] *Sulmoque proximum fluvio* B.'s comments on Ovid and Sulmo clearly demonstrate his direct observation of the site. The citations are *Fasti* 4.79–80; 81–83; see Weiss, *Discovery*, 121, on the fifteenth-century cult of Ovid at Sulmona. The *opifices* are the goldsmiths for which Sulmona was famous in the fourteenth and fifteenth centuries.

Monasterium . . . quod frater Petrus de Morrono . . . inhabitabat The Abbey of S. Spirito in Badia Morronese, five km. north of Sulmona, is where Pietro Angeleri of Isernia came as an anchorite; the obscure hermit known as Pietro da Morrone became Pope Celestine V (who reigned for five months in 1294 before his incompetence resulted in his abdication and return to his

former life). The abbey is now a penitentiary. Near it is the actual chapel with the hermit's cell from which Charles II of Naples summoned the future pope. Celestine's ashes are in the church of Sta. Maria di Collemagino at L'Aquila.

[398E] *sub ipso monte Maiella adiacet monasterium* B. describes from direct observation. The restored medieval church of S. Liberatore a Maiella is visitable today. The previous building was one of the oldest abbeys of the Benedictines of Cassino; B. would have visited its eleventh century reconstruction. Despite their importance for medieval architecture and art, B. gives no description of the buildings.

[398G] *Ortona* The most important harbor on the coast of Abruzzo. B. passes up an opportunity to glorify Alfonso, who besieged Ortona in 1442 and built (1448–1452) a castle there whose remains are still on site.

[399C] *Iacobi Caudolae* A condottiere, Jacopo Caldora, from a family powerful in the area. The abbey of S. Spirito (see **[397D]**) contains a chapel of the Caldora.

[400G] *Difficiliorem vero habet haec regio* One of the few instances in which B. finds Pliny's division of the regions of Italy to be inconvenient, for it proceeded according to the watershed of the Apennines and the hydrographic net provided by the major rivers. At this point, however, rivers divided by the Apennines flow into the lower part of Samnium but are common also to the region of Campania, treated in the following chapter.

[400H] *Livius in septimo* . . . Actually Livy 10.1.1–2.

[402E] *monasterium Casinense* The famous monastery of Montecassino which B. definitely visited, as we know that he found there a codex, now lost, of a regionary of Rome. Although he used it as a source for *Roma instaurata*, he erroneously attributed it to Sextus Rufus; see Clavuot, *Biondos »Italia illustrata«*, 164 n. 103; Fubini, *DBI*, 547.

[402F] *Urbs vero . . . in Casino monte* The text of Livy is vexed here and B. has read, with many of the mss., *Casinum* for the colony mentioned in Livy 9.28.7–8. Conway and Walters, with Sigonius, have *Interamnam*; and with Mommsen relying on Pliny, *Sucasinam*. Their result is *Volsci Pontias, insulam sitam in conspectu litoris sui, incoluerant. Et Interamnam Sucasinam ut deduceretur colonia, senatus consultum factum est*. . . . However, B.'s addi-

tions of *vicerunt*, and *sicut* for *senatus consultum*, create nonsense in his citation.

[402G] *Fregellas fuisse quem nunc Pontem Corvum dicimus satis constat.* Destroyed in 125 B.C. by the Romans as punishment for rebellion, ancient Fregellae is now thought to have been located between the modern Ceprano and Isoletta.

[402H] *ex more nostro non liceat descriptionem . . . a fonte incipimus* B. refers to his customary procedure of following rivers from their mouths upward, describing towns and cities along their banks.

[403B–C] B. mistakenly locates Ailano halfway between Lago del Matese and the Volturno; and names Pratellus the river Lete.

[404F] *Antoninus Pius . . . ad Mercurialem primum . . . posuit* The Santuario di Monte Vergine. Here the reading of the Basle (1559) edition, *ad magnam partem*, is surely wrong, and the Verona (1482) edition's reading correct: *ad Magnam Matrem*. Both the Antonine *Itinerarium* and the *Tabula Peutingeriana* show "Ad Magnam Matrem" as a stopping-place near Aeclanum (Eclano). It occurs between Equum Tuticum and "Ad Columna, id est Traiectum" (Cuntz, 15); and in the *Tabula Peutingeriana* on the route from Capua to Venosa. Apropos of the latter map (102 in his edition) Miller, col. 377, notes that the temple of the Dea Magna stands on the Via Appia near Eclano and the station on the *Itinerarium* noted as "Ad Magnam Matrem" should be located here.

[405C] *Saepinum* B. is far off in citing as Livy, book 21, what is actually the narrative at 10.45.12–13 of the consul L. Papirius Cursor's capture of Samnite Saepinum in 293 B.C. B. also severely abridges Livy's text, and his text of Livy does not make sense in the final sentence, the enumeration of the slain and captured, *septem milia quadringenti caesi, capta minus tria milia hominum*. The import of this sentence is to show the courage and desperation of the Samnite inhabitants of the town, who preferred death to capture.

After the capture of Saepinum, a Roman *municipium* arose in the first c. A.D. on the plain near the site of the original Samnite town, but this was sacked in the ninth c. by Arabs (although its ruins have been excavated and can be visited). What B. names here is probably the more recently founded (and also extant) settlement on a nearby hill, for he does not identify the site as in ruins, merely as having an ancient name.

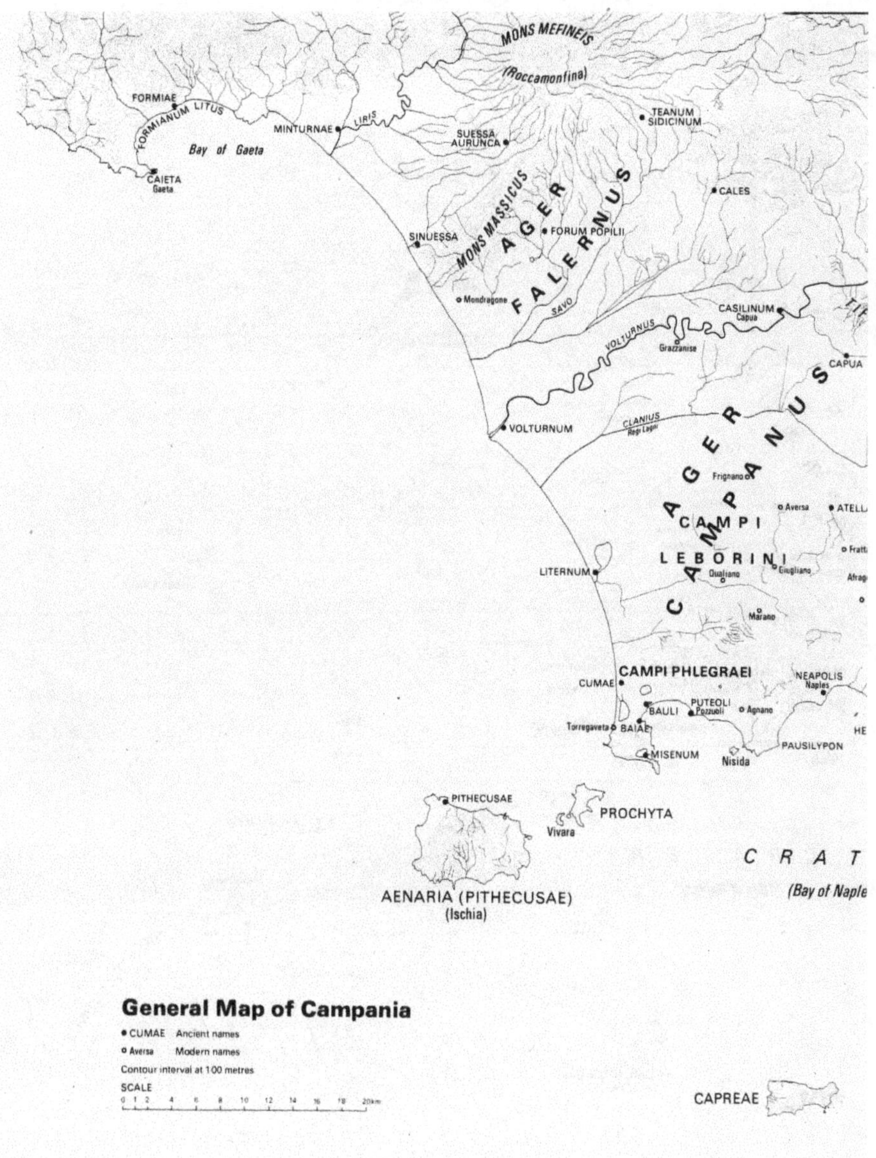

Plate V. General map of Campania. Reproduced from M. W. Frederiksen, *Campania* (British School at Rome, 1984) by permission of Dr. Nicholas Purcell.

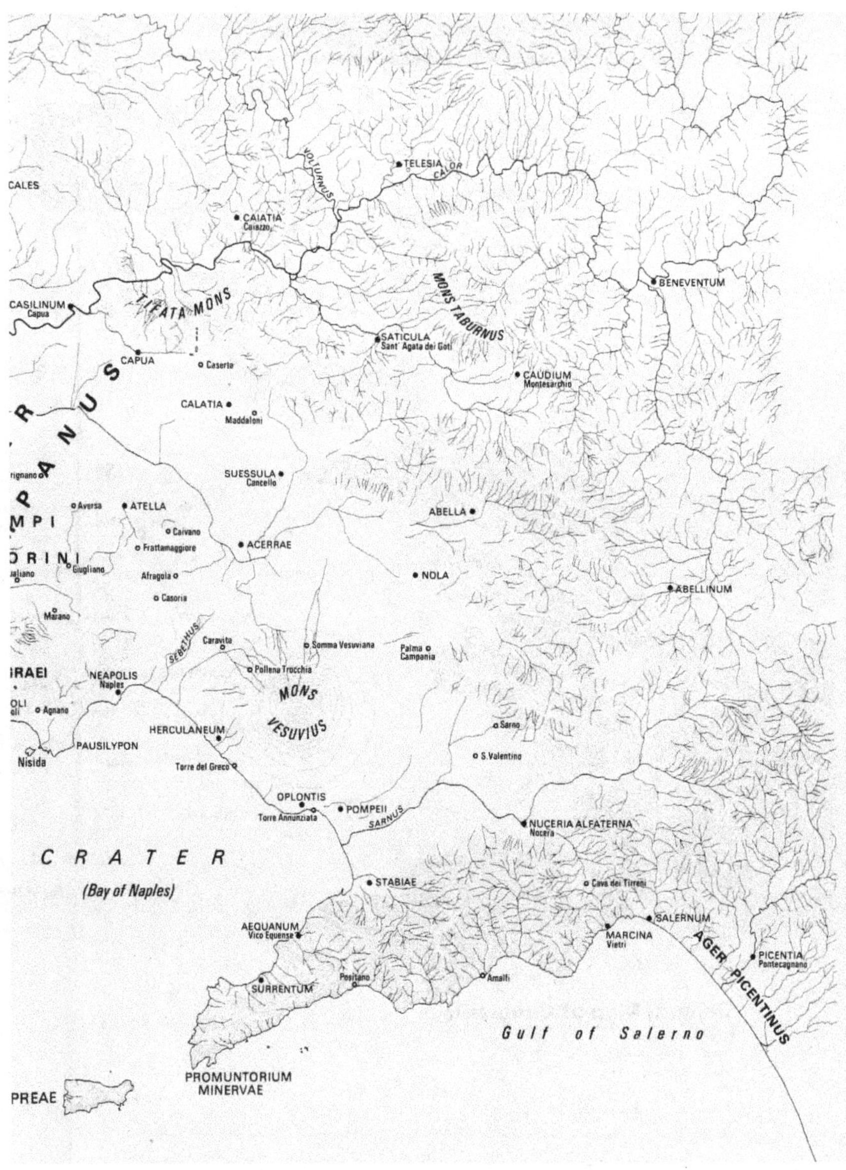

Plate VI. General map of Campania. Reproduced from M. W. Frederiksen, *Campania* (British School at Rome, 1984) by permission of Dr. Nicholas Purcell.

Thirteenth Region, Campania Commentary

Campania is one of the regions whose boundaries Biondo does not initially delineate clearly or completely. He gives as boundary for the region of Campania only Monte Massico, the northern boundary of the Campanian plain. Although adhering for the most part in *Italia illustrata* to the Augustan definitions of the regions as Pliny describes them in his third book, Biondo splits into two regions the Augustan region I, *Latium et Campania*. The boundaries of Campania in ancient times were the Vulturnus River in the north; the mountains of Surrentum and Nuceria in the south; M. Tifata and M. Vergine in the east; and the Tyrrhenian sea in the west.

In the region of Campania are found many of Italy's most ancient settlements and important archaeological sites. From Biondo's descriptions of the ruins of Cumae, Baiae, and Puteoli we can probably gauge the state of antiquarian knowledge in the 1400s, a consequence of the renewal of interest in classical antiquity. Both Petrarch and Boccaccio had anticipated Biondo in antiquarian visits to the Campi Flegrei. Biondo's choice of sites to treat with expanded descriptions reflects the importance placed on the ruins of that area: antiquarians and humanists of his time considered them second only to those of Rome, indeed a lesser version of the monuments visible to them at Rome. Today, of course, thanks to the work of scholars too numerous to list in a commentary of general scope, among them Maiuri and Frederiksen, we are privy not only to archaeological discoveries (the site of ancient Herculaneum, for example, was rediscovered in 1709 by a farmer who was digging a well and bumped into the stage of its theatre), but to comprehensive studies of sites, of the rise and fall of their fortunes in relation to the expansion of Roman power, data integrated from archaeological, historical, numismatic, epigraphical, and geomorphological research. Biondo's methodology, however, heralds in primitive form this integrative approach.

In addition, the history and archaeology of Campania are rich in Greek artifacts, somewhat less so in Etruscan (but see J. Heurgon, *Recherches sur l'histoire, la Religion et la Civilisation de Capoue Préromaine*, Bibliothèque

des Écoles Françaises d'Athènes et de Rome 154 [Paris: Boccard, 1942] 153 n.1., on the Etruscan origin of the name Vulturnus). Greeks settled the area in the eighth century B.C., and Greek names and Greek sources (e.g., Neapolis; Timaeus of Tauromenium) are fundamental to an understanding of the region's history. Yet Biondo was deficient, admittedly in the Greek language and, like other humanists of his time, in knowledge of Greek activities in Italy (not to mention Campania's Oscan history), an ignorance which causes his account of the region to appear poor to modern readers, even as we appreciate his personal observation of many sites (Liternum; Cumae; Baiae) which was in part the result of his hopeful and lengthy cultivation of the patronage of Alfonso of Aragon, king of Naples from 1443 to his death in 1458. The humanist's visit to Naples in 1452 must be the basis for his remark at **[409B]** on a road *qua nuper Neapolim ivimus ipsi*. White, "Critical Edition," 279, endorses Nogara's conclusion (*Scritti inediti*, CXXIV): "over the period from the latter half of 1452 to early in 1453 in Naples and back in San Biagio (cf. **[353C]**, vol. 1, pp. 74–76), he worked on and completed *Regiones* XII–XIII (Abruzzo and Campania) and part of Regio XIV (Puglia). . . ."

If chapters III ("Lazio,") and VI ("Romagna") of *Italia illustrata* can be read as tributes to Prospero Cardinal Colonna and Malatesta Novello of Cesena, respectively, "Campania" approaches the status of a tribute to Alfonso, although it was never formally dedicated to him. Alfonso was the inspiration for *It. ill.*, originally conceived as a catalogue of famous men of the time; as Fubini comments (*DBI* 548), Alfonso probably envisioned a work like *De viris illustribus* which Bartolomeo Facio (cf. **[299C]**, vol. 1, pp. 27; 244–5), the Genoese Alfonso chose as his court historian, composed later (1455–57) and dedicated to Alfonso (indeed Alfonso's was the last of Facio's sixty-three biographies of famous men). Whatever his specific intention, in 1447 Alfonso had asked, in Biondo's words, *ut . . . vetustis Italiae locis, populis nominum detur, novis auctoritas, deletis vita, memoriae deinde ut obscuritas, illustretur a nobis* (in Nogara, *Scritti Inediti*, CXXII n. 155). The *Proemium* which Francesco Barbaro wrote in 1451 in Biondo's name was addressed to Alfonso. In Biondo's correspondence can be traced the progress of his unsuccessful attempts to elicit from Alfonso himself materials on the history of the Regno for use in this chapter. At two points in the chapters on southern Italy, once in "Abruzzo" **[393D]** and once in "Campania" **[417D]**, Biondo indulges in the expected praise, even flattery, of Alfonso.

Even Biondo's use of Latin sources with which he was very familiar-mostly Livy on the Hannibalic War and Cicero's speech against the agrarian proposal of Servilius Rullus-are, more than elsewhere, a patchwork of citations with little awareness of background, complexity, context, or source problems (e.g., Livy's changes to his own sources). Biondo shows no awareness of the turbulence and civil instability for which Campania was famous in the late Republic and early Empire. He seems unaware also of Campania's rich cultural legacy, mentioning in this regard only—and disapprovingly—the Atellan farce **[411C]**; in regard to other cultural legacies of Campania which drew moralising comments in antiquity (notably its τρυφή), he copies selected passages, but does not focus his own comments on the ethical associations for the Romans of Campanian luxury. In addition, there is nearly nothing here of the inspiration for *Italia illustrata*, and an important element in its chapters on northern and central Italy: biographical notices of the region's famous men. Biondo has very little to say about famous Campanian contemporaries; although he mentions intellectuals at the court of Naples, he limits his biographical notices to famous Romans, Petrarch and King Robert, and Alfonso.

The question of whether an early group of cartographers was an element of the intellectual circle around King Robert arises with mention of King Robert d'Anjou and his court at Naples, an issue important to a consideration of the sources of *Italia illustrata* because of the tantalizing remarks B. makes at **[353C–D]** (vol. 1 p. 76) and **[355D]** (vol. 1 p. 84), both concerning the course of the Po. The first, in the change in the river's course, relies on personal observation and a reference to the map of King Robert and Petrarch ([*Padi cursus*] *quem nunc . . . secus villam Belreguardam desiccatum videmus. Nam pictura Italiae, quam in primis sequimur, Roberti regis Siciliae et Francisci Petrarchae eius amici opus, Vicuentiam Viceriamque et Conam vicos profluenti Pado appositos habet*). The second occurs in his description of the "rotta di Ficarolo," a branch of the Po: *Hunc vero Ficaroli ramum intra centum proximos annos inchoasse, ideo non dubitamus, quia Roberti regis Neapolitani, et Francisci Petrarchae pictura Italiae, qua nos sequi supra diximus, ipsum non habet ramum.*

Biondo appears to be our only informant about this map's existence. Several scholars have examined the evidence about the Neapolitan court during Robert's reign (1309–1343), where a circle of intellectuals was active. Petrarch's admiration for the king is well-known; he chose him to be his examiner preliminary to his being crowned at Rome in 1341. Petrarch

himself was sufficiently expert in topographical matters to write an itinerary, *Itinerarium Syriacum*, and to display an impressive knowledge of the Ligurian coast in his passage in the *Africa* on the death of Mago (6.839–918); cf. Clavuot, *Biondo's »Italia illustrata«*, 142 n.13, for details of the evidence of Petrarch's geographical interests. Although Robert was a patron of culture and the arts as well as of scholarly learning, his own interests tended towards philosophy, theology, and law; despite the existence of records from his library which allow us to know what he purchased or had copied, there is no evidence to corroborate B.'s suggestion that the "Re Savio" was an amateur of cartography. What he himself wrote appears to have been on moral and civil themes.

The map itself vanished long ago from the Biblioteca Estense in Modena. Perhaps the most definite conclusion possible is the suggestion of Clavuot (*Biondo's »Italia illustrata«*, 140–141, based on B. Degenhart and A. Schmitt, "Marino Sanudo und Paolino Veneto. Zwei Literaten des 14. Jahrhunderts in ihrer Wirkung auf Buchillustrierung und Kartographie in Venedig, Avignon und Neapel," *Römisches Jahrbuch für Kunstgeschichte 14* [1973] 1–137) that Paolino Veneto (aka Fra Paolino Minorita), bishop of Pozzuoli, may be identified as somehow contributing to the creation of this map through his association with the circle of intellectuals around King Robert.

The lack of prosopographical notices in "Campania" has two possible causes. First, Biondo claims to have been forced to premature publication by the plagiarism of an early version of the work. The three chapters on the regions of southern Italy, "Abruzzo," "Campania," and "Puglia," betray great haste in composition, notably in the abrupt ending to the last of these chapters, which is also the concluding chapter. Second, in the Quattrocento the south of Italy was (except for the court at Naples) less productive than the northern regions of citizens famed for political, legal, or intellectual accomplishments; and when we consider that B. tends to include a large number of fellow humanists in the catalogues of a region's famous men, the lack of biographical notices in the chapters on southern Italy is understandable.

[406E] *Lucanus, et umbrosae Liris* Lucan, *De bello civili* 2.424–425; see my comments on **[299C]**, vol. 1, pp. 243–244.

[406E–F] *Ausones* The name was given the natives by the Greeks. Livy 9.25.1, tells of the (314 B.C.) beginning of the campaign against the Ausones, also called the Aurunci: *Consules ab Sora profecti in agros atque*

urbes Ausonum bellum intulerunt. Clavuot, *Biondo's »Italia illustrata«*, 217, calls attention to B.'s exemplary paraphrase of this sentence as a reduction of Livy's sentence to the kernel of its content. As E. T. Salmon (*Samnium and the Samnites* [Cambridge: Cambridge University Press, 1967]) 238, describes the end of the Ausones:

> The victorious consuls promptly attacked the insurgent Aurunci and made them pay dearly for their revolt: it was the Romans, now in 314 . . . who were responsible for the massacres and other harsh measures that put an end to the existence of the Aurunci as a separate, identifiable nation.

B. then cites Livy 9.25.3, and paraphrases 25.6–9. Modern editors of Livy read *Vescia* instead of B.'s *Vestina*; Clavuot (*Biondos »Italia illustrata«*, 201 and n.4) adduces this reading as an indication that B.'s text belonged to the Symmachean-Nicomachean tradition (we cannot identify the ms. B. used beyond that it was probably a contaminated Italian one of the late fourteenth or fifteenth century). The Vestini, attested in Juvenal 14.181, were part of the Sabellic League along with the Marsi, Peligni, and Marrucini, located in the central and eastern part of central Italy. The *Vescinus ager*, however, is located near Suessa Aurunca, and was the territory of the Aurunci, and therefore more appropriate to the part of Italy B. is describing at this point.

Marica: an Italic goddess of fertility. M. W. Frederiksen, *Campania* (ed. Nicholas Purcell [Rome: British School at Rome, 1984]), 76 and n. 150, relates a report that the people of Minturnae stole from Cumae a statue of Artemis and worshipped her under the name of Dea Marica (scholiast to Augustine, *de civ. Dei* 2.23, explaining Marica as another name for Diana).

[406G–H] *Minturnae . . . exstat theatrum paene integrum* . . . An important city of the Aurunci, Minturnae was famous for the episode of Marius' capture and escape, in Valerius Maximus, *Factorum Dictorumque Memorabilia* 1.5.5. Minturnae was devastated by the Lombards in 590. Subsequent to Gregory the Great's merging of the two churches, Minturnae's people abandoned the site and moved to a nearby hill. This settlement became the medieval town of Traetto, a name derived from the crossing there of the Garigliano, which had taken the place of the Roman bridge on the Appian Way, which had collapsed. In 883, Traetto was conquered by the Saracens. After the battle of the Garigliano in 915, which B. recounted in book 12 of *Historiarum Decades*, Traetto became part of the duchy of Gaeta, and the

seat of a Lombard count. In the early twentieth century it reassumed the classical name of Minturno.

Livius septuagesimo For this B. has copied the *Periocha* of book 77 of Livy (B.'s text is, for the most part, the same as that of O. Rossbach, ed., *Titi Livi Ab Urbe Condita Libri* Pt. 4 [Stuttgart: Teubner, 1972] p. 85).

Historiarum John X, pope from 914 to 928, succeeded for a few years in motivating the Roman aristocracy to unite to defeat the Saracens in central Italy.

[406H] *Mons ... Gaurus* The toponym, derived from the Greek for "proud," "majestic," has been popularized into Monte Barbaro.

[407A] *Sinuessa* B. erroneously identifies ancient Sinuessa with Mondragone, a common error; Sinuessa is actually north of modern Mondragone.

Livius etiam, XXII B. must here paraphrase Livy 22.14.1. The two appearances in Livy of the toponym *Massicus* are 22.14.1 and 22.14.3.

[407B] *Valerius Martialis poeta*. Martial 13.83.1:

> Caeruleus nos Liris amat, quem silva Maricae
> protegit: hinc squillae maxima turba sumus.

[407B–C] *M. Cicero in oratione contra legem agrariam ... De lege agraria* 2.14.36: B. reproduces accurately Cicero's list of Campanian places which the decemvirs planned to sell, but reads or writes *sileta* where modern editions have *salicta*, "willow-beds."

[407D] *molle Calenum* B. is in error in his attribution to Horace of this phrase from Juvenal, *Sat*. 1.69: the matron who poisons her husband's wine (*molle Calenum*) with toad venom furnishes an example of the corruption that moves Juvenal to write satire.

viis cavis These sunken roads or "cupe," a topographical feature still visible in Campania, exist around Naples today.

[408E] *Calenum primo, sive Carinula ... Cales sive Calvi* Cf. **[407A]**, where B. identifies *Calenum oppidum* as *nunc Carinulam*. B. here (mistakenly) names the same city with two different toponyms, giving the impression that he is listing two different cities. He may be following Pliny, who uses the adjectival form Calenum (derived from the name *Cales* at 3.63). Strabo (E.3.9) also calls Cales "the city of the Caleni" (Ἡ τῶν Καληνῶν).

Idem in decimo Samnitium legions I have given the modern text of Livy 10.31.4–7, bracketing B.'s omissions, as an example of how B. abbreviates and selects only what he finds relevant (the text is, however, disputed at one of B.'s omissions):

> Samnitium legiones, cum partem Ap. Claudius praetor partem L. Volumnius pro consule sequeretur, in agrum Stellatem convenerunt. [Ibi ad Caiatiam omnes considunt et Appius Volumniusque castra coniungunt.] Pugnatum infestissimis animis, [hinc ira stimulante adversus rebellantes totiens, illinc ad ultimam iam dimicantibus spem.] Caesa [ergo] Samnitium sedecim milia trecenti, [capta duo milia septingenti; ex Romano exercitu cecidere duo milia septingenti.]
>
> The praetor Appius Claudius was pursuing some of the Samnite legions; the proconsul L. Volumnius was pursuing others of them. [There they came together in the plain of Stella and they all encamped at Caiatia where Appius and Volumnius set up a combined camp.] There was a fierce battle, [with the Romans on one side motivated by their anger against the Samnites who habitually rebelled, the Samnites on the other side motivated by desperation to fight until the last hope was gone.] 16,300 of the Samnites, accordingly, were slain, [and 2,700 captured; from the Roman army were lost 2,700 men.]

[408E–F] B. summarizes the story of Hannibal's misguided march to Casilinum as told in Livy 22.13.1–14.1; it occurs also in Plutarch, *Fab. Max.* 6. As Frederiksen, *Campania*, 238, notes, this story, that because of his accent Hannibal was misdirected to Casilinum when he had requested direction to Casinum, "is too picturesque to be true. . . . The anecdote probably arose in an attempt to excuse the temporising policy of Fabius Maximus Cunctator." Again, as with all anecdotes from this source, B. had access to the Latin translation of Plutarch by his friend Pier Candido Decembrio, in this case the *Life* of Fabius Maximus which we know Decembrio translated (see below, **[409D]**).

[409B] *qua nuper Neapolim ivimus ipsi* . . . B. alludes to a recent trip to Naples, probably in 1452; see White, "Critical Edition," 278, cited above.

Urbs . . . ipsius nomine Vulturnum appellata . . . Frederiksen, *Campania*, 18, notes that the Roman colony of Vulturnum was settled in this place "to pro-

tect the river-mouth against sea-marauders, just as the later fort of Castelvolturno, on the same site, was a defence against Saracen raids. . . ."

[409C–D] *vicos Cancellum et Arnonum fuisse Casilinum* Cancello ed Arnone is today considered one site. Ancient Casilinum, known as the site of the battle in the second Punic War, was located where Arnone is today. B. places the site of ancient Casilinum at the small town of "Castellutium," location unknown to us. Worth summarizing here are Clavuot's comments on this identification (*Biondo's »Italia illustrata«*, 193 and n. 213), which provide a general analysis of B.'s method of identifying ancient with contemporary sites. In the case of his Castellutium-Casilinum identification, B. relies on the proof of phonetic similarity of the ancient and modern toponyms, and evidence from the literary tradition.

Clavuot (201) concludes that although we cannot in general be certain what manuscript of Livy B. used, his citations suggest he consulted a corrupt Italian ms. of the later 14th or 15th century; and, more specifically, that B.'s text for Livy's third decade goes back to a lost codex from the cathedral library at Chartres. In regard to this site, Clavuot states (192) that B. was misled by a corrupt passage in Livy into locating Casilinum (actually three miles from Castel Volturno) at the mouth of the Vulturnus river. This corrupt passage Clavuot refers to must be 25.20.2; however, B.'s problem is one not of corruption but of reading with erroneous punctuation:

> Capua a consulibus iterum summa vi obsideri coepta est, quaeque in eam rem opus erant comportabantur parabanturque. Casilinum frumentum convectum; ad Volturni ostium, ubi nunc urbs est, castellum communitum. . . .
>
> The consuls renewed the siege of Capua, and all things necessary for it were provided and brought together. The grain was stored at Casilinum; a fortress was set up at the mouth of the Vulturnus river, where there is a now a city. . . .

Immediately after this point, Conway and Walters infer a missing line; but this example of corruption is not needed to explain B.'s error here. B. neglected to punctuate after *convectum*, thus reading that Casilinum was at the mouth of the Vulturnus, whereas modern editors place a semicolon after *convectum*, sensibly considering the *urbs* to be Castel Volturno.

Stubbornly insisting on his identification, however, B. must then forestall the objection that few ancient ruins had been found in Castellutium, while a

good number had been found in Cancello ed Arnone nearby. In an argumentative maneuver fairly common for him, B. explains that Casilinum was a small city (clearly relying on Livy 23.17.12, *tam exigua moenia*) without extensive walls. Still trying to rationalize information from Livy, B. emphasizes Cancello ed Arnone's location more than three miles inland and thus the impossibility of considering them to be on the delta of the ancient Vulturnus. As often, B. sets aside archaeological evidence when it does not fit with his opinion. Clavuot describes B.'s methods of proof here as arbitrary, but credits him with breadth of argumentation and an attempt to connect arguments from topography and literature instead of viewing each in isolation.

[409D] *Petrus noster Candidus* Pier Candido Decembrio may have repeated the ancient identifications of this famous problem of the Campanian coast, its *importuosum litus*, in Livy 10.2.4; Tac. *Ann.* 4.67; and Pliny *Ep.* 6.31.17.

sed id unum in Casilini praeconium . . . ut salva fuerit ab Hannibale res Romana may be an allusion to Ennius, *Ann.* 370 Vahlen, *Unus homo nobis cunctando restituit rem*. The heading beside this fragment in Vahlen: PRAECONIA FABII MAXIMI. If these words are in the text which transmits this fragment of Ennius, B. would have just been reading about Fabius Maximus' leading troops on the ridges of Mt. Massicus; he has used *praeconium* in close conjunction with the statement that the *res Romana* had been made *salva*, a paraphrase of Ennius' tribute to Fabius; and this entire sentence is reminiscent of the tradition about Fabius Maximus. I have noted at least one other reminiscence of Ennius in *It. ill.*, *per ora virum volitare*, in B.'s commemoration of Bartolo da Sassoferrato **[337B]**.

[410D–E] *aucupium . . . apud Arnonum* B. mentioned birdcatching in his description of Neptunnium.

[410E] *falconis avis aereae et rapacissimae aucupium* This digression exemplifies B.'s methods of deduction and how seriously he took, in a typically humanist way, even ancient poetry as factual testimony. He bases his conclusion in an *argumentum ex silentio* from Pliny and Servius, and finds a confirmation in Virgil's description of the hunt of Dido and Aeneas, a literary passage not on the same factual level as the former authors.

[410E–F] *urbs Capua* Heurgon, *Capoue*, 441, summarizes Capua's advantages as vulnerabilities: location in the middle of a fertile plain, near a sea which made possible imports from Greece; but by virtue of these same

privileges, Capua was easily invaded because not defended by natural fortifications; and desirable prey to people from the less hospitable mountain regions.

[410F] *vetustae urbis fundamenta* ... Ancient Capua was an Oscan settlement, then became an Etruscan city in the second half of the sixth c. B.C. The Julian Law of 59 B.C. established a colony at Capua. Its site lies under the modern town of Sta. Maria Capua Vetere. B. foretells this evolution in his mention of the name of the church of Sta. Maria delle Grazie. This church may have given the name to the *borgo* of Sta. Maria Suricorum, which later evolved into Sta. Maria Maggiore and became, at the end of the mediaeval period, the site of the resurgence of Capua (cf. Heurgon, *Capoue*, 126). Nowhere in his discussion of Capua does B. mention the Seplasia, the famous quarter of the perfumesellers, which had already in antiquity (in the writings of Varro [*Sat. Men.* 7, 3], unknown to B., and Cicero, familiar to him) become synonymous with Capuan τρυφή. Cf. B.'s display of personal knowledge of the quarters of the city of Padua (**[382E]**; vol. 1, pp.196–198).

B. concludes this summary of Livy 23.1.5–2.1 and 23.18.9 with *exercitus ille Campanis emarcuit deliciis*, using a verb not found in Livy, and a rare, usually figurative, post-Augustan usage. Beyond this expression B. declines to summarize 23.18.10–16, Livy's moralizing description of the degenerate pleasures which supposedly destroyed the Carthaginians' hardness for battle; intent on quarrying Livy for topographical details, B. excludes consideration of the moralizing fundamental to the work of the man he ranks as the greatest ancient historiographer.

[410G–H] *Marcus autem Cicero cum legem agrariam supradictam dissuaderet* In his connection of citations from Livy with excerpts from Cicero's speeches *De lege agraria*, B. approaches most nearly to a moralizing comment on Capua and its reputation for luxury. Clavuot, *Biondo's »Italia illustrata«*, 104, accurately characterizes B.'s thought process in the connection between Capua's history in the second Punic War and the four citations from Cicero's speeches against establishment of a colony there: B. is progressing in an associative way, the common elements being the characteristic *arrogantia* and *luxuria*, rather than attempting a balanced historical account of the city. Clavuot compares B. in his procedure here to an artist cutting a silhouette from wood, creating a profile from salient features.

[411A] *rex Vandalorum Gensericus* In 456, as part of Genseric's and the Vandals' raids on Italy, facilitated by their recent occupation of North Africa, during which (455) they sacked Rome.

libro septimodecimo ... B. mentions Livy's book 17 as a source but appears to disregard the fundamental Pliny *NH* 18.109–114, especially 111.

pars eius quae Leboriae vocatur ... The Campi Leborini, according Pliny *NH* 18.111, were located between the roads from Capua to Puteoli and Capua to Cumae. This was the southern part of the *ager Campanus*, later called Terra di Lavoro, traditionally considered the most fertile area in Campania.

[411B] *a Tiphatis monte* In antiquity, the name Mons Tifata was a collective toponym designating the group of mountains now distinguished as Monte Tifata, Montevergine, and Monte Calvi.

[411C] *haec Atellanarum carminum lasciviam ... invenit.* Atella was an ancient Oscan-speaking town, near (south-east of), but not identical with, what is now Aversa. (B.'s identification of ancient Atella with modern Aversa may have stemmed in part from the use of building materials from ancient Atella in Aversa's religious buildings.) The *locus classicus* for the Atellan farce, a popular preliterary form of drama, Livy 7.2.12 distinguishes the Atellan as the fifth stage in the development of the *ludi scenici* which were instituted to appease the wrath of the gods manifested in a plague.

[411D] *Aversa* B.'s etymology, although picturesque, does not accord with conventional historical accounts, which credit Rainulf Drengot with the "foundation" of Aversa (in fact, a monument in Aversa commemorates Rainulf Drengot as founder); Rainulf was actually given Aversa by Duke Sergius IV of Naples, and Rainulf built its walls. Robert Guiscard arrived in Italy only in 1046, and the foundation of Aversa as the first Norman lordship in Italy is a major event attested as happening in 1030.

Vergilius Clanius non aequus Acerris B. cites Virgil, *Geo.* 2. 224–225,

> talem dives arat Capua et vicini Vesaevo
> ora iugo et vacuis Clanius non aequus Acerris.

The variant *Nola* for *ora* and its explanation are from Gellius 6.2.1 and Servius, *ad Geo.* 2.224 (Thilo-Hagen 3.1.2, 240). Gellius recalls finding in a commentary that *Nola* was what Virgil first wrote and recited; but that af-

terwards the poet asked the people of Nola for permission to lead off a watercourse onto his property. When the Nolans refused, the angry poet removed the name of their town from his poem and in its place inserted *ora*. Clavuot, *Biondo's »Italia illustrata«*, 235, attributes B.'s explanation to his reliance on Servius, *ad Geo.* 225, who comments that the Clanius flowed past Acerrae and weakened it with frequent flooding. The Clanius (Clanio Vecchio) is no longer visible, but its name is reflected in the local term "Regi Lagni" ("royal channels") for the canals built by the rulers ("regnanti"), starting in the sixteenth century, to drain the area. Frederiksen, *Campania* 20, comments on the innocuous appearance today of the Campanian rivers, which have shrunk so that none of them is navigable, and two are no longer recognizable as rivers at all. It is therefore difficult to appreciate the problems that they presented to the ancient inhabitants of the area.

[412E] *in ruinis Linterni Scipionis Africani villae aedificata.* B.'s description of Liternum is an important example of his argument from both ancient sources and direct observation for the identification of an ancient site. For this reason, it is the methodological centerpiece of "Campania." But his erroneous reading of Livy 22.16.4 causes him to isolate this passage as differing to other sources in locating the site of ancient Liternum on the north side of the Volturno river. Because B. reads, in the description of Hannibal's plight, *inter fortunae minas ac Linterni arenas per horrida situ* (the reading of P) he places Liternum *ad Falerni agri partem*. Modern (and better) texts read *Inter Formiana saxa ac Literni arenas stagnaque et per horrida silvas*. Fortunately this is not an instance in which B. blindly follows a mistaken reading to insist on an erroneous conclusion. The preponderance of sources combine with his personal observation to direct him to the correct conclusion about the location of ancient Liternum. As Clavuot (*Biondos »Italia illustrata«*, 165) notes, B. relies on the lists of the geographers (e.g., Mela 2.4.70; Pliny, *NH* 3.61), who place Liternum between Vulturnum and Cumae. Although Petrarch had in 1343 met with frustration due to the inhospitable terrain in his attempt to visit the tomb of Scipio Africanus (hero of his epic *Africa*), B. does not allude to his predecessor's account.

Now located near the modern Lago di Patria, what had for centuries been pointed out as the burial monument of Scipio at Liternum is recognized today as an altar at the site of the ancient forum of an imperial town (covered in sand dunes, then destroyed in the seventeenth to eighteenth centuries). Here Scipio retired to avoid the continuous charges in the 180s against his

brother Lucius and himself of financial misconduct in Asia; cf. Livy 38.52.1, *Postquam cum invidiam et certamina cum tribunis prospiceret . . . in Literninum concessit.* Persistent local tradition has it that this area was named "Patria" after Scipio's defiant rejection of burial at Rome, *ingrata patria ne ossa quidem mea habes* (Valerius Maximus 2.10.2); the name Patria seems to have been mentioned in the sixth c. A.D. Cf. Frederiksen, *Campania*, 71, "To the north of Cumae there now lies the large sand-locked lagoon of the Lago di Patria, yet in ancient times, before the formation of the sandbar, this was an open and probably marshy bay. . . ." Lago di Patria was previously a swamp called Palus Liternia, and modern geology confirms B.'s description of the fifteenth-century site as marshy and sandy, as does the toponym "Arenata di Patria" used of a part of the left shore of the Lago di Patria. Seneca, *Ep.* 51 cited here by B., confirms the difficulty of the terrain: *Severior loci disciplina firmat ingenium aptumque magnis conatibus reddit. Literni honestius Scipio quam Bais exulabat: ruina eiusmodi non est tam molliter conlocanda.* Like the area around Ferrara in north-central Italy, the modern history of this area has been in large part determined by the success or failure of reclamation projects, which have over the years drained the marshes marking the course of the ancient Clanius. In the matter of Liternum, B.'s use of Livy as a reliable source for topographical identification, in combination with personal observation, stands him in good stead. At 38.32, *ipsi vidimus*, we find a rare instance of Livy's own recounting of direct observation of a site. Livy says that he has seen the tomb of Scipio and the statue on top of it, which had already been damaged by weather. B. also noticed, in confirmation of his identification of the site of Scipio's villa, the sour-tasting spring (*fons acidula*) mentioned by Pliny as near the site of the villa and the tomb of Scipio (*NH* 14.14). From Pliny's description arose the popular toponym "la fonte di Scipione." Cf. Vitruvius 8.3.20, *eam aquam sine vino potantes fiunt temulenti.*

[412H] *villa . . . Servilii Vatiae* This villa has been located on a small promontory south of Lago di Fusaro, next to the present Torregaveta. See Mariarosaria Borriello and Antonio d'Ambrosio, *Baiae-Misenum* (Forma Italiae, Regio I, v. 14 [Florence: Olschki, 1979]), 166. B. misunderstands the import of Seneca's comment, *Ep.* 55. 3–4, *Nam quotiens aliquos amicitiae Asinii Galli, quotiens Seiani odium deinde amor merserat (aeque enim offendisse illum quam amasse periculosum fuit), exclamabant homines, "o Vatia, solus scis vivere."* B.'s characterization of Seneca's examples as *occu-*

pati does not quite do justice to Seneca's point: those who have been involved in politics in dangerous times, and ruined by dangerous associations, recall enviously Vatia's detachment from politics.

[412H–418G] **The Campi Phlegraei**. At this point B. begins an expanded treatment, marked, as was his description of Liternum, by evidence of his direct observation of the area. Clavuot, *Biondo's »Italia illustrata«*, 196, interprets B.'s treatment of the famous area as an attempt to bring his personal observations into accord with the testimony of ancient authors. Here he follows in general the emphasis of humanists, even of Petrarch, in their interest in the sites of ancient Cumae (Cuma), Mt. Misenum (Miseno), Baiae (Baia), Puteoli (Pozzuoli), and Neapolis (Naples); with Liternum, B.'s discussion of these sites is among the most extensive in *It. ill.* Boccaccio, too, has the hero of *Filocolo* visit the Campi Phlegraei: sites he visits in common with B.'s treatment are Puteoli, Baiae, the grotto of the Sibyl, Mt. Misenum, Lake Avernus, the Piscina Mirabilis, the baths at Tritoli, and the temple of Apollo. Ancient testimony describing these sites combined with impressive remains still visible to early modern times created awareness among humanists of their importance in antiquity and their evocative effect on the emotions. Noticeable is B.'s interspersing of citations from Livy, his most frequently-cited source in *It. ill.,* with descriptions of the sites of the Campi Phlegraei from many other ancients, in particular Suetonius' biographies of the emperors.

Cumae The foundation of Cumae probably by colonists from Kyme in Chalcis in Euboea, around 740 B.C. Although B. cites only Livy (8.22.6), Strabo E.4.4 is also an important source.

[413A] *Arces quibus altus Apollo praesidet*... Virgil, *Aen.* 6.9–10:

> At pius Aeneas arces quibus altus Apollo
> praesidet horrendaeque procul secreta Sibyllae.

pinnae cernuntur murorum excelsae. B. stays within the Virgilian context by using *pinnae* for battlements or walls; cf. *Aen.* 7.158–159:

> . . . primasque in litore sedes
> castrorum in morem pinnis atque aggere cingit . . .

The context is a description of Aeneas at the site of Rome marking his walls for his fort with a shallow trench, then putting up earthworks with battlements, like a camp, their first settlement on the shore.

antrum Sibyllae B. seems to have anticipated Maiuri's identification of the cave of the Sibyl with the "long, trapezoidal gallery that runs along the western side of the hill . . . the actual site of her cave . . . remains uncertain . . ." (Frederiksen, *Campania,* 76).

Prosper Camuleius One of the few mentions in "Campania" of contemporary humanists, so prominent a feature of B.'s chapters on regions in northern and central Italy. Unfortunately, this person cannot be securely identified; Clavuot, *Biondo's »Italia illustrata«*, 50 n. 90, notes that this excursion likely took place on the occasion of B.'s visit to Naples early in 1452; and that it is unclear whether B. intends to name Prospero Camogli, secretary to the Duke of Milan, or Prospero Schiaffino da Camogli.

[413A–B] *Hamarum locus sacer* A federal cult was centred at Hamae. Frederiksen, *Campania*, 33, identifies the site with the modern Torre San Severino.

Tripergula The medieval village of Tripergola continued the tradition of baths and later evolved into a social point for the Aragonese court. See Fikret K. Yegül, "The Thermo-Mineral Complex at Baiae and De Balneis Puteolanis," *Art Bulletin* 78.1 (1996) 137–161, 148: "In 1298, Charles II founded a hospital for hydrotherapy at the village of Triepergula (Tripergole) near Lake Avernus . . ." B. was probably one of the last antiquarians to inspect the ancient baths of Tripergola, for not long after his generation, in 1538, they were destroyed by the eruption and formation of Monte Nuovo; see Antonio Scherillo "Vulcanismo e Bradisismo nei Campi Flegrei," *I Campi Flegrei nell'archeologia e nella storia* (Rome: Accademia nazionale dei Lincei, 1977), 81–116; 96.

[413C] Baiae.

For the ruins B. describes at Baiae in general, see Borriello and d'Ambrosio, *Baiae-Misenum*. B. cites semi-accurately Horace, *Epistle* 1.1.83, but shows little understanding of its meaning or context.

> "Nullus in orbe sinus Bais praelucet amoenis"
> si dixit dives, lacus et mare sentit amorem. . . .
> If a rich man has said, "No bay in the world outshines pleasant
> Baiae," the lake and sea feel the heat of his love. . . .

The variability of human interests is Horace's topic; he goes on to describe the rich man ordering his workmen to Teanum (inland, about 30 miles north of Baiae, and thus a contrast) the day after he has employed them to work on his villa at Baiae. B. misunderstands the line as Horace's own praise of Baiae, whereas it illustrates not the absolute supremacy of Baiae among seacoast resorts, but the fickleness of human preferences; Baiae is simply a well-known example of a type of place.

Mare . . . vix tria milia passuum et sexcentos ex Suetonii Tranquilli in vita Caii Caligulae sententia . . . B. cites here, and below at **[414H]** *Caligula* 19.1; he seems to find Misenum and Baiae interchangeable as end points for measuring the width of the Bay of Baia to Pozzuoli. The text of Suetonius: *Baiarum medium intervallum ad Puteolanas moles, trium milium et sescentorum fere passuum spatium.*

[413B–D] *Misenum* The area around the village of Misenum was developed by the Romans as a result of their predilection for seaside vacation amenities and Augustus' basing the fleet there. The Piscina Mirabilis accurately described by B. (but mistakenly identified with the Villa of Lucullus; see Clavuot, *Biondo's »Italia illustrata«*, 195–196) was the water-supply for the colony; its site correlates with the modern Bacoli. Cf. Velleius 2.81.2 for an account of the development under Augustus of naval bases at Misenum and Portus Iulius.

[413C] *Baiae . . . civitas opulenta* B. obviously observed the topography and investigated the ruins of the entire region of the Bay of Baia. Clavuot, *Biondo's »Italia illustrata«*, 196, emphasizes how here, more than in most of the other descriptions in *It. ill.*, B. strives to conform his personal impressions to the literary tradition.

[413D] *Et quia in loco* . . . P. C. Decembrio's translation of Plutarch's *Life* of Lucullus is a likely Latin source for B.'s rendition of this anecdote.

[414E] *continuatam . . . urbem* Cf. **[310H]**, the amplification of Ocriculum, with the same expression, the trope of the city's appearing to continue beyond its limits due to the grandeur of the architecture in the outlying areas.

fabrefecerit a very rare word.

[414G] *Lucrinus, de quo in Virgiliani versus expositione* . . . B. refers here to Virgil, *Geo.* 2.161–164:

Plate VII. Projection of Lacus Lucrinus and Portus Iulius in antiquity. Reproduced from M. W. Fredericksen, *Campania* (British School at Rome, 1984) by permission of Dr. Nicholas Purcell.

an memorem portus Lucrinoque addita claustra
atque indignatum magnis stridoribus aequor,
Iuliaque ponto longe sonat unda refuso
Tyrrhenusque fretis immittitur aestus Avernis?

Or should I tell of the harbours and the barriers at Lucrinus, and the angry seething of the sea, where the Julian wave crashes as it is pushed back and the Tyrrhenian Sea is let in to Lake Avernus?

B. cites Virgil in reference to the constructions of Agrippa in 37 B.C., man-made barriers placed between Lake Lucrinus and the sea, and a shipping channel cut through them. A channel was also cut to connect Lake Lucrinus and Lake Avernus. The phenomenon of bradyseism, in this case a slow sinking of the land on the coast, caused the submersion of the piers of the structures forming the sides of this navigable canal. For Lucrinus, Portus Iulius, and Avernus, see Plate VII.

Portum Iulium Suetonius, *Aug.* 16. The Portus Iulius was the naval port constructed in Lake Avernus by Agrippa in 37 B.C.

Avernus The information that birds fell dead if they flew over this lake goes back to Hellenistic sources. Strabo mentions it disbelievingly as a fiction (E.4.5) purveyed by local inhabitants. But B. accepted the idea, and even reported at **[311C–D]** that he and Prospero Colonna witnessed at Anzio this phenomenon which, according to modern geology, is possible given the production of anhydride sulfates from mephitic pools.

[414H] "*Acheronte refuso*" Virgil, *Aen.* 6.107, in the description of the underworld, the dark swamp created by Acheron's flooding:

. . . hic inferni ianua regis
dicitur et tenebrosa palus Acheronte refuso, ...

Bauli At Bauli, attested in a long list of ancient sources, Hercules was said to have shut up the cattle taken from the giant Geryon in Spain. The proposed identification of Bauli with modern Bacoli has not been universally accepted.

[415C–D] *Livius in quarto* This is actually Livy 24.7.10–11.

Puteoli In general, B. seems oblivious to the significance of ancient Puteoli, which grew from a colony established in 194 B.C. to one of the largest and

most famous towns in Italy, due in great part to the importance of its port, which replaced that of Cumae.

[416E] *ea est cuius ruinae ingentes balneo supereminent Agnani dicto* . . . B. identifies Agnano as the site of the villa of Lucullus. Varro *d. r. r.* III. 17.9 and Pliny *NH* IX, 54 refer to Lucullus' construction of a canal which joined with the sea the *piscinae* of his villa. Great baths existed here, still reported in late antiquity, and were erroneously thought to be the ruins of the villa of Lucullus. B. transmitted the tradition, and Leandro Alberti followed him, that the lake of Agnano was identical with these *piscinae*.

[416F] *Sequitur Neapolis* . . . Seneca *Ep.* 57. The Crypta Neapolitana, dug in the first century B.C., is still visitable in the Parco Virgiliano. It connected Naples and Puteoli.

Livius in octavo . . . Livy 8.22.5. Except for the transposition of *procul* and *inde*, B. finds Livy's description apt for his own time, as Naples, unlike many smaller Italian towns of the seacoast, had (and has) not changed its location.

quod sepulcrum nequivimus invenire . . . Local tradition persists in the name "tomba di Virgilio" (qualified in more reliable guidebooks by "cosidetta") for an Augustan *columbarium*, or niche for a cinerary urn. Donatus' biography of Virgil is the source for the story that Virgil's ashes were taken to Naples, where they were placed in a tomb on the Via Puteolana at a point between the first and second milestones; Statius, *Silvae* IV.54–5, records his visit to the tomb. But Petrarch (*Itinerarium Syriacum*) is B.'s likely source, as Petrarch, like B., refers to the tomb in connection with the *crypta puteolana*.

[416G] A series of errors in the location of passages in Livy. First, *Ipse per agrum Campanum* is 23.1.5–6. *Hannibal Capua recepta* is Livy 23.14.5–6.

Et infra, quarto As this citation is Livy 24.13.7, B. must have intended *vigesimo quarto*.

[416H] *Franciscus quoque Petrarcha* Petrarch was examined by King Robert d'Anjou at Naples for his coronation (1341) on the Campidoglio at Rome. A fuller picture of the relationship and activities of Petrarch and King Robert is desirable, but unlikely due to the lack of new evidence. Petrarch's interest in geography is clear from his treatise *Itinerarium Syriacum* (1358). From B.'s reference to the map made by the two, some have deduced the existence

within the *cenacolo* around King Robert of a group of cartographers, or proto-humanists interested in cartography. (But see J. d'Amato, "Cicero's Villa in the Phlegraean Fields," *Viator* 24 (1993): 385–419, 395; apropos of King Robert the Wise, "Conforming to conventional methodology, scholars still maintained an approach that centred on literary rather than archaeological evidence or direct observation.") The most detailed case for this interest is made by Degenhart and Schmitt, "Marino Sanudo und Paolino Veneto," on which see my fuller comments above in the introduction to the commentary on "Campania."

[416H] *Servius in Virgiliani versus expositione . . . abibis Oebale* Virgil, *Aen.* 7.733–735:

> Nec tu carminibus nostris indictus abibis,
> Oebale, quem generasse Telon Sebethide nympha
> fertur, Teleboum Capreas cum regna teneret. . . .

The stream Sebethus at Naples was named for the river god Sebethus; his daughter, the nymph Sebethis, was mother of Oebalus, whose band of warriors Virgil describes as augmenting the forces of the Italians.

[417D] *Castellum Novum* The Castel Nuovo, the most important secular building of the Angevin and Aragonese city. On the site of the Angevin building of the 13th century, which had been nearly destroyed by disasters, Alfonso I of Aragon decreed in 1443 the restoration of the palace in the context of a fortress. The Catalan architect Guillermo Sagrera had charge of the renovations (1449–1450). At the back (west) entrance is the triumphal arch of Alfonso I which celebrated his entrance into Naples in 1443, as well as providing access to the city. Despite his two flattering mentions of Alfonso's triumph B. cannot mention this arch, which was built between 1453–1468 and thus postdated the first publication of *It. ill.*

[418G] *Vesevum vero montem . . . nunc appellant summum. . . .* In the 17th century Vesuvius was still known by the name "la montagna di Somma." Cf. Frederiksen, *Campania*, 12, ". . . by observing scrupulously the stratification of small and large *lapilli*, and by examining their chemical composition, studies have supported the older view that what we now know as the peak of Vesuvius was non-existent or small in antiquity, and that the main volcano was contained in the crater of Monte Somma." The peak at the left is Monte Somma, the cone on the right Vesuvius itself (the only active crater in recorded historical times).

[418H] *Talem dives arat . . . Geo.* 2.224–225; cf. on **[411D]** above.

[419A] *Vulturnum superius omissa repetenda sunt.* B. has described the towns and cities along the greater part of the east-to-west (middle) section of the Volturno river; now he turns to the north-to-south (upper) section, where the Volturno makes a right-angled bend and a junction with the Calore near Telesia. In this first part of B.'s treatment of the areas along the Volturno in Abruzzo, the areas defined by the course of the Volturno correspond to the ancient land of the Caudini, western Samnium, "among the mountains that ringed the plain of Campania (the Mons Taburnus and the Monti Trebulani) and in the valley of the River Isclero and the middle reaches of the Volturnus" (Salmon, *Samnium*, 46).

Isclerus An ancient equivalent for this river's name is unknown.

Mons nunc Tabor, olim Taburnus . . . quem Servius Virgilium in Georgicis exponens . . . Geo. 2.38:

> . . . iuvat Ismara Baccho
> conserere atque olea magnum vestire Taburnum.

Cf. Wilkinson *ad* 2.38 who notes Virgil's inclination to couple places in the Greek world famous in myth, song, or history with familiar Italian places.

Virgilii Aeneidos XII Ac velut ingenti Sila summove Taburno, This is *Aen.* 12.715–719:

> ac velut ingenti Sila summove Taburno
> cum duo conversis inimica in proelia tauri
> frontibus incurrunt, pavidi cessere magistri,
> stat pecus omne metu mutum, mussantque iuvencae
> quis nemori imperitet, quem tota armenta sequantur.

Gambi's remark is appropriate here, ("Cosa era la Padusa," 6, apropos of Virgil *Aen.* 9.680, *sive Padi ripis Athesim seu propter amoenum* [cf. **[375C]**, vol. 1, p. 170 on the Athesis [Adige] river), that Virgil's use of two toponyms in his similes is in the Alexandrian tradition and taste for variety (the Sila mountains are actually in Bruttium). B. takes literally and seriously ancient authors' uses of toponyms as strictly accurate evidence for location and geographical proximity.

[419D] *Sulla Nolam* B. actually summarizes part of *Periochae* 86, (Rossbach p. 93), *Sylla Nolam in Samnio recepit. XLVII legiones <in> agros captos deduxit, et eos his divisit.*

[420E] *nocturnae aurae editor a Lucano appellatus* B. is in error: it is the Vulturnus, not the Sarnus, to which Lucan refers in 2.423.

Livius libro XXII Again B. is off; the reference in Livy is to 27.3.

Virgilius … et qua rigat oppida Sarnus The modern Sarno still flows between Naples and Salerno. B. is obviously citing from memory here Virgil, *Aen.* 7.738, naming the people named after this river: *Sarastis populos et quae rigat aequora Sarnus.*

[420F] *Amalphim civitatem … spoliasse* Clavuot, *Biondo's »Italia illustrata«*, 203, corrects B.'s information: Amalfi existed as early as the sixth c., and was sacked during the Italian campaigns of Lothar of Supplinberg (1125–1137).

Fourteenth Region, Puglia
Commentary

The region of Puglia, the fourteenth and briefest of the eighteen projected regions, is incomplete and its brevity betrays shows both Biondo's haste to finish the work and his unfamiliarity with the region. Biondo broke off the work on his historical topography with its premature publication, ostensibly to forestall the appearance of a plagiarized copy which an enemy in the Curia was about to publish. His unfulfilled promise to describe the coast of Puglia **[422H]** after the description of Mte. Gargano indicates that he did not have time to complete even the brief treatment he had envisioned for this region. See Clavuot, *Biondos »Italia illustrata«*, 51–52, who suspects that, while there is no need to disbelieve Biondo's claim, other motives may also have operated to cause the premature publication of the incomplete work: by 1453 Biondo's interest was occupied with the Turkish threat and work on *Roma triumphans*; discouraged, he was probably glad to leave off work on the portion of the treatise which treated southern Italy, because he had not received from Alfonso I the hoped-for materials (history, topographical description, and a map) which he had requested. Nor had Biondo traveled extensively in the region, so he could not describe it from personal observation.

Pliny includes Apulia in the second Augustan region, "Apulia et Calabria" and Biondo follows the Augustan demarcation of the Tifernus River as the northern boundary, although Apulia had by Biondo's time extended to cover part of the area known in classical antiquity as Calabria. It is likely that Biondo resorts to Ptolemy for a description of the region in terms of its native populations because Pliny is not much help in defining the boundaries of the region.

[421A] "*Diomedis ad urbem*" B. has greatly abbreviated Servius's explanation *ad Aen.* 8.9, *mittitur et magni Venulus Diomedis ad urbem*.

[421C] *Livius libro viginti duo* . . . An example of B.'s extreme abbreviation of a literary source in order to sift out and retain only topographical informa-

tion, with the result that the excerpt makes little sense. Livy 22.18.7–8 reads in Walters and Conway's Oxford text: *Ex Paelignis Poenus flexit iter retroque Apuliam repetens Gereonium pervenit, urbem metu, quia conlapsa ruinis pars moenium erat, ab suis desertam; dictator in Larinate agro castrum communivit.*

> Hannibal next changed direction out of the territory of the Peligni, and returning into Apulia reached Gereonium, a town abandoned as unsafe by its inhabitants, as part of its walls had collapsed. The dictator fortified a position for a camp, near Larinum.

The name of the town is vexed. B. reads *Galeranum*; Walters and Conway adopt Alschefski's emendation *Gereonium.* Long after B. read this passage, Sigonius interpolated *Gerunium* from Polybius (3.100.1). In addition, B. adds *ad* before *urbem*, and omitting the detail of the city's desertion joins this phrase with the element of Fabius's making camp, thereby causing redundancy with *ad urbem* and *in Larinate agro*.

[421C] *Neapolitani oratores venerunt Romam.* Cf. Clavuot, *Biondo's »Italia illustrata«*, 202 n. 6: the different traditions in the mss. of Livy that B. (and Lorenzo Valla) were working with are apparent in B.'s variant in citing Livy 22.32.4, *oratores*, instead of *legati*, read by Valla (*Antidotum in Facium* 4.5.21), the main textual tradition, and modern editors.

[421D] *Garganus mons* The sanctuary of St. Michael Archangel who, according to legend, at the end of the fifth century appeared to rescue the city of Siponto from barbarian attack. The sanctuary was destroyed and rebuilt several times in the medieval period, then became a stronghold of the Latin church, and then of the Normans, against the Byzantine Empire. After the Normans took it over, it became a famous destination for pilgrimages.

[422E] *Tirium* Modern Rodi; it is actually Pliny's Vria (*NH* 3.103).

[422F] *Diomedum ferunt deificatum* . . . Tradition told that the deified Diomedes was buried on the island named after him; his companions, changed into birds, receive peacefully any Greek or descendant of Greeks, but attack all other strangers. B. relates this from Augustine, *De Civitate Dei* 18.16.9–12, 15–23. Marine birds of the stormy petrel type are still called "le Diomedee."

Central and Southern Italy
Bibliography

(For full bibliographical entries of items cited in Volume 2 which were previously cited in the Introduction and Commentary to Volume 1, the reader should consult the Bibliography to Volume 1.)

PRIMARY SOURCES

Annali Aretini (1192–1343). In Bini, Arturo, Giovanni Grazzini, and Pasqui Ubaldo, edd., *Annali Aretini Documenti per la storia della Città di Arezzo*, v. 4. Arezzo: Bellotti, 1904.

Biondo Flavio. *Italy Illuminated.* Edited and translated by Jeffrey A. White. The I Tatti Renaissance Library. Cambridge, MA: Harvard University Press, 2005.

Cuntz, Otto. *Itineraria Romana*. Leipzig: Teubner 1929. Volume I: *Itineraria Antonini Augusti et Burdigalese*.

Cyriac of Ancona. *Cyriac of Ancona: Later Travels*. Edited and translated by E. Bodnar with Clive Foss. Cambridge, MA: Harvard University Press, 2003.

Ennius. *Ennianae poesis Reliquiae*. Edited by J. Vahlen. Amsterdam, 1967.

Livius. *Ab urbe condita libri*. Pars 4. Periochae. Edited by O. Rossbach. Stuttgart: Teubner, 1972.

Pliny the Elder. *Pline l'Ancien Histoire Naturelle Livre III*. Edited and translated by Hubert Zehnacker. Paris: Société d'Édition »Les Belles Lettres«, 1998.

Ranzano, Pietro. *Descriptio totius Italiae* (*Annales, XIV–XV*). Edited by Adele di Lorenzo, Bruno Figliuolo, and Paolo Pontari. Florence: Sismel, 2007.

Servius. *Servii Grammatici qui feruntur in Vergilii carmina commentarii*. Edited by Georg Thilo and Herman Hagen. Hildesheim: Olms, 1961.

Strabo. *Strabonis Geographica.* Vol. II, books III–VI. Edited by F. Sbordone. Rome 1970.

Valerius Maximus. *Factorum et dictorum memorabilium libri novem.* Edited by C. Kempf. Berlin 1854. Reprint 1976 Hildesheim & New York: Georg Olms.

BOOKS

Annechino, Raimondo. *Agnano: L'origine del nome e del Lago.* Collezioncina flegrea no. 7. Naples: Tipografia unione, 1931.

Barraclough, Geoffrey. *The Medieval Papacy.* Harcourt, Brace & World, 1968.

Bentley, Jerry H. *Politics and Culture in Renaissance Naples.* Princeton: Princeton University Press, 1987.

Cameron, Alan. *Claudian: Poetry and Propaganda at the Court of Honorius.* Oxford: Clarendon Press, 1970.

Cammarosano, Paolo. *Storia dell'Italia medievale: Dal VI all'XI secolo.* Bari: Laterza, 2001.

De Marchi, Andrea. *Gentile da Fabriano: Un viaggio nella pittura italiana alla fine del gotico.* Milan: Federico Motta Editore, 1992.

DeVoti, Luigi. *Splendori dei castelli Romani: Espressioni artistiche dal secolo XVII al secolo XX.* Velletri: Edizioni tra 8 e 9, 1992.

Droandi, Enzo. *Guido Tarlati di Pietramala, Ultimo Principe di Arezzo.* Cortona: Calosci, 1993.

Franchetti Pardo, V. *Arezzo.* Le città nella storia d'Italia. Rome and Bari: Laterza, 1986.

Frederiksen, M. W. *Campania.* Edited by Nicholas Purcell. London: British School at Rome, 1984.

Gordan, Phyllis Walter Goodhart. *Two Renaissance Book Hunters: The Letters of Poggius Bracciolini to Nicolaus De Niccolis.* New York: Columbia University Press, 1991.

Gothein, Everardo. *Il Rinascimento nell'Italia Meridionale.* Florence: Sansoni, 1915.

Grafton, Anthony. *Leon Battista Alberti: Master Builder of the Italian Renaissance.* New York: Hill and Wang, 2000.

———. *What Was History? The Art of History in Early Modern Europe.* Cambridge: Cambridge University Press, 2007.

Grendler, Paul F. *Schooling in Renaissance Italy: Literacy and Learning 1300–1600*. Baltimore and London: Johns Hopkins University Press, 1989.

Hermansen, Gustav. *Ostia: Aspects of Roman City Life*. Edmonton, Alta.: University of Alberta Press, 1981.

Heurgon, J. *Recherches sur l'histoire, la Religion et la Civilisation de Capoue Préromaine*. Bibliothèque des Écoles Françaises d'Athènes et de Rome 154 . Paris: Boccard, 1942.

Husslein, J. C. *Flavio Biondo als Geograph des Frühhumanismus*. Würzburg, 1901.

Kidwell, Carol. *Pontano: Poet and Prime Minister*. London: Duckworth, 1991.

Lancellotti, Francesco. *Dizionario Storico degli uomini illustri di Ancona*. Fermo, 1796. Reprinted 1983 Arnaldo Forni.

Loud, G. A. *The Age of Robert Guiscard: Southern Italy and the Norman Conquest*. Essex, UK: Pearson Education, 2000.

Mack, Charles R. *Pienza: The Creation of a Renaissance City*. Ithaca, NY: Cornell University Press, 1987.

Maiuri, Amedeo. *The Phlegraean Fields: From Virgil's Tomb to the Grotto of the Cumaean Sibyl*. Translated by V. Priestley. Rome: Istituto poligrafico dello stato, 1937.

Meiggs, Russell. *Roman Ostia*. 2nd ed. Oxford: Clarendon Press, 1973.

Miller, Konrad. *Itineraria Romana: Römische Reisewege an den Hand der Tabula Peutingeriana*. Rome: L'Erma di Bretschneider, 1964.

Morghen, Raffaello. *Bonifacio VIII e il Giubileo del 1300 nella storiografia moderna*. Quaderni della fondazione Camillo Caetani. Roma: Edizioni dell'elefante, 1975.

Richardson Jr., L. *A New Topographical Dictionary of Ancient Rome*. Baltimore and London: Johns Hopkins University Press, 1992.

Salmon, E. T. *Samnium and the Samnites*. Cambridge: Cambridge University Press, 1967.

Sherwin-White, A. N. *The Letters of Pliny: A Historical and Social Commentary*. Oxford: Oxford University Press, 1966.

Smith, Denis Mack. *Medieval Sicily 800–1713*. Volume 2 of M. I. Finley and D. Mack Smith, *A History of Sicily*. London: Chatto and Windus, 1968.

Tarassi, Massimo. *Incisa in Val d'Arno: Storia di una società e di un territorio nella campagna fiorentina*. Florence: Salimbeni, 1985.

Tomassetti, G. *La Campagna Romana.* 7 vols. Volume 4, Via Latina. 2nd ed. Edited by Luisa Chiumenti and Fernando Bilancia. Florence: Olschki, 1979.

Touring Club Italiano. *Abruzzo e Molise.* 4th ed. Milan: Centro Grafico Ambrosiano, 1979.

———. *Basilicata Calabria.* 4th ed. Milan: Centro Grafico Linate, 1980.

———. *Campania.* Milan: Centro Grafico Linate, 1981.

———. *Lazio.* Milan: Centro Grafico Ambrosiano, 1981.

———. *Marche.* Milan: Centra Grafico Linate, 1979.

———. *Napoli e Dintorni.* Milan: Centro Grafico Ambrosiano, 2001.

———. *Puglia.* Milan: Centro Grafico Linate, 1978.

———. *Umbria.* Milan: Centro Grafico Linate, 1978.

Uccelli, G. *Le Navi di Nemi.* Rome, 1927.

ARTICLES

Alfieri, Nereo. "La Battaglia del Metauro (207 a.C.)." *Picus* 8 (1988): 7–35.

———. "Le Marche e la fine del mondo antico." 9–34 in *Istituzioni e società nell'alto medioevo marchigiano.* Atti del Convegno, Ancona-Osimo-Jesi, 17–20 ottobre 1981. Ancona 1983.

Boskovits, M. "Giotto di Bondone." *DBI* 55 (2000): 401–423.

Calasso, F. "Bartolo da Sassoferrato." *DBI* 6 (1964): 640–669.

Cherici, Armando. "Arretium." *JAT* (*Journal of Ancient Topography*) 7 (1997): 77–128.

Clavuot, Ottavio. "Flavio Biondo's »Italia illustrata«: Porträt und historisch-geographische Legitimation der humanistischen Elite Italiens." 55–75 in *Diffusion des Humanismus: Studien zur nationalen Geschichtsschreibung europäischer Humanisten*, edited by J. Helmrath et al. Göttingen: Wallstein Verlag, 2002.

———. "Italien entdeckt sich selbst- Über die historischen und antiquarischen Studien des Biondo Flavio (1392–1463)." 145–159 in *Feconde venner le carte: Studi in Onore di Ottavio Besomi.* Bellinzona: Casagrande, 1997.

D'Addario, A. "Acciaiuoli, Agnolo." *DBI* 1 (1960): 77.

D'Amato, Jean. "Cicero's Villa in the Phlegraean Fields." *Viator* 24 (1993): 385–419.

D'Amelio, G. "Castro, Paolo di." *DBI* 22 (1979): 227–233.

Dykmans, M. "Conti, Lucido." *DBI* 28 (1983): 449–451.
Falaschi, P. L. "Fortebraccio, Andrea." *DBI* 49 (1997): 117–127.
Fiorelli, P. "Accorso." *DBI* 1 (1960): 116–121.
Hyman, I. "Brunelleschi, Filippo." *DBI* 14 (1972): 534–545.
Lugli, G. "La Villa Sabina di Orazio." *Monumenti Antichi* 31 (1926): 458–598.
Mack, C. R. "The Bath Palace of Pope Nicholas V at Viterbo." In *An Architectural Progress in the Renaissance and Baroque.* Edited by H. Millon and S. Munshower, 100–119. Papers in Art History VIII. University Park: The Pennsylvania State University, 1992.
———. "The Wanton Habits of Venus: Pleasure and Pain at the Renaissance Spa." *Explorations in Renaissance Culture* 26 no. 2 (2000). 257–276.
Mallett, M. E. "Conti, Giovanni." *DBI* 28 (1983): 415–417.
Mazzarino, S. "La regione umbra nella cultura romana." 227–247 in *Problemi di Storia e Archeologia dell'Umbria.* Atti del I convegno di studi Umbri. Gubbio, 1964.
Monfasani, John. "The Fraticelli and Clerical Wealth in Quattrocento Rome." 177–195 in *Renaissance Society and Culture; Essays in Honor of Eugene F. Rice, Jr.* Edited by John Monfasani and Ronald G. Musto. New York: Italica Press, 1991.
Paci, Gianfranco. "Schede per l'identificazione di antichi predii in area Picena." 163–198 in Janni, Pietro and Eugenio Lanzillotta, edd., ΓΕΩΓΡΑΦΙΑ. Atti del secondo Convegno Maceratese su Geografia e Cartografia Antica. Rome: Bretschneider, 1988.
Pellegrini, Giovan Battista. "Appunti di Toponomastica Marchigiana," *Atti e Memorie Istituzioni e Società nell'Alto medioevo Marchigiano* 86 (1981) Pt. 1. Atti del Convegno. Ancona: Deputazione di Storia Patria per le Marche, 1983: 217–300.
Petrucci, F. "Colonna, Antonio." *DBI* 27 (1982): 267–270.
Pignatti, F. "Fiocchi, Andrea." *DBI* 48 (1997): 80–81.
Pontari, P. "Gli artisti nel Catalogus Virorum Illustrium dell' Italia illustrata di Biondo Flavio." *Letteratura e Arte* 1 (2003): 80–110.
Rao, Ennio. "Alfonso of Aragon and the Italian Humanists." *Esperienze Letterarie* 4 (1979): 43–57.
Scherillo, Antonio. "Vulcanismo e Bradisismo nei Campi Flegrei." 81–116 in *I Campi Flegrei nell'archeologia e nella storia.* Rome: Accademia nazionale dei Lincei, 1977.

Strnad, A. A. "Capranica, Angelo." *DBI* 19 (1976): 143–146.

———. "Capranica, Domenico." *DBI* 19 (1976): 147–153.

Sassi, Romualdo. *Documenti sul soggiorno a Fabriano di Nicolò V e della sua corte nel 1449 e nel 1450*. Ancona: Deputazione di Storia Patria per le Marche, 1955.

von Falkenhausen, Vera. "Rocca Niceforo: Un Castello Normanno in Calabria." *Bollettino della badia greca di Grottaferrata* N.S. 54 (2000): 227–237.

Ward-Perkins, B. "Luni: The Decline and Abandonment of a Roman Town." *Papers in Italian Archaeology* 1 pt. 2 (1978): 313–321.

Weiss, Roberto. "Iacopo Angeli da Scarperia (c. 1360–1410–11)." In *Medioevo e Rinascimento: Studi in onore di Bruno Nardi* II, 803–817. Florence, 1955. Reprinted in R. Weiss, *Medieval and Humanist Greek: Collected Essays by Roberto Weiss*. Medioevo e Umanesimo 8. Padua: Antenore, 1977.

Yegül, Fikret K. "The Thermo-Mineral Complex at Baiae and De Balneis Puteolanis." *Art Bulletin* 78.1 (1976): 137–161.

General Index

Aborigines, 61
Acciaiuoli, Agnolo, 25, 363
Accius, 177
Accolti, *family*
    Benedetto, 41, 369
    Francesco, 41, 369
Accorso, Francesco, 21, 362, 364
Accursius, see Accorso, Francesco
Achaeans, 43
Acron, 167, 169
Actia, 95
Ademar of Chabannes, 408
Aelius Paetus, C., 323, 339
Aelius Pertinax, *emperor,* 193
Aelius Spartianus, 5, 63, 85, 107, 233, 321, 323
    Life of Hadrian, 81
Aemilius, Mamercus, 133
Aemilius Barbula, Q., 349
Aemilius Cerretanus, Q., 347
Aeneas, 63, 67, 73, 85, 93, 95, 105, 243, 257, 297, 299, 377, 427, 432
Aeneas Silvius Piccolomini, see Pius II, *pope*
Aequi (Aequicoli), 63, 103, 107, 109, 163, 245
Agnolo di Ventura, 368
Agostino di Giovanni, 368
Agrippa, 436
Agrippina, 321
Alaric, *king of the Goths,* 207, 402
Alberico da Barbiano, *count of Cunio,* 57, 389
Alberti, Leandro, 365, 437
Alberti, Leon Battista, 25, 129, 384
    De re aedificatoria, 127, 364, 386
    Della famiglia, 364
    Navis, 386
Alcuin, 21
Alexander, *king of Epirus,* 65, 207
Alexander II, *pope,* 17, 213
Alexander III, *pope,* 37, 217, 351
Alexander IV, *pope,* 223
Alexander Severus, *emperor,* 131
Alexander the Great, 77, 345
Alexius, *Byzantine emperor,* 213, 215
Alfonso of Aragon, *king of Naples,* 225, 227, 297, 331, 390, 405–409, 412, 415, 420–421, 438, 441
Alighieri, Dante, 21, 362
    De vulgari eloquentia, 389
    Inferno, 361
Allecto, 71
Allobroges, 113
Almaricus, *king of the Ostrogoths,* 49
Amalasuntha, *queen of the Ostrogoths,* 49
Amatus of Montecassino, 408–409
Amiternini, 227
Ammianus Marcellinus, 49, 392
Anacletus, *antipope,* 217
Ancus Marcius, *Roman king,* 63, 285
Angeli da Scarperia, Jacopo, 25, 364
Angevin kings, 225, 411
Anguillara, Orso, 59
Annali Aretini, 368
Antoninus Pius, *emperor,* 81, 85, 325
    Itinerarium, 271, 416

Antonius, L., 45, 371
Antonius, M., 45, 73, 99
Apelles, 21
Apollo, 55, 311
Apostolic See, 215
Appius Claudius, 289, 425
Aprutini, 295
Apuani, 5, 7
Apuli (Apulians), 347, 349
Aquinas, Thomas, 261
Arabs, 65, 85, 191, 209, 305, 329, 331, 353, 355, 416
Arcadians, 163
Arcadius, *Roman emperor,* 3
Aristides, 399
Aristius, 163
Armenians, 23
Arnolfo di Cambio, 361
Arpinates, 259
Arretines, 39, 41, 43, 367
Arruns, 5, 358
Artemis, 423
Arverni, 113
Ascanius, 93
Asians, 23
Asisinates, 389
Astures, 73
Atellan farce, 421
Atinius, 323
Atintani, 9
Atri, *dukes,* 201
Atticus, 41
Attius Tullius, 101
Augustine, St., 111, 353
    De civitate Dei, 75, 423, 442
    De trinitate, 15
Augustus, *emperor,* 41, 45, 49, 63, 95, 99, 179, 199, 313, 323, 341, 361, 367, 372, 434
Aulus Cerretanus, Q., 243
Aulus Gellius, 305
Aurelian, *emperor,* 63
Aurelius Antoninus (Marcus Aurelius), *emperor,* 119
Aurunci, 77, 279, 281, 283, 285, 423
Ausones, see Aurunci
Avicenna, 389
Azzo, Giovanni, 181, 399

Baglioni, Braccio, 47
Baios, 311
Balbus, 95
Banderesi, 411
Barbaro, Francesco, 407, 420
Bargio, Benedetto, 47
barilotto, xii, 187, 400–401
Bartolo da Sassoferrato, 45, 183, 399, 427
Bartolomeo, *bishop of Corneto,* 13
Beatrice of Barcelona, 223
Becarda, *bishop of Formiae,* 281
Beccadelli, Antonio (Panormita), 412
Belisarius, 133, 177, 179, 191, 329, 331
Bellini, Jacopo, 401
Benedict, St., 115, 153, 261
Benedict VI (VIII), *pope,* 123
Benedict VII (IX), *pope,* 125
Benedictines, 415
Benzi, Ugo, 37
Berardo, *bishop of Spoleto,* 161
Berengar II, *king of Italy,* 5, 358
Bernard, *king of Italy,* 11, 13
Bernardino, St., 37, 239
Bescavettus, *Moorish prince,* 213
Bessarion, *cardinal,* 33, 125, 363
Bettieminus, 213
Betutius Barrus, T., 203
Bini di Prato, Angelo, 368
Biondo Flavio, *works*
    Additiones correctionesque Italiae illustratae, 367

De verbis Romanae locutionis, xii, 363, 399
Historiarum Decades, 3, 11, 17, 25, 47, 139, 147, 177, 179, 189, 197, 207, 209, 225, 273, 283, 329, 343, 351, 376, 397–398, 407–408, 424
Italia illustrata, 355, 366, 368, 370, 378, 382, 384, 397, 405, 408, 412, 414, 419–421, 427, 432, 434, 438
Roma instaurata, 15, 23, 61, 113, 393, 415
Roma triumphans, 441
Bituitus, *king of the Arverni,* 113
Boccaccio, Giovanni, 31, 362, 391, 419, 432
Boethius, 103
Boniface, *count of Pisa,* 187
Boniface IV, *pope,* 109, 381
Boniface VIII, *pope,* 99, 364, 380
Boniface IX, *pope,* 333
Braccio da Montone, 47, 145, 389, 392, 403, 414
Bracciolini, Poggio, 31, 362, 384, 391
Brennus, *Gallic chieftain,* 171
Bretons, 57, 93
Brunelleschi, Filippo, 21, 357, 361
Bruni, Leonardo, 1, 19, 29, 33, 41, 49, 361–362, 367, 369
Bruni, Leonardo, *works*, 357
Bruttians, 273
Byzantine Church, 409
Byzantine Empire, 442
Byzantine Greeks, 209, 409

Cadalus of Parma, *antipope,* 17
Caecilius Pinna (Caecilius Pius, Q.), 111
Caeculus, 117
Caelius Antipater, L., 155
Caesar Vopiscus, 157, 391
Caesius Sabinus, 165
Caetani, Onorato I, *count of Fondi,* 87, 97
Caieta, 85
Caldora, Antonio, 251
Caldora, Jacopo, 249, 251, 275, 415
Caligula, *emperor,* 319, 386, 434
Calixtus II, *pope,* 215
Calixtus III, *pope,* 372
Callimachus, 147, 151, 389
Camerti, 195
Camertini, *family,* 149
Camilla, 93
Camillus, 51, 53, 55, 131, 183
Camogli, Prospero, 313, 433
Campani, 303
Campanians, 273, 301, 311, 313, 339
Campobasso, *counts,* 351
Campofregoso, Tommaso, 5, 359
Canonics, 353
Capitani, *Roman barons,* 211
Capranica, *family*
Angelo, 115, 381–382
Domenico, 115, 381
Nicolò, 115
Paolo, 115, 381–382
Capuans, 289, 299
Capys, 299, 303
Carthaginians, 428
Carvilius, Sp., 257
Cassius, C., 257
Castor and Pollux, 65, 83, 377
Cataneo, Malatesta, 141
Catiline, 19, 361
Catillus, 91, 105
Catullus, 151
Caudini, 439
Cecco d'Ascoli, see Stabili, Francesco
Celestine II, *pope,* 217
Celestine III, *pope,* 219

Celestine V, *pope,* 101, 103, 243, 414–415
Cerretani, 151, 390
Charlemagne, 3, 5, 9, 11, 21, 239, 355
Charles I of Anjou, *king of Naples and Sicily,* 7, 73, 223, 225, 351, 411
Charles II of Anjou, *king of Naples and Sicily,* 225, 411, 415, 433
Charles Martel, 225, 412
Chiavelli, *family,* 185
  Battista, 185
  Chiavello, 401
Christ, 19
Chrysogonus, 159
Chrysoloras, Manuel, 362–363
Cicero, M. Tullius, 23, 73, 83, 113, 123, 159, 259, 285, 291, 301, 303, 305, 315, 317, 325, 333, 358, 379, 383, 390, 403, 424, 428
  Ad familiares, 362
  Brutus, 203, 360
  De lege agraria, 87, 421, 428
  De legibus, 259
  De oratore, 87
  Disputationes Tusculanae, 360
  Pro Murena, 91
  Pro Roscio comoedo, 391
  Pro Sestio, 390
Cinna, 63, 67, 97
Circe, 75, 111
Ciriaco d'Ancona, see de' Pizzicolli, Ciriaco
Cistercians, 97
Civil War, 367
Claudian, poet, 362
Claudius, *emperor,* 15, 63, 107, 109
Claudius Marcellus, M., 337, 341
Claudius Nero, C., 11, 175, 179
Clement III, *pope,* 217
Clement IV, *pope,* 223, 369, 411
Clement V, *pope,* 99
Cleopatra, 99
Clitarchus, 77
Clodius Albinus, *emperor,* 63, 105
Code of Justinian, 399
College of Cardinals, 381
Colonna, *family,* 97, 123, 375, 380–381
  Antonio, 73, 375, 378
  Jacopo, 73
  Lorenzo, 131
  Odoardo, see Martin V, *pope*
  Pietro, 123
  Prospero, *cardinal,* xii, 53, 67, 91, 115, 123, 127, 372, 373, 375–376, 378, 380, 383–384, 387, 400, 406–407, 420, 436
  Sciarra, 99, 119, 380
  Stefano, 117
Coluccio, Pietro, see Nicholas V, *antipope*
Conon, 189
Conrad IV, 221
Conradin (duke of Swabia), 73, 221, 223, 225, 411
Constance, *queen of Sicily,* 219, 411
Constance of Aragon, 73, 221, 225
Constantine, *emperor,* 49
Constantius, *emperor,* 49, 51, 392
Coppoli, Ivone, 47
Corax, 91
Cornelii Scipiones, *family*
  Lucius, 33, 235, 309, 431
  Publius, 3, 41, 87, 153, 195, 233, 307, 309, 323, 339, 430–431
Cornelius, P., 333
Cornelius, Sp., 235
Cornelius Arvina, P., 99
Cornelius Cethegus, C., 77
Cornelius Fulvius (Fulvius, Cn.), 253
Cornelius Nepos, 379
Cornelius Scapula, P., 135
Corpus iuris civilis, 362

Corsicans, 65
Corybantes, 71
Council of Clermont, 215
Council of Constance, 333, 381, 401
Council of Ferrara-Florence, 363, 381
Council of Lyons, 411
Council of Melfi, 215, 410
Crescentius, 165
Crescenzi, *family,* 393

da Carrara, Ubertino, 389
da Varano, *family,* 195
Giulio Cesare, 195, 402
Rodolfo, 195
Damocles, 360
Danae, 73
Daunians, 347
Daunus, *king,* 347
David, *prophet,* 111
de'Pizzicolli, Ciriaco (Ciriaco d'Ancona), 191
Commentaries, 402
Decembrio, Pier Candido, 297, 425, 427, 435
Decius Mus, P., 145, 183, 389
de'Conti, *family,* 105, 381
Alto, 105, 381
Giovanni, 105, 381
Lucido, 105, 381
degli Ubaldi, Baldo, 45
degli Uberti, Farinata, 21, 361
della Pergola, Angelo, 183
della Torre, Giacomo, 37
dell'Anguillara, Orso, 373
dell'Asti, Nicolò, 193
delle Torre, Giacomo, *bishop,* 408
Demetrius of Epirus, 65
d'Este, *dukes,* 369
d'Este, Leonello, 376, 380, 386
Diana, (Cynthia, Trivia), 95, 125, 131, 165, 423
Dido, 299, 427
dies Alliensis, 171
Dino da Mugello, 25
Diomedes, 139, 271, 347, 353, 442
Domitian, *emperor,* 155
Donatello, 25, 363–364, 392
Donatus, 157, 325, 437
Drengot, Rainulf, 409, 429
Drusus, 65
Durand, Guillaume, 181, 398

Egeria, 95
Eleutherius, *exarch,* 179
Ennius, 309, 391, 399, 427
Enzo, *king of Sardinia,* 221
Erasmus, St., 83, 281
Ethiopians, 23
Etruscan empire, 1
Etruscan League, 359
Etruscans, 1, 3, 5, 15, *35,* 39, 41, 47, 51, 57, 59, 65, 95, 139, 183, 195, 299, 358
Eugenius III, *pope,* 9, 165, 217
Eugenius IV, *pope,* xi, xii, 23, 35, 37, 47, 61, 97, 141, 195, 353, 359, 361, 363–364, 372, 375–376, 381, 390, 397, 402
Eusebius, 147, 177
Eutychianus, *pope,* 5
Evander, *king,* 163

Fabii (Fabians), 53, 59
Fabius, Q., 53
Fabius Ambustus, Cn. 79
Fabius Ambustus, M., 195
Fabius Maximus Allobrogicus, Q., 113
Fabius Maximus Verrucosus ("Cunctator"), Q., 81, 161, 265,

267, 283, 289, 291, 293, 295, 297, 323, 425, 427, 442
Fabius Maximus Rullianus, Q., 43, 45, 57, 183, 388–389
Facio, Bartolomeo, 407, 412, 420
Faunus, 169, 279
Faustinus, 81
Federigo da Montefeltro, 141, 177, 179, 181, 387–388
Ferentani, 227
Fidenates, 51, 133
Fidentinus, 370
Fieschi, Sinibaldo, *cardinal,* 219
Filelfo, Francesco, 195
Fiocchi, Andrea, 25, 363–364
  De magistratibus sacerdotiisque Romanorum, 363
Flaminius, C., 27, 29, 43
Flavius Eutropius, 9, 63
Florentine Republic, 17, 21
Florentines (Fluentini), 7, 11, 17, 19, 33, 37, 43, 333
Formosus, *pope,* 15
Fortebraccio, Carlo, 145
Fortebraccio, Niccolò, 121, 145
Fortebraccio, Poncelletto, 119
Fortuna, 65, 117, 377
Francesco da Fiano, 51
Francis of Assisi, St., 143, 400
Franciscan order, 185, 235, 400–401
  Spiritual Franciscans, 185, 187, 400–401, 403
Franks, 207, 355
Fraticelli, see Spiritual Franciscans
Frederick I Barbarossa, *Holy Roman emperor,* 37, 107, 123, 219, 353
Frederick II, *Holy Roman emperor,* 73, 219, 221, 257, 411
Frederiksen, Martin, 419
French, 227
Frentani, 229, 241, 243, 245, 295, 349
Frontinus, 81
Fulvia, 45, 99
Fulvius, C., 251
Fulvius Flaccus, Q., 133, 273
Fundanians, 85
Furconenses, 227
Furius, L., 121

Galba, *emperor,* 87, 101
Gaspare da Volterra, 33
gastald, 3
Gattamelata (Erasmo da Narni), 161, 392
Gauls, 15, 39, 77, 131, 171, 183, 185, 327
Gelasius II, *pope,* 75, 89, 131
Gellianus, 109
Genseric, *king of the Vandals,* 303, 329, 429
Gentile da Fabriano, 185, 189, 361
  Adoration of the Magi, 401
Gentile da Foligno, 143, 388–389
Genucius, L., 255
Georgians, 23
Gerard, *bishop of Florence,* see Nicholas II, *pope*
Germanicus, 65, 243
Germans, 93, 225, 227, 241, 386
Ghibellines, 398
Gian Pietro da Lucca, 19, 361
Giotto di Bondone, 21, 361
Giovanna da Corvara, 185
Giovanni, *cardinal of Taranto,* 109
Giovanni da Capestrano, St., 187, 235, 401, 414
Giovanni da Ravenna, 358
Gisulf, 211
Gnatho, 151, 390
Gnathonici, 151, 390
Goths, 3, 17, 19, 103, 147, 189, 191
Gracchi, 153, 390
Gratiosus, *bishop,* 165

Greeks, 1, 9, 65, 105, 189, 305, 311, 325, 377, 410, 420, 442
Gregory I The Great, St., *pope,* 55, 423
  Register, 165, 281
Gregory IV, *pope,* 85
Gregory VII, *pope,* 13, 47, 175, 213, 261
Gregory IX, *pope,* 219, 257
Grimoald, *king of the Lombards,* 353
Guaimar, *prince of Salerno,* 209, 211
Guarini, Guarino, 376, 382, 391, 399
Guidantonio, *count of Urbino,* 17
Guidi, *counts,* 31
Guido d'Arezzo, 41
Guido of Ravenna, 253, 307
Guinigi, Paolo, 17
Guiscard, Robert, see Hauteville, *family*

Hadrian, *emperor,* 5, 15, 63, 81, 107, 213, 233, 325
Hadrian II, *pope,* 273
Hadrian IV, *pope,* 217
Hannibal, 3, 17, 27, 29, 39, 55, 71, 73, 81, 109, 121, 133, 135, 155, 159, 161, 175, 207, 227, 229, 263, 265, 267, 271, 277, 283, 289, 291, 293, 297, 299, 301, 307, 323, 327, 335, 337, 339, 341, 349, 365, 413, 425, 430, 442
Hanno, 271, 273
Hasdrubal, 65, 81, 175, 179, 181, 398
Hauteville, *family,* 331
  Bagelardus, 211
  Bohemond, 215
  Drogo, 209
  Geoffrey, 213
  Godfrey, 211, 239
  Humphrey, *count,* 211
  Robert Guiscard, 175, 211, 213, 215, 239, 261, 305, 410, 429
  Roger I, *count of Sicily,* 211, 213, 410
  Roger II, *king of Sicily,* 215, 217, 219, 343, 411
  Tancred, 207, 209, 211, 405, 409
  Tancred, *son of Roger II,* 217, 219
  William, *duke of Apulia,* 215
  William I, *king of Sicily,* 211, 217, 411
  William II, *king of Sicily,* 217, 273, 351, 353, 411
Henry, *senator,* 223, 225
Henry I, *Holy Roman Emperor,* 21
Henry (II), *Holy Roman Emperor,* 123
Henry II (III), *Holy Roman Emperor,* 211
Henry III, *Holy Roman Emperor,* 95, 213, 409–410
Henry IV, *Holy Roman Emperor,* 213
Henry VI, *Holy Roman Emperor,* 219, 411
Henry VII of Germany, 221
Heraclius, *emperor,* 181
Hercules, 321, 365, 436
Hernici, 61, 99, 101, 103, 269
Hippolytus, 95
Hirpiae, *families,* 55
Hirpini, 157, 271
Hirtius, A., 241
History of the Roman church, see *Liber Pontificalis*
Hohenstaufen, 409, 411, 414
Honorius, *Roman emperor,* 3
Honorius II, *pope,* 215
Honorius III, *pope,* 219
Horace, 41, 65, 87, 123, 163, 287, 315, 327, 377, 424, 433, 434
  Epistles, 167, 169, 393, 433
  Odes, 55, 169, 171, 368, 393
Hormisda, *pope,* 103

Hostiario, Pandolfo, 123
Hugh of Arles, *king of Italy,* 358
Hungarians, 5, 241
Hyginus, 71, 307

Iapygians, 339
Innocent II, *pope,* 215, 217, 343
Innocent III, *pope,* 99
Innocent IV, *pope,* 219, 221, 411
Ioannes Paleologus, *Byzantine emperor,* 23
Islam, 409
Isocrates, 361
Italians, 151, 265, 331
Iulius Iulianus, L., 392

Jacobites, 23
Jacopo, *bishop of Perugia,* 43
Jacopo della Marca, 201, 401, 403
Jason, 109
Jerome, St., 317
Joanna I, *queen of Naples,* 225
Joanna II, *queen of Naples,* 225
John, *king of Jerusalem,* 221
John X, *pope,* 5, 283, 329, 331, 424
John XV, pope, 165
John XVIII, *pope,* 35
John XIX, *pope,* 123
John XXII, *pope,* 185, 187, 400–401
John XXIII, *pope,* 333
Julia, 95
Julian Law, 303, 428
Julius Caesar, 81, 125, 129, 227, 229, 241, 293, 303, 317, 319, 321, 358, 361
  Commentaries on the Civil War, 191, 197, 349
Julius Capitolinus, 63, 105, 111, 119
Junius Bubulcus, C., 347
Juno, 131
  Juno Sospita, 67
Jupiter, 79
  Juppiter Clitumnus, 390
Justin, 1, 9, 43, 339
Justinian, *Byzantine emperor,* 103, 189, 329, 372
Juvenal, 7, 189, 261, 305, 423–424

Labicani, 103, 135
Labienus, 191
Laconians, 83
Ladislaus IV, *king of Naples,* 43, 225, 333, 412
Laelius, 87
Lalage, 169
Landgrave of Thuringia, 221
Lando, *pope,* 173
Larinates, 227, 229, 241, 245, 349
Lateran Council, 175
Latin League, 383
Latins, 61, 67, 71, 77, 89, 97, 121, 131, 311
Lavinia, 93
Leborini, 303
Lelli, *family,* 231
  Simon, 231
  Teodoro, 231
Leo II (V), *pope,* 73
Leo IV, *pope,* 65, 331
Leo V (IX), *pope,* 211
Leo IX, *pope,* 409–410
Lepidus, M., 45
Leto, Pomponio, 393
Libanius, 399
Liber Pontificalis, 11
Liburnians, 227, 229
Libyans, 23
Licinius Mucianus, C., 379
Ligorio, Pirro, 386
Ligurians, 9
Lingones, 370
Livius, C., 339

Livius Salinator, 175, 179
Livy, 1, 3, 7, 9, 11, 15, 17, 25, 27, 29, 33, 39, 41, 43, 45, 47, 55, 57, 59, 61, 63, 65, 67, 75, 79, 81, 85, 87, 91, 93, 95, 97, 101, 103, 107, 109, 111, 113, 117, 119, 121, 125, 131, 133, 135, 139, 143, 145, 147, 153, 155, 159, 161, 171, 175, 177, 179, 181, 183, 195, 203, 207, 229, 233, 235, 245, 251, 253, 255, 257, 259, 261, 263, 265, 267, 269, 271, 273, 277, 279, 281, 283, 285, 287, 289, 291, 293, 295, 297, 299, 301, 305, 307, 309, 311, 313, 323, 325, 327, 333, 335, 337, 339, 341, 345, 347, 349, 359, 365, 377–378, 380, 387–389, 398, 412, 414–416, 421–423, 425–432, 436–437, 442
Periochae, 424
Lombards, 3, 17, 57, 109, 143, 179, 185, 193, 237, 239, 261, 303, 406, 423
Lothar, *king of Italy,* 5, 358
Lothar I, *Holy Roman Emperor,* 191
Lothar III, *Holy Roman Emperor,* 217, 343, 440
Louis, *king of the Franks,* 207
Louis I, *emperor,* 3
Louis IV, *Holy Roman Emperor,* 185, 369, 400
Louis IX, St., *king of France,* 223
Lucan, 5, 9, 81, 117, 129, 147, 149, 177, 179, 241, 255, 279, 341, 353, 358, 389–390, 422, 440
Lucanians, 273
Lucilius, 83
Lucius II, *pope,* 217
Lucius III, *pope,* 17, 217
Lucretius Asella (Lucretius Ofella, Q.), 119
Lucullus, L., 123, 315, 317, 325, 403, 434, 437
lucumones, 1
Lydians, 1, 109

Macrobius, 41, 305
Maecenas, 41, 169, 368
Mago, 3, 422
Maharbal, 289, 291
Maiuri, Amedeo, 419, 433
Malaterra, Geoffrey, 408
Malatesta, Domenico (Novello), 375, 387, 406–407, 420
Malatesta, Malatesta, 177
Malatesta, Paola, 177
Malatesta, Sigismondo, 183
Mammea, 131, 321
Manetti, Giannozzo, 25, 363–364
Manfred, *king of Sicily,* 37, 221, 223, 225, 411
Manlius, Cn., 53
Manlius of Tusculum, 121
Manlius Torquatus, 131
Marcacci, Niccolò, 368
Marcellinus, *pope,* 281
Marcellus Claudius, M., 269
Marcius, *aedile,* 107, 113
Marcius Rutulus, C., 267
Marcius Tremulus, Q., 99
Margaritus, *king of Epirus,* 219
Maria of Hungary, 225
Marica, 279, 283, 285, 423
Marius, C., 33, 63, 67, 97, 117, 119, 259, 281, 367, 423
Marquis of Ferrara, 17
Marrucini, 111, 227, 229, 233, 239, 241, 245, 349, 413, 423
Marruvians, 109
Mars, 185
Marsi, 41, 63, 111, 115, 229, 233, 245, 413, 423
Marsuppini, Carlo, 41
Marsyas, 109

Martel, Charles, 35
Martial, 5, 15, 35, 43, 81, 85, 91, 93, 97, 105, 141, 145, 147, 153, 161, 165, 175, 285, 358, 360, 366, 370, 372, 388, 392–393, 424
Martin III, *pope,* 159
Martin IV, *pope,* 181, 398
Martin V, *pope,* 65, 97, 115, 375, 378, 381–383, 401
Matilda, *countess of Tuscany,* 13, 39
Matteo da Corvara, 185
Mauruzzi, Niccolò, see Niccolò da Tolentino
Mazzancolli, Giovanni, 159
Medea, 109
Medici, *family,* 25, 363
  Carlo, 23
  Cosimo, 23, 357, 363
  Giovanni, 23
  Piero, 23, 357
Melissus, 147
Melo, 409
Memmius, L., 53
Menapians, 360
Merculinae (Mercorini), *faction,* 49
Mettius Fufetius, *king of Alba,* 51
Mezentius, *king,* 15
Michael Archangel, St., 351, 442
Michael IV, *Byzantine emperor,* 209
Michelotti, Biordo, 47
Michelotti, Ceccolino, 47
Minerva, 75, 165, 321
Minorita, Alberto, 39
Minorites, 185
Minucius, Q., 81
Montagano, Jacopo, 349
Montevecchio, Ugone, 183
Morroni, Tommaso, 155, 391
Mucianus, 77
Muffatae (Beffata, Muffati), *faction,* 49
Murena, *family,* 67, 91
  Lucius, 89
Mussolini, Benito, 377, 386

Narses, 17, 133, 147, 179, 191, 303
Neapolitans, 327, 329, 331, 341
Nepos, Cornelius, 41
Nero, *emperor,* 67, 133, 319, 327, 377
Niccoli, Niccolò, 23, 363
Niccolò Mauruzzi da Tolentino, *condottiere,* 195, 402
Nicetas, *Byzantine admiral,* 11
Nicholas II, *pope,* 37, 211, 213, 239, 410
Nicholas III, *pope,* 203
Nicholas IV, *pope,* 411
Nicholas V, *pope,* 369–370, 372, 373, 378, 382, 400
Nicholas V, *antipope,* 185, 187
Nicola da Tolentino, St., 195
Nicolò da Furca Palenae, 247
Nile, St., 383
Nolans, 430
Nonius Marcellus, 145
Normans, 209, 211, 213, 217, 227, 239, 408–410, 414, 442
Novello, Guido, *count,* 29
Nucerini, 341
Numa Pompilius, *Roman king,* 95, 165

Ocriculani, 161
Octavius, C., 95, 341
Oddo, Pietro, 167, 393
Oebale, 329
Oebalus, 438
Oenotri, 163
Oliva, Alessandro, 183, 399
Opimius, 85
Oppianus, 35
opus quadratum, 237
Ormisda, 51

Orsini, *family,* 15, 59, 107, 171
Orso, *count,* 239
Ortonenses, 295
Osci, 77
Ostrogoths, 49, 133, 191, 303
Otho, *Roman emperor,* 101, 380
Otto IV, *Holy Roman Emperor,* 219, 343
Ovid, 71, 95, 151, 167, 189, 241, 406, 414
Fasti, 243

Pallas, 163
Palma, 81
Pandoni, Porcellio, 412
Pandulf, *prince of Capua,* 209
Paolino Minorita (Paolino Veneto), 422
Paolo di Castro, 49, 372
Papirius Crassus, L., 85
Papirius Cursor, L., 277, 416
Parthians, 203
Paschal I, *pope,* 57
Paschal II, *pope,* 3, 123
Patrizi, Francesco, 37, 366
Paul, St., 125
Peligni, 183, 227, 229, 241, 243, 245, 247, 249, 293, 349, 413, 423, 442
Pelops, 9
Pentri, 253
Perotti, Nicolò, 183, 399
Perses, 159
Perseus, 73
Persians, 51
Persius, 33
Perusini, 45
Pescennius Niger, *emperor,* 261
Peter of Aragon, *king of Sicily,* 73, 225
Petrarch, Francis, 21, 23, 59, 225, 327, 329, 361–362, 373, 419, 421, 432
Africa, 422, 430
Itinerarium Syriacum, 422, 437
Petrileoni, Peter, see Anacletus, *antipope*
Petruccio, Giovanni, 47
Peuceti, 347
Philip of Swabia, 219
Phocas, *Byzantine emperor,* 109, 381
Piccinino, *family*
Carlo, 145
Francesco, 47, 145
Jacopo, 47, 145
Niccolò, 17, 25, 41, 47, 145
Picenes (Picentes), 41, 175, 203, 227
Pietro da Morrone, see Celestine V, *pope*
Pinna (Cornelius Cinna, L.), 111
Pinnenses, 227
Pippin, 239
Pisans, 33, 217
Pius II, *pope* (Aeneas Silvius Piccolomini), xi, 37, 366–367, 383
Commentaries, 383–384
Pius VI, *pope,* 392
Plato, 253, 259
Plautius, P. (Publilius Philo, Q.), 327
Plautius Proculus, P., 135
Plautius Venox, L., 85
Plautus, 167, 393
Pliny, 7, 11, 13, 15, 17, 19, 39, 43, 49, 51, 53, 55, 63, 67, 69, 71, 73, 77, 89, 93, 97, 105, 107, 109, 113, 115, 117, 119, 121, 131, 133, 139, 141, 149, 155, 157, 159, 161, 171, 175, 177, 181, 189, 197, 227, 229, 231, 233, 235, 239, 243, 245, 247, 251, 255, 261, 271, 283, 287, 297, 307, 309, 313, 317, 325, 335, 339, 341, 351, 357, 359–361, 370, 372, 376, 378–379, 389–391, 405, 413, 415, 419, 424, 427, 429–431, 437, 441–442
Pliny the Younger, 15, 141, 388

Plutarch, 315, 325, 361, 399
    Life of Cicero, 25, 364
    Life of Fabius Maximus, 425
    Life of Lucullus, 434
    Parallel Lives, 297
Poetelius, C., 135, 257, 339
Poetelius, M., 255, 271
Polybius, 33, 399, 442
Pompeius Strabo, Gn., 203, 403
Pompeius Trogus, 1, 139
Pompey, 241, 315, 325, 358
Pomponius Mela, 13, 307, 359
Pontano, *family,* 151
    Giovanni Gioviano, 151, 390
    Lodovico, 151, 390
    Paolo, 151
Pontius, C., 269
Porcii Catones, 123
Porsenna, *king of Clusium,* 39, 95, 97, 370
Postumius, Sp., 269
Postumius Megellus, L., 47, 349
Postumus, A., 97
Praetutians, 227, 229, 233, 235, 245, 413
Priors of the Guilds, 21
Privernates, 85
Propertius, xii, 145, 151, 389
    Elegies, 147
Ptolemy, 13, 231, 239, 245, 247, 271, 307, 309, 347, 351, 353, 359, 441
Publilius Philo, Q., 347
Punic War, second, 41, 197, 233, 421, 426, 428
Pyrrhus, 207
Pythagorean school, 83

Quinctius, 169
Quintus Ovidius, 161, 165

Radagasius, *king of the Goths,* 25
Rainone, 123
Reguardati, Benedetto, 153
René of Anjou, *king of Naples,* 225, 331
Robert of Anjou, *king of Naples,* 225, 327, 329, 331, 373, 421–422, 437–438
Roman Church, 75, 273, 392, 409–410
Roman Curia, xii, 99, 127, 185, 223, 231, 364, 372, 381, 398–400, 409, 441
Roman Empire, 1, 3, 313, 329, 333
Romans, 3, 7, 39, 49, 51, 53, 55, 57, 59, 65, 67, 71, 73, 77, 79, 85, 87, 93, 97, 99, 101, 103, 109, 113, 119, 125, 133, 147, 163, 175, 177, 179, 183, 185, 197, 203, 215, 225, 229, 255, 263, 269, 273, 281, 289, 293, 295, 297, 299, 303, 313, 327, 329, 333, 339, 341, 347, 358, 364, 377, 392, 416, 421, 423, 425, 434
Romanus, *pope,* 55
Romulus, 51, 163
Roscius Amerinus, Q., 159, 391
Rossellino, Bernardo, 367
Rossoni, Dino, 364
Rubens, Peter Paul, 369
Rullus Cornelius (P. Servilius Rullus), 87, 285, 291, 301, 333, 341
Rutilius Claudius Namatianus, 377
Rutuli, 15, 61, 71

Sabellic League, 423
Sabines, 139, 141, 145, 163, 171, 173, 175, 388, 392
Sabinian, *pope,* 57
Sacrani, 71
Sagrera, Guillermo, 438
Salentini, 347
Sallust, 237, 361
    War with Catiline, 25
Sallusti, Sallustio, 47

Salutati, Coluccio, 23, 362
Samnite Wars, 388
  Samnite War, second, 389, 402
Samnites, 89, 135, 183, 227, 235, 253, 255, 257, 259, 263, 265, 267, 269, 271, 287, 289, 291, 299, 337, 339, 341, 347, 406, 425
Santa of Aragon, *queen of Naples,* 331
Saracens, 13, 83, 213, 219, 223, 273, 423–424
Saturn, 61
Savelli, *family,* 95, 171
Scalamonti, Francesco, 191, 402
Scalamonti, Niccolò, 191, 402
Scarampi, Ludovico, 95
Scribonius Curio, C., 197
Sebethis (Sebetris), 329, 438
Seguani, 5
Sempronius Gracchus, Ti., 273, 307, 339
Sempronius Longus, Ti., 17
Sempronius Tuditanus, M., 7
Seneca, 165, 325, 431–432
  Epistles, 309, 325
Serafino, 179
Sergius, *pope,* 191
Sergius IV of Naples, 429
Sertorius, Q., 153
Servilius Ahala, C., 79
Servilius Cornelius, 255
Servilius Vatia, 309, 431–432
Servius, 61, 63, 71, 73, 75, 79, 83, 93, 95, 99, 105, 109, 125, 131, 145, 153, 157, 159, 163, 167, 171, 271, 279, 297, 311, 317, 319, 321, 329, 337, 339, 347, 353, 379, 381, 390, 427, 441
Severa, St., 15
Severus Alexander, *emperor,* 321
Sextilius, M., 135
Sextus Rufus, 415
Sextus Tarquinius, 131
Sforza, *dukes,* 369
Sforza, Francesco, 195, 199, 392, 397–398
Sforza, Galeazzo, 388
Sforza, Muzio Attendolo, 389, 414
Sicilian Vespers, 411
Sicilians, 189
Sidicini, 133, 285, 339
Sienese, 13
Sigismund, *Holy Roman Emperor,* 333
Sigonio, Carlo, 442
Silverius, *pope,* 103
Simplicius, pope, 107
Sixtus IV, *pope,* 382
Social (Marsic, Italian) War, 41, 61, 111, 233, 265, 271, 341
Socrates, 259
Solymus, 243
Soter, *pope,* 89
Spaniards, 343
Spoletans, 151
Stabili, Francesco (Cecco d'Ascoli), 203, 403
Standard-Bearer of Justice, 21
Statius Trebius, 271
Statius, *poet,* 437
Stefano da Montefortino, 105
Strabo, 61, 63, 65, 67, 71, 73, 75, 77, 83, 85, 87, 91, 105, 107, 113, 115, 117, 119, 121, 123, 125, 175, 279, 283, 285, 360, 376–379, 382–384, 424, 432
Strozza, *family,* 21
Strozzi, Palla, 25, 363
Suetonius, 101, 109, 125, 155, 293, 303, 313, 319, 321, 323, 327, 341, 380, 386, 391, 432, 434
  Life of Caligula, 315, 319, 435
  Life of Tiberius Caesar, 81, 133
  Life of Titus, 335

Sulla, 33, 41, 113, 117, 119, 159, 271, 341, 367
Sulpicius, 233
Sulpicius Longus, C., 255, 271, 347
Sulpicius Priscus, Q., 103
Superaequani, 243, 247, 249
Sveva, *countess of Alba of the Marsi,* 115
Sylvester, *pope,* 53
Symmachus, 103

Tabula Peutingeriana, 416
Tacitus, 177
Tagliacozzo, *battle of,* 411
Tarlati di Pietramala, Guido, *bishop of Arezzo,* 31, 41, 141, 357, 366–367, 369
Tarquins, *family,* 359
  Tarquinius Priscus, 13
  Tarquinius Superbus, 13, 97, 121, 131, 285, 311
Tatius, T., *king of the Sabines,* 163
Tellus, 203
Terence, 390
Terentius Varro, C., 39, 175
Thelesius, 119
Thelo, 329
Theodatus, *king of the Goths,* 103
Theoderic, *king of the Ostrogoths,* 147
Theodora, 55
Theophrastus, 77
Theopompus, 77
Thermus Minucius, Q., 197
Tiberius, *emperor,* 61, 63, 65, 129, 323, 363, 386
Tiburtines, 381
Tiburtus, 91, 105
Tiferni, 347
Tiguli, 5
Timaeus of Tauromenium, 420
Titus, *emperor,* 155, 335
Tortelli, Giovanni, 43, 369
Totila, *king of the Ostrogoths,* 19, 133, 177, 179, 207, 261, 273
Trajan, *emperor,* 15, 189, 360, 386
Trojan War, 33
Tullus Hostilius, *king of Rome,* 51, 53
Turnus, 15
Tusculans, 121, 123
Tyrrhenians (Tyrrheni), 33, 43
Tyrrhenus, *king,* 1

Ubaldini, *family*
  Bernardino, 181
  Ottaviano, 181, 399
Ugo, *cardinal,* 215
Ulysses, 75, 311
Umbrians, 1, 139, 143, 145, 183, 389
University of Bologna, 364, 399
University of Naples, 411
University of Perugia, 399
Urban II, *pope,* 215
Urban III, *pope,* 217
Urban IV, *pope,* 223
Urban V, *pope,* 49
Urban VIII, *pope,* 398

Vacuna, 165, 392
Valentinus, *emperor,* 275
Valerius Corvus, M., 337
Valerius Maximus, 281, 423, 431
Valerius Maximus, M., 35
Valignani, *family,* 239
Valla, Lorenzo, 442
Vandals, 429
Varro, 39, 53, 75, 155, 157, 305, 370, 378–379, 428
  Antiquitates rerum divinarum, 165, 392
Veientes, 51, 53, 59
Venetians, 105, 145
Ventidius Bassus, P., 203, 403

Venus, 165
Verulani, 103
Verus Caesar, 119
Vespasian, *emperor,* 155, 179
Vesta, 73
Vestini, 89, 227, 255, 279, 283, 285, 423
Veturius Calvinus, T., 269
Virgil, 11, 13, 15, 25, 49, 53, 57, 63, 73, 75, 79, 85, 91, 93, 95, 99, 105, 117, 131, 133, 139, 145, 153, 157, 159, 163, 171, 237, 257, 297, 307, 311, 313, 317, 319, 321, 325, 327, 329, 337, 341, 353, 427, 429–430, 434, 437–440
  Aeneid, 61, 63, 71, 83, 107, 109, 125, 155, 163, 269, 271, 279, 337, 347, 379, 391, 432, 435, 439
  Bucolics, 339, 391
  Georgics, 149, 159, 327, 335, 337, 390–391, 435, 439
Visconti, Filippo Maria, 397
Visconti, Giovanni Avello, 197
Vitalianus, *pope,* 105
Vitelleschi, Giovanni, 13, 359, 397
Vitelli, Nicolò, 141
Vitellius, 177
Vitruvius, 431
Vitruvius Bacchus, 85
Vittorino da Feltre, 19, 361, 399
Volaterrani (Volterrans, Volienses), 11, 33
Volcacius Tullus, 145
Volscians, 61, 77, 93, 261, 285
Volumnius, L., 253, 289, 425

William of Apulia, 408–409
William of Holland, 221

Xerxes, 325

Zacchi, Gaspare, 366
Zeuxis of Heraclea, 25

Index of Places

Abruzzo, xi, xii, 201, 207, 213, 227, 229, 239, 247, 253, 255, 295, 337, 347, 405–408, 412, 414–415, 420, 422, 439
Abruzzo e Molise, *region,* 405
Acarnania, 213
Accumoli, 201
Acerra (Acerrae), 307, 335, 337, 429
Acheron, *river,* 157, 319, 435
Acquafondata, 263
Acqualagna, 179
Acquamela, 343
Acquapendente, 47
Acuto, 103
Ad Aquas Salvias, *marsh,* 125
Adige (Athesis), *river,* 439
Adria, 1
Adriatic Sea, 1, 139, 175, 193, 253, 275, 343, 351, 353, 397, 405–406
Adversa, see Aversa
Aenaria, 311
Affile, 115
Africa, 41, 71, 153, 195, 223, 233, 235, 281, 313, 329, 422, 429
Agillina, 3, 15, 360
Agnano, 403
  baths, 325
  lake, 325, 437
Agnone, 251
Ailano, 267, 416
Airola, 337
Alanno, 235
Alatri, 103
Alba, 53, 93, 125, 255, 265
Alba, *river,* 239
Alba dei Marsi, 113
Alba Fucens, 113
Alban Hills, 384
Alban Mount, see Monte Cavo
Albano, 95
Albula, *river,* see Vibrata
Albunea, *spring,* 105
Alento, *river,* 243, 245
Aletrium, 99, 101
Alexandria, 362
Alfedena (Aufidena), 251, 253
Algidus, *mountain,* 97, 103, 121, 131, 135
Alifanum, 263
Alife (Allifae), 135, 267, 287, 289, 293, 295
Allia, *river,* 167, 171, 173
Allifae, see Alife
Alps, 1, 9, 365
  Liburnian, 207
Altavilla, 271
Altilia, 277
Altino, 249
Altopascio, 19
Alvito, 257
Amalfi, 343, 440
Amandola Salvi, 197
Amaseno (Amasenus), *river,* 93
Amatrice, 201, 203, 229
Amelia (Ameria), 49, 59, 159, 391
Amiternae, 71

Amiternum, 235, 237
Ampsanctus, *lake* (LeMofete, Lago d'Ansante), 391
Ampsanctus, *valley,* 155
Amyclae, 77, 83, 379
Anagni (Anagnia), 99, 101, 121, 135, 380
Ancarano, 229
Ancona, 143, 185, 189, 191, 402
Anghiari, 41, 47, 369
Aniene (Anio), *river,* 51, 107, 115, 131, 133, 137, 141, 145, 161, 173, 175, 387
Anjou, 223
Anser, 191
Anticoli Corrado, 115
Antioch, 215
Antrodoco, 155
Anxur, see Terracina
Anzio (Antium), xii, 53, 63, 65, 67, 69, 71, 73, 378, 384, 436
  Castor and Pollux, *temple,* 65, 377
  Rostra, 65, 377
Apennines, 1, 5, 17, 19, 25, 47, 63, 107, 113, 141, 143, 145, 153, 155, 163, 175, 177, 181, 185, 189, 193, 195, 197, 199, 201, 203, 231, 233, 235, 239, 243, 247, 251, 253, 255, 257, 263, 265, 267, 271, 275, 277, 279, 343, 357, 387, 389, 397, 405–406, 414–415
Apice, 275
Apiro, 191
Appignano, 233
Apricena, 351
Aprilis, see Laguna di Orbetello
Aprutium, 227, 406, 412
Apsa, *stream,* 177
Apulia, see Puglia
Apulia et Calabria, *region,* 441
Aqua Marcia, 113
Aqua Virgo, 123
Aquae Foetidae, 91
Aquae Sinuessanae, 283, 291
Aquaviva Picena, 201
Aquila, see L'Aquila
Aquino (Aquinum), 213, 261, 263
Arbia, *river,* 37
Arce, 259
Archi, 249
Ardea, 71, 73, 125, 378
Arezzo (Arretium), 3, 21, 25, 27, 29, 31, 33, 35, 39, 43, 45, 141, 357–358, 369–370, 372
  Palazzo del Comune, 367
  Piazza Grande, 367
  S. Maria in Gradi, *church,* 41, 367–368
  S. Pietro Maggiore, *church* (Duomo), 368
Argyripa, 347, 353
Ari, 247
Ariano Irpino (Ara Iani), 275
Ariccia (Aritia), 95, 97, 125, 129, 376, 379–380
Arielli, 247
Arienzo, 339
Ariminum, see Rimini
Arno, *river,* 9, 19, 25, 29, 31, 33, 365
Arpaia (Hirpinum), 269, 271
Arpi, 267, 271, 339, 347, 413
Arpini, 277
Arpino (Arpinum), 259, 261
Arquà, 21
Arquata del Tronto, 201, 203
Arretium, see Arezzo
Arrone, 155
Arsoli (Carseoli), 109
Artena (Montefortino), 105
Arzilla, *river,* 179, 397

Asciano, 13
Ascoli Piceno (Asculum), 175, 203, 229, 397
  Piazza Ventidio Basso, 403
Asia, 431
Asia Minor, 1
Aso, *river,* 199, 201, 398
Asola, *stream,* 193
Aspio, *river,* 191
Assisi (Assisium, Axis), 143, 145, 147, 333, 389
Astura, *river,* 378
Atella, 291, 303, 305, 307, 323, 341, 429
Aterno, *river,* 227, 235, 239, 243
Aternus, *river,* see Pescara *and* Aterno
Atessa, 251
Athens, 77, 187
Atina, 71, 257
Atri (Hadria), 233
Aurunca, see Sessa
Auser, *river,* see Serchio
Ausonia, 77, 279
Ausonian Sea, 77
Auximum, see Osimo
Avellino (Abella, Abelinum), 271
Aventino, *river,* 247, 249
Avernus, *lake,* see Lago di Averno
Aversa, 303, 305, 307, 323, 335, 409, 429
Avezzano, 113
Avignon, 187

Baccano, 59
Bacoli, 435–436
Badia Morronese, 414
  S. Spirito, *abbey,* 414–415
Bagni S. Filippo, 47
Bagno a Acqua, 366
Bagnoli del Trigno, 251
Bagnoli Irpino, 275
Bagnone, *stream,* 5
Bagnoreggio, 49
Baia (Baiae), 309, 311, 313, 319, 325, 329, 331, 419–420, 432–435
  Baia, *gulf,* 315, 317, 321, 323, 435–436
Balneum Rusellarum, 35
Bandusia, *spring,* 171
Baranello, 349
Barbarano Romano, 59
Barberino Val d'Elsa, 31
Barga, 17
Bari, 347
Basilica, 251
Basilicata Calabria, 207, 405
Bauco, 103
Bauli, 321, 436
Belforte, 195
Belforte all' Isauro, 181
Belgermano, 323
Bellante, 231
Belmonte, 199
Beneventana, *region,* 405
Benevento (Beneventum), 73, 211, 215, 223, 227, 265, 271, 273, 275, 277, 347, 381, 411
  S. Martino, *church*, 273
Berarda, 381
Bettona, 145
Bevagna, 145, 147, 149, 151, 389
Bibbiena, 31
Bientina, 19
Bientina, *swamp,* 19
Biferno, (Tifernus), *river,* 245, 253, 347, 349, 351, 405–406, 414, 441
Bisegna, *fortress,* 231
Bisenti, 233
Bisenzio, *river,* 19
Blera, 57
Bocchignano, 167

Bojano (Bovianum), 135, 251, 253, 257, 273, 349, 351
Bologna, 25, 37, 49, 221, 362
Bolsena (Vulsinia, Volsinii), 3, 35, 45, 47, 49, 358
Bomba, 249
Bonito, 275
Borghetto, 43
Borgo, 31
Borgo San Lorenzo, 25
Borgo Sansepolcro, 23, 41, 47, 141, 189, 367, 388
Bovianum, see Bojano
Bovillae, 103, 341
Branca, 141
Brasticaria, 181
Broccostella, 255
Brundisium, 83
Bruttium, xii, 207, 209, 213, 227, 271, 273, 329, 405, 412, 439
Bucchianico, 245
Bucine, 369
Buggiano, 19
Buonalbergo, 275
Buonanotte, 249
Buonconvento, 13
Bussi, *castle,* 235
Busso, 349

Cabum, see Monte Cavo
Caecuban Mount, 89
Caecubum, 89
Caere, 358–360
Cagli, 179
Cagnano, 351
Caianello (Calicula), 287, 289
Caiazzo (Calatia, Caiatia), 269, 287, 289, 341, 424
Caieta, see Gaeta
Calabria, xii, 209, 211, 213, 215, 217, 261, 410, 441
Calcinaia, 33
Caldarola, 195, 402
Calentino, *river,* 165, 167
Calenum, see Carinola
Calenzano, 19
Calicula, see Caianello
Callicula, *mountain,* 293
Calore, *river,* 157, 265, 271, 273, 275, 439
Calvi (Cales), 133, 165, 287, 289, 291, 424
Camerino, 141, 149, 195, 389
Campagnano di Roma, 59
Campagnatico, 33
Campania, xi, xii, 69, 77, 79, 105, 135, 157, 207, 253, 255, 263, 277, 279, 283, 285, 289, 291, 295, 297, 299, 301, 303, 305, 317, 327, 329, 333, 335, 337, 339, 347, 405–406, 408, 415, 420–422, 424, 429, 433, 438–439
Campania and Marittima, 61, 63, 137
Campi Flegrei (Campi Phlegraei), 357, 419, 432, 433
Campi Palentini, 225
Campiglia Marittima, 11
Campli, 231
Campo Marino, 349
Campobasso, 351
Campodipietra, 351
Campolattaro, 277
Campotosto, 233
Cancello, 337, 339
Cancello ed Arnone, 297, 426–427
Candida, 273
Candigliano, *river,* 179
Canne (Cannae), 119, 123, 209, 271, 297, 327
Cannale, 211
Cannara, 143, 145
Cantalupo, 107, 239

Cantiano, 179
Cantiano, *river,* 179
Canzano, 231
Capalbio, 13
Capestrano, 235, 414
Capistrello, 255
Capo d'Acqua, 235
Capo d'Orso, 343
Capodacqua, 149
Capodimonte, 49
Capracotta, 251
Capranica, 59
Capranica Prenestina, 381
Caprese, 369
Capri, 329, 341
Capua, 61, 133, 273, 277, 287, 291, 293, 295, 297, 301, 303, 305, 307, 311, 323, 327, 335, 337, 339, 341, 409, 416, 426, 429
  Madonna delle Grazie, *church,* 428
  S. Maria delle Grazie, *church,* 299
  S. Maria Maggiore, 428
  S. Maria Suricorum, 428
  Seplasia, *quarter,* 428
Caramanico Terme, 239
Carapelle Calvisio, 235
Carinola (Calenum), 283, 287, 291, 424
Carmagnano, 19
Carmon, see Chiusi
Carnaro (Flanaticum), *gulf*
  Carnaro, *promontory,* 207
Carola, 181
Carpineto Sinello, 251
Carpino, 351
Carrara, 5
Carrara Lunigiana, *mountains,* 7
Carthage, 349
Casa Castalda, 143
Casacalenda, 349
Casacanditella, 247
Casal di Janni di Reino, 275
Casalanguida, 251
Casalbordino, 251
Casalbore, 275
Casalciprano, 253
Casalduni, 277
Casale, 249
Casali di Sessa, 285
Casalvieri, 257, 259
Casanova, *abbey,* 235
Casape, 115
Cascano, 287
Cascia, 189
Casciana, 23
Casciana Terme, 33, 366
Casentino, *region,* 23, 25, 31, 189
Caserta, 337
Casilinum, 119, 269, 287, 289, 291, 293, 295, 297, 299, 307, 424, 426–427
Casinum, see Cassino
Casole d'Elsa, 31
Casperia, 163
Cassano Irpino, 275
Cassia, 151, 153, 155
Cassino (Casinum), 135, 223, 261, 263, 289, 415
Cassiopa, 213
Castel del Giudice, 249
Castel delle Ripe, 399
Castel di Romena, 31
Castel di Sangro, 251, 295
Castel di Sessola, 135, 263, 269, 305, 337, 341
Castel Durante (Urbania), 181, 398
Castel Fiorentino, 31
Castel Focognano, 369
Castel Menardo, 245
Castel S. Flaviano (Castrum Novum), 231
Castel Savelli, 95
Castel Volturno (Vulturnum), 295, 299, 329, 426, 430

Castelbottacio, 253
Castelfidardo, 191
Castelfranco di Sopra, 31
Castelfranco in Miscano, 275
Castelgandolfo, 129
Castellamare di Stabia, 333
Castellano, *river,* 203, 229
Castellina, 31
Castellino del Biferno, 349
Castello della Rancia, 195
Castellone, 87
Castellonorato, 87
Castelluccio, 251, 355
Castellum Firmanum, see Porto S. Giorgio
Castellutium, 291, 295, 297, 299, 426–427
Castelnuovo, 17, 31, 247
Castelnuovo di Farfa, 163
Castelnuovo di Garfagnano, 5
Castelnuovo di Porto, 55
Castelpoto, 269
Castelvecchio, 231
Castelvetere sul Calore, 275
Castiglion Aretino, 41
Castiglione, 235
Castiglione del Lago, 43
Castiglione della Pescaia, 11
Castiglione Messer Raimondo, 231
Castignano, 199
Castilenti, 233
Castro, 49, 105
Castrocaro, 23
Castropignano, 253
Castrum Novum, 13, 227, 359–360
Castrum Pili, 249
Castrum Reparum, 398
Castrum Trove, 11
Catillus, *mountain,* 91
Caudine Forks, 269, 337, 339
Caudine mountains, 269
Caudine Valley, 269, 271, 337
Caudium, 269
Cava, 343
Cave, 97, 123
Ceccano, 105
Cecinna, *river,* 11
Celano, 113
Celenza, 355
Celle, 109
Cellino Attanasio, 233
Centum Cellae, see Civitavecchia
Cepagatti, 235
Ceprano (Fregellae), 89, 103, 135, 227, 257, 261, 263, 416
Cercemaggiore, 351
Ceretano, *river,* 15
Cermignano, 233
Cerreto, 31
Cerreto di Spoleto, 151, 155
Cerreto Laziale, 115
Certaldo, 31
Cerveteri (Caere, Caere Servatorum), 15
Cesano, *river,* 183, 397
Cesena, 375
Cetona, 39
Chalcis, 311, 432
Chartres, 426
Chiana, *river,* 39, 43, 49
Chiana, *swamp,* 39
Chianciano, 39
Chiaravalle, *monastery,* 197, 403
Chiascio, *river,* 143, 145, 159
Chienti, *river,* 193, 195, 398, 402
Chieti (Teate), 213, 239, 347
Chiusano di S. Domenico, 275
Chiusci, 369
Chiusi (Clusium), 3, 33, 35, 39, 358
Ciciliano, 115
Cimera, see Monte Conero
Ciminian Forest, 57, 358

Ciminus, *mountain,* 55, 57
Cingoli, 191
Circeian fortress, 75
Circello, 275
Cisterna, 47
Città della Pieve, 43
Città di Castello (Tifernum Tiberinum), 41, 141, 181, 388
Città S. Angelo, 233
Cittareale, 155
Civita Castellana, 51
Civita Indivina, 91, 378
Civitaluparella, 249
Civitanova Alta, 193
Civitanova del Sannio, 251
Civitas Bucelli, 249
Civitate, 410
Civitavecchia (Centum Cellae), 13, 15, 360
Civitella, 115, 231, 247, 251
Civitella del Vescovo, 41
Clanio, *river,* 305, 307, 337, 429, 431
Clanis, see Clanio, *river*
Clanius, see Clanio, *river*
Clitumnus, *river,* see Clitunno
Clitunno, *river,* 149, 389–390
Clusium, see Chiusi
Coffiano, 275
Colchis, 109
Colfiorito, 149
Collatia, 257
Colle Alto, 259
Colle d'Anchise, 253
Colle di Macine, 249
Colle di Mezzo, 249
Colle di Val d'Elsa, 31
Colle Plinio, 388
Colle Sannita, 275
Collecorvino, 235
Collepardo, 103
Collescipoli, 163
Colletorto, 351
Collevecchio, 167, 231
Collina, 31
Collis Pacis, 337
Collodi, 19
Collodi, *river,* 19
Colonella, 229
Colonna, 97, 103
Columnae, 271
Comino (Plaga Comminium), 257
Comitatus Aprutinus, 406
Compsa, 271
Compulteria, 265
Comunanza, 199
Conissa (Leonessa, Gonessa), 153, 391
Constance, 381
Constantinople, 51, 209, 213
Controguerra, 229
Cora, 91
Cordova, 355
Corese, *river,* 167, 171
Corfinium, 229, 241, 349
Corinalto, 183
Corneto, 13, 359
Corno (Corvus), *river,* 151, 153, 390
Corropoli, 229
Corsano, 275
Corsica, 11
Corsignano, see Pienza
Corsolona, 31
Cortona, 23, 39, 43, 333
Cosa, 11
Cosenza, 211
Cossignano, 199
Costacciaro, 143
Cottanello, 167
Cotulo, *fortress,* 47, 177
Crecchio, 247
Cremera, *river,* 53, 59, 372

Crepacorius, 275
Crustumium (Crustumerium), 51, 71, 171, 173
Cuma (Cumae), 307, 311, 323, 325, 329, 337, 419–420, 423, 429, 431
Apollo, *temple,* 311, 313, 432
cave of the Sibyl, 313, 432–433
Cumae, see Cuma
Cures, see Torri
Cusano, 239, 269, 275
Cutilia, 155

Dalmatia, 191, 229
Daunia, 347
Deruta, 159
Digentia, 167
Donadeum, 169
Dovadola, 23
Drumentum, river, 343
Ducaria, *stream,* 25
Dugenta, 337
Durazzano, 337
Durazzo, 213

Eclano (Aeclanum), 416
Egypt, 17, 362, 402
Elba, *island,* 11
Elice, 233
Elsa, *river,* 31
Empoli, 21, 31
Epirus, 213, 219
Equum Tuticum, 416
Era, *river,* 31
Esino, *river,* 185, 189, 398
Ete Morto, *river,* 199, 402
Ete Vivo, *river,* 195, 197, 402
Euboea, 311, 432
Euganean Hills, 21
Europe, 23, 151
Evreux, 382

Fabriano, 143, 185, 189, 195, 399–400
Faesulae, see Fiesole
Faicchio, 269
Faleria, 3
Falerii, 55
Falernian territory, 281, 287, 289, 291, 295, 307, 349
Faliscan territory, 55
Fallascoso, 249
Fallo, 249
Fano, 179, 183
Fara S. Martino, 245, 247
Fara, *castle,* 167
Farfa (Fabaris, Farfarus), *river,* 163, 167, 393
Farnazzano, 177
Feltrino, *river,* 247
Ferentillo, *monastery,* 155
Ferentina, *river,* 101
Ferentino (Ferentinum), 101, 135, 380
Fermignano, 181
Fermo (Firmum Picenum), 197, 199, 403
Ferrara, 363, 376, 431
Fiano, 51
Fiastra, *stream,* 195
Fiastro, 195
Fibrenus, *river,* 259
Fidenae, 51, 53, 133, 173
Fiesole (Faesulae), 3, 21, 25, 29, 35, 41
Figline, 29
Filattiera, 5
Filettino, 103
Filetto, 247
Fino, *river,* 233
Fiuggi, 103
Fiumicino, *stream,* 231
Fivizzano, 5
Florence, 3, 19, 25, 27, 29, 31, 35, 37, 39, 43, 49, 223, 357–359, 363–364, 372, 376, 397, 402–403

Laurenziana, *library,* 363
Ognissanti, *church,* 362
Palace of the Priors, 21
Palazzo di Parte Guelfa, 361
S. Marco, *library,* 23
S. Marco, *monastery,* 23
S. Maria del Fiore, *cathedral,* 361
S. Miniato, *church,* 21
Uffizi, *museum,* 362, 401
Via Larga, 23
Flumeri, 275
Foglia, *river,* 177, 181, 397–398
Foligno (Fulgineum, Fulginia), 143, 145, 149, 389
Fondi (Fundi), 85, 87, 89, 97
Fontana, 259
Forano, 167
Forca di Presta, 201, 203
Force, 199
Forcella, 231
Forchia, 271
Forcona (Furconium), 237
Forino, 339
Formelo, 295
Formia (Formiae), 77, 83, 85, 329, 331
Fornelli, 265
Foro, *river,* 245
Fortore, *river,* 275, 351, 355, 410
Foruli, 163, 265
Forum Appii, 97
Forum Flaminii, 143
Fosdinovo, 5
Fossa Nova, *monastery,* 97
Fossacesia, 247
Fossalto, 251
Fossato di Vico, 143, 185, 189
Fossombrone, 179, 181
Fragneto l'Abate, 277
Francavilla (Frentana), 243, 245
France, 217, 223, 333
Frascati, 123, 315, 383–384
Frasso Sabino, 169
Fratta, 89, 145
Fregellae, see Ceprano
Freteale, 279, 283
Frisa, 247
Frondarola, 231
Fronzòla, 369
Frosinone (Frusinum), 103, 135, 380
Fucine Lake, 101, 109, 113, 255, 376
Fumone, 101, 103
Furca Palenae, 247, 249, 295
Furcae, 249
Furlo, 179
Gola del Furlo, xi, 179, 398

Gabii, 97, 115, 121, 131, 135, 380
Gaeta (Caieta), 83, 87, 89, 201, 329
Gaeta, *gulf,* 85
Gaeta, *duchy,* 423
Gaiano, 113
Galeria degli Orsini, 59
Gallese, 55
Gallicano nel Lazio, 97, 131, 135, 380
Gallicanus, *mountain,* see Monte Barbaro
Gallinaro, 257
Gallo, 267
Galluccio, 217
Gambassi, 31
Gamberale, 249
Garfagnana, *valley,* 17
Garganus, *mountain,* see Monte Gargano
Garigliano, *river,* see Liri
Gaul, 313
Gaurus, *mountain,* see Monte Barbaro
Gavignano, 105, 167
Gello Biscardo, 31
Genazzano, 115

Genoa, 5, 7, 127
Genzano di Roma (Cynthianum), 125, 127, 129
Gerano, 115
Gereonium, 327, 349, 442
Germany, 57, 219, 221, 223, 323, 333, 414
Gessopalena, 249
Gildone, 351
Gioia Sannitica, 269
Giovenco (Juvencus), *river,* 113
Gissi, 251
Gragnana, 17
Gragnola, 5
Graviscae, 13
Greece, 3, 23, 187, 209, 213, 215, 327, 377, 401–402, 427
Gripta, mountain, 337
Grosseto, 13
Grottaferrata, 383–384
    monastery, 123, 383
Grottaminarda, 275
Grottammare, 201
Grotte, 47
Guadagnolo, 115
Gualdo Tadino (Tadinum), 143, 189, 388
Guardiagrele, 247
Guardia Vomano, 231
Guardialferia, 253
Gubbio, 141, 143, 179, 388
Guiglionesi, 253
Guiletti, *monastery,* 277
Guilmi, 213, 239, 251

Hadria, 413
Hamae, 313, 433
Herculaneum, 285, 333, 335, 419
Hesperia, 343
Hirpinum, see Arpaia
Hungary, 5, 225, 412

Iapygia, 353
Ida, *mountain,* 243
Idaspis, see Apsa, *river*
Imelle, *river,* 163, 165
Incisa in Val d'Arno, xi, 27, 29, 365
Interamna (Umbria), see Terni
Interamna Lirenas, see Pignataro Interamna
Interamna Praegutiorum, see Teramo
Ionian Sea, 211, 353
Ioveniscum, 349
Isaurus, see Foglia, *river*
Ischitella, 351
Isclero, *river,* 337, 439
Isernia (Aesernia), 265, 289
Isola, 13
Isola di Liri, 259
Isola Farnese, 372
Isoletta, 259, 416
Istia d'Ombrone, 13
Istria, 207
Italy, 1, 3, 5, 13, 17, 29, 37, 39, 43, 55, 57, 61, 65, 67, 69, 71, 75, 77, 87, 89, 95, 109, 111, 125, 139, 149, 151, 153, 155, 157, 159, 161, 189, 193, 199, 201, 207, 209, 211, 213, 215, 223, 225, 227, 233, 235, 237, 245, 279, 283, 287, 289, 291, 299, 303, 311, 313, 315, 321, 329, 331, 333, 343, 345, 358, 363, 368, 370, 390, 397, 401, 405–406, 408–412, 415, 422–424, 429, 431, 433
Itri, 87
Iuvanum, 247
Iuvatinus [Batinus], *river,* 227

Janiculum, 53
Jerusalem, 223
Jesi, 185
Jesi, *river,* 185

Kyme, 432

La Vene, *river,* see Clitunno
Laconia, 83
Lago del Matese, 416
Lago di Albano, 125
Lago di Anguillara, 59
Lago di Averno (Lake Avernus), 313, 315, 317, 321, 323, 432–434, 436
Lago di Bolsena, 13, 47, 55
Lago di Fondi, 87
Lago di Fusaro, 431
Lago di Lésina, 351
Lago di Lucrino (Lake Lucrinus), 313, 317, 321, 323, 434–436
Lago di Nemi, xii, 125, 364, 375–376, 384, 386
Lago di Patria (Palus Liternia), 430–431
Lago di Piediluco (Velino, *lake*), 155, 157, 161, 163
Lago di Pilato, 199
Lago di Varano, 351
Lago di Vico, 57
Lago Regillo, 97, 121
Laguna di Orbetello, 11
Lake of the Marsi, see Fucine Lake
Lake Trasimene (Lago di Perugia), 43, 147, 175, 229, 365
Lake Vadimonis, 3, 59
Lama dei Peligni, 247
Lamoli, 181
Lanuvium, 67, 89, 91, 133, 378, 380
Lapio, 275
L'Aquila (Aquila), 37, 211, 227, 235, 237, 239, 241, 410, 414
  S. Maria di Collemagino, *church,* 415
Larchiano, *stream,* 31
Larino (Larinum), 349, 406, 442
Laterina, 31, 369
Latium et Campania, *region,* 419
Laurentinum, 11
Laurentum, 87, 378
Lautulae, 79, 255
Lavinium, 63, 67, 95
Lazio (Latium), xi, xii, 51, 61, 63, 89, 97, 103, 105, 113, 115, 131, 133, 135, 137, 139, 141, 173, 175, 364, 373, 375–376, 380, 384, 397, 401, 406–407, 419
Leborini Campi, see Campania
Leonessa, 155
Lésina, 351
Lete (Pratellus), *river,* 265, 267, 416
Lettopalena, 247
Liburnian Sea, 207
Licenza, 393–394
Licenza (Digentia), *river,* 393
Liguria, 7, 17, 27, 29
Limatola, 277
Limosano, 253
Linari, 31
Liri (Garigliano, Traetto, Liris), *river,* 87, 89, 101, 115, 135, 137, 255, 257, 261, 263, 279, 281, 283, 285, 287, 423–424
Liternum, 293, 307, 309, 329, 420, 430–432
Livorno, 9, 11
Lombardy, 223
Loreto, 235
Lucania, xii, 157, 207, 209, 265, 329, 345, 405
Lucca (Luca), 3, 7, 17, 19, 29, 33, 37, 358
Luceoli, 179, 181
Luceria, 269, 273, 413
Lucignano, 39, 369
Lucito, 253
Luco, 239
Lucretilis, *mountain,* 169
Lucrinus, *lake,* see Lago di Lucrino

Lucullanum, *villa,* 123
Lumenico, 19
Lunatula, 337
Luni (Luna), 3, 5, 9, 358–359
  Luna, *harbor* (La Spezia), 7
Lunigiana, *region,* 5
Lupara, 253
Lycaeus, *mountain,* 169
Lydia, 1
Lyons, 219

Macchia, 351
Macerata, 193
Macchia da Sole, 229
Maddaloni, 337
Maenza, 93
Maeonia, 1
Magliano, 33
Magliano de' Marsi, 113
Magliano Sabina, 163, 165, 167
Magra, *river,* 1, 5, 357
Maida, 211
Maiori, 343
Maleventum, 271
Malgrate, 5
Mandela, 167
Manoppello, 239
Mantua, 177, 367
March of Ancona (Picenum, March of Fermo), xi, xii, 147, 149, 175, 177, 185, 191, 193, 197, 199, 201, 203, 213, 227, 229, 359, 387, 397–398, 406
Mare Morto, 313
Marigliano (Merelanium), 335, 339
Marina, *stream,* 19
Marino, 89, 91, 95, 123, 125, 135, 376, 383–384
  church, 380
Marta, 49
Marta, *river,* 13, 49
Martirano, 211
Mascioni, 233
Massa Marittima, 5, 15, 33
Massa Trabaria, 181, 399
Mastrata, 265
Matelica, 189, 193
Mauritania, 329
Mediterranean Sea, 402
Melfa, *river,* 257, 259, 261
Melfi, 209, 215, 409–410
Melito, 275
Mendoso, 183
Mentana (Nomentum), 39, 165, 376, 393
Mera, *river,* see Serchio
Mercatello sul Metauro, 181
Mercato S. Severino, 343
Mercogliano, 271
Mercuriale, 271
Meronida, 337
Messapia, 347
Messina, 213, 217, 329, 410
Metauro (Metaurus), *river,* 179, 181, 183, 388, 398
Mevania, see Bevagna
Miano, 231
Miglianico, 245
Mignano Monte Lungo, 287
Mignone (Minio), *river,* 13
Milan, 360, 362, 376, 397
  Pinacoteca di Brera, *museum,* 401
Minerva, *promontory,* 343
Minori, 343
Minturnae, see Minturno
Minturno (Minturnae), 83, 87, 279, 281, 283, 329, 331, 423–424
Mirabella Eclano, 275
Miraldella, 181
Misa, *river,* 183, 398

Miscano, *river,* 275
Miseno (Misenum), 313, 315, 317, 319, 323, 432, 434
Modena (Mutina), 177, 397
Biblioteca Estense, 422
Modigliana, 23
Molinara, 275
Mombaroccio, 179
Mondavio, 183
Mondragone, 283, 295, 424
Mons Grumus, 275
Mons Nitidum, 273
Monsummano, 19
Montagano, 349, 351
Montagna del Matese (Mt. Tifernus), 253
Montagna della Maiella, 239, 243, 245, 247, 251, 414
Montalcino, 35, 37, 47
Montalto, 199
Montalto di Castro, 13
Montaniola, 57
Montaquila, 263
Monte Amiata, 47
Monte Argentario, 13
Monte Asdrubaldo, 181, 397
Monte Barbaro, 283, 285, 293, 419, 424, 427
Monte Bodio, 183
Monte Bufario, 229
Monte Calvi, 429
Monte Cascano, see Monte Barbaro
Monte Cassino, 261
Monte Cavo (Alban Mount), 61, 75, 121, 129, 131, 382–384
Monte Circeo (Circeii), 75, 77
Monte Compatri, 97, 103
Monte Conero, 189
Monte Corno, 231, 233
Monte del Matese, 267, 269
Monte di Bibona, 211
Monte Gargano, 273, 347, 351, 353, 355, 441
S. Michael Archangel, *sanctuary,* 442
Monte Leone, 155
Monte Massico (Massicus), 283, 286, 287, 291, 419, 427
Monte Nero (Severus), 163
Montepagano, 231
Monte Pallano, 251
Monte S. Giovanni (Tetrica), 163
Monte S. Giusto, 31, 195
Monte S. Maria, 167
Monte S. Maria in Gallo, 199
Sibyl's Cave, 199
Monte S. Martino, 197
Monte San Savino, 369
Monte Sant'Angelo, 351
Monte Taburno (Taburnus, *mountain*), 337, 439
Monte Terminio, 271, 273
Monte Tifata, 271, 303, 339, 341, 419, 429
Monte Toro, 355
Monte Vergine, 419
Monte Vettore, 201
Montebuono, 163
Montecalvo, 275
Montecarlo, 19
Montecassino, *monastery,* 261, 415
Montecatini, 19
Montecchio, 193
Montecosaro, 193
Montedinove, 199
Montedoglio, 141
Montedorisio, 251
Montefabbri, 177
Montefalcione, 273
Montefalco, 145
Montefalcone, 179, 199, 355
Monteferrante, 249

Montefiascone (Mons Faliscorum), 49
Montefiore, 199
Montefortino, 197
Montefredane, 271
Montefusco, 273
Montegualtieri, *fortress,* 233
Montelabbate, 177
Montelapiano, 249
Monteleone, 389
Montella, 275
Montelupo, 31
Montelupo Fiorentino, 19, 27
Montemalo, 275
Montemonaco, 199
Montemurlo, 19
Montenero, 11, 251, 263
Montenerodomo, 249
Monteprandone, 201
Montepulciano, 39
Monterappoli, 31
Montereale, 239, 241
Monterosi, 59
Monterotondo, 51, 171, 173
Monterubbiano, 199
Montesanto, 193, 229
Montescudo, 397
Montesilvano, 235
Montespertoli, 31
Montevarchi, 31
Monteverde, *fortress,* 233
Montevergine, *mountain,* 271, 429
    monastery, 271, 416
Montevettolini, 19
Monti Trebulani, 439
Monticchio, 233
Montolmo, 193
Montone, 47, 145, 231, 389
Montopoli, 31
Montopoli di Sabina, 167
Montorio al Vomano, 231
Monzone, 5
Morcino, 199
Morcone, 277
Morò, *river,* 245, 247
Morocco, 313
Morolo, 105
Morro d'Oro, 229, 231
Morrone del Sannio, 349
Morrovalle, 193
Mosciano Sant'Angelo, 231
Moscufo, 235
Motrone di Versilia, 7
Mottola, *fortress,* 233
Mt. Pontighinus, 43
Mt. Severus, see Monte Nero
Mte. Massico, see Monte Barbaro
Mucata, *river,* 211
Mugello, *region,* 25
Mugello, *valley,* 25
Mugnone, *river,* 19, 25
Musone, *river,* 191, 193, 398
Mutusca, see Trevi

Naples, 209, 219, 221, 225, 233, 293, 299, 305, 325, 327, 329, 333, 335, 341, 343, 349, 373, 405, 408, 420–422, 424, 432–433, 440
    Castel Nuovo, 331, 412, 438
    Crypta Neapolitana, 325, 437
    Parco Virgiliano, 437
    S. Chiara, *monastery,* 331
    S. Martino, *monastery,* 331
Naples, *kingdom,* xii, 73, 207, 405–407, 420
Narni (Nequinum, Narnia), 49, 161, 392
Narnia, see Narni
Natoronum, *river,* 297
Nemi, 125, 127, 129, 376, 386
Nemorensis, 125
Nepi (Nepesum), 55, 59
Neptuninus, *spring,* 155

Nequinum, see Narni
Nera (Nar), *river,* 145, 151, 153, 155, 157, 159, 163, 195, 391
Nereto, 229
Nerola, 167
Nettuno (Neptunnium), 67, 69, 427
Nicastro, 211
Nicolaium, 25
Ninfa, *river,* 121
Nocera Inferiore, 333, 341, 343, 388, 419
Nocera Umbra 143, 149, 193
Nola, 269, 271, 305, 327, 337, 339, 341, 429
Nomentum, see Mentana
Nora, *river,* 235
Norcia (Nursia), 151, 153, 189, 199, 201, 235, 387, 390
Notaresco, 231
Noto, 410
Novilara, 179
Nuceria, see Nocera
Numana, 191
Numicus, *river,* 71, 73, 125
Nursia, see Norcia
Nuzzo, 275

Ocriculum, 49, 51, 392, 435
Oenotria, 163
Ofanto, *river,* 209, 275
Ofena, 235
Offida, 199
Olevano Romano, 115
Olivento, 209
Ombrone, *river,* 11, 13, 19, 39
Opi, 251
Orsogna, 247
Orta, *river,* 239
Orte (Orta), 49, 55
Ortona, 245, 247, 415
Ortonovo, 5
Orvieto, 49
Osento, *river,* 251
Osimo (Auximum), 191
Ostia, 15, 61, 63, 65, 67, 137, 319, 360, 377
Otranto, 191
Otricoli, 161, 163, 392

Pacentro, 241, 243
Padua, 25, 372, 392, 428
Arena Chapel, 362
Padule, 275
Paestum, 165
Paganico, 33, 181
Paglia, *river,* 39, 47, 49
Paglieta, 249
Pago Veiano, 277
Palaepolis, 325, 327
Palani, mountain, 249
Palazzolo, 383, 385
Palena (Pelignum), 247
Palermo, 217, 219, 410–411
Palestrina (Praeneste), 97, 99, 115, 117, 119, 123, 131, 165, 382
Paliano, 103, 123
Palombara Sabina, 171
Palombaro, 247
Palus (Perga), 15
Panicale, 43
Paris, 362
Parma, 177, 221
Parthenope, see Naples
Passignano sul Trasimeno, 43
Passo Corese, 167
Paterno, 113
Patrica, 105
Patrimony of St. Peter, 13
Pausilypon, 325
Peccioli, 33
Pedaso, 199
Penna, 197, 245, 251, 271

Pennadomo, 249
Pennapiedimonte, 247
Penne, 235
Percile, 107
Pereto, 109
Pergola, 183
Perugia (Perusia, Augusta Perusia), xii, 3, 35, 39, 43, 45, 47, 143, 145, 147, 333, 358, 372
Arco Augusto, 372
Perusia, see Perugia
Pesa, *river,* 31
Pesaro (Pisaurum), 177, 179, 197
Pescara (Aternus, Aterno), *river,* 227, 233, 235, 237, 239, 241, 243, 245, 414
Pescasseroli, 251
Pescia, 19
Pescia, *stream,* 13, 47
Pesco Sannita, 277
Pescocostanzo, 249
Pescopennataro, 249
Pescosolido, 255
Pesolia, 269
Petraroia, 269
Petrella Tifernina, 349
Petrioli, 33, 366
Petritoli Piceno, 199
Pettorano, 243
Peucetia, 347
Phenne (Falacrinae), 155, 391
Pianello, 143
Pianello Cerratina, 235
Piano delle Cinquemiglia, 243, 249
Picinisco, 257
Pieca, *plain,* 195
Piediluco, 155, 163, 169
Pienza (Corsignano), 39, 367
Pietracatella, 351
Pietraferrazzana, 249
Pietranico, 235
Pietransieri, 249
Pietrasanta, 7
Pietrelcina, 277
Piglio, 103, 123
Pignataro Interamna (Interamna Lirenas), 135, 259, 263
Piomba, *river,* 233
Piombino, 11
Pirlo, 181
Pisa, 3, 7, 9, 21, 23, 29, 31, 217
Piscianum, 115
Piscina Mirabilis, 315, 432, 435
Pistoia (Pistoria), 3, 19, 189, 361
Pithecusae, 311
Pizzoferrato, 249
Plaga, 257
Po, *river,* 9
Ficarolo branch, 421
Po Spinetico, 139
Pofi, 103
Poggibonsi, 31
Poggio, 169
Poggio Cancelli, 233
Poggio Mirteto, 167
Poggio Moiano, 169
Poggio Umbricchio, 231
Poggiomorretto, 231
Poli, 115
Policorvo, 251
Polimarzo, 57
Pollutri, 251
Polystephanum, see Palestrina
Pompeii, 333, 335, 341
Pomptine fields, 77, 93
Pomptine Marshes, 77, 79, 81, 95, 131
Ponsacco, 33
Pontassieve, 27
Ponte, 151, 155
Ponte Biferchia, 277
Ponte Landolfo, 277
Ponte Patulli, 143

Ponte S. Giovanni, 143
Ponte Valleceppi, 143
Pontecorvo, 89, 135, 261, 263
Pontedera, 31
Pontignana, 31
Pontremuli, 5
Ponza (Pontiae), 87, 261
Ponzano Romano, 51
Pópoli, 241, 243
Poppi, 31
Populonia, 3, 9, 11, 358
Porciano, 31
Porciliano, 103
Porcina, 265
Portici, 23
Porto Baratti, 11
Porto d'Ascoli, 201
Porto S. Giorgio, 197, 199
Porto Sant'Angelo, 233
Portoferraio, 11
Portus Herculis, 13
Portus Iulius, 434–435
Porzio, 89
Posta Fibreno, 255
Potentia, 193
Potenza, *river,* 193, 398
Pozzuoli (Puteoli), 315, 317, 319, 323, 325, 329, 419, 429, 432, 434–435, 437
Praeneste, see Palestrina
Praetutian territory, 227, 229
Prato, 19, 29, 265
Pratola, 241
Pratolino, 141
Pratovecchio, 31
Presenzano, 287
Priverno (Privernum), 85, 93, 379
Proceno, 47
Provence, 223, 358
Puglia (Apulia), xi, 41, 157, 207, 209, 211, 213, 215, 217, 227, 229, 241, 253, 255, 261, 269, 271, 275, 295, 345, 347, 349, 353, 406, 410–411, 413, 420, 422, 441–442
Puglianello, 269
Pupinia, 135, 389
Puteoli, see Pozzuoli
Pyrgo (Pyrgi), 15, 360

Quadri, 249
Quarata, 31
Quintucium, 347

Radicofani, 39, 47
Raiano, 235
Rapino, 231, 245
Rasino, *stream,* 249
Rasinum, river, 295
Raspagatti, 181
Ratinum, 349
Ravello, 343
Ravenna, 21, 125, 139, 141, 388
Reate, see Rieti
Recanati (Ricinetum), 193, 359
Reggio di Calabria, 211, 213, 329, 410
Regi Lagni, 430
Reino, 275
Riano Flaminio, 55
Ricinetum, see Recanati
Rieti (Reate), 155, 161, 163, 185
Rimini (Ariminum), 139, 179, 183, 197, 271
Rio Sole, *stream,* 167
Riofreddo, 107, 109, 263
Ripa, 231
Ripafratta, 17
Ripatransone, 199, 201
Ripattoni, 231
Ripi, 103
Rivisondoli, 249
Rocca, 183, 249, 251
Rocca di Cava Capranica, 115

Rocca di Cave, *citadel,* 117
Rocca di Papa, 123, 383–384
Rocca Lerici, 115
Rocca Mondragone, 285, 287
Rocca Niceforo, 213, 215
Rocca S. Giovanni, 247
Roccagiovine, 393
  Vacuna, *shrine,* 393
Roccagorga, 93
Roccamontepiano, 245
Roccamorice, 239
Roccantica, 167
Roccaraso, 249
Roccaravindola, 263
Roccascalegna, 249
Roccasecca dei Volsci, 93, 261
Roccaspromonte, 253
Roccavivara, 251
Rocchetta (Aprutium), 231
Rocchetta (Apulia), 349
Rocciano, *fortress,* 231
Rocha Mutiorum, 115
Rodi, 351, 442
Roiate, 115
Romagna, 23, 141, 181, 207, 209, 358, 375, 397, 406–407
Rome, 3, 7, 11, 15, 21, 23, 43, 45, 49, 51, 53, 55, 57, 59, 61, 65, 67, 71, 77, 81, 83, 89, 91, 101, 103, 105, 107, 111, 113, 115, 117, 121, 123, 125, 129, 131, 133, 135, 139, 141, 147, 151, 155, 159, 163, 167, 171, 173, 179, 181, 183, 185, 211, 213, 215, 223, 237, 239, 245, 247, 279, 281, 293, 297, 303, 315, 323, 327, 329, 331, 333, 349, 357–359, 362–364, 373, 376–377, 380, 389, 400–401, 411, 413, 415, 419, 429, 431, 432
  Aventine Hill, 273
  Caelian Hill, 93
  Campidoglio, 437
  Castel Sant'Angelo, 13, 165, 213
  Castel Sant'Angelo (Mausoleum of Hadrian), 39
  Castro Crescenzio, 165
  Forum Romanum, 257, 377
  Ponte Mammolo, 131
  Porta Capena, 309
  Porta Flaminia (Porta Fluentana, Porta del Populo), 55, 213
  Rostra, 65
  S. Maria in Cosmedin, *church,* 381
  S. Maria Rotonda, *church* (S. Maria ad Martyres, Pantheon), 109, 381
  Ss. Peter and Paul, *basilica,* 331
  St. John Lateran, *church,* 217
  Vatican library, 360
  Vatican museum, 392
Ronciglione, 59
Rondine, 369
Ronta, *river,* 25
Rosciano, 235
Roseto, 231, 355
Rosia, 157
Rosulanus, 157
Rubicon, *river,* 81
Rufento, *river,* 239
Rusellae, 35, 39, 358
Rusellana, 3

S. Agata dei Goti (Saticula), 269
S. Angelo d'Alife, 267
S. Angelo di Pesco, 249
S. Angelo in Vado (Tifernum Metaurense), 181, 388
S. Apollinare, 247
S. Benedetto del Tronto, 201
S. Biagio, xi, 420
S. Croce del Sannio, 275
S. Domino, *island,* 353

Diomedes, *temple,* 353
S. Donato 31
S. Donato Val di Comino, 257
S. Egidio, 229
S. Elia, 261, 263
S. Elpidio al Mare, 195
S. Felice Circeo, 75
S. Fiora, 47
S. Germano, 215, 261, 263
S. Gimignano, 31
S. Ginesio, 195
S. Giovanni, 31
S. Giovanni, *monastery,* 247
S. Giovanni in Campo Orazio, 123
S. Giuliano di Puglia, 351
S. Godenzo, 25
S. Gregorio (Abruzzo), 275
S. Gregorio (Lazio), 115
S. Iona, 113
S. Liberatore a Maiella, *monastery,* 243, 406, 415
S. Lorenzo in Campo, 183
S. Lorenzo Nuovo, 47
S. Lorenzo Maggiore, 277
S. Lupo, 277
S. Marco, 355
S. Marco Argentano, 211
S. Maria, 249, 275
S. Maria, *church,* 305
S. Maria and S. Eutimo (S. Euthymius), *church,* 165
S. Maria Casanova, *abbey,* 413
S. Maria de Oliveto, 263
S. Maria in Cassiano, 193
S. Maria in Giorgio (Tignium), 197
S. Martino in Valle, *monastery,* 247
S. Martino, 271
S. Miniato, 31
S. Notoria, 149
S. Omero, 229
S. Pelino in the Fields, 241
S. Pietro, 167
S. Pietro Avellana, 251
S. Potito, 113
S. Quirico, 39
S. Severino Marche, 193
S. Severo, 351, 355
S. Silvestro, *mountain,* 53
S. Stefano in Rivomare, *monastery,* 251
S. Vicenzo al Volturno, 263
monastery, 263, 295
S. Vincenzo, 11
S. Vito, 229
S. Vito Chietino, 247
S. Vito Romano, 101, 115
S. Vittoria in Matenano, 199
Sabato, *river,* 265, 269, 271, 273, 275, 277, 337
Sabina et Samnium, *region,* 405
Sabine region, 163, 165, 169, 171, 173
Sabine territory, 376
Sacriportus, 117
Salcito, 251
Salentini, 207, 405
Salerno, 211, 213, 215, 343, 409, 440
Saline, *river,* 231, 233
Salisano, 169
Sambuca, 31
Sambuci, 115
Samnite mountains, 279
Samnium, 135, 155, 227, 247, 253, 255, 265, 271, 277, 289, 293, 307, 341, 376, 391, 406, 415, 439
Sangemini, 161
Sangro (Saro), *river,* 243, 247, 249, 251, 414
Sannicandro Garganico, 351
Sannio, 261
Sant'Angelo a Scala, 271
Santo Martino, 181
Saonus, see Savone, *river*
Saracinesco, 115

Sardinia, 1, 11, 295
Sarmineta, 91
Sarnano, 195
Sarno, 339
Sarno (Sarnus, Scafati), *river,* 333, 337, 339, 341, 440
Sarteano, 39
Sarzana, 5
Sarzanello, *citadel,* 5
Sarzanello, 5
Sassinoro, 277
Sassoferrato, 183, 185
Satura, 79
Savone, *river,* 291
Scandrilia, 167
Scaphanum and *Gaurianum, tower,* 281
Scarlino, 11
Scarperia, 25
Scerne, 233
Scerni, 251
Scheggia, 141, 143
Scheggino, 155
Schiavi, 259
Scontrone, 249
Scurcola Marsicana, 109, 411
Scurmina, 271
Scythia, 243
Sebethus, *stream,* 438
Seca (Bica), 247
Segni, 105
Sele, *river,* 265, 343, 345
Senigallia (Sena), 183, 185
Sentino, *river,* 183, 185
Sentinum, 183, 185
Sepino (Saepinum), 277, 416
Septempeda, 193
Seravalle, 19
Seravalle di Chienti, 149, 195
Serchio (Auser), *river,* 7, 9, 17
Serenum, 271
Seritella, *river,* 269
Serra S. Quirico, 189
Serracapriola, 351
Serrone, 103
Servigliano, 199
Sessa (Suessa Pometia, Aurunca), 227, 255, 283, 285, 287, 311, 423
Sesto, 287
Settefrati, 257
Sezze (Setia), 93, 133
Sgurgola, 105
Sicily, 73, 209, 213, 217, 219, 221, 223, 225, 408, 410–412
Siena, 21, 29, 31, 33, 35, 37, 39, 366, 372
Sieve, *river,* 25, 27
Sigillo, 143
Signa, 27, 29
Sila, *mountain,* 337, 439
Silva, 233
Silvestro, 55
Sinello, *river,* 251
Sinope, 283
Sinuessa, 61, 77, 83, 89, 283, 285, 287, 289, 295, 307, 329, 424
Siponto, 442
Sirolo, 191
Sisto, *river,* 378
Sitano, *gulf,* 61
Soana, 47
Sonnino, 93
Sora, 255, 257, 259, 279, 281
Soracte, *mountain,* xii, 53, 55, 378, 384
Sorbetolo, 181
Sorbo Serpico, 273
Sordo, *river,* 390
Soritella, *river,* 337
Sorrento (Surrentum), 201, 419
Spain, 233, 313, 355
Spello (Pellium), 143
Sperlonga, 87
Spigno Saturnia, 89

Spina, 139, 388
Spinete, 253
Spoletium, see Spoleto
Spoleto (Spoletium), 147, 149, 151, 153, 155, 159, 229, 387, 389, 413
Spoleto, *duchy,* 139, 141, 151, 175
Spoltore, 235
Squillace, 211
St. Gaudius, 355
Staffolo, 191
Staggia, 31
Stella, *plain,* 287, 289, 291, 293, 425
Stella, *river,* 19
Stia, 31
Stimigliano, 167
Storax (Nymphaeus), *river,* 77, 97
Stroncone, 167
Subiaco (Sublaqueum), 115, 131
Subiaco, *lake,* 115
Suessa Pometia, see Sessa
Suessula, see Castel di Sessola
Sulmo, see Sulmona
Sulmona (Sulmo), 241, 243, 406, 414
Supino, 105
Suriano del Cimino, 57
Sutri (Sutrium), 57, 59, 358
Suvereto, 11

Tagliacozzo, 109, 113, 411
Talamone, 13
Tammaro, *river,* 275, 277
Tarano, 163
Taranta, 247
Taranto (Tarentum), 221, 349
Tarquinia, 13, 358–359
Taurasi, 275
Tavo, *river,* 233, 235
Teano (Teanum Sidicinum), 287, 305, 435
Tegernsee, 414
Telesia, 265, 277, 289, 439
Tenna, *river,* 197, 398
Tennius, *river,* see Topino
Teramo (Interamna Praegutiorum), 231, 406
Termoli, 253
Terni (Interamna Nahars), 159, 161
Terra di Lavoro, see Campania
Terracina (Anxur, Tarracina), 77, 79, 81, 83, 85, 87, 89, 91, 93, 129, 379
Terranuova, 31, 41
Terravecchia, 277
Tesino (Tessuinum), 229
Tessuinus, *river,* 227
Tetrica, see Monte S. Giovanni
Tiber, *river,* 1, 7, 15, 47, 49, 51, 53, 55, 59, 61, 63, 91, 131, 133, 141, 143, 145, 159, 163, 167, 171, 173, 181, 357, 376, 387
Tibur, see Tivoli
Tiburtine mountains, 107
Tifernum Tiberinum, see Città di Castello
Tifernus, *river,* see Biferno
Tignia, see Tenna, *river*
Tinius, *river,* see Topino
Tirium, 351
Tivoli (Tibur), 71, 105, 107, 115, 117, 131, 163, 165, 169, 381
Tocco, 241
Todi (Tuder, Tudertum), 143, 159
Toffia, 167
Tolentino, 195
Tollo, 245
Topino (Tinius, Tennius), *river,* 143, 145, 149
Tordino (Vivantium), *river,* 231
Torgiano, 145
Tornareccio, 251
Torre, 239, 259, 273
Torre Anastasia, 87
Torre Annunziata, 333, 341

Torre Antonelli, 235
Torre d'Astura, 73, 225, 378
Torre del Greco, 333, 335
Torre di Fossato, 181
Torre di Patria, 307, 309
Torre di Sangro, 251
Torre Francolise, 287, 293
Torre San Severino, 313, 433
Torreamando, 275
Torregaveta, 431
Torremaggiore, *castle,* 355
Torri (Cures), 165, 167
Torrice, 103
Torricella Peligna, 249
Torrita da Siena, 39
Tortureto, 229
Traetto, 89, 423–424
Traetto, *river,* see Liri
Tramonti, 341
Transpadane region, 1
Tranum, 291
Trapiata, 265
Trasacco, 113
Trebia, *river,* 365
Trebula, see Trevi
Trevi (Trevia, Trebula Mutusca), 145, 147, 149, 151, 389
Trevi nel Lazio, 103
Trevico, 275
Trieste, *gulf,* 191
Trifanum, 283
Trigno, *river,* 251
Tripalum, 251
Tripergola (Triepergula, Tripergole), 313, 321, 433
Triponzo, 151
Tritoli (Frictolae), 317, 321, 325, 432
Trivento, 251
Trivigliano, 103
Troia, 231, 233
Tronto, 229
Tronto, *river,* 175, 201, 203, 207, 227, 229, 239, 253, 397–398, 405–406
Troyes, France, 223
Truentus, *river,* see Tronto
Tuder, see Todi
Tudertum, see Todi
Tufano, *spring,* 101
Tuscania, 49
Tuscany (Etruria), xi, xii, 1, 3, 5, 7, 9, 13, 15, 19, 23, 31, 33, 35, 39, 43, 45, 47, 55, 59, 61, 101, 139, 141, 173, 181, 267, 333, 357, 360, 375, 378, 380–381, 387, 388, 397, 401, 406
Tusculum, 103, 115, 121, 123, 135, 165, 376, 382, 384
Tyrrhenia, 1
Tyrrhenian Sea, 1, 5, 9, 33, 67, 79, 137, 299, 313, 327, 341, 343, 357, 405, 419, 436

Uffente, *river,* 77, 79
Ufita, *forest,* 275
Ufita, *river,* 275
Umbria, xi, xii, 47, 51, 133, 139, 141, 143, 147, 149, 153, 161, 189, 195, 235, 372, 387–390, 401, 413
Urbino, 177, 179, 181, 388
Urbisaglia (Urbs Salvia), 195, 197, 402
Uzzano, 19

Vacone, 163
Vacri, 247
Vaglio Serra, 233
Vairano, 287
Val di Saline, 211
Valca, 59
Valentinian bridge, 275
Valeria, 109, 406

Valle Castellana, 229
Valle Oscura, 241, 243
Valleromita, *monastery,* 189
Vallerotonda, 263
Vallis Regia, 249, 251
Vallombrosa, *monastery,* 31
Valmontone (Labici), 97, 103, 105, 121, 135, 381
Vasto (Histonium), 251
Vatican, 51, 133
Veii, 51, 53, 125, 133, 173, 358, 372
Velino, *lake,* see Lago di Piediluco
Velino, *river,* 155, 239
Velletri, 71, 91
Venafro (Venafrum), 263, 287, 289, 406
Venice, 353, 361
  S. Giorgio in Alga, *monastery,* 35
Venosa (Venusia), 157, 416
Ventotene, 87
Venusia, see Venosa
Vercelli, 211
Verde, *stream,* 247, 249
Veroli (Verulae), 99, 101, 103
Verrestis, *river,* 121
Verrucola, 5, 19
Vestina, 255, 279, 281, 423
Vesuvius, *mountain,* 283, 313, 335, 339, 438
Vetralla
  S. Maria di Foro Cassio, *church,* 57
Vetulonia, 358
Vezzola, *river,* 231
Via Appia, 79, 81, 83, 87, 89, 93, 95, 125, 133, 275, 285, 287, 319, 323, 379–380, 416, 423–424
Via Arretina, 37
Via Aurelia, 9
Via Cassia, 57, 59, 372
Via Faventina, 25
Via Flaminia, 49, 51, 55, 143, 145, 161, 179, 392
Via Herculanea, 87, 291
Via Latina, 89, 97, 263, 380
Via Nomentana, 133
Via Prenestina, 380
Via Puteolana, 325, 437
Via Salaria, 133
Via Tiburtina, 89, 105, 131, 380
Viareggio, 7
Vibona, 11
Vibrata, *river,* 227, 229
Vicalvi, 257
Vicarello, 59
Vico, 103, 351
Vico S. Leonardo, 51
Vicovaro, 107, 115
Vieste (Vestice), 351
Vietri, 343
Villa, 87
Villa Celiera, 413
Villa S. Maria, 249
Villafranca in Lunigiana, 5
Vinchiaturo, 349
Virgin Mary of Loreto, *church,* 193
Visso, 153
Viterbo (Viturvium), 55
  Bagno del Papa, 373
Vittorito, 235
Volterra (Volaterrae), 3, 29, 31, 33, 35, 358
Volturara, 355
Volturno (Vulturnus), *river,* 263, 265, 267, 269, 287, 289, 291, 295, 297, 299, 303, 305, 307, 337, 416, 419–420, 426–427, 430, 439–440
Vomano (Vomanus), *river,* 231, 233
Vria, 442
Vulci, 358
Vulsinia, see Bolsena

Vulturara, 273
Vulturnus, see Volturno, *river*

Zagarolo, 89, 380
Zancato, 105
Zinzano, 97, 99, 103
Zungoli, 275